READING AS COMMUNICATION
AN INTERACTIVE APPROACH
Second Edition

FRANK B. MAY

Portland State University

Merrill Publishing Company
A Bell & Howell Company
Columbus Toronto London Sydney

Cover Photo: © Norma Morrison

Photo Credits: Brad Eliot—11, 21, 65, 121, 225, 243, 265; Evelyn Liu-Eliot—277, 288, 380, 406, 471, 499; Peace Corps—98; Paul Conklin—160, 322, 342; Strix Pix—181; Merrill Publishing—1, 35, 41, 90, 107, 147, 193, 214, 317, 328, 338, 365, 418, 447, 483

Published by Merrill Publishing Company
A Bell & Howell Company
Columbus, Ohio 43216

This book was set in Aster.

Administrative Editor: Beverly Kolz
Production Editor: Molly Kyle
Cover Designer: Cathy Watterson

Library of Congress Catalog Card Number: 85–51806
International Standard Book Number: 0–675–20405–4
Printed in the United States of America
    4 5 6 7 8 9—91 90 89 88

To Evelyn

She listens to her writer friend,
  like a quiet stream sliding by,
Sometimes praising—
  with a pretty reflection,
  a glint of sunshine.
Sometimes scolding—
  with a popped bubble,
  a splash in the face.
But always with playful joy.

PREFACE

The preface of a textbook is almost always written for instructors rather than students. This preface is an appeal to both: Please let me communicate with you in my own personal style. You see, the major problem for the author of any textbook is one I certainly did not escape; I was expected, and I desired, to write a book that would be highly readable for both undergraduate and graduate students. This in itself has always been a problem for me and other textbook authors I know, but it's not the major problem I'm speaking of. The major problem is that the first reader is the professor! I must satisfy my colleagues (who choose the book) before I am allowed to communicate with students. Which is the way it should be, of course, but it creates a dilemma: If I successfully impress professors, do I confuse their students? If I communicate well with students, do I irritate professors by leaving out ideas, words, studies, or names that any reputable writer in the field of education should have put in?

A famous philosopher once admitted that the first book he published was designed to impress his colleagues. After that, he said, he felt free to write simply and clearly. Well, in a way, without really trying to, I'm afraid I followed his advice. My first book, published in 1967, was *Teaching Language as Communication*, and it evidently pleased many professors. So much so, according to reports from book representatives, that the professors used it for their lecture notes rather than adopt it for their students! Since then, if I may be facetious, I've tried to write with more compassion for *students*.

To Help Children Read was published in 1973 and was followed in 1978 by a second edition. In 1982, after much soul-searching by the publishing staff and myself, and breaking all traditions in the publishing business, we decided to give the third edition a new name, *Reading as Communication*. We did so to emphasize two things: (1) the modular approach with competency objectives was no longer a feature of the text, and (2) I was attempting something nearly impossible—to integrate subskill and psycholinguistic philosophies of instruction. This change pleased some professors and, naturally, bothered others. To some I was "selling out" to the psycholinguists. To some I achieved just the right balance. To others I was tainted by my insistence that no matter how paramount comprehension, phonics instruction still has an important place. (In other words, I "integrated" myself into a very tight corner indeed—one that allowed me to be pummeled from two sides at once.)

What this is all leading to, of course, is my fourth book on reading, which, for good reason, is called *Reading as Communication: An Interactive Approach*, 2nd edition. Although the fourth book is a far cry from the first, it does follow the same belief I've had since 1973: that reading is not an either-or process. Furthermore, every time I've revised this book, I've emphasized that particular axiom even more—or, "The more I teach it, the more I understand it."

In this revision you'll find relatively little emphasis on subskills. I see less and less justification for centering too much instructional time on them. In fact, I think that is what's wrong with much of the reading instruction in schools: too much isolated practice on subskills, not enough integrated practice with guided, whole-passage reading. Unless unconscious biases are clouding my vision, I am seeing more clearly than ever that reading is a highly complex interactive process, involving the reader in hypothesis production and assessment. Both the production and assessment modes require parallel simultaneous data: semantic, syntactic, schematic, and graphophonic. In other words, the reader is called upon to check (through decoding processes) the hypotheses triggered by contextual (comprehension) processes, and vice versa. And this is just *one* example of the interaction that takes place during the reading act.

So, is this book a "top-down" (psycholinguistic) approach? No. Is it a "bottom-up" (decoding-first) approach? No. An interactive approach? To the best of my ability, it is. Why? The rest of the book, particularly Chapter 2, explains my reasons.

Reading as Communication: An Interactive Approach is useful in these ways:

1. As a basic text for an undergraduate course that covers a wide range of concerns related to reading instruction, and allows instructors to require certain chapters and make others optional.

2. As a basic text for a graduate course that offers students an opportunity to get back in touch with a subject they have not formally studied for some time, and offers opportunities for students and instructors to select a core of chapters that meet individual needs.

And now let me praise the prepublication reviewers who devoted so much time and energy providing constructive criticism: Sister Angela Schreiber, The College of St. Catherine; Professor Arlene Saretsky, Chicago State University; Professor Jerry Converse, Cal State, Chico; and Professor Edward J. Earley, Kutztown University. Special thanks to Sam Sebesta of the University of Washington for the enormous patience, refreshing wit, and piquant wisdom in his many letters of advice. Receiving advice from Sam is like taking bitter medicine thoroughly camouflaged by caviar.

Many thanks also go to the editors and their associates at Merrill Publishing Company for their excellent guidance and assistance, especially to Bev Kolz, Executive Editor; Molly Kyle, Production Editor; and Jo-Anne Weaver, Product Manager.

I would also like to thank my wife, Evelyn, not only for her continual encouragement and inspiration, but also for her extremely valuable contributions as research and production associate.

CONTENTS

II READING AS A LANGUAGE PROCESS 99

IV SPECIAL CONCERNS OF THE CLASSROOM READING TEACHER

11 The Content Areas: Continued Growth in Reading and Study Skills 374

12 Increasing Positive Attitudes: Reading in the Affective Domain 412

13 Children with Special Needs: Gifted, English-Deficient, Handicapped 442

14   Becoming a Good Instructional Manager: A Look at the Future   478

APPENDIXES

USING THE PQ3R METHOD IN READING THIS BOOK

Do you have trouble remembering what you read? If you've never used the PQ3R method, you may find it worth a try. This method is described in detail in Chapter 11, but here's the gist of it. Just follow these steps:

1. *Preview:* Read the first paragraph in the chapter, the subheadings, and the last paragraph. This takes only a minute or so and gets your mind ready for the chapter.

2. *Question:* Just before you read each section, change the heading into a question. For example, if the heading is "Reading as Communication," you might change it to "How is reading considered communication?" This gives you a specific reason to read that section.

3. *Read:* Read the section, trying to answer your question thoughtfully.

4. *Recite:* It only takes another few seconds to ask yourself the question again and to answer it in your own words. It may be a good idea to put your answer in writing.

5. *Review:* At the end of the chapter, go back to each subheading, ask your question again, and see if you can recite your answer without looking at your notes. If not, check your notes or scan the section until you can.

Simple, isn't it? And it works. To give you a head start in this book, the preview step for each chapter has been simplified. Just read the Chapter Outline and Chapter Preview before starting the chapter. This will help you get your mind off other things and give you the mental set for understanding what you read. You may find this method works as well for you as it does for many others.

READING AS AN INTERACTIVE PROCESS

CHAPTERS

1 THE NATURE OF READING: WHAT DO YOU THINK?

CHAPTER PREVIEW*

What *you* think about the nature of the reading process may greatly influence the way you teach reading. This chapter may help you begin to make important decisions you haven't had a chance to make before. For instance, are you presently a behaviorist or a gestaltist in your ideas about reading and learning? What difference might it make in the way you teach? Do your assumptions about reading reflect a "top-down" or a "bottom-up" theory? How may those assumptions affect your teaching? Will your

*Research (Thomas & Robinson, 1977) shows that readers who read the subheadings and preview a chapter before they read it, tend to understand a chapter better than those who skip these two steps.

concepts about writing and authors make a difference in your teaching? And what about the process of reading instruction—should it be an operation of "push-pull-click . . . change kids that quick"? Or is it much more a social process, involving children's *feelings*—about themselves, about school, and about reading?

"Uncle Bogglestar?"

"Yes?"

"Do the human creatures on Earth argue as much as we do?"

"Oh yes, even more. Human beings are creatures who argue about everything: who will make the best leader, what's the best headache remedy, was Buck Rogers a jerk or a genius? You name it."

ARE YOU A BEHAVIORIST OR A GESTALTIST?

Thought is the seed of action.

—*Ralph Waldo Emerson*

All our knowledge has its origins in our perceptions.

—*Leonardo Da Vinci*

Thought is the child of action.

—*Benjamin Disraeli*

Man is what he believes.

—*Anton Chekhov*

Behavioral psychology is the science of pulling habits out of rats.

—*Douglas Busch*

Teachers of reading, perhaps more than any other teachers, have daily, almost moment-by-moment decisions to make about learning. When Jodie makes a mistake reading a particular word in a sentence, should you interrupt her? Should you wait until she has read the entire sentence before discussing the word she has missed? Should you let the mistake go if she has substituted a word that means the same thing? Should you stop her immediately after the mistake and have her slowly "sound out" each letter? Or should you have her use a more visual approach of looking for familiar letter patterns? Or maybe you should have her pretend that the word she missed is a blank and ask her to think of all the words that might fit in the blank. I've given you five or six alternatives, all of which require you to make a decision based on your view of learning—as well as your view of the reading act.

According to research (Barr & Duff, 1978; Bawden et al., 1979; Gove, 1983), the way you think learning takes place influences the way you teach. Not that we need research to tell us this. It's just common sense, isn't it? But perhaps you haven't had the chance yet to decide how *you* think learning takes place. Maybe on this topic you've only had the chance to tell a *professor* what you thought he or she wanted to hear; you've yet to decide how *you* think. For instance, do you think like a behaviorist or like a gestaltist?

THE BEHAVIORIST VIEW OF LEARNING AND READING

The behavioristic view of learning and reading processes has been the most dominant view since the 1920s. Every now and then the gestaltist view gets a foothold again, but until the early '80s, it was not very popular. All the most influential behaviorist psychologists, such as Pavlov, Thorndike, and even Skinner, have relied on three variables to explain learning: stimulus, response, and reinforcement. Pavlov spent his free moments ringing chimes whenever he offered food to dogs. You remember, don't you? Before long the dogs would salivate not only when offered food but also when offered nothing more than the sound of a chime. (I do the same thing when it's not my turn to cook and my wife says, "Okay, honey, dinner's ready.") At first the stimulus is the sight and smell of food, but eventually the stimulus becomes the sound of a chime (or a loved one's voice). The salivation (sorry about that repulsive word) becomes the response, and the actual food becomes the reinforcement. The more frequently such a chain of events occurs—stimulus, response, reinforcement—the more firmly established the learning becomes, according to behaviorist theory.

Thorndike liked cats better than dogs. No one knows why, but perhaps it was because cats are cheaper to feed. At any rate, as you remember, he locked them up in wooden boxes, put a catch on the door of the box, and placed a dish of food *outside* the door. (In all other respects, I understand, he was a nice man.) With the sight of the food as the stimulus, a cat thrashed about until eventually it accidentally opened the door (response) and got its reinforcement (the actual food). The next time, though, the cat usually took less time getting out of the box, and eventually it went straight for the latch and opened the door. The frequency of trials, Thorndike surmised, increased the chance that the learning would stick.

Skinner used pigeons. Cheaper yet? I don't know. At any rate, he would wait for one to move in the right direction, then reinforce it by punching a hand-held button that released a tasty pellet. Once, on national television, Skinner taught a pigeon, in less than two minutes, to spin around in a circle. As soon as a partial circular movement had been established, he waited until the pigeon moved even farther in a circular direction before rewarding it with a pellet. In other words, Skinner skipped the type of artificial stimulus used by Pavlov and Thorndike and relied on the pigeon's memory of its own movement (a more intrinsic, natural kind of stimulus). His method was very effective, but I hasten to add that he first starved the pigeon by one-third of its body weight before he trained it. (If I were that starved, I would not only spin around in a circle, I would recite the Gettysburg Address at the same time.)

So you see, Pavlov, Thorndike, and Skinner believed that the frequency of the stimulus, response, and reinforcement encouraged learning to take place. They also believed that complex behavior was nothing more than the adding up of numerous stimulus-response-reinforcement "bonds." If we apply this theory to reading instruction, we would want to teach the smallest, simplest behaviors first and gradually build up to more complex behaviors. Right? We'd teach children letters like *a* and *p* first, wouldn't we, asking them to respond with the middle sound in *cat* every time they saw the stimulus letter *a* and to respond with the sound /p/ every time they saw the letter *p*. And of course we would reinforce them with a smile or a kind word every time they behaved correctly. When we wanted more complex behavior we would teach them to "chain" the two bonds and respond with the sound /ap/ when they saw the letter *a* followed by *p*. And for even more complex behavior, we could eventually get them to respond correctly to *words* such as *cap*, *lap*, and *nap*.

Sounds simple, doesn't it? Teach children letters, then "phonograms" like *ap*, *ip*, or *ite*, then words like *cap*, *lip*, and *kite*, then phrases, then sentences. Thus, according to behavioristic thinking, learning to read becomes a problem of addition. We slowly add up the parts until we get the whole.

THE GESTALTIST VIEW OF LEARNING AND READING

Gestalt is a German word meaning a unified whole, pattern, or form. For gestaltists, learning does not move best from parts to whole but the other way around. Gestaltists have done many experiments with human beings, but the best known have been with ambiguous figures. Do you remember this one? What do you first see inside the rectangle in Figure 1.1?

Some people see a beautiful young woman looking to the left, some see an old woman with a huge nose and jutting chin. What we see is not dependent so much on the stimulus, say the gestaltists, as it is on our *hypothesis* about the stimulus. And that hypothesis depends upon our background, needs, and interests. In other words, we have considerable control over the stimuli in our environment. We usually see what we need or want to see. Furthermore, we tend to perceive the "parts" on the basis of a "whole" (an expectation or theory) in our heads. And we perceive the whole suddenly, all at once, without adding up the parts.

But gestaltists didn't limit themselves to mere humans in their studies. They went back and took a second look at some of the animal experiments the behaviorists had been doing. Kohler (1915) taught chickens to peck at the *darker* of two squares in order to get food. But after responding to the same stimulus numerous times, the chickens switched suddenly to a new stimulus. Why? Because a new square inserted in the cage was even darker than the *old* dark one. Hmmmm . . . what have we here? A thinking bird with a mind of its own? Here we thought the bird had formed a strong bond with a *particular* dark stimulus. Instead it had formed a kind of non-verbal hypothesis (minor though it may be): "Duh, let's see now. Whichever one is darker, I'm supposed to peck at that."

Figure 1.1 *An Ambiguous Figure*

Koffka (1928) repeated some rat-maze experiments that had been performed by behaviorists. He noticed that the rats' solution to the maze was very sudden, as if they had suddenly caught on—as if a brand new nonverbal hypothesis were tried and it worked! This observation seemed to conflict with the notion of frequency—that the more the rat tried the experiment, the faster it would get at reaching the food. Perhaps even rats form a kind of generalization (a whole) that influences the way they perceive the separate stimuli (the parts).

Gestalt psychologists, then, see reading in a different light from behaviorist psychologists: an experienced reader does not perceive letters, then words, then phrases, then sentences, then meaning. For experienced readers, all the meanings they have gathered in the past influence the way they perceive letters, words, and sentences. Take the following sentence, for example: The _____ went sailing across the _____. Your background knowledge and your hypotheses about what the author is telling you make it possible for you to predict the missing words in a variety of ways. We'll get back to this notion in a few minutes, but first let me introduce you to four philosophers from the planet Zania, who will help us understand the debate a little better.

FOUR PHILOSOPHERS FROM PLANET ZANIA DISCUSS READING

Four philosophers from the planet Zania were given permission by Mrs. Kelley, the elementary-school principal, to visit a third-grade classroom to determine what Earthlings were talking about when they used the word *reading*. The four philosophers stumbled down the corridor to room 18, Miss Jerinski's room. Neither their eyes nor their ears had become adjusted to the Earth's heavy atmosphere and pollution; consequently, they could see and hear very poorly. Yet they were determined to examine the phenomenon of reading that seemed to concern so many Earthlings.

Philosopher Alpha studied a child who was being taught by Mr. Blair, an aide to Miss Jerinski. Mr. Blair was showing Cindy that the words *dog*, *dig*, and *dive* all start with the same letter and that this letter represents the same sound in each word. "Aha," said Philosopher Alpha. "Reading is a decoding or deciphering process. When a child learns to read, she is learning to translate written symbols into spoken ones. Reading is nothing more than decoding."

Philosopher Beta examined a child who was being taught by Miss Jerinski. Miss Jerinski was asking Brad some questions before and after he silently stared at each page of a book. "Eureka," said Philosopher Beta.

"Reading is a process of gathering meaning from written symbols. Reading is nothing more than comprehension."

Philosopher Omega scrutinized a "scope and sequence chart" that Miss Jerinski had presented to him. On this chart were phrases such as these:

_____ Decoding the initial consonant letters *h*, *m*, and *p*
_____ Decoding the final consonant clusters *st* and *nd*
_____ Selecting the topic sentence in an information paragraph
_____ Determining when words are used as metaphors

The phrases went on and on. There were handtoes and handtoes of them. (The term *handtoe*, on the planet Zania, refers to a set of twenty.) There were so many different phrases that Philosopher Omega was at first quite confused as to the nature of reading. But suddenly it came to him. "I know exactly what reading is!" he exclaimed. "Reading is one gigantic skill that's made up of many, many tiny subskills. Put all those subskills together and what have you got? Reading!"

Meanwhile, Philosopher Theta was staring at a girl who was, in turn, staring at a book. Every now and then the girl let out a laugh or shook her head, as if disagreeing with someone. Once she even said out loud, "That's a bunch of malarkey!" Several times she wrote down some words that seemed to be similar to, but not the same as, the ones in the book. Philosopher Theta continued to watch in amazement. The girl was totally wrapped up in what she was doing. The book seemed to be entertaining her, sometimes annoying her, and perhaps informing her of something, since she often wrote things down. Theta decided to interrupt the girl and talk to her.

"What is it that you're doing?" he asked.

"I'm reading this book," she said.

Theta scratched his head. "Could you tell me who made that book?"

The girl shrugged her shoulders. "I don't know who made it, but a man named Butterworth wrote it."

Theta squinted at the girl. "Wrote it?"

"Yes," she said. "You know. He made up the story. It's called *The Enormous Egg.*"

Theta nodded his head and stroked his beard. "I see. And when you're reading this story that Mr. Butterworth made up, are you talking with him?"

The girl giggled. "Well, not really," she said. "But in a way I guess I am. It's just as if Mr. Butterworth were telling the story to me."

Theta nodded. "Amazing!" he said. "Truly amazing. Can you read the book in such a way that I might hear what Mr. Butterworth is saying?"

The girl gave Theta a strange look and shrugged her shoulders. "Sure," she said. "I'll read you a little bit of it."

She proceeded to read a short part in which a scientist was explaining how a normal chicken could lay a dinosaur egg. The philosopher gasped and interrupted the girl again. "Are you reading exactly what Mr. Butterworth is saying to you?"

"Sure," she said.

"But how do you know?"

The girl shrugged her shoulders again. "It's right there," she said, pointing to the words on the page. "See these little words here? Mr. Butterworth wrote them down and I'm reading them just the way he wrote them."

Theta smiled. "That's really wonderful, isn't it?"

The girl smiled back. "Want me to read some more?"

Theta said, "Yes, please. But first tell me something. Before you read me more, do you have any idea what the words are going to say next?"

"Oh, sure," she said, and proceeded to predict quite closely what the author then said. After listening to her read more and asking her more questions, Philosopher Theta walked out into the corridor to join his three companions. "Reading is a code-emphasis process!" one of them was shouting. "It's a meaning-emphasis process!" another one said. The third one replied mysteriously, his arms spread outward, as if holding a large globe. "Reading is huge," he said. "It's a gargantuan set of decoding and comprehension subskills!"

"Gentlemen," Theta said softly. "I know exactly what reading is." The others waited, staring at him hostilely. "Reading," Theta said, "is a game!"

"A game!" the others cried.

"A game," he said, with a twinkle in his eyes. "A kind of guessing game. In fact, Earthlings have developed a highly sophisticated set of rules for this game."

"Rules?"

"Yes," Theta replied, chuckling to himself. "Rules about how to think when you want to communicate with someone else. Rules on what sounds you have to make or what symbols you have to write or what order the word-noises have to be in. Rules for what the word-noises will mean."

"Are you saying . . .," Alpha started to ask.

"I'm saying," said Theta, "that reading is a game that a reader plays with an author. It's a guessing game."

"A guessing game!" the other three shouted.

"Exactly," said Theta. "When Earthlings read, they are intelligently guessing what the author is going to say and then confirming their guesses by looking for special clues."

"Impossible," said Omega. "Reading is a vast set of tiny subskills. I can show you right here on this chart . . . ."

"It's nothing more than cracking a code!" said Alpha . . . .

The four philosophers from Zania spent considerable time arguing over their isolated perspectives, then drove off in four rented cars to different schools and universities throughout the country. Several weeks later they met again at the International Airport in Chicago, where their spaceship had been guarded and studied by employees of the Chicago Museum of Science and Industry. I was fortunate enough to be allowed to interview three of the philosophers before they took off for Zania.

My first interview was with Philosophers Alpha and Beta and went like this:

MAY: As I recall, Philosopher Alpha, you were convinced before you left Chicago that reading is more of a decoding process rather than one of gathering meaning. Do you still feel that way?

ALPHA: Yes, I do. To me, reading is primarily the translation of written symbols into speech sounds—a decoding process.

BETA: I beg to differ, Alpha. Reading is the process of getting meaning from those written symbols—it's a comprehension process.

ALPHA: [shaking his head] That doesn't come until the end.

BETA: What do you mean?

ALPHA: I mean, first an Earth child has to notice each letter in a word; then he has to figure out the meaning of that word; then he has to do that for each word in a sentence; and finally he has to figure out the meaning of the sentence. Decoding comes first—then comprehension.

BETA: An Earth child does not read one letter at a time, Alpha—any more than Zania children listen to one speech sound at a time.

ALPHA: Listen, Beta, I've been talking to some professors at the University of Aritexas, or something like that, and they've been using some pretty sophisticated timing devices and cameras. The professors *I* talked to say that Earth people read letter by letter from left to right. The meaning doesn't come until later. (Gough, 1972)

BETA: Well, I've been talking to some professors at the University of Illiana, and they've been using a pretty sophisticated method of studying earth children's reading errors. It's called "miscue analysis," and what they say is, readers don't begin with letters and build up gradually to the sentence meaning. They start with an idea of what the author might say next and check their predictions by sampling from the print.

ALPHA: You mean Theta was right? That reading is a guessing game?

BETA: Well, yes, in a way. It's a very intelligent guessing game based on the Earth child's past experiences and on his ability to notice a variety of clues.

ALPHA: What kind of clues?

BETA: The way a word fits in with the meaning of the *rest* of the sentence. Or the order of the word in the sentence. Or the way the word is spelled.

ALPHA: [laughing] Nah. You've got it wrong. As usual, Beta, you're a romantic. A mystical thinker. It doesn't happen that way at all. Take it from me. The only Earth children who guess are the poor readers, not the good ones. A good reader systematically "plods through the sentence, letter by letter, word by word . . . ." (Gough, 1972, p. 335)

BETA: Until he finally reaches comprehension?

ALPHA: Until he finally reaches comprehension. But decoding is where all the work is—translating those symbols into sounds. Comprehension is secondary, I'm convinced of that.

BETA: Did your professor friends say that—that comprehension is secondary?

ALPHA: No, but I did.

MAY: Thank you gentlemen. This has been most interesting.

BETA: [smiling] You can call Alpha a gentleman if you want to, but I'm female.

MAY: Oh, I'm really sorry. I didn't realize . . .

BETA: [taking off her hat] Zanian females have hair; Zanian males lose theirs when they reach pubescence. That's the only way you can tell us apart.

Decoding: translating written words into spoken or subvocal words

---

After the embarrassing ending to the first interview, I proceeded with more caution in the interview with Omega, who unfortunately was wearing a helmet.

MAY: If you were living on the planet Earth, would they refer to you as Mr. Omega or Ms. Omega or something else?

OMEGA: Dr. Omega.

MAY: Uh, thank you. Tell me, Dr. Omega. Have you changed your mind about the reading process since you left Chicago?

OMEGA: No, I haven't.

MAY: I see. Well, as I recall, you left Chicago believing that reading is nothing more than a vast set of tiny subskills.

OMEGA: [beaming] Yes, vast indeed. Why, in one school system they were teaching children over 300 of them in the first six grades!

MAY: Could you give me a few examples?

OMEGA: Oh, there was one I really liked. It's called "discrimination between the voiced and unvoiced *th* in words like *this* and *thin*." And another one I liked was called "pronouncing the /ō/ sound when it's represented by *oa* in words like *boat* and *oak*." Such precision is really quite beautiful, something I hadn't expected to see on Earth.

MAY: Hmmm. Any comprehension subskills?

OMEGA: Oh yes. Lots of those too . . . like "recognizing when a story is a fantasy and not a true story," and, let's see, like "recognizing the main idea in a nonfiction story."

MAY: You mentioned that this school system is teaching over 300 subskills. Is this a good thing, as far you're concerned?

OMEGA: Certainly. The more subskills your Earth children learn, the more they learn how to read.

MAY: And you're convinced that this is the best kind of reading instruction.

OMEGA: Yes. It reminds me of a club I was in as a boy back in Zania. Every time I learned a new skill, you know, like projecting my voice for a hundred yards, I was given a badge I could wear on my zober-haired sweater.

MAY: [much more relaxed now that I knew what sex he was] What's a zober?

OMEGA: Oh, it's like one of your monkeys, I guess.

MAY: Interesting. So, you'd get a badge for each new skill?

OMEGA: Yes, it was like the way children in your schools get rewarded for passing a subskill test. If they get 80 percent correct, they get their card punched, or their checklist checked, or something definite like that. For example, if they pass a test on "reading words with the digraphs *th* or *sh* in them," they get punched or checked off. Some teachers give them little scratch-and-sniff stickers or maybe a token they can use for buying something later.

MAY: I see. And so you think that reading is a process of learning one little subskill after another until you accumulate enough to be called a reader.

OMEGA: [delighted] Yes, that's it. Like in the Yellow Zobers—that's the name of the boys' club I was in—we were called Banzoombles after we passed all the tests.

MAY: Banzoombles?

OMEGA: Something like your Eagle Scouts.

MAY: Right. And did you find any evidence during your travels that this procedure of teaching and testing subskills produces good readers?

OMEGA: Well, the principals of all the schools I visited were quite enthusiastic about it.

MAY: And the classroom teachers?

OMEGA: Oh, I'd say they believed in it pretty much, although I'd have to say that many of them thought they did things because the principals wanted them to do them.

MAY: How about the reading specialists?

OMEGA: They weren't quite as enthusiastic. Some of them didn't think the subskill method of teaching was all that effective.

MAY: What you've just said about teachers, principals, and reading specialists fits a survey I've seen. (Shannon, 1982)

OMEGA: [showing interest by raising his eyebrows] Yes?

MAY: The survey showed pretty much what you said. The reading specialists were not overly impressed with the validity of the commercial materials the classroom teachers were using—the materials based on the subskill approach to instruction.

OMEGA: Oh?

MAY: But the principals were.

OMEGA: [satisfied] Ah.

MAY: And most of the teachers said they use the subskill materials because the administrators expected them to.

OMEGA: Rightly so.

MAY: Well, what about it, Dr. Omega. Do you think the subskill method is scientific?

OMEGA: What does that mean—*scientific*?

MAY: It means that a large group of children are taught using the subskill approach and their achievement is compared with a large group who did *not* use the subskill approach. It also means that someone can demonstrate that there are such things as subskills that good readers use as they read. John Downing, for example, says that the "so-called reading skills" are "largely mythical" and have "no basis in objective data from studies of actual reading behavior." (Downing, 1982, p. 535)

OMEGA: [smiling] Your notion of *scientific* is amusing to me. On Zania we once had such a notion, but we gave it up.

MAY: Really? Why?

OMEGA: Because too few of us understood it. Oh, many Zanians pretended to understand. But for the most part, they just used the word *scientific* without *being* scientific. So we dropped the idea of *scientific* and went back to *logical*. That's why I'm so impressed with the subskill notion, because logically, every skill can be broken into subskills. And every subskill can be broken into even smaller subskills. If you break a skill down into fine enough subskills, you can gradually teach it to a very young Earth child. Maybe even to a—what do you call it here?—a rug rat.

MAY: No matter what the skill is?

OMEGA: Certainly. Let's take that charming custom you call dancing. You can teach someone how to move his left foot, how to move his right foot, his left arm, his right arm, his head, his hands, his torso, how to hear the beat, how not to grin like an ape . . . then, all he has to do is put them together and he's dancing!

MAY: I can tell you about studies that raise serious questions about the subskill approach to instruction. (Downing, 1982; Stennett et al., 1975)

OMEGA: [smiling] Are they based on your so-called scientific method?

MAY: Yes.

OMEGA: I think my spaceship is about to leave. I've enjoyed our little conversation.

BOTTOM-UP OR TOP-DOWN: WHAT'S YOUR PREFERENCE?

The Michigan Institute for Research (Barr & Duff, 1978; Bawden et al., 1979) conducted several studies to determine teachers' beliefs about the nature of the reading process. They found that their views fell into two major categories. The labels often given to these categories are both descriptive and amusing—"bottom-up" and "top-down." If a teacher indicates that her most important instructional goal is to get her students to "really know the sounds that the letters make," her view of reading would probably be placed in the bottom-up category, since the unit of language she emphasizes is at the "lowest" level. If a teacher says that her most important instructional goal is to get her students "to read more library books," her view would probably be placed in the top-down category, as her emphasis is on "higher" units of language.

Bottom-up approaches to reading include the assumption that reading begins with print and proceeds systematically from letters to words to phrases to sentences to meaning. Top-down approaches assume that reading begins with knowledge and hypotheses in the mind of the reader. You remember that sentence I gave you before: The _____ went sailing across the _____. Now, suppose you were reading a story about a tennis match and you came to these two sentences: Jerry swung the racket. The _____ went sailing across the _____. (I fooled you earlier, didn't I?) As I said earlier, because of your background knowledge and your ability to hypothesize, you would know right away what words to expect in the blank slots. To make sure of your predictions, however, you probably would sample a bit of the print, if it was available to you—something like this: The b––l went sailing across the n––. By checking the print in this way you would confirm your predictions. This way of perceiving the reading process is called the top-down view.

The chart in Table 1.1 was developed by Mary Gove and published as part of an article in *The Reading Teacher* (Gove, 1983). By examining it you can get some idea of where you presently stand on the important issue of

Table 1.1 *Conceptual Framework of Reading*

Concept Areas	Summary of beliefs	
	Bottom-up Conceptual Framework of Reading	Top-down Conceptual Framework of Reading
Relationship of word recognition to comprehension	Believe students must recognize each word in a selection to be able to comprehend the selection	Believe students can comprehend a selection even when they are not able to recognize each word
Use of information cues	Believe students should use word and sound-letter cues exclusively to determine unrecognized words	Believe students should use meaning and grammatical cues in addition to graphic cues to determine unrecognized words
View of reading acquisition	Believe reading acquisition requires mastering and integrating a series of word recognition skills	Believe students learn to read through meaningful activities in which they read, write, speak, and listen
Units of language emphasized instructionally	Letters, letter/sound relationships, and words	Sentences, paragraphs, and text selections
Where importance is placed instructionally	View accuracy in recognizing words as important	View reading for meaning as important
Student evaluation	Think students need to be tested on discrete subskills	Think students need to be tested on the amount and kind of information gained through reading

Reprinted with permission from M.K. Gove and *The Reading Teacher*, 37(1983): 261–268.

what the reading process really is. I hope, though, you'll keep an open mind until you "hear me out" in Chapter 2.

WHAT ARE YOUR VIEWS ON WRITING AND AUTHORS?

Karen is a lucky six-year-old. From the age of one, her parents read books to her. They bought her books. They gave her paper and pencils. They encouraged her scribbling. They praised her when she first wrote her name.

They read everything she wrote with eagerness. Without even trying they were teaching her that reading is a process of communicating with authors. If her teachers continue to teach her this concept, two things will probably happen: (1) she'll stay motivated toward learning to read, and (2) she'll develop the type of mental set that will cause her to read for meaning rather than merely for "sounding out the words" or for "getting the diggy-nabbed assignment done."

On the other hand, if Karen begins to perceive reading as nothing more than sounding out words, filling in blanks, and handing in assignments, you may have a "reluctant reader" on your hands—or at best one who thinks of "school reading" as entirely different from "real reading." From the very beginning of her school days, Karen needs to be helped to perceive reading as an enjoyable process of communicating with authors.

But let's talk about authors for a moment. You've seen many of them, no doubt, on television talk shows or in person. Perhaps you're an author yourself, or you know one personally. At any rate, you would probably agree that authors have very little in common as far as personality or physical characteristics go. But they do have one need in common. They all need to communicate. More specifically, they all need to entertain or inform.

As you could see from my account of four philosophers from Zania, I was trying both to entertain and to inform my readers—as if I were a personal friend, telling them something I knew about reading in as interesting a way as I could. And this is the way most authors seem to look at their writing—as a means of communicating with people by sharing ideas and feelings. This is true whether the author is trying to write a best-selling novel, a cookbook, or a "Dick-and-Jane" story designed to help first graders learn to read. (Even with a "Dick-and-Jane"-type story, created as a teaching device, the author does try to communicate some type of message.) Once teachers thoroughly grasp this point, some interesting things begin to happen: (1) they notice that they are more inclined to have children read to understand the author's message rather than merely to pronounce the words; (2) they find themselves asking children "What does the *author* say?" rather than, "What does the *book* say?"; and (3) they find themselves asking children fewer questions about the extraneous details in a reading passage and more questions about the important ideas or feelings the author wishes to share.

What I'd really like to persuade you to believe (and to pass on to children) is that authors and readers do communicate. You and I are having a form of conversation right now. It's true that we're missing an important ingredient in any good conversation—your ability to influence what I have to say directly. This is unfortunate. If you *could* influence me, I would then modify what I have to say to respond to your ideas and questions—and even your facial expressions. But we *are* having a conversation. You're doing with me just what you do when you chat with other people. You're "listening" to my words; you're predicting what I'm going to say next; you're agreeing or disagreeing with me; and you're even having thoughts about me as a person—"he's nice," "he's obnoxious," "he's interesting," "he's weird," and so on.

As a mature reader, you normally read as if some type of communication were actually taking place. Sometimes this may take the form of imagining yourself listening to the author speaking to you. At other times it may take the form of actually becoming the author—entertaining or informing yourself. This last form is particularly true when you're reading the fast-paced exciting parts of a novel, devouring the words like popcorn. In either case, whether you're "listening" to the author or taking the author's place, you're engaged in real communication.

But what about writing itself? Do you think of this activity as something directly related to reading? Do we read when we write? Does writing help children learn to read better? Is an author, writing for children, better understood by children who write also? The answer to at least the last three questions seems to be a resounding "Yes." In Chapters 3, 5, and 7, I'll be talking to you about this.

SOME OTHER CHOICES TEACHERS MUST MAKE BEFORE READING INSTRUCTION BEGINS

During the weeks before school begins in the fall, and also during the first few weeks of school, teachers have to make many decisions related to their program of reading instruction. In addition to deciding which definition of reading will most influence their instructional practices, they have many other types of decisions to make. Mrs. Blanchard, for instance, teaches in a first-grade, self-contained classroom. This is her second year of teaching, and she is trying to decide whether to continue using a basal-reader program or to begin the year with a language-experience approach. With the basal-reader program, as described in Chapter 9, she is provided with several basal readers, at various levels of reading difficulty, that are full of fictional stories, poems, informational articles, and plays. She has teacher guides and workbooks to go with each basal reader, and tests and other materials that correlate with each of the readers.

On the other hand, she's wondering if she might like to try a language-experience approach, at least as a modification of the basal-reader program. With this approach, as described in Chapter 7, children create much of their own reading material by dictating stories and ideas to the teacher

or teaching aide. With this approach, children can more readily perceive reading as a communication process, rather than a mere "sound-it-out" process.

A second decision Mrs. Blanchard has to make is how to group her students for instruction. She knows that the experience of reading should be success-filled; therefore, she doesn't want to instruct her students with materials that are too difficult. She decides to group her children primarily on the basis of an informal reading inventory. With this technique, described fully in Chapter 10, each child reads a small portion from several of the basal readers. After listening to a child read, the teacher decides which reader is at the appropriate level of difficulty for the child and into which group he should be placed.

A third decision for Mrs. Blanchard, and one she must continue to make throughout the year, is what specific help each child needs in becoming a better reader. This she decides through the administration of diagnostic tests (described in Chapter 10), through observation during lessons, through examination of worksheet and workbook results, through individual conferences (described in Chapter 8), and possibly through the use of a skills-management system (described in Chapter 9).

A fourth decision Mrs. Blanchard faces is that of readiness. How ready are the children for reading instruction? Do they all have good auditory- and visual-discrimination skills? That is, can they tell the differences between letter shapes and sounds? Have they learned good listening skills? Can they follow directions? These questions she'll have to answer by examining the results of reading-readiness tests (as described in Chapter 6), observing during lessons, and generally getting to know each child personally.

Mr. Nicholson and Miss Porter, a fifth-grade teaching team, have no fewer choices to make than does Mrs. Blanchard. Their biggest decision so far has been whether to use an individualized approach, in which children read library books (described in Chapter 8), a basal-reader approach, or a combination of the two approaches. With any of these methods, they need to have a good idea of each child's instructional level. Therefore, like Mrs. Blanchard, they decide to use an informal reading inventory. And, like Mrs. Blanchard, they are concerned about readiness. They realize that readiness is important in all the grades and not just in kindergarten and first grade.

READING AS A SOCIAL PROCESS

Perhaps by now it goes without saying that reading is a social process. That is, it involves the willingness on the part of readers and authors to communicate with each other. The authors have to want to communicate their ideas so badly that they stay up late at night writing, revising, polishing, until the information or entertainment they want (need) to provide seems clear or amusing or beautiful or exciting (or, perhaps, in the case of textbooks, not overly burdensome). The readers, on the other hand, have to want to communicate with the author so badly that they stay up late at night reading, studying, pondering (or, in the case of a good novel, gulping) until the information or entertainment they want (need) also seems clear or amusing or beautiful or exciting (or not overly burdensome).

While the process of reading is a social act, however, the process of learning to read is even more so. Research (Bawden et al., 1978; Bond & Dykstra, 1967; Chall, 1967; Dykstra, 1968; Gove, 1981) shows us again and again that the teacher is the most important variable in how well a child learns to read. The teacher's self-confidence (which comes partly through his or her knowledge of how to teach reading) seems to be an important factor. The teacher's enthusiasm is another. The teacher's organizational ability is a third. And the teacher's communication of warmth or caring is another.

In most cases, but not all, the teacher's ability to communicate with a child seems to be more important than the child's intelligence quotient, the state of his home life, or any other genetic or environmental factor. This presents a tremendous challenge to teachers—particularly in situations in which they do not get as much parental, societal, and administrative support and assistance as they need. But it appears to be a fact of life.

It's teachers who make the difference. It's their enthusiasm for reading good books to themselves and to their students. It's their awareness of strategies—those that encourage children to look for ideas and feelings that authors wish to share and not just those that bind children to filling blanks with correct answers (as useful as this sometimes can be). It's their ability to organize the instructional time and materials in such a way that steady growth in reading ability can take place. It's their concern for children and their future. It's all these things and much more that cause teachers to make the difference. And teachers do make the difference.

SUMMARY OF MAIN IDEAS

The way you think about the reading process will influence the way you teach reading.

A behaviorist, "bottom-up" theory of reading encourages a teacher to emphasize decoding more than comprehension, to be more concerned with word accuracy than with understanding an author's message.

A gestaltist, "top-down" theory of reading encourages more emphasis on comprehension, with less emphasis on subskill practice and tests and on word-by-word accuracy.

Teachers must make many choices before (and during) instruction, and one is the choice of emphasis on units of language.

Teachers make a major difference in children's success or failure to read well.

REFERENCES AND SUGGESTED READING

Artley, A. S. (1980). Reading: Skills or competencies. *Language Arts, 57,* 546–549.

Barr, R., & Duff, G. (1978). *Teachers' conceptions of reading: The evolution of a research study* (Research Series No. 17). East Lansing, MI: Michigan State University, Institute for Research on Teaching.

Bawden, R., Buike, S., & Duffy, G. (1979). *Teacher conceptions of reading and their influences on instruction* (Research Series No. 47). East Lansing, MI: Michigan State University, Institute for Research on Teaching.

Bond, G. L., & Dykstra, R. (1967). The cooperative research program in first-grade reading instruction. *Reading Research Quarterly, 2,* 5–142.

Chall, J. (1967). *Learning to read: The great debate.* New York: McGraw-Hill.

Downing, J. (1982). Reading—skill or skills? *Reading Teacher, 35,* 534–537.

Dykstra, R. (1968). Summary of the second grade phase of the cooperative research program in primary instruction. *Reading Research Quarterly, 1,* 49–70.

Goodman, K. (1971). Reading: A psycholinguistic guessing game. In H. Singer & R. Ruddell (Eds.), *Theoretical models and processes of reading* (pp. 259–271). Newark, DE: International Reading Association.

Gough, P. (1972). One second of reading. In J. Kavanagh & I. Mattingly (Eds.), *Language by ear and by eye* (pp. 331–358). Cambridge, MA: MIT Press.

Gove, M. K. (1983). Clarifying teachers' beliefs about reading. *Reading Teacher, 37,* 216–268.

Gove, M. K. (1981). *The influence of teachers' conceptual frameworks of reading on their instructional decision making.* Unpublished doctoral dissertation, Kent State University, Kent, Ohio.

Harst, J., & Burke, C. (1977). A new hypothesis for reading teacher research: Both teaching and learning of reading are theoretically based. In P. D. Pearson & J. Hansen (Eds.), *Reading: Theory, research and practice,* Twenty-sixth Yearbook of the National Reading Conference. Clemson, S.C.: National Reading Conference.

Koffka, K. (1928). *The growth of mind: An introduction to child psychology.* London: Routledge and Kegan Paul.

Kohler, W. (1915). Opteshe untersuchungen am chimpanse rind am haushuh. *Abhandlungen preussiccche physichemathematishe klasse. Akademic der wisenshaften,* M. 3.

Krechevsky, I. (1932). Hypotheses in rats. *Psychology Reviews, 39,* 516–532.

McNeil, J. D. (1974). False prerequisites in the teaching of reading. *Journal of Reading Behavior, 6,* 421–427.

Otto, J. (1982). The new debate in reading. *Reading Teacher, 36,* 14–18.

Rumelhart, D. (1976). *Toward an interactive model of reading* (Technical Report No. 56). San Diego: Center for Human Information Processing.

Shannon, P. (1982). Some subjective reasons for teachers' reliance on commercial reading materials. *Reading Teacher, 35,* 884–889.

Smith, F. (1971). *Understanding reading.* New York: Holt, Rinehart, & Winston.

Stennett, R. G., Smythe, P. C., & Hardy, M. (1975). Hierarchical organization of reading subskills: Statistical approaches. *Journal of Reading Behavior, 7,* 223–238.

Thomas, E. L., & Robinson, H. A. (1977). *Improving reading in every class.* Boston: Allyn & Bacon.

Weaver, P. (1978). *Research within reach, a research-guided response to concerns of reading educators.* Washington, D.C.: National Institute of Education.

APPLICATION EXPERIENCES FOR THE TEACHER EDUCATION CLASS

A. *What's your opinion?* Discuss why you agree or disagree with the following opinions. If you do this in a small group, compare your decisions with other groups. You are encouraged to use short quotations from the textbook, but most of your discussion should be in your own words. Use your own experiences and observations to help explain your point of view; this will help make the ideas *yours. Making inferences and value judgments is the goal in this experience rather than reciting correct answers.*

1. Teachers should teach according to their beliefs about learning.

2. The author, May, is obviously pushing the behaviorist view of learning and reading.

3. The subskill approach is a bottom-up, behaviorist view of reading.

4. Teaching and testing subskills is the only way to assure that children learn to read well.

5. The gestaltist, top-down view of reading makes more sense than the behaviorist, bottom-up view.

6. The most important influence on the child's reading ability is the home.

B. *Miscue Analysis:* When a reader makes a mistake it is often referred to as a miscue. Find Jennifer's miscues in the following passage. What can you tell about Jennifer's concepts of reading? Does she seem to perceive reading as mostly a decoding operation (translating written symbols into speech sounds) or does she appear to perceive it mostly as a comprehension operation (discovering the author's meaning)? Is reading, to Jennifer, like telling a story?

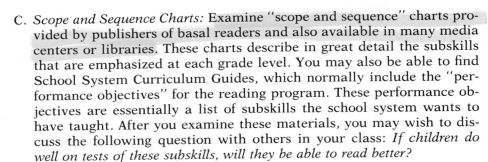

Author*

"I didn't hear you!" Walter said.
"I called and called," his mother said.
"I had the radio on," Walter said. "I couldn't hear you."
"Well, you can now," his mother said.
"I want you to go to the store."

Jennifer, 3rd grade

"I don't hear you!" Walter said.
"I cannot call," his mother said.

"I have a radio on," Walter said. "I cannot hear you."
"Will you come now?" his mother said.
"I want you to go to the store."

C. *Scope and Sequence Charts:* Examine "scope and sequence" charts provided by publishers of basal readers and also available in many media centers or libraries. These charts describe in great detail the subskills that are emphasized at each grade level. You may also be able to find School System Curriculum Guides, which normally include the "performance objectives" for the reading program. These performance objectives are essentially a list of subskills the school system wants to have taught. After you examine these materials, you may wish to discuss the following question with others in your class: *If children do well on tests of these subskills, will they be able to read better?*

FIELD EXPERIENCES IN THE ELEMENTARY SCHOOL CLASSROOM

A. *Informally* interview several children, one at a time, to see if you can determine what their concepts of reading are. Ask them questions such as these:

1. What do you think reading is?

2. When you were younger, did you think reading was something else?

3. Do you think that reading is mainly pronouncing the words or understanding the words?

4. What is an author?

5. When you read, do you try to understand what the author is telling you?

6. Do you have a favorite author?

*Bank Street College of Education, "Walter's Walkie-Talkie Machine," *Green Light, Go,* Rev. Ed. (New York: Macmillan, 1972). Reprinted by permission of the publisher.

7. Do you think reading is like listening to someone tell you something?

8. When you read, do you ever pretend that *you* are telling the story?

9. Do you have a favorite book? Why is it your favorite?

After you have finished each interview, jot down what you think are the child's concepts of reading. If possible, share your results with others in your reading class.

B. As you watch another teacher teach reading, see if you can determine whether that teacher has more of a top-down or bottom-up view of reading. Use Table 1.1 as a guide to your observations. Keep records and compare your findings with others in your reading class.

2 WHAT ARE GOOD AND POOR READERS LIKE? AN INTERACTIVE VIEW

CHAPTER PREVIEW*

When we teach reading, we need to keep models of good readers in our mind—that is, what do good readers do that makes them read with fluency and comprehension? But first in this chapter we'll look at some poor readers, so you'll have a better idea of the kinds of readers you *don't* want to "produce." As mentioned in Chapter 1, teachers can have a major impact on children's success or lack of success in becoming good readers. After we look at both good and poor readers, we'll talk

*Just a reminder that research (Thomas & Robinson, 1977) shows that readers who read the subheadings and preview a chapter before they read it tend to understand a chapter better than those who skip these two steps.

about the way good readers use inferences, "schemata," and metacomprehension to understand what they read. This will lead into an explanation of a major theme of the book—that reading is an interactive process, involving the interplay of several thought processes at the same time and making use of our incredibly complex brain.

Humans are creatures who build roads—and roads—and roads. Since some humans don't know where they're going, I suppose any one of those roads will get them there.

James, a fourth grader who likes to read:
"Reading is when you fall into your imagination."

Margaret, a fourth grader who likes to read:
"The book is putting on a play and you picture it in your head."

David, a fourth grader who hates to read:
"Reading is hard work . . . It's no fun."

Valerie, a poor reader in third grade:
AUTHOR: The rangers had marked off a place for people to cut trees.
VALERIE: "The rangers had market of a plack for people to cut trees."

A LOOK AT POOR READERS

The author I just quoted (Dunkeld, 1979, p. 5) is trying to tell Valerie (in written form) that the forest rangers had marked off a place for people to cut Christmas trees. Valerie, though, is content with her own rendition, that the rangers had *market of* a *plack* for people to cut trees. Why is she satisfied with *market* instead of *marked*, with *of* instead of *off*, with *plack* instead of *place*? Is this because she doesn't *know* the words she has missed? Or is it more complicated than that?

Let's look at her first two miscues, *market of* for *marked off*. The rangers had *market of* doesn't make sense, does it? It doesn't sound right because *market of* doesn't fit the syntax (the order and types of words expected). Valerie would never *talk* this way, but she's content to *read* this way. Why is this? Maybe it's because of her concept of reading. Even though Valerie is only eight years old, perhaps she has already developed too much of a bottom-up view of reading. To her, reading may be a word-by-word operation—to read is to come up with a word for the next set of letters, then the next, and then the next. She doesn't seem to have developed the concept that reading is a process of creating sense out of what an author has written. She doesn't go back and correct any of her three mistakes. She just "plods" on, as Alpha put it, trying to come up with one word after the other, *market* for *marked*, *of* for *off*, and *plack* for *place*.

> **Miscue:** a reader's substitution, omission, insertion, or repetition of a word

Suppose we check our theory about Valerie's miscues by looking at Valerie's third miscue. Here she's content to read: "a *plack* for people to cut trees." But *plack* isn't even a word, you say. Well, actually, *plack* is what they used to call a small coin in Scotland back in the sixteenth century, but I doubt that Valerie had that in mind, don't you? So what does this new evidence tell us? Not only is she willing to substitute words that don't fit the syntax of the sentence, she's also willing to substitute nonsense words. Her problem is worse than we thought, then; for her substitution of *plack* indicates that her concept of reading is quite far from the mark. To her, reading may be merely the process of making wordlike *sounds* in response to sets of letters. But perhaps she has learned to respond according to her training. Is it possible that she's actually been reinforced for coming up with word-noises and meaningless substitutions? If so, then how could such reinforcement possibly take place? In Chapter 3 we will spend a considerable amount of time discussing the answer to this question. For now, though, let's look at what research says about poor readers.

An award-winning study by Beebe (1979–80) shows that those children who are willing to make substitutions that don't fit the syntax of the sentence tend to score low on comprehension tests. Researchers Englart and Semmel (1981) found that the same was true for those willing to make *nonsense* substitutions. Valerie, you'll remember, made both types of substitutions. As these two studies show, poor readers usually concentrate more heavily on decoding (translating print into sound) than on understanding. Valerie, for example, is far less aware than good readers that the purpose of reading is to make sense of a passage.

But how else do poor readers differ from good readers? Let's look at another third-grader named Cora. (Lest you fear from my examples that most poor readers are girls, let me add that the vast majority are boys.) In the same story Valerie read is this passage:

> "What do you mean?" said Pete. "They don't let you just go into the forest and cut trees."
> "Yes they do," said Cathy. "You have to buy a permit first."

Cora read the passage just fine until she got to the word *permit*. For *permit* she substituted the word *permanent*. Because of her particular background, perhaps, Cora chose to talk about buying a permanent rather than a permit, even though the story was about cutting a Christmas tree in the forest. In other words, poor readers are not only willing to ignore the *syntactic* context, they are also willing to ignore the *semantic* context (meaning). In this particular case, the word *permanent* fits the syntactic context all right. "You have to buy a permanent first" *sounds* all right. But it doesn't fit the *semantic* context, since the author is not talking about *hair* at all. Like Valerie, Cora was willing to come up with a *word* she thought was correct even though the *meaning* couldn't be correct.

> So, what do we have so far? Poor readers tend to make the kinds of substitutions when they read that they would never make when they speak. While they treat speaking and listening as meaningful communication processes, they treat reading as a meaningless word-calling task. Reading, to them, is a bottom-up view (of letters) without a top (message) in sight!

While part of poor readers' troubles seems to result from their wrong idea of what reading really is, another part often relates to the very thing they emphasize the most when they read—they concentrate on decoding, but their decoding skills are often weak. Travis, a second-grader, will now demonstrate this for us by reading a story designed for early first grade. Every time Travis defaults on a word for at least five seconds (doesn't say the word), the teacher tells him the word. A default is shown with a d.

Mary has a $\overset{d}{\text{dog}}$. His name is $\overset{d}{\text{Rex}}$. He is little. He is brown. He likes to play.

He likes to run. He runs fast. Mary $\overset{d}{\text{follows}}$ him. Then he stops. He can do

$\overset{d}{\text{tricks}}$. He sits up. He rolls $\overset{d}{\text{over}}$. He $\overset{d}{\text{shakes}}$ hands. He can $\overset{d}{\text{swim}}$. He swims in the river. He gets wet. Mary picks him up. Then she gets wet. She puts

him down. He shakes himself. Then he is dry. "Good dog," says Mary. She

likes her dog.*

Although Travis is now in second grade, he has considerable trouble with this early first-grade story. Why? It's not because he's making unsuitable substitutions. He seems to lack the confidence even to *try* making substitutions. For instance, even after finding out that the dog can do tricks and can sit up, Travis doesn't try to complete this sentence: "He rolls _____." Travis just stares at the page until the teacher gives him the word. And when he finds out that the dog can swim, he confidently reads the next four words but stops on the fifth one: He swims in the r———.

So what's his problem, then? What is he afraid of? As you've probably guessed, Travis is afraid of making a mistake; he's afraid of predicting. But why? Well, for *some* poor readers, especially for those who are extrasensitive, it's because they've been *corrected* every time they've made a mistake. To them, a correction is like a rebuke. For other poor readers, their fear of making a mistake is caused by lack of enough sight words (words that are instantly recognizable). Their visual memory for words has not been sufficiently developed. (Chapter 4 shows how to use games, patterned books, and other activities to help this problem.) And for still others, their fear can be caused by their inability to notice common "phonics" patterns in words and syllables. (Chapter 5 provides ideas for dealing with this problem.)

A poor reader, then, ignores—or doesn't know how to use—one or more of the "cueing systems" that good readers use: *syntax* (the order and type of word expected next), *semantic cues* (the surrounding words that provide context and meaning to the unfamiliar words), and *graphophonic cues* (those cues obtained from spelling patterns and the sounds they represent). But a fourth cueing system is based on background experiences— with things, people, and oral language. The *poor* reader is often quite deficient in this respect. In the next two sections I'll explain these four cueing systems more thoroughly and show how good readers use them.

A LOOK AT GOOD READERS

Author	Bobby
The rangers had marked off	The rangers had market off—had marked off
a place for people to	the place for the people
cut trees.	to cut their trees.

---

*Colin Dunkeld, Portland Informal Reading Inventory, Form P. Unpublished manuscript, Portland State University, School of Education. Reprinted by permission of the author.

Bobby is a good reader in the third grade. He enjoys reading, he reads with good intonation as if he were telling the story himself, and he scores high on reading comprehension tests. And yet, a teacher with a strictly bottom-up view of reading (letters and words are the most important units) might consider Bobby a poor reader. After all, in a twelve-word sentence, he makes four "mistakes." He says *market* for *marked*, he says *the place* for *a place*, he inserts *the* before *people* and *their* before *trees*. Whew, that's a lot of mistakes. But rest assured that good readers don't miscue that often in every sentence. On the other hand, they do tend to make more "errors" than a teacher would like—if the teacher has word-accuracy as his major goal.

Why do they make such errors? Is it because they don't "know" the words? Let's look. At first Bobby says *market* for *marked*. Is this because he doesn't know the word *marked*? No, he knows it, all right. It's just that he allows himself to be fooled for a moment by the two words' great similarity in physical appearance. But only for a split second, and then he corrects himself, probably because *market* doesn't fit the syntactic cues in the passage. *The rangers had market off* simply doesn't sound right, for one thing. And a word like *market* doesn't go with a word like *had* unless you put the word *a* between them (had a market).

So let's look at his second "mistake": *the place* for *a place*. Does Bobby not know the word *a*? A reader with great comprehension and love of reading? Of course he knows it. But in this particular passage he predicts the word *the* will follow *marked off* and come before *place*. And since it works so well, he sticks with it (just the way you and I do when we read). But what about his last two miscues? What two words does he miss? Look back at his rendition and see if you can find the last two words he misses.

Couldn't find two misses, could you? That's right; rather than *miss* two words he *inserts* them—again, just as we do when we're "on a roll" and reading well. According to Bobby's version of the story, the rangers had marked off *the* place for *the* people to cut *their* trees. Did Bobby get the author's message? Was his comprehension good? Yes, on both counts. Otherwise he wouldn't have been able to make such meaningful miscues.

From a bottom-up point of view, Bobby was expected to respond correctly to each word in the sentence. He was not expected to make a self-correction, a substitution, and two insertions. I'm sorry, Bobby, but that's four strikes against you. You had a chance to make 12 points on that 12-word sentence, but you get only 8 points. Eight out of twelve is only 67 percent; not a very good score.

From a top-down point of view, Bobby was expected to make hypotheses about the author's *meaning* as he read the sentence. He was expected to confirm his hypotheses as he sampled from the print. He was expected to understand the author's message. Well, judging from the four meaningful miscues he made, he did make the hypotheses, he sampled

enough of the print to confirm them, and he understood the author's message. Nice going, kid. (But then, you really don't need my praise, do you, since you were rewarded by your success in understanding the story.)

Now that we've had fun with Bobby, let's look at the research concerning good readers. Are these children the bright ones with high IQs? Not necessarily. There *is* a fairly strong relationship between high IQ scores and reading comprehension scores, but there are many children with an average or below average IQ who read quite well—and many with a high IQ who read quite poorly. There are numerous things that differentiate good from poor readers, but one of the most important is that of "reading concept." Good readers perceive reading as a form of communication; that is, they sense that there's a story or message being presented to them, and they use searching-type behavior to "ferret out" what's happening or what's being said.

This kind of hunting behavior leads them to attack a reading passage as if it were a totality—a whole living animal, rather than a pile of separate lifeless bones. Good readers don't slowly pick up each bone, with much phonetic huffing and puffing, and toss it aside, one bone at a time, until they have no bones left. They attack it the way you do when you pick up a newspaper or magazine and read your favorite columnist. With hope! With an expectation of a successful hunt, a hunt that leads to entertainment, information, ideas, good feelings. Part of their expectation comes from things like their home background, intelligence, and personality characteristics, but a great deal of it comes from the concept of reading that *teachers* have helped them develop.

This point, about the importance of teachers, will come up again and again in this book. But for now, let's look at what these expectations on the part of good readers lead to. According to the study by Mona Beebe (1979–80) that I mentioned earlier, children who score high on reading comprehension tests tend to be those who are more willing to risk making a mistake. They'll say something like *market* for *marked*, but as soon as they realize it doesn't fit the context, they'll correct their mistake. In other words, they make plenty of self-corrections as they read, the way you and I do. In fact, they correct twice as many substitutions as do poor readers (Weber, 1970). They also make plenty of substitutions, the kind that don't really change the author's essential message: *this* for *that*, *a* for *the*, *what* for *which*, even *she* for *he*, if they think the subject is a female rather than a male. And, as you'll often see in the examples I use in this book, they also tend to use meaningful insertions and omissions of words. As Karen D'Angelo and Marc Mahlios (1983, p. 778) found in their study, very few insertions or omissions ever distort the author's message. "Omission miscues," they say, "are often deliberate and represent meaningful interaction between the reader and text . . . As a reader develops proficiency, omissions tend to be well known words or redundancies . . . *Insertions increase as a reader gains proficiency.*" (Italics mine.)

THE FOUR CUEING SYSTEMS USED BY THE GOOD READER

As I mentioned, poor readers tend to ignore or have trouble with one or more of the cueing systems. They might pay attention to the letters but not the meaning. They might pay sufficient attention to the author's syntax and meaning but ignore a spelling pattern that would help them decode an unknown word. They may read something letter-perfect, but because of their insufficient background, not understand what it means. Good readers, on the other hand, allow the four cueing systems to interact as they read, thus providing themselves with four avenues of understanding at the same time.

Let's look once more at Bobby's way of describing what the forest ranger did. This time I'll give you a little more of the text and also show you a coding system that some researchers and teachers use:

> **Text:** a portion of a fiction or nonfiction selection

"We can go into the forest," said Cathy, "and cut our own tree." Next

Saturday the whole family drove to the forest. They found the ranger sta-

tion and bought a permit . . . The rangers had (MARKET marked off THE a place for THE peo-

ple to cut THEIR trees.

As this research code shows, Bobby read it this way: The rangers had market off—marked off the place for the people to cut their trees. (The big C around *market* and extended under the word *off* tells you that Bobby substituted *market* for *marked* and went right on to read the next word *off*; he then corrected *market off* to read *marked off*. This is a code you'll become skilled in using as you read the next few chapters. It is summarized in Chapter 10.)

In reading this sentence, Bobby probably used all four cueing systems to deal with the word *marked*. Unfortunately he relied too much on graphophonic cues at first and substituted *market*. But immediately the syntax and semantic cues from the previous sentences and from the words surrounding *marked* told him to make a self-correction. Furthermore, his background experiences must have helped him recognize the need for a self-correction; forest rangers are normally not found in a market, for example. The phrase *market off* is not one he is used to hearing, but *marked off* is one he may have heard in several different contexts. At any rate it is quite likely that Bobby used all four cueing systems to help him determine the author's message.

1. *Syntax cues:* those context hints provided by the *order* of the words in the sentence or by the *type* of word (noun, verb, adverb, adjective) expected in the next "slot." For example, we intuitively expect to read a noun or adjective following the word *the* when we see "The candy is in the _____. It's in the _____ bowl." As another example, we intuitively *expect* to read a verb in the following slot: The car _____ fast!

2. *Semantic cues:* those context hints provided by the meaning of the surrounding words. For example, when we see "The car _____ fast," we expect to read a word such as *moved* rather than *munched*.

3. *Graphophonic cues:* single letters or sets of letters, particularly their positions in words, and the speech sounds they represent. For example, the letter *y* stands for a very different sound at the beginning of a word than it does at the end of a word. If authors use *y* at the beginning, as they would for *yellow*, *yeast*, and *yuck*, they're telling the reader to think of a certain beginning sound. But they don't want the reader to think of the same sound at the end of two-syllable words, as in *belly*, *funny*, and *Betty*. The *position* of a letter is a major phonographic cue. As another example, the letter *a* stands for a different sound in *plan* and *plane*. Confusing the two would certainly make a difference in this sentence: "It's my plan," Jim said, "to sail across the ocean."

4. *Background cues:* memories, mental images, associations, or minitheories about the world that help the reader understand. These cues are based on past experiences and also on the language heard and spoken during those experiences. The word *plane*, for instance, can only be read with meaning after a child has seen a plane and heard the word applied to it: "My mom went on a plane to New York."

DO GOOD READERS DIFFER FROM POOR READERS IN THEIR DECODING SKILLS?

There are still other ways that good readers differ from poor readers. A teacher who wishes to push for a heavy phonics approach to reading instruction can find plenty of studies to show that good readers tend to have better decoding skills than poor readers—for example, they have a better sight vocabulary, better recognition of graphophonic patterns (phonics), and better awareness of suffixes. "Therefore," say some teachers, "just concentrate on sight words, phonics, and suffixes and you'll produce good readers."

Now, there's something a bit tricky here—a little like the chicken and the egg question. Do good readers become good readers because they study phonics, sight words, and suffixes? Or do they pick up phonics, sight words, and suffixes intuitively as they read more and more and more. What is the cause, and what is the effect? At present no one has a definite answer to this, but for now let me admit my bias: It's hard to beat reading as good training for reading.

Furthermore, the majority of good readers do show a better awareness of graphophonic cues, but some of them have learned to ignore them. They've learned to bluff their way through sentence after sentence, relying on background, syntax, and semantic cues, and using little more than first

> From my own experience in working with children and teachers, I'd have to say that teaching "phonics," sight words, and suffixes is indeed very important, but, it is definitely of secondary importance to helping children gain a love for reading and a concept of reading as a sharing of ideas and stories.

letters for their graphophonic cues. This works fine in the early grades, but later the bluffers get caught more and more in a game of wild guessing. By the time they reach high school, it becomes clear that they are not truly "good readers." A good reader learns to use all four cueing systems comfortably and confidently.

METACOMPREHENSION, INFERENCES, AND SCHEMATA

The good reader is not a bluffer in another sense as well. A good reader tends to know what she knows and what she doesn't know. We've already seen how a good reader is willing to use substitutions but self-corrects those which violate syntactic or semantic cues. Self-correcting is an example of knowing what you do and don't know. Another example occurs when a good reader tells herself that she doesn't understand a sentence or paragraph she has just read, so she goes back and reads it again. This type of self-correction is called *comprehension-monitoring* and is part of a process called *metacomprehension*. (The prefix "meta" means *after* or *along with*.) All of you reading this book are undoubtedly good at metacomprehension or you wouldn't be so successful in understanding what you read. By the time good readers get into sixth grade, many of them are already experienced with this process. In Chapter 3, we'll talk about helping poor and average readers learn it too.

The good reader also tends to be better than poor readers in making inferences as he reads. Researchers Diane Lapp and James Flood (1984) have found, in fact, that a good reader processes *inferences in his head* even more than he processes sentences on paper. Let me give you an example of this from our now famous story of the forest ranger. When we last left Cathy and Pete, they had bought a permit and were ready to cut down their own Christmas tree.

"Look at that one," said Cathy. "It's perfect."
"No, it's not," said Pete. "It's way too small."

To understand these two sentences, you must make several inferences. You might infer, for example, that Cathy is pointing to some kind of evergreen tree when she says, "Look at that one." When she says, "It's perfect," you might infer that it has a conical shape, that its color is pleasing, that it's a good size for your living room, and so on. And when Pete says, "It's way too small," you might infer that it's a "baby tree" or it's about three feet high or that Pete is just envious because Cathy found it first. At any rate, you would make numerous inferences just in understanding those two simple sentences. Not that you would make such inferences consciously. The good reader makes them instantaneously and intuitively (Lapp & Flood, 1984). Unfortunately, the poor reader often does not (Carr, 1983), although it is possible, as we'll see in Chapter 3, to do something about this problem.

This leads us to one other way that good readers shine and poor readers don't. There's a special type of inferring that *you* do, I'm sure, whenever you read a story. You infer that it's going to follow some kind of pattern you've run across before—such as boy meets girl, they fall in love, boy loses girl, boy gets girl back again, and they live together happily ever after (even though sometimes they live together for ten years and then get a divorce). In other words, in your head you carry around several outlines or organizations for stories. Reading researchers call a mental outline like this is a *schema*; when they talk about more than one schema, they use the word *schemata*, the plural of schema. These schemata are minitheories that help us predict what is coming next when we listen to or read a story. At the beginning of a story we expect the main character or characters to appear in some kind of setting. We expect some kind of problem to arise before too long, and we expect the characters to react to the problem. As we read the written material (called *text* by researchers), we wait expectantly for our minitheories to be confirmed. As Marshall puts it, "The closer the reader's organization is to that of the text, the greater comprehension is likely to be" (1983, p. 616).

We use schemata when we read story text and when we read informational text. For purposes of reading a story the schema in our head is a little like the outline or "query letter" an author sends to an editor to pique her interest. Whereas the outline provides the editor with descriptions of characters, scenes, and the order of the action, a schema provides the *reader* with *anticipations* of those story elements. For purposes of reading *informational* text, however, the schema in our heads is more like a page from a *College Outline* book, but with lots of "empty slots" for us to fill in. In other words, as we read more and more informational text, we get used to the ways authors describe or explain things to us. We wait with mild (perhaps meager) anticipation for the author to fill in those slots that lie empty in our schema.

Lapp and Flood (1984) report that good readers are quite adept at predicting how authors are going to present what they have to say, whether

the authors are telling a story or providing information to the reader. Flood presented this sentence to good readers: "Christmas always meant going to Grandma's house," and asked them to write a second sentence to go with it. What do *you* think the second sentence should be like? Should it be like this: "There we ate turkey, pumpkin pie, and cranberry sauce, and played with all the farm animals"? If so, your schema for this scene would include the notion that grandmothers live on farms and love to stuff their guests with delicious food. Actually this is the *type* of sentence that Flood got from his subjects—a sentence that was highly descriptive "about the event of Christmas." Then he asked his subjects to respond to this sentence: "One of the oldest drinks known to man is milk." What kind of second sentence do you think they wrote? Should it be like this: "Maybe this is because milk is so nutritious"? Flood (1976) found that all the subjects came up with an informative second sentence that tied in with the first, indicating that good readers can use their background schemata to anticipate the kind of text that will be coming—narrative, nonnarrative, formal, informal, humorous, serious. Again we see that good readers *attack* what they read, armed with schemata, with hypotheses to confirm or deny, with "empty slots" they expect the author to fill in with informational or story-type data. Good readers are active hunters and gatherers, with purposes of their own.

AN INTERACTIVE THEORY OF READING

> Tell me, I'll forget. Show me, I may remember. But in-
> volve me and I'll understand.
>
> —*Chinese Proverb*

The schemata that help to guide us as we read are not limited to scen-
arios or outlines or expectations about the styles that authors will use. They
seem to be much more pervasive than that. When a little girl says to her
mother, "My legs are all out of breath," we know exactly what she means,
don't we? And we know intuitively how she came up with her conclusion—
her past experiences of "running out of breath" acted as a kind of filter for
understanding the sensations in her legs. The phrase "out of breath" became part of a schema or minitheory for explaining what happens whenever she exerts herself.

This is the way many of our schemata form as we grow up and learn
about the world. We put two and two together and sometimes, if we're
lucky, it comes out four the first time. Other times it comes out five or three
and we have to wait for other experiences to teach us that we were wrong.
Bobby, the good reader who seemed to realize that a forest ranger would
be more likely to *mark* something than to market it, must have already
developed a schema related to "forest ranger." This schema might include
the ideas that a forest ranger wears a khaki uniform, fights fires, collects
money from campers, and even marks off a place for cutting Christmas
trees. And with this "forest ranger" schema and other schemata (such as a
minitheory on the nature of Christmas trees and where they might be
found), he was able to predict what the author was going to say and to
understand what he did say.

> **Schemata:** minitheories about things, people, lan-
> guage, places, and other phenomena in our back-
> ground of experiences (Plural of *schema*)

Rumelhart (1984) has been engaged in schemata research for several
years at the Center for Human Information Processing at the University of
California at San Diego. Besides his contributions related to schemata, he
has often been given credit for developing a major "interactive theory of
reading." In this section of the chapter, I will explain this theory to you
and invite you to consider it as a possible guide to your own teaching of
reading. Actually, I've been explaining his interactive theory throughout

the chapter, but now that we've talked about schemata, you'll be able to understand his theory even better. I like some of the examples Rumelhart uses. For instance, what schemata are set in motion in your head as you read these next two sentences?

> "Mary heard the ice cream truck coming down the street. She remembered her birthday money and rushed into the house." (Rumelhart, 1984, p. 1)

All right, let's check your schemata. How old do you think Mary is? Jot down her age if you wish, and we'll see if you change your mind later. Okay, why do you think she rushed into the house? If you have your answer clearly in mind, then we're ready to move on to the next two sentences:

> "Mary heard the bus coming down the street. She remembered her birthday money and rushed into the house." (Rumelhart, 1984, p. 1)

How old is the Mary in *this* scene? And why did this Mary rush into the house? Did your answers change? Did you find that Mary got older and that her reason for rushing into the house changed, even though we only changed *ice cream truck* to *bus*?

Let's try it again. Instead of changing the ice cream truck to a bus, we'll leave the ice cream truck alone. Here are the next two sentences:

> "Mary heard the ice cream truck coming down the street. She remembered her gun and rushed into the house." (Rumelhart, 1984, p. 2)

How did your answers change this time? Did Mary's age change again? And what was she going to do that the other two Marys had no intention of doing? What really happened when we changed *birthday money* to *gun*?

Rumelhart feels that when we read something like these sentences, we put our schemata (the minitheories in our head) to work to help us make inferences about what's really happening. If we read that Mary heard the ice cream truck coming down the street, we immediately make inferences about her age, about the nature of the truck, and the nature of her desires. It's no surprise to read that she remembered her birthday money and rushed into the house. It's quite easy to infer that her birthday money is hers to spend any way she wishes and that she is about to make excellent use of it.

On the other hand, if we read that Mary heard the *bus* coming down the street, we make use of a different set of schemata. Now, instead of a little girl eager for sugary delights, we might infer things about an older girl or a woman waiting for the bus to take her to work. So we retrieve those schemata related to such things as waiting for buses, ignoring the stares of strangers, and so forth. But the author comes up with "Mary remembered her birthday money . . . ." Now we're forced to change our hypothesis and make new inferences. Maybe her decision to take a bus was a sudden one and she has no money with her. Maybe her birthday money is all she has to her name, poor soul.

In the third pair of sentences we read that Mary heard the ice cream truck coming down the street. So we get set with our schemata related to ice cream trucks and little children longing to dirty up their T-shirts. But the author comes up with "She remembered her gun and rushed into the house." This requires a severe shift in our schemata, doesn't it? Instead of thinking about birthday money in a nice little girl's treasure box, we have to shift our thinking to something like a .25 automatic pistol in a not-so-nice older girl's bureau drawer. Having changed our schemata, we now change our inferences as well. Instead of inferring that Mary is merely going to *purchase* a creamsicle, we now infer she's going to steal one—along with all the money in the till.

> From an interactive viewpoint, the words "rushed into the house" change in meaning as the author changes *ice cream truck* to *bus* or as he changes *birthday money* to *gun*. If you merely think about each *word* in the phrase "rushed into the house," you can't arrive at the author's meaning. The author's meaning is *outside* the words. It's in your head, where you've stored those types of organized hunches we're calling schemata. There is an interaction between the words of the author and the schemata of the reader.

According to Rumelhart, a reader is "constantly evaluating hypotheses about the most plausible interpretation of the text. Readers are said to have understood the text when they are able to find a configuration of hypotheses which offer a coherent account for the various aspects of the text" (1984, p. 3).

Of course, if a reader's experiences have not yet resulted in schemata necessary for making the right inferences, she will fail to comprehend what the author has said. Nearly every experience we have as we grow up helps us to develop minitheories or schemata. We create schemata about cars, for example—what they're for (to take daddies and mommies to work and children to the beach) and how they run (there's a big noisy gizmo under the hood that drinks gasoline and forces the wheels to go around). We create schemata about mommies too—what *they're* for (to take care of kids when they're lonely or hungry) and how *they* run (they have two fast-moving legs and a face that smiles or frowns at us, and they don't need help in getting dressed or parting their hair). We create thousands and thousands of schemata about things, people, actions, places, *and about language*. And as we grow older and wiser we keep modifying those schemata to make them match the new information we receive. Then, when we read, we apply our schemata to the written text. Our schemata help us to make inferences (about what's between the lines), to predict what the author is going to say next—even the order in which it will be said, and to understand the message (what the author means).

So by now you may understand better what I'm talking about when I say that reading is an interactive process. For one thing, an interaction takes place between the words we see in print and the way our mind has been storing and organizing our background of experiences. Earlier in the chapter I referred to this background as one of the four cueing systems. Now I think it would be more accurate to call it the *schematic cueing system*. We can say, then, that there's an interaction between the letters (graphophonic system) and the schematic system. But that's not all; remember that we have two other systems--the syntactic and semantic systems. It is Rumelhart's belief, and that of many other researchers (Brewer, 1972; de Beaugrande, 1984; Englert & Semmel, 1981; Goodman, 1971; Jones, 1982; Smith, 1979), that all four systems are constantly interacting as good readers read.

I think the best way to complete my explanation is to use you, the reader, as an experimental subject. First, I'll give you a sentence, then I'll ask you predict the next sentence—one word at a time. All right? Here's the first sentence:

Mary looked down the snowy hillside and saw a lake.

What do you think the first word of the next sentence will be? Jot down your answers, please, before reading any further. Some people say "She," some say "It," some say "The." The author used the word "Three."

What word do you think will follow"Three?" (You might jot the entire sentence down as you create it. So far you would have "Three _____ . . .") If you've written down your prediction for the second word, you're ready to read on. Some people predict *skaters*, some say *birds*, some predict *deer*. What did you say? What made you say it?

Okay, the second word is *ducks*. Now here we go with the third word, but this time I'll give you a hint from each of the four cueing systems before you make your prediction:

Syntactic cue: The author has already said, "Three ducks . . ." What kind of word would you intuitively expect next? A verb like *paddle?* A noun like *water?* An adjective like *pretty?* An adverb like *noisily?* If you decide on a verb, should it be in the present or past tense?

Semantic cue: What verb goes best with "Three ducks. . .?

Schematic cue: What minitheories do you have about ducks, snow, and lakes that help you predict whether the verb will be *swam* or *waddled* or *slid* or *quacked?*

Graphophonic cue: Suppose I give you just the first letter. It's an *s.*

What do you think the third word is? "Three ducks s_____ . . ." Did you predict *skated?* Some people do. How about *slid* or *sat?* What if I give you a better graphophonic cue: the first *two* letters are *sw.* "Three ducks sw_____ . . . ." You're right, the first three words are "Three ducks swam . . . ." The fourth word is *in,* so what do you think the fifth word is? Both the semantic and syntactic cues would help you predict the word *the,* right?

So now we have: "Three ducks swam in the . . . ." And I'll bet you predict that the next word is *water,* right? Sorry, not right. The next word starts with the letter i_____. If you use your schematic cues, you'll come close, but let me give you a syntactic one as well. Here's the way the entire text looks so far:

Mary looked down the snowy hillside and saw a lake. Three ducks swam in the i_____ _____.

You're right. "Three ducks swam in the icy water." What you just demonstrated to yourself is the way a good reader must allow all four cueing systems to interact in order to read with accuracy and comprehension. In Figure 2.1 you can see how a child read the same two sentences. But she had it easier than you did, since both sentences were there to look at from the very beginning.

INTERACTIVE READING AND THE BRAIN

You are justified in asking how the human mind can possibly do so much as it helps us read. "To do all that," you might say, "would take a computer the size of a building." And you would be correct. It *would* take a computer that size to read with the intelligence that humans display when they read. Although computers have been "taught" to read (Dehn, 1984; Estes, 1983), they seem to get pretty mixed up if you give them text that is not extremely predictable. You can program them ahead of time with "schemata," but it would be difficult to program them with as many as human beings carry around in their heads. Furthermore, it would be difficult to program them to apply sufficient judgment as to which schemata really best fit the text.

Our brain, on the other hand, is quite capable of shifting gears numerous times during all those processes of helping us shift hypotheses, reminding us of previous experiences, feeding us ready-made schemata, and helping us pay attention to all four cueing systems *at the same time.* Our brains are much, much better in most respects than the best computers yet built and will probably outperform them indefinitely when it comes to creative thinking, judgment, and inferential thinking. It is now fairly well established that the human brain contains at least 100 billion neurons (nerve cells). That, in itself, is awe-inspiring, considering that this is one million times as many units as most computers have and that the brain only weighs about three pounds. Yet even more awe-inspiring is the idea that the number of interconnections among the brain's 100 billion neurons is, as Anthony Smith writes in *The Mind*, ". . . about as infinite as anything we know" (1984, p. 6). "It is certainly larger than the number of atoms presumed to exist in the entire universe . . ." (p. 4). But as a reading teacher, all you need to realize is that each one of those interconnections can provide the mind with another unit of information—a word, a memory, a speech sound. And several of these interconnections, probably working in concert, can provide us with an almost instantaneous schema.

Not that the brain is terribly fast. It's not as fast as electricity by any means, since the speed of transference between neurons is only around 200 miles per hour or roughly 300 feet per second. Is this really fast enough to do all the things I said a reader could do as she reads? Well, let's look at the brain a bit closer and see. When we get inside the brain we find a scene not at all like you see when you examine a computer chip through a magnifying glass. The computer chip looks like a well-laid-out set of city streets. The brain looks more like a mass—in miniature—of hopelessly tangled spaghetti and broccoli florets and extremely elongated parsley leaves. Each neuron has hundreds of thousands of "fingers" (dendrites and axons) reaching out in all directions toward other neurons. Some of them fold back and forth and are extremely long. And each one carries nerve impulses that jump to other dendrites or axons and excite other nerve cells. Sometimes the nerve impulse travels only a few inches before connecting with another nerve cell; sometimes several feet.

Let's do some imagining together for a moment. Suppose that during each second of time we will permit only *one* isolated nerve cell to be stimulated through our senses (a ridiculously impossible limitation). But as this lonely nerve cell is stimulated, it sends out nerve impulses at 300 feet per second along thousands of dendrites and axons toward other nerve cells. Are you with me so far?

Now let's suppose that the average distance for a nerve impulse to travel before it connects with (and stimulates) another nerve cell is about one foot. This would mean, at 300 feet per second, that we would have time

Mary looked down the snowy hillside and saw a lake. Three ducks swam in the icy water.

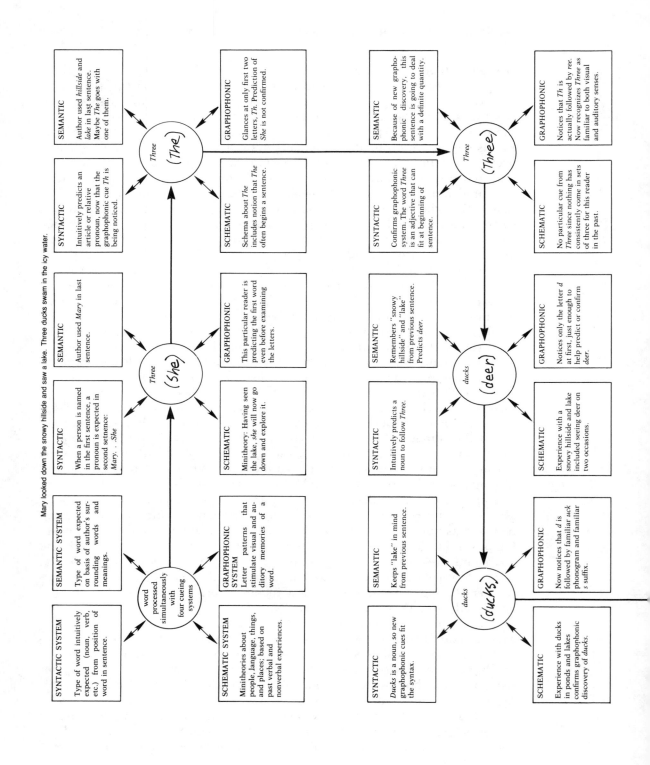

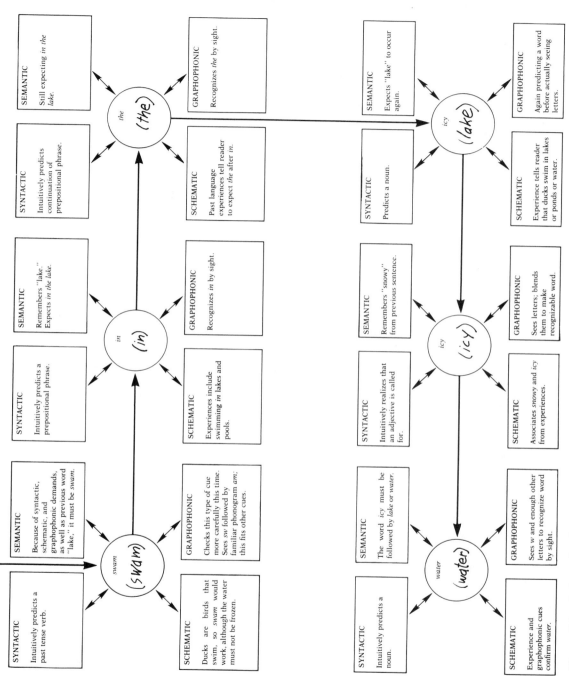

Figure 2.1 A Sample of Interactive Reading

for 300 interconnections with other nerve cells during a period of one second. Still with me?

All right. Let's bring in a child to read for us. But first we'll give him some rules. "Sorry, Johnny, but for every second that you read, we'll permit you to have only one brain cell stimulated by your senses." Johnny, being a compliant child, agrees to our limitation. So we give him one more rule. "Furthermore, Johnny, it's all right for that one nerve cell to send out impulses that stimulate other nerve cells, but no fair letting the other ones stimulate still other nerve cells." Johnny nods his head, and we're ready to begin.

Now, we know from research that the average elementary school child reads about two words per second (Sticht, 1984).* Can our subject, Johnny, maintain that reading rate with only 300 interconnections allowed per second? Well, it might be possible—since at two words per second he can *still* make 150 interconnections on each word that he reads. And with these 150 bits of information per word coming in, he might still get enough graphophonic, semantic, syntactic, and schematic cues to determine the pronunciations and meaning of the word.

We watch him with baited breath, our stopwatches poised to record his time. After five minutes we stop him and count the number of words he says he has read. *Voilà!* Still two words per second!

We're impressed, but the look in Johnny's eyes tell us that maybe he cheated. Maybe he didn't really restrict his senses from stimulating only one nerve cell per second. Maybe he didn't really restrict all those nerve cells from interacting with each other.

After reading up on this subject a little more, we decide to forgive Johnny. He couldn't really help himself from cheating. He might have *tried* to limit himself, but he had many, many more than 150 bits of information to work with on each word. For, with two words per second stimulating his mind, it's obvious that more than one nerve cell would be stimulated by the senses each second. More likely, thousands of cells would each be stimulating thousands of others during a one-second interval. Research on the retina of the eye shows that the amount of information our brain can generate in one second is indeed quite massive. Jeanne McDermott, in the April 1985 issue of the *Smithsonian*, reports that the retina (working with the brain) performs the equivalent of 10 billion calculations per second!

Are you convinced then, that our brain, with the help of our eyes, has the capacity to carry on interactive reading? Naturally, I hope so. But to me the rapid operation of the brain is only the tip of the iceberg. It is just one aspect of the total entity we call a human being. And the interactive

---

*Average high school student, 3 words; average college student, 4 words.

nature of the reading process, as marvelous as it is, is just one example of the potentially incredible capabilities of the learner.

SUMMARY OF MAIN IDEAS

Poor readers, on the average, tend to view reading incorrectly as primarily a decoding, word-calling process.

Poor readers are generally deficient in their concept of reading, their ability to use all four cueing systems in an interactive way, their visual memory of sight words, and their recognition of graphophonic patterns.

Good readers tend to view reading as a communication process between author and reader.

Good readers score high on comprehension tests, but in the process of comprehending a passage, they often make meaningful substitutions, self-corrections, omissions, and insertions. Teachers with a bottom-up theory of reading tend to view these miscues mistakenly as reading errors.

Good readers allow four types of cues to interact as they read: syntax cues, semantic cues, graphophonic cues, and schematic cues.

Schemata are minitheories of how our world—and all the ingredients important to us—operate. These schemata interact with the cues from the author's text to help the reader make hypotheses, inferences, and predictions.

The human brain permits so many interconnections per second among its nerve cells that it is easy for a good reader to pay attention to all four cueing systems in a way that seems simultaneous.

REFERENCES AND SUGGESTED READING

Beebe, M.J. (1979–80). The effect of different types of substitution miscues on reading. *Reading Research Quarterly, 15,* 124–136.

Brewer, W.F. (1972). Is reading a letter-by-letter process? In J. Kavanagh & I. Mattingly (Eds.), *Language by ear and by eye* (pp. 359–365). Cambridge, MA: MIT Press.

Carr, K.S. (1983). The importance of inference skills in the primary grades. *Reading Teacher, 36,* 518–522.

D'Angelo, K., & Mahlios, M. (1983). Insertion and omission miscues of good and poor readers. *Reading Teacher, 36,* 778–782.

de Beaugrande, R. (1984). The literacy of reading: Fact, fiction, or frontier? In J. Flood (Ed.), *Understanding reading comprehension* (pp. 45–74). Newark, DE: International Reading Association.

Dehn, M. (1984). An AI perspective on reading comprehension. In J. Flood (Ed.), *Understanding reading comprehension* (pp. 82–100). Newark, DE: International Reading Association.

Dunkeld, C. (1979). Portland informal reading inventory, Form P. Unpublished manuscript, Portland State University, School of Education.

Englert, C.S., & Semmel, M.I. (1981). The relationship of oral reading substitution miscues to comprehension. *Reading Teacher, 35,* 273–280.

Estes, T.H. (1983). A commentary on *Reading and Understanding: Teaching from the perspective of artificial intelligence. Reading Teacher, 36,* 483–490.

Flavel, J.H. (1979), Metacognition and cognitive monitoring: A new area of cognitive-developmental inquiry. *American Psychologist, 34,* 906–911.

Flood, J.E. (1978). The influence of first sentences on reader expectations within prose passages. *Reading World. 17,* 306–315.

Goodman, K. (1971). Reading: A psycholinguistic guessing game. In H. Singer & R. Ruddell (Eds.), *Theoretical models and processes of reading.* Newark, DE: International Reading Association.

Jones, L.L. (1982). An interactive view of reading: Implications for the classroom. *Reading Teacher, 35,* 772–777.

Lapp, D., & Flood, J. (1984). Promoting reading comprehension: Instruction which insures continuous reader growth. In J. Flood (Ed.), *Promoting reading comprehension* (pp. 273–288). Newark, DE: International Reading Association.

Marshall, N. (1983). Using story grammar to assess reading comprehension. *Reading Teacher, 36,* 616–628.

Rumelhart, D.D. (1984). Understanding understanding. In J. Flood (Ed.), *Understanding reading comprehension* (pp. 1–20). Newark, DE: International Reading Association.

Smith, A. (1984). *The mind.* New York: Viking.

Smith, F. (1979). *Reading.* Cambridge: Cambridge University Press.

Sticht, T.G. (1984). Rate of comprehension by listening or reading. In J. Flood (Ed.) *Understanding reading comprehension* (pp. 140–160). Newark, DE: International Reading Association.

Thomas, E.L., & Robinson, H.A. (1977). *Improving reading in every class.* Boston: Allyn & Bacon.

Weber, R.M. (1970). First graders' use of grammatical context in reading. In H.D. Levin & J.P. Williams (Eds.), *Basic studies in reading* (pp. 147–163). New York: Basic Books.

APPLICATION EXPERIENCES FOR THE TEACHER EDUCATION CLASS

A. *What's your opinion?* Discuss why you agree and/or disagree with the following opinions. If you do this in a small group, compare your decisions with other groups. You are encouraged to use short quotations from the textbook, but much of your discussion should be in your own words. Use your own experiences and observations to help you explain your point of view; this will help make the ideas *yours. Making inferences and value judgments is the goal in this experience rather than reciting correct answers.*

1. More than anything else, poor readers need to learn more sight words and phonics.

2. Good readers would tend to treat reading situations in about the same way they would treat listening situations.

3. Children should be encouraged to make any substitutions they wish.

4. Semantic cues are the most important cues for the reader.

5. Good readers are good simply because they've learned more words and more phonics.

6. The interactive theory of reading means that good readers just mix phonics with their background of experience and whiz right along.

7. Those schemata things are nothing more than our past experiences.

B. *Miscue Analysis:* With at least one other person, find the different ways Amy miscues in the following "text."

Author's Text	***Fifth Grader Amy's Miscues***
One cold (winter) day, a friend	Omitted *winter*
went into Dr. Jenner's small	No miscues in this line
office to talk over a problem. He	No miscues in this line
found the young scientist busy at *(that / science)*	Substituted *that* for *the* and *science* for *scientist*
his desk, working in his overcoat, *(as)*	Substituted *as* for *in*
gloves and boots, his nose red with *(He had)*	Inserted *He had* and treated comma as period
the chill. Dr. Jenner's friend	No miscues in this line

^R ^{rest}
could not resist the temptation

Repeated *could* and substituted *rest* for *resist*

^R
to laugh.

Repeated *to*

Do you think Amy repeats a word so as to give herself more time to think? Which of Amy's substitutions didn't change the author's meaning? How did the other three substitutions fit the syntax cues but not the semantic cues? Did Amy's omission and insertion change the author's meaning? Is Amy's concept of reading that reading is a process of getting an author's meaning? What do you think her concept is?

C. *Reading a Story Written in Applebet:* With the entire class or a small group, study the alphabet in Figure 2.2. You will use this alphabet, called *applebet*, for your graphophonic cueing system in reading the story in Figure 2.3 (on pp. 56–59) called "The Sam Trap." Before you

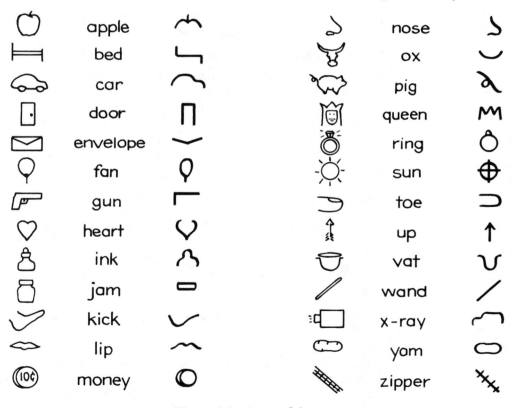

Figure 2.2   An Applebet

read this story, get to know the "applebet" better by writing your first and last names with it; then have at least three other students read your name. Then try reading "The Sam Trap" together.

D. *Discussing the Problems of a Beginning Reader:* Discuss the frustrations and feelings you had as you were reading "The Sam Trap." How might they be similar or different from beginning readers' experiences? Now discuss how you used the four cueing systems as you read. Share your examples with other people in the class.

FIELD EXPERIENCES IN THE ELEMENTARY SCHOOL CLASSROOM

A. Listen to one or more children read who are above their grade level in general reading ability. Then listen to one or more children read who are below their grade level in general reading ability. Compare the types of miscues they make. Do the high level readers make meaningful substitutions and self-corrections? What kinds of substitutions do the lower level readers make? If possible, use a tape recorder for this experience.

B. Informally interview several children to determine the development of their schemata—their minitheories about various aspects of the world. For instance, you might ask them about people of different occupations; for example: What is a farmer? What do farmers do? What is a secretary? What do secretaries do? What is a housewife? A teacher? A jockey?

Try other categories of schemata such as *wearing apparel* (Why do people wear different kinds of hats?) or the *transportation* category (Why do some people drive to work and others take a bus or a train?) Try the *time* category; for example: How long is a moment? A generation? A while?

Figure 2.3 THE SAM TRAP (A Primer in Applebet)

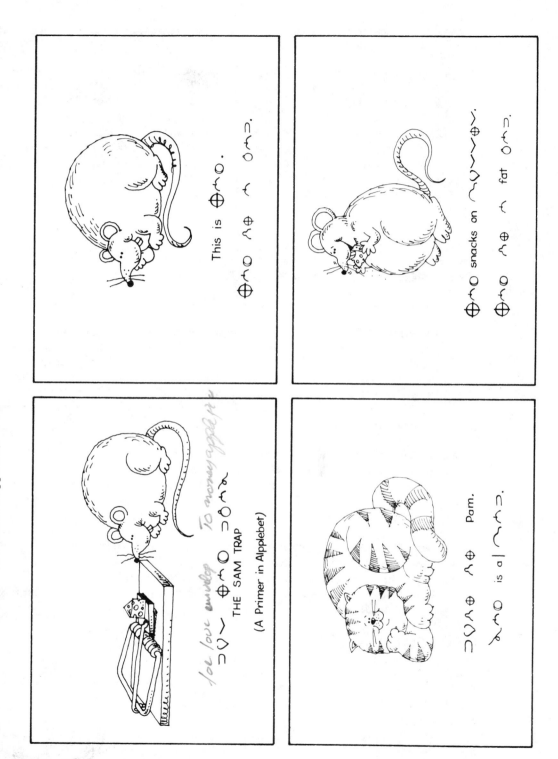

56

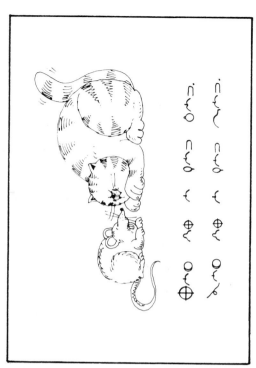

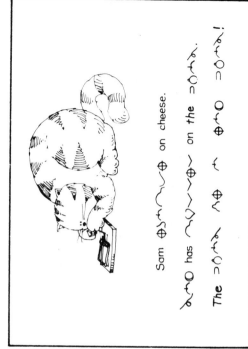

Sam ⊕ on cheese.

has on the

The !

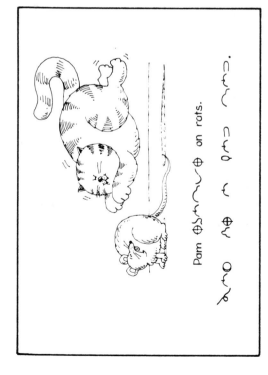

Pam ⊕ on rats.

Pam, the , has a

The is rat

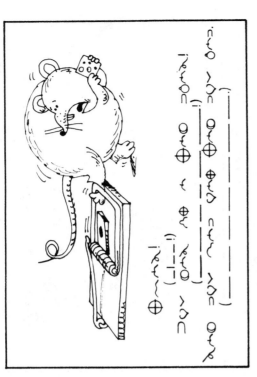

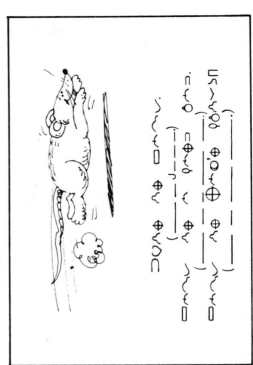

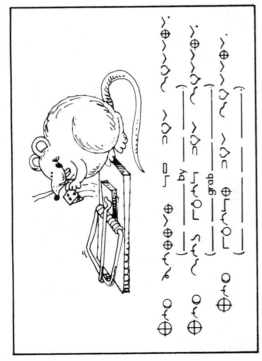

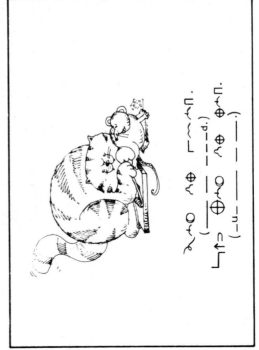

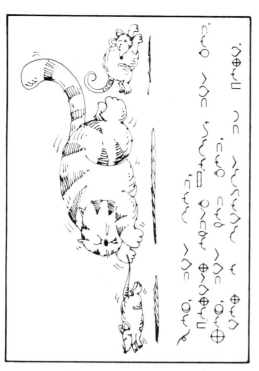

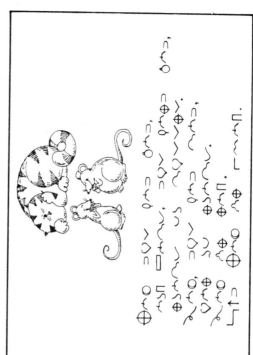

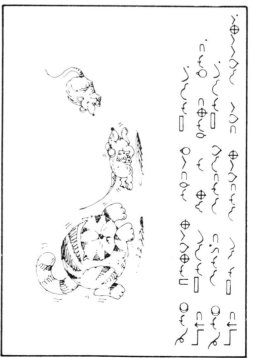

3 READING FOR COMPREHENSION: WHAT TEACHERS CAN DO

CHAPTER PREVIEW

In the last chapter we talked about some differences between good and poor readers and how good readers use interactive processes as they read. In this chapter we'll move our discussion into the classroom and see how teachers can help all readers use interactive processes in comprehending what they read. We'll see that teachers, simply in the way they think of reading, influence children's comprehension a great deal. We'll see that memory and comprehension are related, but not the same thing—and this insight will help us to use questioning strategies that teach instead of test. We'll also see how important it is to help children use and enhance their schemata to read inferentially, as mature readers do. And finally we'll see how children can be encouraged to "monitor" their own comprehension rather than rely on teachers to do it for them.

Humans seem to learn from their yesterdays but not from their yesteryears.

The child should never be permitted to read for the sake of reading as a formal process or end in itself . . . Word pronouncing will therefore always be secondary to getting whole sentence meanings, and this from the very first.

—*A teachers' guide in 1895*

TEACHER-MADE CONSTRAINTS ON COMPREHENSION

In Chapter 2, we saw that Valerie was content to read that "the rangers had *market of* a *plack* for people to cut trees." We left our study of Valerie with the question: "Is it possible that she's been actually reinforced for coming up with word-noises and meaningless substitutions? If so, then how could such reinforcements possibly take place?"

Let's see if we can answer that question right now. As Jerome Harste and Robert Carey (1984, p. 32) have confirmed through their research, what the teacher believes about the process of learning to read "strongly affects what instructional strategies are employed." If the teacher believes, for example, that learning to read requires correction of each word a child reads "wrong," she will probably emphasize *word* correction more than *meaning* correction. This emphasis will in turn produce what Harste and Carey refer to as an "instructional constraint." An instructional constraint is something in the teaching-learning environment that limits what is learned. For example, the teacher just mentioned will probably have students who will learn to concentrate on one word at a time rather than on the author's message. A child like Valerie, then, becomes willing to plug in *market* for *marked*, *of* for *off*, and even *plack* for *place*, since *plack*, after all, sounds like a word.

But why are children, especially young children, so eager to concentrate on what they think the teacher wants? You probably already know the answer to this question. All of us, as we grow up, are placed in situations in which we're dependent upon another person for affection, for a sense of belonging, for a feeling of importance. In the classroom, the teacher is usually the major "giver"—the major person to meet children's needs. Is it any wonder that children try to please the teacher? Not that there's anything wrong with trying to please. Even as adults we keep right on trying. (I like to please my wife, for example, by having tea ready for her in the morning, or by yawning more softly than I'd like to, so I don't hurt her ears.)

A word-emphasis by the teacher, a particularly damaging kind of instructional constraint, tends to encourage what Frank Smith (1979) refers to as "tunnel vision." The children concentrate so hard on each word, they ignore the rich matrix of surrounding words that provide semantic and syntactic cues to meaning. They become, as Dasch puts it, "overly concerned with the visual information . . . and try to decode letters and words rather than (to) process units of meanings. They [fail] . . . to use prior knowledge to make sense of the text" (Dasch, 1983, p. 428).

Perhaps the worst side effect of the word-emphasis constraint is the erroneous concept of reading that children develop as a result. In the process of trying to please the teacher, they gradually come up with a schema (a minitheory) about reading that may slow down their growth in reading ability for years. Once they get the notion that reading is a process of word-calling rather than a search for meaning, it may take a great deal of time and effort (usually by a remedial reading teacher) to undo the damage.

As I said, one way children acquire the wrong concept of reading is by having teachers correct them for each mispronounced word—even when their substitutions, insertions, and omissions are completely in line with the author's meaning! And even though, given half a chance, and an emphasis by the teacher on meaning, they will usually go back and self-correct miscues that don't make sense.

*Author**	*Melody*
"Walter!" Walter's mother called again. Walter did not answer. "Walter!" Still no answer.	"Walter!" Walter's mother called again. Walter didn't answer. "Walter!" He still didn't answer.

What do you think you would do in this situation? Would you be tempted to stop and correct her (in spite of what has been said in this chapter and the last)? If so, don't feel bad. Experienced teachers often tell me it has taken them awhile to break an old habit. (After all, how many times were *they* corrected for a "wrong word" when they were learning to read?)

Now let's see what you would do with Dena.

*Author**	*Dena*
Next Saturday the whole family drove to the forest. They found the ranger station and bought a permit.	Next Saturday the whole family *droove* to the forest. They found the ranger station and *brought* a permit.

What should you do this time? Should you stop her at the end of the first sentence, or at least at the end of the paragraph? Should you gently say something like this: "Okay, Dena, what do you think the first sentence is about?" (If she says, "I don't know," what might you say that would help her understand the first sentence?) What would you do about the second sentence?

What are some other teacher-made constraints on comprehension? Another is the *time* teachers choose to ask comprehension questions. Many teachers ask no questions until *after* the children have read an entire selection. This is fine if you want to see what they *remember*, but memory and comprehension are not the same thing (Smith, 1979). Andy might have good comprehension of a story but poor memory of it; Robert may have both poor comprehension and poor memory of the story. If you, the teacher, check only on memory, how will you know how to help Andy and Robert? With Andy, you'll want to help him learn how to retain key features of a story, so that he can talk about them later (see the discussion of metacognition and comprehension monitoring.) With Robert, you'll want to concentrate first on helping him *comprehend* what he reads, then concentrate later on his ability to remember what he reads.

---

*Colin Dunkeld, Portland Informal Reading Inventory, Form P. Unpublished manuscript Portland State University, School of Education. Reprinted by permission of the author.

Unless you check on comprehension *while they read,* however, you won't know how to help either of them. Nor will you be able to encourage interactive reading by helping Robert to use all four cueing systems. Not every selection they read should be handled this way, of course, but you will need to use the "while-they-read" approach enough to allow you to *teach comprehension* rather than merely testing memory *after* they read.

So the *timing* of your questions is another constraint—another influence on how well students learn to comprehend what they read. Still another instructional constraint would be the people Andy or Robert would be expected to read *to*—to themselves, to the teacher, to their peers. Andy might comprehend equally well in all three situations. Robert, on the other hand, might comprehend nothing if he has to read in front of his peers. It's not unusual for a child to do poorly with his peers and teacher, yet comprehend quite well when reading out in the hall with a teacher aide.

Another constraint is the *way* teachers ask questions. If they ask them as if they were administering an oral examination, some children comprehend, or remember, nothing more than the intensity of the teacher's voice,

or perhaps the impatience in her eyes. If, however, teachers use questions informally—and merely to stimulate children's thinking—both Robert and Andy might do quite well. But equally important is the *type* of questions teachers ask. If they ask only literal questions rather than questions that require inferential (interpretive) thinking, students "become adept at searching for the correct answer and ignore the whole story" (Swaby, 1982).

The point of all this, of course, is that comprehension can't be thought of as something isolated from what teachers do in the classroom. I may have given you the false impression in Chapter 2 that interactive reading is a natural process that good readers engage in and poor readers don't, but as you can see, teachers have a great deal to do with how "natural" it is. As Peter Mosenthal put it, "the most important context influencing reading comprehension in classroom lessons may be the interaction between the teacher and the students" (1984, p. 17).

PREDICTABLE TEXT FOR TEACHING INTERACTIVE PROCESSES

So how can teachers encourage the interactive processes of reading so that children read for comprehension? For one thing, they can be sure to use highly predictable reading materials, especially for beginners or poor readers. When I speak of predictable materials, I'm not referring to instructional materials with predictable spelling patterns: "Pat sat on that mat. That mat is Pat's mat. That rat on Pat's mat is fat." What I'm talking about is predictable *language*. "That mat is Pat's mat" is *not* predictable language—no one talks that way—it's unnatural. And no authors write that way when they want to entertain or inform.

Predictable language can be found in children's speech, for example. That's why the language experience approach, an approach in which children dictate or write their own reading materials, works so well. (See Chapter 7.) Since the materials have been written by the children themselves, they tend to be highly predictable.

Predictable language can also be found in many Mother Goose rhymes.

Jack and Jill went up the hill to fetch a pail of water.
Jack fell down and broke his crown and Jill came tumbling after.

While it's true that such rhymes do not imitate natural speech, they have a rhythm, a pattern, *and a plot* that sticks in the mind. It is easy for most children to remember some of them well enough to chant them with other children or to read along with the teacher or with other children.

The most abundant source of predictable language, other than language experience stories, is the library. For the teacher interested in the interactive approach to reading, there is no shortage of books. There are literally hundreds of patterned stories, many in picture-book form, that can provide the necessary predictability. I'll give you just a few examples here; there are many more in Appendix P. One of the favorites of children I've worked with, both in the primary (1–3) and intermediate grades (4–6) is Rose Bonne's version of *I Know an Old Lady*. You remember this old-time jingle, don't you? Here's the first verse:

I know an old lady who swallowed a fly.
I don't know why she swallowed a fly.
Perhaps she'll die.

And here's the third verse:

I know an old lady who swallowed a bird.
How absurd to swallow a bird.
She swallowed a bird to catch the spider.
That wriggled and jiggled and tickled inside her.
She swallowed the spider to catch the fly.
But I don't know why she swallowed a fly.
Perhaps she'll die.

For younger children, there are many predictable (or "patterned") books by Bill Martin. A very simple one is his *Brown Bear, Brown Bear, What Do You See?* Here's a piece of it:

Brown bear, brown bear, what do you see?
I see a red bird looking at me.
Red bird, red bird, what do you see?
I see a yellow duck looking at me.

. . .

This pattern is repeated more than a dozen times as the book continues.

An example of a more difficult patterned book (with a more interesting plot) is Stephen Kellogg's *Can I Keep Him?* In this book a little boy (with a vivid imagination) keeps bringing home a different kind of pet to show his mother. "Can I keep him?" he asks each time. And each time his mother gives him a new excuse, such as "Your grandmother is allergic to cat fur." The story is touching and humorous, with insights into both children and mothers, and has similar words and sentence patterns throughout. It's a delightful book that children can enjoy reading again and again.

Patterned books and other predictable materials, then, take a variety of forms. Some, like *I Know an Old Lady* and *Brown Bear, Brown Bear*, sweep you along with their catchy rhythm and rhyme. Others, like *Can I Keep Him?* or *Alexander and the Terrible, Horrible, No Good, Very Bad Day*, grab the reader with repeated phrases and a repeated plot. You can't wait to see what animal the little boy is going to bring to his mother next; you can't wait to see what horrible terrible thing Alexander will experience next. And you can't wait to say with Alexander, "This would be a terrible, horrible, no good, very bad day . . . I think I'll move to Australia." But don't forget that other type of highly predictable story, the language experience story that children write or dictate themselves. With these stories the children have a very good idea of what's going to happen next because they are the authors.

Now that you know what I mean by "patterned books" and other predictable materials, we can move on to the advantages of using them. Remember that with the interactive approach, the student will be engaged in making hypotheses as she reads. Her procedure will be to predict what the author is going to say next and to sample enough of the print to confirm her predictions. The trick is to find those materials that cause the student to use this procedure without getting bogged down in decoding each word separately.

With predictable materials, the child, from the very first day of school, can learn that reading depends on other cues besides letters. She can learn intuitively that reading is very much like something she's been doing for years: *listening*. Whether a person listens or reads, she pays attention (without thinking about it) to the syntactic and semantic cues in the language, and to the schematic cues that reside in her mind. Just as we hypothesize when we listen, so we hypothesize when we read. What is the speaker saying? What is the *author* saying? What does the speaker mean? What does the *author* mean?

Bridge asks, "Is it possible for the novice reader to learn to read by reading?" (1979, p. 503). She justifies her question by saying: "It is only through practice in reading that children can learn to be efficient predictors of meaning and economical users of visual information (print)" (p. 504). And finally, she answers her question this way: "When given structured language patterns it is possible, even from the beginning stages, for readers to use their predictive abilities . . . They are role playing themselves as readers and thus have taken a giant step toward becoming successful readers" (p. 505).

"Role playing themselves as successful readers"—that's a very important teaching strategy for those interested in the interactive approach. When children are asked to "sound out" each word as they read, they are *not* role playing as successful readers, *they are practicing poor reading.* A successful reader is a fluent reader, not a halting, stuttering reader, puffing and growling his way through pieces of language that might as well be Latin or Greek. As adults, how would we like it if we were taken to, say, the Soviet Union, plunked down in a "little reading circle" with other frightened adults staring at us, and made to "sound out" word-by-word a story written in Russian (with the Russian alphabet as well)? I don't think we would think of ourselves as fluent, successful readers. I don't think we would go home with joy shining from our faces and say: "I can't wait to go back to school tomorrow."

In "Fluency: The Neglected Reading Goal," Allington (1983) argues for predictable materials as an answer to a prevalent problem in the schools: reading that is not fluent—that is, it is not smooth and expressive; nor does it show that the author is understood. You see, we have convinced ourselves in the schools that when Clifford passes lots of miniature tests on even more miniature subskills (for example, "the student will be able to decode words that rhyme with the phonogram *ame*"), he is automatically becoming a reader. Nothing could be further from the truth. Sooner or later, someone notices that Clifford can pass all the tests, but his fluency is very poor. And, as Allington says, this diagnosis "often leads to further instruction in letters, sounds, or words in isolation" (Allington, 1983, p. 557). Yet, if we look at the research on this problem, we find that children who are guided into reading-for-fluency increase their reading *comprehension* considerably more than children who are taught to concentrate on word accuracy (Allington, 1983).

The following list of ideas for using patterned books to develop fluent natural reading with beginners can also be used with older readers who need to change their concept of reading.

1. After reading the title of the book to them and showing them the pictures on the cover, ask them to predict what the book will be about.

2. After reading three or four pages *to them*, ask them what they think will happen next, or what they think a particular character will say next.

3. Have children explain their reasons whenever they make predictions; for example: Why do you think that will happen? Why do you think those words will come next? Have you seen those words before in this book? Is that the kind of thing he would say? Why do you think so?

4. Follow each set of predictions and reasons with a chance for the children to confirm or disconfirm their predictions.

5. Read the rest of the story to them and ask them to join in whenever they think they know the words.

6. On the second day, read the story to them again, allowing them plenty of opportunities to join in, as well as some opportunities to say the next line before you read it.

7. Using either a large wall chart or individual dittoed booklets, have the children take turns or use their own booklets to point to the words as you read the story again.

8. On the third or fourth day, after they have had enough time following along, ask for volunteers to read parts of the story.

9. When they have learned the story well, let them take the booklets home (with their own illustrations, if you wish) and read them to their parents.

10. Please don't follow these steps slavishly. You'll be more successful adjusting them to the students you're working with.

"CLOZE" PLUS CHORAL, ECHO, REPEATED, AND MODELED READING LEAD TO INTERACTIVE READING

In Chapter 4 we'll talk about the use of predictable materials in teaching sight words. For now, though, let's look at other ways to encourage interactive rather than word-by-word reading:

When children read orally in front of each other, don't permit word-correction or any other form of criticism. The worst case of this I've seen was in a third-grade classroom I visited. Every time a child corrected another child for his "mistakes," he was handed a token by the teacher. When he had accumulated enough tokens, he would receive a prize! Instead of encouraging such negative "correction," let's foster a positive spirit with teacher-comments like these: "Good, Ben, you read that just as though you were telling it to me!" or, "I could almost hear the author talking when you read that!" or, "I'll bet the author would be proud of you for the way you read that!"

Try modeling for 100 words or so before asking children to read. Read those 100 words as if you had written the story yourself.

Read to the children for enjoyment each day. Show them what good reading sounds like.

"Echo reading" is an excellent way to build confidence and fluency. Have the children repeat each sentence you read, following along both times with their copy—first when you say it, and then when they say it. Let them point with their fingers as they follow along. Have more experienced readers repeat an entire paragraph. After they have repeated it as a group, allow the eager ones to repeat it "solo."

"Choral reading" is great for reading patterned books together and for very short stories or poems. At first everyone reads together and follows along with the printed page. As confidence builds, have the children try to break the text into parts and decide which smaller group or pair or individual will read each part. Practice the selection together until it sounds like something more communicative than a hive of droning bees. (Tell them to pretend they're on television.) If you're working with only one child who needs this kind of help, the two of you can still use choral reading, even to the extent of dividing up the parts. The point is to emphasize fluency, to build confidence, and to make reading a successful experience.

Try "repeated readings." With this technique the student or small group rereads a short meaningful passage until reaching fluency— smooth, expressive language that sounds as though the author were doing the talking. When the student or small group has been successful, it's time to move on to a new selection, but don't forget to send a copy home for them to read to their parents. Samuels (1979) reports that an experimental group who tried a similar technique as an adjunct to regular instruction made significantly greater gains in both comprehension and speed as compared to a control group who did not use the technique.

The most important step in any of these suggestions so far, including the use of patterned books, is that of *choosing the selection.* As Louritzen suggests, having no doubt learned from her experience as a remedial reading teacher, "the choice of reading material and the method of presenting it are crucial to success" (Louritzen, 1982, p. 457). My own experience with these techniques reminds me that the *selection* must be the major source of motivation, rather than tokens, progress graphs, or "scratch-n-sniff" stickers. If you find that a selection doesn't excite them on the first reading, put it aside and try your next choice. Don't continue with the procedure until you find one that produces a glow of excitement. As you search for selections of this type, look for those with a definite rhythm, with repeated phrases or sentences, or at least with very similar sentence patterns (rhyme is not necessary). The sequence of events must have a pulling quality—one that makes you want to go on (for example, to see what else the Old Lady will swallow.) The books listed in Appendix P have those qualities, but don't be limited by that list. There are hundreds more!

The "cloze" technique is one of the most versatile teaching tools. As you'll see throughout this book, it can be used for a variety of purposes. In this chapter we'll limit its use to teaching children how to pay more attention to syntactic, semantic, schematic, and graphophonic cues. Suppose you're preparing a group of second graders to read a story about two boys who try to build a playhouse, which eventually crashes to the ground.

Step A: You will probably first talk about this kind of building project to refine their schemata about playhouses, building materials, and building tools.

Step B: Then you might want to *show them*—in an intuitive rather than analytic way—the importance of the four cueing systems by using the *cloze* technique (omitting certain words or letters). The first two sentences in the story go this way: "Bob and Paul had been sawing and hammering all day. They were building a playhouse." Before you tell them what the story is about, and before they have a chance to read these sentences, write the following on the board and read it to them (say "blanking and blanking"): Bob and Paul had been _____ ing and _____ ing all day.

Step C: Now ask them for words that end with the /ing/* sound that could fit in the blanks. Make a list of their suggestions. They might give you words like these:

fighting	running
pounding	sawing
singing	yelling
building	hammering

If they don't give you words right away, start listing some and have them add more as they gain confidence.

Step D: Build their "syntax sense" by asking them whether *these* words will work: happying, funnying. Tell them that the story is going to be about two boys who try to build a playhouse. Ask them to choose two /ing/ words from their list that will best fit the story they're going to read. This will help build their "semantic sense."

---

*When you see a pair of slash marks like this, read the *sound* inside the marks rather than the letters. Say "/ing/" rather than "*i–n–g.*"

Step E: Add a few graphophonic cues such as these to the blanks:

> Bob and Paul had been s __ __ ing and ham __ __ __ ing all day.

Ask them again to "guess" what the two words will be in the story. List any words they predict. Now let them confirm their predictions by having them read the story.

This should give you some idea of the versatility of the *cloze* technique. The blanks you use depend on your good judgment. You'll simply ask yourself: What kind of cues are they ignoring the most? If they're using graphophonic cues too much, for example, save them for last. If they're using them too little, use them first.

Although the "lesson" I just demonstrated for you was designed for children in second or third grade, the cloze technique can be used with early first graders as well. Whenever you read to them and leave out a word for them to guess, you are using the *oral cloze technique.* And whenever you rewrite the language experience stories they've dictated and substitute a word here and there with a blank, you are using the cloze technique. You can also do the same type of rewriting with basal reader stories. Take a look, for example, at some of the possibilities for this preprimer story: Can you see at what points syntactic, semantic, schematic and graphophonic cues are called for?

> Bill saw a box. It was big. He opened it. He got in. He sat down. Dan saw the _____. He opened it. He _____ in too. He sat down. They sat still. They were h __ ding. Susan was looking for them. She looked up. She looked d __ __ __. She kept look __ __ __. She saw the __ __ __. She did not see them. Bill and Dan saw S __ __ __ n. Then they laughed. She heard them. Then she f __ __ __ __ them.*

By putting a story like this on a chart or ditto, you can use the cloze technique to help children use syntactic, semantic, and graphophonic cues interactively. But don't forget the schematic cues. As I'll explain in the next section, they're as important as the others, if not more so.

---

*Colin Dunkeld, Portland Informal Inventory, Form P, unpublished manuscript, School of Education, Portland State University, with permission from the author.

SCHEMATA ENHANCEMENT AND INFERENTIAL READING

Before asking children to read a selection, the teacher needs to ask himself, "What schemata do they need in order to understand it?" Even for the simple story about the two boys in a box, they need to have developed a schema about hide-and-seek. Since the author never even mentions this game, they will certainly need minitheories about its objective and its rules, or the point of the story will be lost on them. They'll also need a schema about boxes that allows them to imagine a child getting inside one—or two children getting inside one.

Should the teacher tell them ahead of time? "Boys and girls. Today you're going to read a story about three children playing hide and seek." Well . . . that would help them understand the story, all right, but it would also spoil the fun the author had in mind for the readers. And besides, the chances are quite good that they've already played hide-and-seek. A better approach, since the box is so important in the story, would be to talk about various sizes of boxes and what might fit inside a big one. "Could you fit a bicycle inside a big box? Could you fit a child? Two children?" Then you might get them interested in the story: "This story is about a big box. And it's also about a game some people like to play. After you're all through reading the story, I'll let you whisper to me what you think the game is."

Why do we need to worry so much about children's schematic backgrounds *before* asking them to read a selection? Because without adequate development of their schemata, they will find it difficult or impossible to make *inferences* as they read. Let me give you an example of this. The story I'm going to ask you to read doesn't stimulate the schemata in your mind that you'll need to infer what's going on. Try it, and you'll see what I mean:

> This operation is really not that difficult. First you remove them from the room you've just used and take them into the other room. Next you remove the material you no longer want and place each one in the appropriate place. Don't worry if this sometimes seems difficult. In time you'll get used to all the possibilities that are available to you. After you're satisfied with the arrangement, just follow the directions on the front and you'll be finished for awhile. Later, when you have a need for them again, you can use them directly or put them away and use them some other time. It's true that you have to repeat the operation many times in the course of living but I'm sure you'll agree that it's worth it.

Did you understand the author's message? Most people find it extremely difficult to comprehend until I tell them to use their schemata related to washing dishes in the dishwasher. Then, when they read it again, it makes sense.

Going back to our hide-and-seek story, you can imagine how difficult it would be for a child to comprehend it if he had never played hide-and-seek, or if he had never developed a schema about boxes that included the possibility of hiding inside one. He could use every syntactic cue, every semantic cue, and every graphophonic cue available and still not understand the story. Without the appropriate schemata he could not make the necessary inferences, and without inferences, there is no real reading (Carr, 1983; Dehn, 1984; Hansen & Pearson, 1980; Rumelhart, 1984; Smith, 1979).

> Studies indicate that inferences play a major role in reading comprehension. Research results also support the theory that the reader constructs inferences during reading to make the story coherent. (Carr, 1983, p. 520)

Not only do readers need to make one *large* inference related to what the story is about, they also need to fill in "empty slots" with inferences as they read from sentence to sentence. Let me show you what I mean using the familiar story of "The Three Bears." When authors write stories, they don't tell you everything; they leave empty slots for your imagination to fill in. Even "The Three Bears" usually has one or two empty slots between each sentence. For example, between the following two sentences, we can find at least two:

> One morning the mommy bear put some hot cereal into three bowls— a great big bowl, a middle-sized bowl, and a wee little bowl.

> *Empty Slot #1:* Where were the bowls? *Inference:* On the kitchen table.
> *Empty Slot #2:* Who were they for? *Inference:* Daddy, mommy, and baby, in that order.

> The cereal was too hot to eat, so the three bears went for a walk in the forest.

> In other words, when people read, they *must* read between the lines to understand the text. They must infer what the author didn't actually say. Such inferences are based on the reader's schemata, which in turn are based on the reader's background experiences. *The teacher who ignores this basic component of the reading act cannot hope to teach reading comprehension.*

Yet, in observations of elementary school classrooms, Durkin (1978–79, 1984) found that helping children develop the necessary background before they read an assigned selection was the one step teachers most consistently omitted. The reason? "It takes too much time."

RESEARCH ON INFERENTIAL READING

Research has borne out the importance of background knowledge in making inferences. But background can be enhanced by the teacher, and so can children's ability to read between the lines (applying their background as they make hypotheses about the author's message). Research tells us the following:

Poor readers and very young readers have the most trouble reading inferentially (Holmes, 1983). This trouble is directly related to background deficiency. In fact, background knowledge "seems to account for text difficulty to a greater degree than . . . sentence length and word frequency" (Lipson, 1984).

Very young readers have trouble reading many "basal readers" (the books they are given for reading instruction) because authors who write the stories are not allowed to use very many words. Thus, the words are not as precise as they should be and leave gaps that the beginning readers have to fill in with their own background. Thus, they "have to use more inferencing than older children—at a time when they are less equipped to infer than older children" (Beck et al., 1981).

Children need much more than the experience of defining words before they read a selection. Equally important are discussions on why people behave in certain ways in certain situations. Comprehension of stories requires considerable understanding of human nature—emotions, customs, roles, goals, and ways of achieving those goals (Dehn, 1984). Jane Hansen (1981), for example, was successful in using this approach in a ten-week study with second graders. After working with new vocabulary in each story to be read, she discussed three ideas important to the story, first in relation to the children's own experiences and then in relation to their predictions of what was going to happen in the story. For example, the main character in one story looked at his feet when he was embarrassed—an important clue to the reader. The children might have missed it without a discussion first of what people do when they feel embarrassed. The group who had the benefit of this type of discussion raised their standardized reading score considerably more than did a control group; they also made greater improvements on tests of inferential thinking.

Mere practice in answering inferential-type questions before, during, and after reading can improve your students' reading ability, whether the students are poor readers (Holmes, 1983) or average readers (Hansen & Pearson, 1980).

Science and social studies should not be omitted from a busy schedule just to provide more time for "reading" instruction. These two areas of the curriculum are vital in developing children's backgrounds and schemata (Kellogg, 1971).

Creative drama is an excellent medium for developing the schemata necessary for inferential thinking (Manna, 1984). In addition to using spontaneous drama, teachers may wish to use published plays for children. (See Appendix F.)

QUESTIONING STRATEGIES: D–R–T–A (DIRECTED READING– THINKING ACTIVITIES)

How to help children think inferentially and to read between the lines is a major concern of the teacher who understands the interactive nature of reading. There are a variety of ways to improve children's inferential thinking, one of which we just discussed—namely, the enhancement of their background schemata before they are asked to read. Another way is how we experience a reading selection *with them:* probing their thoughts about what they're reading, asking questions that stimulate further thinking, praising them for their insights. In a moment we'll watch a teacher who is using a venerable method labeled by Stauffer (1975) as "Directed Reading-Thinking Activities" (D–R–T–A). In this method of guiding children's reading, children are first asked to predict what each page or two is going to be about, then are directed to read *silently* to check on their predictions, and finally, they are asked to prove their interpretations of what the author said. In a nutshell, the teacher asks, in a variety of ways: "What do you think? Why do you think so? Can you prove it?"

Several studies have shown that the D–R–T–A method results in higher levels of comprehension than those methods that test only the children's memory at the end of their reading. One reason for this success might be that the D–R–T–A method recognizes that each child differs, which a testing approach to comprehension does not. "Children differ not only in motivation, attitude, and purpose but in the ability to grasp, assimilate, retain, and use information as well" (Stauffer, 1975, p. 3). Because of these differences, teachers should not expect all children to give the same answers to questions. Teachers who use the D–R–T–A method properly don't even *ask* the same question of each child. Their interaction with children is dynamic, rather than a static relationship based on expected answers listed in a teacher's guide.

Magic Doors*

Johnny's mother asked him to go to the big new store at the corner.
His little brother Howie said, "I want to go too! I want to go too! I'll be good."
So Johnny took his little brother to the big new store.
There were two big doors.
One door had the word IN on it. The other door had the word OUT. Johnny and Howie went to the IN door. Whish! The door opened all by itself!
Howie said, "Look at that. It's magic!"
"You are silly!" said Johnny. "It isn't magic. The new doors work by electricity."

MRS. S: [before the children read] Look at the title of this story and tell us what you think the story is going to be about.
JACKIE: Maybe about some doors that open by magic when you say "Open Sesame," and inside the doors you find gold and jewelry and things like that.
MRS. S: That's an interesting idea, Jackie. What makes you say that?
JACKIE: Well, I remember this story my Daddy read to me once, and that's what happened.
MRS. S: All right. Who has another idea?
BONNIE: I think it's going to be about some doors in a closet that lead into another land with witches and elves and things.
MRS. S: Well, that sounds possible. Why do you think your idea is right?
BONNIE: Umm, well . . . I heard a story like that once.
MRS. S: I'll bet you did. There's a story like that called "The Lion, the Witch, and the Wardrobe."
RONNIE: Yeah, maybe that's the one.
MRS. S: Turn the page and look at the picture on the next page. Maybe that will give you another idea of what this story is going to be about."
DAVID: Oooh, I know.
MRS. S: David?
DAVID: It's a picture of a supermarket. I'll bet the magic doors are those doors that open all by themselves.

---

*Bank Street College of Education, *Uptown, Downtown*, rev. ed. (New York: Macmillan, 1972). Reprinted by permission of the publisher.

MRS. S: Do you see anything else in the picture that makes you think that David is right?

SANDRA: There's a lady walking through one of the doors and she's not pushing on it or anything.

MRS. S: Yes, you did some very careful looking, Sandra.

RONNIE: Maybe she already pushed the door and it's just staying open for a while.

MRS. S: Yes, that's quite possible, Ronnie. Well, why don't you read the first two pages to yourself, and see if you can find out why the author called the story "Magic Doors."

MRS. S: [two minutes later] Were you right, Jackie? Are they going to find gold and jewelry behind those magic doors?

JACKIE: [shaking her head] No, but they'll find ice cream.

MRS. S: [laughing] How do you know?

JACKIE: Because those doors go inside a supermarket, and that's where we buy our ice cream.

MRS. S: You can tell it's going to be a supermarket by the picture. Is that how you knew?

JACKIE: Yes.

MRS. S: Can you find something the *author* tells you that makes you sure it's a supermarket?

JACKIE: [looking] Oh, here it is. It says, "One door had the word IN on it. The other door had the word OUT."

MRS. S: Good. Can you find another clue from the author, Bonnie?

BONNIE: [long hesitation]

MRS. S: What about the first sentence. Why don't you read it to us.

BONNIE: [reading] "Johnny's mother asked him to go to the big new store at the corner."

MRS. S: Does that sentence give you an idea of where Johnny will be going?

BONNIE: [smiles] To the grocery store.

MRS. S: Why?

BONNIE: Because that's where my mother always wants *me* to go.

MRS. S: Good. You didn't really need the picture of the supermarket did you?

BONNIE: No.

MRS. S: Okay then . . . David? Why don't you tell us what the magic doors were.

DAVID: [proudly] Just what I said. They're doors that open by themselves.

MRS. S: You were sure right, David. But what really makes the doors open? Is it magic, Ronnie?

RONNIE: No. It's an electric motor or something.

MRS. S: Can you find a sentence that proves it?

RONNIE: The last sentence says, "The new doors work by electricity."

MRS. S: But how in the world did you read that big word?

RONNIE: [smiles] I thought it was *energy* the first time. But then I saw it was *electricity*.

MRS. S: How did you know it wasn't something like . . . *electronically?*

RONNIE: [says nothing and smiles]

MRS. S: Suppose I read the last sentence this way: "The new doors work by *electronically.*"

RONNIE: [laughs] That sounds funny!

MRS. S: You're right, it does. But how did you know it was *electricity* and not *energy?*

RONNIE: [shrugs] I don't know.

SANDRA: I know. Because you can see the word *city* at the end of it.

MRS. S: Good . . . Jackie, what else can you see that makes you sure it's *electricity* and not *energy?*

JACKIE: [studies page but makes no response]

MRS. S: What two letters does *electricity* start with?

JACKIE: It starts with *e–l.*

MRS. S: And what would *energy* start with?

JACKIE: With *e–n.*

MRS. S: Very good. David, do you agree with Ronnie? Do you think that electricity makes sense in that last sentence?

DAVID: [smiling] Sure. I know it's electricity. It's not magic.

MRS. S: Right. So now before you read the *next* two pages, what do you think will happen to Johnny and Howie in the big new store?

As you watch Mrs. Stineberg, you notice that she doesn't constantly refer to her teacher's guide as she leads the children through the selection. Not that she hasn't studied it *before* the discussion; she has—to reread the story, the recommended questions, and the teaching suggestions—but she doesn't follow it slavishly as she works with the children. Instead she interacts with each child in such a way that she accomplishes several teaching objectives:

She gets the children to make hypotheses and predictions, to read silently to confirm or disconfirm them, and to prove their ideas, either by reading orally, by remembering what they read, or by relating the text to their own experiences.

She keeps the children focused on reading as a thinking and communication act rather than strictly a decoding act.

She prepares them for the selection by enhancing their schemata. She does not omit the crucial "background step."

She responds to them humanly, with interest, rather than mechanically, with prepackaged questions; thus, she models reading as a learning experience rather than one of coming up with "right" answers for the teacher.

She encourages them to use all four cueing systems; schematic, syntactic, semantic, and graphophonic.

She guides them toward reading inferentially rather than merely literally and considers filling in the author's "empty slots" more important than repeating the author's exact words.

She *teaches* comprehension rather than merely *testing* memory.

QUESTIONING STRATEGIES: INTERACTIVE PROCESSES VS. ISOLATED SUBSKILLS

The complex skill we're calling "reading comprehension" is really quite similar to listening comprehension. When a good listener listens, he concentrates not so much on the sounds as he does on word order (syntax) and the speaker's implied meanings (semantics). But in doing this, he must rely heavily on the schemata he has developed through past experiences. Yet, reading comprehension is more difficult than listening comprehension. For one thing, the written symbols stand in the way, and for another thing, the listener gets to watch the speaker's facial expressions and body movements—something the reader is deprived of.

Although we educators have been sensible enough not to create long lists of tiny subskills related to listening comprehension, we have not been able to resist the temptation with reading. The thinking goes something like this: since reading is a difficult skill for children to learn, let's make it easier by breaking it into subskills. And let's break *those* into even tinier subskills. Then, as children master each of them, it will be like building a reading castle: with each new brick (subskill) the castle will get stronger and stronger; the reading will get better and better.

A nice thought, but alas, it doesn't work that way with reading any more than it would with listening or speaking. No parent I know attempts to teach his child oral language that way. In fact, that method doesn't even work with something like tennis. You could have John McEnroe or Chris Evert-Lloyd show your students how to hold the racquet, how to rotate the wrist, how to hold the ball for a serve, and so on. Then you could have them test the kids on how well they can do each of the dozens of so-called subskills. And finally, you could provide them with a court and watch them play. But don't expect much. They would need to *play* tennis to learn how to play tennis, just as they have to *read* books to learn how to read books. A list of subskills looks impressive in school-district curriculum guides and in publishers' scope-and-sequence charts, but it doesn't really guide the teacher as to how to teach. For example, here is just a sample of thinking operations referred to as subskills:

A. Literal-Thinking Operations

   1. Translating text into mental images

   2. Following sequence of events, ideas, or cause and effect

   3. Recollecting significant details

B. Inferential-Thinking Operations

   1. Making predictions

   2. Reading between the lines

   3. Recognizing main ideas

C. Critical-Thinking Operations

   1. Distinguishing factual from nonfactual

   2. Detecting author bias

   3. Evaluating according to criteria

D. Creative-Thinking Operations

   1. Inventing flexible alternatives to authors' ideas or characters

   2. Applying old ideas to a new situation

   3. Translating ideas read about into an artistic medium

Now, there's nothing wrong with coming up with a list of thinking operations. Such a list can help a teacher decide whether she's asking too many of one type of question and too few of another. But the evidence for reading as a set of exact subskills is sadly lacking (Downing, 1982). The subskills have been invented through logic, but they haven't been verified by experimental research. No one, to my knowledge, has been able to produce a list of subskills, teach them, and then demonstrate that this approach produces better readers than those students who "merely" spend their time reading books.

The important thing is not the list of subskills itself, but how it's used. As a guide for selecting workbooks and tests for children, it has doubtful value. I have yet to find a body of research that demonstrates that isolated tests and workbook exercises on single isolated subskills will cause children to read better. On the other hand, there does seem to be evidence (Baker & Brown, 1984; Carr, 1983; Hansen, 1983; Hansen & Pearson, 1980) that when teachers teach comprehension in an integrated, interactive way, with an emphasis on inferential thinking and the interaction of the four cueing systems, comprehension can be improved.

As Wilson (1983) points out, comprehension seems less a set of isolated subskills then a process of connecting text information to the information stored in the reader's head. For the reader to make this connection, he has to confront a set of problems, such as decoding a strangely spelled word like *pseudoephedrine,* or seeing a word like *home* in a verb slot rather than a noun slot, as in "'Home it!' the catcher screamed to the pitcher." If there *are* separate subskills involved in reading (and right now we really don't know), they must be thinking or problem-solving operations that are constantly changing and interacting as we confront the text and try to make sense out of it.

In the following episode, you'll see how a teacher can encourage through her questions the interaction of such problem-solving operations. This teacher is working with a small group of fourth graders who are going to read a short article about a snowstorm that hit New York City. You"ll want to read the article so you can see how she prepares them for it and guides them through it, teaching comprehension as she goes rather than merely testing later for memory.

In 1888 a terrible snowstorm hit New York City. Tall poles snapped, and electric wires fell into the street. People were killed by electric shock. Some were killed by the falling poles. And nearly a thousand died in the fires that broke out.

The mayor saw that he must do something to make his city a safe place to live. He asked electricians to put electric wires safely underground. Then the mayor sent men out to take down the wooden poles.

These electric wires were the beginning of America's amazing underground city in New York. Today the narrow streets and the sidewalks hide more than four million miles of wire. In some places there are so many wires and pipes that two fingers cannot be pushed between them . . . .*

TEACHER: Do you know what kinds of things you can find underneath the streets here in New York City?

BARBARA: Oh, I know. Subways!

TEACHER: That's right. Can anyone think of something else you might find underneath the streets? [Operation D_2]

DONALD: There are all kinds of pipes under the streets. I know, because my dad told me. And they're full of water.

JANET: I know what's under there. Monsters!

TEACHER: Well, I hope that's not true.

BILL: Aren't there wires and things like that under there?

---

*From page 250 of "Air Pudding and Wind Sauce," *Keys to Reading* (Oklahoma City, OK: Economy Company, 1972), adapted from "Amazing Underground City," by Edward Hymoff (*Boy's Life,* August 1963).

TEACHER: Yes, there are over four million miles of wire under our streets. That's enough wire to go around the world over 160 times! Do you know why that wire is there?

KEN: It's for sending messages.

BILL: Naw. It's for telephones.

TEACHER: What do you think it's for, Janet? [Operation B_1]

JANET: Electricity.

BARBARA: Yeah, electricity.

TEACHER: Well, I'll tell you what. I'd like you to find out why that wire was put down there in the first place. Read the article to yourself and then let's stop and talk about it.

TEACHER: Well, now you know why they put the wire under the streets. What do you think it looks like under the streets? Can you get a picture in your mind? [Operation A_1]

BILL: I think it looks like spaghetti.

TEACHER: [joins in the laughter] You may be right, Bill. What do you think it looks like, Barbara?

BARBARA: I don't know, but I know it doesn't look like spaghetti.

TEACHER: Who can find a sentence on this page that tells what it looks like? [Operation A_3]

KEN: Oh, I know. It's the last sentence. It says, "In some places there are so many wires and pipes that two fingers cannot be pushed between them . . . ."

TEACHER: Yes, and maybe that's why Bill said it must look like spaghetti down there. [Operation A_3]

BILL: Yeah, like a whole bunch of spaghetti all squished together.

TEACHER: Would it be like uncooked spaghetti that comes out of the box all straight, or would it be like cooked spaghetti that's all piled up on your plate? [Operation A_3]

JANET: Oh, I know. It would be like uncooked spaghetti when it comes out of the box.

TEACHER: [nodding approval] Why do you think so, Janet?

JANET: Because that's what they do with wires and pipes.

TEACHER: They lay them out straight?

JANET: Yes.

TEACHER: Have you seen people do it that way?

JANET: Yes, That's the way they do it. They don't bunch it all up like cooked spaghetti.

TEACHER: [laughing] I'm sure you're right. Has anyone else watched people put in wires and pipes anywhere?

BILL: Yeah, I have. My uncle does that kind of thing for a living. He puts wires in buildings.

TEACHER: He's an electrician?

BILL: Yeah.

TEACHER: All right. Now let me ask you something else. Did they take down the wooden poles before or after they put the wires under the street? [Operation A_2]

KEN: They took 'em down and then put the wires under the street.

TEACHER: Well, Ken, let's pretend you were the mayor of New York at that time. If you told them to take down the poles and then had them put the wires under the street, wouldn't you have people get angry with you?

KEN: [laughing] Oh yeah. They wouldn't have any electricity if I had 'em take down the poles first.

TEACHER: [smiling] So what do you think would be the smart thing to do, as Mayor of New York? [Operation C_3]

KEN: I'd put the wires under the streets, and then when they're all fixed up and the lights and everything working, then I'd do it.

TEACHER: Do what, Ken?

KEN: Have 'em take down the poles.

TEACHER: That makes sense. What do you suppose they used all those poles for? Do you have an idea, Donald?

DONALD: I don't know. Maybe they built log cabins with them.

TEACHER: That's a good idea. Any other ideas?

BARBARA: Oh, I know! They could use them for fuel!

TEACHER: Another good idea. We only have a minute or two left. Why don't we see how many ideas for using those poles we can think of in that time? [Operation D_1]

QUESTIONING STRATEGIES: STORY GRAMMAR AS A FRAMEWORK

I've given you two strategies for inventing your own questions when you are helping children comprehend what they read—the D–R–T–A Approach and the interactive processes approach. Having your own strategies for inventing questions is important; otherwise, as Mary Shake and Richard Allington (1985) found in their study, when teachers *don't* use the teacher's guide, their questions tend to focus "on trivial information or defining unfamiliar words" (p. 437).

Let's look at a third strategy, that of using story grammar. I mentioned earlier that we all carry around a set of schemata that help us know what type of text to expect as we read—story type, information type, persuasive type, and so on. Once we know it's going to be story type, we employ a particular schema for that type of text, a minitheory that tells us we're going to have a main character, a place and time, a plot and so on. As we read a story, then, we expect these elements to show up. This expectation, if fulfilled, helps us to comprehend the story.

When writing a story, an author normally follows an intuitive *story grammar*, a set of rules as to what must be included to comprise a real story. There must be a setting, including a main character (Goldilocks in the forest); there must be an initiating event to get the story going and to cause some sort of conflict (the three bears go for a walk and leave the house unguarded); there must be a response by a main character (she sneaks into the bears' house); this response should lead to further problems or conflict (she makes the bears very upset); there should be a resolution (Goldilocks manages to escape rather than being thrown in jail for trespassing); usually there is supposed to be some kind of theme (bears are only human after all, or look what happens when you leave your front door unlocked).

For the past several years, teachers and researchers have been attempting to teach story grammar to children with the idea that it would improve children's prediction power and therefore their reading comprehension (Dreher & Singer, 1980; Gordon & Braun, 1983; Rumelhart, 1984). But as the research results come in, it has become apparent that direct teaching of story grammar is probably not a consistently effective means of improving children's comprehension. Explaining the story grammar of a particular story might increase their understanding of it, but there seems to be little carry-over to other stories (Dreher & Singer, 1980; Marshall, 1984; Rand, 1983; Rumelhart, 1984).

Two indirect approaches to story grammar, however, may enhance children's ability to read stories with better comprehension. One approach is that advocated by Muriel Rand (1983): "having many experiences with well-formed stories" (p. 381). In other words, children will develop better schemata for stories if they have many stories either read to them or given to them to read. My recommendation is that you read stories to them often, preferably every day, and that you sometimes talk informally about the components of those stories: "Who's the most important person in this story? What problems does he have? What's going to happen? How will he feel if it happens?"

The other approach is to use story grammar as a framework for inventing the questions you ask children before, during, and after a story you have assigned them. For instance, if you want to emphasize those components of story grammar that Sadow (1982) uses, you would ask questions about the *setting*, the *initiating event*, the main character's *reaction* to that event, the *action* of the main character, and the *consequence* of his or her reaction. Sadow shows how to use this story grammar with *Charlotte's Web* by E.B. White:

1. What is a runt-pig? Who is Fern? Where does she live? (Setting)

2. What was Fern's father going to do? Why was Fern's father going to 'do away' with the pig? (Initiating Event)

3. How did Fern feel when she learned that her father was going to kill the pig? (Reaction)

4. What did Fern do about it? (Action)

5. How did her father respond to her? (Consequence)

Marshall (1984) advocates a similar approach, suggesting that direct teaching of story grammar is not necessary, since children come to school with an intuitive grasp of story grammar already. "Bringing intuitive knowledge to the level of consciousness does not change the comprehension process" (p. 617). Marshall suggests instead that we simply use questions that touch on each of the major components of a story grammar. Based on her ideas, I recommend the following set of questions to consider when discussing a story:

Setting: Where is this taking place? When? If it happened at another place or time, would it make a difference?

Character: What kind of person is she? What makes you think so? Why do you think she did what she did?

Theme: What does she learn in this story?

Conflict: What problem does she face? How do you think she will solve it?

Reaction: What are her feelings about the problem?

Attempts: What does she do first? What do you think she'll do next? Why did the first attempt fail?

Resolution: How was the problem solved?

Reaction: How did she feel about the way it was solved? What are some other ways it might have been solved? What do you think she will do now that the problem has been solved?

These questions provide a framework not only for helping students understand a particular story but also for reading other stories. (Notice how inferential-type questions are mixed in with those that require only literal thinking.) I am not recommending, of course, that you use these questions rigidly story after story. I'm only suggesting them as one of the many ways you can help children increase their predictive power—by using one set of schemata they have already intuitively developed.

QUESTIONING STRATEGIES: TIME TO THINK AND GROW

The three frameworks I've mentioned for asking questions —D–R–T–A, interactive operations, story grammar—are subject to potential misuse, unless the teacher has a clear idea of what the questioning is for. As John Pikulski (1983) says, "unfortunately, most of the questions we ask in the name of comprehension do little to stimulate thought or to *teach* reading comprehension. Most tend to *test* children's memory for facts contained in the materials they have read" (p. 111). Research backs him up on this (Durkin, 1978–79, 1984; Gambrell, 1980, 1983). It's almost as if the teacher says to himself, "I must test these kids on this story. Otherwise, what good has it been for them to read it?"

> Crafton (1982) makes this point: "We have to ask ourselves what intellectual purpose is served when students are asked to answer questions unique to one text. It's *using* the information learned from reading that counts" (p. 296). In most respects I agree with her. Sharing what they are reading or have read should provide children with an opportunity for personal growth. If all they get to do is answer questions delivered in a testlike atmosphere, they have been deprived of a major value of reading—to learn more about the world and about themselves.

Comprehension should not be seen as a minute point in time (Johnny got 7 out of 10 questions right on that selection). It should be seen as a long-range process. Answering questions on one selection should not always lead to answering questions on the next selection, as if the children were working on an assembly line for producing answers. There's something very "right" about having children extend the comprehension of a topic by finding other books on the topic, or by changing a story into a play so they can *feel* what the characters in the story felt, or by creating their own book of stories similar to the story they've just read, or merely by talking about experiences they've had that were similar to those of the main character. We who teach children must create time for this. *We should take the time to model the process of learning from reading*, otherwise we are modeling only the process of testing.

We encourage mass production of question answerers rather than thoughtful readers by the *way* we ask questions. Not only are most questions of the literal- rather than inferential-thinking type, but "American teachers allow an average of only one second of think-time" (Gambrell, 1980, p. 143) after they ask a question. If the child doesn't come up with an answer in that time, the teacher tends to ask another child or ask another question or repeat the original question. Furthermore, questions are often asked in a formal way (sometimes straight from the teacher's manual), thus causing some children to feel highly threatened.

Some teachers, however, have mastered the art of questioning. Knowing that a question can be perceived unconsciously as an instrument of power, they ask their questions as indirectly as possible. For instance, Mary Farrar (1983) suggests that instead of asking questions directly, we should use a more informal, indirect approach.

> *Direct:* What reason did the author have for giving the story this title?

> *Indirect:* Do you think the author had a special reason for giving the story this title?

Farrar also recommends taking the time to give children a hint when they are having trouble. As she puts it, we have traditionally had "the notion that the best questions are *demanding* as well as being clear, concise, and complete. This concept of teacher questions is mistaken, however, because it fails to account for the social aspects of language use" (p. 371). A good point, I think, and kids are no different from adults in this respect—they don't respond well under bright interrogation lights. Not that teachers intend to make the question period an interrogation; it's just that, because teachers are so busy, there's a temptation to read the questions from the teacher's guide as if one *were* interrogating instead of teaching. (I've been guilty of yielding to the same temptation.)

Some teachers have not only mastered the art of questioning, they've also mastered the art of providing time for children to think. Those who have trained themselves to wait for five seconds after asking a question receive these rewards for their patience: (1) students give longer responses; (2) students give more correct responses; and (3) students take more risks and dare to speculate (Rowe, 1978).

METACOGNITION AND COMPREHENSION MONITORING

"Whew!" you must be saying. "There's an awful lot to think about when you're teaching comprehension." True. And to make matters even more confounding, I feel obligated to mention one more type of thinking operation you need to encourage—one I mentioned briefly in Chapter 2 called

metacognition. This is a fancy (but accurate) word that researchers use to refer to "knowing about knowing" (Guthrie, 1983, p. 478).

As adults we tend to know when we know something and when we don't—when we understand what we're reading, for example, and when we don't understand, or why we know something and why we don't know, or exactly *what* we know. This kind of thinking develops slowly. Children in the primary grades (K–3), for instance, often can't explain why they're having trouble understanding something (Baker & Brown, 1984). By the time they reach the intermediate grades (4–6), however, good readers can begin to verbalize the problem—"I don't know what that word means," or "I've never heard about this stuff before," or "I don't know how to pronounce that word" (Baker & Brown, 1984). Poor readers, however, need considerable help in developing their metacognitive skills.

Baker and Brown have been studying metacognition at the University of Illinois Center for the Study of Reading for many years. Their major concern has been to determine how well children "monitor" their own reading comprehension. "Comprehension monitoring entails keeping track of the success with which one's comprehension is proceeding, ensuring that the process continues smoothly, and taking remedial action if necessary'' (Baker & Brown, 1984, p. 22). In other words, when good readers know they don't understand something, they do something about it.

The major reason for Baker's and Brown's concern about comprehension monitoring is this: Teachers and researchers have been concentrating on children's memory (*after* they read) rather than their comprehension (*while* they are reading). These researchers have been trying to make clear to us that reading comprehension is a *process*, not a product that can be measured by how many questions are answered correctly. It is a process of assuring yourself *while* you read that you are communicating with the author. It involves *monitoring activities* such as these:

1. *Establishing your purposes* for reading a particular text. Unless a reader knows what he's looking for and why he wants it, reading becomes nothing more than allowing the eyes to scan the print. (This is similar to the way I used to read a dull textbook as a college student, glancing at the clock every few minutes and counting the number of pages still to be "covered.")

2. *Modifying your reading rate and strategies* to match your purpose. Should you just scan for certain details? Should you just skim to get the gist? Should you read slowly, making sure you understand each sentence? If it's a story, should you read fast so as to merely follow the plot, or slow down to appreciate the character development? According to research, even many college students do not set their own purposes or vary their reading rates (Baker & Brown, 1984).

3. *Using your background of experience* (and your schemata) to understand what the author is talking about.

4. *Paying attention to the sequence* of events, steps, or logic (depending on the kind of text). Without following the author's order, the reader usually gets lost.

5. *Going back and rereading* something that wasn't clear the first time.

6. *Self-correcting words* that didn't fit the context at the first reading.

7. *Getting help with words* that are crucial to successfully understanding the author's message (asking a friend or teacher, consulting a dictionary, waiting to see if the author explains the word in the next few sentences). Poor readers are less likely than good readers to do these things (Baker & Brown, 1984).

You can see, then, that if reading comprehension includes these kinds of monitoring processes, teachers must do more than merely ask testlike questions after children finish a selection. The *process* of comprehension must be taught *while* children read and *before* children read (as shown in the episode on pp. 78–80). They should be helped to develop *purposes* for reading what they're about to read. They need to see demonstrations of how to change one's reading pace to fit one's purposes (see Chapter 11 for more about this). They must be given time before they read to activate and enhance their schemata (as shown on pp. 83–85). They should be given practice, during actual reading experiences, in following sequences (as shown on pp. 84–85). They need to be given abundant opportunities to go back and reread passages that were not clear, and also to see teachers modeling this behavior. They should be praised for their self-corrections. They must be *shown* how to use a dictionary with ease (see Appendix N), how to use context clues, how to search for an author's definition of a strange word, and how to get help from others. If teachers will do these things for children, they will be *teaching* comprehension.

Research demonstrates (Baker & Brown, 1984) that the metacognitive process of comprehension monitoring can be taught, even to poor readers. The pages I have referred you to in the last paragraph let you see teachers doing this. To conclude this chapter, though, I'd like to show you one more example based on a study by Jane Hansen and Ruth Hubbard (1983, p. 587). Notice how the teacher in this example tries to make a group of poor readers in fourth grade *conscious* of part of the comprehension process so they can use it with other selections. The "part" I'm referring to is that of bringing their own past experiences to bear on understanding what the author is describing. Studies consistently demonstrate that many children don't realize they're *supposed* to do this (Baker & Brown, 1984).

TEACHER: For many weeks now we've been doing something special before you read each new story. Do you remember what it is?

SALLY: Talking.

TEACHER: Yes. What special kind of talking?

JOHNNY: Comparing.

TEACHER: Yes, that's the word we've been using.

PHYLLIS: Ooh, I know. Comparing what's happened in our lives to what will happen in the story.

TEACHER: You're absolutely right. And why have we been doing this?

JAY: So we'd . . . so we'd get an idea of what the story's going to be about.

SALLY: To help us understand the story better.

TEACHER: Uh-huh.

PHYLLIS: So we'd remember it better.

TEACHER: Yes, those are all good reasons. Now, last time we met I had you imagine the kind of comparisons you would make if you were going to read about some children flying kites. Remember?

CHILDREN: Yes.

TEACHER: Well, today, let's imagine that you're going to read in your social studies book about some schools in Japan.

PHYLLIS: Oh good.

TEACHER: [smiling] Okay, what might you think about before you read and as you're reading? What *comparisons* would you make?

JOHNNY: I'd think about our class.

JAY: I'd think about this school, and about my old school too.

PHYLLIS: We could see if their school is like ours.

JOHNNY: It'd be different, I'll bet.

SUMMARY OF MAIN IDEAS

When teachers correct each "mistake" children make as they read, even when their miscues are completely in line with the author's meaning, it can have a negative influence on children's growth in comprehension.

To *teach* comprehension instead of merely testing memory, the teacher must frequently guide children before and during the time they engage in silent reading. Discussing a selection only after they have finished reading it is not as effective.

By using reading materials with predictable language, teachers can provide children with practice in fluent, successful reading, thus helping them to develop an effective concept of the reading process.

Isolated exercises on comprehension subskills (which may or may not exist) are less effective than integrated interactive experiences with guided reading.

There are numerous ways to encourage interactive reading, such as the cloze technique, choral reading, echo reading, teacher modeling, repeated readings, and praising children's meaningful renditions of text.

Schemata enhancement before children read an assigned story is essential for good comprehension. Vocabulary discussion is insufficient.

Inferential thinking is an essential ingredient of reading comprehension. Schemata enhancement techniques and questioning strategies can be an effective means of teaching children to create inferences as they read.

Four effective questioning strategies include the D-R-T-A approach, the use of interactive processes, story grammar, and giving children more time to think about and learn from what they read.

Comprehension monitoring, a form of metacognition that can be taught, is an important partner in the comprehension process.

REFERENCES AND SUGGESTED READINGS

Allington, L. (1983). Fluency: The neglected reading goal. *Reading Teacher, 36,* 556–561.

Baker, L., & Brown, A. L. (1984). Cognitive monitoring in reading. In J. Flood (Ed.), *Understanding reading comprehension* (pp. 21–44). Newark, DE: International Reading Association.

Beck, I. L., McKeown, M. G., & McCaslin, E. S. (1981). Does reading make sense? Problems of early readers. *Reading Teacher, 37,* 116–121.

Bridge, C. (1979). Predictable materials for beginning readers, *Language Arts, 56,* 503–507.

Carr, K. S. (1983). The importance of inference skills in the primary grades. *Reading Teacher, 36,* 518–522.

Crafton, L. K. (1982). Comprehension before, during, and after reading. *Reading Teacher, 36,* 293–297.

Dasch, A. (1983). Aligning basal reader instruction with cognitive stage theory. *Reading Teacher, 36,* 428–434.

Dehn, N. (1984). An AI perspective on reading comprehension. In J. Flood (Ed.), *Understanding reading comprehension* (pp. 82–100). Newark, DE: International Reading Association.

Downing, J. (1982). Reading—skill or skills? *Reading Teacher, 35,* 534–537.

Dreher, M. J., & Singer, H. (1980). Story grammar instruction unnecessary for intermediate grade students. *Reading Teacher, 34,* 261–272.

Duffy, G. G., Roehler, L. R., & Mason, J. (1983). *Comprehension instruction: Perspectives and suggestions.* New York: Longman.

Durkin, D. (1978–79). Reading comprehension instruction. *Reading Research Quarterly, 14,* 495–527.

Durkin, D. (1984). Is there a match between what elementary teachers do and what basal manuals recommend? *Reading Teacher, 37,* 734–744.

Farrar, M. T. (1983). Another look at oral questions for comprehension. *Reading Teacher, 36,* 370–374.

Fitzgerald, J. (1983). Helping readers gain self-control over reading comprehension. *Reading Teacher, 37,* 249–253.

Gambrell, L. B. (1980). Think-time: Implications for reading instruction. *Reading Teacher, 34,* 143–146.

Gambrell, L. B. (1983). The occurrence of think-time during reading comprehension instruction. *Journal of Educational Research, 77,* no. 2, 77–80.

Gordon, C. J., & Braun, C. (1983). Using story schema as an aid to reading and writing. *Reading Teacher, 37,* 116–121.

Guthrie, J. T. (1983). Children's reason for success and failure. *Reading Teacher, 36,* 478–479.

Hansen, J. (1981). An inferential comprehension strategy for use with primary grade children. *Reading Teacher, 34,* 665–669.

Hansen, J. (1983). Poor readers can draw inferences. *Reading Teacher, 37,* 586–589.

Hansen, J., & Pearson, P. D. (1980). *The effects of inference training and practice* on young children's comprehension (Technical Report No. 166). Urbana: Center for the Study of Reading, University of Illinois.

Harste, J. C., & Carey, R. F. (1984). Classrooms, constraints, and the language process. In J. Flood (Ed.), *Promoting reading comprehension* (pp. 30–47). Newark, DE: International Reading Association.

Holmes, B. C. (1983). A confirmation strategy for improving poor readers' ability to answer inferential questions, *Reading Teacher, 37*, 144–148.

Jones, L. L. (1982). An interactive view of reading: Implications for the classroom. *Reading Teacher, 35*, 772–777.

Kellogg, D. H. (1971). *An investigation of the effect of the science curriculum . . . on gains in reading readiness.* Unpublished dissertation, University of Oklahoma.

Lee, G. (1982). Playing about a story: Its impact on comprehension. *Reading Teacher, 36*, 52–55.

Lipson, M. Y. (1984). Some unexpected issues in prior knowledge and comprehension. *Reading Teacher, 37*, 760–764.

Louritzen, C. (1982). A modification of repeated readings for group instruction. *Reading Teacher, 35*, 456–458.

Manna, A. L. (1984). Making language come alive through reading plays. *Reading Teacher, 37*, 712–717.

Marshall, N. (1984). Discourse analysis as a guide for informal assessment of comprehension. In J. Flood (Ed.), *Promoting reading comprehension* (pp. 79–96). Newark, DE: International Reading Association.

Miller, G. M., & Mason, G. E. (1983) Dramatic improvisation: Risk-free role playing for improving reading performance. *Reading Teacher, 37*, 128–131.

Mosenthal, P. (1984). Reading comprehension research from a classroom perspective. In J. Flood (Ed.), *Promoting reading comprehension* (pp. 16–29). Newark, DE: International Reading Association.

Paris, S. G., & Lindauer, B. K. (1976). The role of inference in children's comprehension and memory for sentences. *Child Development, 8*, 217–227.

Pikulski, J. J. (1983). Questions and answers. *Reading Teacher, 37*, 111–112.

Rand, M. K. (1983) Story schema: Theory, research and practice. *Reading Teacher, 37*, 377–382.

Rowe, M. B. (1978). Wait, wait, wait . . . . *School Science and Mathematics, 78*, 207–216.

Rumelhart, D. E. (1984). Understanding understanding. In J. Flood (Ed.), *Understanding reading comprehension* (pp. 1–20). Newark, DE: International Reading Association.

Sadow, M. W. (1982). The use of story grammar in the design of questions. *Reading Teacher, 35*, 518–523.

Samuels, S. J. (1979). The method of repeated readings. *Reading Teacher, 32*, 403–408.

Shake, M. C., & Allington, R. L. (1985). Where do teachers' questions come from? *Reading Teacher, 38*, 432–439.

Smith, F. (1979). *Reading without nonsense.* New York: Teachers College Press.

Stauffer, R. G. (1975). *Directing the reading-thinking process.* New York: Harper & Row.

Swaby, B. (1982). Varying the ways you teach reading with basal stories. *Reading Teacher, 35*, 676–680.

Tompkins, G. E., & Webeler, M. B. (1983). What will happen next? Using predictable books with young children. *Reading Teacher, 36*, 498–502.

Whaley, J. F. (1981). Story grammars and reading instruction. *Reading Teacher, 34*, 762–771.

Wilson, C. R. (1983). Teaching reading comprehension by connecting the known to the new. *Reading Teacher, 36*, 382–390.

APPLICATION EXPERIENCES FOR THE TEACHER EDUCATION CLASS

A. *What's your opinion?* Discuss why you agree or disagree with the following opinions. Use both the textbook and your own experiences.

1. Teachers should correct every reading error a child makes, otherwise the child will learn to read words incorrectly.

2. The best time to ask questions of children is after they have finished reading a selection; otherwise, continuity and comprehension suffer.

3. The D-R-T-A strategy of asking questions is better than the Story Grammar Strategy.

4. Predictable materials may improve children's fluency, but they don't really help children to read better. They're not reading; they're just memorizing.

5. The cloze technique actually teaches children to make wild guesses rather than to use the four cueing systems.

6. It's impossible to read more than three sentences with understanding without relying on inferential thinking.

7. Comprehension and comprehension monitoring can't really be separated.

B. *Miscue Analysis:* Study Christopher's miscues and decide what cueing systems are most important to him. What might his concept of reading be? What influences might have caused him to have this concept? What are some things you would do to help change his concept? (Circled words are omissions.)

Pete   cut   it   down.   They   loaded   it   *on*   to   the   roof   [*loaned*]

of   the   car   and   drove   home.   When   they   got   home

Cathy's   tree   was   too   big   to   go   *through*   the   door.   [*thruff*]

They   had   to   cut   *about*   a   foot   off   the   bottom.*   [*of*] [*bottle*]

*Text by Colin Dunkeld, Portland Informal Reading Inventory, Form P, Unpublished Manuscript, School of Education, Portland State University.

C. *Using the Cloze Technique:* With a partner, rewrite the previous story text as the author wrote it, but use blanks that will encourage each of the four cueing systems. Compare your use of the cloze technique with that of others in the class.

FIELD EXPERIENCES IN THE ELEMENTARY SCHOOL CLASSROOM

A. Use the cloze technique in the same way called for in Application Experience C. Use either the selection you already prepared or prepare another selection more appropriate for the children you are working with. For each blank, have the children tell you why they wish to fill it in the way they do.

B. Select a patterned picture book and try out some of the procedures discussed on pages 69–70. Discuss your results with your class.

C. Write a brief report on the "instructional constraints" on reading comprehension that you notice in the classroom in which you are assisting. Which of these constraints might you reasonably change if you were in charge of the class? (Refer to pages 62–66 for assistance.)

READING AS A LANGUAGE PROCESS

4 READING VOCABULARY: THE CUEING SYSTEMS' CATALYST

Chapter Preview

Chapters 1 and 2 gave you an idea of what your ultimate goals in reading instruction might be. Chapter 3 showed you some ways to accomplish those goals as you concentrate on reading comprehension rather than word-by-word reading. In the next three chapters we're going to back up for awhile and look at some of the language tools children need to enable them to use the cueing systems with skill and comfort. Our first and perhaps most important language tool is a reading vocabulary. In Chapter 4 we'll look at how one's vocabulary triggers the four cueing systems and enables us to read fluently and with comprehension. We'll see that vocabulary growth is not a goal in itself, but the means by which we understand authors and communicate with others.

We'll look at a list of words that will help children read more fluently. I'll show you how children can master these words by sight through patterned books and basal readers, through vocabulary games, and through direct spelling lessons with the teacher. We'll also discuss ways of expanding vocabulary through "key words," language experiences, dictionaries, vicarious and direct experiences, library books, lessons on derivatives, semantic mapping, and through instruction in the use of context clues. Throughout this discussion I'll be reminding you that we increase reading vocabulary so that children can read more interactively and successfully.

On the planet Earth, words have almost the same value as money.

VOCABULARY AND COMPREHENSION

Thorndike (not the same one who experimented with cats) gathered information in 15 countries on 100,000 students. What he found agreed with the findings of many other researchers: there is a fairly high correlation between students' scores on vocabulary and comprehension. (Those who score high on one tend to score high on the other.) He concluded that his results showed "how completely reading performance is determined by word knowledge" (Mallet, 1977, p. 62).

Why does this relationship between vocabulary and comprehension exist? Anderson and Freebody (1981) tell us there are three views on this matter. The "instrumentalist position" is a very practical view: no matter how a reading vocabulary is obtained, it's the main *cause* of good comprehension. According to this position, one should teach vocabulary directly rather than expect children to pick up words incidentally through reading.

The "aptitude position," on the other hand, is that a good vocabulary is merely the reflection of a quick mind—a mind that soaks up words as a person reads. Therefore, teach vocabulary by providing children with plenty of opportunities to read. To help beginners and poor readers, however, you should also provide a great deal of drill on quick recognition of words.

The "knowledge position" is that good comprehension is not *caused* by good vocabulary; instead, both comprehension and vocabulary abilities are caused by abundant knowledge about one's environment and culture. A good vocabulary is a reflection of one's general knowledge. According to this position, attempting to have children acquire more vocabulary without the experiences and concepts to go with it is at best an inefficient operation. The best way to increase vocabulary, therefore, is to provide more experiences to talk and write about, thus developing more schemata. This in turn enables children to learn new meaningful words *during* their experiences and to retain those words for use during the reading act. For example, a teacher might bring to the classroom several objects that relate to baking muffins—a tablespoon, measuring cup, a muffin pan, muffin liners, shortening, an actual muffin, and so on. The children could then experience the production of muffins and learn a set of related words, such as *tablespoon, muffin, shortening,* and so on. They would use these words in writing or dictating about their experience and purposefully review them later by reading their own and others' writing.

My observations in both American and British classrooms, as well as my examination of research reports, warns me to be cautious about pushing one of these positions much more than the others. All three seem to have something to say for them. I would, however, suggest a fourth position for your consideration, one I'll call an "interactive position." The other three positions seem to overlook the importance of *all four* cueing systems working together to produce good comprehension. We don't comprehend a passage by adding up all the separate word meanings in the passage. We comprehend, as you've seen in the previous chapters, by hypothesizing, predicting, and confirming, with the four cueing systems interacting as we go.

Let's look at another example of the way vocabulary and comprehension are interdependent:

> Jake was beating the batter happily. The muffins were going to be great! Suddenly he smelled something. One of the *liners* was smoking. Quickly he grabbed a pair of *tongs* and threw the *smoldering* liner into the sink. He had left on the rear burner underneath the muffin pan!

I've italicized three words that are unfamiliar to Nancy, the reader of this passage. She can use the graphophonic cues to help her pronounce them, but she doesn't know their meanings. Suppose that when she first reads that one of the liners is smoking she imagines a *liner* to be some type of person who smokes. But then, when Jake throws the liner into the sink, she knows her hypothesis is wrong. At this point, let's say she tries out another schema related to her experiences of watching her mother baking muffins and other baked goods. She remembers the "paper things" her mother puts in muffin pans—things she only thought of before as "pretty." Now she has another hypothesis and tries it out by rereading some of the passage. This time her hypothesis is confirmed. The semantic and syntactic cues the author provides (and that Nancy recognizes as easy words) help her realize that the *liners* must be "those paper things" and the *tongs* must be something to hold the liner so Jake won't get burned. And the word *smoldering?* It must mean about the same as *smoking.* Without an ample reading vocabulary (in this passage only three words were unknown), Nancy would have had a very hard time making use of the semantic and syntactic cues to help her determine what was happening in the passage. Without the schematic cues that she brought to the passage, however, all the reading vocabulary in the world wouldn't have helped her comprehend this passage. *Vocabulary and schemata must interact for comprehension to take place.*

Now let's return to Thorndike's study of 100,000 students in 15 countries. As I said, there was a fairly high correlation between vocabulary and comprehension scores, but despite the high correlation, vocabulary apparently accounts for only 50 percent of a person's comprehension ability.* That still leaves 50 percent that hasn't been accounted for. Some of this remaining 50 percent is probably due to chance factors, but I suspect that part of it is due to schematic factors. Words are important, but so are schemata. Comprehension is not simply a result of "knowing a whole lot of words." It's much more likely to be a result of a student's using all four cueing systems skillfully and interactively. This skillful use of the four systems depends on the development of both schemata and vocabulary.

WANTED: VOCABULARY FOR ASSISTING THE CUEING SYSTEMS. APPLICANT MUST COMMUNICATE WITH THE AUTHOR.

> The qualities a reader brings to a book can have as much to do with its worth as anything an author puts into it.
>
> —*Norman Cousins*

In the previous section we saw how Nancy used her reading vocabulary to understand the semantic cues the author was giving her. Knowledge of the words *muffins, smelled, grabbed, threw, sink,* and *burner* helped her figure out the unknown words and to comprehend the author's message. But how did her reading vocabulary help her notice the syntactic cues as

---

*Computed by squaring the average correlation of 0.71 in Thorndike's study.

well? First of all, she knew all of the "function words" the author used—these italicized words:

> Quicky he grabbed *a* pair *of* tongs *and* threw *the* smoldering liner *into the* sink.

If you're not already convinced that function words are an important part of one's vocabulary, try that sentence again without them:

> Quickly he grabbed pair tongs threw smoldering liner sink.

A bit harder to read that way, isn't it? (Especially if you hadn't already known what the message was.) Your reading vocabulary of function words helps you use syntactic cues. Your reading vocabulary of *derivatives* also helps. For example, if you know that *beating* is a derivative of *beat*, and *happily* is a derivative of *happy*, you'll understand this sentence better:

> Jake was beating the batter happily.

There are other ways your reading vocabulary aids the syntactic system, which we'll discuss in Chapter 6 when we talk about things children need in order to be ready for reading instruction.

What about the graphophonic and schematic cues? Does your reading vocabulary help these systems as well? Yes. If you already know a word like *coin*, for instance, this helps you to pronounce an unfamiliar word like *foin* (a thrust, as in fencing). And if *foin* were already part of your reading vocabulary, it would probably trigger the appropriate schema related to your fencing experiences, thus enabling you to understand this:

> His foin was wide of the mark.

Your reading vocabulary, then, aids the graphophonic cueing system by reminding you of words with similar spelling patterns: it aids the schematic systems by reminding you of schemata that have developed as a result of past experiences. Vocabulary is indeed a major element in the reading process.

ESSENTIAL READING VOCABULARY

By now you've probably determined, in context, that a reading vocabulary refers to those words the reader can pronounce and understand in a particular context. If a reading vocabulary makes such important contributions

to children's use of the four cueing systems, on what words should the teacher concentrate? There are over 500,000 words in some dictionaries. We need some way to select words that will make the most impact in the shortest time on the reading process. The words that seem worthy of special, concentrated attention are those that are most common to children's speaking vocabularies; those most frequently encountered in printed materials; those that are generally most difficult to learn; and those that particular children cannot remember.

First, why should we be concerned with a child's speaking vocabulary? Simply because decoding, at the initial stage of learning to read, involves the translation of print to speech (vocal or subvocal). If a word already occurs frequently in a child's speaking vocabulary, the decoding process will lead instantly to comprehension and to an increase in fluency. This greater fluency will in turn lead to quicker comprehension of sentences and longer passages.

For example, read the following sentence: *I want to give you this ring for your birthday.* All the words in that sentence are generally quite common to a school child's speaking vocabulary. Suppose we leave out the two most difficult words and assume that the rest are sight words.

I want to give you this _____ for your _____.

We can see that a large proportion of the meaning of the sentence has already been established and that the tough job of decoding and comprehending has been reduced to only two words, both of which can be partially decoded by using the context clues the sight words provide.

As for the second criterion—frequency of the word in printed materials—its significance in the selection of those words that should have special attention is probably obvious. But what may not be obvious is how the classroom teacher can take on the Herculean task of determining those words that are most frequently encountered in print, in addition to determining the most common words in children's speaking vocabularies. Fortunately, both of these jobs have already been done for you. Back in the 1930s, Dolch (1936) compiled a list of 220 "basic sight words," mainly by selecting "tool words" (words other than nouns) that were common to three very comprehensive lists developed in the 1920s. Along with the list of basic sight words, Dolch prepared a list of "ninety-five common nouns" that were common to all three lists. The 220 basic sight words, he then discovered, comprised anywhere from 52 percent to 70 percent of all the words children generally encountered in their assigned reading materials. Thus, by learning these 220 words, the children would have more than half the battle won.

For many years these 220 basic sight words—and to a lesser extent, the 95 common nouns—have been important ingredients in reading programs for children. More recently, however, numerous specialists in the field of reading have developed more up-to-date basic lists of words for children to learn. Table 4.1 summarizes eight of those lists.

As is to be expected, these word lists do not agree with each other (although there is remarkable consistency if one looks at only the first 100 high-frequency words in each list). On the one hand, I'm inclined to agree with Johnson that the list of basic sight words developed by Dolch "has perhaps outlived its usefulness" (Johnson, 1971, p. 30). On the other hand, those who have been using Dolch's basic list can rest assured that a large proportion of the words on his list have not gone out of style. In fact, none

Table 4.1 *Lists of High-Frequency Basic Sight Words*

Compilers	Sources
Barnard and DeGracie (1976)	Kindergarten and first-grade basal readers from eight different series (found 103 words common to all eight series)
Dolch (1936)	"Basic sight words" based on compilations done in the 1920s
Hillerich (1974)	School texts in grades three through nine Creative writing of children in grades one through eight Adult printed material Primary grade library books Dolch lists
Johns (1974a)	School texts in grades three through nine Primary grade library books Adult printed material Speech of kindergarten and first grade children
Johns (1974b)	Forty-six nouns common to the high frequency words in three out of four of the compilations examined in Johns's 1974 study.
Johnson (1971)	Adult printed material Speech of kindergarten and first-grade children
Moe and Hopkins (1974)	Speech of kindergarten, first- and second-grade children living in middle-class neighborhoods
Sherk (1973)	Speech of four-, five-, and six-year-old children living in lower-class neighborhoods

of them has gone out of style; it's just that some of them can no longer be considered to be words of high frequency.

About 75 percent of Dolch's 220 basic sight words can be found on the Johnson list, for example. Words such as *the, go,* and *of* are on both lists and are entitled to be called "basic" sight words. Words such as *clean, wash,* and *shall* appear only on Dolch's list and probably should be retired as basic sight words—as should most of Dolch's "ninety-five common nouns." Only about 30 percent of his nouns can be found on the Johnson list. Some of the words that were on Dolch's list of nouns, such as *cow, chicken, corn, duck, farm, farmer,* and *stock* are not to be found on the Johnson list. Instead, you find nouns like *people, world, city,* and *group.*

So, which list should a teacher use? If Dolch's list is out-of-date, is Johnson's list a better one to use? Is Johns's "Word List for the 1970s" the answer? How about Fry's or Mitzel's? One could become slightly neurotic trying to choose from among all the excellent lists that have been compiled.

It seems probable that the nature of today's reading instruction makes all the lists obsolete for some purposes. Dolch's list was popular at a time when the majority of teachers were using the "look-say method" of teaching reading. Words were presented over and over again until children knew the words "by sight." Consequently, visual memory was called upon more than phonics. Only after children had learned a large body of words by sight was phonics introduced. And often phonics was introduced in an incidental fashion, rather than as a systematic form of instruction.

Today, judging from examination of the most popular reading programs and from observations in classrooms, phonics is a major component of reading instruction (sometimes *too* major for those of us who view reading as an interactive process). Since about three-fourths of the words in high-frequency lists have regular (phonetic) spelling—words such as *hit* and *lunch*—children will normally encounter these words during phonics instruction. Consequently, it might seem better to concentrate on those high-frequency words that have irregular spellings, such as *any*, *friend*, and *thought*.

If the teacher concentrates only on irregular words, however, she will overlook an important fact: three-fourths of the 100 *most frequent words* in the English language have regular spellings. Furthermore, these 100 words "make up about 50 percent of all written material" (Fry et al., 1984, p. 22). Amazing, isn't it? We have over a half-million words to communicate with, but half of everything we write and read depends on the hundred most frequent ones. (This count includes derivatives as well; for example, *ring*, *rings*, and *ringing* all count as one word in this list of 100 words.) Furthermore, the first 10 words make up 24 percent of all written material (Fry, 1980). These ten words could win any popularity contest:

the	of	and	a	to
in	is	you	that	it

Just try writing a ten-word sentence without using one of them.

I'm going to recommend, then, that teachers concentrate on a combination of two lists when teaching a reading vocabulary. One is the first 100 words in the list developed by Elizabeth Sakiey and Edward Fry (1979). The Sakiey-Fry list was created from a much longer list (Carroll et al., 1971), produced by taking 500-word samples from 1,045 books in 12 subject areas in grades three through nine. Samples were also taken from library books and magazines.

The second list (that I've combined with the Sakiey-Fry list of 100 words) is one I developed several years ago to show teachers those high-frequency words that need to be learned through visual memory rather than phonics because of their irregular spelling. The 96 words in that list were chosen not only because they were irregular in spelling (*one*, *brought*), but also because they were found on at least two of the eight lists already described in Table 4.1. As a list, those 96 words represented oral vocabularies as well as written vocabularies, adults as well as children, lower-income neighborhoods as well as middle-income neighborhoods, and various geographic areas.

Table 4.2 shows the combination of the Sakiey-Fry list and the earlier May list. Because of the importance of these 165 words in children's ability

Table 4.2 *Essential Reading Vocabulary**

anything	give	great	Mrs.	says	very
and	at	when	about	time	than
a	could	group	night	should	want
because	do	have	nothing	some	water
in	be	can	out	has	first
again	does	head	of	something	was
is	this	use	then	look	called
almost	done	knew	brother	the	were
another	door	heard	on	sometimes	wanted
that	or	an	them	more	oil
always	buy	know	off	their	what
it	had	each	these	write	its
any	enough	light	one	they	where
are	four	only	long	who	thought
he	by	which	so	go	now
been	from	dog	other	there	father
for	but	she	her	see	down
both	friend	many	own	through	goes
brought	full	might	people	to	work
as	words	how	make	number	day
house	don't	money	put	together	you
with	not	if	like	no	did
city	live	mother	right	today	would
come	gone	Mr.	said	two	your
his	all	will	him	way	get
year	they're	school	our	there's	once
I	we	up	into	my	find
made	may	part			

*Teaching goal: to have children recognize these words through visual memory within one second, preferably by the end of second grade or not later than than third. Good testing procedures require that these words be arranged in random rather than alphabetical order. Have the child being tested read each row from left to right.

to read and write with fluency, I'd like to suggest that you *concentrate* on teaching these words during the first two or three grades. I'd also like to recommend that you teach them through the visual memory techniques I'll describe in this chapter, rather than wait for the regular (phonetic) words in the list to be learned through phonics lessons. Naturally, children will be learning many other words during the first three grades, but these 165 words deserve special attention through games, patterned books, spelling lessons, and numerous writing experiences.

ESSENTIAL READING VOCABULARY: BASAL READERS VS. PATTERNED BOOKS

As you can see from Table 4.2, the essential reading vocabulary consists of words that most children already use in their listening and speaking vocabulary by the time they reach school age. Consequently, teachers need to concentrate on helping children recognize them by *sight* rather than dwelling on their meanings. Sight recognition should be within one second, so that the cueing systems that depend upon the essential vocabulary can interact quickly and the reading can be fluent. (Fluency, remember, is crucial for good comprehension.)

Basal readers can serve as one medium for teaching the essential vocabulary and other high-frequency words. Basal readers, as you probably know, are books of stories, plays, poems, and informational articles; they're facetiously called "Dick and Jane books." These books are designed to introduce a few new words in each selection; they also provide a great deal of repetition of the new words. A new word may be repeated as many as 20 to 30 times in the first selection that features it, and then repeated in later selections. Some children learn the words strictly from the practice provided by the basal reader. *Many children need more practice than this.*

One of the best forms of additional practice can be found in the predictable patterned books I mentioned in the last chapter. Researchers (Bridge et al., 1983) have found that patterned books might work even better than basal readers in teaching sight words. My hunch is that children like the *rhythm* found in patterned books but not often found in basal readers. Perhaps this rhythm-pattern approach activates the right side of the brain, which in turn assists the left side of the brain to learn and store words. (For thousands of years the human race has known that rhythm and rhyme help people remember better.)

In the study by Bridge, Winograd, and Haley (1983), experimental and control groups of first graders were taught the same 77 words, with the experimental group using patterned books and the control group using basal readers. Both control and experimental groups consisted of below-average learners. The teaching occurred for 25 minutes a day, five days a week, for only four weeks. Here are the results:

Groups	Pretest	Posttest	Gain
Patterned books	15	52	37 words
Basal readers	23	35	12 words

As you can see, the patterned-book group gained 37 words in four weeks; the basal-reader group gained only 12. The differences between the two groups on the *pretest* were not statistically significant, whereas on the posttest they were. But even more important is the effect the patterned books had on children's strategies and attitudes. Many of the children who had the benefit of using patterned books changed their strategy, from slowly sounding out each word to greater reliance on context clues. By skipping a hard word and reading on, many found they could then figure out the word. Furthermore, when asked how they felt about reading out loud in their reading group, this group was more positive than the basal-reader group. You might like to try the procedures the teacher used in this study. (You will need more than one day.)

1. Teacher selects enjoyable patterned books that emphasize the "target words." (In this study, four Bill Martin books were used: *Brown Bear, Brown Bear, What Do You See?*; *Fire! Fire! Said Mrs. McGuire*; *The Haunted House*; and *Up and Down the Escalator*. The other two books were by Bruno Munari: *Jimmy Has Lost His Cap, Where Can It Be?* and *The Elephant's Wish*.)

2. Teacher reads book out loud.

3. Teacher reads book again, with the children joining in whenever they can predict what comes next.

4. Children take turns with echo and choral reading.

5. Teacher reads the text from teacher-made charts with no picture clues. Then children read with the teacher.

6. Children place matching sentence strips on charts. (Teacher has made charts so that a sentence strip can be taped under a sentence on the chart.)

7. Children later place matching *word* strips on charts, saying the word as they match it. (Teacher has children match words in correct order the first time this is done; later in random order.)

8. Children and teacher chorally read the entire story.

9. Teacher places word strips in *random order* at the bottom of the chart. Children come up and match the strips to words in the story, saying each word as they match it to one in the story.

10. The only step I would add to this excellent set of procedures is to have the children *write* the target words as well as read them. Research shows that writing words "helps the child to commit them to his sight vocabulary" (Bond & Dykstra, 1967, p. 124).

One tricky part to using patterned books this way is finding books that contain the exact words you want to teach. Actually, though, this is less a problem than you might imagine, since the Essential Reading Vocabulary is composed of such high-frequency words. Thus, most patterned books use many of the words from the list. However, there are times when you may want to create your own patterned stories, which you can do by adapting a patterned story that already exists. For instance, the following story is one I adapted from Bill Martin's *Brown Bear, Brown Bear, What Do You See?* It features 13 words from the Essential Reading Vocabulary, as well as three repetitions each of several three-word phrases: *hungry bird, stalking cat, barking dog,* and so.

"Little Bug, Little Bug, What Do You Fear?"*

Little bug, little bug, what do you fear?
A hungry bird might come for me. That's what I fear.
Hungry bird, hungry bird, what do you fear?
A stalking cat might come for me. That's what I fear.
Stalking cat, stalking cat, what do you fear?
A barking dog might come for me. That's what I fear.
Barking dog, barking dog, what do you fear?
A teasing child might come for me. That's what I fear.
Teasing child, teasing child, what do you fear?
My angry brother might come for me. That's what I fear.
Angry brother, angry brother, what do you fear?
A scary night might come for me. That's what I fear.
Scary night, scary night, what do you fear?
A friendly sun might come for me. That's what I fear.

---

*A patterned story for teaching sight words, and for enjoyment.

Friendly sun, friendly sun, what do you fear?
NOTHING!

READING TO YOUR STUDENTS

Another way to use patterned and other books is more casual than the
methods I've been describing. Reading books of various kinds to your students is an excellent way of modeling good reading, inspiring them to read
on their own, sharing a common experience, and teaching vocabulary. With
any book, you can stop for a moment and discuss an interesting word and
write it on the chalkboard, then go back to the sentence in the book and
read the word in context. With patterned books you can look at the book
ahead of time to see which words are repeated many times. In some of the
more interesting patterned books for children beyond grade two, for instance, you may find only four or five words like this. Just write these
words on the board before you read the book to your students. Then, whenever you come to them in the book, casually point to the board and encourage the children to read them. With one book, for instance, they will have
many opportunities to read these particular words: "terrible, horrible, no
good, very bad day" *(Alexander and the Terrible, Horrible, No Good, Very
Bad Day)*.

ESSENTIAL READING VOCABULARY: GAMES VS. WORKSHEETS

Teachers often use games for teaching essential sight words, but there's
always that fear that maybe the children aren't really learning anything
important when they play games. "Aren't they just having fun?" one
teacher asked me. And another asked, "Don't the games distract them from
really learning?" Well, I can understand fears like this, because I've often
had them myself. (The Puritan ethic is still strong enough in our society to
make us feel guilty for enjoying ourselves too much.) Fortunately, research
shows that the use of games to reinforce sight vocabulary can work quite
well—in fact, even better than traditional workbooks or worksheets. One of
the best studies on this was conducted by Dolores Dickerson (1982), who
compared the effectiveness of games with worksheets, using 274 first graders from 30 classrooms in a large urban school system. Those children who

knew more than 25 percent of the sight words before the experiment began were eliminated from the study. After six weeks the results looked like this:

	Active Games		Passive Games		Worksheets	
	Boys	Girls	Boys	Girls	Boys	Girls
Pretest	4	4	4	3	2	3
Posttest	35	34	30	27	21	21
Gain	31	30	26	24	19	18
Gain one week later	32	31	27	25	20	20

Those are pretty impressive differences. The passive-games approach brought about a 30 percent greater gain than the worksheet approach; the active-games approach, a 53 percent greater gain.

What made the difference? Well, the worksheets involved *one individual* in matching exercises and sentence completion exercises. The games, on the other hand, involved *two or more* individuals in a social situation rather than an isolated situation. The games also necessitated abundant feedback of an instantaneous and highly specific type ("No, that's not *thought*; that's *through*; you have to go back a step.") The active games included Word Toss, Words in a Circle, See the Same, Word Point, and Stepword from *Teaching Slow Learners through Active Games* (Humphrey & Sullivan, 1970). Another active game was "a variation on the commercial game *Twister* from Milton Bradley . . . Passive treatment games were Go Fish, Word Checkers, The Snoopy Game, Concentration, Word Rummy, and Word Dominoes" (Dickerson, 1982, p. 47). Other studies have shown that using games can be an effective instructional approach to teaching sight words (Hunter, 1975).

Dickerson's advice, however, might prove valuable to you: "Incorporating games into regular lessons and not as adjunct activities increases the value of the game, since its objective reinforces the lesson" (p. 49). I would also advise that you schedule the additional game playing so that each child can only play a particular game a few times before moving to another game. Children tend to keep returning to the same game again and again because of their familiarity and success with it, so the teacher needs some way to challenge them to gain greater breadth of practice. You may wish to use some kind of merit stickers or tokens for those games they have completed.

In the list of suggested readings at the end of this chapter, you'll find several books and articles that will give you ideas for games. Also take a look at Appendix A for many more games.

DIRECT LESSONS ON ESSENTIAL VOCABULARY

Some children may need very direct lessons on essential words they are not learning. The following sample lesson involves spelling and writing the words. As I mentioned, having children *write* the words they are attempting to learn to read seems to aid their visual memory of the words.

Step 1: Introduce the words in context. About two to five words is enough. If you introduce more, it will be difficult for the children to master them. (Normally you will be working with a small group of children, rather than the entire class. It is assumed that they have already learned how to write each letter of the alphabet.)

  A. Write sentences containing the words on the chalkboard, using a form of printing. Underline the particular words you will be emphasizing.
     "Who has my ball?" Jim asked. "I want it back."
     "There it is," Janet said. "Your coat is on top of it."

  B. Read the entire "story" to your students.

  C. Have the children echo-read each sentence the second time through.

  D. Write each word on the board, using lowercase letters.

  E. (Optional Step) Point to one of the words, pronounce it, and ask a child to make up another sentence using the same word. Have a different child do the same with each word.

  F. Point to one of the words, pronounce it, and ask a child to spell it out loud. Have her pronounce it after she has spelled it. Have a different child do the same with each word.

Step 2: Have the children enhance their visual memory and auditory memory of the word.

  A. Have them look at one of the words and spell it to themselves. (By having them spell the word out loud and to themselves, you are helping them enhance their auditory as well as visual memory of the letters in the word.)

  B. Have them close their eyes and imagine themselves writing it on their paper.

  C. Ask them to look at the board to see if they have it correct.

Step 3:   Ask them to write the same word from memory.

    A. Have them look at the word again and spell it to themselves.

    B. Cover the word on the chalkboard and ask them to write the word on their papers.

    C. Uncover the word and ask them to check to see if they have it correct.

    D. Check each child's paper to make sure she has the word correct.

Step 4:   Repeat Steps 2 and 3 for each of the underlined words.

Step 5:   Have them practice recognizing the words in isolation.

    A. With the words written on flash cards, expose each one for about one second to the group and ask them to say it out loud together.

    B. Expose each one again to one child at a time.

Step 6:   Repeat Step 5 with the first letter of each word capitalized (Who, There, Want, Your).

Step 7:   To ensure that positive transfer takes place, arrange for them to practice the words in context.

    A. Go back to the sentences you put on the board at the beginning of the lesson and ask the children to read them without your help.

    B. Have them search for the words in their basal reader or other reading material; give them page numbers.

Step 8:   Distribute the practice with games and activities over several days and weeks. There are a variety of ways to make the practice sessions different each time. Here are examples of some "practice" sessions:

A. Play the number-line game.

    1. Draw a number line from zero to ten for each child who will play the game.

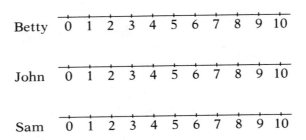

2. Prepare a stack of about thirty three-by-five cards, some with + + +1, some with + + +2, and some with + + +3 on them. Place them face down.

3. Flash a word card for one second to each child in turn, who must read the card to be permitted to draw a number off the top of the number stack. (She misses her chance if she cannot say it within three seconds after you've flashed the card.)

4. The child must then place an X above the correct number on the number line.

5. The first one to get to the 10 wins.

B. Before the children get to go somewhere—lunch, recess, home— they have to tell you the "password," which is simply a word on one of the flash cards.

For children who are slow or disabled learners, these steps may be insufficient. Chapter 13 provides information and guidance on working with these children. For most children, however, the steps provide a good way of learning essential sight words.

PERSONALIZED KEY WORDS AND OTHER LANGUAGE EXPERIENCES

In addition to having the children learn the Essential Vocabulary shown in Table 4.2, you will also want them to learn words that have more meaning to them. The words in the Essential Vocabulary list tend to be mostly "function words" that *help* people communicate but say very little by themselves—words like *from*, *your*, and *in*. Children need "meatier" words to work with as well, such as *love*, *fight*, *money*, *bus*, *crash*, and *kiss*. But herein lies a problem. What's meaningful to one child may not be meaningful to another. And the more meaningful the words, the easier they are usually learned. (*Mother* is an easier word to learn than *said*.)

Many years ago Sylvia Ashton-Warner discovered (or rediscovered) a way of motivating children in New Zealand to learn words rapidly. She called this the "key words" method, by which each child would accumulate his own word cards based on his own needs for words that were important to him (Aston-Warner, 1963).

This method is being used today in many language experience programs and has been advocated for many years by Jeannete Veatch, a strong advocate for individualized reading instruction. We'll talk more about her ideas in Chapters 7 and 8, but for now let me summarize the steps that she and others recommend for developing a key-word vocabulary (Veatch et al., 1979).

1. Each day the child whispers his special word into the teacher's ear.

2. The teacher prints the word on a large card, saying the letters as she writes.

3. The child traces the word with his finger, then talks briefly with the teacher about the word and why it's important to him.

4. The child is now reminded of possible things to do with the word, such as writing it on paper, drawing a related picture, writing it on the chalkboard, making sentences with several of his cards, and so on, depending on the child's wishes and the facilities in the classroom.

5. About every two or three days, the child brings his words to the teacher and reads them as quickly as he can. The words he can say within one or two seconds, he gets to keep; the teacher keeps the others. (My own preference is to put a check mark on those he missed and give him a second or third try the next time; if he misses some the third time, he's probably not very interested in them.)

6. Gradually children engage in more and more writing, using their key words and any other words they have learned to write about their own lives.

Some teachers use other language experiences for developing vocabulary. Instead of using key words, children dictate a story to the teacher, who then duplicates the story and provides each child with a copy the next day. The child receives a word card for those words in the story she still remembers. These word cards are then used in much the same way as those developed through the key word approach.

Chapter 7 will give you many more ideas on how to use language experiences to teach reading. The important thing to know is that language experience approaches that emphasize reading materials created through children's own writing or dictation can be as effective as basal reader approaches. In Kelly's study (1975), for example, below-average third graders who were given 15 weeks of instruction through language experiences gained 22 percent more sight words than a control group given instruction through basal readers. (See Chapter 7 for more research on language experience approaches.)

WHEN DO WE KNOW A WORD?

We've been talking about teaching sight words from the Essential Reading Vocabulary and from children's own private key words. These words, however, are those that children already comprehend the moment they decode them. Let's talk, instead, about words your students encounter as they read and aren't too sure of their meanings. As reading teachers, we have to help children *understand* words as well as pronounce them. But when is a word understood?

Let's begin by talking about "nambol." I've given you only one of the four cueing systems you need to read this word. The word *nambol* can be decoded (translated from print to sound) by using only graphophonic cues.

You can see from the spelling patterns that there will be two distinct syllables when you pronounce the word: /nam/ and /bol/. You can also tell that *nam* will probably rhyme with *ham*.

So do you know this word now? Hardly. You have only a good idea what it sounds like. All right, then, let's introduce a bit of syntax. This time let's say "The nambol" instead of just "nambol." Now do you know the word better? Yes; by placing the word *the* in front of it, we've given *nambol* a position. It's no longer an isolated word. It's probably a nounlike word (The nambol is . . .) or maybe an adjective-type word (The nambol bogitt is . . .).

So now do you know the word? Only a little better. All right, let's introduce the semantic cueing system. We'll insert a word that adds meaning rather than mere position: The muddy nambol . . .

Do you know the word now? At this point, most readers are ready to make a hypothesis about its meaning. The word *muddy* means *wet, squishy dirt*. But good readers don't think like a dictionary and stop with "wet squishy dirt." Instead, they use their personal schemata about mud, such as "found in a river," or "found all over the bodies of pigs," or "scraped from a little boy's clothes." It is this ability to combine all four cueing systems that enables good readers to *know* a word.

In actuality, good readers are open-minded about what they know. We may hypothesize that a nambol is a river, but as we read further, we may change our hypothesis. If we read "The muddy nambol licked . . ." we may quickly hypothesize that it's not a river; it's probably a creature of some sort. The word *licked* has given us more pieces of the puzzle. The syntactic position of the verb *licked* assures us that *nambol* is indeed a noun; the -*ed* at the end of *lick* has told us that an action has already taken place. Semantically speaking, we know that a nambol is a creature with a tongue. But schematically speaking we also now suspect from our past experiences that a nambol is a dog or cat—or something similar. Only when we read the complete sentence do we feel we *know*: "The muddy nambol licked its feet and purred."

The point I'm making here is that a word is seldom "known" in isolation. When words are used for communication, they are known or understood in *context*. Goodman (1983) demonstrated with 100 first-, second-, and third-graders that children can miss many words they attempt to read on a list, then turn around and read three-fourths of the missed words correctly in a story. When the children in Goodman's study had all four cueing systems available to them, they could read the words quite well! Other researchers have had the same results (Highes, 1977; Hudelson-Lopez, 1977; Pearson, 1978; Veatch et al., 1979).

So, going back to our original question, when do we know a word? From the standpoint of reading, one answer would be: when all four cueing systems lead us to its meaning in a particular passage. But my hunch is that you'd like a more definite answer. All right, let's look at the problem from a different angle. Suppose we ask ourselves how we might measure a child's *reading* vocabulary. Of course, we could do what is so often done— we could give her a multiple choice test. For each word, there would be four alternative definitions, and all she has to do is select the right definition for each word. What could be simpler? But what's wrong with that idea? Is that what teachers should be doing in classrooms? Teaching and testing words in isolation? No. By now I'm fairly sure you're with me on this. Teachers are expected to produce readers, not parrots. Reading is an intelligent, active process of observing, predicting, and confirming, not a passive one of being filled with words and definitions.

MEASURING CHILDREN'S VOCABULARIES

A child's *sight* vocabulary is fairly easy to measure. If you flash a printed word in front of a child for a duration of only one second (assuming she has no vision problem), and she can instantly pronounce the word, that word is part of her sight vocabulary. Your only problem is deciding which words are essential for her to have in her sight vocabulary and determining which of those she already knows through visual memory.

Measuring a child's *reading* vocabulary, on the other hand, is not so easy. How do you know that Sally understands a word? Well, we might say she understands the word *piano* because she can point to it. When we say *piano* to her, she doesn't point to her big sister's trumpet, or to the refrigerator, or to the piano bench. In addition to pointing to a piano, she can tell you something about it ("My brother plays it. You can play tunes on it, like 'Mary Had a Little Lamb.' If you hit it up here, it makes a high sound. If you hit it down here it makes a low sound.")

But suppose you ask her to "name a large musical instrument with eighty-eight keys." She may draw a blank if she doesn't know what *keys* are, or what *musical instrument* means, or even what the number *eighty-eight* means. In short, she doesn't understand the word *piano* that well. You can see, then, that whether or not a child understands a word depends partly on what the measurer means by "understands." Unless teachers keep the concept of communication in mind, it is possible for them to get confused on this matter and to reinforce learning that does not lead to better reading.

From the teacher's standpoint, all that should matter is that the children comprehend a word well enough to help them comprehend the author's message. The word *piano*, like so many words in the English language, has many shades of meaning, depending on how technical or detailed one wishes to be. But one can communicate about a piano without knowing all the intricacies of the strings and soundboard. Generally speaking, it is both inefficient and unwise for the reading teacher to dwell very long on the meanings of words *in isolation*. Remember, from an interactive standpoint, the author's *message* is the important focus, rather than the author's words.

The notion that a large vocabulary demonstrates superior intelligence still lingers on in our society. We are still apt to be impressed by those who use "big words," rather than by people who communicate simply, clearly, and thoughtfully. Such a notion about intelligence easily creeps into our thinking as we work with children. Our goal sometimes becomes one of increasing their vocabulary rather than increasing their ability to communicate. Unfortunately, our tendency to set the goal of a large vocabulary is encouraged by the fact that vocabulary growth is so much easier to measure than communication growth.

This is not to say that teachers shouldn't spend a considerable amount of time strengthening children's vocabularies; I only wish to urge teachers to use the concepts of cueing systems and communication as guides in determining how much time to spend on learning the meanings of particular words. Vocabulary is only part of the picture. One may understand every word in a message in the greatest detail and still not understand the message.

USING DALE'S CONE OF EXPERIENCE

Dale (1969) developed a useful model for teachers to use when planning vocabulary building experiences. This model, the "Cone of Experience," is shown in Figure 4.1. In essence, Dale's theory goes like this: Children learn at the deepest and most intense level through direct, purposeful experiences, the base of Dale's cone. They learn at the shallowest and least intense level through sheer verbal experiences, the tip of the cone. In between the base and the tip of the cone are vicarious (indirect) experiences that provide different depths and intensities of learning. Next to a direct experience of driving a car, for instance, the deepest and most intense experience would be that of a contrived experience with a mock-up car, one that simulates a road, other cars, a crash, and so on.

In theory at least, the information we receive at the verbal level (including new words) often goes in one ear and out the other, sticking inside just long enough to use it for passing a test. Information we receive at the direct level of experience (such as the word *hot* the moment we touch a hot stove) tends to stay with us longer and to become a part of our readily available source of words or concepts.

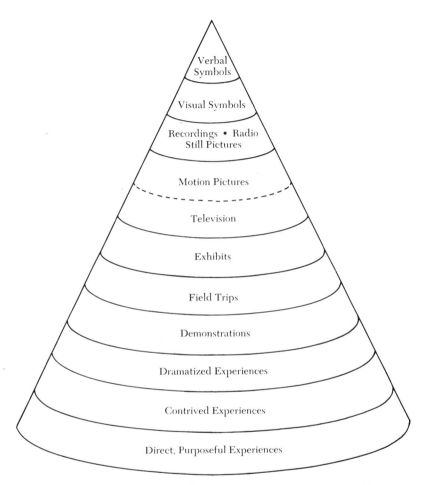

Verbal
Symbols

Visual Symbols

Recordings • Radio
Still Pictures

Motion Pictures

Television

Exhibits

Field Trips

Demonstrations

Dramatized Experiences

Contrived Experiences

Direct, Purposeful Experiences

Figure 4.1 *Dale's Cone of Experience. From* **AUDIOVISUAL METHODS IN TEACHING,** *Third Edition by Edgar Dale. Copyright 1946, 1954,* © *1969 by Holt, Rinehart and Winston. Reprinted by permission of Holt, Rinehart and Winston.*

Let's take the words *rozaga hunt* as an example. The best way to teach David about a rozaga hunt would be to take him on one. Let him get up with you in the middle of the night, carry one of the four-celled flashlights in one hand and the sharpened spear in the other, and stumble through the woods toward the swamp. Let him listen to the hurrumping of the bull frogs, the hooting of the owls, and that eerie low whistle of the rozaga. Let him shiver with fright as he unexpectedly comes face to face with one, its fangs and yellow eyes highlighting the swanlike neck covered with dark leathery scales, its snakelike tongue darting in and out of its mouth only three feet away from David's right arm. Let him hear your shout of warning and feel his tight-muscled arm jab the spear through the vital spot, right through the neck. Do you have any doubt that David will forget the word *rozaga?* (Be assured that there are no rozagas lurking about; the rozaga is a creature of the author's imagination.)

Assuming for a moment that the rozaga is a real animal, let us suppose you are teaching a social studies unit on the rozaga hunters of North Borneo. You are trying to show how these people have adapted to their environment, and since rozaga hunting is their chief means of survival, it is important that your students understand the words *rozaga hunt.* Since you plan to discuss these people on and off for the next few weeks, you want your students to make the words *rozaga hunt* part of their vocabulary. What should you do?

Obviously you can't provide them with the direct experience of rozaga hunting. So, looking at Dale's Cone of Experience, what would be the next best learning experience? A contrived experience would probably be out because of the time and expense. (Although taking apart and putting together a plaster model of a rozaga would be one type of contrived experience.)

What about a dramatized experience of a rozaga hunt? This would be excellent after children have developed some simpler ideas of what a rozaga is and how a rozaga hunt is carried out. In fact, telling the students that they will eventually get to enact a rozaga hunt will spur most of them on to finding out more about a rozaga hunt.

The next layers of the Cone of Experience suggest the use of demonstrations, field trips, and exhibits. Having someone (such as the teacher) who has seen a movie of a rozaga hunt provide a demonstration of the hunt would help the children get a deeper understanding of the concept. A field trip, in this case, would be impractical, unless you were able to take them to a museum showing exhibits related to the rozaga hunt. At an exhibit, they would be able to see the weapon and perhaps a stuffed rozaga close at hand.

A movie or a televised documentary, although not providing the close-at-hand experience of the exhibit, would provide the emotional impact that has so far been missing in your attempts to get them to understand a rozaga hunt. But if nothing else is available, perhaps you'll at least have some still pictures showing the rozaga and the hunters and perhaps a recording of someone describing an actual rozaga hunt.

As you can see, we've reached the top of the Cone of Experience with nothing left but visual symbols (such as diagrams or maps) and verbal symbols (words and definitions). You could simply write the word *rozaga* on the board and say, "A rozaga is an amphibian with dark leathery scales and a swanlike neck living in the swamps of North Borneo." That would take a lot less time than all the vicarious experiences we've been discussing. And there are plenty of times when that's all a word deserves. But if you truly want the children to make a word part of their vocabularies, you have to back up the verbal experience with one or more nonverbal ones.

USING THE DICTIONARY

Must all words for a semantic vocabulary be developed through direct or vicarious experiences? What about the "good old dictionary," or just picking up new words in context as the child begins to read for recreation and information? An important point: to learn all words through direct or nearly direct experiences would require the nine lives of a cat. Many words must be added to one's reading vocabulary just through reading and discussion, looking up words in a dictionary, and through wide, thoughtful reading. And yet, an understanding of dictionary definitions depends upon prior experiences—direct, vicarious, and verbal.

For instance, if you look up the word *excursion* in a dictionary, you may find as one meaning, "a short journey or trip." Now, having the children look up this word in a dictionary is a much quicker and more sensible way of getting them to discover its meaning than packing them up and taking them for an excursion— providing you're sure of two things: (1) the children have all experienced a journey or trip, and (2) they have all heard (and preferably spoken) the word *trip* or *journey* in this context. (If Bobbie has only heard the word *trip* in connection with drugs, she may be somewhat puzzled.)

One secret to success in teaching children to use a dictionary is to avoid assigning dictionary tasks that are too difficult. Too often children are asked to use dictionaries before they are ready to use them, and this leads to plenty of frustration for children and teachers alike.

Let's take the word *fatigue*, for example. Suppose you ask Henry to look up this word and tell the class how to pronounce it. What skills does he need to do this quickly and correctly? Assuming he knows where to find the dictionary (an assumption that could easily be erroneous), he should know first of all that since the word starts with *f*, he will need to open the dictionary somewhere in the first part of the book. If he opens it to words beginning with *g*, he must know that he should now go toward the front of the book rather than toward the back. As soon as he finds the *f* pages, he shouldn't look randomly for the word *fatigue*; he should head toward the first *f* pages, since the second letter in *fatigue* is *a*. To put it another way, he should know alphabetical order perfectly. As Henry continues his search, his eyes should only be scanning the top of each page rather than the whole page, since at the top he will find two guide words that indicate the first and last entries for the page.

Now that he's finally found the word, he should study the respelling in parentheses. In this case it's (fə/tēg'), rather than (fat'/ig/yū), which is what he thought it was going to be. Suppose he's thrown by the pronunciation of (fə), the first syllable. Then he should glance immediately to the bottom of the page at the "Concise Pronunciation Key" to find that (ə) is equal to *a*, as in *alone*. Now, by paying attention to the diacritical mark over the *e*, by noticing the syllabication and the accent mark, and by employing his phonics knowledge, he is ready to tell the class how to pronounce it.

You can see, then, what you've really asked Henry to do! In list form, to be able to decode a word "simply" through the use of a dictionary, he must be able to do these things:

1. Locate the appropriate section of the pages

2. Determine whether the first letter of the word is before or after the page he is reading

3. Determine whether the second letter of the word is before or after the page he is reading

4. Determine whether the third or possibly the fourth letter of the word is before or after the page he is reading

5. Locate the guide words (entry words) that "enclose" the word he's seeking

6. Locate and use the Concise Pronunciation Key, if necessary, to determine the pronunciation of each syllable

7. Use the diacritical marks to determine the pronunciation of certain graphemes (letters that stand for speech sounds)

8. Interpret syllabic division correctly

9. Interpret accent marks correctly

10. Employ his knowledge of phonics

But that's not all! Suppose you want Henry to find the *meaning* of the word as well? Then the poor kid has to go through each of the definitions (and some words have dozens) to find the one that matches the context of the sentence he's looking at. Perhaps it's clear, then, that before asking children to use dictionaries, it would be wise to teach them each of the operations involved in looking up a word. Appendix N offers suggestions you may wish to follow with your students: a sample lesson on the front, middle, and back of a dictionary; ideas for teaching alphabetical order; a sample lesson on guide words; and some ideas for teaching the use of a pronunciation key.

LEARNING WORDS THROUGH READING

A large number of new words that children add to their vocabulary is acquired through actual reading—of their basal readers, their library books, and their textbooks in the content areas. Before children read a selection in their basal reader or social studies textbook, for instance, the teacher usually clarifies the meaning of important words in the selection. This tends to increase their understanding not only of the words themselves but of the entire story or article.

Sometimes teachers discuss far too many words before they have the children read, often because teachers' editions of the basal reader or content-area textbook list too many for the teacher to discuss. But whatever the reason, it is usually impossible to do justice to more than four or five words in the time available. Many of the words that teachers explain to children can be comprehended through context clues; to clarify these words ahead of time is to deprive the children of the opportunity to practice this valuable skill. Therefore, when selecting key words for prereading discussion, try to choose those that meet more than one of these criteria:

1. Words that cannot be comprehended through the context clues provided in the selection

2. Words that are crucial to providing the necessary experiential background for the selection (an article about telephone repairs, for instance, might require an explanation of the word *splicing*)

3. Words that may be difficult to decode as well as comprehend

Besides learning new words through assigned reading, children may learn numerous words through their informal reading of library books. They pick up most of these words through context clues and through repetition. The more children read on their own like this, the more their reading vocabulary generally grows.

LEARNING DERIVATIVES

Many children delight in creating new words out of old. Mrs. Johns asks, "How many new words can we get from the word *paint*?" Her fourth graders wave their hands frantically to get her attention. "Painter," says one child, and writes it on the chalkboard under the word *paint*. "Painting," says another, and takes her turn at the board. And on it goes, with *paints, painters, paintings, painted, unpainted, repaint, repainted*. Building derivatives is the name of the game, and this group of children seems to love it.

Sometimes, though, Mrs. Johns has her charges reverse the process and search for the root. "What's the root of this word?" she says, pointing to *refurnishing*. When they agree on the root, she asks them how the meaning changes when the prefix and ending are added. They don't seem to enjoy this process quite as much, but they're getting skilled at it.

Another teacher, Miss Tevlin, does something similar with her first graders. Whenever children learn a new word, she often asks them, "What would happen if we put an *s* on the end of this word? How would you say it now? What does it mean now?" And sometimes she does the same thing with *-ing*, *-ed*, *-er*, *-ly*, and *-est*. These six are the most common endings for words in the English language (Fry, 1980). Mrs. Jones and Miss Tevlin are both helping their students build their reading vocabulary.

LEARNING WORDS THROUGH CONTEXT CLUES

Context analysis (using the author's semantic and syntactic cues) is probably the most important tool for learning new words. Yet, unless you demonstrate how to use context, many children skip over "hard words" like foot soldiers dodging land mines. A few dutifully plow through a dictionary at the slightest difficulty, thus slowing themselves down far more than necessary.

During regular reading instruction, there are many opportunities to show children how to make an intelligent guess of a word's meaning. Perhaps the best way to motivate children to learn from your demonstration, though, is first to list the words on the board before they begin reading a selection. Then, for the first word, tell them only the page number and challenge them to "see who can discover what it means by reading the words around it." If a child gets the correct meaning, have him explain his "secret method" of finding out what it means. Then do the same for each of the other words.

On the occasions when students can't discover a secret method, you'll need either to teach them a method, explain the word's meaning with vicarious and verbal experiences, or help them use a dictionary or glossary. Here are some of the "secret methods" you may wish to teach:

"Place" clues: Here we try to get them to notice syntactic cues intuitively without getting into a formal discussion of syntax. For example, suppose they're about to read a selection that includes a sentence similar to the one we've already discussed: "The muddy *nambol* licked its paws and purred." Ask them questions like these: "Do you think *nambol* is an action word or a name of something? How can you tell? What would happen if we put *nambol* in a different position in the sentence?" (Try it: "The nambol muddy . . . ." Also try presenting one word at a time as I did for you on pages 121–122.) In addition, you might ask them to list words that could fit in *nambol's* place.)

"Memory" clues: Here we try to have them notice semantic cues that trigger schematic cues. Ask them: "What does the word *muddy* make you remember? Do you think *that* memory will help you figure out what *nambol* means? What about the word *licked*? What does *that* word remind you of? Will it help you decide what *nambol* means?"

"Double-comma" clues: children usually enjoy searching for these. They're straightforward and easy to spot—even by the reluctant reader.

The *gully*, a deep ditch, was full of water.

The *galloon*, or braid, was made of silver thread.

"Definition" clues: these are usually easy and need very little demonstration by the teacher.

"The kind of *poke* I'm talkin' about is a small bag."

An *ophthalmologist* is a doctor who treats eye diseases.

"Mood" clues: these are much more difficult to use and may require several demonstrations by the teacher.

The house was dark. The wind was howling through the cracks like ghosts. I was *terrified*.

First he'd lost his best friend. Then he'd lost his bus fare. He was totally *depressed*.

"Building-block" clues: These are simply derivatives—words built by adding suffixes and other word parts to an original word.

She *unwillingly* walked to school. (*willing*) + (*un*) + (*ly*)

He was *unfastening* his seat belt.

"Interpreter" clues: these are clues derived from the reader's interpretations or inferences and are the most difficult to demonstrate.

His *opponent* for the boxing match looked much stronger and bigger.

He was so angry his face was *florid.*

By teaching more words through context analysis, teachers can provide children with long-range strategies for learning new words by themselves. And, of course, by concentrating more on context analysis, you will also be emphasizing reading as an interactive rather than word-by-word process.

LEARNING WORDS THROUGH SEMANTIC MAPPING

Perhaps the best way for you to understand or review the concept of semantic mapping is to complete the semantic map shown in Figure 4.2. Just fill in the blanks.

When you've completed it, you can see that semantic mapping is a procedure for extending the meaning of a word by showing the categories of words that relate to it. Semantic mapping is based on the premise that everything we learn must be related to something else that we already understand. If I want to teach the meaning of the fictitious word *rozaga,* for instance, I may relate it to words such as *fangs, swan, leather, snake, hunting, spear, swamp,* and so on.

The advantage of the semantic-mapping process is that it enables a child not only to visualize relationships, but to categorize them as well. Such categorization reinforces both the understanding of the word in question and the child's ability to perceive similarities and differences in the environment.

The steps one might use for semantic mapping with children are these:

1. Select a word you want them to understand in greater depth.

2. Provide direct and vicarious experiences related to the word.

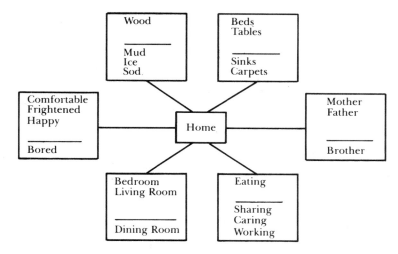

Figure 4.2 *Semantic Map*

3. Have each child write down as many words as she can that she thinks have some relationship to the word.

4. Map and categorize the words together on the chalkboard.

5. Have them create a title for each category.

THE MAIN IDEAS IN THIS CHAPTER

Good vocabulary may not *cause* good reading comprehension directly. Good vocabulary and comprehension may both be reflections of rich background experiences and schemata.

For comprehension to take place when one reads, vocabulary and schemata must interact. Vocabulary is the trigger or catalyst that enables all four cueing systems to interact.

The "Essential Reading Vocabulary" is a list of high-frequency words combining part of the Sakiey-Fry List and the May list. It is designed to show teachers which words to help children learn by sight as early as possible in the primary grades.

Highly effective means of teaching essential sight words include the use of patterned books, active and table games, and direct lessons involving spelling.

Personalized "key" words and other language experiences help children develop a reading and writing vocabulary of highly meaningful words.

Our goal as reading teachers should not be to help children develop huge vocabularies of isolated words. (Teachers shouldn't be in the trivia business.) Our goal should be to help children unlock authors' messages by *using words* to trigger the interaction of the four cueing systems.

There are a variety of ways to build your students' reading vocabulary: through specific training in dictionary use; through direct and vicarious experiences; through reading to them and providing ample opportunities to read; through expanding their word power with derivatives; through semantic mapping; and through language experiences at every grade level. But the most important way to help them build their *own* vocabulary and their *own* ability to use interactive processes is to teach them to use context clues.

REFERENCES AND SUGGESTED READINGS

Anderson, R., & Freebody, P. (1981). Vocabulary knowledge. In J. Guthrie (Ed.), *Comprehension and teaching* (pp. 77–177). Newark, DE: International Reading Association.

Ashton-Warner, S. (1963). *Teacher.* New York: Simon & Schuster.

Barnard, D.P., & DeGracie, J. (1976). Vocabulary analysis of new primary reading series. *Reading Teacher, 30,* 177–180.

Bond, G.L., & Dykstra, R. (1967). The cooperative program in first grade reading instruction. *Reading Research Quarterly, 2,* 5–142.

Bridge, C.A., Winograd, P.N., & Haley, D. (1983). Using predictable materials vs. preprimers to teach beginning sight words. *Reading Teacher, 36,* 884–891.

Brown, B. (1981). Enrich your reading program with personal words. *Reading Teacher, 35,* 40–43.

Burie, A.A., & Heltshe, M.A. (1975). *Reading with a smile: 90 reading games that work.* Washington D.C.: Acropolis Books.

Carroll, J.B., Davies, P., & Richman, B. (1971). *The American Heritage word frequency book.* New York: Houghton-Mifflin.

Ceprano, M.A. (1981). A review of selected research on methods of teaching sight words. *Reading Teacher, 35,* 314–322.

Dale, E. (1965). Vocabulary measurement: Techniques and major findings. *Elementary English, 42,* 895–901, 948.

Dale, E. (1969). *Audiovisual methods in teaching.* New York: Holt, Rinehart and Winston.

Dickerson, D.P. (1982). A study of the use of games to reinforce sight vocabulary. *Reading Teacher, 36,* 46–49.

Dolch, E.W. (1936). A basic sight vocabulary. *Elementary School Journal, 36,* 456–460.

Durr, William K. (1973). Computer study of high frequency words in popular trade juveniles. *The Reading Teacher, 27,* 37–42.

Eeds, M. (1985). Bookwords: Using a beginning word list of high frequency words from children's literature K–3. *Reading Teacher, 38,* 418–423.

Fry, E. (1980). The new instant word list. *Reading Teacher, 34,* 284–289.

Fry, E.B., Polk, J.K., & Fountoukidis, D. (1984). *The reading teacher's book of lists.* Englewood Cliffs, NJ: Prentice-Hall.

Goodman, K.S. (1965). A linguistic study of cues and miscues in reading. *Elementary English, 42,* 639–643.

Goodman, K.S. (1983). A linguistic study of cues and miscues in reading. In Gentile, L.M., Kamil, M.L., & Blanchard, J.S. (Eds.), *Reading research revisited* (pp. 187–192). Columbus, OH: Charles E. Merrill Publishing.

Harris, A.J., & Johnson, M.D. (1982). *Basic reading vocabularies.* New York: Macmillan.

Highes, M.A. (1977). *Word identification and comprehension in learning to read.* Unpublished doctoral dissertation, University of Toronto.

Hillerich, R.L. (1974). Word lists—getting it all together. *Reading Teacher, 27,* 353–360.

Hudelson-Lopez, S. (1977). Children's use of contextual clues in reading Spanish. *Reading Teacher, 30,* 735–740.

Humphrey, J.H. (1967). The use of the active game learning medium in the reinforcement of reading skills with fourth grade children. *Journal of Special Education, 1,* 369–372.

Humphrey, J.H., & Sullivan, D.D. (1970). *Teaching slow learners through active games.* Springfield, IL: Charles C. Thomas.

Hunter, D.L. (1975). Spoken and written word lists: A comparison. *Reading Teacher, 29,* 250–253.

Johns, J.L. (1974a). *Updating the Dolch basic sight vocabulary for the schools of the 1970's.* Paper presented at the annual convention of the International Reading Association. New Orleans, Louisiana.

Johns, J.L. (1974b). Dolch list of common nouns—a comparison. *Reading Teacher, 28,* 538–540.

Johnson, D.D. (1971). The Dolch list reexamined. *Reading Teacher, 24,* 449–457.

Johnson, D.D. (1971). A basic vocabulary for beginning reading. *Elementary School Journal, 72,* 29–34.

Kelly, A.M. (1975). Sight vocabularies and experience stories. *Elementary English, 52,* 327–328.

Mallet, J.J. (1977). *101 make-and-play reading games for the intermediate grades.* Englewood Cliffs, N.J.: Center for Applied Research in Education.

McCormick, S., and Collins, B.M. (1981). A potpourri of game-making ideas for the reading teacher. *Reading Teacher, 34,* 692–696.

Moe, A.J., & Hopkins, C.J. (1975). The speaking vocabularies of kindergarten, first-grade, and second-grade children. ERIC Document Reproduction Service No. ED 105 465.

Otto, W., & Chester, R. (1972). Sight words for beginning reading. *Journal of Educational Research, 65,* 435–443.

Pearson, P.D. (1978). On bridging gaps and spanning chasms. *Curriculum Inquiry, 8,* 353–362.

Russell, D.H. et al. (1975). *Reading aids through the grades: A guide to materials and 440 activities for individualizing reading activities.* New York: Teachers College Press.

Sakiey, E., & Fry, E. (1979). *3,000 instant words.* Highland Park, NJ: Drier Educational systems.

Sherk, Jr., J.K. (1973). *A word count of spoken English of culturally disadvantaged preschool and elementary pupils.* Columbia: University of Missouri.

Snyder, G.V. (1981). Learner verification of reading games. *Reading Teacher, 34,* 686–691.

Thorndike, R.L. (1973). *Reading comprehen-*

sion education in fifteen countries. New York: Wiley.

Veatch, J.; Sawricki, F.; Elliott, G.; Falke, E.; & Blakey, J. (1979). *Key words to reading.* Columbus, OH: Charles E. Merrill.

Wood, M.N. (1976). *A multivariate analysis of beginning readers' recognition of taught words in four contextual settings.* Unpublished doctoral dissertation, Texas Women's University.

APPLICATION EXPERIENCES IN THE TEACHER EDUCATION CLASSROOM

A. *What's your opinion?* Discuss why you agree or disagree with the following opinions. Use both the textbook and your own experiences.

1. A good reading vocabulary is all you need for good reading comprehension.

2. Key words are more important than the words in the Essential Reading Vocabulary in Table 4.2.

3. Vocabulary games provide the teacher with a better teaching method than do patterned books for teaching words from the Essential Reading Vocabulary in Table 4.2.

4. Reading comprehension is really a matter of intelligence. Smart kids understand what they read; the others don't.

5. Schemata development is more important than vocabulary development.

6. The ten most frequent words in the English language make up 24 percent of all written material, and we can prove it!

B. *Miscue Analysis:* Study Matt's miscues and decide how his reading vocabulary helped him use the cueing systems to comprehend the author's message. For example, what enabled him to self-correct his substitution of *swimming* for *sawing*? Was it just his use of graphophonic cues? (A large *C* means a self-correction.)

Bob and Paul had been ⌈Swimming⌉ sawing and hammering all day. They were building a play house . . . ⌈They⌉ The boys finished the frame but they did

A

not nail any boards across the frame to make it strong. Instead, they started work on the roof.*

---

*Colin Dunkeld, Portland Informal Reading Inventory, Form P. Unpublished manuscript, Portland State University, School of Education. Reprinted by permission of the author.

C. *Essential Reading Vocabulary:* With a partner or small group, make a list of the nouns from the Essential Reading Vocabulary in Table 4.2. Why are these nouns of such high frequency in our language? How might they be important to children in their writing?

D. *Planning for Teaching:* Decide with a small group how you might use some ideas in this chapter (including Dale's Cone of Experience) to help you enhance children's schemata before they read a selection about living on a farm in 1880. Three of the words in the story are *plow*, *oxen*, and *yoke*. You have allowed no more than ten minutes to prepare them for reading the selection. (You discover that one of the sentences in the selection is "Jake attached the yoke to one of the oxen, but the other ox started to move away.")

FIELD EXPERIENCES IN THE ELEMENTARY SCHOOL CLASSROOM

A. With two or more children, try out the direct lesson approach to teaching three or four sights words from the Essential Reading Vocabulary in Table 4.2.

B. Prepare two or more children for reading a selection from a basal reader, social studies textbook, or science textbook. Spend ten to fifteen minutes on schemata enhancement and on vocabulary. Make sure you introduce at least one of the new words through context analysis.

C. Use a patterned book to teach one or more children several sight words from the Essential Reading Vocabulary in Table 4.2. For a list of patterned books, see Appendix P. (Bring an extra patterned book or two in case the children don't care for the one you have chosen.)

D. Use one of the games in Appendix A to teach one or more children some of the sight words from the Essential Reading Vocabulary in Table 4.2. The first time or two you play the game, you should help the children with words they don't know, or you may wish to play the game after you've taught the words through direct lessons.

5 GRAPHOPHONIC PATTERNS: THOSE NECESSARY CONFIRMATIONS

CHAPTER PREVIEW

In Chapter 4 we discussed vocabulary, one of the language tools children need for using the four cueing systems effectively and communicating with authors. In this chapter we're going to study the graphophonic cueing system—a tool that the other cueing systems require for confirmation of predictions. We'll see that graphophonic analysis is an intelligent, primarily right-brain process of recognizing patterns, rather than one of merely sounding out words letter by letter or memorizing verbal rules. We will look at five ways to help children acquire these patterns; two ways have an auditory emphasis and three a visual emphasis. Then we'll see how children's knowledge of patterns can be applied to words with more than one syllable. We'll also look at an important but commonly ''underlearned'' part of the graphophonic cueing system, namely *punctuation* and other graphic devices the author uses to communicate with the reader. But most importantly, we will see that graphophonic analysis can be practiced in the context of actual interactive reading experiences guided by the teacher.

Huemuns spell wirds in a flitey inkunsistent wae. This must make it hard for yungstirs too lirn too rede.

THE PLACE OF GRAPHOPHONIC ANALYSIS IN INTERACTIVE READING

It wouldn't surprise me if researchers were to find that the most common phrase children hear as they're learning to read is "Sound it out." This three-word imperative sentence might not be as common in a child's life as "Drink your milk" or "Eat your spinach" or "Don't bother me," but it is delivered quite freely by a child's parents, relatives, and teachers. Yet, it is probably one of the poorest pieces of advice ever passed on from one generation to the next.

There are several reasons that it's poor. First of all, if you give this advice often enough, it can profoundly affect a child's concept of reading—and therefore his strategies for reading. Imagine, for example, that Tyrone is reading this sentence: "The bicycle hit the hole and Dan went flying over the handlebars." He points to *flying* and asks you what this word is. If you say, "What word would make sense in that sentence?" you are telling Tyrone that *making sense* is what reading is all about. If instead you say, "Sound it out" you are telling him that *pronouncing words* is what reading is all about.

Second, by telling Tyrone to "sound it out," you are missing a chance to help him see that reading is an interactive process with *four* cueing systems rather than one. Why not encourage him to use one of the abundant schemata (minitheories) he has no doubt developed by this time in his life; for example, "Have you ever been riding a bike, Tyrone, and all of a sudden

140

you hit a curb or a bump—or a hole in the street?" With this kind of question you'll probably be talking in a moment about the time he or one of his friends had a temporary catastrophe. If you don't have time for that type of schema building, you could just ask him more questions: "What happened when you hit it, Tyrone? What do you think is happening to Dan in this story? When you fell from your bike was it a little bit like flying for a moment? Do you suppose that *flying* is the word in this sentence? What sound does flying begin with? What letter stands for that sound? What happens when we take the *ing* off the word flying?" And so on. By now, I'm sure you see how a teacher can encourage interactive predicting and confirming rather than the mechanical sounding out of letters. And you can see how a teacher can encourage the use of graphophonic cues as an aid to predicting and confirming. As one remedial reading teacher said to me, "There's no sorrier sight than a poor reader who has become a slave to phonics. He's just *got* to sound it out, that's all there is to it—even though he could easily predict the word by using his intelligence and his past experiences."

GRAPHOPHONIC ANALYSIS—WHAT IS IT?

Is graphophonic analysis merely the process of "sounding out words"? No, it's much more sophisticated than that. Take the nonsense word *cibby*. When we come across a hard word like this, do we "sound out" each letter one at a time—first the sound of *c*, then the sound of *i*, then the sound of *b*, then the sound of *b*, again, then the sound of *y*—and then we put all the sounds together? Well, if you've been *taught* to do that, you might. But good readers don't do it that way. Instead they look for letter *patterns*. As Glass and Burton (1973) found in their study, 85 percent of the decoding done by successful readers (second and fifth graders in their study) consists of recognizing *groups* of letters.

What patterns or groups do we notice in the word *cibby*? Some people will intuitively notice the *ci* pattern, indicating that the *c* probably has a soft sound as in *city*. Some will intuitively notice the double consonant letter *bb* in the middle of the word, indicating that the *i* sound will probably be short as in *kitty*. Some will intuitively notice the vowel-consonant pattern *ib*, indicating that the *i* sound will most probably be short as in *it* or *fib*. And most will intuitively notice that the *y* comes at the end of a two-syllable word, indicating a long *e* sound as in *baby* or *daddy*.

For good readers, graphophonic analysis is *not* sounding out words letter by letter; it's a process of decoding new words by means of recognizable or spelling patterns in known words. From our memory of *city*, for example, we can take the *ci* pattern and apply it to *cibby*. Or from our memory of *fib* we might take the *ib* and apply it to *cib*. Or from *tubby* we might take the *bb*. And so on. Eventually, as we learn to read, we get so good at this that we recognize spelling patterns by sight and do very little thinking about them. The patterns have become as easily recognized as sight words.

Certainly we do not sound out words like *knight*. Try it, and you'll see why this word, although once pronounced just the way it's spelled, has been simplified over time. What we do today, because the old spelling has remained, is to recognize the combinations *kn* and *ight* as in *knife, knee, right,* and *tight*. So basically, what good readers do when they use graphophonic analysis is to (1) visually recognize known patterns of letters; (2) translate those patterns into the sounds they represent; and (3) blend the sounds together to form the correct pronunciation. This, as you can see, is not the same as "making a sound for each letter."

PATTERNS AND THE BRAIN

> Quite apart from anything the teacher does . . . the student, being human, is a pattern-finder and a pattern maker . . .
>
> —*David B. Bronson (1977, p. 453)*

As you know, the left and right sides of our brains perform different functions. The right side is generally responsible for pattern decoding and encoding (recognizing or producing a pattern). While the right side specializes in dealing with such nonverbal aspects of the individual's environment, the left side specializes in verbalizing about it (Hart, 1983; Smith, 1984). For an efficient reader, for example, it's my guess that the right side has the main responsibility for graphophonic and syntactic cues while the left has more responsibility for the semantic and schematic systems. This is only a guess, of course, since our knowledge of the brain is so limited—first by the difficulty of examining it while a person is using it and second by its incredible complexity.

At any rate, though, there seems to be little doubt that human beings have survived and evolved as a pattern-seeking being (Hart, 1983; Smith, 1984). It is only wise, therefore, for a teacher to take advantage of this natural inclination when teaching reading. In earlier chapters we talked about children's recognizing syntactic patterns as they read. We also discussed their use of schemata, which at first may be mere hypotheses but in time may become fairly rigid memory patterns that help them explain their world and what they read as they experience it. In much of this chapter, then, we'll look at ways of encouraging children to recognize graphophonic, right-brain patterns as they read.

LEARNING GRAPHOPHONIC PATTERNS THROUGH AN AUDITORY EMPHASIS

First, I'm going to show you two ways of teaching graphophonic analysis that emphasize the auditory (phonic) mode of learning more than the visual (graphic). It's not that these two methods are the best; in fact, I doubt that they are—it's just that they're used so often and have such a strong tradition behind them.

The Analytic Method

Suppose several of your students are having trouble decoding the digraph *sh*, as in *shell* or *dash*. (A *digraph* means two letters standing for one sound, such as the *th* in *thin* or the *oa* in *boat*. For other "phonics words" you don't understand from context clues, please refer to the "Graphophonic Terms" in Table 5.3. You have already used the *th* lessons in the basal reader teacher's guide, so you decide to make up another one for these children. Here are some planning steps you might follow to use the analytic method.

Planning Steps

1. Make a list of easy words that include the digraph *sh*. To have every list a teacher might conceivably need when teaching graphophonic analysis, you may some day want to order a copy of *The Reading Teacher's Book of Lists* (Fry et al., 1984). In the meantime, words ending with *ash* would give you a start in your planning for this lesson: *cash, dash, gash, hash, lash, mash, crash,* and so on. Those ending with *ish* might also be listed—*dish, fish, wish*—as well as some beginning with *sh: shell, shut, should,* and *ship.*

2. Write one sentence for each word you plan to use in your lesson. Usually four or five words are enough, unless you decide to have one sentence for each child in the group. If possible, you can weave the sentences together to make a very short story, like this:

   "I like <u>hash</u>," Dan said.

   "I like <u>fish</u>," Nan said.

   "What <u>should</u> we do? Dan said.

   "I know what we can do," <u>she</u> said. "Let's eat <u>fish</u> <u>hash</u>!"

Try to make the words in the sentences simple and meaningful to the children. The context words that surround the "target words" (underlined) should not be more difficult than the target words themselves. After you've put your story on butcher paper or the chalkboard, you're ready for the third planning step.

3. Find other *sh* words in their basal reader (or another book they use in common) and write down the pages on which the children can find the words later.

4. Plan on an auxiliary visual-emphasis method you can use as well as a game or activity that will provide them with more practice.

5. Make a list of words you can read to the children for Step 8 of your lesson (shown in the next section).

Teaching Steps

Now that you've done your planning, here are some actual teaching steps you can try:

1. Read the sentences out loud to the children, smoothly and informally, as if you were speaking to them.

2. Have them echo-read each sentence after you.

3. Have them say each target word together after you.

4. Have each child say a target word after you and then use it in a sentence.

5. Say all the target words to them again. Then ask them what letters are the same in each word.

*6. Ask them what sound is the same in each word. Have them make the sound with you.

*7. Ask them what sound they should think of when they see the letters *sh* together.

8. Have them close their eyes and raise their hands whenever they hear a word that has the /sh/ sound in it. Read several words to them, with about half of them containing the /sh/ phoneme (sound). Words like *ship* and *chip* might be used, for example, or *back* and *bash*, or *glass* and *flash*.

---

*Some teachers and programs avoid having children pronounce letter sounds in isolation. Instead, children are asked to notice that the words all have the same sound in them and then asked to think of other words that include that sound.

9. Return to the sentences and have the children first read them together and then individually read them.

10. Use one of the other practice activities described later in this chapter.

As you can see, the analytic method starts with several target words imbedded in contextual sentences. It requires the children to analyze the target words to determine the common grapheme (such as *sh*) and the phoneme (such as /sh/) that the grapheme stands for. The children learn this grapheme-phoneme connection (letters and corresponding sounds) through discovery rather than through being told by the teacher ahead of time.

Phoneme: a distinctive speech sound that can contrast one word with another, e.g., hip, lip.	**Grapheme:** one or more letters used to represent a phoneme.

Synthetic Method

Whereas the analytic phonics method has children break words down into grapheme-phoneme units, the approach referred to as "the synthetic method" has them build words up from grapheme-phoneme units. Basically, with the synthetic method, children learn first to decode letters in isolation and then learn how to put them together to make words. As I did with the analytic approach, I'll give you one type of sample lesson plan that uses the synthetic phonics method. (There are many other types.)

Let's again suppose that several students are having trouble decoding the digraph *sh*. Let's also imagine that some of them are also having trouble with the short *a*. Assume also that you've already used the lessons in a basal reader on these two graphemes. This time, in planning a lesson for these children, you would make a list of one syllable words that include the two graphemes *a* and *sh*, such as *shack, ash, bash, cash,* and so on. Now you're ready to begin your lesson using the synthetic approach. Here are some teaching steps you might follow:

1. Write *sh* and *a* on the board. Point to each one and tell the children what sound they are to make when they see it. (Refer to the letters as the "short *a* sound" and the "*sh* sound.")

2. Have the children make the *sh* sound /sh/ and the short *a* sound /a/ whenever you point to the letters. Make sure each person in the small group can say them.

3. Review the sounds of the graphemes *b, h, m,* and *ck* in the same way, using steps 1 and 2.

4. Have each child write the *sh* and *a*, first on the board and then on their paper. Have them point to what they've written on the board and say the sounds (not the letters).

5. Remind them how to blend sounds together by using a word they already know, such as *mess*. Write it on the board and have them say it slowly: "mmmeeesss." Then have them say it fast: "mess."

6. Point to the isolated graphemes that you've put on the board (*sh, a, b, h, m, ck*). Tell them they "are now going to blend these together to make some words. Whenever I point to one of them, you make the right sound."

7. Point to three graphemes (from left to right) that will produce a word, such as *b, a,* and *sh*, and have them make the appropriate sounds as you point to them /b/ + /a/ + /sh/. Point to the sequence of three graphemes several times, each time faster than the previous time. Finally tell them to "say it fast."

8. Write the word you've just produced, in this case, *bash*. Have each child "say it slowly" then "say it fast."

9. Do the same thing with other possible words: *hash, mash, shack*.

10. Finish the lesson by using some of the words in context with them; for example, "Do you like to eat *hash?*"

Maybe you've noticed from the sample lesson plan some advantages and disadvantages of the synthetic method. On the plus side, the children are told what sound is associated with what letter or letter pair. They don't have to discover it on their own through the analysis of whole words. Those who have trouble learning to decode through the analytic method often are able to learn to decode with the synthetic method (Bond & Dysktra, 1967; Dykstra, 1968; Weaver, 1978).

But we should look at the minus side as well. Unfortunately, by learning to decode letters in isolation, the child is not learning to use graphophonic analysis in the most efficient way. Many letters do not stand for sounds when they're all by themselves. They must be seen in a spelling pattern before they can be properly decoded. The letter *a*, for example, stands for a different phoneme in *can* and *cane*. It's the spelling pattern that makes the difference. In the word *can*, we see the VC (vowel-consonant) pattern, whereas in *cane*, we see the VCE (vowel-consonant-final *e*) pattern. Furthermore, the *c* in *cane* has a different sound from the *c* in *city*, because of the letters that follow the *c* in each case. In addition, many groups of letters in our written language have to be seen as patterns for correct decoding, such as the *ight* in *night*, the *ch* in *church*, the *ai* in *wait*, and so on.

Furthermore, concentration on sounds in isolation may increase a child's difficulty in blending sounds. For example, if *b*, *a*, and *sh* are first presented as a whole word, the child learns the proper blending of sounds from the very beginning. If these same graphemes are sounded out separately, however, the child is actually trying to blend four phonemes, rather than three: /b/ + /u/ + /a/ + /sh/. The reason there are four phonemes here is that it is nearly impossible to produce most consonant sounds without an accompanying vowel sound.

Nonetheless, despite the disadvantages of the synthetic phonics method, research shows that it works reasonably well for some children (Bond & Dykstra, 1967). Many teachers recommend it for children who are having trouble learning the analytic method. All reading teachers should become familiar with this method, so they can use it with any child who simply is not getting it any other way. After all, it's terribly important that each child learn *some* form of graphophonic analysis.

Rather than rely on either the analytic or synthetic method alone, however, I strongly urge you to combine one of the methods with one or more of the visual-emphasis methods I will describe. I also recommend that you combine either method with a language experience approach (see

chapter 6) so that children do not get the wrong idea of what reading really is. It's so easy for some children to learn the wrong thing—that reading is a process of making word-sounds rather than creating meaning.

LEARNING GRAPHOPHONIC PATTERNS THROUGH A VISUAL EMPHASIS

Now let's look at three methods that emphasize the visual rather than the auditory mode of learning. Whenever I've asked groups of people to indicate whether they prefer the visual or auditory mode of learning, most people choose the visual mode. Yet, when I ask them to remember a telephone number that I write on the chalkboard and then erase, nearly everyone combines visual memory with auditory memory in one way or another. For instance, if I were to give you the number 847-5329, you might remember part of it visually and the other part by reciting it over and over to yourself.

Like adults, children too have preferences for the visual or auditory mode of learning certain things. Besides preferences, they also have learning-mode strengths and weaknesses. Some children's auditory memory may be quite weak when it comes to words or phonemes; for instance, they may have trouble thinking of rhyming words or coming up with words that begin with a particular phoneme you give them, such as the /m/ sound. Others may even have trouble telling the difference between certain phonemes, such as the vowel sounds in *bed* and *bad;* their auditory *discrimination,* as well as auditory memory, may be weak.

All children can probably benefit from the use of *both* visual and auditory modes of learning graphophonic analysis—particularly children who have trouble with auditory discrimination and memory. Since the analytic and synthetic methods rely more on the auditory than the visual mode, it seems advisable to supplement them with one or more of the methods that emphasize the visual mode.

Phonogram Method

For purposes of reading instruction, the following clusters of letters are called "phonograms": *ack,* as in *back, sack,* and *pack; ip,* as in *hip, ship,* and *lip; ake,* as in *cake, make,* and *lake; ight,* as in *fight, night,* and *light.* These letter sets are extremely handy in teaching children how to use graphophonic cues. Why?

> They have a reasonably consistent pronunciation from one word to the next (Jones, 1970; Wylie & Durrell, 1970).

They seem to be a kind of pattern that children notice naturally, even with little or no instruction (Cunningham, 1975–76).

Teaching children to read phonograms may allow teachers to move more quickly into teaching words of more than one syllable (Groff, 1971). The word *hobbit*, for example, includes the familiar *ob* and *it* phonograms found in *job, rob, sob* and *bit, hit, sit*.

Suppose we've just used the analytic method to teach a group of children to decode the *sh* grapheme. Since the analytic method has an auditory emphasis, let's now switch to a visual emphasis by using the phonogram method. This may seem strange, since by now you may be convinced that the phonogram method merely uses rhyming words (which would involve *auditory* memory rather than visual.) This impression isn't quite true. With the phonogram method, the teacher *uses* rhyming words but does not *ask* for rhyming words. Instead, the teacher writes two words on the board, such as *bash*, and *cash*, and asks for more words that end with the same three letters—*a–s–h*. To make the experiences even more visual, this is how the teacher writes the words the children give her:

	V C C
b	a s h
c	a s h
d	a s h
l	a s h
s l	a s h
g	a s h
t r	a s h
r	a s h
h	a s h

A vertical line separates the phonogram from the other letters, or the phonogram is underlined with different colored chalk. This helps the children to learn the phonogram by visual memory, just as if it were a sight word to be learned through abundant repetition. It also helps them see the vowel letter in a pattern rather than in isolation. In this case, for instance, the letter *a* is seen in a VCC pattern (vowel-consonant-consonant), indicating that the *a* probably has a short sound. This visual presentation also helps children learn or review the initial consonant letters *b, c, d, l, g, r,* and *h* and the consonant cluster *sl* and *tr*. If the teacher wishes, he can also have them look at words like *crashing* and *smashing* so they can see the value of the phonogram in multisyllable words. Table 5.1 shows a list of phonograms that will be valuable to your teaching.

Table 5.1 *Phonograms* with Ten or More Rhyming Words*

Short A:	VC:	ab, ad, ag, am, an, ap, at
Short A:	VCC:	ack, amp, and, ang, ank, ash
Long A:	VCE:	ace, ade, ake, ame, ane, ate, ave
Long A:	VVC:	ail, ain
Long A:		ay
Irregular A:		all, ar, are (dare), ark, aw
Short E:	VC:	ed, en, et
Short E:	VCC:	ell, end, ent, est
Long E:	VCE:	unusual pattern for long *e*
Long E:	VVC:	eak, eal, eam, eat, eed, eep, eet
Irregular E:		ear (fear), ew (few)
Short I:	VC:	id, ig, im, in, ip, it
Short I:	VCC:	ick, ill, ing, ink, int
Long I:	VCE:	ice, ide, ime, ine, ive
Long I:		ight
Long I:		ind (find)
Short O:	VC:	ob, od, og, op, ot
Short O:	VCC:	ock, ong
Long O:	VCE:	oke, one, ope
Long O:		old, ow (low)
Diphthong O:		ow (cow)
Irregular O:		ore, orn
Short U:	VC:	ub, ug, um, un, ut
Short U:	VCC:	uck, uff, ump, ung, ush, unk
Long U:		none with ten

Other phonograms with five or more rhyming words:	aft, air, age, aid, air, alk, ance, ant, ape, art, ask, awn, ast, atch, ead (head), ean, eek, eel, een, eer, ess, ife, ift, ike, ile, ipe, ire, irt, isk, itch, ite, oat, ode, oil, ole, oll, olt, ook, ool, oom, oon, oop, oot, ort, ose, oss, ought, ound, ouse, out, owl, own (down), oy, ry (cry), ud, ude, udge, ull, umb, unch, unt, ur, ust.

Example: Phonogram *ab.* Rhyming words: cab, gab, jab, tab, crab, drab, grab, scab, slab, and stab.

**Definition:* For purposes of teaching reading a phonogram is being defined as a combination of at least one vowel letter and at least one consonant letter at the end of a one-syllable rhyming word.

Substitution Method

Again, suppose we've just taught some students by one of the auditory methods (analytic or synthetic) to decode the digraph *sh;* that is, to think of the /sh/ sound whenever they see the letter *s* and *h* together. This time, when we supplement the lesson with a visual approach, we'll use the substitution method instead of the phonogram method. To plan for this part of the lesson you'll need to list several pairs of words on a chart or on the board. Each pair of words will show *minimal* contrast, such as *he* and *she*. On page 108 of *The Reading Teacher's Book of Lists* (Fry et al., 1984), I find a list of *sh* words that include *she, shell, ship,* and *shot,* among many others. This is how I would pair these four words to use the substitution method:

he	she
sell	shell
hip	ship
hot	shot

And here's how you could use these pairs with your students. Moving your hand from left to right for each pair, you might say: "This word is *he,* and it's spelled *h-e.* But the word next to it is spelled *s-h-e.* What sound does *sh* stand for? . . . That's right. So if this word is *he,* then what word is next to it? . . . Yes, if this word is *he,* then this word must be *she.*" Follow the same procedure for the other pairs in your list. *You* tell them the word on the left, *they* tell you the word on the right. Whenever they have trouble, show them the difference in the spellings of the two words.

When they seem to understand the procedure, you can introduce some more difficult *minimal contrasts,* such as those at the *end* of words:

hat	hash
fib	fish
track	trash
win	wish

When children have difficulty seeing the minimal contrast, you can also place the pairs vertically as well as horizontally, like this:

h a|t	f i|b	t r a|c k	w i|n
h a|sh	f i|sh	t r a|sh	w i|sh

Just to make sure you understand the substitution method, let me ask you a question. If you wanted to teach the *st* cluster with the substitution method, which of the following pairs of words would show the *minimal contrast* in letters that you need to show?

mist	mast
stick	stack
fast	fan
mash	mast

Which pair did you choose?

The first pair would be useful for teaching the short *a*, since that's what you're contrasting with the short *i*. Do you see what I mean? The second pair would be useful for teaching the short *a* again. The third pair would be good for teaching the decoding of *n*, although if the pair had been reversed, it could have been used to teach *st*. Only the last pair is appropriate for teaching children to decode the *st* grapheme. ("If this word is *mash*, and the second word ends with *st* instead of *sh*, then what is this second word?")

The Vowel Pattern Method

Vowels are the most difficult to decode because vowel sounds can be spelled so many different ways. The long *e* sound, for example, can be spelled seventeen ways, as in *see, team, equal, he, key, Caesar, e'en, deceive, receipt, people, demesne, machine, field, debris, amoeba, quay, pity.* Fortunately, though, there are only two or three *common* ways for each vowel sound. For long *a* there are two: *made* (VCE) and *maid* (VVC); in *made* we have the (vowel + consonant + final *e*) pattern, more easily referred to as the VCE pattern. In *maid* we have the (vowel digraph + consonant) pattern, referred to as the VVC pattern.

To use letters to designate the vowel pattern, simply start with the first vowel letter and add the letters to the right, as we see in Table 5.2. (This works for all patterns except the CV pattern.)

June Knafle (1978) found that children taught to recognize vowel patterns did better in reading words than those in a control group. This doesn't surprise me, since my university students and I have had similar results with children above second grade. What does surprise me is how few experimental studies have been done on this seemingly very effective method. Patrick Groff (1971a) because of his own research and research reviews (1971b) has been advocating the use of vowel patterns and phonograms since 1971, but few have taken up the call to examine its effectiveness in classroom situations.

A large part of the effectiveness of teaching vowel patterns depends, of course, on *how* you teach them. The methods I'm going to explain are those that my students and I have found to be the most enjoyable and productive. As you may have already noticed, when you teach phonograms you are already beginning to teach vowel patterns. When you use the *et* phonogram with words like *bet, let,* and *met,* you are already demonstrating the VC vowel pattern. All you have to do is incidentally place a VC above the column of words and mention that all the words end with a vowel letter followed by a consonant letter. (Children seem to like using the letters VC better than the words "vowel-consonant.") Thus by the time you use *direct*

Table 5.2 *Words for Teaching Vowel Patterns*

Short VC	Short VCC	Long VCE	Long VVC	Long CV
in	ink	ape	eat	he
p in	sink	cape	heat	she
at	ill	ate	aid	go
c at	pill	plate	paid	me
th at	spill	note	mail	by
d ot	blank	lake	soak	fly
c up	dash	like	boat	try
ch ip	bell	five	feet	no
top	send	came	road	Hi
not	lamp	rope	train	my
bud	best	nine	green	be
fun	sick	flame	jail	we
bed	bang	time	beak	so
sad	spring	poke	pain	pro
spin	hint	bone	mean	sky
pet	sock	kite	clean	spy

teaching of the vowel patterns, they will have already learned a great many phonograms and developed an idea of what the vowel patterns are.

Steps for Direct Teaching of Vowel Patterns

Step 1: Display on a chart or chalkboard the first eight words from the VC column in Table 5.2. Use a vertical rectangle to separate the phonograms from the initial consonant letters or digraphs. Write the letters VC above the rectangle.

Step 2: Read the first eight words to the children and point out that each word ends with a vowel followed by a consonant. Tell them that "these words are all VC words." Think of this as more a right-brain *intuitive* learning experience than one that takes a lot of left-brain verbal analysis.

Step 3: Hand each of the children five cards, each of which has a word from one of the five columns (lower half). For example, you might hand Bernice these five: *top, send, came, road,* and *Hi.* Ask them to find the one card that is like the words on the board.

Step 4: Have them all show you this card at the same time. Ask them to check their card to see if it ends with a vowel letter followed by a consonant letter. (If necessary, remind them what the vowel letters are.) Have them hold up their cards again. Those who have the wrong pattern should be asked to look again at their cards.

Step 5:   When they all have the correct pattern, have them each try to read their word (with your help, if necessary) and place it on the chalkboard railing. As each one comes to the board, ask him what kind of word he has (VC word) and have him first point to the vowel letter and then to the final consonant letter.

Step 6:   Have the children play a game with the VC words. For example, you might play a game of concentration by having two cards for each of 10 words in the VC column. This will give you four rows of five cards. For a more difficult game, use more of the words. (See Appendixes A and B for instructions on Pattern Concentration and other pattern games: Wild Things, Three of a Kind, Maybe One More, Steal the Words, and Word Chase.)

Note: Adapt steps 1–6 to fit the age, abilities, and interests of your own students.

After the children have thoroughly learned the VC vowel pattern, you're ready to use the direct teaching approach with the VCC pattern. As soon as you think they're ready, you can have them work with both patterns at once. For example, instead of their finding a VC word in their stack of five cards, they now find both a VC and a VCC card. If you wish to make this more challenging, you can give them more than five cards to deal with. After they have mastered the VC and VCC patterns, gradually teach them the VCE, VVC, and CV patterns, in that order. You'll find that the activities and games become increasingly interesting and challenging to them as they deal with more and more patterns.

Most second graders we've worked with seem able to handle the first three patterns, but only if they've first had considerable experience with phonograms. Without numerous phonogram experiences (including incidental teaching of vowel patterns), it would be well to postpone *direct* teaching of the vowel patterns. By the time children reach third grade, most can handle all five patterns, if introduced after previous ones have been mastered. Many children get into grades four through eight without really mastering the vowel patterns. This is unfortunate, since without this mastery their access to graphophonic cues is limited, which in turn limits their ability to confirm the predictions they make through syntactic, semantic, and schematic cues. As remedial reading teachers so often tell me, "they just don't *know* their vowel patterns."

PATTERNS VS. RULES

Is it "better" for children to learn vowel patterns than rules?

"When two vowels go walking, the first one does the talking."

"When there are two vowels, one of which is final *e*, the first vowel is long and the second is silent."

Experience and research (Cunningham, 1975–76; Glass & Burton, 1973) tell me "Yes." Learning graphophonic analysis, as I mentioned, seems to be largely a right-brain phenomenon that relies on a great many experiences in decoding words. In fact, many children teach the vowel patterns to themselves, simply by reading and writing.

If we can rely on what children tell us, they do not recite rules in their heads as they decode. They see clusters of letters that remind them of known words or known phonograms or known vowel patterns. Downing (1969) put it well: "very young children perform wonders in manipulating . . . language, without anyone telling them the rules or their being able to describe them . . . It is quite unnecessary for rule following behavior to be based on verbal formulation of the rule" (p. 226).

Tovey (1980) demonstrated that Downing was correct. When Tovey administered a phonics test consisting of nonsense words to children in grades two through six, he found they did quite well in pronouncing the words correctly, with scores ranging from 55 percent to 83 percent. When they were asked to *verbalize* their phonics knowledge, however, extremely few of them were successful. A study by Rosso and Emans (1981) was even more revealing. They also gave children a phonics test, this one consisting of 14 words that represented 14 phonics rules. Each student was then asked to give a rule for the words he had pronounced correctly. An average of 75 percent of the children pronounced each of the words correctly, but an average of only 14 percent could explain the rule for their correct pronunciation.

So we see, then, that children can learn the patterns quite well in an intuitive, nonverbal, nonrulelike manner. But how reliable are the five patterns in predicting the correct pronunciation of words? The answer depends upon a very important concession. To treat these patterns as reliable, one must concede that it's necessary to teach children some major exceptions. The so-called "bossy *r*" is one of them. When this letter follows a vowel, both the rules and patterns crumble. The word *car*, for instance, can't be placed in the VC column, indicating a short *a*. The short /a/ heard in *can* is very different from the /a/ heard in *car*. So when a child wants to put a word like *car* or *fur* or *her* in the VC column, just calmly put it in a new column called "the r column" and show her how the vowel sound differs for words that end in *r*. Words placed in the VC or VCC columns *must have a short vowel;* this means that words that rhyme with *find* shouldn't be placed in the VCC column. Sorry, but the *ind* phonogram is a loner and a spoilsport.

Now let's look at a major exception in one of the long-vowel columns, namely the renegade VVC column. In this column we find a fairly consistent long sound if we stick to the *ea, oa, ai,* and *ee* pairs, as in "Eat toad tails? EE!" But stay away from those inconsiderate pairs, *ei, ie, ou, oi* and *oo.* To teach *oi, oo,* and *ou,* you'll need the phonogram method and these phonograms: *oil, ook, ool, oom, oon, oop, oot, out.* As for *ei* and *ie,* the few words that contain these strange digraphs should be learned as visual memory sight words or through regular spelling lessons—and through regular reading. (How many words with *ie* or *ei* can you think of that children really need, besides *friend, piece,* and *Leif Ericson?*) There is one other major exception in that VVC column. The *ea* digraph works just fine for the phonograms *eak, eal, eam, eat,* and *ean*—as in *leak, seal, seam, seat,* and *bean*—but don't count on the *ead* phonogram, as in *dead head.* It has a short sound and needs to be learned via the phonogram method, all by its nasty little self.

If at times you become a little discouraged with our crazy spelling (especially when a student points out inconsistencies like *bone, done,* and *gone*) rest assured that it's not as bad as it may seem. Just smile and remember that there's also *cone, drone, hone, phone, shone, stone, tone,* and *zone.* Look at it this way: about three-fourths of the time, our spelling is consistent with the way words sound (Bailey, 1967; Burmeister, 1968; Clymer, 1963; Emans, 1967; Greif, 1980). Wouldn't you rather have kids decode words with a three-out-of-four-chance for success than with only a random chance?

TEACHING GRAPHOPHONIC ANALYSIS WITH MULTISYLLABIC WORDS

One of the most important advantages of teaching phonograms and vowel patterns is the contribution they make toward determining the pronunciation of words with more than one syllable. In examining hundreds of miscue analyses on poor readers, I've often noticed the paralysis that sets in for these children whenever they reach "big words." Sometimes it's paralysis; other times it's a frantic display of bravado, throwing out any big word starting with the same letter:

bulletin
The car was speeding down the boulevard.

And then there are times when the child invents a new word right on the spot, as when Brenda read *hillycopy* for "helicopter."

How can a knowledge of phonograms and vowel patterns help this situation? Let's assume for a moment that *rabbit, basket,* and *robin* are not part of Randy's sight vocabulary. One glance at *rabbit* and he's got the familiar phonogram *ab,* which children who have been taught phonograms will associate with *cab, grab* and other *ab* words; he's also got the familiar phonogram *it,* which he will have associated with *bit, sit,* and many others. It's quite true that the second syllable in *rabbit* contains a schwa vowel sound rather than a short *i* sound, but research has shown that this is really not a problem. Wylie and Durell (1970), for example, have found that 95 percent of the phonograms in the words used in primary grade books can be read intelligibly by ignoring the schwa sound and using a short or long vowel instead.

Looking at the word *basket,* Randy will find the high-frequency phonogram *et,* but also the phonogram *ask*—one with considerably lower frequency. If Randy has learned vowel patterns, however, he can intuitively see that basket can be broken up mentally into two VC patterns, *bas* and *ket;* or it can be broken into a VCC pattern, *bask,* and a VC pattern, *et.* Either form of syllabication will work fine; the point is that with both phonogram and vowel-pattern knowledge, Randy has an excellent chance of decoding the word with minimal discomfort.

What about a harder word, like *robot* or *robin?* Using a rule once taught to me, I would divide *before* the consonant. It works with *robot* but not with *robin.* Despite whatever rule you might have learned, the fact is that dividing before the consonant letter works 50 percent of the time and dividing after the consonant letter works 50 percent of the time (May, 1985). But more importantly, it's doubtful that children should be straddled with *any* syllabication rules. Instead of rules, they need strategies for finding recognizable clusters of letters in words; teaching them vowel patterns provides them with a strategy. With words like *robin* and *robot,* for example, we can encourage them to "try pronouncing the word both ways."

V C   C V   V C   C V
Try r o b/i n and r o/b i n. Try r o b/o t and r o/b o t.

Whichever sound "rings a bell" or seems right in context is the one to use. In other words, instead of teaching children syllabication rules, teach them to keep right on using the four cueing systems, but armed with knowledge of phonograms and vowel patterns.

If you want children to understand this concept more thoroughly, here's one way to demonstrate it. Have them read each word *out loud* both ways and then tell you which one sounds right in the sentence.

V C	C V	
m i n/e r	m i/n e r	The miner is in the pit digging coal.
V C	C V	
c e d/a r	c e/d a r	The blankets are in the cedar chest.
V C	C V	
C h i n/a	C h i/n a	China is a country in Asia.
V C	C V	
s t a p/l e r	s t a/p l e r	Use a stapler to put the pages together.

MAKING SYLLABICATION A CONTEXT STRATEGY AS WELL

You probably recall that a dictionary presents two ways of dividing each word, first according to printing convention and then according to the need of the reader; for example, risk/y (ris'/kē) and drift/er (drif'/tər). It would be helpful for the reading teacher to look at word division in this same way— as two separate conventions. As a reading teacher, of course, you're only concerned with the decoding convention and not the printing convention.

You see, a secretary or printer divides words according to *printing* conventions and not according to what's helpful to the reader. For example, a printer would divide the word *hoping* this way: hop-ing. A reader who divides it mentally that way would come up with *hopping;* and, through contextual analysis, he'd know that he'd divided it the wrong way. If he then switches to ho-ping, he'll come up with a better pronunciation and the right meaning.

Syllabication, then, becomes a tool for the reader who is searching for meaning—searching for the message the author is presenting. Syllabication should not be a "busywork" exercise of merely drawing lines between syllables.

COMBINING GRAPHOPHONIC ANALYSIS WITH CONTEXT ANALYSIS

Studies show that more time in classrooms is spent on isolated phonics lessons and practice than on any other aspect of reading instruction (Durkin, 1978–79). The fact that insufficient time is spent on comprehension is something we'll talk more about in Chapter 14. Right now, let's just say that much practice time on graphophonic analysis needs to be carried on in the context of regular reading, guided by a skillful teacher. This would be the best way to encourage interactive reading. If children spend most of their time on phonics lessons worksheets, they are simply not going to have enough time *applying* what they've supposedly learned from those lessons. No matter how well they score on phonics subskill tests, they are not demonstrating growth in actual reading.

Here is one example of a teacher's skillfully combining instruction in context and graphophonic analysis, helping children use all four cueing systems:

BENNY: [reading] The man aimed his rifle and shot the deer.

TEACHER: [for the benefit of the group] How did Benny know that last word was *deer* and not *desk*?

MARTHA: [laughing] Because *deer* doesn't end with *sk*.

TEACHER: Good, you noticed one of the clues. Now what's another clue? George, do you know why that last word couldn't be *desk*?

GEORGE: Because . . . uhh . . .

TEACHER: Why don't you try reading Benny's last sentence again, but this time use the word *desk* instead of *deer*.

GEORGE: The man . . . the man aimed his rifle and shot the *desk*. [laughs out loud] You can't shoot a desk!

MARTHA: Yes you could. You could shoot a desk.

GEORGE: Yeah, but it would be silly, and . . . and besides this man's out in the woods. There wouldn't be any desk out in the woods!

TEACHER: All right. Good work, both of you. You paid attention to the letter clues, but you also paid attention to what the author *meant*. Lucilla, why don't you read the next page.

LUCILLA: When the man reached the dead deer, he looked at the an . . .

TEACHER: [after several seconds] Try that trick I showed you.

LUCILLA: With a blank?

TEACHER: Yes, the blank trick.

LUCILLA: When the man reached the dead deer, he looked at the blank and saw that he had killed a five-point buck. His family would eat well this winter.

TEACHER: Now go back to your blank and see if you can fill it in.

LUCILLA: [after a few seconds] Antelope?

TEACHER: Try it out.

LUCILLA: When the man reached the dead deer, he looked at the antelope and . . . Oh no, that wouldn't make sense.

TEACHER: [smiling encouragement] How about the last part of that sentence? What does it say after your blank?

LUCILLA: And saw that he'd killed a five-point buck.

TEACHER: Do you remember what we said a buck is?

LUCILLA: A male deer.

TEACHER: That's right. And what part of a male deer would have five points on it?

LUCILLA: Oh, I know. That thing on top of his head. His horns.

TEACHER: That's right. And those horns have a special name.

GWEN: I know what they are.

TEACHER: Lucilla, would you like Gwen to tell you what she thinks they are?

LUCILLA: [smiling] Yes.

GWEN: They're antlers.

LUCILLA: Oh yeah, antlers.

TEACHER: All right, Lucilla, try your sentence again, and fill in the blank.

LUCILLA: When the man reached the dead deer, he looked at the antlers and saw that he had killed a five-point buck.
TEACHER: Did it make sense this time?
LUCILLA: Yes.
TEACHER: So how do we check to see that our guess is a good one?
LUCILLA: Check the letters.
TEACHER: Right. How do we know that word is really *antlers.* Do you see any group of letters that you recognize?
LUCILLA: Oh, I see *a-n-t.*
TEACHER: Good. And how do you say that part of the word?
LUCILLA: Ant.
TEACHER: Yes, and what about the second part?
LUCILLA: Lers.
TEACHER: Fine. That was good checking. Now let's have Judd read the next page for us.

PUNCTUATION IS PART OF THE GRAPHOPHONIC CUEING SYSTEM

From the very beginning of instruction in reading, children need to learn that those little ink blots (punctuation marks), wiggly letters (italics), and other graphic signals help the reader know how to "say it the way the author would say it." Most of us adults forget how important those insignificant-looking graphic cues are.

Suppose someone asks you this question in a letter: "Are you going there?" Which one of these is probably meant by the question?

Are *you* going rather than someone else?

Are you *going* there or have you already been there?

Are you going *there* instead of somewhere else?

Are you going there, or are you just bluffing?

It depends, of course, on which word the letter writer meant to stress. And your comprehension of the intent depends on which word you stress. If the writer meant for you to accent *there,* and you accented *you,* a serious misunderstanding could ensue. ("What does she mean, am *I* going? Doesn't she think I'm good enough to go?")

We've talked about how a person's reading comprehension is influenced by her understanding of words and sentences. Now we need to look at another component of the comprehension process—the component often referred to as "expression." *Expression* is a general term that covers three specific signals: stress, pitch, and pause. Without the proper use of these three signals, it can be quite difficult for one person to comprehend another person's speech or writing. You've seen one example of this difficulty already. Now look at this one. A scribbled note from your friend says, "Come join us at the park buy some ice cream sandwiches and pop." Which of these did your friend probably mean?

> You're to join them at the park but first buy some ice cream, sandwiches, and pop.
>
> Join them at the park but first buy some ice, cream, sandwiches, and pop.
>
> Join them at the park but first buy some ice-cream sandwiches and some pop.

You decide that your friend meant the third alternative; you buy the stuff and drive to the park in your hot car. By the time you get there, the ice-cream sandwiches look like burnt toast floating in a puddle of milk. Your friend laughs hysterically and says, "I didn't want you to bring us anything. I just meant you could buy some ice cream, sandwiches, and pop for yourself—here—at the park!"

Quite likely you can think of other incidents when confusion arose over misplaced stress or pauses. During a conversation you have with another person, that person's intonation, gestures, and so on usually provide the clues that are necessary for comprehension to occur. But when a person is reading what another has to say, he has to provide his own interpretation of what the stress, pitch, and pause patterns should be. And sometimes the reader makes the wrong interpretation, as in the case of the melted ice-cream sandwiches.

Teachers will sometimes say to children, "Read it with more expression, Susan!" or "Read it as if you were just talking to us, Ronny." In most cases this probably demonstrates the teacher's understanding of how important pitch, stress, and pauses are to good reading comprehension. But just telling children to "put more expression into it" is often not enough. Instead, they need to be shown why expression is important, what it sometimes "looks like" in print, and how one can determine the proper pitch, stress, and pauses that are necessary for reading with comprehension.

First task: Showing them why expression is important. This can be handled in a manner similar to the way I tried to show you why it is important. For instance, suppose you and the pupils come across this passage in a story from a basal reader:

Bill watched Jim throw the ball.

Bill called, "Hey! Show me how to throw, Jim."

By reading the second sentence out loud to the children in a variety of ways, you can help them see the relationship between expression and comprehension. Some of the ways this sentence can be read as follows:

Bill called, "Hey! Show me how to *throw*, Jim."

Bill called, "Hey! Show *me* how to throw, Jim."

"Bill!" called Hey. "Show me how to throw *Jim*."

Bill called, "Hey! Show me how to throw Jim?"

Bill called, "Hey! *Show* me how to throw Jim!"

Bill called, "Hey! Show me how to throw *Jim*."

Just by reading this sentence in a variety of ways—and letting them try their hand at it—you can help them discover intuitively why pauses, pitch changes, and stress variations are important.

Second and third tasks: Showing them what symbols are used in print to indicate expression. Showing them how to determine the proper pitch, stress, and pauses. The need for printed symbols for stress, pitch, and pauses becomes evident to children during an experience like the one just described. The importance of commas seems obvious to them when they realize that without them *Jim* is thrown instead of the ball and *Bill* is called by *Hey* instead of calling "Hey!" himself. Likewise, they can see that a period, a question mark, and an exclamation point are not just simple stops like commas, but indicators of pitch changes as well.

With a language experience approach (described in Chapter 7), the teacher can casually show the children how to use punctuation and underlining as she takes dictation of their stories. Suppose one of the children dictates this, for instance:

Bob said, "Did you take my hat?"

The teacher can show in a natural way how to separate the speaker's message from the actual speaker, and how to use capital letters, commas, quotation marks, and question marks. As the children read what they have dictated, the teacher helps them notice the graphic expression marks so they can read the message in the way they, as the authors, intended the message to be read. This type of experience demonstrates vividly to children the importance of expression to reading comprehension. Sometimes, of course, stress is indicated by letters in italics or uppercase: "I want *you* to eat it. I've had ENOUGH!" But often a reader is expected to provide her own italics, as in the case of the following passage:

Bill watched Jim teaching Harry how to throw.

Bill called, "Hey! Show me how to throw, Jim."

In a case such as this, the child must learn to rely on context for a clue as to which word to stress. Since Bill has been watching Jim teach Harry how to throw, it is likely (but not certain) that Bill would say, "Hey! Show *me* how to throw, Jim."

In addition to the types of experiences with stress, pauses, and pitch I've described, the teacher can provide the children with dittoed stories that are completely lacking in punctuation and ask them to insert capital letters, periods, commas, question marks, and exclamation marks and to underline the word in each sentence that should be given the most stress. You may want to try this example yourself.

I'll do it Roy shouted Terry you run back to town and get some copper wire clippers and some electricity tape tell them Roy sent you and tell them we'll be needing more copper wire soon.

Children can get excellent practice in reading with expression by reading plays to each other—or stories that have a lot of dialogue. Whatever practice materials are used, however, positive reinforcement should be given for meaningful expression and not just for interesting variations in pitch or stress. Some children can appear to be reading with magnificent expression, yet show through their answers to questions that they had very little idea of what they were reading. The goal of communicating with the author should always be paramount.

A GLOSSARY OF GRAPHOPHONIC TERMS

When teachers share ideas for teaching graphophonic analysis, they use certain terms—the jargon of the trade. These terms are used by authors of basal reader teacher's guides, by remedial reading teachers, by speech therapists, and by other people in the profession. You've already read many of these terms in context; you can review them in Table 5.3.

Table 5.3   A Glossary of Graphophonic Terms

Sample Words	Letter Symbols	What to Call the Letters that Represent the Sounds	What to Call the Sounds	Sound Symbols
hat	a	Vowel letter	Short vowel sound	/a/
wait	ai	Vowel digraph	Long vowel sound	/ā/
hobby	y	Vowel letter	Long e sound	/ē/
yell	y	Consonant letter	Consonant sound	/y/
shake	sh	Consonant digraph	Consonant sound	/sh/
stop	st	Cluster or blend	Cluster or blend	/st/
boy or now	y or w	Glide	Glide	/y/ or /w/
cow boy / out oil	ow oy / ou oi	Diphthong	Diphthong (vowel sound + glide)	/ow/ or /oy/
pencil, about	i, a, e, u, o	Vowel letter	Schwa sound	/ə/

Note 1: If you see /sh/, say the *sound*. If you see *sh*, say the two letters.

Note 2: Linguists, speech therapists, and reading educators don't always agree on terms. For example, many linguists use the word *blend* to indicate a word produced by joining parts of other words, e.g., *smoke* joined to *fog* yields *smog*. (Terms are often more historical than rational.)

THE MAIN IDEAS IN THIS CHAPTER

Phonics and reading are not the same thing. Graphophonic cues are only one of four types of cues used in the reading process. The teacher's overemphasis on phonics can cause reading problems.

Athough graphophonic analysis should be seen through the perspective of the total reading act, it *is* an important and sophisticated process, much more complex than sounding out letters one at a time.

It is natural for children to look for patterns in their environment. By teaching children with the phonogram and vowel pattern methods, we may be able to enhance this natural inclination.

The analytic and synthetic methods of teaching graphophonic analysis emphasize the auditory mode of learning more than the visual mode. They should be supplemented with methods that emphasize the visual mode, such as the phonogram, substitution, and vowel pattern methods.

The only purpose of teaching syllabication strategies is to help children apply graphophonic analysis to the syllable units. Syllabication instruction can coincide with or follow instruction on phonograms, vowel patterns, and suffixes.

Graphophonic analysis is probably more a right- than left-brain operation. This belief coincides with research showing that it is easier for children to learn graphophonic patterns intuitively than to learn phonic rules verbally.

Practice in graphophonic analysis should be combined with context analysis more often than conducted in isolation.

REFERENCES AND SUGGESTED READINGS

Bailey, M. H. (1967). The utility of phonic generalizations in grade one through six. *Reading Teacher, 20,* 413–418.

Bond, G. L., & Dykstra, R. (1967). The cooperative research program in first-grade reading instruction. *Reading Research Quarterly, 2,* 5–142.

Bronson, D. B. (1977). Towards a communication theory of teaching. *Teachers College Record, 78,* 447–456.

Burie, A. A., & Heltshe, M. A. (1975). *Reading with a smile: 90 reading games that work.* Washington, DC: Acropolis Books.

Burmeister, L. E. (1968). Usefulness of phonic generalizations. *Reading Teacher, 21,* 349–356.

Clymer, T. L. (1963). The utility of phonic generalizations in the primary grades. *Reading Teacher, 26,* 252–258.

Cunningham, P. M. (1975–76). Investigating a synthesized theory of mediated word identification. *Reading Research Quarterly, 11,* 127–143.

Downing, J. (1969). How children think about reading. *Reading Teacher, 23,* 217–230.

Durkin, D. (1978-79). What classroom observations reveal about reading comprehension instruction. *Reading Research Quarterly, 14,* 481–527.

Dykstra, R. (1968). Summary of the second-grade phase of the cooperative research program in primary reading instruction. *Reading Research Quarterly, 1,* 49–70.

Emans, R. (1967). The usefulness of phonic generalizations above the primary grades. *Reading Teacher, 20,* 419–425.

Fry, E. B., Polk, J. K., & Fountoukidis, D. (1984). *The reading teacher's book of lists.* Englewood Cliffs, NJ: Prentice-Hall.

Glass, G. G., & Burton, E. H. (1973). How do they decode? Verbalizations and observed behaviors of successful decoders. *Education, 94,* 58–64.

Greif, I. P. (1980). A study of the pronunciation of words ending in a vowel-consonant-final E pattern. *Reading Teacher, 34,* 290–292.

Groff, P. (1971a). Dictionary syllabication—How useful? *Elementary School Journal, 72,* 107–117.

Groff, P. (1971b). *The syllable: Its nature and pedagogical usefulness.* Portland, OR: Northwest Regional Educational Laboratory.

Hart, L. A. (1983). *Human brain and human learning.* New York: Longman.

Jones, V. W. (1970). *Decoding and learning to read.* Portland, OR: Northwest Regional Laboratory.

Knafle, J. D. (1978). Word perception: Cues aiding structure detection. *Reading Research Quarterly, 8,* 502–523.

Mallett, J. J. (1977). *101 make-and-play reading games for the intermediate grades.* West Nyack, NY: Center for Applied Research in Education, 1977.

May, F. B. (1985). A case for vowel pattern instruction. In process.

Rosso, B. R., & Emans, R. (1981). Children's use of phonic generalizations. *Reading Teacher, 34,* 653–658.

Russell, D. H., et al. (1981). *Reading aids through the grades.* New York: Columbia University Teachers College.

Smith, A. (1984). *The mind.* New York: Viking.

Tovey, D. R. (1980). Children's grasp of phonics terms vs. sound-symbol relationships. *Reading Teacher, 33,* 431–437.

Weaver, P. (1978). *Research within reach.* Newark, DE: International Reading Association.

Wylie, R. E., & Durrell, D. D. (1970). Teaching vowels through phonograms. *Elementary English, 47,* 787–791.

APPLICATION EXPERIENCES FOR THE TEACHER EDUCATION CLASSROOM

A. *What's your opinion?* Discuss why you agree or disagree with the following opinions. Use both the textbook and your own experiences.

1. When a child doesn't know a word, just tell him to sound it out.

2. A child should learn as many phonics rules as possible.

3. Children should have the opportunity to learn graphophonic analysis techniques with more than one method.

4. The synthetic method is superior to the analytic method.

5. The substitution method is superior to the phonogram method.

6. The nonsense word *cobanantopes* must be syllabicated like this in order to pronounce it: co/ban/ant/o/pes. There is no other way.

B. *Miscue Analysis:* Scotty is a third grader. Analyze his miscues in this passage. Does he appear to be using graphophonic cues in a way that leads to comprehension? Does he need any particular help on graphophonic analysis? (A check means a long hesitation; a large C, a self-correction.)

Bob and Paul had (been sawing) [BEAN WATCHING] and hammering all day. They were building a play house . . . Mr. Krämer, who lived next door, had [✓] [HAD] [HE'D]

given them some lumber from an old garage. He had also given them [A]

some bricks to make a (solid) floor.* [SOLD]

C. Teach two different vowel patterns from Table 5.2, using children in grade four or up as your students. (See "Steps for Direct Teaching of Vowel Patterns" on pages 153–54.)

D. *Teaching Vowel Patterns:* Using Tables 5.1 and 5.2, decide on some of the phonograms you should probably teach before teaching them the difference between the VC and VCE patterns. How would you teach those phonograms?

---

*Colin Dunkeld, Portland Informal Reading Inventory, Form P. Unpublished manuscript, Portland State University. Reprinted with permission from the author.

FIELD EXPERIENCES IN THE ELEMENTARY SCHOOL CLASSROOM

A. Teach a consonant letter, digraph, or cluster, using one auditory-emphasis and one visual-emphasis method. Discuss your procedures and results with at least one other person. (You will find a list of consonant letters, digraphs, and clusters in Appendix H.)

B. Teach three different phonograms related to the same vowel pattern from Table 5.1. Then play a game of "Steal the Words" with one or more children, using one-syllable words that have those three phonograms as endings. (See the directions for "Steal the Words" in Appendix A.)

C. Teach two different vowel patterns from Table 5.2, using children in grade four or up as your students. (See "Steps for Direct Teaching of Vowel Patterns" on pages 153–154.)

6 LANGUAGE AND READING READINESS: THE INTERACTING LANGUAGE ARTS

CHAPTER PREVIEW

Now that you've looked at the four cueing systems, and at comprehension, vocabulary, and graphophonic analysis, the concept of reading readiness will probably make some sense to you. I didn't want to bring it up before, because it's difficult to really understand "readiness" until you know what you're getting children ready *for*. How we get children *ready* to use the four cueing systems in an interactive way is basically what this chapter is about. And essentially, we get them ready by starting with the language abilities they already have and providing them with opportunities to *extend* those abilities. Much of the chapter will be about language development—because, to start where children are, you need a pretty good idea of what they already know about language before they get into your classroom. You also need a pretty good idea of how and why children *differ* in their language abilities, and what the home and school have to do with those differences.

Children come to kindergarten and first grade with anywhere from two thousand to five thousand words they can understand and use in their speech. That's a good start, but naturally they're going to need to hear and speak and write and read—and learn— a lot more words while they're in school. Children come to kindergarten and first grade using syntax pretty well. But there are some difficult syntax patterns they'll need to get used to hearing and speaking before they'll be able to read them with understanding. And children come to kindergarten and first grade already knowing how to read some words by sight, but their recognition of graphophonic patterns is usually pretty meager, and some will need a lot of help in learning to spot those phonograms and vowel patterns. To get ready to spot them, they may even need some practice in making visual and auditory discriminations or in communicating about letters by name or even in recognizing that we use separated words when we speak and write. But even more importantly, they may need language experiences that help them realize how ideas can be changed from speech to print and then changed back again into speech, and that this is one way human beings communicate with each other.

Getting human beings ready for something is often like getting a cat ready for a bath.

Eventually I believe we must abandon our concentration on words . . . and develop a theory of reading and a methodology which puts the focus where it belongs: on language.

—*Kenneth S. Goodman*

THE CONCEPT OF READING READINESS

The concept of reading readiness includes several ideas: getting children ready to receive reading instruction for the first time, getting them ready to receive further reading instruction, and getting them ready to read particular text from a particular author. Although these states of readiness may seem to be separate and discrete, they are really not. Before children engage in any learning experience, whether it's one of learning letters in the alphabet or one of reading assigned text, they need a body of experiences, schemata, and vocabulary to which they can relate the new knowledge. New ideas must be based on old—that's the nature of the human mind. In this sense, the concept of readiness can't be separated from the concept of difficulty, for without sufficient readiness, a new learning experience becomes too difficult, and both frustration and lowered self-esteem may occur, rather than learning.

"Reading readiness" has sometimes been partitioned off into its own little sideshow, usually reserved for five- and six-year-olds and often consisting of colorful workbooks in which they may mark as directed by the teacher. Such exclusiveness is no worse, however, than the view, occasionally expressed by teachers of older children, that reading readiness is something those teachers of five- and six-year-olds "didn't do a very good job on." As one teacher of nine-year-olds put it, "I really can't understand what some of these kids did in the lower grades. They obviously are not ready for fourth-grade work!" To avoid belaboring this point, let's just remind ourselves that reading readiness is everybody's territory. The teacher who refuses to take Johnny where he is—at this particular moment—is not sufficiently concerned about a basic concept of teaching that applies to all levels and all subjects: readiness.

Those of us who write about reading readiness have sometimes confused the issue by making it seem as though reading and reading readiness were two distinct subjects with which teachers need to concern themselves. In reality a child's "readiness for learning to read" and his actual "learning to read" are part of the same operation. This is true whether we're talking about six-year-olds or twelve-year-olds. In either case, the teacher, to teach successfully, must be concerned with what the learner has already learned. Whether the teacher wishes to teach a six-year-old how to decode the letter *t*, or a twelve-year-old to differentiate between facts and opinions, the same principle applies.

Nearly everything a child does before learning to read for the first time is a readiness experience—every time an infant raises an object to her eyes and examines it like a geologist examining rocks from Mars, every time she tests its true character by placing it in her mouth. Every time a preschooler runs fast, feeling the wind rush against his cheeks—and falls flat, feeling the sidewalk scrape against his nose. Every time he creates a one-word imperative sentence (Swing!) and gets a rewarding response from an adult. Every time new experiences are stored in the child's mind and new schemata and language possibilities are developed. Language—that's what reading is a piece of. Reading is nothing more and nothing less than an extension of those plentiful language experiences a child has had on her long five- or six-year journey to school.

To get children ready for learning to read for the first time, or for receiving further reading instruction, or for understanding a new reading selection, a teacher needs to know what related *language* experiences they've had and what related *language* experiences they require. Before children arrive at school for the first time, the schematic, semantic, and syntactic cueing systems have been developing without the help of teachers. Every oral language experience (listening and speaking) provides them with practice in "reading" the semantic and syntactic cues built into our language and applying their own personal schemata to those cues. When someone tells them that "Grandma likes to eat rabbit," no teacher has to be standing by to give them a syntax cue, explaining that Grandma will eat the rabbit and not to worry—the rabbit won't eat Grandma. No teacher has to provide them with minitheories about rabbits. They've developed their own from pressing their noses against pet store windows. Children come to school (whether at the age of five or ten) *bursting* with language and minitheories.

MODERN IDEAS ON LANGUAGE ARTS INSTRUCTION

Slowly, ever so slowly, reading is coming to be viewed by classroom teachers and other educators as one of the language arts (speaking, listening, writing, reading) rather than as an isolated subject of its own. The idea waxes and wanes according to educational fashion and society's fears. As people entertain such fears ("Our children aren't as well-educated as children used to be" or "The Russians are ahead of us" or "Teachers aren't well trained"), there tends to be a corresponding pressure on the schools to teach reading with more rigor—more structure, more isolation, more sub-subskills, more "accountability." But on the whole, from my own limited perspective, and from reading historical accounts of schooling (Robinson, 1977), there appears to be a growing conviction by educators that reading cannot be taught well without making it an integral part of the language arts curriculum, as well as part of the total school curriculum.

In the schools of the early 1900s, the language arts were referred to as "English" and consisted primarily of lessons on grammar, handwriting, spelling, punctuation, and rhetoric (literary composition). Since the end of World War II, however, changes in thinking (if not always in practice) have gradually taken place. These changes have often reflected the rediscovery of ideas expounded by educational philosophers such as Dewey and Froebel, powerful ideas about the nature of children: Dewey realized for instance, that children need to talk if they are to learn; Froebel observed that children, like the young of other species, learn naturally through play.

Thus, the language arts, in the classrooms of teachers who understand these two principles, have become infused with experiences in oral language (speaking and listening) as well as experiences that have the element of playful, yet intense, learning. And more recently, educational researchers have been backing up the intuitive insights of such teacher/philosophers. We know from research reports (Anderson & Freebody, 1981), for example, that oral language development is conducive to better writing and reading. As children learn to speak and listen better, their ability to write and read improves. Therefore, if teachers want children *ready* for higher quality writing, they need to give more guided practice in speaking and thinking rather than more drill on writing. If teachers want children *ready* for higher quality reading, they often need to increase the number of guided listening and thinking experiences.

For example, if a teacher wants to *get children ready* for recognizing the sequence of major events in a story, he can use what Cunningham (1982) calls a "listening-reading transfer lesson." For a listening lesson, Cunningham explains, the children might *hear* a selection and then rearrange sentence strips on which the teacher has written its major events. Following this, the children would *read* a different selection and then arrange a new set of sentence strips. Ellis and Preston (1984) propose another way that oral language experiences can get children ready for reading experiences. They suggest the use of wordless picture books that require youngsters to think about what is happening and to create their own story. In this way, they can develop their thinking skills *before* they must apply them during the reading process.

It may be apparent from the previous discussion that in speaking of "language arts," I'm not referring to the outmoded notion of "English" *products*, such as "good grammar" or "fine penmanship," but to the *processes* of speaking, listening, reading, and writing. It's no doubt apparent, also, that these processes are not separate entities but interrelated and often interacting means of communicating and discovering. As one example of such interaction let's watch the fictitious William Robert Sherman Thomas, III, a child in the second grade, as he attempts to read the following sentence written by one of his classmates:

"It looks like steam is coming out of that whale!"

How do the language arts interact as WRST III attempts to read this sentence? Let's take just the first word in the sentence, the word "It." A simple enough word. Yet, by itself, the word has no meaning. The word *it* is a chameleon, changing its color as conditions change. If the sentence were simply, "Look at it," then WRST, III, might be able to figure out that "It" refers to *whale* or *steam*. But the sentence is not that simple—especially since the child who wrote this sentence wrote it in a natural way, as if she were speaking. And when we *speak* we often use the word "it" in an indefinite way; for example, "It is raining."

So how does poor WRTS III determine what *it* means as he reads? He doesn't really *have* to determine what the word means, does he? He *knows* what it means simply because he has spoken the word and listened to it in this type of sentence pattern numerous times before. Thus, when he translates the written sentence into a spoken (or subvocal) sentence, the meaning becomes instantly clear. Without such previous experience, though, little WRST III would be unable to *read* the word *it* with understanding.

THE NATURE OF LANGUAGE

Language arts instruction has also been changing as a result of information provided by linguists about the nature of language and the way children learn it. Children don't learn language, for instance, merely by imitating adults. If this were so, then teaching language skills would be much simpler and less challenging than it is. Children learn language primarily by using their powers of observation and creativity. They observe and listen to people speak, to be sure, but they also observe how people *react* when they, the children, do the speaking. Do Jamie's parents get him a little round sweet thing when he says "cookie"? Do they rush him into a special little room whenever he utters a sound like (pŏt'ē)? Do they pick him up and cuddle him and coo in his ear when he utters nothing more than "up"? In other words, Jamie gains language power by trying out sounds and noticing their effects. If a sound like "gickle" doesn't get him what he wants, he tends not to use it again. As children try out various sounds, they often demonstrate creativity by the use of *overextension*. A child sees an orange, for instance, and calls it a ball. If an adult picks up the "ball" and hands it to the child, the child's overextension becomes reinforced. A similarly creative overextension, referred to as overregularization, continues later as children regularize verbs that are irregular. Thus, *come*, in the past tense, is changed to *comed; give* is changed to *gived; break* becomes *breaked.*

Children likewise employ creativity as they attempt to produce sentences. At first the sentences are no longer than one word that signals many words. For example, Sandy says "Mommy" as she points to a dress draped over a chair; translated, this might mean, "There's Mommy's dress." At another time Sandy hands her grandfather a box of cookies and says, "Open!" This may have much richer meaning, such as: "If you want me to continue adoring you, Grandpa, open up this confounded box so I can greedily gobble up as many as I want!"

After Sandy has acquired around fifty or more single words in her vocabulary (Dale, 1976), she will begin to use her creative powers to combine those words. For example:

Mommy open!

No Mommy!

Open myself! [Rip! Tear!]

(The last sentence, of course, would occur only after the child has gained in self-confidence and digital strength.)

An even greater instance of children's creative power with language occurs when they generate sentences that no one else would have even thought of. Braine (1963) provides three examples of this:

"All gone sticky!" [after washing hands]

"More page!" [a request to continue reading]

"All gone outside." [after front door has been closed]

Philip Dale (1976) claims that this type of creativity with sentence production is not really that unusual. When we use language, he says, we can't help but be creative. More often than not the sentences we utter are novel ones.

Why is this so? Why is it that the number of *words* in our language is limited but the number of sentences is, for all practical purposes, limitless? There are roughly 500,000 words available to English-speaking people; yet the availability of English *sentences* is probably well beyond the storage capacity of most home computers. The possible *ways* of combining those 500,000 words approaches the infinite. Let's take this one "message" as an example: *Sam sold Joe the diamonds*. Here are just a few ways to express the same message:

Sam sold Joe the diamonds

He sold Joe the diamonds.

He sold him the diamonds

He sold 'm the ice.

It was him what sold them diamonds to Joe.

The diamonds were sold by Sam to Joe.

The diamonds were sold to Joe by Sam.

The ice went through Sam to Joe.

Sam disposed of those diamonds via Joe.

Spade threw the rocks at Lewis. (secret code)

Joe he buyed da rocks offa Sam.

Perhaps by now the point is clear: the use and development of one's own language is a highly creative process. Growth in language seems to require an attitude of playfulness and experimentation, a freedom to express oneself without too much feeling of danger. (The child who said, "All gone sticky!'' after washing his hands is an example of one who feels such freedom.) But let's talk more about this kind of freedom and how it might or might not be available in the home and school environments.

EFFECTS OF HOME ENVIRONMENT ON LANGUAGE GROWTH

Several factors in the home environment can affect children's language development:

The number of adults and siblings present in the home.

The birth order and spacing of the children.

The nature and the amount of conversations.

The interest and affection shown by adults.

While some studies (Aserlind, 1963; Harris & Sipay, 1980) show that "only" children tend to be more mature in language development than children with siblings, a very large study (Zajonc & Markus, 1975) suggests that the firstborn of four may have, on the average, the greatest advantage. Both the only child and the firstborn child tend to be more influenced in their language growth by the adults in their home environment than are later children. A third child out of five, for example, may grow up in a home environment heavily influenced by four other minds that are *relatively* immature and language-deficient compared to the adults in that same environment. (Fortunately for some children in this type of environment, other factors intervene, such as sensitive parents who provide special educational opportunities for each child.) The child who is first of four, on the other hand, not only has unobstructed access to adults during that crucial first year or two, he also has a chance to be the most sought-after language teacher for three others.

Spacing seems to be another major factor that influences children's language growth. Children spaced no more than a year apart tend to develop language at a slower *rate* than children who are spaced farther apart (Zajonc & Markus, 1975). Twins and triplets ("spaced" only a few minutes apart) often have the most difficulty in this respect. Zajonc and Markus found that twins score lower on the average than do singletons on intelligence tests. They also found that when a twin is stillborn or dies within a month of birth, the test scores of the surviving twin approximate those of singletons. Other studies have shown similar results, although most show that twins usually catch up to singletons later in childhood (McCarthy, 1954).

Numerous research reports, however (Saltz, 1973; Watts et al., 1974; Whitehurst et al., 1972) show that *quality* of adult contacts is just as important as quantity. Esther Milner (1951), for example, found that first graders who attained high scores on the language part of an intelligence test had many more conversations with adults in the home than children who attained low scores. The high scoring children received more encouragement to interact with the adults in the home, more affection, and thus more freedom to experiment with language.

Such freedom is not as abundant in the home of many children who become stutterers. Most investigations of this phenomenon have found that parents' attitudes and behavior contribute to the onset of stuttering. They've found, for instance, that parents of stutterers typically disagree on how to discipline their child. Furthermore, they tend to use harsh disciplinary measures such as corporal punishment, threats, or humiliation; they are often inconsistent in their demands on the child for sleeping and eating; and most significant, perhaps, they tend to scold and call attention to their children at the time of the child's stuttering (Moncur, 1971). They also rely more on rejection (Kinstler, 1961) and on criticism (Moll & Darley, 1960). As a result of this kind of pressure, stutterers, looking back on their childhood, often feel that their parents never understood them, showed disappointment in them, were often nervous, and seldom provided enough affection (Duncan, 1949).

It is reasonably evident that deficient oral language abilities, when not physiologically caused, are often related to the quality of a child's home environment. Children who do not have these deficiencies tend to come from homes in which parents have positive feelings toward themselves, accept their children and display affection toward them, maintain consistent but mild discipline, avoid setting impossible standards for them, and provide ample opportunities for them to speak without being under tension. It is likely that these criteria for a good home environment also apply to the school environment.

EFFECTS OF SCHOOL ENVIRONMENT ON LANGUAGE GROWTH

The school environment for a particular child is greatly influenced by her peers, who come to school with a wide range of linguistic abilities. Furthermore, many aspects of language are habitual by the time she enters kindergarten or first grade. Templin (1957) found that after the age of three, there is little change in the parts of speech children use, and that the greatest growth in accurately pronouncing the forty or so speech sounds in our language takes place between the ages of three and four. Chomsky's research (1969) on children from five to ten, however, shows that the process of learning to construct sentences *does* continue actively during the early school years.

Menyuk (1984) describes three areas in which language development continues during children's school years:

Pragmatics—Children continue to learn how to influence other people's behavior with commands, requests, questions, and refusals; how to converse and keep track during a conversation; and how to interpret intonation.

Semantics and Syntactics—Children learn to use thousands of new words in sentences, in addition to the few thousand words they could already use in sentences when they started school. They learn a variety of meanings for some words instead of the single meaning they might have when they start school. They also learn a variety of syntactic and semantic ways of saying things in sentences.

"Morphophonological" Elements—Children learn how to use different verb tenses from those they have been used to and how to stress different syllables in order to move from one part of speech to another (re*cord* to *rec*ord). They also learn how to produce rhyming words and words with the same initial sounds and how to discriminate among different phonemes and blends. Although they know a great deal of language when they start school, they have much more to learn.

Differences in schemata, though, between teachers and students can sometimes interfere with learning. Salus and Salus (1984) point out that the meanings children have for words may be quite different from the meanings adults have. The word *fish*, for example, might mean one thing to a child and quite another to an adult. An adult may think of a chunk of frozen halibut at the grocery store, while a child may think of those creatures she's seen in an aquarium. Thus, in communicating with children about words, teachers need to find out what meanings the *children* have.

Through specific instruction, then, teachers can have an impact on children's language development. A teacher who expects her students' language to improve simply through listening to her everyday speech (no matter how good it might be) will probably be disappointed. This is particularly true if the teacher does most of the talking during the day. One study found that teachers spoke an average of 72 percent of the words in the classroom (Bellack & Davitz, 1963). Such a verbal barrage hardly gives students much time to practice oral language skills, especially when they have to share the airwaves with 30 other students.

Teachers' leadership patterns, though, may have a significant impact on language growth. Lippitt and White (1958), in their classic boys' club study, found that a democratic leadership style encouraged friendly discussion, joking, asking opinions, and making suggestions. The authoritarian style resulted in either apathetic withdrawal (which would hinder oral language practice) or aggressive resistance (which would channel oral language into narrow destructive uses). Similarly, Ryans (1961) found that teachers who were understanding and friendly, yet organized and stimulating, encouraged productive and confident participation. Other researchers have found that when teachers make use of their students' ideas and opinions, the students tend to score higher on tests of language skills (Morrison, 1966; Nelson, 1964). Christensen discovered that vocabulary growth was

significantly greater under teachers whose pupils rated them high on a "warmth scale." Other have speculated that a teacher's expectations of how well a child is going to learn may influence his growth in language skills (Braine, 1963; Rosenthal & Jacobson, 1968; Snow, 1969).

OBJECTIVES OF LANGUAGE ARTS INSTRUCTION

The language arts—reading, writing, listening, speaking—are not generally considered in the same category as the content areas such as science, social studies, and mathematics. Yet they are often treated in elementary schools as if they were. Teachers give tests on grammar, spelling, and reading comprehension, for example, with the implication that information covered by the tests is as important to understand and remember as knowledge presented in science and social studies textbooks. Because of the importance of language skills, there may be some justification for this practice.

On the other hand, the language arts should probably more often be treated as "mediators" rather than mere subjects in and of themselves. Each of the language arts—writing, speaking, listening, reading—provides a medium of exchange for ideas, feelings, and information. In other words, the language arts are the mediators of *communication;* therefore, one would expect the objectives of language arts instruction to relate to the larger goal of helping children become better communicators.

For science instruction, for instance, teachers may have the following as one of their objectives: "To understand that air has weight and exerts pressure in all directions." For language arts instruction, on the other hand, teachers might have more mediating objectives such as these: "To express ideas orally with self-confidence, to read for the purpose of understanding an author's ideas, to listen for people's feelings as well as their words, to describe events in writing in a sequence that communicates to others." All four of these mediating objectives emphasize processes necessary for communicating with others, rather than, say, scientific knowledge that one should absorb to understand and appreciate one's environment.

Once teachers understand the mediating, communicating nature of language arts instruction, they can be freer and more flexible in their thinking about instructional activities and materials. Rather than thinking in terms of *quantities* of language arts information to pass on to children (as if children were small jars to be filled from a large jar via a funnel), they will realize that language arts instruction should be a catalytic, growth-producing process and not a funneling, filling up process. Rather than filling them up with workbook and textbook pages, teachers can feel more open to consideration of questions such as these:

1. What communication skill do many of my students need to learn better? How can I get them ready to learn it?

2. Can I find or adapt an experience or activity that will teach that skill and provide a meaningful opportunity to communicate with at least one other person (peer, adult, author)?

3. Does this activity in which I'm now engaging the students have any potential for teaching other communication skills they need?

4. Can I expand on this language arts textbook or workbook idea so that my students can engage in more actual communication and language experimentation rather than just fill in blanks?

5. Is there some way for me to capture the moment (the enthusiasm, the *need* to learn, the novelty) and to use language as a medium for learning?

6. Instead of always imposing a language arts assignment on my students, is there some way we can use language together?

READINESS FOR DIFFICULT SYNTAX PATTERNS

Now that I've reminded you of the importance of language development to reading progress and of the role of your language arts program in that development, let's investigate some specific readiness experiences that children may need to achieve greater success in learning to read well. Please recall as we talk about these experiences, though, that we're not limiting them to kindergarten and first grade. Many of them need to continue throughout children's elementary school education.

In Chapter 4 I talked about the importance of a sizable reading vocabulary to reading comprehension. A mature reader, however, relies on more than his vocabulary to understand a passage. Like the musician who reads musical phrases as well as notes and measures, the good reader reads not only letters and words, but sentences as well. José may know all the words in a sentence and still not be able to read it with comprehension. Why is this? Simply because the pattern of the words doesn't make sense to him; that is, he is not used to that particular order or arrangement of words.

Ted, for example, was quite capable of reading "He found his ball there." When he was later confronted with the sentence, "There he found his ball," however, he said it didn't make sense. He could read each word all right, but the sentence had no meaning for him. Not having spoken this pattern alteration before, his vocalization of the printed sentence provided him with no memory clues. It was "a silly sentence" as far as he was concerned. Research indicates that this boy's problem is not an isolated instance: reading comprehension and sentence-structure understanding are significantly related.

Studies by Pavlak (1973), Reid (1970), and Ruddell (1965) all demonstrate that reading comprehension depends to a great extent on the similarity between the sentence patterns in the reading material and the sentence patterns children normally use in their oral language. For example, if Tommy is not used to using the passive voice in his speech, his comprehension will suffer when he is faced with a sentence like this one: "The hamburger was gobbled up by the hungry dog." Since Tommy is used to using the active voice, he would have less trouble if the sentence were written: "The hungry dog gobbled up the hamburger." Other studies by Gibbons (1941), MacKinnon (1959), and Strickland (1963) also show the strong relationship between sentence structure and reading comprehension. Several researchers, in fact, have presented evidence that complex syntactic structures can interfere with children's reading comprehension (Bormuth et al., 1970; Fagan, 1971; Richek, 1976). One of these difficult patterns has a name more difficult than the pattern: the "subordinate sentence, tense shift, *if* clause structure," for example, *If you had a car, you would drive it.* Another difficult syntax pattern is called the "relative clause without deletion structure," as in *The man who is driving the car is my father.* A third difficult pattern is called the "subordinate sentence, simultaneous structure," as in *When I came in, my brother yelled.*

The fact that reading comprehension depends on even more than vocabulary and schemata development makes it necessary for teachers to understand certain aspects of the structure of our language. Linguists have discovered, for example, that nearly all English sentences can be "generated" (created) by using or transforming a small number of basic sentence patterns. Six patterns that are common in materials written for elementary-school children can be found in the following "story."

The coyote was in the barn. The man came quickly. The man looked angry. The coyote was his enemy. The man shot the coyote. The man gave his wife the tail.

The six patterns are these:

1. Noun + Be verb +   The coyote was in the barn.
   Prepositional phrase

2. Noun + Intransitive verb +   The man came quickly.
   Adverb

3. Noun + Linking verb +   The man looked angry.
   Adjective

4. Noun + Linking verb + Noun	The coyote was his enemy.
5. Noun + Transitive verb + Noun	The man shot the coyote.
6. Noun + Transitive verb + Noun + Noun	The man gave his wife the tail.

Most children have listened to these patterns so often, they arrive at school already able to recognize them reasonably well. These patterns can be altered and expanded in countless ways, however, and this is where children may have trouble. If they are not accustomed to hearing particular alterations or expansions, many sentences may not make any sense to them in print.

Just hearing the pattern alterations or expansions on TV often doesn't seem to be enough. To make them part of their speaking and reading tools, children need to hear themselves utter the alterations and expansions and need to be reinforced or assisted by others. In a home in which verbal fluency is considered highly desirable, this type of assistance occurs quite often. The infant says, for example, "Daddy shoes," and the mother spontaneously replies, "Do you see daddy's shoes? I see his shoes, too." Thus the child learns in a natural way to refine and alter a basic sentence pattern. In a home in which verbal fluency is not considered highly desirable, such reinforcement and teaching seldom takes place.

For many children, then, the teacher must provide oral-language experiences that complement and supplement those received at home.

Teaching Procedures

Much of the teaching related to comprehension of sentence patterns, alterations, and expansions can be integrated with regular instruction in reading or with the learning experiences the teacher instigates in her language arts program. Suppose, for example, that the teacher and children were reading a story from a first-grade basal reader and came to this passage:

> Soon Mr. Green came.
> He went into the street,
> and he made the car stop.
> Then hop, hop went the rabbit
> out of the street.
> And hop, hop it went
> off into the trees.*

---

*From page 72 of "Green Feet," *Keys to Reading*. (Oklahoma City, OK: Economy Company, 1972).

By asking the children to think of other ways to say each sentence, the teacher can help them become more aware of various patterns, alterations, and expansions. The first sentence, for instance, could be modified to read "Mr. Green came soon" or "Mr. Green came very soon." The third sentence might be modified to read "Then the rabbit went hop, hop out of the street," or "Then the rabbit hopped out of the street," or "The little frightened rabbit then hopped right out of the street and into the bushes," and so on. Once children get used to this procedure, such "incidental" learning need take no more than an additional minute or two in an occasional reading lesson. This same procedure, of course, can be used with upper-grade children, many of whom delight in creating interesting alterations and expansions.

More direct teaching may be utilized in a teacher's language-arts program. Odegaard and May (1972) for example, in a study of children's creative composition, found that third-grade children gained significantly from direct instruction in sentence patterns and pattern modifications. At the end of a series of brief lessons, the children were found to be using a greater number of patterns and alterations in their writing, and their written stories were considered by independent judges to be more creative than those of a control group.

Direct instruction should be oral at first, with reading and writing coming later. Experience indicates that informal lessons of about five to ten minutes work best. It's best not to analyze the sentences with the children by talking about nouns, verbs, and so on. *Sentence alterations and expansions are something they must gain intuitively* through a great deal of listening and speaking. When you try analyzing the sentences with them, their interest in learning sentence alterations and expansions seems to diminish.

The procedures for direct instruction can be similar to the following. (These procedures seem to be suitable for any grade level, including kindergarten, providing the teacher relies on oral rather than written language.)

Step 1:   Introduce the children (preferably a small group) to a set of model sentences. Do this first orally by reading the model sentences to them. (Later, in the same lesson, you can present them in writing providing they are reading at the second grade level or above.) You might start with Pattern 5, shown below, since that seems to be the one with which most children are quite familiar:

The boy ate the apple.

The girl threw the apple.

The horse bit the apple.

The man smashed the apple.

Table 6.1 *Some Common Pattern Alterations and Expansions of the Sentence: The man shot the coyote.*

Alterations	
1. present	The man shoots the coyote.
2. future	The man will shoot the coyote.
3. present perfect	The man has shot the coyote.
4. past perfect	The man had shot the coyote.
5. future perfect	The man will have shot the coyote.
6. progressive	The man is shooting the coyote.
7. infinitive	The man had to shoot the coyote.
8. affirmative	The man did shoot the coyote.
9. plural subject	A man shoots. Men shoot.
10. passive	The coyote was shot by the man.
11. pronoun	He shot him.
12. Did?	Did the man shoot the coyote?
13. negative	The man did not shoot the coyote.
14. What?	What did the man shoot? The coyote?
15. When?	When did the man shoot the coyote?
16. There	A coyote is here. There is a coyote here.
17. sequence	The man came quickly. Quickly the man came.

Expansions	
1. adjective	The angry man shot the coyote.
2. prepositional phrase	The man with the gun shot the coyote in the head.
3. adverb	The man shot the coyote quickly.
4. compound subject	The man and the boy shot the coyote.
5. compound predicate	The man shot and killed the coyote.
6. relative clause	The man who had a gun shot the coyote.
7. compound sentence	The coyote was here and the man came quickly.
8. dependent clause	Because the coyote was his enemy, the man shot the coyote.

Step 2: Have them "make up sentences that sound like these."* This should be done orally at this point. One or two written sentences might be required from the children at the end of the lesson, if you wish to evaluate how well each child comprehends the pattern (but go easy on this or you'll kill their interest). If a child states a sentence that doesn't fit the pattern, simply say something like this: "You're close, Jerry. You're almost in the Pattern Club, but not quite. Listen some more and then try again in a few minutes." In this way, all they have to think of at first are a simple subject and verb. Then you can have them modify the sentences they have created—first by changing *The* to words like *this, that, your, my, his, her,* and *a;* then by changing *apple* to words like *ball, rider, car,* and so on. ("That horse bit his rider.")

Step 3: After they are all "in the Pattern Club," show them the model sentences in writing or read them to the children one at a time again. After each one, have them "listen to how I change it." For example:

> The boy ate his apple. . . . The boy eats his apple.
>
> The girl threw the ball. . . . The girl throws the ball.

After you've read two or three of these pairs of sentences, read them another one and challenge them to "change it in the same ways." Like this:

TEACHER: The horse bit his rider.
CHILD: The horse bites his rider.

This part of the exercise, then, becomes an opportunity for children to get into a "New Pattern Club."

Step 4: After they are in the New Pattern Club, challenge them to get into one more pattern club. This time expand your pattern rather than alter it. Like this:

TEACHER: The boy ate his apple. . . . The hungry boy ate his apple.
TEACHER: The girl threw the ball. . . . The happy girl threw the ball.
TEACHER: The horse bit his rider.
CHILD: The angry horse bit his rider.
TEACHER: Good. You're in the club.

---

*Note: It's a good idea to accept other words for *The,* such as *A, His, Her, That.* It's also a good idea to accept other words for *apple.* But don't accept verbs that aren't in the past tense; just say, "I'll call on you again, after you've changed the third word in your sentence." Don't accept plural nouns.

Noyce and Christie (1981) have expanded on the Pattern Club method by using children's literature for the modeling step. By selecting patterned books carefully, a teacher can provide the children with a greater variety of examples of the pattern as well as an enjoyable story. For example, since Noyce and Christie wished to teach the "subordinate sentence, tense shift, *if* clause structure" (*If you had a bicycle,* you would ride it.), they chose the patterned book entitled *"You Look Ridiculous," Said the Rhinoceros to the Hippopotamus* by Bernard Waber to read to their students. (Having been told by the rhinoceros that she looks ridiculous, the hippo wanders around the jungle feeling sorry for herself. "If only I had handsome spots like the leopard, I wouldn't look ridiculous," she says after seeing the leopard.) They also chose the book entitled *If I Found a Wistful Unicorn* by Ann Ashford as another book for modeling the same syntactic structure.

After step (1), listening, the teachers had the children engage in (2) speaking activities such as the Pattern Club, (3) writing activities such as producing a book similar to one of the model books, and (4) reading activities such as reading on their own other books that have the same syntactic pattern. These are a few other books they recommend: *If All the Seas Were One Sea,* by Janina Domanska; *If I Had . . .,* by Mercer Mayer; *If I Were a Toad,* by Diane Peterson; *If You Were an Eel, How Would You Feel?* by Nina and Howard Simon.

PRINT AWARENESS AND OTHER READINESS EXPERIENCES FOR GRAPHOPHONIC CUES

To most adults graphophonic analysis is no big deal. Just isolate those spelling patterns they've often seen in familiar words and the battle is almost won. But a great many children between four and six don't have a very clear idea of what a word is (Downing, 1973–74). Ask them how many words there are in this sentence, for instance: "The dog is in the house." Some will count the number of rhythmic beats and come up with "three." The *dog* . . . is *in* . . . the *house* (Hare, 1984). Or ask how many words they see when you put these words on the board: *cat and dog.* Some will count the letters and tell you "nine."

In one study (Clay, 1972) only half the children were successful at the end of first grade in sliding a card across a line of print to demonstrate to the tester what "just one word" looked like. They could not tell where one word left off and another started, nor could they show the tester "just one letter" or "just the first letter of a word." So you see, the "print awareness" that adults and older children carry around with them is not something we can necessarily expect from kindergartners or first graders. Instead, it's often something that teachers have to *teach* children.

"But," you say, "my four-year-old can read all kinds of signs and brand names. Is he a genius or something? He's got *great* P.A. (print awareness)." Well, your child may be a genius, all right, but for other reasons. Many children can "read" Stop signs as well as "McDonald's" and "Coca-Cola" and all kinds of other logos. Marilyn Goodall (1984) found that preschoolers could do quite well in reading words as long as the words were part of a photograph that included an "environment" for each word—such as McDonald's golden arches. In fact the children could either say the pictured word or come close on 69 percent of them. When she showed them the same words with the "environment" in the photograph masked, however, they got only 32 percent of them. Furthermore, the strategies the children used when they couldn't read the isolated words showed Goodall that most children do not develop readiness for using graphophonic cues merely from being exposed to signs and logos. Evidently additional readiness experiences are required.

We can see, then, how a young child may recognize the word "Stop" when it's printed on a stop sign but not necessarily recognize it when it's written on the chalkboard or printed in a book. Furthermore, if the word is printed in a sentence, the task may be even more difficult: "The man couldn't see the stop sign." To many children, this sentence might as well be written like this: Themancouldn'tseethestopsign. They simply haven't learned yet to use the spaces between the words.

This is not to imply that *all* first graders have trouble with print awareness. In a study by Virginia Mickish (1974), 117 first graders were asked to divide this sentence into words: Thecatandthedogplayball. Those children who had been placed in "readiness" groups weren't successful, but those placed in average groups were more capable of doing it, and those placed in advanced groups were much more capable still.

Perhaps by now my point has been made. Children come to school with varying levels of awareness of the nature of printed language. Many come with little awareness of what a *word* is, what a *letter* is, what a *letter sound* is, what a *sentence* or *phrase* is. These are all concepts that have to be learned through readiness experiences that teachers provide. After all, the children have been hearing *spoken* language for years, and here is how spoken language would be printed if we were faithful to our ears: "Yawan-nagowithme? Getsumcanny? Helpmefinesummunnysowekingitgoin."

Here are some readiness experiences the teacher can provide children in kindergarten and first grade that will develop greater language and print awareness:

Produce language experience charts together, letting the children dictate things they have done as a group (see Chapter 7 for numerous ideas). As you take their dictation, talk about the language and the print. Say things like, "This one is a big word. It has six letters in it!

One-two-three-four-five-six . . . This word is a little word. It has only two letters in it . . . Whew, let's count the words in that last sentence . . . Should I allow more space between these two words so we can tell that they're two different words?"

Same as above, but do it with a page from a patterned book you've finished reading to them.

Put sentences on the board. After you read one of them, have children come up one at a time, circle a word, and tell you what they remember it saying.

Place removable labels on important things in the room. Each day you can select a different one for a child to bring up to the front of the room to read in isolation. Then talk about the letters in the word, how many there are, which is the first letter, and whether someone's name starts with the same sound or letter.

Use the "key word" approach described on pages 191–192. Have the children use the word cards to create sentences together.

Use logos and brand names in producing language experience charts (Wepner, 1985).

Give each child a sentence strip to cut up into word strips.

In addition to print-awareness experiences, the teacher will also want to provide kindergarten and first grade children with other types of experiences to help them get ready for using graphophonic cues in reading longer text. Three other types of abilities—auditory discrimination between phonemes, visual discrimination between graphemes, and letter recognition—have been shown to correlate significantly with early reading achievement (Barrett, 1965; Bond & Dykstra, 1967; deHirsch et al., 1966; Durrell & Murphy, 1962; Wingert, 1969). Furthermore, some of the reading programs that emphasize these readiness skills appear to have been more successful than those that do not (Dykstra, 1966; Karnes et al., 1968; King, 1964; Sivaroli & Wheelock, 1966). Other researchers, though (Downing & Thackray, 1971) cite studies demonstrating that no advantage (on reading-achievement scores) was gained by children given *formal instruction* in letter recognition. Although the presently available research on this matter is conflicting, it seems likely that most children will benefit from the inclusion of these three types of experiences, at least in kindergarten and first grade.

There are other types of language experiences that may also influence later success with graphophonic analysis. Although the research results are not as consistent with these, they will be included in the sample readiness experiences that follow.

Visual Discrimination

Visual discrimination is the ability to notice differences between graphemes. This is a rather fundamental ability, of course, for without it a child can't learn to decode at all. Fortunately, studies show (Deutsch, 1964; Loban, 1963; Lyon, 1977) that a majority of children can discriminate visually by the time they enter kindergarten. The teacher's job, then, becomes one of providing practice for those who aren't in the majority.

For many years it was thought that visual discrimination between letters and words should be preceded by having children notice differences in pictures and geometric shapes. Research (Ritz, 1969; Wingert, 1969) demonstrates, however, that such experiences do not significantly influence reading readiness. Only experiences in which children make discriminations between letters and words actually make a difference in how well they are prepared for phonic analysis. These are the types of experiences you might use:

1. "On the chalkboard are two sentences. Let's see how many differences we can find between these two sentences. The first one says 'Sam is a rat.' The sentence right underneath says 'Pam is a cat.' Do you see any differences between these two sentences?" (Talk about concept differences as well as grapheme differences.)

2. "On the chalkboard are two pairs of words: *happy—happy* and *lazy—sleepy*. Will one of you put a circle around the pair that is the same? All right. Now here are some more pairs [on the chalkboard or on a worksheet] for you to look at. Circle only the pairs that are the same." (For the pairs that are different, use words that have gross differences, such as *hope—run, elephant—turtle*.) For children who have trouble with this exercise, be sure to point out the differences in words: the different lengths of the words, the different number of letters, even the names of the different letters if they've learned them. If you don't do this, you are merely testing the children, rather than teaching them.

3. Same as #2 but use words that differ only in the initial grapheme or cluster, such as *hope—rope, beer—deer, there—where*.

4. Use words that differ only in the final grapheme or cluster, as in *hop—hot, bang—bank, mold—mole*.

5. Use words that differ only in a medial grapheme or cluster, as in *hat—hot, rubber—rudder, master—masher*.

6. Use pairs of letters instead of words, starting first with unlike pairs that are grossly different, such as *m—p*, and moving to unlike pairs that require finer discrimination, such as *m—n*, or *d—b*.

7. Same as #6, but use cutouts of letters, so that children who are having trouble making discriminations can try fitting one letter on top of another.

8. Same as #7, but use dotted letters and have the children trace over each pair before deciding whether to circle it.

9. "On the chalkboard is a list of words. I'd like you to circle those that begin (or end) in the same way as the first word."

10. Same as #9, but emphasize medial graphemes instead of initial or final ones.

11. Same as #9, but use letters instead of words. "Circle those letters that are the same as the first one."

12. Same as #9, #10, and #11, but have them find the word or letter that is different from all the rest.

Letter Recognition

Letter recognition is the ability to communicate about the names of letters. There is no clear-cut evidence that children must know the letters of the alphabet before they can learn to read. In fact, it would be quite possible to learn to read without ever knowing the names of the letters as long as one knew what sounds to associate with the letters. However, letter names are handy tools for teachers and children to use during reading instruction. Most teachers will tell you it's easier to teach reading when children know the letter names.

What this means in practice is that we would like children to know the letters in a very practical sense. When a teacher points to a letter, the children will be able to say its name, and vice versa; when she says its name, they will be able to point to it. When the teacher asks, "What letter do you see that is the same in all three of these words?" the children will be able to recognize the common letter and to say its name. While some teachers work on letter recognition alone, many teachers combine lessons on letter recognition with lessons on visual memory. With this approach, the children are taught to write the letters as they are learning to recognize them. There is probably considerable justification for this, as writing tends to reinforce one's memory of letter shapes. The following exercises, however, are for letter recognition only:

Play matching games in which the children match their letter cards to a letter card that the teacher or leader holds. Be sure to have them say the letter name as they match them.

Use the letter names as a "password." Hold up a letter card and have the children name the letter before they can pass from one activity to the next.

Put a new letter on the board each day, in both lowercase and uppercase. Several times during the day, ask someone to tell what the letter is. Review with flashcards those letters that have been on the board on previous days.

Encourage children and parents to watch "Sesame Street" together and to play games that require use of the alphabet.

Write the names of several children on the chalkboard. Have each child in the group compare and contrast his name with one or two other names: length of names, number of letters, number of different letters, the names of the exact letters that are different, and so on. (This gives them practice on both letter recognition and visual discrimination.)

Visual Memory

Visual memory, when applied to reading readiness, is the ability to recognize, recall, and produce graphemes and grapheme sequences. This ability is more complicated than either visual discrimination or letter recognition and is based on the acquisition of these two simpler skills. With visual memory the child not only must be able to tell the differences between letters and know their names, she must also be able to write the letters—from memory—both in isolation and in sequence. Furthermore, she must be able to remember sequences that are actual words.

In Chapter 4, we discussed ways of using visual memory to teach children irregular words we would like them to have as part of their sight vocabulary. As you recall, this procedure required the children to look at the letters of the word and say them; close their eyes and imagine the letters while they say them silently; look at the letters again to see if their visual memory was correct; write the letters of the word in sequence without looking at them; and check once more to see if they have written the word correctly. Readiness experiences to use in preparation for this type of procedure include these:

Help each child spell his own name orally and in writing.

Teach children to write each letter by introducing two or three letters at a time in the context of a word. For example, to teach the letters *s* and *e*, introduce them in the context of the word *see (SEE)*. After they learn to write the *s* and *e*, both in uppercase and lowercase form, have them write the word in both forms: *see* and *SEE*.

Help them learn to spell and write their key word for the day. (See pages 119–120 for a review on "key words.")

Help them spell and write the words they need from the Essential Reading Vocabulary in Table 4.2. (See the steps for learning these in Chapter 4.)

Auditory Discrimination

Auditory discrimination is the ability to notice differences between phonemes. Whereas studies show that most children have sufficient ability to discriminate visually by the time they enter school, many children, particularly those who rely on nonstandard dialects for most of their communication, need considerable help in improving their auditory-discrimination abilities (Deutsch, 1964; Loban, 1963; Lyon, 1977). Some children who are weak in auditory discrimination can be helped through specific exercises. Others, however, do not seem to gain significantly from specific instruction and may need to be taught graphophonic analysis partially through the visual approaches discussed in Chapter 5. Generally speaking, though, most children, whether they speak a standard or nonstandard dialect, seem to gain from a multisensory approach in which visual, auditory, and writing approaches are used. Thus, it is necessary to provide assistance in both auditory and visual discrimination, especially in conjunction with actual reading instruction. The following experiences may be used in developing improved auditory discrimination:

1. Same as #1 under *Visual Discrimination*, but this time have them *listen* for differences in the two sentences, "Sam is a rat . . . Pam is a cat."

2. "Close your eyes and listen to these words: *hair, dare.* Keep your eyes closed and raise one finger if you think the words are the same. . . . Now listen to some more pairs of words. Each time you hear a pair of words that are the same, raise your finger." (Use pairs whose initial consonant phoneme is either the same or different, such as *far—car, head—head, that—bat.* Discuss immediately any pairs that cause trouble.)

3. Same as #2, but use pairs whose final consonant phoneme is either the same or different, as in *bag—back, man—map, run—run.*

4. Same as #2, but use pairs whose medial vowel phoneme is either the same or different, as in *here—hair, flip—flip, clip—clap.*

5. "Listen to these three words: *tiger, table,* and *top.* Can you think of some words that begin in the same way?" (Give positive reinforcement for any word that begins with the /t/ phoneme. Do other initial phonemes in the same way.)

6. Same as #5, but use words whose final phonemes are the same ("words that end in the same way"), such as *map, trip, tulip, flop.*

7. Same as #5, but use words whose final phonograms are the same ("words that rhyme"), as in *hall, ball, stall.* (Do the same thing for other phonograms.)

Auditory Memory

Auditory memory is the ability to recognize or recall phonemes and phoneme sequences. Whereas auditory discrimination requires only the ability to notice that one phoneme has a different sound from another, auditory memory requires that the child be able to concentrate on one phoneme at a time and to reproduce that phoneme in his own speech. At times he may be required to reproduce only one phoneme; at other times he may be required to reproduce a sequence of phonemes. For instance, a teacher may ask Ricardo to repeat the /a/ sound; or she may ask him to think of another word that starts with the /a/ sound; or she may have him think of a word that ends in the same way as *bat* and *cat*, thus requiring him to remember the sequence of the /a/ and /t/ sounds.

Children with a high level of auditory memory seem to be able to learn well through the analytic method described on pages 143–145. Children with a low level of auditory memory will need to have their lessons reinforced through the substitution and phonogram methods described on pages 148-152. They may also gain from readiness experiences such as these:

1. "I'm thinking of something in this room that begins in the same way as the word *church*. What is it? That's right: *chalkboard*." (Do the same for other initial phonemes.) After the children understand the game, let them take turns being a leader. (Or whoever answers correctly gets to be leader.)

2. Same as #1, but use blends instead of single phonemes.

3. "I'm thinking of something in this room that rhymes with *hall*. That's right: *ball*." (Do the same with other phonograms such as *ill*, *at*, *ape*, *ap*, and so on.) After the children understand the game, let them take turns being leader.

4. "Who can make exactly the same sound I'm making: /a/? Now who can make this sound: /e/? Who can make this sound: /p/? Who can make this sound /m/?"

5. "Who can say these letters in exactly the same order as I say them: *p—b—a?*" (Do the same with other three-letter or four-letter sequences that do not spell an actual word.) The child who answers correctly can be the next leader.

Letter-Sound Association

Letter-sound association is the ability to communicate about the most common sounds associated with letters in the alphabet. This ability requires the combination of several visual and auditory abilities. When the teacher points to the letter *t*, and asks Wanda, "What sound does this letter stand for?" Wanda has to be able to do several things. She has to use her visual abilities to recognize that this letter differs from other letters like *l*, *i*, or *f*. She has to use her auditory abilities to recall that this letter stands for the sound /t/ and to be able to reproduce that sound. Her ability to do all these things will make it easier for her to be taught either through the analytic or the synthetic method. Children who have trouble with this ability may be assisted through the substitution and phonogram methods. They may also be assisted through the following readiness experiences:

> As children learn to recognize and say the letters of the alphabet, they are often taught the sounds of the letters at the same time.
>
> As children learn to write the letters of the alphabet, they are often taught the sounds of the letters at the same time.
>
> Children may use their "key words" to associate with each letter as they learn how to say and write them. For instance, when they learn the letter *p*, they can associate it with a pig. This "key word" then reminds them that *p* usually stands for the sound heard at the beginning of *pig*.
>
> "I'm going to point to a letter and then I'm going to call on someone to tell me what sound the letter usually stands for."

Auditory Blending

Auditory blending is the ability to place phonemes in a sequence and to recognize the word thus produced. If Michael decodes *a* as /a/, *n* as /n/, and *d* as /d/, he should recognize that he has produced the word *and*. As strange as it may seem, many children cannot do this without a considerable amount of help. They may be able to make the /a/ sound all right, the /n/ sound, and the /d/ sound, but these three phonemes remain in the child's mind as separate distinct sounds. They do not become blended together into a recognizable word.

For this reason, synthetic phonics programs such as DISTAR have sometimes been recommended. These programs actually teach children how to blend phonemes together to make words. They are taught, for example, to say a word like *sun* very slowly, like this: /sssss—uuuuu—nnnnn/; then to say it faster:/sss—uuu—nnn/; and finally to say it "the right way": /sun/. For a reminder of how this method works, see pages 145–148.

On the other hand, synthetic phonics programs may sometimes cause the very trouble they are designed to cure. By having children learn letter-sound correspondences first and then put them together to produce words, this type of program may actually teach children to perceive a word as a set of distinct phonemes. To exaggerate my point a bit, the word *bat* may be misperceived by some children as /buh/ + /a/ + /tuh/ and actually thought of as "buhatuh." You can see then why it is so important, when using a program such as DISTAR, not to neglect the exercises on blending.

To help children learn auditory blending, it is probably advisable to use a synthetic phonics method only for those children who do not seem to respond well to the more popular analytic method. In addition, you may wish to reinforce the analytic method with the substitution and phonogram methods described in Chapter 5. By using visual approaches alongside the analytic method, you will be teaching children to see the spelling patterns that make up many words and to see the minimal contrasts between one letter-sound correspondence and another. Thus you will reduce the amount of auditory blending the child needs to do to decode unknown words. Readiness experiences such as these may also help:

> As much as possible, teach letters and letter sounds in the context of whole words. For example, teach the letter *p* and the letter sound /p/ in association with pictures and words such as *pig*, *pie*, and *puppy*. Avoid overemphasizing letters and letter sounds in isolation.

> If a child does pronounce isolated consonants, have him place his hand under his chin and press upward. This technique will minimize the added vowel sound. Or, have him clench his teeth. Avoid having him add the short *u* sound /u/ to consonants.

> If possible, avoid the notion of "sounding out" words. This procedure for decoding words should be taught only as a last resort to those who have trouble learning common spelling patterns (such as phonograms, VCE, VC, and so on). It is far better, for instance, to teach *cap* as /k/ + /ap/ than as /kuh/ + /a/ + /puh/.

> If you do plan to use the synthetic phonics method, be sure to prepare the children for this type of instruction by teaching them how to blend phonemes to make a word. Start with words they already have in their oral vocabulary and have them say them slowly, faster, and fast. The word *much*, for instance, would be said: /mmmmm—uuuuu—chchchchch/, then mmm—uuu—chchch, then /much/. Use words with fricatives such as /s/, /z/, /ch/, /sh/, /j/,/θ/, and /th/, or nasal sounds such as /m/, /ng/, or /n/: *sing, zing, chin, shush, judge, thin, them.* In this way, you can exaggerate the phonemes without adding a vowel sound to the consonants.

Left-to-Right Orientation

Occasionally a child will demonstrate difficulty in adopting our habit of reading from left to right and from top to bottom. Most children, though, seem to have little trouble picking up the habit of reading from left to right and from top to bottom, probably because parents and teachers have conditioned them to expect to decode words and sentences that way. After all, it would be quite possible to read from right to left and from bottom to top.

One of the easiest ways for a teacher to condition children to our left-to-right convention is to develop experience charts with them. These are simply sentences dictated by the children and written in print by the teacher on a large piece of paper. The children watch the teacher write the "story" from left to right and from top to bottom. After writing each sentence, the teacher reads it and has the children say it with her, passing her hand under the words in a left-to-right direction. Since the sentences are usually based on children's personal experiences, an experience chart seems to be a meaningful way to develop not only the concept of left-to-right, but also the useful concept that "reading is something like changing written words back into spoken words."

Some activities for encouraging a left-to-right and a top-to-bottom orientation are these:

1. When reading stories to children, occasionally turn the book around so the children can see it; point to the words as you read.

2. As you read to the children, ask them occasionally, after you've turned a page, where you should start reading.

3. Create language experience stories with them.

4. Provide children with a sheet of paper (or space on the chalkboard) that has three rows of four rectangles. Write two sentences on the board containing a total of twelve words. Write these twelve words from left to right in three rows. Have the children copy the words in the same sequence, using the rectangles as their guide.

5. Read two or three of the Sunday "funnies" with a small group of children. Place the comic strip up on the board and point to the pictures as you read the words in the "balloons."

6. Same as #5, but block out the words in the "balloons" and have them make up their own words.

7. Have a primary-level typewriter or a word processor available in the classroom for their use.

Following Oral Directions

Before children can learn skills in graphophonic analysis (or any other skill, for that matter) they need to learn how to follow the oral directions that teachers give them. Many times we may think that a child has reading problems, when in reality he simply doesn't understand the directions (or pay enough attention to them). One of the reasons Carl may not have paid attention is that he may not have been taught how to follow oral directions. Another reason is that his teacher may talk too much. Let's look at these two reasons one at a time.

For some children, following directions is easy because they have such good auditory memory. As they hear a set of directions, they store it in memory and then re-hear it as they prepare to follow what they're supposed to do. Children with poor auditory memory, however, need to compensate by using visual memory as well. Therefore, a teacher needs to teach children how to create "pictures in your mind" while listening to directions.

Suppose, for instance, the teacher wants the children to find all the pictures with objects that start with the /s/ sound, circle those pictures, and draw a line from each circled picture to the large S at the top of the page. Some children could do this with only oral instructions. Many, though, will need to develop a picture in their minds of what they are to do. One way to help them develop that picture, of course, is to illustrate the directions graphically on the board or on the page of a workbook. But that is often not enough for some children. In addition to illustrating it graphically, it's a good idea to have them close their eyes and imagine themselves doing each of the three things in sequence: finding a picture, circling it, drawing a line from the picture to the large S. In this way, you will not only help them follow these particular directions, you will be teaching them a valuable scheme for following directions in general.

The second reason Carl may not have paid attention to the directions is that the teacher talks too much. No one likes to listen to the same voice all day long. No matter how good a voice you may have, children will tire of it. Studies have shown (Devine, 1978) that teachers often speak 50 to 80 percent of the words heard by the entire group in a classroom. Is it any wonder that kids sometimes tune out?

Here are some experiences that may increase children's ability to follow directions given orally:

1. Let children take your place as teacher as often as possible. For instance, let an older child sometimes read a story; have a child in the class lead the Pledge of Allegiance; have another child take lunch count, and so on.

2. Make your instructions a game as often as you can. Challenge them to follow the instructions "after I've told you only once." Praise those who succeed. Those who don't get your instructions should come to your desk—or to another student—for another quiet explanation. Don't force the entire class to listen to your instructions again in a loud, irritated voice.

3. Sometimes when you give instructions, you can ask children to complete the last word of each sentence. This provides novelty as well as a cloze-type experience.

4. Pantomime some of your instructions so that the children actually end up verbalizing them.

5. Give them a sequence of three numbers and have them repeat them in the exact order. Gradually work up to five or more numbers. The child who repeats the sequence successfully gets to be the next leader.

6. Same as #5, but use "action words" instead, such as *jump, eat,* and *swim.* The use of action words will help them use their visual memory as well as their auditory memory.

7. Same as #6, but have them pantomime the action words after you give them all three at once.

8. Occasionally play "follow-the-directions games" such as "Simon Says" or others that you make up: "The first one to do all three things and in the right order gets to be the next leader . . . You can't start until I tell you all three things and say 'go' . . . Turn all the way around three times . . . Bend at the waist and touch your toes . . . Say your last name twice."

Oral Vocabulary

Decoding printed words into spoken words is partly dependent upon sufficient experience with spoken words and with those things or concepts the words represent. Most children could decode simple regular words like *cat* or *run* without prior experience in speaking or listening to them; that is, they could pronounce the correct phonemes in response to the graphemes, even though comprehension would not follow. This would not be "reading," however, as defined in this book. And they certainly would have difficulty decoding more complex words or irregular words without acquiring them first as part of their oral vocabulary. A two-syllable word such as *robin,* remember, could be decoded as (rō'bən) rather than (rob'ən), unless the word were already in the decoders' reservoir of speaking and listening words. And an irregular word such as *one* would readily be decoded as (ōwn), were it not for the check provided by their oral vocabulary. So once again we see the interaction between decoding and comprehension and the interplay among the various communication skills. For children unhampered by major speech and hearing defects, the development of skill in decoding appears to be partially dependent upon the development of oral vocabulary. The following types of experiences may help in this development:

A major means of fostering oral-vocabulary growth, as well as growth in other reading skills, is to provide children with a solid science program, particularly in the kindergarten through third-grade years. Such science programs as Science—A Process Approach II (SAPA-II), Science Curriculum Improvement Study—Beginnings (SCIS), Elementary Science Study (ESS), and the Biological Sciences Curriculum Study—Elementary School Sciences Program (BSCS-ESSP) provide children with firsthand experiences in problem solving, producing knowledge, locating information, remembering, inferring, predicting, classifying, and in developing such concepts as *far/near, to/from, top/bottom, first/last,* and so on. Several studies (Ayers & Mason, 1969; Bethel, 1974; Kellogg, 1971; Ritz, 1969) have shown that participation in such systematic science programs has contributed to the growth of children's oral language and their readiness for reading.

Provide abundant verbal and nonverbal experiences so that concepts can be developed and associated with words:

When a child has the chance to hear one good story after another, day after day, he is being taught to read. When his . . . year is a series of mind-stretching eye-filling trips, helping him know more solidly his world, he is being taught to read. When a child hears good adult language, he is being taught to read. When he creates with blocks, when he communicates with paint, when he uses his body freely as a means of expression, he is being taught to read. When a child stares, fascinated, at a picture—when he looks ever so carefully at the scale in his store or at the life in his aquarium, he is being taught to read. When he hammers ever so carefully at the workbench, fashioning his battleship, this too teaches him to read. When he uses his whole body—two eyes, two hands, two arms, two legs and knees and feet—to pull himself up a scary slanted climbing board, he is being taught to read. (Hymes, 1968, p. 156)

Provide some type of show-and-tell experience for each child at least once a week. Encourage each child to participate, even if it means calling parents to get their help.

See Chapter 4 for many more suggestions on developing vocabulary.

DIAGNOSTIC TESTS FOR READING READINESS

In some school districts, children are administered a reading-readiness test during their kindergarten year. The usefulness of such a test depends largely on the precautions teachers take in interpretation. For one thing, the time between administration and interpretation is highly significant. Unless teachers interpret and act within a month or two after the test is administered, they are likely to make serious errors in their instructional strategy for a particular child. What often happens is that children are tested in April or May of their kindergarten year, and the test is interpreted in September or October by the first-grade teacher. For many children, a lot of learning and forgetting has gone on in the meantime.

For another thing, what the teacher chooses to interpret is also highly significant. Often only the total score is noticed, and the child is put into group A, B, or C accordingly. The assumption seems to be that the total score is a good predictor of an individual's capacity to learn to read. This may be wishful thinking. Since most of the correlations between total scores and subsequent reading achievement range between .50 and .60 (Harris & Sipay, 1980), it can only be concluded that total scores on readiness tests are not very good for predicting an individual's achievement. They are pretty good for helping researchers compare the average score of one group with the average score of another group, and they are pretty good for separating the few extremely ready from the few extremely unready. On the other hand, for helping a teacher decide what specific skills to teach Bobby Smith, total scores are nearly useless.

To get much use out of standardized tests, teachers must use them as diagnostic tools, studying the subtests or the items themselves and making notations on the specific skills a student lacks. Most readiness tests, for example, provide a measurement of children's visual- and auditory-discrimination skills, and some provide information on their letter knowledge. By looking at the subtest scores and by noting the types of mistakes made on the subtests, teachers can then plan specific lessons for specific children.

Some of the commonly administered reading-readiness tests are:

Clymer-Barrett Prereading Battery, Personnel Press

Gates-MacGinitie Readiness Skills Test, Teachers College Press

Gesell Institute Readiness Tests, Harper and Row

Harrison-Stroud Reading Readiness Test, Houghton Mifflin

Lee-Clark Reading Readiness Test, California Test Bureau

Metropolitan Readiness Test, Harcourt Brace Jovanovich

Murphy-Durrell Diagnostic Reading Readiness Test, Harcourt Brace Jovanovich

Reading Aptitude Tests, Houghton Mifflin

If you do not have standardized test results available (or if you want to check their validity with your own individual assessment), you may wish to develop some informal tests.

For letter knowledge—Test each child individually by having him tell you the names of the letters you have on a dittoed sheet. The letters should not be in alphabetical order, as a child can "know" the alphabet by rote but be unable to recognize specific letters. Both capital and small letters should be listed. Simply circle the letters the child cannot name.

For visual discrimination—Use as your model for test items the visual-discrimination exercises described earlier. This test can be made a group test by asking the children to circle their answers on a dittoed sheet.

For auditory discrimination—Use as your model for test items the auditory–discrimination exercises described previously. This also can be made a group test.

For left-to-right orientation—Whether you need to test for this before phonics instruction begins is debatable. If you are curious about the left-to-right orientation of some children, however, a simple test is to hand them individually a cartoon from the Sunday "funnies." This should be a cartoon with several pictures in three or more rows and one that can be interpreted without reading the captions. Ask the child to tell you "what is happening in each picture" and observe the direction in which the child tries to "read" the pictures.

For oral vocabulary—Some children's deficiencies or strengths in oral vocabulary can be observed during a show-and-tell period, while they are playing on the playground, when they are listening to the teacher read a story, and so on. But if you wish to be more certain about particular children, you can set up a situation like this one on an individual basis.

For each of three or four pictures you present to them, ask them to tell you (1) what is happening, (2) what they think happened just before, and (3) what they think will happen next. Their responses will give you a fair idea of how much extra time you should spend with them on developing their oral vocabularies. All children, of course, need continued assistance in developing their speaking and listening vocabularies. Some children, though, may be disadvantaged in this respect and need extra stimulation.

A FINAL NOTE ON READING READINESS

Thelma Zirkelbach (1984), after examining the history of preschool reading programs and researchers' recommendations, came up with a resounding *no* to certain reading readiness experiences. She came up with a vigorous

yes to other reading readiness experiences. I would like to extend her recommendation to apply all the way through kindergarten and the first half
of first grade.

The Negative Recommendations

Working in workbooks

Decoding isolated words with no emphasis on meaning

Labeling children who do not read before first grade as failures

The Positive Recommendations

Reading to children

Helping them create language experience stories

Drawing their attention to the wealth of reading material around
them

Providing them with materials and activities for reading and writing
as they desire them

Engaging them in experiences to increase their vocabularies

Engaging them in experiences to stimulate their thinking

Allowing them the freedom to read when and if they are ready

THE MAIN IDEAS OF THIS CHAPTER

Reading is an extension of earlier language experiences provided by
the home or school. Reading readiness should be based on the knowledge and skill gained from those earlier experiences.

Reading is one of the four language arts and should be taught as an
integral part of the language arts program. Improving children's reading skill often requires particular readiness experiences in listening,
speaking, or writing.

The development of language is a highly creative rather than an imi-
tative process. Teachers and school administrators should attempt to
provide more opportunities for this natural creative process to occur

and not treat the language arts, including reading, as a subject to be learned only through memorization, drill, and testing.

Children who are free from major language deficiencies tend to come from homes that amply provide affection, consistent but mild discipline, and opportunities to speak without tension. These same characteristics are probably equally important in the school environment.

Although children come to school with a considerable knowledge of language, they depend upon the school for opportunities to increase their vocabulary, syntax sense, schemata, and graphophonic awareness.

Special readiness experiences can help prepare children for the processes involved in reading. These experiences are designed to enhance kindergarten and first-grade children's print awareness, visual discrimination, letter recognition, visual memory, auditory discrimination, auditory memory, letter-sound association, auditory blending, left-to-right orientation, ability to follow oral directions, and oral vocabulary.

If teachers are to benefit from the use of standardized reading readiness tests, they must have access to subtest scores and children's responses to individual items. Total scores are essentially useless for teaching purposes.

Reading readiness should concern all teachers at all grade levels. Basically, reading readiness means inspiring children through provision of background knowledge and language skills that help them *want to read.*

REFERENCES AND SUGGESTED READING

Anderson, R. C., & Freebody, P. (1981). Vocabulary knowledge. In J. Flood (Ed.), *Comprehension and teaching: Research reviews* (pp. 77–117). Newark, DE: International Reading Association.

Aserlind, L., Jr. (1963). *An investigation of maternal factors related to the acquisition of verbal skills of infants in a culturally disadvantaged population.* Unpublished doctoral dissertation. University of Wisconsin.

Ayers, J. B., & Mason, G. E. (1969). Differential effects of science–A process approach upon change in Metropolitan Readiness Test scores among kindergarten children. *Reading Teacher, 22,* 435–439.

Barrett, T. C. (1965). The relationship between measures of prereading visual discrimination and first-grade reading achievement: A review of the literature. *Reading Research Quarterly, 2,* 51–76.

Bellack, A. A., & Davitz, J. R. (1963). The language of the classroom. Cooperative Research Project No. 1497. New York: Institute of Psychological Research, Teachers College, Columbia University.

Bethel, L. J. (1974). *Science inquiry and the development of classification and oral communication skills in innercity children.* Unpublished doctoral dissertation. University of Pennsylvania.

Bond, G. L., & Dykstra, R. (1967). The cooperative research program in first-grade reading instruction. *Reading Research Quarterly, 2,* 5–142.

Bormuth, J., Carr, J., Manning, J., & Pearson, D. (1970). Children's comprehension of between- and within-sentence syntactic structures. *Journal of Educational Psychology, 61,* 349–357.

Braine, M. D. S. (1963). The ontology of English phrase structure: The first phase. *Language, 39,* 1–13.

Brophy, J. E., & Good, T. L. (1970). Teachers' communication of differential expectations for children's classroom performance: Some behavioral data. *Journal of Educational Psychology, 61,* 365–374.

Chomsky, C. (1969). *The acquisition of syntax in children from 5–10.* Cambridge: Massachusetts Institute of Technology.

Christensen, C. M. (1960). Relationship between pupil achievement, pupil affect-need, teacher warmth, and teacher permissiveness. *Journal of Educational Psychology, 51,* 169–174.

Clay, M. M. (1972). *Reading: The patterning of complex behavior.* Aukland, New Zealand: Heinemann Educational Books.

Cunningham, P. (1982). Improving listening and reading comprehension. *Reading Teacher, 35,* 486–488.

Dale, P. S. (1976). *Language development.* New York: Holt, Rinehart, & Winston.

deHirsch, K., Jansky, J., & Langford, W. S. (1966). *Predicting reading failure: A preliminary study.* New York: Harper and Row.

Deutsch, C. P. (1964). Auditory discrimination and learning: Social factors. *Merrill-Palmer Quarterly of Behavior and Development, 10,* 277–296.

Devine, T. G. (1978). Listening: What do we know after fifty years of research and theorizing? *Journal of Reading, 21,* 296–304.

Downing, J., & Thackray, D. (1971). *Reading readiness.* London: University of London Press.

Downing, J. (1973–1974). The child's conception of "A Word." *Reading Research Quarterly, 9,* 568–582.

Duncan, M. H. (1949). Home adjustment of stutterers versus nonstutterers. *Journal of Speech and Hearing Disorders, 14,* 255–259.

Durrell, D., & Murphy, H. (1962). Reading in grade one. *Journal of Education, 146,* 14–18.

Dykstra, R. (1966). Auditory discrimination abilities and beginning reading achievement. *Reading Research Quarterly, 1,* 5–34.

Ellis, D. W., & Preston, F. W. (1984). Enhancing beginning reading using wordless picture books in a cross-age tutoring program. *Reading Teacher, 37,* 692-698.

Fagan, W. T. (1971). Transformations and comprehension. *The Reading Teacher, 25,* 169–172.

Gibbons, H. D. (1941). Reading and sentence elements. *Elementary English Review, 18,* 42–46.

Golden, M., Bridger, W. H., & Montare, A. (1974). Social class differences in the ability of young children to use verbal information to facilitate learning. *American Journal of Orthopsychiatry, 44,* 86–91.

Goodall, M. (1984). Can four year olds "read" words in the environment? *Reading Teacher, 37,* 478–482.

Hare, V. C. (1984). What's in a word? A review of young children's difficulties with the construct "word." *Reading Teacher, 37,* 360–364.

Harris, A. J., & Sipay, E. R. (1980). *How to increase reading ability.* New York: David McKay.

Hess, R., & Shipman, V. (1965). Early experience and the socialization of cognitive modes in children. *Child Development, 36,* 869–886.

Higgenbotham, D. C. (1961). *A study of the speech of kindergarten, first, and second grade children in audience situations with particular attention to maturation and learning as evidenced in content, form, and delivery.* Unpublished doctoral dissertation. Northwestern University.

Hymes, J. L. (1968). Early reading is very risky business. In V. M. Howes & H. F. Darrow (Eds.), *Reading and the Elementary School Child* (pp. 153–157). New York: Macmillan.

Karnes, M. B., et al. (1968). An evaluation of two preschool programs for disadvantaged children. *Exceptional Children, 34,* 667–676.

Kellog, D. H. (1971). *An investigation of the effect of the science curriculum improvement study's first year unit, material objects, on gains in reading readiness.* Unpublished doctoral dissertation. University of Oklahoma.

King, E. M. (1964). Effects of different kinds of visual discrimination training on learning to read words. *Journal of Educational Psychology, 55,* 325–333.

Kinstler, D. B. (1961). Covert and overt maternal rejection in stuttering. *Journal of Speech and Hearing Disorders, 26,* 145–155.

Lippitt, R., & White, R. K. (1958). An experimental study of leadership and group life. In E. E. Maccoby et al. (Eds.), *Readings in Social Psychology.* New York: Holt Rinehart & Winston.

Loban, W. (1963). *The language of elementary school children.* Urbana, IL: National Council of Teachers of English.

Lyon, R. (1977). Auditory-perceptual training: The state of the art. *Journal of Learning Disabilities, 10,* 564–572.

MacKinnon, A. R. (1959). *How do children learn to read?* New York: Copp Clark.

McCarthy, D. (1954). Language development in children. In L. Carmichael (Ed.), *Manual of Child Psychology* (pp. 492-630). New York: John Wiley & Sons.

Menyuk, P. (1984). Language development and reading. In J. Flood (Ed.), *Understanding reading comprehension* (pp. 101–121). Newark, DE: International Reading Association.

Mickish, V. (1974). Children's perception of written word boundaries. *Journal of Reading Behavior, 6,* 19–22.

Milner, E. (1951). A study of the relationship between reading readiness in grade one school children and patterns of parent-child interaction. *Child Development, 22,* 95–112.

Moll, K. L., & Darley, F. L. (1960). Attitudes of mothers of articulatory-impaired and speech-retarded children. *Journal of Speech and Hearing Disorders, 25,* 377–384.

Moncur, J. P. (1951). Environmental factors differentiating stuttering children from non-stuttering children. *Speech Monographs, 18,* 312–325.

Morrison, B. M. (1966). *The reactions of children to patterns of teaching behavior.* Unpublished doctoral dissertation. University of Michigan.

Nelson, L. N. (1964). The effect of classroom interaction on pupil linguistic performance. *Dissertation Abstracts International, 25,* 789.

Noyce, R. N., & Christie, J. F. (1981). Using literature to develop children's grasp of syntax. *Reading Teacher, 35,* 298–302.

Odegaard, J. M., & May, F. B. (1972). Creative grammar and the writing of third graders. *Elementary School Journal, 73*, 156–161.

Pavlak, S. A. (1973). *Reading comprehension—a critical analysis of selected factors affecting comprehension.* Unpublished doctoral dissertation. University of Pittsburgh.

Reid, J. (1970). Sentence structure in reading. *Research in Education, 3*, 23–27.

Richek, M. (1976). Effect of sentence complexity on the reading comprehension of syntactic structures. *Journal of Educational Psychology, 68*, 800–806.

Ritz, W. C. (1969). *The effects of two instructional programs (Science—a process approach and the Frostig program for the development of visual perception) on the attainment of reading readiness, visual perception, and science process skills in kindergarten children.* Unpublished doctoral dissertation. Buffalo: State University of New York.

Robinson, H. A. (1977). *Editor, Reading and writing instruction in the United States: Historical trends.* Newark, DE: International Reading Association.

Rosenthal, R., & Jacobson, L. (1968). *Pygmalion in the classroom.* New York: Holt, Rinehart & Winston.

Ruddell, R. B. (1965). The effect of oral and written patterns of language structure on reading comprehension. *Reading Teacher, 18*, 270–275.

Ryans, D. G. (1961). Some relationships between pupil behavior and certain teacher characteristics. *Journal of Educational Psychology, 52*, 82–90.

Saltz, R. (1973). Effects of part-time 'mothering' on IQ and SQ of young institutionalized children. *Child Development, 44*, 166–170.

Salus, P. H., & Salus, M. W. (1984). Word finding, word organizing, and reading. In J. Flood (Ed.), *Understanding reading comprehension* (pp. 122–139). Newark, DE: International Reading Association.

Sivaroli, N. J., & Wheelock, W. H. (1966). An investigation of auditory discrimination training for beginning readers. *Reading Teacher, 20*, 247–51.

Snow, R. E. (1969). Unfinished pygmalion. *Contemporary Psychology, 14*, 197–199.

Strickland, R. G. (1963). Implications of research in linguistics for elementary teachers. *Elementary English, 40*, 168–171.

Templin, M. C. (1957). *Certain language skills in children: Their development and interrelationships.* Minneapolis: University of Minnesota Press.

Watts, J. C., Halfargood, C., & Chan, I. (1974). Environment, experience and intellectual development of young children in home care. *Journal of Orthopsychiatry, 44*, 773–781.

Wepner, S. B. (1985). Linking logos with print for beginning reading success. *Reading Teacher, 38*, 633–639.

Whitehurst, G. J, Novak, G., & Zorn, G. A. (1972). Delayed speech studied in the home. *Developmental Psychology, 7*, 169–177.

Wingert, R. C. (1969). Evaluation of a readiness training program. *Reading Teacher, 22*, 325–328.

Zajonc, R. B., & Markus, G. B. (1975). Birth order and intellectual development. *Psychological Review, 82*, 74–88.

Zirkelbach, T. (1984). A personal view of early reading. *Reading Teacher, 37*, 468–471.

APPLICATION EXPERIENCES FOR THE TEACHER EDUCATION CLASSROOM

A. *What's your opinion?* Discuss why you agree or disagree with the following options. Use both the textbook and your own experiences.

1. Listening experiences might be important readiness experiences for reading, but speaking experiences can't really get you ready for reading.

2. By the time children get to school they've already learned all the language skills they need. The teacher should concentrate instead on having them learn facts and ideas.

3. Patterned books can be extremely useful in getting children ready for reading experiences.

4. Language arts is a subject in the elementary school curriculum—like science, math, social studies, and that kind of thing.

5. The best way for teachers to develop children's language abilities is to model good language at all times. There are no other really effective ways.

6. There must be at least a dozen different ways of saying anything. (Use this sentence to prove or disprove what you believe: "Into the valley, their horses steaming, the enraged warriors thundered." Now decide what this had to do with the ideas in Chapter 6.)

B. *Miscue Analysis*—What specific readiness experiences might Betty, a first grader, need before she can be more successful with text such as the following? (A *d* over a word means the child defaulted and the teacher had to pronounce the word. A large *C* around a word means a substitution has been self-corrected.)

Mary (*is* has a dog . . . He swims in

the river. *d* He gets wet . . . He

shakes himself *d* . . . Then he is

dry . . . "Good (*boy* dog," says Mary.

She likes her dog.*

Question: How does Mary's dog get dry after he's been swimming?

Betty's answer: Mary dries him with a towel.

Question: Why does Mary tell him he's a good dog?

Betty's answer: Because he doesn't bark?

*Colin Dunkeld, Portland Informal Reading Inventory, Form P. Unpublished manuscript, Portland State University. Reprinted with permission from the author.

    C. *Reading Readiness Materials*—With a partner or two, examine either a reading-readiness workbook and the accompanying teacher's guide or a reading-readiness test and the accompanying manual. What abilities are emphasized? What abilities discussed in this chapter are not emphasized? How do these materials relate or not relate to language and the four cueing systems?

FIELD EXPERIENCES IN THE ELEMENTARY SCHOOL CLASSROOM

    A. Record the various ways that language skills were strengthened (or could have been strengthened) during a one- to three-hour period of observation in an elementary school classroom. How often did these occur informally? How often did these occur as part of formal instruction? What opportunities were taken by the teacher to encourage "talk" and "language experimentation" in such a way that language could be further developed? What opportunities might have been missed?

    B. Carry on an informal conversation with two children at different times—one child whom the teacher thinks has highly developed language skills and one whom the teacher feels has poorly developed language skills. What specific differences do you notice? If you discover anything about the children's background of experiences in the course of your conversation, what differences between the two children do you notice?

    C. Develop a brief reading-readiness test and administer it to one or more children. You may wish to use some of the ideas on pages 192–202.

    4. Analyze how another teacher determines whether children are ready for a reading experience she is planning to give them. Also observe how she provides necessary readiness experiences. Does she sometimes provide oral-language experiences before similar reading experiences? What changes in her "readiness" procedures would you make?

INTEGRATING THE THREE MAJOR APPROACHES TO READING INSTRUCTION

7 WRITING AS AN AID TO READING: LANGUAGE EXPERIENCE APPROACHES

We saw in Chapter 6 how important it is for the teacher to view reading as one of the language arts. In this chapter we'll look at specific language arts methods of developing children's reading skill, particularly the contributions that writing experiences can make toward growth in reading ability. Although the idea of teaching reading through writing experiences has been around for a long time (Sylvia Ashton-Warner used writing as a natural medium for children to learn to read), only recently has writing "taken hold" during formal education as a process that shouldn't be separated from reading. I feel comfortable in predicting that the schools of the future will give writing a much more dominant place in the curriculum than it has today. We'll examine in this chapter how teachers can use the language of children as a stimulus for both writing and reading. We'll find that when a child sees his verbal expression translated into print, and then sees the print translated back into speech, the reading process begins to make sense to him. This cooperative writing-reading process is a natural one and is the basis for the variety of language experience approaches that can be used in the elementary school. This chapter will also show you specifically what to do when using children's written or dictated ideas as a medium for teaching reading. You'll learn how to stimulate children's writing, how to teach vocabulary and phonic patterns through the use of their writing, and how to combine language experiences with other instructional approaches.

On any planet—even Earth—the young are often their own best teacher.

THE INTERACTION OF WRITING AND READING PROCESSES: AN EXAMPLE

Mrs. Friedman read several poems to her fourth grade class that day. "It was just one of those poetry days," she said later. The sun hadn't been out for three days straight, Billie Jean had thrown up in the cloakroom, and Mrs. Friedman had forgotten to turn in her lunch count, thus getting a mild reprimand over the public address system. "If ever humorous poetry was called for," she said, "it was that day."

Shel Silverstein came to the rescue with his poem about Peggy Ann McKay, who was able to find sixteen chicken pox on her body, along with a sunken belly button and twenty-five other ailments that were sure to keep her from going to school. And there was his poem about the peanut butter sandwich that locked the jaws of a silly young king. And, of course, the one called "Stone Telling."

> How do we tell if a window is open?
> Just throw a stone at it.
> Does it make a noise?
> It doesn't?
> Well, it was open.
> Now let's try another . . .
> *CRASH!*
> It wasn't!*

*"Stone Telling" from WHERE THE SIDEWALK ENDS by Shel Silverstein. Copyright © 1974 by Snake Eye Music, Inc. Reprinted by permission of Harper & Row, Publishers, Inc.

Among all the poems read that day was my own opinionated one that "Waffles Are Better." The students in Mrs. Friedman's class enjoyed this poem, and there was quite a discussion about the virtues of pancakes versus waffles. She realized, while the children were engaged in debate, that this poem would be a useful model for their own writing.

Waffles Are Better*

Some favor pancakes
Fried in a pan,
Then piled high,
Slathered in butter
Drowned in syrup!
. . . But not I.

I favor waffles.
Waffles are something
You never fry.
You pour in the batter,
You put down the lid,
And my oh my!

You wait and you wait,
Your patience so thin,
Your hopes in the sky,
While the magic takes place,
While waffle elves work,
And eternity goes by.

You watch and you stare
Through mystical steam
At the little red eye.
"Will it ever go off?
Will it ever turn dark?"
You cry . . . then sigh.

But at last the aroma!
And the steam disappears.
The red light does die.
You open the lid
And the magic is done.
It's time to pry.

Out pops the disk
As gold as the sun,

---

*Copyright © 1986 by Frank B. May.

As round as a pie.
On goes the butter
Like molten lava
From mountains high.

Then on with the syrup
Into valleys so deep
You try and you try
To fill every one . . .
And not miss a peak:
A feast for the eye!

Now gobble that moonscape
Demolish that city
Let no building lie.
You could have had pancakes
So flat and so smooth
And delicious—but why?

So, the next day, when things were running smoothly once more, she showed them the poem, now written on a large chart. She invited them to join her in a choral reading of the poem, with Mrs. Friedman reading every other verse by herself (to provide modeling) and the children reading the alternating verses as a group. Then she asked them to tell her how the poem had been written. Through skillful questioning she helped them come up with these characteristics that she wrote on the chalkboard:

1. Two favorite things were compared.

2. Every third line rhymed.

3. The rhyming sound was always the same.

4. One of the favorite things was shown to be better.

5. The rhythm throughout the poem was the same.

With these characteristics on the board, the children then attempted to write a similar poem as a group. Janet suggested that they compare eggs with bacon, but Kim thought they were too different and suggested chicken with steak. Nancy waved her hand wildly and said, "Oh, I know! Let's compare an ice-cream cone with a candy bar!" This idea met with approval from the entire class, but now they had a bigger problem to solve: which one would they show to be better? The vote was close, but the ice-cream cone won. To diminish the candy lovers' disappointment, Mrs. Friedman told them they could write the parts of the poem in praise of the candy bar.

Now they had to select a rhyming sound that would be the same on every third line. In response to the teacher's question, "What are some words that rhyme," Dennis came up with *cat, bat*, and *sat*. The list of *at* words on the board grew from three to eighteen, and they decided they had enough. Mrs. Friedman wrote the first line and invited the candy bar lovers to describe a candy bar in such a way that everyone in the room would want one.

"Some like candy bars," she wrote, then waited for a response. "Filled with nuts and covered with chocolate," Robin said. The teacher wrote:

> Some like candy bars,
> Filled with nuts
> And covered with chocolate.

This version met with instant protest, since the third line didn't end with the rhyming sound of /at/. Mrs. Friedman asked for another third line.

"Pat, pat, pat," Cindy said, smiling and patting her hand on her desk. Mrs. Friedman smiled back. "You mean as if someone is patting the nuts into the candy bar?" Cindy assured her that this was exactly what she had in mind!

The teacher changed the third line by drawing lightly through it and writing the new third line off to the side. In this way, she knew she wouldn't lose the contribution that had been made earlier about the candy bar's being covered with chocolate. The poem now read:

> Some like candy bars,
> Filled with nuts.
> Pat, pat, pat.

Mrs. Friedman said, "Since we're putting all those nuts into the candy bar, perhaps we need a word that's stronger than 'filled'."

"Smashed," David said.

"Mooshed," Diane said.

"Crammed," Bobbie said.

And on through their poem they plunged and weaved and slashed, the teacher contributing a line now and then to keep them going, until thirty-five minutes later the tired poets rested:

Ice-Cream Cones Are Better!*

Some like candy bars,
Crammed with nuts,
Pat, pat, pat.

---

*Copyright © 1986 by Frank B. May.

Some like candy bars
Mooshed with cream,
Fat, fat, fat.

Most like candy bars
Smothered with chocolate,
Imagine that!

With so much sugar
It can sweeten up
The meanest brat.

But I like ice-cream cones,
So smooth and round,
Not bumpy and flat.

You stand at the counter
With noses pressed to the glass,
You and Shelly and Nat.

And you wait and you wait
As she scoops it up,
Pat, pat, pat.

Finally yours is ready
And you take a secret nibble,
Feeling like a rat.

You know you should wait
For your friends to get theirs.
So you anxiously chat

About weather and school,
About cabbages and kings,
About zit, zoom, and zat.

And finally you've got them
Enclosed in your fists,
The ball and upside-down hat.

Only one more choice to make:
To lick, lip, or bite.
Oh, drat!

WHAT DOES WRITING INSTRUCTION CONTRIBUTE TO READING GROWTH?

Durkin (1966) studied "early readers" for six years in California and for three years in New York City. One of her conclusions was that the scribbling and writing experiences these early achievers had before starting formal schooling had made an important contribution to their success in learning to read at an earlier age than most children. One implication she drew from her research was that writing and reading should be taught together. Other researchers have drawn the same implication from their research (Chomsky, 1971; Graves, 1979). Loban (1976), for example, found in his 13-year study of children's development that children who did well in writing tended to do well in reading, and vice versa. Although this does not demonstrate a cause and effect relationship between the two language processes, it is likely that the two skills enhance each other's growth. Several researchers have found a significant relationship between children's reading achievement and the syntactic complexity of their writing (Evans, 1979; Evanechko et al., 1974; Lazdowski, 1976).

Dionisio (1983) found that teaching reading through writing was the best approach for her sixth-grade remedial readers who were "turned off to reading." By modeling both writing and revising behavior with the students and giving them plenty of opportunity to read each other's work (as well as their own), she was able to help them improve in their reading abilities—even without providing them with formal reading instruction. Graves and Murray (1980) had similar results with their writing programs for children.

The ways of teaching reading through writing are as varied as the individual teachers. It's true that some of the "reading through writing" programs have become somewhat formalized, but people in the "ed business" are always trying to put good ideas into neat little commercial packages—often with the assumption that all teachers and students are alike. You, as an individual teacher with children who are each different from the others, will no doubt think of many ways of combining reading and writing as you teach. Perhaps the only principle you need to remember is that writing experiences frequently need to *precede* reading experiences. This is different from the way many of us in this country are used to thinking about teaching. As Graves pointed out in his 1978 Ford Foundation Report:

> Although reading is valued in other countries, it is viewed more in the perspective of total communication . . . Our anxiety about reading is a national neurosis . . . Concern about reading is today such a political, economic, and social force in American education that an imbalance in forms of communication is guaranteed from the start of a child's schooling. (Graves, 1978, p. 3)

I talked earlier about Sylvia Ashton-Warner and her followers who have had considerable success using the writing of "key words" as a beginning to the process of learning to read. The approach I'll be talking about most in this chapter is the "language experience approach," which also involves considerable experience in writing before reading. No, I don't mean that writing is taught and then reading is taught. It's just that a writing experience often precedes a reading experience by a few minutes. The two experiences *together* provide a better basis for learning than the two in isolation (again, the interaction principle of communication). But before we talk about language experience approaches, let's first look at a more familiar approach.

TEACHING READING THROUGH THE WRITING OF PATTERNED BOOKS

In previous chapters we've discussed the use of patterned books to help children develop the concept of reading as a process of predicting and confirming. We've also talked about using these books for readiness experiences and as media for teaching sight words and graphophonic patterns. In this chapter I'd like to show you another use for them. Let's watch a teacher in Vancouver, Washington, using a patterned book to teach reading and writing to three first graders in her "learning disabled classroom." The teacher, Brenda Louthan, chose Steven Kellog's book, *Can I Keep Him?* The main character is an imaginative boy who keeps telling his mother about a new animal he's found and asking her if he can keep it. The mother, of course, has an appropriate excuse for each one of her denials. Here's the way Mrs. Louthan describes her experience:

Day one: I read the book to the children. I then read it again and asked them if they had noticed anything that had happened over and over in the story. They were able to see the pattern in which Arnold tries to bring home pet after pet and his mom always tells him, "No, dear. You can't keep him."

Day two: I read the book again and we made a list on the board of all the animals that Arnold had brought home. We went back through the book and checked to see if we had gotten all of them.

Day three: I read the book again and we made a list of all the other animals that Arnold could have brought home. They really enjoyed this and came up with a long list.

Day four: I read the book again and we made a list of all the reasons Arnold's mom gave him for not keeping the pets. We also looked closely at the illustrations this time, as they showed clearly what Arnold's mom was talking about.

Day five: At this time I told the three children to each choose one animal from our long list that they would like as a pet. They chose a hippo, a bald eagle, and a worm. We then made a list, for each animal, of reasons a mom might give for not keeping these pets.

Day six: I read the story again and we made a list of all the reasons Arnold gave his mom for keeping the animals. We then made a list for each of *our* three animals. We also made a list of all the places these animals might be found, and each child got to choose one for his animal.

Day seven: I read the book again and discussed the pattern of mother's replies to Arnold. We looked back to the list we had made on day five (containing reasons for not keeping animals) and chose three of them for each of our animals. We then put these reasons into sentences, using the pattern of the mother's words. We also chose our main character, who turned out to be a boy named Fred.

Day eight: I read the book again and this time we discussed the pattern of Arnold's words. We then looked back at the list we had made on day six (containing reasons for keeping our animals) and chose three of those for each of our animals. We then put these reasons into sentences, using the pattern of Arnold's words and including where our animals had been found.

Day nine: On separate pages I wrote out each sentence we had developed. We read these together and the children illustrated two pages each.

Day ten: We talked about the ending of the story where Arnold tries one more time to bring home a pet. There is only a picture of this event, so each of the children drew a picture of what animal they thought Fred might bring home. We then made a cover for our book and each child drew a picture of one of our three animals on it.

Day eleven: I had made copies of the book and we read it together. The children then colored the pictures and took the books back to their other rooms to share. They were really thrilled that they could "write" a book, and I felt it was a very positive learning experience.

SOME GENERAL ADVICE ABOUT WRITING INSTRUCTION

Producing patterned books is only one type of valuable writing and reading experience for children. Even something as simple as scribbling pretend words (usually between the ages of three and five) is a readiness experience for reading. When children pretend to write, they are beginning to catch on to that vital connection between two communicating human beings, one of whom is writing, the other reading. The same is true when children ask you to write something *for* them—a letter to grandma, their own name for them to copy, a label for their favorite stuffed animal "so when she gets lost someone can tell her how to get home." And when they move from their own pretend words to their own invented spellings for words, they are coming even closer to being ready for the reading process. Graves (1979) says, teachers should be quite tolerant of children's invented spelling, because it is a natural and vital step toward mastering our difficult and complex spelling system.

There's something marvelously inspiring about watching children invent language of *any* kind, whether it be their own or their verson of an English sentence. Remember what I said in Chapter 6—that the oral production of a sentence is a very *creative*, inventive act, since there are so many different ways of saying the same thing. But when a child willingly, "wantingly" puts that sentence on paper, he is reaching for adulthood as he's never reached before. He is reaching out to adults to show him how to record his ideas, and is thus unconsciously moving toward the concept of what reading is all about—the sharing of our recorded ideas.

In a few moments, we'll look at ways to hasten children's natural drive to communicate and to record and share their ideas. In a school setting these processes usually fall under the label of "language experience approaches." But before we examine language experience approaches to the teaching of reading—all of which involve a considerable amount of writing—it would be wise to look at some of Graves's (1975) findings:

1. Children tend to respond better to choice than to assigned writing. When they can decide whether to write and what to write, they tend to write more often and at greater length.
2. In informal classroom environments, children do not seem to need motivation or supervision in order to write.
3. Large amounts of assigned writing inhibit the range, content, and amount of writing.

Graves's findings are definitely something to keep in mind when one embarks on language experiences that bring writing and reading together. In our enthusiasm to have children do more writing (to "get 'em to read better"), we have to remember that writing, like so many other human characteristics, is a slow development process that takes not only time but also plenty of enthusiasm within the writer.

LANGUAGE EXPERIENCE APPROACHES: IN A NUTSHELL

While most elementary-school teachers use one of the basal-reader approaches to teach reading, a growing number are using one of the language experience approaches either as a substitute or a supplement. Rather than rely upon basal readers as the medium of instruction, they rely as well (or instead) upon the language of their students. Children dictate or write their own reading selections and thereby learn in a practical way that reading is a form of communication and that authors and readers are truly communicators. Teachers use the selections created by their students as instructional material for readiness, decoding, and comprehension experiences. They keep track of children's progress through a skills-management system or some other form of careful observation.

STUDENTS WHO CAN LEARN FROM A LANGUAGE EXPERIENCE APPROACH

A variety of types and ages of students are being taught successfully through a language experience approach. Many kindergarten teachers use a language experience approach to get children ready for more formal instruction in first grade. Children in small or large groups dictate their ideas to the teacher, who immediately prints them, exactly as dictated, on the chalkboard or on tagboard charts. The teacher reads the ideas back to the children and then encourages them to "read" (say) the ideas with her, thus getting the kindergarten children used to the idea that printed words can represent spoken words. A left-to-right reading orientation is developed; letter names are taught or reviewed; visual and auditory discrimination are reinforced—all through the use of such "experience charts."

In first grade, such an approach is taken several steps further. Children not only *dictate* their thoughts, they begin to write them as well. In addition, they learn from dictation and writing to recognize numerous words by sight, as well as common suffixes and graphophonic patterns. As the year progresses, they read not only their own and their peers' written accounts, but the stories and descriptions of adult authors as well. Library books, and even basal readers normally used for instruction, become opportunities to apply the communication skills they have gained through creating and reading their own "stories" and "books."

In the second grade and later, language experience approaches are used to enrich children's understanding gained through more formal reading instruction, and through the social studies, science, and other areas of the school curriculum. The children create charts, stories, magazines, newspapers, and books as records of what they are learning, experiencing, and feeling. These materials then provide enrichment-reading experiences for the children.

Children who need remedial instruction, at any grade level, can be helped through a language experience approach. This is especially true of those youngsters in grades three through twelve who have been "turned off" by too many previous experiences with completing worksheets and drilling on subskills. For many remedial readers, a language experience approach can provide a first glimpse into the real meaning of reading. Tyrone, for example, was a leader of a small "gang" of third-grade boys who hated "readin' and goin' to school." Their teacher decided in desperation to try a language experience approach. Her husband came to school one morning and gave Tyrone's gang an exhilarating ride around the playground in his sports car. When they got back, the teacher took dictation while they excitedly took turns telling her about their adventure. When their story was finished, they read it with the teacher and then proudly to the entire class. For the first time, reading made sense!

Tyrone's teacher duplicated their story so they could take it home to read to their parents. She then formed a special reading group, appropriately called "Tyrone's Gang." This reading group created numerous experience stories, gained reading skill through the use of the stories, and gradually joined the world of book readers.

Children who do not speak Standard English can be taught at first through a language experience approach. In this way their own language is not denigrated, but used as the first building block toward learning to read. Since early reading is primarily a matter of translating print into speech, it is highly important that such print represent the way children normally speak. (This type of language experience approach is discussed in further detail in Chapter 13 and also in this chapter.)

RATIONALE AND RESEARCH RELATED TO LANGUAGE EXPERIENCE APPROACHES

By now you can probably write your own rationale for the use of a language experience approach. A language experience approach uses the child's present language. It does not rely on language created by adults. Thus, the translation of print back into speech (or subvocal thought) is usually natural and meaningful. Furthermore, children quickly learn the most important concepts about the reading process: (1) it involves communication with a person who wrote down his thoughts; and (2) it is not a subject in school, a torturous process of "sounding out" words, or an endless conveyer belt of worksheets and workbook pages. In addition, a language experience approach does not separate the language arts into separate skill areas of reading, writing, speaking, and listening. All four avenues of language are used in combination to take advantage of children's natural desire to communicate.

A vast majority of the research studies on language experience approaches have demonstrated that they are as effective as basal-reader approaches and may even have special advantages (Hall, 1978). Perhaps the greatest fear educators and parents have about the use of a language experience approach is that children will not gain as much in vocabulary as will children who are taught through other approaches. Hall summarizes the research on vocabulary this way:

> A persistent criticism of language experience instruction is that students may not develop a satisfactory reading vocabulary, since the lack of vocabulary control and the lack of systematic repetition may be detrimental to learning. The research refutes this criticism. Language experience instruction presents learners with meaningful vocabulary, and a reading vocabulary *is* acquired by learners through the use of LEA. (Hall, 1978, pp. 27–28)

Others have been afraid that a language experience approach would not expose children to the graphophonic regularities in our language (such as the change in meaning and pronunciation between *can* and *cane* and the consistency in pronunciation of phonograms such as *ill*, *at*, and *ap*). In a study by Dzama (1975), however, it was discovered that the words used by first graders in language experience programs provided ample examples for learning such regularities. Other studies (Bond & Dykstra, 1967; Dykstra, 1968) have shown that LEA students tend to learn graphophonic decoding skill about as well as those students in basal programs. Furthermore, studies (Chomsky, 1971) have shown, not surprisingly, that LEA students usually become better spellers than students taught by a basal approach.

A WORD OF CAUTION

If a language-experience approach works so well, why aren't the majority of elementary-school teachers using it to teach reading? Probably for three reasons:

> Most textbook authors and reading professors have advocated it in a serious way only in the past decade or two (Hoover, 1971). Perhaps it took the research report by Stauffer and Hammond (1967) to convince many of us of its effectiveness.

> Because of the fear some teachers and principals have of public criticism for not using a more "systematic" basal approach.

> Because it takes more skill and work to teach reading this way than it does with basal reader programs. With a language experience approach, the teacher must do much more of the daily planning. With a basal-reader approach, the teacher is given an assist by the Teacher's Guide.

Because it is such an important approach, however, an increasing number of teachers and principals are accepting it, at least as a supplementary procedure (Staton, 1974). We will discuss techniques of using a language experience approach in an auxiliary in a later section. Right now, let's look at some actual procedures for working with children in a full-fledged LEA program.

PROCEDURES FOR CREATING GROUP EXPERIENCE CHARTS

Group experience charts may be created with the entire class on some occasions, such as following a field trip to a farm or zoo. But to get every student involved, it is best to develop most experience charts in smaller groups of ten or fewer. When you do this, however, I would not put all your confident language users together in one group and your quiet ones in another group. Children with low self-confidence seem to need the company of their more confident peers as language models.

Experience charts are generally created and used in this order:

1. Developing interest about an experience or topic

2. Discussing the experience or topic

3. Dictating and writing the chart

4. Reading the chart

5. Using the chart to teach and learn reading processes

The length of time for each of these steps varies a great deal. The experience you write about may take five minutes, several hours, or no time at all, if it's one the children have had outside of the classroom. Normally, however, steps 2–4 are completed during one "sitting" of about 30 minutes.

Developing Interest

The LEA approach, like any other, can become dull and lifeless if the teacher does not concern herself enough with motivational principles. The experiences and topics selected by the teacher, and the procedures she uses in communicating about them, should provide novelty, meet basic needs, and fit the appropriate level of difficulty for the children. To be successful in using a language experience approach, it is extremely important for the teacher to plan stimulating *experiences* and topics for children to talk and write about. These are some sample experiences and topics:

The hamster in our classroom

What things are blue?

Our biggest wishes

What we like to do after school

The movie we saw about stars

The experiment we did about air

How it would feel to be a balloon

Halloween is coming!

What we think of ghosts

What teachers do

What parents do

Our favorite foods

Our trip to the supermarket

What makes us mad

How yesterday is different from tomorrow

Stone Soup

What we do on the playground

What it might be like to be deaf

Mike Mulligan and His Steam Shovel

A daydream we just had

This is just a tiny sample of the possibilities for experience stories. You may wish to examine the *Peabody Language Development Kits* by Dunn and Smith (1965, 1966, 1967) as well as Van Allen's *Language Experiences in Reading* (1974), and Hall's *Teaching Reading as a Language Experience (1981)*. All contain numerous ideas for language experience activities. You'll also find many more ideas in Appendix D.

Discussing the Experience or Topic

Some teachers get in a hurry when using an LEA and have children start dictating or writing too soon. In most cases it works much better to have a general discussion of the topic or experience before writing about it. Such a discussion usually gets the ideas flowing, as one thought stimulates another. Research on creativity (Torrance, 1962) shows that this type of verbal stimulation before compositions are expected can actually produce more creative and longer compositions than you would get by simply having the children write or dictate without discussion. Teachers often worry that a discussion will lead to everyone's saying or writing the same thing when it comes time to produce the actual composition. Some of this "copycat" behavior will occur, it's true, but this is far better than having several children not communicate at all. Remember, the purpose in developing experience charts is to teach the communication skills of speaking, listening, writing, and reading rather than to produce "original" compositions. As usual, process counts much more than product.

It would be difficult to emphasize this point too much: the oral language experiences that children engage in are just as important for the development of reading skills as the actual reading experiences. Oral language growth at any grade level is a major factor in producing greater growth in both reading and writing. In the case of experience charts (or personal stories), a good oral discussion usually leads to easy and natural dictation or writing, *followed by easy and natural reading of the composition.*

The two stages of developing interest and carrying on a discussion preceding story production are inseparable. The teacher can develop interest and start the discussion, for instance, by asking an open-ended question about a caged animal she has brought in:

TEACHER: What do you think this hamster feels about your looking at him?

JERRY: I think he's happy.

TEACHER: Why, Jerry?

JERRY: Because he has someone to play with.

TEACHER: [nodding appreciatively] He doesn't seem very frightened, does he?

MONA: He's got long whiskers.

TEACHER: Yes, they're quite long. How long would you say they are? Are they as long as this pencil?

FRANK: [laughing] They're not that long. They're as long as . . . as long as my little finger.

TEACHER: Yes, I think you're right, Frank. What else do you notice about this little hamster . . . Stephen?

STEPHEN: He's got sharp teeth.

TEACHER: How can you tell?

STEPHEN: Because . . . because they're pointed and because he can chew up those little round things real fast.

TEACHER: Yes, he can, can't he? Those little round things are sometimes called *pellets* and they're what he likes to eat. Do you know what they're made of?

STEPHEN: I don't know. Nuts maybe.

TEACHER: Well, in a way, you're right! They're made from the seeds of wheat and barley and other grains like that. Since nuts are a kind of seed, Stephen, you were almost right!

STEPHEN: [smiling] Yeah.

TEACHER: What do you think he'll do when we each hold him?

Dictating and Writing the Story

After the discussion (and experience) have continued awhile, the teacher begins the dictation period by moving to a tagboard chart and asking something like this: "Who would like to begin today? We need a sentence at the top that will remind us what we've been doing just now . . . Julie?"

JULIE: We've been lookin' at a funny little hamster.

TEACHER: All right, let's write that down. I'll start way at the top and way over on the left side. I'll start with a capital letter. [She writes: We've been looking at a funny little hamster.] That's what Julie said: "We've been looking at a funny little hamster." Who would like to have the next turn . . . Stephen?

STEPHEN: He has real sharp pointed teeth.

The dictation continues until everyone has had a turn or until the group feels that the "story" is complete. Here's an example of what a finished chart may look like:

A Funny Little Hamster

Julie says: We've been looking at a funny little hamster.
Stephen says: He has real sharp pointed teeth.
Frank says: He has whiskers as long as my little finger.
Mona says: He lives in a wire cage, and he keeps looking at us.
Marilyn says: The funny little hamster runs races with himself.
David says: The funny little hamster ain't got a friend to live with.
Francis says: But we can be his friends. We'll feed him and give him water and play with him.

When taking dictation the teacher usually avoids the temptation to edit the children's language. In other words, if a child says "ain't," the teacher writes "ain't." She does not attempt to control the vocabulary or sentence structure or grammar in any way. The only modification she would make is in spelling; when a child mispronounces a word, she doesn't spell it according to the mispronunciation. The teacher spells it correctly and lets him read it any way he wishes later.

One reason the teacher avoids editing grammar, vocabulary, and sentence structure, of course, is to make sure the child perceives reading as a true communication process, rather than a process of pleasing adults. Teachers who edit more than spelling will find that children are less willing to volunteer their ideas. Since the teacher's use of standard spelling does not seem to inhibit children's communication, it is probably wise to avoid nonstandard spelling. Some children will take offense if they discover you've been misspelling words to allow for their peculiar way of pronouncing them.

Another reason the teacher avoids editing grammar, vocabulary, and sentence structure is that children tend to read their sentence as they have dictated it, rather than as the teacher has edited it. Thus, the important link between print and speech has been broken, causing children to have more difficulty developing a sight vocabulary and a feeling for the importance of reading for comprehension. We will talk more later about working with children who speak in a nonstandard dialect.

Reading the Chart

The chart that children create is read many, many times, both by the teacher and by the students—but each time in a slightly different way. Some teachers read the chart as they write it, word by word. Some wait until an entire sentence has been written and then read it back to the children. Some do both and then read the entire thing to the children after it has been completed. In any case, a successful teacher reads the "story" to the children before asking them to read it with her or to read it by themselves.

After reading the chart to the children, the teacher then asks the children to read it with her. Next she calls on children to read one or more sentences by themselves, helping them as soon as they run into trouble. The important thing is that the reading experience is an enjoyable, successful one. (One way of assuring this success is to have each child read by herself only the sentence she dictated. Later, after the story has become more familiar, each is asked to try other sentences.)

Using the Chart to Teach and Learn Reading Skills

The day following the creation of a chart, the children are usually shown the tagboard version of the "story" and presented with a dittoed personal copy as well. The teacher has also prepared a word card for each word in the story. These materials, along with others, are used for the purpose of developing vocabulary, decoding skill, comprehension skill, or possibly readiness. Each of these will be discussed separately in later sections.

PROCEDURES FOR CREATING PERSONAL EXPERIENCE STORIES

After children have become familiar with the process of developing group-experience charts, they are usually given opportunities to develop their own personal stories. At first these stories are dictated to the teacher or another person (hired teaching aide, parent, volunteer aide, teacher trainee, child from another room). Gradually, as children develop writing skills, the stories are written entirely by the children themselves.

Motivation for developing such personal stories arises from many sources. Often a small-group or total-class experience story can lead to additional stories created by each child in the classroom. Following the group-experience story on the hamster, for example, the teacher could have inspired children in small groups each to write a brief, separate story—one each about what the hamster eats, how it plays, how it sleeps, what its mouth and nose are like, what its eyes and ears are like, and so on. Or she might have inspired each child to write a brief adventure of "the funny little hamster."

Other possible motivations for writing personal stories might include these:

A picture the child has drawn or painted while working in the "art corner"

A class discussion on a peculiar object the teacher has brought to school

A follow-up on having a turn during a show-and-tell period

A special trip taken over a weekend or holiday

An illustration the child has made of a group-experience story

A show seen on television

A response to seeing a photograph of himself

A picture book read either by the teacher or by the child

A "big plan" for making something

A chance to contribute a page to a group-produced book

Essentially the same procedures used for developing group experience stories are used for personal stories. Interest is developed in creating the story; the topic is discussed with the teacher or another person; the story is dictated or written; the child experiences himself and other people reading his story; the teacher uses the story to provide practice in interactive reading and lessons on vocabulary and graphophonic patterns.

TEACHING VOCABULARY

Vocabulary development is a very personal process. The words that relate to a child's own experience, particularly when those experiences have been highlighted by either positive or negative emotions, are those that are learned and retained most easily (Olson & Pau, 1966; Veatch et al., 1979). Sylvia Ashton-Warner (1963), in her successful attempt to teach Maori children of New Zealand, found that one child who had great difficulty learning words such as *come* and *look*, could quite easily learn words like *kill*, *knife*, and *gaol (jail)*.

Because of the personal nature of vocabulary building, teachers who use a language experience approach usually try to personalize the acquisition of vocabulary. To do this, the teacher asks each child to develop a personal "word bank." A word bank usually takes the form of small cards kept by the child in a small box or on a ring. A word is written for the child on a card whenever she demonstrates that she can read it. After the teacher passes out a dittoed copy of a group experience chart, for instance, children are asked to underline the words they know. If Barbara successfully reads her underlined words to the teacher, the teacher makes out a card for each word and gives them to her for her word bank. The same procedure of underlining and presenting word cards is also used for personal experience stories. Other words children learn, such as personal "key words" or those gained from noticing the labels the teacher has taped up in the room, can also be added to their individual word banks.

The individual word banks have several major functions:

To serve as a *record* of the reading vocabulary of individual children (helpful to child, teacher, and parents)

To serve as references for creative writing and spelling

To provide reinforcement through repeated exposure to words

To serve as stimulus words for examples during skill instruction

To provide independent activities with word games, matching activities, and sentence building

To provide examples for group language study (Hall, 1981, p. 61)

The children keep the word banks at their desks to practice with each other, to match with the words in their dittoed stories, and to play games suggested by the teacher. They bring them to the small-group meetings to use as their own suggested examples of a graphophonic pattern (such as words with a VC spelling pattern) and to help the group create "group word banks."

Group word banks are created by both the small groups and the entire class. This type of word bank is designed to help children become more aware of word categories and sentence patterns. Examples of group word banks are Color Words, Action Words, Sound Words, Names of Animals, Homophones, and Feeling Words. This type of "bank" is often printed on large tagboard charts so the children can refer to them when they are producing stories. Sometimes the words are also printed on cards and placed in boxes so the children can use them for independent activities suggested by the teacher.

The words in the group word banks are accumulated gradually throughout the year. One way to begin them is to ask children in a small group to look through their personal word banks and find all the color words (or action words or whatever category the teacher wishes to emphasize). After the group word banks are printed on tagboard, they become a quick reference for various activities such as producing group stories or creating sentences. In creating sentences, a child can select, for example, an animal word and an action word (Dogs dig . . .). The rest of the group then tries to alter and expand this basic sentence (The frisky young dogs dug deep holes all over the garden).

TEACHING DECODING AND COMPREHENSION SKILLS

In addition to teaching vocabulary through children's writing and word banks, the teacher can also use these materials for teaching the usual lessons on phonics, context clues, suffixes, and comprehension. Whenever the teacher feels these materials are not providing enough practice, she can use the teacher's guide to the basal readers the children would normally read at the particular grade level. In the teacher's guide, she'll find numerous ideas for skill lessons to supplement those based on children's group charts and personal stories.

When using a group chart, for example, a natural phonics lesson occurs whenever the teacher has the children notice how letters represent sounds and how spelling patterns determine sounds. For instance, the teacher may indicate three words in a story that all start with the letter *p*, then pronounce the three words with the children, and next ask the children what sound they hear at the beginning of each word. He may also find two words with the same final phonogram, such as *night* and *fight*. This could lead to a short lesson on the *ight* phonogram. He may point out the difference between the words *hat* and *hate* in a story, and how the VC pattern and VCE pattern predict different sounds. Having introduced a particular graphophonic concept through a story, the teacher would later review this concept, either by using later stories or by follow-up skill lessons.

Derivatives are taught by having children notice compounds, contractions, roots, suffixes, and prefixes in their stories and word banks. Contrasts are made, for instance, between such words as *happy* and *unhappy*, *happy* and *happiness*, *fast* and *faster*. Context analysis is taught by blocking out words in a story and asking children to predict the word or words that would fit in the blank. This activity is usually followed by a brief discussion of the clues that enabled them to make such good predictions.

A language experience approach provides a firm foundation for developing comprehension skill because of its total emphasis on meaning and communication. After a story has been completed, however, the teacher can have the children think of a title that "really shows what your story is about," thus engaging them in thinking of main ideas. She can ask them about specific details ("Who can show us what Frank said about how long the hamster's whiskers are?"). She can have them alter and expand some of the sentences in the story. She can have them read with the proper intonation. (See Appendix L for other comprehension activities.)

DEVELOPING READINESS

A language experience approach provides numerous opportunities for getting children ready for the world of print. By emphasizing meaning and communication from the very beginning, it prepares children for reading in the true sense of the word. By emphasizing oral language skills, it prepares children for natural and meaningful translation from print into speech. And by placing an emphasis on communication, it also avoids such readiness blocks as the concept of reading as "sounding out words" or reading for words rather than ideas.

Specific readiness cues can be taught in the same way that decoding cues can be taught. The experience stories provide the examples; the teacher helps the children notice the appropriate cues. Children can be asked, for example, to match word cards to words in the story, thereby emphasizing visual discrimination. "Letter cards" can be used in the same way. Visual memory, to take another example, can be developed by holding up a word card, then covering up the card and asking a child to find the word in the story. Finer discrimination can be taught by using a group word bank of children's names. Names that look alike, such as *Timmy* and *Tammy*, can be compared. While teaching visual discrimination and memory, the teacher can also help them learn (or review) the names of letters. Auditory discrimination and memory can be reinforced by having children think of words that "start in the same way" or words that rhyme. The left-to-right orientation is taught through the natural development and "reading" of an experience story.

THE VARIETY OF LANGUAGE EXPERIENCE APPROACHES

The language experience concept is flexible and creative, and does not require some kind of lockstep procedure day after day. One of the most heartening things I've witnessed in my observations of both British and American schools has been the variety of methods teachers have invented to apply the language experiences idea to their own classrooms.

Wright and Laminack (1982) describe an innovative practice in which a first-grade teacher used a language experience approach to teach his students about television commercials. The children learned a great many "commercial words" such as "fresh" and "product" and other favorites of advertisers and wrote many language experience "stories" to describe how they tested the advertiser's claims.

Exhibit A

We listened to a cat food commercial. They say that it is sealed in a pouch . . . On TV when the man opens the pouch a voice says, "Fresh!"

Cammie tried this at home. Her cat food did not say, "Fresh!"

Exhibit B

We put water into two small cups. Next, we put a Mounty paper towel in one cup and a plain paper towel in the other cup . . . We could lift a cup with a wet Mounty. The plain paper towel fell apart.

Exhibit C

Z-soap will make you feel awake. Meredith tried Z-soap. She said that she did not feel any better. We did not see her jump up and down.

Mallon and Berglund describe a language experience approach that differs from the sequence I offered:

Day 1: A stimulus is introduced followed by discussion. The stimuli might include toys, books, trips, pictures, special events, or a retelling of a story. After discussion a list of children's suggestions for stories are put on a chart.

Day 2: Yesterday's discussion is reviewed. Each child draws a picture of his idea and begins writing or dictating, depending on his skill.

Day 3: Each child reads her story to the teacher independently. Known words are underlined by the teacher. Other students are either finishing their stories and illustrations, reading their stories to each other, working in a center, or completing other work.

Day 4: Children read their stories to the teacher again—independently. The teacher underlines words again, including those already underlined, that the child knows. Some words now have two lines under them.

Day 5: This is skill development day. Children make cards for words that have been underlined twice. These cards are then used for lessons on graphophonic clues, vocabulary, and other decoding and comprehension skills.

If you'd like to see how one teacher taught reading through LEA for the first time, read the article by Allen and Laminack (1982) in the March 1982 *Reading Teacher.* This article excerpts Mr. Laminack's journal in which he describes his stumbling but very successful first year with an LEA program. If you're interested in trying the language experience approach, I think you'll find this seven-page article quite inspiring.

Lancaster (1982) got her second graders to write three times a week by following Chomsky's advice (1971) to let children spell the words the way they thought they should be spelled rather than the way the teacher told them to spell. The only help the teacher gave the children was to occasionally ask them what letter they thought came first, what letter they thought came next, and so on. Most of the time, however, the teacher simply refused to do anything but encourage them to try it themselves. Gradually the calls for help diminished and most of the children's energy was put into getting down their thoughts. The longest stories they wrote were their retellings of favorite folktales the teacher had read to them.

As the program evolved, four principles or procedures seemed to emerge:

Writing three times a week was just about right.

A teacher-led discussion before the children wrote was very important.

Having the teacher circulate around the room to encourage and help children with their thoughts was essential.

The children's writing needed to be shared in some way—especially by reading it aloud to the class after lunch and *by having the stories typed and made into a book.*

Virginia Morrison, a teacher in Saline, Michigan, has put her micro-computer to good use in a language experience program. Rather than write her children's stories on a chart or chalkboard, she uses word processing software to take dictation. The child or children whose story is being dictated can watch their story unfold on the video screen. Their story can be stored on the disk for future use and printed up whenever needed. Children

can edit their own stories as they dictate them by asking the teacher to make the appropriate changes, or the stories can be edited at a later date after a discussion of ways to make the story even better. "Together the teacher and student or group of students can move words around on the video screen to improve the quality of the expression" (Morrison, 1983, p. 448). The children's word banks can also be stored on disk and printed out whenever needed.

In contrast to Morrison's informal approach to the use of word processors is the formalized program Martin (1984) developed, the "Writing to Read System." This program is a highly systematized preplanned set of computer-directed activities designed to teach young children a phonetic alphabet and how to create words and sentences with that alphabet. Each computer lesson teaches three words and the phonemes that make up those words. It then evaluates the child's understanding with a mastery test and concludes with a "Make Words" section that encourages the child to recombine the phonemes to create new words. While this program seems to be an effective teaching device that you may want to look into, it lacks the spontaneity possible with one of the informal language experience approaches.

Gillet and Gentry (1983) have developed a controversial method of using an LEA to teach reading to children who speak a nonstandard dialect. First they have the children read their stories exactly as dictated until they can read them fluently in their own dialect, enabling them to make that necessary connection between speech and print, as well as helping them develop the concept of reading as communication. Then the teacher rewrites the story (out of the children's view) and presents it as "another story about the funny fruit." After the children have learned to read the second story, the teacher now brings out the original story and helps each child to make his contribution longer and to "think of another way to say it." Finally the children learn to read the third story. Here's an example of an original story (about two kiwi fruit) and the two transformed stories.

Original Dictated Story

Mandy said, "They was in a bag—a lunch bag."

Kareem said, "They was some kind of fruits."

Tonya said, "Teacher say feel it."

Jerome said, "They was real squishy."

Teacher's Story

> Mandy, Kareem, Tonya, and Jerome learned about some funny fruit. First we looked at a lunch bag. Second, we each felt the funny fruit. Then, we talked about the fruit. We tried to guess what the fruit was. Last, we wrote a story about the funny, squishy fruit.

Children's New Story

> Mandy said, "First we looked at the lunch bag."
>
> Kareem said, "There were some fruits in the bag."
>
> Tonya said, "Our teacher said to put in your hand and feel around but don't tell what it is."
>
> Jerome said, "The fruit felt squishy and sort of round."

What do you think of Gillet's and Gentry's method? Can you see some advantages? Disadvantages?

KEEPING TRACK OF CHILDREN'S PROGRESS

Evaluation of children's progress in learning to read can be accomplished in somewhat the same way used with a basal approach. A skills-management system can be used, such as the "Wisconsin Design" (Otto & Askov, 1973), the "Prescriptive Reading Inventory" (1972), or one from a basal series. Appropriate assessment and retention tests are administered throughout the year and records are kept on each child. For teachers who wish to use a more informal approach, a skills-management checklist is kept on each child, and a checklist is completed on the basis of both tests and classroom observations. Tests are used only for those skills on which teachers observe children having trouble. Following the tests or observations, the children are provided with remedial learning experiences. (These procedures are explained in more detail in Chapter 9).

COMBINING LANGUAGE EXPERIENCES WITH OTHER APPROACHES

Many teachers use a language experience approach as a supplement to their regular reading program. Some first grade teachers, for instance, use language experience approaches during the first semester and then switch the children gradually into a basal program. At the end of the first semester, children are administered informal reading inventories and other placement tests provided by the basal-series publisher. Because of most children's progress, though, very few will have to start at the earliest level of the basal program.

Other first-grade teachers use a language experience approach right along with a basal reader program from the very first. The two programs can be quite compatible if the teacher uses the basal program primarily for skill development and the language experience approach primarily for developing the concept of reading as communication.

Many teachers rely upon language experience stories to augment the stories provided by basal readers. Word banks are derived from both basal and experience stories. In this way, the teacher can combine both the element of structure provided by a basal approach and the elements of communication, writing, and creativity provided by a language experience approach.

Teachers of the upper grades often use experience stories as a method of personalizing what children learn through the social studies, science, and other areas. In one class, for example, Mr. Walters encouraged his fifth graders to develop personal and group-written books on their imagined life in the Middle Ages. In another, Mrs. Fredekind had one group of fourth graders make an experience chart listing the steps for a science experiment they had "invented." The rest of the class used this chart to "replicate the study."

HANDLING THE LIMITATIONS RELATED TO LANGUAGE EXPERIENCE APPROACHES

Perhaps the greatest limitation to a language experience approach is not inherent in the approach itself but in the transition to another approach. Some children who have started out learning to read "à la-LEA" become frustrated after moving into a basal program. Their frustration is quite understandable and usually occurs when the teacher using a basal program does not provide ample time for writing creatively and expressing oneself in group discussions. (It's a little like giving an adult a job, respecting her ideas and opinions for a year, giving her many choices for her own way of handling things, and then suddenly presenting her with a very autocratic boss who wants things done exactly his way.) As I've implied, this limitation is not as strong when the teacher using a more structured approach provides numerous opportunities for the children to express themselves in discussions and through writing.

A second major limitation is the resistance parents sometimes offer. Some parents become confused by a language experience approach and get the idea that children are "not really learning how to read—they're just memorizing little stories that they're making up. Why, my Johnny can't even sound out words yet." Such criticism is bound to be discouraging to teachers. Most teachers, though, avoid criticism by carefully explaining their instructional approach at the beginning of the school year—either in a letter to the parents or in a general meeting with them. This is followed up with newsletters that explain the language experience approaches in more detail. Children are also asked to take home certain experience stories to read to their parents. The first stories selected for this honor are usually those that contain mostly words the child already has in his personal word bank. Furthermore, they are stories that do not contain nonstandard grammar. As the year progresses, however, and the parents seem to understand the program more thoroughly, the stories are selected with less scrutiny. Conferences are usually scheduled with parents of each child so that the teacher can show them the stories their child can now read, the word bank he has developed, the assessment and retention test results, and the checklist of mastered skills.

THE MAIN IDEAS IN THIS CHAPTER

Skill in reading and writing should probably be developed at the same time, with writing experiences often coming immediately before reading experiences.

Having children learn to write their own patterned book is an excellent way to teach reading.

Language experience approaches use a child's own language to teach him how to read. Group experience charts and personal experience stories, along with individual and group word banks, provide the major instruction media.

The usual order for developing charts and stories is to:

1. Develop interest in a topic

2. Have a thorough discussion of the topic

3. Provide time for dictating or writing about the topic

4. Read the story created

5. Use the story to teach decoding and comprehension skills

There are a great variety of language experience approaches, all of which involve the four language arts: listening, speaking, writing, and reading.

A skills checklist or skills management system is often used alongside a language experience approach.

Many teachers combine language experience approaches with a basal reader program.

REFERENCES AND SUGGESTED READING

Allen, E. G., & Laminack, L. L. (1982). Language experience reading—It's a natural! *Reading Teacher, 35*, 708–714.

Ashton-Warner, S. (1963). *Teacher.* New York: Simon and Schuster.

Bond, G. L., & Dykstra, R. (1967). The cooperative program in first grade reading instruction. *Reading Research Quarterly, 2*, 5–142.

Chomsky, C. (1971). Write first, read later. *Childhood Education, 47*, 396–399.

Cramer, R. L. (1970). An investigation of first-grade spelling achievement. *Elementary English, 47*, 230–237.

Dionisio, M. (1983). Write? Isn't this reading class? *Reading Teacher, 36*, 746–750.

Dunn, L. M., & Smith, J. O. (1965, 1966, 1967). Peabody language development kits, Levels I, II, III. Circle Pines, MN: American Guidance Service.

Durkin, D. (1966). *Children who read early: Two longitudinal studies.* New York: Teachers College Press.

Dykstra, R. (1968). Summary of the second-grade phase of the cooperative research program in primary reading instruction. *Reading Research Quarterly, 4*, 49–70.

Dzama, M. A. (1975). Comparing use of generalizations of phonics in LEA, basal vocabulary. *Reading Teacher, 28*, 466–472.

Evans, R. V. (1979). The relationship between the reading and writing of syntactic structures. *Research in the teaching of English, 13*, 129–135.

Evanechko, P., Ollila, L., & Armstrong, R. (1974). An investigation of the relationship between children's performance in written language and their reading ability. *Research in the Teaching of English, 8*, 315–325.

Gillet, J. W., & Gentry, J. R. (1983). Bridges between nonstandard and standard English with extensions of dictated stories. *Reading Teacher, 36*, 346–360.

Graves, D. H. (1975). An examination of the writing processes of seven-year-old children. *Research in the Teaching of English, 9,* 227–241.

Graves, D. (1978). *Balance the basics: Let them write.* New York: Ford Foundation Report.

Graves, D. H. (1979). Research update: What children show us about revision. *Language Arts, 56,* 312–319.

Graves, D. (1980). Research update. A new look at writing. *Language Arts, 57,* 913–918.

Graves, D. H., & Murray, D. H. (1980). Revision in the writer's workshop and in the classroom. *Journal of Education, 162,* 38–56.

Hall, M. A. (1981). *Teaching reading as a language experience.* Columbus, OH: Charles E. Merrill.

Hall, M. A. (1978). *The language experience approach for teaching reading, a research perspective.* Newark, DE: International Reading Association.

Henderson, E. H., et al. (1972). An exploratory study of word acquisition among first-graders at midyear in a language experience approach. *Journal of Reading Behavior, 4,* 21–31.

Hoover, I. (1971). *Historical and Theoretical Development of a language experience approach to teaching reading in selected teacher education institutions.* Unpublished doctoral dissertation, University of Arizona.

Lancaster, W., Nelson, L., & Morris, D. (1982). Invented spellings in Room 112: A writing program for low-reading second graders. *Reading Teacher, 35,* 906–911.

Lazdowski, W. F. (1976). *Determining reading grade levels from analysis of written composition.* Unpublished doctoral dissertation, New Mexico State University.

Loban, W. (1976). *Language development, kindergarten through grade twelve.* Urbana, IL: National Council of Teachers of English.

Mallon, B., & Berglund, R. (1984). The language experience approach to reading: Recurring questions and their answers. *Reading Teacher, 37,* 867–873.

Martin, J. H. (1984). Writing to read—Challenging an age-old tradition. *Electronic Education, 3,* (Feb.), 21–22.

Morrison, V. B. (1983). Language experience reading with the microcomputer. *Reading Teacher, 36,* 448–449.

Olson, D. R., & Pau, A. S. (1966). Emotionally loaded words and the acquisitions of a sight vocabulary. *Journal of Educational Psychology, 57,* 174–178.

Otto, W., & Askov, E. (1973). *Rationale and Guidelines.* The Wisconsin Design for Reading Skill Development, National Computer Systems.

Prescriptive reading inventory. (1972). New York: CTB/McGraw-Hill, 1972.

Staton, J. (1974). *Initial reading practices in open education environments in the midprairie states.* Unpublished doctoral dissertation, Oklahoma State University.

Stauffer, R. G., & Hammond, W. D. (1967). The effectiveness of language arts and basal reader approaches to first grade reading instruction. *The Reading Teacher, 20,* 740–746.

Stauffer, R. G. (1980). *The language experience approach to the teaching of reading.* New York: Harper & Row.

Torrance, E. P. (1962). Creative thinking of children. *Journal of Teacher Education, 13,* 448–460.

Van Allen, R. (1974). *Language experiences in reading.* Chicago, IL: Encyclopedia Britannica Press.

Veatch, J., et al. (1979). *Key words to reading.* Columbus, OH: Charles E. Merrill.

Wright, J. P., & Laminachk, L. (1982). First graders can be critical listeners and readers. *Language Arts, 59,* 133–137.

APPLICATION EXPERIENCES FOR THE TEACHER EDUCATION CLASSROOM

A. *What's Your Opinion?* Use your own experiences as well as the textbook to help you defend your opinion:

1. Writing experiences can help children realize that reading is a communication process.

2. Writing involves the same cueing systems as reading does.

3. Mrs. Friedman, the teacher described on page 219, was teaching poetry. She wasn't really teaching reading or writing.

4. Learning to write and read are essentially oral language experiences.

5. Teaching reading with a basal reader program designed by experts would be more effective than teaching reading through language experience approaches.

6. Having each child write or dictate his own stories makes more sense than having a small group dictate or write one together.

7. The LEA method of Gillet and Gentry is the best way to work with children who speak nonstandard English.

B. *Miscue Analysis:* Holly is in fourth grade. In what ways do you think her natural language differs from the author's? Rewrite the paragraph the way you think she might have written it in her own language. What does this tell you about the process of teaching reading?

Next Saturday the whole family (drove to *down* the forest. They found the (ranger *a large* station and bought a permit. (It cost a *It's close to* dollar. The ranger had (marked *a* off a place for people *where the* to cut trees. *could*

C. *Teaching Skills with a Language Experience Story:* With a partner or a small group examine the experience story called "A Funny Little Hamster" on page 235. Make a list of specific things you may be able to teach through the use of this story. For example, could you teach a lesson on contractions? Which ones? Compare your list with lists made by others in the class.

D. *Use a Group Experience Chart:* Divide up the class into several groups and assign a topic to each group for the development of a group-experience chart. Each group should appoint one person as their teacher-recorder. Go through the five stages of development suggested on pages 231–236. Then share your stories with other groups. Here are some topics you may want to use:

Here's how you make muddy gravel soup

Here's why applesauce can be dangerous to your health

Here's how to scratch your back, eat chocolate pudding, and read a textbook assignment at the same time

The monster who ate important belongings of college students

What students know about teachers

What teachers know about students

FIELD EXPERIENCES IN THE ELEMENTARY SCHOOL CLASSROOM

A. Help a few children develop a group experience story. (What highly interesting, but brief, experience can you help them have first?)

B. Help a small group of children bind a book that they have created. Simple means of binding books are described in the books by Van Allen, Hall, and Dunn and Smith, and also in the free booklet called *Cover to Cover* published by the Encyclopaedia Britannica Press, 425 North Michigan Avenue, Chicago, IL 60611. Most libraries also have other books on this subject.

C. Come up with a writing experience of your own that you can turn into a reading experience for one or more children.

8 PRACTICING REAL READING: WITH REAL BOOKS

CHAPTER PREVIEW

> The medium is the message.
>
> —*Marshall McLuhan*

I think McLuhan was right. The medium *is* the message. When we use the medium of

instruction discussed in Chapter 7 (children's own language), what message do we present to children? That their own language is important. That what they have to say is worth writing and reading. But suppose we were to use children's choices of library books as a major medium of instruction? What message would we be sending to children? That searching for books to read is fun. That their decisions do matter. That reading *books,* not workbooks, is what it's all about.

This chapter is about the use of real books as a medium—and as a message. We'll talk about the differences in children's abilities and interests and how difficult it would be to find teaching materials that fit each child if it weren't for children's literature (the books publishers call trade books and librarians call library books). We'll discuss the various things teachers can do to encourage children to practice real reading with real books. Then we'll zero in on a particular type of "individualized reading" that relies exclusively on library books for reading instruction. What we're leading to, by the time we finish Chapter 11, is that there are four major media for reading instruction—children's own language, library books, textbooks, and basal readers. Why not use them all!

On Planet Earth children are kept so busy learning how to read, they seldom have time to read.

THE REALITY OF INDIVIDUAL DIFFERENCES

There was a time in educational writing when the term "individual differences" could be found in just about every paragraph. The term implies something teachers have always known—even back in the cave clan days of teaching children to catch fish with their bare hands and scare woolly haired bears with fire. People learn at different speeds and in different ways. How easy that is to say! And yet how very difficult to do anything about it. Basal-reading programs, for example, allow for different *speeds* of learning, but none of them allows adequately for different *ways* of learning. Most teachers become adept at pacing the learning differently for different individuals, but few become adept at the far more difficult process of varying the learning style.

The problem of individual differences can be quite severe when it comes to reading instruction. We know, for instance, that teachers working in self-contained classrooms usually have students whose general reading abilities vary by several grade levels. A fifth-grade teacher may have to work with children whose reading-achievement grade-level scores range from 2.0 to 8.0. At the same time, each child's specific reading abilities may also vary by several grade levels. Let's compare Sally's scores with Virginia's scores as an example. Sally and Virginia both had a general-ability total score of 5.0. But here's how they scored on the specific subtests:

	Sally	*Virginia*
Vocabulary (isolated)	4.7	3.4
Vocabulary (in context)	5.1	5.1
Paragraph understanding (literal)	5.2	4.5
Paragraph understanding (interpretive)	2.7	5.9
Phonics knowledge	6.3	4.5
Phonics application	5.8	2.6
Morphemic analysis	3.5	7.8
Total score	5.0	5.0

In spite of such differences between Sally and Virginia, however, they would most likely be placed in the same reading group and assigned the same basal reader. To make matters worse, Sally is crazy about animal stories—horse stories and dog stories in particular—and almost any stories dealing with the great outdoors. Virginia, on the other hand, does not care for this kind of story at all. Virginia likes stories of teenage romance, as well as realistic stories about racial strife and other social phenomena.

CHILDREN'S LITERATURE TO THE RESCUE

What can a teacher of reading do about such differences? One possibility is to ignore the differences and assume that "what's good for one is good for all." But, of course, this approach only leads to frustration. Another possibility is to individualize your skill instruction, which we'll talk about later. A third possibility is to put more planning time and energy into your "children's literature program." For some teachers, this may mean teaching reading through library books. For others, it may mean decreasing the amount of time on basal readers and workbooks and increasing the amount of time spent with what children often refer to as "real books."

High quality "trade books" (library books) have much to offer children and their teachers: (1) Opportunities for personal growth; (2) Motivated practice of interactive reading; (3) Enrichment of the social studies, science, and other areas of the curriculum; (4) Models and inspiration for creative writing and (5) Esthetic experiences.

Let's look briefly at each of these potential virtues.

Opportunities for Personal Growth

Psychologists tell us that one of the chief ways in which people develop values, ambitions, and a self-concept is through emotional identification with another person—by imagining ourselves to be that person or by becoming like that person. Trade books, particularly biographies and fiction, offer infinite opportunities for such identification. A single book, of course, is not likely to provide as powerful a model as, say, a likable teacher or an admired parent. Yet thinking about your own experience with books would probably cause you to remember the times that books made a difference in how you felt—about yourself, about human behavior, about animals, or about beliefs you once held. Even if a book doesn't cause any permanent change in behavior, it can at least reinforce one's developing values or make one question these values.

Motivated Practice of Interactive Reading

From either a subskill or interactive point of view, trade books also provide motivated practice of those comprehension and decoding skills the teacher wants her students to acquire. The practice is "motivated" by the fact that children are reading books of their own choice, and, if the books are the right choice, they are giving them pleasure. Today, even first graders can find series they will enjoy enough to motivate reading practice.

One of these series is the *Beginning Books* series, including the first one in the series entitled *The Cat in the Hat* by Dr. Seuss. And for the true neophyte, there's the series called the *Beginning Beginner Books*. One of the books in this series—*Bears on Wheels* by Stan and Jan Berenstain—has only fourteen different words, and surprisingly enough, is usually fun for both children and adults to read. Another series is the *I Can Read* books, including *Frog and Toad Are Friends* and *Frog and Toad Together*—the first of which was a 1971 Caldecott Honor Book and the second of which was a 1973 Newbery Honor Book. There is also an *Early I Can Read* series, including the book on a favorite children's topic: *Dinosaur Time*. In addition, there are the *Giant First Start Readers*, including *Double Trouble* (34 different words), *Yummy Yummy* (37 different words), and *The Tooth Fairy* (49 different words). For an excellent list of nonseries books, see Roser and Friths' *Children's Choices* (1983), International Reading Association, 800 Barksdale Road, Newark, DE 19711.

Enrichment of Other Curriculum Areas

Without using trade books (children's literature), it would be nearly impossible to achieve some of the objectives of the newer social studies and science programs. In the social studies area, for example, the teacher is usually trying to help children identify with the problems, values, and life styles of different people. Simply reading about these people in a textbook will not accomplish this aim. Social studies textbooks, because of their wide coverage, tend to be somewhat shallow and explanatory. It is difficult for children to identify with the people talked about in the textbook, and it is also difficult for them to find enough meaningful associations and examples. They need more learning in depth and more emotion. Films and other audiovisual media help a great deal, but trade books—fictional, informational, biographical—offer vital opportunities for emotional involvement and intensive study.

Models and Inspiration for Creative Writing

As a model and inspiration for children's own creative writing, it is hard to beat children's literature. I've always had such interesting, highly motivated writing occur in the classroom following the conclusion of books I've read aloud. Numerous teachers have had the same experience. If the teacher has helped the children become aware of an author's use of words, the characters' personalities, and the subtleties of the plot, many children will be bursting with ideas for extending the story, changing its ending, or even writing a sequel. Similar enthusiasm—although not always as strong—often follows the conclusion of a book they have read by themselves. Whether this same enthusiasm for expressing themselves in an interesting way carries over into speech is difficult to measure. My own experience tells me that a "touch of grandeur" lingers, for a while at least, as children try out new phrases, new words, and new ways of arranging them. (This same phenomenon often occurs with adults after they've watched a Shakespearean drama or listened to poetry read aloud.)

Aesthetic Experiences

This leads us to another virtue of high-quality trade books—the aesthetic experience provided by the book itself. Some of the best writing and graphic art today is found between the covers of a children's book. (And probably some of the worst as well, I admit.) Marguerite Henry's *King of the Wind*, to take just one example, is rich in beautiful prose, sensitive characterization, and subtlety of plot development. To read a book such as this is to achieve that intangible something called an *aesthetic experience*. One feels better for the experience, and perhaps that is enough justification for reading any book. Then, too, there is the aesthetic experience provided by the superb illustrations in many picture books and other children's books today. Offset printing has made it possible for artists to use freely and creatively any graphic media they wish. A look at some of the books illustrated by Ezra Jack Keats, Symeon Shimin, Leo Lionni, and Marcia Brown offers the opportunity to test this assertion.

The Newbery and Caldecott Medals

Two coveted awards have been associated with, and perhaps partly responsible for, the aesthetic quality of children's books. One is the John Newbery Medal, presented each year to "the author of the most distinguished contribution to American literature for children." The book whose author will receive the award is selected by a committee of the Children's Services Division of the American Library Association. This committee selects the book it considers to be the best one published the previous year, and also a number of Honor Books for that year. A list of the winners since 1922 may be found in Appendix J. It should be emphasized that not all of the award-winning books are enjoyed by children, and some of them are better read aloud by the teacher because of their difficulty.

The other highly coveted award is the Caldecott Medal, presented each year to "the artist of the most distinguished American picture book for children." The winning book and illustrator, along with several Honor Books are selected by the same committee that selects the winner for the Newbery award. A list of the winners since 1938 may be found in Appendix J.

To limit one's selection of books to the winners and runners-up for the Caldecott or Newbery awards, however, is to make the error of attributing godlike power to the committee of human beings who make such awesome decisions each year. On the other hand, it is probably wise to read several of them to sharpen one's own awareness of the qualities that make certain books seem great and others mediocre.

TYPES OF TRADE BOOKS AVAILABLE

In many libraries, "juvenile" circulation accounts for at least one-half the total circulation. This is a distinct rise from 1939, when juvenile circulation accounted for only one-third the total (Huck, 1976). Part of this increase probably comes as the result of the vast growth in the publication of juveniles—from 852 new titles in 1940 to over 3000 in recent years. Along with this quantitative growth has come an increase in the variety of children's books available. The ever-popular mysteries and fantasies now must compete for shelf space with fictional stories of ever-increasing realism, with informational books on nearly every conceivable subject, and with a host of other types.

Teachers who wish to foster children's growth through reading should be aware of these various types of trade books so they can participate in the process of getting the "right" book to the "right" child at the "right" time. But perhaps you're already aware of the various types. To test your

The Type You Will Look for When . . .

_____ 1. Fictional book that portrays people coping with universal problems of life as these problems exist in modern times

_____ 2. Fictional story that concentrates on finding clues to discover why and how an incident took place

_____ 3. Book of short selections, most that describe the essence of something—sometimes in colorful language, sometimes in rhyming or rhythmic patterns of words

_____ 4. Book in which story is told or information given in two ways, both at the same time—one way is through words, the other is through numerous illustrations

_____ 5. Fictional story of an adolescent coping with universal problems of love

_____ 6. Book of legends, fables, tall tales, epics, myths, old fairy tales, or other traditional stories formerly handed down by word of mouth

_____ 7. Fictional story in which situations or characteristics, usually of a realistic nature, are exaggerated to the point of amusement

_____ 8. Fictional book in which an animal, such as a dog or horse, becomes a heroic figure in a realistic way

_____ 9. Fictional book based on principles or possibilities of nature, often involving future times, space travel, other worlds

_____ 10. Nonfictional book about a noteworthy person

_____ 11. Fictional story in which success in an athletic game is an important element of the conflict and is generally related to the "game of living"

_____ 12. Book of fictional stories written in drama format, nearly all dialogue

_____ 13. Nonfiction book that explains natural and social phenomena or suggests experiments, activities, or procedures

_____ 14. Fictional book emphasizing historical settings and usually historical characters or events

_____ 15. Fictional story involving danger, courage, and a struggle with the natural elements

_____ 16. Fictional story created in writing rather than handed down orally in which events are not only improbable but seem impossible, e.g., talking animals, magic wands, tiny people, events conflicting with present scientific knowledge

A Child Needs or Wants a

a. picture book

b. book of folktales

c. sports story

d. biography

e. historical fiction book

f. science fiction book

g. realistic fiction book

h. mystery story

i. animal story

j. fantasy

k. informational book

l. outdoor/adventure story

m. teenage romance story

n. book of poetry

o. humorous story

p. book of plays

Answers

| 1—g | 2—h | 3—n | 4—a | 5—m | 6—b | 7—o | 8—i | 9—f |
| 10—d | 11—c | 12—p | 13—k | 14—e | 15—l | 16—j | | |

Figure 8.1 _A Matching Exercise_

awareness, try the matching exercise in Figure 8.1. See if you can "find" the type of books that "a child needs." (Feedback and immediate reinforcement can be obtained by checking the answers at the end of the matching exercise.)

If you got twelve or more correct, you should probably celebrate this event in some way, for these sixteen categories and their descriptions are slightly ambiguous and rely upon subtle distinctions. Some teenage romance stories, for instance, could be classified as realistic fiction. Some science fiction could be classified as fantasy, to take another example. Precisely how one decides to classify a particular book, of course, is not very important. What is important is that you become familiar, if you're not already, with the various types of books available for children at various age levels.

Joseph Leibowicz (1983), in his summary of research on children's reading interests, found that no single story structure is an exclusive favorite. Children have a wide range of interests, just as adults do. Greenlaw (1983), on the other hand, found that certain types of books are more consistent favorites than others. "Funny" books are a distinct favorite among primary-grade children, followed by Make-Believe, People, and Animals. Among intermediate-grade children, the most consistent favorite is the "Adventure" type of book, followed by Jokes and Humor, Informational, and Fantasy. Greenlaw's data are based on the choices of about 60,000 children all over the country between 1973 and 1979. It is quite conceivable that by, say, 1990, children's interest in various types of books will change. Greenlaw's research shows that such changes have taken place in the past. On the other hand, the category of "Funny" has remained constant for many years among primary-grade children. "Animals" has also remained in the top four categories.

For intermediate-grade children, the only category that has remained consistently popular through the years has been "Adventure." Don't worry; this doesn't mean that children in grade four and up aren't interested in "funny" books, they're just more selective. If you'd like a list of almost-sure fire funny books for children of this age, here are some books culled from a list prepared by John and Priscilla Bennett (1982). I chose from their list only those that *every* child in their small sample said were funny:

Bunnicula: A Rabbit-Tale of Mystery by Deborah Howe

Fat Men from Space by Daniel Manus Pinkwater

Help! I'm a Prisoner in the Library by Eth Clifford

Jim Bridger's Alarm Clock and Other Tall Tales by Sid Fleischman

Johnny May by Robbie Branscum

Konrad by Christine Nostlinger

The Mark of Conte by Sonia Levitin

My Mother is Not Married to My Father by Jean Okimoto

Pippi on the Run by Astrid Lindgren

Superfudge by Judy Blume

Think About It. You Might Learn Something by Robyn Supraner

Now let's return for a moment to the sixteen types of children's books described in Figure 8.1. Naturally, if you're teaching second graders, you can forget about the teenage romance stories, but all the other types have been published for children of this age. Teachers in the intermediate grades will want to become familiar with all sixteen types—even the picture books, many of which have been published for children beyond the primary grades.

The best way to become truly familiar with children's books is *not* to read anthologies or reviews, but to read and enjoy the books themselves. (It's probably a good idea to keep a card file on the books you read to jog your memory later.) When you read children's books, you may want to follow these suggestions:

Read books for a wide range of age levels. Remember that children at any grade level vary tremendously in their reading abilities and interests. Carolyn Haywood's books, for instance (e.g., *B is for Betsy, Eddie and His Big Deals*) are excellent for the average reader in grades two and three. But some children at this grade level will be reading fourth- and fifth-grade books, such as *Henry Huggins* by Beverly Cleary or *Little House on the Prairie* by Laura Ingalls Wilder, while others will be reading simple picture books like *Where the Wild Things Are* by Maurice Sendak or *Millions of Cats* by Wanda Gag.

Read a variety of book types. In this way you can be more helpful even to the child who is looking for "a real good sports story."

Read them with a sense of involvement from cover to cover. Skimmed books are as bad as poorly digested meals. Only by reading books thoroughly can you prepare yourself to share them honestly with children.

Start by reading several that are considered by many to be of "good" quality. Then when you come across poor-quality books, you will recognize them almost instantly; you will thus avoid wasting your own time and be able to recommend high-quality books to children. In the references at the end of this chapter, you will find sources (Arbuthnot, 1971; Huck, 1976; Norton, 1983; Spache, 1974; Sutherland, 1977) that will help you decide which books are likely to be worthy of your time. Appendix I is "A Starter List of Good Books for Children" which may help you with your selection.

PROVIDE TIME FOR READING

There are several ways to encourage children to make use of trade books. One is simply to allow plenty of time for them to read. In spite of the hustle and bustle of a modern classroom, it is often a better place in which to read than the home. At home, remember, reading must frequently compete with the omnipresent television and its tempting tidbits of instant culture and instant action.

Numerous studies have shown that the average elementary school child watches television more than we would like them to. Long and Henderson (1973) studied the activities of fifth graders when they were not in school. The average time per week spent reading was three hours; the average time per week with television was thirty hours. You can see, then, that to give children enough interactive reading practice, you'll need to schedule time for it during the school hours.

Many teachers sincerely believe they offer their students enough time to read trade books during the school day but when pressed to define what they mean by "enough time," some of them answer like this: "I let them read all during the day. Whenever they get their assignments done, they're supposed to get out a library book and read quietly." What this generally means in practice is that the same three of four students who always get their assignments done early are doing about 90 percent of the reading. Most of the others either spend all their time on the textbook-workbook assignment or, if they finish early, have so little time to read before the next assignment befalls them that they usually decide not to bother.

A first-year teacher wanted to know why his fifth-grade students didn't seem to want to read. When he was asked how much time they had for "free reading," he said, "Well, whenever they finish their other assignments—and sometimes I give them a ten-minute free-reading period before lunch." It was suggested to him that he try something for two weeks: giving them two thirty-minute periods a week for free reading. In two weeks time, he had changed his mind about most of his students: "It takes some of them five to six minutes to get started, but once they get going, I can't tear them away from their books."

THE SSR APPROACH

Many years ago Fader and McNeil (1968) provided one answer to the time problem in their book *Hooked on Books: Program and Proof.* They recommended a timed approach in which, during the first week, only five minutes a day is set aside for intensive silent reading. This time is gradually increased until the children are reading for thirty minutes or more a day. Fader and McNeil claimed considerable success, even with children who were reluctant to read. Their name for this approach was "Uninterrupted Sustained Silent Reading" (USSR), but for obvious reasons this has been changed over the years to the "SSR Approach."

Research on SSR provides only mediocre support; however, as Spiegel (1983) points out, researchers on the whole have tried the approach for only a month or two before checking for signs of children's progress on achievements tests. (It's funny about our society. When a new football coach is hired, the fans usually give him a year or two to shape up the team. When a new idea is tried in a classroom, the teacher is expected to produce results in two months!) Donald Pfau (1966) had the right idea. He studied the effects of an SSR program that was carried on for one or two years instead of months. Children who engage in a long-range program of sustained silent reading, he found, do perform better on achievement tests than those who don't.

As much as I want to encourage the use of an SSR program, however, I should caution you not to consider it a panacea. It's not some kind of cure-all; it's just a good supplement to a strong instructional program in interactive reading. True, daily periods of library book reading are what children need for *practicing* what teachers teach them. On the other hand, children who have not mastered the use of all four cueing systems may be practicing the wrong thing! For the child who is relying solely on graphophonic cues, giving him 30 minutes of timed practice may be consigning him to a half-hour in Hades.

Poor readers need a great deal of *guided* as well as independent reading. Some of this guided reading should be oral, some silent. In either case, the teacher should be directly involved in asking questions, clarifying meanings, and *showing* the children the cues available to them, both from the author and from their own schematic background. Furthermore, poor readers need more help than other children in selecting interesting and *easy* books to read on their own. The practice they have on independent reading must be successful—just having them "read" is not enough.

Moore, Jones, and Miller (1980) reviewed the research on SSR and other forms of "recreational reading" and came up with two conclusions (italics mine): (1) "SSR has a positive effect on student *attitude* toward reading" and (2) "SSR has a positive effect on reading ability *when com-*

bined with a regular program of reading instruction" (p. 448). McCracken and McCracken (1978) investigated several SSR programs that were doing *poorly* and found these common characteristics:

The teacher did *not* read during the SSR period

The troublemakers did *not* read during the SSR period

A visiting adult or an aide did *not* read during the SSR period

The SSR period was too long for the particular children involved

There were not enough books available

The teacher was impatient and didn't want to give the program time to work

Let me add two characteristics based on my own observations:

Many children were attempting to read at their frustration level rather than their independent level: the teacher had not helped them find books that were interesting and *easy.*

Many children had not been given sufficient direct instruction in using all four cueing systems.

PROVIDE ENOUGH BOOKS

A second way to encourage children's use of trade books is to provide them with a wide choice. This can usually be accomplished in various ways, depending on the school and municipal facilities. Many schools today have their own libraries. Some teachers take their children to nearby municipal libraries to check out a collection which they then take to the classroom. A vast number of teachers encourage their students to purchase their own paperback books at a reasonable price from one of the Scholastic Book Clubs. These books, and other paperbacks available from bookstores, are usually printed from the same plates as the original hardbound copies, and the quality of selections is generally high. A few publishers have come out with fairly large classroom collections of paperbacks designed for an "individualized reading program." One example is the *Reading Spectrum* published by Scholastic* and the *Pal Paperback Kits* published by Xerox. School libraries, municipal libraries, county libraries, state libraries, book

---

*For a list of Scholastic book collections write to: Scholastic's Readers' Choice, 904 Sylvan Avenue, Englewood Cliffs, NJ 07632.

clubs, bookstores, publishers—a resourceful teacher can find some way to provide students with a variety of trade books.

HELP THEM FIND EASY BOOKS

Another way to encourage trade-book reading is to help children find books that are not too difficult. Children can easily become discouraged if one book after another offers them little more than frustration. Teachers who

make it a habit to read children's books themselves have little trouble offering children guidance in this respect. There are also numerous lists of easy-reading books for children whose interests are beyond their reading skills. One of the most complete lists is given in Spache's *Good Reading for Poor Readers* (1974), which has been frequently revised to keep it up-to-date. Other lists include Spache's *Good Reading for the Disadvantaged Reader* (1970) and *Easy Reading* (1979), a list of series for grades four through eight by Graves, Boettcher, and Ryder. You'll find another list in Appendix I.

LEARN CHILDREN'S INTERESTS

A fourth way to foster the habit of reading trade books is to suggest books to children that may seem to relate to their needs and interests. Gradually during a school year a teacher can get to know his pupils' interests, hobbies, and personal problems—through informal conversations and observations, and sometimes through a formal interview or questionnaire. The teacher who also becomes familiar with children's books is in the enviable position of being able to suggest specific books to specific children for particular interests or problems. Perusal of book reviews is also helpful to the teacher in this respect. Excellent reviews can be found in books by Arbuthnot (1971), Sutherland (1977), Huck (1976), and Norton (1983), and in *Hornbook Magazine*. Some of the basal reader publishers now have incorporated book reviews in their teacher's guides. *Reading Teacher*, the monthly journal of the International Reading Association, publishes an annotated list each October of "Classroom Choices: Children's Trade Books." This list is comprised of books selected primarily by children and includes annotations that tell how each book fits into the school curriculum.

PROVIDE SHARING OPPORTUNITIES

Still another way to promote trade-book reading is to establish means for sharing books or reacting creatively to them. The old-fashioned book report, it goes without saying, doesn't generally meet this need. A better approach—one that many teachers have found much more successful—is to encourage various types of sharing and creative projects following completion of a book. In Appendix F you will find about seventy "Book Projects for

Children and Teachers,'' which you can modify to fit the age level and interests of your particular students. All have been tested in classrooms and appear to be interesting and worthwhile to children.

Of course, the guidance the teacher offers is often the key factor in making them interesting and worthwhile. Simply passing out a list of projects is not very motivating. Probably the most effective form of guidance is that of reading children's books and carrying on some of the projects yourself. For instance, one of the oral projects suggested is to ''put on a puppet play about one part of the book.'' You can imagine what an inspiration your sharing a book in this way could be for children to read ''your'' book or to share theirs in a similar fashion. Don't make your presentation so awe-inspiring, though, that they'll be afraid to emulate you. Use a simple scene and puppets that the children could easily make themselves. Along with the more creative approaches, just chatting a bit about a book you have read will usually encourage many in the class to read the same one. Besides guiding by showing, however, the teacher can occasionally meet with individuals for a few minutes to talk about books they have recently read and ways they may share them with others. (Incidentally, sometimes a child prefers simply to share his book with you alone.) Or, you can have children get together in small groups once a week or so to talk about books they have been reading.

Although the children usually carry on oral, arts-and-crafts, and drama projects with great enthusiasm, teachers report that they often greet the written projects at first with something less than spontaneous joy. Here again, the teacher's leading the way sometimes helps immensely. A special bulletin board or ''class book'' for written projects is generally a must. Here others may see the teacher's and children's written projects that have been donated. (Again, however, don't overawe them with your writing powers, or yours will be the only one there.) For children below the fifth grade, special praise in front of the class may also work in inspiring the ''writing road to fame.''

USE INSTRINSIC AND EXTRINSIC MOTIVATORS

A final way to instigate the trade-book habit is to use extrinsic forms of positive reinforcement. We've already talked about intrinsic forms, such as finding books that are easy enough, making a wide choice available, and providing avenues for sharing and reacting creatively. All of these are directly involved with the act of reading itself. But sometimes this isn't enough, and you may have to use some type of symbolic or even tangible reward.

One form of extrinsic reward is simply to have the children keep a personal record of the books they read. By checking these records with the children every few weeks and by praising them for the quality or variety, or, in some cases, the quantity of reading they have done, you can often spur children on to further reading. Some teachers like to add a bit of spice to the recordkeeping by providing small rectangles (about one-half inch by four inches) of colored paper that represent book spines. On each slip of paper the child writes the title and author of the book she has just finished; then the slip of paper is pasted on a dittoed "shelf," and the ditto sheet is placed in her folder or notebook.

Along with an individual-record scheme such as the one just described, you may wish to keep a class record of "Books We Have Read." Note, however, that this does not refer to a competitive form of record, such as a chart of names with so many stars after each name. Such a record may easily do more harm than good, since the slowest readers have no chance to "win" and because many children will falsely claim to have read certain books just to win it. What we are referring to is a cooperative record similar to the thermometer graph so often used for community chest or blood bank drives. Or you may wish to construct a "class bookshelf," using different-colored paper for different types of books. You can have the children put the title and author on the front of the piece of paper and their name on the back; these "books" can then be "taken off the shelf" and returned in an envelope to each child at the end of the year.

Some teachers give symbolic tokens for books that children say they have read; some prefer to give them only for books shared through projects. Whatever tactic teachers use, though, they shouldn't defeat the purpose by becoming too serious or demanding about it. Encourage rather than nag, inspire rather than require, help them cooperate rather than compete— these should be the mottoes of a teacher who desires to foster the reading of trade books for information and pleasure.

USING CHILDREN'S LITERATURE IN AN "INDIVIDUALIZED READING PROGRAM"

Some teachers choose to go all the way with trade books and use them as the major instructional material for teaching reading skills. With this approach, the children do the actual selection of materials to read. To differentiate this approach from other ways of individualizing reading instruction, let's call it the "trade-book individualized reading program" or the TBIR program. The TBIR program is based on three principles espoused several decades ago by the child-development specialist, Willard C. Olson.

The three principles are *seeking, self-selection,* and *self-pacing.* In essence, Olson was saying that children, by nature, are "seeking organisms" who are curious about their environment and want to learn about it. This learning is best motivated and maintained when children are given many opportunities to select their own stimuli and experiences and to explore at their own individual pace. Olson felt these principles applied to the processes of learning to read, and thus supported the TBIR movement. Similar views of learning were advocated before Olson by Dewey, Froebel, Rousseau, and other educational philosophers.

Research on TBIR programs (Johnson, 1965; Macdonald et al., 1966; Safford, 1960; Thompson, 1975; Vite, 1961) has had inconclusive results. In general it appears that the success of such a program depends upon the skill and enthusiasm of the teacher. It is likely that those who are successful in using a TBIR program are knowledgeable about the nature of reading, the various ways of teaching it, the means of managing such a flexible program, and the ways of finding books that fit children's needs and interests. It is definitely not a program to enter casually without adequate preparation.

TEACHING SKILLS THROUGH A TRADE BOOK INDIVIDUALIZED READING PROGRAM

Many people think of a TBIR program as one in which children are taught reading skills in a one-on-one manner during individual reading conferences. This is not the case. Although it may be a romantic notion to have the teacher on one end of the log and the attentive student on the other, this type of teaching has only limited possibilities in a classroom full of thirty active and ego-oriented children.

Most teachers who use a TBIR program employ a great many group-teaching techniques. Athough they may teach some skills during an individual conference, most of the skill instruction is carried on with small groups of children who have similar skill deficiencies. Mrs. Spiegal, for instance, may determine during an individual conference that Sandra needs help on decoding vowel patterns. Although she may spend a moment teaching one of those patterns, she will also make a record of Sandra's problem and make sure she later receives instruction along with other children who are having similar problems. (Occasionally, the teacher may decide the entire class needs instruction on the same skill.)

Because of the availability of skills-management systems (discussed in Chapter 9), it is now somewhat easier to manage the skill-development component of a TBIR program than it used to be in the '50s and early '60s.

An SMS provides the teacher with assessment tools, instructional materials, and recordkeeping devices—all of which had to be invented or "scrounged up" by the pioneers of the TBIR program. With an SMS, a teacher can test her children to see what skill lessons they need. She can then divide children into temporary groups in order to teach those skill lessons. And she can keep reasonably accurate records of children's progress by using post tests and skill checklists.

The skills-management system, as you may recall from Chapter 7 can be purchased by the school district from systems publishers; or an SMS sold with a basal reader program can be used. McGraw-Hill, for example, publishes a system, independent of basal readers, called *PRI Reading Systems* (1972). Other examples of independent systems are the *Wisconsin Design* (Otto & Chester, 1976) and the *Fountain Valley Teacher Support System in Reading* (1971). As we'll discuss in Chapter 9, however, a skills-management system attached to a basal reader program can also be used as an independent system. The teacher simply uses the skill lessons in the teacher's guides and the various forms of tests provided by the publisher. The basal readers themselves then serve primarily as anthologies of stories that children may or may not read depending on their own desires (although they are also used to teach comprehension and decoding skills.)

There are, of course, all sorts of ways to schedule the skills instruction. One fifth grade teacher, for example, schedules seventy-five minutes of individual conferences with her students three days a week and seventy-five minutes of small-group instruction two days a week. (On these two days she meets with three groups for about twenty-five minutes each.) Another teacher does it this way:

Monday: Individual conferences—50 minutes; skill group A—25 minutes

Tuesday: Individual conferences—50 minutes; skill group B—25 minutes

Wednesday: Individual conferences—30 minutes; skill group C—20 minutes; skill group D—20 minutes

Thursday: Individual conferences—30 minutes; skill group C—20 minutes; skill group D—20 minutes

Friday: Individual conferences—50 minutes; book sharing—25 minutes

In addition to this type of scheduled instruction, the teacher using a TBIR program usually carries on spontaneous instruction during some of the conferences. Frequently after a conference in which a particular skill has been discussed, he will assign a brief skill worksheet for the child to take back to her desk.

MANAGING INDIVIDUAL CONFERENCES

The most common questions about individual conferences seem to be these:

How long should they be?

How often should they be?

What should happen during a conference?

Unfortunately, there are no easy answers to these questions; they depend on your purpose for a particular conference with a particular child. You may decide to give Jerry two conferences a week of about fiften minutes each; Patricia, one conference a week of about ten minutes; and Randy, one conference every two weeks for five to ten minutes. Jerry, you see, is so far behind the rest of the class in skill development that you decide he needs a lot of individual help. Patricia is doing reasonably well in skill development and responds well to the small-group instruction she has been receiving. Randy is so advanced in his skill development that your major purpose in meeting with him is to provide praise and show interest in what he has been learning about through his reading.

Some teachers, on the other hand, feel it's important to give each child the same number of conferences and about the same amount of time. Consequently they schedule each child for one conference a week for about ten minutes each. With thirty students, this adds up to 300 minutes per week or one hour per day.

As to what happens during a conference, this, of course, varies widely with the different needs of the children, whether it's early in the school year or later, and with what the teacher has planned to emphasize during a particular week. Early in the school year, the first few conferences are often used for administering informal reading inventories and diagnostic tests. This enables the teacher to determine what instructional books to use for each child and to assess his strengths and deficiencies.

Once the testing has been completed, the individual conferences can be used for a while to help children develop skill in selecting their own library books. This is usually done by listening to a child read out loud to see how difficult a book she has already selected seems to be for her, and by providing praise and encouragement. During these early conferences, the teacher often tries to determine some of the child's reading interests, which he then records in a notebook or folder for further reference. This enables him to help each child find appropriate books when the class uses the library.

CHECKING BOOKS FOR READABILITY

Some teachers teach their students to use a rule of thumb that a book will be too difficult if there are more than three or four "hard words" per page. (I can recall teaching that rule myself the first time I used a TBIR program. Fortunately the children ignored my rule and selected their books on the basis of interest, print size, book thickness, and the myriad of standards that children use for selecting books.) This rule would only make sense if every page of every book had the same number of words on it. A better way to help children select books of the right difficulty is to put some type of mark inside the front cover of a book to indicate its approximate level. You can do this (with the librarian) to the catalog in the school library by marking an A for books of grades one to two reading level, a B for books of grades three to four reading level, and so on. You can determine the levels by referring to *Good Reading for Poor Readers* (Spache, 1974) or by obtaining lists from publishers listed in Appendix E.

Another way to determine reading levels of books is by means of a "readability formula." Many such formulas have been invented but none has proved better than the estimates made by teachers who are knowledgeable about children and children's books. One of the best ways to determine whether a book is suitable for an "average" second grader, for instance, is to ask an experienced second-grade teacher. Most of the formulas, moreover, take far more time than it's worth to estimate a book's grade level. One "formula," though, that is relatively easy and quick to use is the graph developed by Edward Fry, shown in Figure 8.2.

Directions for Using the Readability Graph

1. Select three one-hundred-word passages near the beginning, middle, and end.

2. Count the total number of sentences in each hundred-word passage (estimating to nearest tenth of a sentence). Average these three numbers.

3. Count the total number of syllables in each hundred-word sample. Average the total number of syllables for the three samples.

4. Plot on the graph the average number of sentences per hundred words and the average number of syllables per hundred words. Most plot points fall near the heavy curved line. Diagonal lines mark off approximate grade-level areas.

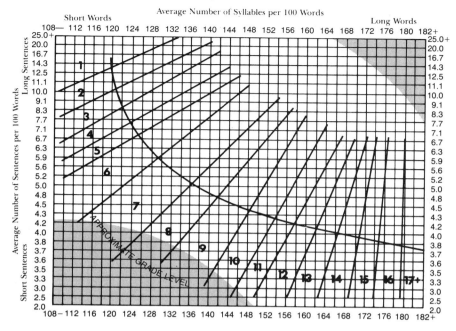

Figure 8.2 *Fry's graph for estimating readability. (From Edward Fry, "A Readability Formula that Saves Time," Journal of Reading 11 [April 1968]:513.)*

For example,

		Sentences per 100 words	Syllables per 100 words
100-word sample	Page 5	9.1	122
100-word sample	Page 89	8.5	140
100-word sample	Page 160	7.0	129
		3)24.6	3)391
	Average	8.2	130

Readability Level: fifth grade

A quicker method for estimating readability levels is to use one of the "readability scales" now available.* With a readability scale, no computation is necessary. Essentially all you do is to compare a passage from your book with a set of graded passages already prepared for you. If your pas-

----

*A scale takes schemata into account much more than a formula does.

sage seems to be most similar to the fourth-grade passage, for instance, you would rate your book as "fourth-grade readability level." If you'd like to have one of these scales for your own use, you may want to order the one prepared by Jean Chall and her colleagues (1983), McGraw-Hill Book Company, 1221 Avenue of the Americas, New York, NY 10020. Ask for the Chall, Bissex, Conrad, and Harris-Sharples *Readability assessment scales for literature, science, and social studies.*

Having labeled the library books by level, you can advise each child as to the approximate level for him. Be sure, however, to give such advise loosely rather than firmly. Children can often read books that would otherwise be too difficult except for the fact that the subject is so interesting. Most children eventually become adept at selecting books at the appropriate level, partly through their own experience, and partly by finding out in sharing periods what other children have been reading successfully.

OTHER USES FOR CONFERENCES

Another thing one often does during a conference with a child is to encourage her to vary her reading interests. If Debbie has been reading nothing but horse stories, you may try to interest her in another type. Sometimes you can suggest a specific book, such as one that includes horses in the *setting* of the story but emphasizes a different theme. Other times you can use some type of extrinsic reward for reading several types of books. A "story train" is one example of this kind of reward: each child has her own story train (made during an art lesson) consisting of construction-paper cars, engine, and caboose, each of a different color. Each color represents a different type of book—fantasy, sports, information, and so on. Whenever the child completes a particular type of book she gets to place a star on the appropriate train car. The goal is to have at least one star on each car by the end of the year. (The story train is kept in the child's folder rather than on a group chart; a group chart usually encourages negative competition and negative self-images.)

Conferences are often used as a time to reinforce a skill or a word that was taught to the child during a recent small-group lesson. You can reinforce spontaneously or by asking the children in a small group to "look for an example in your library books of what you've learned today; write down the page number, and show me the example during your next conference with me."

An individual conference is an excellent time to encourage interactive reading. You can do this simply by letting the child retell what he's read, however he wishes, while showing enthusiasm for his way of retelling. You can also have the child read her book out loud to you. Her first selection should be one she has practiced for the occasion so you can provide her with praise. The second selection should be one you select "magically" by simply giving her a page number at random. Whenever the child makes a self-correction, praise her specifically for coming up with a word that "makes more sense." Whenever she comes up with a substitution that doesn't make sense and is *not* self-corrected, wait until she has read the paragraph or page, then return to the uncorrected miscue. Read the sentence the same way the student read it, then ask her to find the word that didn't make sense. Talk informally about all the things that are different between the "author's word" and her original substitution. For example, to help her see intuitively the importance of schemata, you might ask her to tell you what pictures she gets in her mind when she reads the author's word. Then ask her what pictures she gets when she uses the word she substituted.

Conferences are also part of the very important process of building enthusiasm for school, for learning, and for reading. They are among the few times the child has the chance to relate to the teacher all by himself. As one teacher put it: "Through individual conferences, I've come to know each child quite well!"

QUESTIONS TO ASK DURING A CONFERENCE

Conferences are also used for developing thinking skills. In this regard, a teacher's questioning strategies are just as important with the TBIR program as they are with a basal reading program. In either type of program, your purpose is to enhance children's communication with an author and to develop their thinking skills. Asking questions that only tap literal thinking is equally poor for both types of programs. If you always ask a child "Who is the main character of this story?" or "What is this story about?" you are merely encouraging him to read for shallow details. If you want him to read with greater depth, try to vary the questions each time and to use plenty of questions at the inferential, evaluative, and creative levels. Here are a few examples of open-ended questions at these levels that can be used for any book (for more on questioning, see pages 244–45):

Inferential Questions

You say this story is about Jeff Roberts? Is Jeff struggling against another person, against himself, or against nature? Why do you think so?

Can you tell me about something in this book that makes the title of the book a good one?

You've read about half the book now. What do you think is going to happen next?

What did you have to picture in your mind before you could understand that sentence?

Critical Questions

Is the story you're reading a real-life story or a make-believe story? What makes you think so?

Would you say this book (nonfiction) is full of facts or opinions? Can you give me an example of a fact that author gives? Can you give me an example of an opinion?

Do you think this author is biased in any way? (Or, for younger children): How do you think the author feels about _____? Do you think she likes them?

Do you think Jeff Roberts (the main character) did anything that showed he was strong (or fair, or kind)?

Creative Questions

Jeff Roberts had a problem in this story. What was it? If you were Jeff Roberts, how would you solve that problem?

Do you have any problem in your life that is like the one Jeff Roberts had? How do you think you might solve that problem?

Now that you've finished this book, what kind of book project would you like to do about it? Is there a project you've never tried before?

TEACHING VOCABULARY

Teachers using a TBIR program often have children keep track of the unfamiliar words they run across during their reading. One teacher, for example, has children made a bookmark for each new book. On the bookmark, the children write down each word that causes them trouble. Then, during an individual conference, they talk about the words that are difficult to decode or understand.

Another teacher, who is concerned that children always learn words in context, has the children keep track of "hard words" by writing down on a sheet of paper the page number, the entire sentence, and the underlined word. Another teacher uses the bookmark idea but has the children write both the word and the page number. That way the child doesn't have to write the entire sentence, but the teacher can have him find the word again during the conference and help him use context clues to discover the meaning.

RECORDKEEPING

Recordkeeping is a vital component of a TBIR program. Without adequate records, teachers won't know what skills to emphasize for each child, what reading interests each one has, how much a child has read during the year, how deeply she is comprehending and thinking about what she reads, and what to tell parents during parent conferences. (Some parents may be worried, anyway, when they discover that basal readers and workbooks are not being used as they once were. Thus it is highly important to communicate with parents about the program and about their child's progress.)

A folder is usually kept for each child with his SMS checklist of skills, his test results, samples of his responses on worksheets, notes on his reading interests, a list of new words he is mastering, and a record of his actual reading. Each child often keeps this record himself. Each time that Janet reads a new book, for example, she fills in information on her Book Record sheet, as in Figure 8.3.

<table>
<tr><td colspan="5" align="center">Reading Record</td></tr>
<tr><td colspan="2"><u>Name</u>: Janet Fromkin</td><td colspan="3" align="right"><u>Year</u>: 1982–83</td></tr>
<tr><td align="center">Author</td><td align="center">Title</td><td align="center">Pages Read</td><td align="center">Rating 0–5</td><td align="center">Project</td></tr>
<tr><td>Buck</td><td>The Big Wave</td><td>All</td><td>4</td><td>Oral #3</td></tr>
<tr><td>O'Dell</td><td>Islands of the Blue Dolphins</td><td>All</td><td>5</td><td>Drama #6</td></tr>
<tr><td>Jones</td><td>All about Tar</td><td>6</td><td>0</td><td>None</td></tr>
<tr><td>Baker</td><td>Walk the World's Rim</td><td>All</td><td>4</td><td>All (My own idea)</td></tr>
<tr><td></td><td></td><td></td><td></td><td></td></tr>
<tr><td></td><td></td><td></td><td></td><td></td></tr>
<tr><td></td><td></td><td></td><td></td><td></td></tr>
<tr><td></td><td></td><td></td><td></td><td></td></tr>
<tr><td></td><td></td><td></td><td></td><td></td></tr>
</table>

Figure 8.3 *Book Record Sheet*

EASING INTO AN INDIVIDUALIZED PROGRAM

As you can see by now, a TBIR program can be an exciting and worthwhile form of reading instruction. At the same time, it requires a considerable amount of knowledge and management capability on the part of the teacher. For most first-year teachers, it is probably not the approach to take. By the second year, however, you may wish to ease into this type of individualized program. Some teachers try it for the first time by having only the "top group" engaged in the TBIR program while the other groups continue in the basal reading program. Then, as the teacher gains experience, she has other groups gradually join the top group.

Another way to break into the TBIR program is to use it only one day per week at first, but with the entire class. As you develop skill in handling the program on a once-a-week basis, you can then increase the program to two days per week, and so on. This approach is more satisfying to teachers who don't wish to single out the children in the top group as "privileged." In either case, whether you break in with one group or with one day per week, some kind of gradual adjustment to an individualized program is advisable.

THE MAIN IDEAS IN THIS CHAPTER

An individualized program in which children read library books rather than basal readers can be an exciting and worthwhile way to teach reading—requiring skill, knowledge, and management capability on the part of the teacher.

Whether a teacher uses a trade book or a more traditional approach, encouraging library book reading is essential to a successful reading program. It's easy for teachers to get so wrapped up in teaching isolated subskills that they can forget to give their students practice in reading real books.

Many children today do not seem to have enough time outside school to practice real reading. They must have that practice during the school hours.

Teachers can do many things to encourage children to read books at school. Hickman (1983) gives suggestions that correspond to the main ideas in this chapter. Her criteria for classrooms that help children *want* to read are these:

The teachers love books and show their love for them.

A large supply of books is readily available in the school and in the classroom.

Frequently-changed book displays entice the children to read.

The teacher introduces and discusses books that are new to the room.

The teacher reads to the children every day.

There are opportunities to work on and share book projects.

REFERENCES AND SUGGESTED READINGS

Arbuthnot, M. H. (1971). *Children's books too good to miss.* Ashtabula, OH: Western Reserve Press.

Barbe, W., & Abbott, J. (1975). *Personalized Reading Instruction.* New York: Parker.

Bennett, J. E., & Bennett, P. (1982). What's so funny? Action research and bibliography of humorous children's books—1975–80. *Reading Teacher, 35,* 924–927.

Berglund, R. L., & Johns, J. L. (1983). A primer on uninterrupted sustained silent reading. *Reading Teacher, 36,* 534–539.

Chall, J. S. (1983). Readability and prose comprehension: Continuities and discontinuities. In J. Flood (Ed.), *Understanding reading comprehension* (pp. 233–246). Newark, DE: International Reading Association.

Criscuolo, N. P. (1976). Mags bags, peg sheds, crafty crannies and reading. *Reading Teacher, 29,* 376–378.

Cunningham, P. (1983). The clip sheet: When is reading? *Reading Teacher, 36,* 928–933.

Fader, D. N., & McNeil, E. B. (1968). *Hooked on Books: Program and Proof.* New York: G. P. Putnam's Sons, 1968.

Fountain Valley teacher support system in reading. (1971). Huntington Beach, CA: Richard L. Zweig Associates.

Graves, M. F., Boettcher, J. A., & Ryder, R. J. (1979). *Easy reading: Book series and periodicals for less able readers.* Newark, DE: International Reading Association.

Greenlaw, M. J. (1983). Reading interest research and children's choices. In N. Roser & M. Firth (Eds.), *Children's choices: Teaching with books children like* (pp. 90–92). Newark, DE: International Reading Association.

Hickman, J. (1983). Classrooms that help children like books. In N. Roser & M. Frith (Eds.), *Children's choices: Teaching with books children like* (pp. 1–11). Newark, DE: International Reading Association.

Huck, C. S. (1976). *Children's literature in the elementary school.* New York: Holt, Rinehart, and Winston.

Hunt, L. (1970). The effect of self-selection, interest, and motivation upon independent, instructional, and frustration levels. *Reading Teacher, 24,* 146–151, 158.

Individualized reading from Scholastic. Englewood Cliffs, NJ: Scholastic Book Services.

Johns, J. L., & Hunt, L. (1975). Motivating reading: Professional ideas. *Reading Teacher, 28,* 617–619.

Johnson, R. H. (1965). Individualized and basal primary reading programs. *Elementary English, 42,* 902–904.

Lapp, D. (Ed.). (1980). *Making reading possible through effective classroom management.* Newark, DE: International Reading Association.

Leibowicz, J. (1983). Children's reading interests. *Reading Teacher, 37,* 184–187.

Long, B. H., & Henderson, E. H. (1973). Children's use of time: Some personal and social correlates. *Elementary School Journal, 73,* 193–199.

Macdonald, J. B., et al. (1966). Individual versus group instruction in first grade reading. *Reading Teacher, 19,* 643–647.

McCracken, R. A., & McCracken, M. J. (1978). Modeling is the key to sustained silent reading. *Reading Teacher, 31,* 406–408.

Moore, J. C., Jones, C. J., & Miller, D. C. (1980). What we know after a decade of sustained silent reading. *Reading Teacher, 33,* 445–450.

Norton, D. E. (1983). *Through the eyes of a child: An introduction to children's literature.* Columbus, OH: Charles E. Merrill.

Otto, W., & Chester, R. D. (1976). *Objective based reading.* Reading, MA: Addison-Wesley.

Pfau, D. W. (1966). *An investigation of the effects of planned recreational reading programs in first and second grade.* Unpublished doctoral dissertation, State University of New York at Buffalo.

Prescriptive reading inventory. (1972). New York: CTB/McGraw-Hill.

Roser, N., & Firth, M. (Eds.). (1983). *Children's choices: Teaching with books children like.* Newark, DE: International Reading Association.

Sadoski, M. C. (1980). Ten years of uninterrupted sustained silent reading. *Reading Improvement, 17,* 153–156.

Safford, A. L. (1960). Evaluation of an individualized reading program. *Reading Teacher, 13,* 266–270.

Schaudt, B. A. (1983). Another look at sustained silent reading. *Reading Teacher, 36,* 934–936.

Spache, E. (1976). *Reading activities for child involvement.* Boston: Allyn and Bacon.

Spache, G. D. (1970). *Good reading for the disadvantaged reader.* Champaign, IL: Garrard.

Spache, G. D. (1974). *Good reading for poor readers.* Champaign, IL: Garrard.

Spiegel, D. L. (1983). *Reading for pleasure: Guidelines.* Newark, DE: International Reading Association.

Sutherland, Z. (1977). *Children and books.* Chicago: Scott, Foresman.

Taylor, F. D., et al. (1972). *Individualized reading instruction, games and activities.* Denver: Love Publishing Company.

Thompson, R. (1975). Individualizing reading: A summary of research. *Educational Leadership, 33,* 57–63.

Veatch, J. (1966). *Reading in the elementary school.* New York: Ronald Press.

Vite, I. W. (1961). Individualized reading— the scoreboard on control studies. *Education, 81,* 285–290.

APPLICATION EXPERIENCES FOR THE TEACHER EDUCATION CLASS

A. *What's your opinion?* Use your own experiences as well as ideas from the textbook to help you defend your decisions.

1. A tradebook individualized reading (TBIR) program is better than a language experience program for teaching reading.

2. Kids are kids. We worry too much about how they differ from each other. When it comes to reading instruction, we should be more concerned about how similar they are.

3. It's smarter to spend your time as a teacher reading books from the "Children's Choices" list than from Newbery or Caldecott Award lists.

4. There really is no good way to advise a child as to what library book to read.

5. The SSR approach is the way to go; it helps children get used to reading library books. Timing kids is probably even more important than allowing them choices.

6. Book projects are really no better or worse than book reports.

B. *Miscue Analysis:* How can you tell from Steve's miscues that this little first grader already enjoys the process of reading (in spite of eight miscues) and is interested in this story?

Mary has a dog. His name is Rex. He is little. He is brown. He likes to *(had)* *(Its)* *(His little)*

play. He likes to run. He runs fast. Mary follows him. Then he stops. *(holds)*

He can do tricks. He sits up. He rolls over. He shakes hands. He can *(still)*

swim. He swims in the river.* *(walk)* *(splashes)*

C. *Simulation of an Individual Conference:* Carry on an individual conference with a partner about a book (preferably a children's book she has just read or is in the process of reading). If your partner has not read one recently, she can use a movie or television show as a substitute. (Again, a children's book would be best, however.) Ask your partner a few of the questions from our examples of inferential, critical, and cre-

---

*Colin Dunkeld, Portland Informal Reading Inventory, Form P. Unpublished manuscript, Portland State University. Reprinted by permission of the author.

ative questions. Also discuss an unusual word she came across in her reading (or viewing). Check her comprehension of one or two paragraphs after she has read them silently. In addition, check her decoding skills by having her read two or three paragraphs out loud. Keep notes on the conference.

D. *Planning for an Individual Conference:* With a partner, make up three open-ended questions that could be used in an individual conference for any book a child has read. The questions should include one that helps a child develop images or associations about what she has read (or is now reading), one that helps her follow a sequence of events or ideas, and one that helps her think about specific and important details.

FIELD EXPERIENCES IN THE ELEMENTARY SCHOOL CLASSROOM

A. Conduct an individual conference with one child related to a library book he has been reading. Ask him some questions you made up in your teacher-education class for Experience D. Also ask a few questions from the list of examples. Check his comprehension of one or two paragraphs after he has read them silently. In addition, check his reading skills by having him read two or three paragraphs out loud. Keep notes on the conference. If possible, share these notes with another teacher who has been working with the same child.

B. Examine the school library to see whether it has developed any system for helping children find books at the right level of difficulty. If there is no system, think about a system that could be used. If there is no school library, find out what other ways teachers in the building help children get access to a variety of library books.

9 BASAL READER PROGRAMS: USES AND MISUSES

CHAPTER PREVIEW

At least four out of every five teachers in the elementary grades use basal readers, rather than library books or children's writing, as their *primary* medium of reading instruction.

As you know, basal readers are books that contain stories, articles, plays, and poems that children read under the guidance of their teacher. The teacher generally uses a "teacher's guide" or "manual" to help her guide the children's reading and teach them lessons on specific skills.

As far as *types* of books that adults select, basal readers may be the most popular type in our country, next to cookbooks and romance novels. And yet, joking aside, there are perfectly good reasons for their popularity, and we'll look at some of those reasons in this chapter. We'll also see what a modern basal reader program looks like, its advantages and disadvantages, and some of the organizational plans teachers use while teaching with basal readers. We'll especially look at how teachers can combine a basal reader program with intensive use of library books and language experiences to provide children with the rounded program they need to perceive reading as a communication process.

For humans to feel secure, they need either a
security blanket or a copy of "Emily Post."

THE POPULARITY OF BASAL READER PROGRAMS

The basal reader became a popular teaching medium with the introduction of the *McGuffey Series* around 1840. Today basal reader publishers still follow McGuffey's main plan: to present children with books of stories, articles, poems, and plays whose vocabulary increases in difficulty with each new book. McGuffey controlled the vocabulary of the books by controlling the length of the words, beginning with the two- or three-letter words and leading up to longer and longer ones.

Today publishers control the vocabulary in three ways:

1) By using high-frequency words at first *(the, you)* and gradually introducing words of lower frequency *(view, deal)*

2) By using mostly regular words at first *(bone, cone)* and gradually introducing words whose spelling pattern is irregular *(one, done)*

3) By using a great many high-interest words at first *(mom, dad, eat)* and gradually introducing words that are more abstract and less relevant to children's immediate concerns *(opposite, molecules)*

This systematic approach toward helping children learn to read has great appeal. And for good reason, since it tends to work much better than presenting children with something too difficult, like the Bible or *Pilgrim's*

Progress—two books favored by educators in our country before the advent of basal readers.

Most people can see the commonsense rationale for controlling vocabulary in *some* way; in fact, those who advocate a language experience approach can say, "This is exactly what happens with LEA. The children control the vocabulary by using their own words!" Those who advocate a free-choice library books approach might say, "Children control the vocabulary by choosing books that are interesting and easy enough to enjoy." So you see, we're not really talking about vocabulary control, we're talking about who does the controlling—the children or the reading experts. And who can do it best is a difficult question to answer without dozens of qualifying amendments.

No, the popularity of basal reader programs must be caused by factors in addition to the importance of vocabulary control. I have no statistical evidence to prove what I'm going to propose, but my guess is that basal reader programs are popular because they provide so much security to adults—the parents, teachers, and administrators who are concerned about the children under their care. I certainly don't mean anything negative by this; after all, a sense of security is important to all humans, children or adults. And probably with our large, urbanized, chain-of-command school systems, we must accept security as a major concern of all adults who work in a system or send their children into a system.

Let's look, then, at why basal reader programs might provide some of this needed security. First, basal reader programs have a *logical* organization. They are organized from easy to difficult and from simple to complex. This kind of logic rightfully feels good to most adults. Second, basal reader programs are broken into manageable units. Those interacting cueing systems we've been talking about are broken into hundreds of decoding and comprehension situations that are labeled "subskills" and presented to children in hundreds of "skill lessons" and worksheets. Even the phrase itself, *manageable units*, has a nice ring to it for adults. In fact, philosophers and psychologists have indicated that the older we get, the more we crave both order and manageable units.

Third, the *sequence* of basal reader programs is written down in an organized fashion. And, as any psychologist will tell you, a definite sequence does provide security. Children move through a basal reader program sequentially from one selection to the next, one skill lesson to the next, one worksheet to the next, and one test to the next, according to the written sequence. The fact that the sixteen basal reader publishers in the United States don't agree on the proper sequence doesn't bother adults who are concerned with only one school district—it's the continuity within a single district that matters. The fact that no research has been done to compare the effectiveness of one basal program sequence to another also doesn't seem to matter. (And again, I don't mean this in a negative way.) What matters is that those who purchase the program and teach with the program and send their kids off to use the program all have a written sequence to point to. And it feels right.

People's trust in basal reader programs might seem a little amazing to you, especially since the "First Grade Studies" and the "Second Grade Studies" of the sixties (Bond & Dykstra, 1967; Dykstra, 1968) showed that no matter what media teachers used (language experience stories, basal readers, phonics workbooks, whatever), it really made no significant difference. Children's reading achievement was about the same. It wasn't the materials that made the difference, they found; *it was the teachers*. To put it another way, good teachers, given any materials, any sequence, will still teach reading well. Aukerman (1984) has discovered that in addition to the 16 basal reader programs, there are 165 experimental programs being tried, all of which have been considered highly successful by those using them.

I apologize for burdening you with what appears to me to be the truth about the very natural human need for security. As one teacher-education student said to me, "I don't want to know the truth. I want to feel that the adults who have gone before me have solved things—so I can go out there

and teach and get on with my life." My answer was like this: "Adults before you *have* solved things, in the best ways they could. They've put a lot of thought into preparing instructional materials they think will help children learn to read. And there's nothing wrong with your using basal reader programs to teach reading, as long as you control the materials and they don't control you. No one knows better than the teacher what reading experience Johnny needs to have next. No reading expert from afar. No written sequence. No teacher's guide. No principal. No superintendent. Your sensitivity to the child and your own good judgment should be your major guides in the classroom."

But before we go on to look at basal reader programs, let me mention one more reason why basal programs are so popular. They save time—a precious commodity for harried teachers. The teacher's guides today are so elaborate, it takes very little preparation time to get ready to teach a reading lesson. Many teacher's guides even tell you exactly *what to say*—an obnoxious imposition to some, a gift to others. To put it succinctly, they are cookbooks *extraordinaire*. For the beginning teacher, this can be a godsend. After a few years, however, most teachers alter the recipes (Durkin, 1978–79; Shake & Allington, 1985).

A GENERAL DESCRIPTION OF A BASAL READER PROGRAM

There are about 16 basal reading programs on the market today. Publishers of these programs will be happy to send you a brochure describing their series if you don't have access to them in an elementary school or a university media center. (See Appendix K for a list of the publishers.) Looking at the actual books, especially the teacher's guides, is the best way to understand a basal program, also referred to as a *basal series*.

Most basal reader publishers today use a "continuous progress" format. Rather than producing one book for each of the eight grades in the elementary school, the authors and editors prepare instructional materials for about seventeen *levels*, ranging from readiness materials for kindergarten and first grade all the way up to literature and informational selections for seventh and eighth grades. This multilevel approach is designed to encourage teachers to instruct a class at various levels at the same time, rather than instruct all those in the same grade with the same book.

In a first-grade classroom, for instance, some children who are weak in auditory discrimination, visual discrimination, or other prereading skills may be working at Level A with a set of prereading or readiness materials. This set of materials helps a teacher determine children's specific reading-readiness deficiencies and provides instructional plans and activities for remediation of those deficiencies. Other children in the same first-grade class-room may be working at level B with materials at a slightly higher level. The level B materials might help the teacher make sure that children develop abilities such as paying attention to spoken context clues, learning letter names and sounds, and reading a small set of high-frequency words. By the end of the first grade, some children may be working as high as level F, with a hardbound book and other materials. By this time, the children might be concentrating on such skills as decoding vowel patterns, paying attention to commas, and getting the main idea. As you can see, then, today's basal reading programs do permit a moderate degree of flexibility and individualization.

TYPES OF MATERIALS

The range of instructional materials available to the teacher using a modern basal series is quite extensive. Here are a few of them:

Readers (softbound and hardbound books of stories, poems, plays, and articles)

Teacher's Guides (manuals that contain precise lesson plans, review and enrichment activities, games, annotated lists of children's library books, scope-and-sequence charts for teaching skills, and other information)

Practice Books (workbooks for reinforcing skills and concepts that have already been taught by means of the reader's and the teacher's guides)

Testing materials (tests, inventories, and recordkeeping devices that allow teachers to determine each child's reading levels, strengths, and weaknesses, and to assess his progress as he moves through the program—the SMS or skills management system)

*Ditto masters (for reproducing worksheets that help the teacher not only reinforce reading-skill development and provide extra practice for those who need it, but also provide enrichment experiences in spelling, writing, and other language skills)

*Instructional aids such as charts, word cards, "Big Books" (large reproductions of readers at the lower levels), game boxes (designed for

---

*Many school districts do not have funds for these.

the teacher who doesn't make her own), and computer games and exercises

*Supplementary paperback library books

*Dictionaries

Some companies also sell cassettes and sound-filmstrips for children to use at classroom listening stations or for teachers to use with small and large groups. These cassettes and filmstrips are designed to reinforce earlier lessons and to provide enrichment experiences (such as listening to an author read her own book while the child reads along).

CRITERIA FOR GOOD BASAL READER PROGRAMS

To be competitive, publishers of basal programs must meet a number of standards that teachers and other educators demand. Before I discuss these standards with you, let me put them in the form of questions you can use in examining basal series:

A. Questions about the basal readers

1. Do the illustrations and content represent both sexes proportionately and without stereotyping?

2. Do the illustrations and content represent different groups that children can learn to appreciate (multicultural, elderly, gifted, handicapped)?

3. Are the selections interesting and well written?

4. Do the illustrations foster art appreciation through different techniques and styles?

5. Do the selections represent a large variety of "genre"? (See Figure 8.1 for a list of literature categories.)

B. Questions about the teacher's guides

1. Does it show ways to develop the ability to use all four cueing systems?

2. Does it show ways to encourage inferential, critical, and creative thinking?

3. Does it show how to use oral and silent reading experiences for a variety of instructional purposes?

4. Does it show how to teach reading in the context of all four language arts?

5. Does it provide ideas for working with gifted, handicapped, and English-deficient students?

Now let's examine each of the less obvious criteria from this list.

Representation of Both Sexes

Representing both sexes fairly and without stereotyping has been a serious challenge to publishers of modern basal series. In the past, the majority of books, both basal readers and library books for children, have been biased against women and girls (NEA, 1977). Several studies have shown how men and boys have been far more frequently given story roles calling for courage, honesty, intelligence, and creativity, while women and girls, both in illustrations and content, have more often been portrayed as timid, unimportant, or nonexistent (O'Donnel, 1974).

To give you just a notion of the extent of this bias, I have examined Walker's (1979) list of 1000 words that have occurred most frequently in both voluntary and assigned reading (including basal readers) in grades three through nine in the United States. By looking just at these high-frequency words, we can get a good idea of the degree to which our written language has been reinforcing the notion that males in our society are more important than females. The following words appeared in Walker's list of high-frequency words and were selected as objective indicators of sex bias: *girl* vs. *boy; man + men* vs. *woman + women + lady; he* vs. *she; her* vs. *his; father* vs. *mother; daughter* vs. *son; sister* vs. *brother.* Table 9.1 shows the results of the comparisons between "male words" and "female words."

Table 9.1 shows that the word *girl* was found only 45 percent as often as the word *boy* in Walker's list of high-frequency words. The combination of the words *woman, lady,* and *women* occurred only 22 percent as frequently as the combination of *man* and *men.* (The words *gentleman, gentlemen,* and *ladies* did not occur as high-frequency words in Walker's list.) Further examination of Table 9.1 reveals that "female words" occurred much less frequently than "male words" in every comparison except the one between *mother* and *father.* Even when the *mother—father* comparison is included, however, male words were used almost three times as often as female words.

It may be tempting to overlook the comparison between male and female pronouns, since it is often assumed that male pronouns can be "generic" and refer to both males and females. It may also be tempting to omit and words *man* and *men,* since they are also considered "generic" at times. However, studies show that such so-called generic words as *he, him,* and *man* are not truly generic. Many people, contrary to popular opinion, will

Table 9.1 *A Comparison of the Frequencies of Female Words and Male Words Found in Walker's List of 1000 High-Frequency Words Occurring in Both Voluntary and Assigned Reading in Grades Three through Nine in the United States.*

Female Words (F)	Male Words (M)	Female Percent of Male Words
girl 2,357 (occurrences)	*boy* 5,222 (occurrences)	45
woman + *lady* + *women* 2,296	*man* + *men* 10,645	22
she 14,111	*he* 47,665	30
her 11,444	*his* 29,387	39
mother 3,806	*father* 3,691	103
daughter (less than 534)	*son* 965	55
sister 612	*brother* 1,205	51
total 35,159	total 98,780	36
total without *mother* 31,353	total without *father* 95,089	33
total without *she* and *her* 10,604	total without *he* and *his* 21,728	49

not think of women and girls when confronted with such words; they think specifically of men and boys. Ernst (1977), for example, investigated masculine "generic" pronouns and nouns with 418 students ranging from preschool through college to determine whether masculine generic terms were interpreted as referring to females to the same extent as males. Results indicated that with both nouns and pronouns, the receiver of the language was more likely to interpret it as referring to males than to females. Harrison (1975) found that junior-high students visualized predominantly more males when presented with masculine generic terms such as *man, mankind*, and *he* than they did when presented with terms that were inclusionary, such as *humans, people*, and *they*. Kidd (1971) found similar results with college students when they were confronted with masculine generic pronouns.

It's likely that any aspect of society, including its language, that supports and maintains the negative stereotype of women as inferior to men is detrimental to society. It's detrimental toward the development of healthy self-concepts as girls mature into women. It's detrimental toward the development of positive relationships between the sexes. And it's thus detrimental toward the development of mentally healthy people in a mentally healthy community.

The direct referral to males more than females in basal readers and other children's books, and the use of so-called generic language that is not truly generic, are outdated customs that may someday be relegated to historical documents. Alternate use of *he* and *she* along with *her* and *him*, substitution of plural nouns followed by *they* for singular nouns followed by *he*, and a conscious attempt by authors to place females in the center of the stage as often as males—these are minor but important changes that are gradually being made in basal readers and other books. They need to be made, not just to satisfy the child in all of us who demands fairness, but to help achieve our need for people to grow up with healthy self-images, the ability to view the opposite sex without stereotyping, and a desire to relate with compassion toward all other human beings, regardless of gender.

An illustration of a story that portrays a girl as courageous, intelligent, and creative is the one by Esther Wood Brady in the Houghton Mifflin reader called *Gateways*. The story is entitled "My Name is Tolivar, Sir," and tells of Ellen Toliver, who is given the responsibility of carrying an urgent message to General Washington during the Revolutionary War. Using her wits and her "whistle-a-happy-tune" sense of bravery, she manages to get aboard a redcoats' boat, stand up to a bullying soldier, and accomplish her mission. As Figure 9.1 shows, she even manages to get a lift into the redcoats' boat—but only because the bullying soldier wants to get her bag of bread. Little does he realize that the message to Washington is buried in the bread.

Representation of Different Groups

Some stories found in older basal readers and other children's books can encourage the very thing that an education is supposed to discourage, namely, stereotyping. Rather than setting minds at liberty to think about individuals, some books and stories encourage the freezing of minds instead, causing children to view people of different cultures, races, or ages as homogeneous and inferior rather than as heterogeneous and equal. Let's look at some of the specific characteristics of books and stories that encourage stereotyping.

1. *Fake authenticity.* This characteristic often appears when authors attempt to make their characters and setting more believable (without doing sufficient homework). An interesting example can be found in an early edition of *Mary Poppins*. In the chapter called "Bad Tuesday," the author, Pamela Travers, tried to add authenticity by putting these words in the mouth of a black woman:

But these were British soldiers. How could she trust the enemy?

Before she could decide what to do, she felt a tug at her blue bundle. It was the man called Dow. "Smells like fresh bread there," he said. Quickly, Ellen snatched the bundle away. Then suddenly she felt herself grabbed around the waist by two big hands and whisked across the side of the boat. She was too surprised and frightened to make a sound.

The man with the red cheeks laughed as he set her down on the bench beside him. "No noise from you," he growled.

Figure 9.1 *A sample page from a basal reader selection. (From Esther Wood Brady, "My Name Is Tolivar, Sir," in Gateways, Boston: Houghton Mifflin, 1981, p. 177.)*

"Ah bin 'specting you a long time, Mary Poppins," she said, smiling. "You bring dem chillun dere into ma li'l house for a slice of watermelon right now. My, but dem's very white babies. You wan' use a li'l bit black boot polish on dem. Come 'long, now. You'se mighty welcome."

2. *Nonproportional representation.* This characteristic used to show up in stories about children in a large city. Whereas you would expect some of the characters to be black, some to be Asian-American, some white, some Puerto Rican, and so on, you would find only white characters or perhaps a token black shining shoes or a Chinese laundryworker.

3. *White paternalism.* A good example of this characteristic can be found in the 1923 Newbery Award winner, *The Voyages of Doctor Dolittle*, by Hugh Lofting. In Isabelle Suhl's review of this book for the Council on Interracial Books, she illustrates Lofting's white paternalism this way:

Doctor Dolittle . . . arrives on Spidermonkey Island off the coast of Brazil in search of the "Red Indian," Long Arrow, the world's greatest naturalist. On his first day on the Island, Doctor Dolittle rescues Long Arrow and a group of Indians entombed in a cave and brings fire to the heretofore fireless Indians of Popsipetel. This makes him so popular that he is constantly followed about by crowds of admirers. "After his fire-making feat, this childlike people expected him to be continually doing magic." He solves problem after problem for the Indians and eventually they ask the "Mighty One" to become "the King of the whole Spidermonkey Island." Dolittle, as the Great White Father, dutifully accepts his new role as king, but after a while he wants to go home. But, in the words of Dolittle, "these people have come to rely on me for a great number of things. We found them ignorant of much that white people enjoy. . . . I cannot close my eyes to what might happen if I should leave these people and run away. . . . They are, as it were, my children. . . . I've got to stay."

Such blatant white paternalism is difficult to find in children's stories today, but it's still there in more subtle form. In *Josie's Handful of Quietness*, for example, a white man attaches himself to a Chicano migrant family and causes their lives to change for the better. One can easily infer from this book that the Chicano family couldn't have improved their lives without the wisdom of this fatherly white man. Some stories with a central-city setting have a standard character—the Great White Father or Mother, in the garb of a kindly social worker, who somehow manages to keep the minority child out of trouble.

As an example of a basal reader story that is nonbiased toward specific groups, let's look briefly at the Houghton Mifflin story, "Are Your Arms a Hundred Years Old?" This story is part of a Newbery Medal Honor Book written by Sharon Bell Mathis and portrays a loving relationship between a young boy named Michael and his great-great Aunt Dew, who happens to be 100 years old. And she can "prove it," too, since she has a box with a hundred pennies in it, one for each year of her life. As Michael slowly counts each penny, she tells him an important event in her personal life and in the life of the country for each year since her birth. Although Aunt Dew speaks in her own "black dialect" and Michael speaks in his own "standard dialect," there are no communication barriers between them. Michael, more than anyone else in his family, understands Aunt Dew and her vital secret—that if you want to live to be one hundred, you first "have to have a hundred penny box. . . . Somebody special got to give it to you. . . . And soon as they give it to you, you got to be careful 'less it disappear."

As shown in Figure 9.2, Michael didn't want to take any chances on losing his good friend, Aunt Dew. From his way of thinking, the best way of keeping Aunt Dew around for a long time was to hide that penny box!

Selections That Are Interesting and Well Written

Most basal programs today include numerous selections by writers noted for their craftsmanship and creativity. Portions of the following books, for example, have been incorporated in the Houghton Mifflin readers; these books have been recognized by the Association for Library Service to Children for their "originality, excellence of literary style, respect for the personality of the reader, and acceptance by children":

> . . . and now Miguel by Joseph Krumgold
>
> And Then What Happened, Paul Revere? by Jean Fritz
>
> Annie and the Old One by Miska Miles
>
> Beyond the High Hills by Knud Rasmussen
>
> Dragonwings by Laurence Yep
>
> The Endless Steppe by Esther Hautzig
>
> Flashlight and Other Poems by Judith Thurman
>
> Flower Moon Snow by Kazue Mizumura
>
> Founding Mothers by Linda Grant DePauw
>
> The Foundling by Lloyd Alexander
>
> Frog and Toad Together by Arnold Lobel

He'd tell Aunt Dew right now that they had a good place to hide the hundred penny box. The best place of all.

Michael got down from the huge bed and walked quietly back down the hall to his door and knocked on it very lightly — too lightly for his mother to hear.

Aunt Dew didn't answer.

"Aunt Dew," he whispered after he'd opened the door and tiptoed up to the bed. "It's me. Michael."

Aunt Dew was crying.

Figure 9.2 *A sample page from a basal reader selection. (From Sharon Bell Mathis, "Are Your Arms a Hundred Years Old?" in Gateways, Boston: Houghton Mifflin, 1981, p. 336.)*

As another example, selections by the following well-known writers are among those chosen for the Economy Company's *Keys to Reading* basal-reading program:

Mary Austin	Frank Baum
Betty Baker	Nathaniel Benchley
Michael Berenstain	Lilian Moore
Harold Berson	Ogden Nash
Barbara Brenner	Mary Peacock
James Buechler	Miriam Clark Potter
Marchette Chute	Christina G. Rosetti
Crescent Dragonwagon	Allen Say
Benjamin Elkin	Miriam Schlein
Eleanor Farjeon	James E. Seidelman and
Rose Fyleman	Grace Mintonye
Wilson Gage	Marjorie Weinman Sharmat
Joan Hanson	Shel Silverstein
Homer	Liesel Moak Skorpen
Rachel Isadora	Robert Louis Stevenson
Bil Keane	Jane Thayer
Joe Lasker	J. R. R. Tolkien
Helen Louise Miller	Janice May Udry
A. A. Milne	

Figure 9.3 provides an example of the criterion of "interesting and well written." This illustration is from a story in the Economy Company reader, *A Hundred Circling Camps*. In this story, "The Treasure of Sumiko's Bay," the author, Barbara Chamberlain, portrays an exciting scene with imagery, naturalness of thought and language, and with insight into human nature.

Illustrations That Foster Art Appreciation

The illustrations in most basal series today often include some that many of us would call "works of art." Part of this is the result of more sophisticated printing techniques, which allow artists to use nearly any technique and medium. Part of it is the result of better selection of artists by publishers. Many series, for instance, include illustrations by winners of the Caldecott Medal. Furthermore, to provide novelty from one story to the next, most publishers of basal reading programs use hundreds of different illustrators, with their own particular styles and choices of media. Figures 9.4 and 9.5 are samples of the variety and quality of illustrations included in most basal series today.

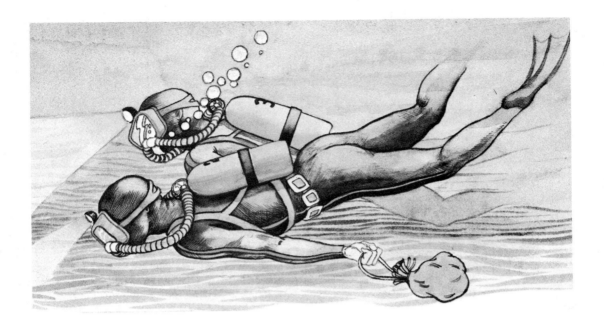

There was a chance to do something! She raced home to tell her plan to Grandmother.

After their plans were finished, Sumiko and her grandmother spent five nights on the beach, sleeping when they could. During the day Sumiko tried ways of slipping quietly through the water, not making a splash or sound. Knowing that she could swim better than anyone in the village lessened her fears of being caught when the robbers *did* come.

"I may have to give up tomorrow, Sumiko. My old bones like to sleep in our home," her grandmother said. "And now that the moon has left, we can't see very well."

Sumiko had been sleeping for only a short time when a sound from the bay woke her. She heard splashing from the direction of the oyster rafts. "Of course! They waited for a dark night!" She whispered to her grandmother to awaken the people of the village. Then Sumiko slipped silently into the water.

Figure 9.3 *A sample page from a basal reader selection. Adapted from "The Treasure of Sumiko's Bay" by Barbara Chamberlain, Jack and Jill magazine, copyright © 1975 by the Saturday Evening Post Company.*

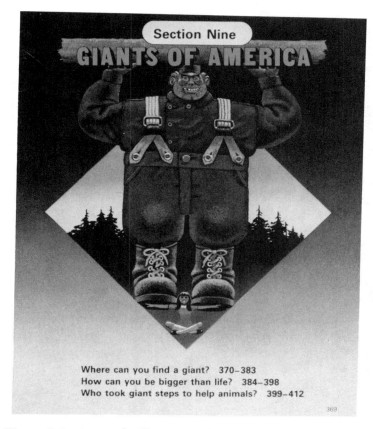

Figure 9.4 *A sample illustration from a basal reader. From*
Wonders and Winners, Focus, Reading for Success by Rich-
ard L. Allington et al., copyright 1985 by Scott, Foresman and
Company. Reprinted by permission of the publisher.

A BALANCE AMONG THE FOUR CUEING SYSTEMS.

There have been periods of time in the history of basal readers when some
of the cueing systems were considered more important than the others. Visual memory of sight words was glorified during the "look–say" era; words
were supposed to be learned as visual units, and graphophonic cues were
not given much significance. This was good for encouraging children to rely
more on syntactic, semantic, and schematic cues, but it caused children to
ignore graphophonic cues.

Figure 9.5 *A sample illustration from a basal reader. From
"The Elves and the Shoemakers," From* People and Places
HBJ Bookmark Reading Program, Eagle Edition, *by Margaret Early et al., copyright 1979 by Harcourt Brace Jovanovich, Inc. Reproduced by permission of the publisher.*

Phonics was king during another era (and still is with a few of the basal reader series). This approach provided children with a more effective way to confirm predictions, but it caused many teachers and pupils to concentrate on word-by-word instead of interactive reading. During one era, on the other hand, whole sentences rather than words or letters were considered the basic units of instruction. That kind of emphasis no doubt encouraged interactive reading among those who had discovered the graphophonic system on their own; on the other hand, it again gave students one less method for confirming their predictions and also encouraged them to "make up their own story" rather than communicate with the author.

Today several publishers are moving toward a better balance among the cueing systems, although they vary in their emphasis on meaning vs. decoding. We will use the Houghton-Mifflin Program as an example of a "meaning emphasis" type of program. In each teacher's guide of this series, the teacher will find context analysis emphasized somewhat more than graphophonic analysis, because of the authors' and editors' stated belief that, through an emphasis on context, "students are conditioned to expect and look for meaning as they read."

In Level A, for instance, children are first taught to anticipate words that will make sense in sentences the teacher reads to them (a type of oral "cloze" exercise). The teacher reads, for example, "Ivan poured a glass of _____ for the baby." The children select appropriate answers from pictures of a hook, water, milk, and comb. As children go through the Level A reader, they learn the skill of associating sounds with letters, but this is always tempered with the need to pay attention to context clues. As an example, the Teacher's Guide to *Getting Ready to Read* suggests that the letter *d* be decoded in the context of a meaningful sentence: "I helped Mom put the _____ into the dishwasher." The guide suggests that the teacher ask the children why they wouldn't choose the word *dentist* instead, thus making sure the children think about what word makes sense rather than what word starts with *d*.

ENCOURAGEMENT OF INFERENTIAL, CRITICAL, AND CREATIVE THINKING

Publishers were traditionally reluctant to put too many questions in the teacher's guides that asked for inferential or critical thinking—perhaps because so many teachers told them they were too hard for children, perhaps for other reasons. If you look at teacher's guides of the past, you will usually see that the questions were mainly of the "who did what" variety. Today the picture has changed for the better, with most guides encouraging higher-level thinking from the earliest grades on up.

In 1985 Scott, Foresman published a new basal reader series called *Focus*, designed for poor readers. It is interesting to note that, contrary to what many people would expect, this program does not assume that poor readers should have *less* time on higher-thinking skills than good readers. Instead, the *Focus* program seems to assume that although inferential, critical, and creative thinking are more difficult than literal thinking, they are vital processes in communicating with an author. For an example of how the *Focus* program emphasizes these thinking skills, you will want to study

Setting Purposes

Have pupils turn to page 150 in their books. Have pupils read the title. ("The Fire") Then have them look at the illustration. Ask:
• Kathy and Ruth are now near the neighborhood hall. Who has come to help? (firefighters)
• Do you think the firefighters got there soon enough to keep the hall from burning to the ground? (Answers will vary.)
• Let's read the story to find out if Kathy and Ruth's fast thinking and quick action saved the hall.
• Remember to use all of the story clues you are given both in the pictures and in the words to figure out the story.

Pupils who are capable of reading the selection independently should read silently to find out if Kathy and Ruth's fast thinking saved the hall. After they have finished reading, ask:
• Did Kathy and Ruth's fast thinking save the hall? (yes) What actions did they take that you should take in case of a fire? (They smelled smoke, saw smoke, and went for help to call in the alarm.)

For pupils who need more guidance, see the Guiding Reading suggestions below. Both groups of pupils should be asked *Checking Comprehension* questions at the end of *Guiding Reading*.

Guiding Reading

As you guide reading, have pupils read silently first. If you wish to have pupils read orally during the guided reading, you may ask them to read sentences to answer questions you ask. For other oral reading suggestions, see *Oral Reading*.

Pages 150–151

Have pupils read these pages to find out about the fire trucks and the firefighters. Tell pupils they will see some secret words. They will be able to figure out the word because they know the words to which the endings -er, -est have been added.

When they have finished reading, ask:
• Let's talk about the firetrucks. How many trucks came? (three)
• Which truck was the fastest? (the smallest truck)
• Who was in the smallest truck? (the Fire Chief)
• What did the firefighters from the smallest truck do? (hooked up a hose to spray water)
• What did most people think would happen to the hall? (It would burn to the ground.)
• Did the hall burn to the ground? (no) How do you know? (It says the fire did not last much longer.)

Oral Reading

Have pupils take turns rereading page 150 as though they were television reporters reporting the news. Emphasize using strong, clear voices.

The Fire

Kathy and Ruth met back near the hall. Soon they could hear sirens. Three fire trucks came, one large truck and two <u>smaller</u> ones. The Fire <u>Chief</u> was in the smallest truck. That truck was fastest. It seemed to fly by the stopped traffic with its siren going.

150   UNIT 13

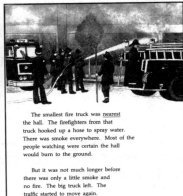

The smallest fire truck was <u>nearest</u> the hall. The firefighters from that truck hooked up a hose to spray water. There was smoke everywhere. Most of the people watching were certain the hall would burn to the ground.

But it was not much longer before there was only a little smoke and no fire. The big truck left. The traffic started to move again.

UNIT 13   151

235

Figure 9.6 (pp. 304–305) *Teacher's Guide pages from Scott, Foresman's Focus series. From Teacher's Edition, Focus, Whistles and Dreams, Reading for Success by Richard L. Allington et al., copyright 1985 by Scott, Foresman and Company. Reprinted by permission of the publisher.*

Figure 9.6, which shows you two pages from a teacher's guide to a second grade reader.

Notice under "Setting Purposes" how children are prepared to think *before* they read the story. Although the questions under "Guided Reading" are mostly at the literal (memory) level, the questions under "Checking Comprehension" involve mostly inferential (interpretive), critical (evaluative), and creative thinking.

Figure 9.7 shows the next page in the teacher's guide. Notice under "Checking Skill Growth" and under "Reviewing Skills" how two types of inferential thinking are encouraged. Under "Checking Skill Growth," chil-

Pages 152–153
Have pupils read these pages to find out where the Fire Chief went the next day and what he did.

When they have finished reading, ask:
• Where did the Fire Chief go the next day? (to Ruth and Kathy's school)
• What did the Fire Chief do? (He talked to the children in the school hall.)
• What did the Chief tell the children about what to do in a fire? (think fast, get out of the building, and go for help or go to a fire-alarm box)
• Why did Ruth and Kathy get a reward? (for their fast thinking)
• What was their reward? (They each got a firefighter's hat.)
• Which reward would you have liked best, a button, a T-shirt, or a firefighter's hat? (Answers will vary.)

Oral Reading
Have pupils pretend to be the Fire Chief talking to the children in the school hall and read the last paragraph on page 152 and the first two paragraphs on page 153. Remind children to watch for the quotation marks showing the beginning and end of exactly what the Chief is saying. Encourage them to speak loudly and clearly for the whole class to hear.

The Chief asked, "Who pushed the alarm button? This fire would have been awful if it had burned longer."

The policewoman said, "Chief, Ruth and Kathy each called in an alarm."

The Chief said, "It's sad that the neighborhood hall won't open today. However, thanks to Ruth and Kathy's fast thinking, it will open soon."

The next day the Chief went to Ruth and Kathy's school. All the children met in the big school hall.

The Chief said, "We would all have felt awful if the new hall had burned to the ground. Ruth and Kathy's fast thinking saved the hall. If you are ever in a building and you smell smoke, you should think fast and get out,

152 UNIT 13

even if you don't see the fire. Then you should call for help or go to a fire-alarm call box. But always think before you run."

The Chief said, "As a reward for their fast thinking, I am giving Ruth and Kathy firefighter hats."

Ruth and Kathy were surprised. Firefighter's hats were even better than T-shirts or buttons.

UNIT 13 153

Checking Comprehension
The bulleted questions reflect the major skill focuses of this Unit.

Questions and Answers
• 1. The story never really says that the hall didn't burn all the way to the ground. How do we know it didn't? (The firefighters put the fire out quickly. The neighborhood hall will open soon. If the hall had burned down, it couldn't open soon.) (draws conclusions; interpretive)
2. What was the most important thing Ruth and Kathy did? (They thought before they ran to get help.) (details; literal/evaluative)
• 3. How do we know the Fire Chief liked what Ruth and Kathy did? (He came to their school to give them a reward and tell other children to act the same way in an emergency.) (draws conclusions; interpretive)
4. What would you do if you smelled smoke and saw a fire? (Answers will vary but should include the safety steps given in the story.) (creative)
○ 5. [Write the words *smaller, longer, lower,* and *greater* on the board.] What ending is at the end of these words you know: *smaller, longer, lower, greater?* (-er)
○ 6. [Write the words *smallest, longest, fastest,* and *nearest* on the board.] What ending is at the end of these words you know: *smallest, longest, fastest, nearest?* (-est)

236

Figure 9.6 *(continued)*

Checking Skill Growth

Draws Conclusions

For pupils who will benefit from additional instruction, do the following:

Have pupils turn to page 151. Say:
• I know by the end of this page that the fire is over. Read the last paragraph for some clues that help me figure this out.
• When a fire is over, the smoke usually goes away. It says: . . . *there was only a little smoke* . . . This is my first clue.
• When a fire is over there are no flames. It says: . . . *and no fire*. This is another clue.
• When a fire is over, the fire truck usually goes back to the station. What clue tells me this? *(The big truck left.)*
• When a fire is over, it is usually safe for cars and trucks to go by again. Read the clue that tells me this. *(The traffic started to move again.)*
• All of these clues help me figure out that the fire is over.
• Remember that a story might not say exactly what is going on, but you can usually find many clues in the story to help you figure out what is happening.

For pupils who need further teaching, see *Reteaching Skills: Draws conclusions.*

Endings -er, -est

smaller (150), **nearest** (151)   These are secret words. If pupils read these words without difficulty, they are applying the word study skill of this Unit. For pupils who need additional practice, write the words *smaller* and *nearest* on the board. Say:
• This is a word you already know, but it has a new ending. [Frame the word *small*.] What is it? (small) **What is the word with the ending?** [Point to the word *smaller*.] (smaller)
• **What is the ending on the word** *smaller?* (-er)
• This is also a word you already know with a new ending. [Point to the word *nearest*.] **What is the word with the ending?** (nearest)
• **What is the ending on the word** *nearest?* (-est)

For pupils who need further teaching, see *Reteaching Skills: Endings: -er, -est.*

Reviewing Skills

Cause and Effect

Remind pupils that in any story things happen, and to understand the story, they need to know why things happen. Tell pupils that sometimes the words *because* and *so* help them find out what is happening and why.

Use Chart 71 or write the following on the board.

Chart 71

> 1. The firefighters went to the hall because the hall was on fire.
> 2. The firefighters hooked up a hose so they could spray water on the fire.

Have pupils read the first sentence. Ask:
• **What happened in this sentence?** (The firefighters went to the hall.) **Why?** (because the hall was on fire)
• The word *because* tells you the why part is coming up.
• Read sentence two and tell me what the firefighters could do. (spray water on the fire)
• The word *so* lets us know what happened.
• When something happens, it may cause something else to happen. Or something happens because something else has already been done. In these sentences, there was a fire so the firefighters came. By hooking up the hoses, the firefighters were able to spray the fire.

Looking Back

To provide children with a quick review of the Unit, say:
• This story was about an emergency and how people acted in an emergency. What was the emergency? (fire)
• What was important for Ruth and Kathy to remember before they did anything to help? (to think quickly)
• What will you remember to do if you are ever needed to help in an emergency? (to think quickly first, then act)

You may want to have children think about ways to prevent fires. Have them learn all they can about fire prevention by talking to adults, interviewing a firefighter, going to the library. Then have them report to the class on what they have learned. Allow pupils to use what they have learned to make fire safety and prevention posters.

Further Practice

Workbook, page 101 (Selection questions)
              page 102 (Cause and effect relationships)
              page 103 (Vocabulary)
Masters,   page 101 (Drawing conclusions)
              page 102 (Cause and effect relationships)
              page 103 (Vocabulary)

Assessment
Unit Test 13

UNIT 13

Figure 9.7 *Teacher's Guide page from Scott, Foresman's Focus series. From* **Teacher's Edition, Focus, Whistles and Dreams, Reading for Success** *by Richard L. Allington et al., copyright 1985 by Scott, Foresman and Company. Reprinted with permission of the publisher.*

dren are shown how to *read between the lines.* Under "Reviewing Skills," they're shown how to use word clues to determine the *cause and effects* the author had in mind.

ORAL AND SILENT READING EXPERIENCES

Many of today's basal reading series are designed to encourage teachers and children to put more emphasis on the communication aspects of reading. There is more emphasis, for example, on silent reading than on oral reading. This in itself communicates to the child that reading is a thinking, communicating process, rather than a mechanical, sounding-it-out process.

But even oral reading, in many of today's programs, is treated differently (Heinrich, 1976). No longer are teachers encouraged to stop a child every time he makes a reading error. Instead teachers are encouraged in most teacher's guides to use oral reading practice for various purposes. If children are to read to each other in an actor-audience situation, they are given time to practice what they will read; those who are not reading look at the "actor" rather than at their books. In this way reading becomes a communication process—one that can entertain and inform others. If children are to read orally so the teacher can check on their decoding and comprehension skills, the teacher will first have them read the story silently and then reread the story out loud, either as a play or as a challenge to them to prove the hypotheses and predictions they have made. In any case, the emphasis is on understanding or appreciating what the author says. (Only if the teacher were trying to test a child on decoding skills would she have him read out loud to her without first having him read a selection silently.)

Looking again at Figure 9.6, you can see two examples of imaginative "Oral Reading" that involve communication rather than word-by-word reading. Rather than read around a circle ("round-robin reading"), stumbling over their words and waiting impatiently or fearfully for their turn, children are asked first to read a story silently and then to read it orally for purposes of improving expression, comprehension, and thinking abilities.

READING IN THE CONTEXT OF LANGUAGE ARTS

Here we have a criterion that is often given lip service by basal reader publishers but seldom any real emphasis. The Economy Company has attempted to build language experience stories into one of its series, The Keytext Program. Other companies from time to time have made similar attempts. But in general, we're talking about something that's very hard to do with a basal reader series itself. Basal reader programs tend to be highly structured and do not lend themselves easily to spontaneous sessions of listening and speaking to each other or to writing about ideas that are timely or personal. The teacher generally has to impose such timeliness and personal expression onto the program. A story the children have read may, for example, inspire a lengthy discussion only if the teacher permits this change in her schedule. An informational article can inspire a trip to the library or the neighborhood for more information only if the teacher thinks such a spontaneous journey is called for. A poem can inspire a poem book by the children only if the teacher is willing to alter her plans for the day.

The nature of language experiences is that they are normally quite spontaneous, rather than structured by experts from afar (basal reader authors and editors). Whenever experts try to build in multiple language use, it comes out looking like leftover lettuce, limp and yellowed before its time. Trying to build in language experience stories, for instance, can sometimes lead to pretty deadly and uninspired writing or dictating if the topics have been preselected by authors and editors who live in some other place and some other moment in time.

Nevertheless, most basal reader programs do try to incorporate the other three language arts in their suggestions in the teacher's guides. At the end of each unit the teacher will usually find a section called "Enrichment Activities." These generally call for one of four kinds of experiences:

1) Relating what the children have read to another area of the curriculum, especially science or social studies

2) Discussions

3) Creative Writing

4) Independent Reading

For example, in "The Big Enormous Carrot," a story in Scott, Foresman's second grade reader, Victor grows a giant carrot that he plans to enter in a fair. Unfortunately, Mr. Jones's pet rabbit eats it, and Victor is sure his plans for a trophy are doomed. Mr. Jones offers to let Victor enter the rabbit instead, and of course, Victor gets his trophy. The enrichment section in the teacher's guide calls for several related activities to promote speaking, listening, and writing skills (see Figure 9.8).

COMMON LESSON PROCEDURES

Most basal reading lessons follow a fairly similar format:

1. A few new words are introduced before the children read a selection so that these words don't become stumbling blocks during their reading. (Please refer to pages 129–32 for ideas on making this part of the lesson successful.) I'm particularly concerned that you remember to examine some of the words together with the children by looking at the actual sentence and paragraph in which each word occurs. This will give them the kind of practice they need in interactive reading.

Enrich

Plants and seeds   If possible, obtain a seed catalog for pupils to look at. Help them examine the types
of seeds and what the various plants will look like when
they are grown. Point out that a single fruit, vegetable,
or flower may come in many different varieties. To
illustrate this, you may want to bring in several varieties
of the same fruit or vegetable such as apples, onions,
pears, or lettuce.

Creative writing   Invite pupils to pretend that each
one of the following animals is their pet. What would
they name each pet? Why?

a white rabbit	a canary or parakeet
a black horse	a cat
a large dog	a very small dog

Have each pupil choose one of the above pets and
write a poem or story about it.

Independent reading   You may wish to read to pupils
The April Rabbits by David Cleveland (Coward, 1978);
Pieter Brueghel's the Fair by Ruth Craft (Lippincott,
1975)—childlike verses accompany reproductions of
Brueghel's painting; and *Babar's Fair* by Laurent de
Brunhof (Random House, 1956).

Figure 9.8   *An Enrichment Section from a Teacher's Guide*

2. After new words are introduced, the teacher "motivates" the children
   to read one or more pages silently. It's very important, though, that
   you remember what we talked about earlier: children need to be prepared for a selection not only through vocabulary development but
   also through schemata development.

3. After the children have read a page or two silently, the teacher checks
   and *develops* their comprehension for those pages. As I mentioned,
   however, you'll want to do more than merely test the children by
   reading questions from a teacher's guide. You'll also want to sometimes *model* good comprehension by showing them how you, the
   teacher, would use all four cueing systems to understand what they
   just read. You'll also want to have them try what you've modeled
   when they read the next page or two.

4. The sequence of motivation, reading, and comprehension teaching then continues until the whole selection has been read.

5. Oral reading sometimes follows and sometimes coincides with the silent reading. For example, when the teacher wishes to use the D-T-R-A approach and have children "prove their point," she will have them read small portions orally as they go through the selection. If, on the other hand, she wishes to use the selection to develop greater expressiveness, or to have them change the selection into a read-aloud play, or to have them simply read to each other for enjoyment of a favorite story, the oral reading will follow the silent reading—either on the same day or the next time the group meets. (See Chapter 14 for more ideas on when to use silent vs. oral reading.)

6. A skill lesson is often taught on a different day. This lesson is one described in a teacher's guide and usually emphasizes a particular decoding or comprehension subskill, such as "reading the *ap* phonogram" or "recognizing details that support main ideas." The skill lesson is often followed by the explanation of a workbook assignment.

7. Review lessons or enrichment experiences, described in the teacher's guide, usually occur on a different day. It is unfortunate that some teachers feel too rushed to allow time for these types of experiences—especially the enrichment type. (See Chapter 14 for ways to manage time for them.)

ORGANIZATIONAL PLANS FOR USING A BASAL READING PROGRAM

Teachers and administrators have developed numerous ways to allow for the variations among children, teachers, space, time, and materials, when using basal readers as the basic medium of reading instruction. It would be difficult to recommend one of these ways over any of the others, since their utility depends so much on the particular conditions of learning in a particular school. Let me simply describe them for you so that you can contribute toward making an intelligent choice of plans in whatever school situation you find yourself.

The Self-Contained Plan

With the self-contained plan, each teacher divides her group of approximately thirty children into two to four (and most often three) reading-instruction groups. This comes after administering informal reading tests or looking at other information about each child's general reading ability. In a self-contained classroom, the same teacher teaches all the groups, which usually represent the "above-average," the "average," and the "below-average" students in the class. The reading groups meet with the teacher at different times of the day or week. While one group meets with the teacher, the other groups work on workbook assignments, reading enrichment activities (such as library book reading), or even complete work in another subject such as mathematics.

The main advantage of this approach is that one teacher can usually obtain a good understanding, during the entire year, of each child's reading strengths and weaknesses—particularly since she instructs him in most of the other subjects as well. The main disadvantage is that children may be placed in a reading group that is too far above or below their abilities simply to make it more possible for a teacher to manage an instructional program for everyone. For instance, if the general reading range in the class is all the way from Level F to L, and the teacher feels he can only handle three groups, the children in Level L may have to work in materials below their abilities and the children at Level F may have to work in materials above their abilities.

The Joplin Plan

The "Joplin Plan" is sometimes referred to as the "Cross-Grades Plan." Instead of one teacher's trying to handle three groups of children who are at very different levels, the teachers in a school building all teach reading at the exact same time; each works (during that time only) with children who are reading at about the same level. At nine o'clock, say, a bell rings and all the children go to their reading teacher. For a few children this may mean staying in their homeroom, but for most children, it will mean going to another teacher for forty-five minutes or more. Mrs. Jones may teach only Levels A and B; Miss Franklin may teach only Levels C and D; Mrs. Char may teach only Level E (since so many children are reading at that level); Mr. Webster may teach Level F, G, and H (because there are so few children reading at those levels), and so on, down the halls of the school building. There are many versions of the Joplin plan, but this gives you a rough idea of how it works.

The main advantage of the Joplin Plan is that it drastically reduces reading abilities a single teacher has to face. The main disadvantage is the potential lack of transfer from reading instruction to actual reading of library books, social studies texts, and other texts in other subjects. Johnny's reading teacher seldom has the opportunity to see to it that he practices, in actual reading situations, the skills she has taught him. Johnny's homeroom teacher, unless she communicates extremely well with his reading teacher, is often not fully aware of Johnny's reading strengths and weaknesses during the time she has him read materials related to other subjects.

The Track Plan

The "track plan" can be used alongside either the Joplin plan or the self-contained plan. With this approach, the school district makes available to the teacher not just one basal series, but two or three (or in some cases an "advanced form" and an "easy form" of the same series). This approach increases the flexibility of grouping children. Let's take the extreme situation, for example, in which the teacher wishes to move a child back one or two levels from the one he was in at another school in another city that used the same basal series. In other words, she feels he has been pushed too fast and needs to gain skills he's missed along the way. Rather than have the child read exactly the same reader he has already read in the other city, she'll put him, along with a few other children, in another series that he hasn't seen before. As you can well imagine, there are numerous variations of the track system, depending upon the needs of the teachers and children.

The main advantage of the track system, as already mentioned, is the flexibility of grouping that such a system provides. The main disadvantage is that the teacher now has to become familiar with two or three series rather than one. This can be quite a burden, particularly to the beginning teacher; but wherever a particular school population is highly mobile, it may be one of the most reasonable solutions.

The Staggered-Day Plan

Instead of the usual three groups found in most self-contained classrooms, the staggered-day plan divides pupils into four groups of about six to nine pupils each. Two of these four groups come to school one hour earlier than the other two groups. These twelve to eighteen "early birds" receive instruction in reading until the "late birds" arrive. In the afternoon the early birds leave school one hour before the late birds do. The late birds, who are also divided into two groups, stay behind to receive their reading instruction.

The main advantage of the staggered-day plan is that the teacher has more time to give individual attention to children in a subject that is so vital. The main disadvantage is that this plan works well only in schools to which children walk rather than take a school bus. In "consolidated" schools that ship children in from all over the city, the extra cost of transportation the staggered-day plan requires can be prohibitive.

There are numerous other plans for organizing reading instruction, such as the variety of plans created through team-teaching situations. However, all of them attempt to provide greater individualization of instruction—some through more homogeneous grouping, some by providing greater choice of basal readers, and some by working with fewer children at one time.

USING A SKILLS MANAGEMENT SYSTEM WITH A BASAL PROGRAM

All basal reader publishers will provide teachers (at the school district's expense) with tests and recordkeeping devices to accompany the teacher's guide. This set of materials is often referred to as a skills management system, or SMS. Most skills management systems have these components:

Placement tests for determining what book to provide each child for instructional purposes

A checklist for recording each child's test performances

A very brief test for each "subskill" taught in the program

Longer tests to check on retention of subskills

The placement tests are sometimes in the form of an individual informal reading inventory containing selections similar to those in the basal readers. These selections are read orally until the teacher notices that a child is frustrated and stops the testing. (This procedure will be discussed more fully in Chapter 10.) The placement tests are sometimes in the form of a group test, similar to the multiple-choice tests university students know so well. The content of the group test is usually vocabulary and certain reading subskills considered important by the program's authors.

After children are placed, teaching the basal reader units can begin. A unit usually consists of one or two lessons involving silent and oral reading of a selection in the reader, one or two skill lessons, and one or two opportunities for review or enrichment. (Unfortunately the *poor* readers get the review and the good readers get the enrichment, even though the poor readers need motivation and real-reading practice the most.) At the completion of the unit many teachers give a short test consisting of five to twenty items related to one or more subskills. Children who don't score high enough on this test usually receive extra instruction.

After several units are completed, a retention test is often administered and further instruction provided for those who seem to need it. After scoring the retention test, the teacher usually records the scores on each child's checklist (see Figure 9.9). Some basal programs are designed for easy access to computers that will not only score the various tests but also print out a prescription for review lessons or practice worksheets.

LIMITATIONS OF BASAL PROGRAMS

Basal reader programs have two kinds of defects—one that is inherent in the very idea of a basal reader, and the other in the way basal readers are

B: BEARS	FORM CSA	FORM B	TBRS CS
Date			
Word Recognition			12
1. Digraph *th* D1·7b	4		4
2. Following Directions CA1·1	4		4
* 3. Comma of Address C4·2a			
4. End Sounds *l, t* D1·7c	4		4
5. End Sounds *n, p* D1·7c	4		4
6. Letter Sounds & Context D1·7	3		4
7. Digraph *sh* D1·7b	4		4
8. Word Referents C3·1a	3		4
* 9. Exclamation Mark C4·1c			
10. Cluster *fr* D1·7d	3		4
11. Drawing Conclusions CA5·2	3		4
* 12. Clusters *lp, mp* D1·7e			
* 13. Intonation			
14. Predicting Outcomes CA6·2	2		4
15. Cluster *st* D1·7d, e	3		4
16. Noting Details CA2·1	2		4
17. Categorizing CA10·2	3		4
18. End Sounds *m, d, g* D1·7c	4		4

C: BALLOONS	FORM CSA	FORM B	TBRS CS
Date			
Word Recognition			12
1. Noting Correct Sequence CA3·3	2		4
* 2. Contractions with *'s* D1·7f			
* 3. Sound Association for *x* D1·7c			
4. Plurals D1·7h	4		4
* 5. Verbs Ending with *s* D1·7g			
6. Clusters *sw, fl* D1·7d	2		4
7. Letter Sounds & Context D1·7	3		4
8. Cause-Effect Relationships CA7·2	2		4
9. Word Referents C3·1a	3		4
10. Main Idea CA4·2	2		4
11. Digraph *ch* D1·7b	4		4

D: BOATS	FORM CSA	FORM B	TBRS CS
Date			
Word Recognition			12
1. Following Directions CA1·1	3		4
* 2. End Sounds *nt, nk* D1·7e			
* 3. Ending *ing* D1·7g			
4. Digraphs *th, sh, ch* D1·7b	4		4
5. Predicting Outcomes CA6·2	2		4
6. Sound Associations *c/s/* D1·7n	3		4
* 7. Ending *ed* D1·7g			
8. Noting Important Details CA2·1	3		4
9. Clusters *fl, sw, fr, pl* D1·7d	2		4
10. Multi-meaning Words C1·1c	2		4
11. Categorizing CA10·2	2		4
* 12. Reviewing Endings *s, ed, ing* D1·7g			
13. Word Referents C3·1a	3		4
14. Drawing Conclusions CA5·2	3		4

E: SUNSHINE	FORM CSA	FORM B	TBRS CS
Magazine 1 **Date**			
Recognizing High-Frequency Words			12
1. Cause-Effect Relationships CA7·1, 2	2		4
2. Short *a* Sound D1·7l	4		4
3. Long *a* Sound D1·7l	4		4
* 4. Quotation Marks, Comma CA4·8a			
5. Correct Sequence CA3·3	2		4
6. Doubling Consonants Before Endings D1·7j	4		4
7. Sound Associations for *y* D1·7l	2		4
8. Dropping Final *e* Before Endings D1·7j	4		4
Magazine 2 **Date**			
Recognizing High-Frequency Words			12
* 9. Contractions with *'s, n't, 'll* D1·7f			
10. Sound Associations for *oo* D1·7m	2		4
11. Compound Words D1·7o	2		4
12. Ending *er* D1·7g	2		4
13. Predicting Outcomes CA6·2	2		4
14. Short *e* Sound D1·7l	3		4
15. Long *e* Sound D1·7l	3		4
* 16. Intonation			
17. Sound Associations for *ai, ay* D1·7m	3		4
18. Drawing Conclusions CA5·2	2		4
Magazine 3 **Date**			
Recognizing High-Frequency Words			12
19. Short *i* Sound D1·7l	3		4
20. Long *i* Sound D1·7l	3		4
* 21. Sound Association for *kn/n* D1·7b			4
22. Multi-meaning Words C1·1c	3		4
23. Main Idea CA4·2	2		4
24. Short and Long *a, e,* and *i* D1·7l	4		4

KEY

1. Digraph *th*   D1·7b

Skill Description ← (Digraph *th*)   Skill Reference Number ← (D1·7b)

Basic Reading Skill Lesson

Figure 9.9 *Sample progress checklist. (From Cumulative Individual Reading Record Folder, Boston: Houghton Mifflin, 1981, p. 2.)*

sometimes used (or abused). The inherent weakness in basal readers is the idea that children can be best motivated and instructed through a highly systematic, adult-structured set of procedures and materials. There seems to be little doubt among educators that a basal approach can motivate and instruct moderately well, but many of us have nagging doubts about its being the best approach for all children. These doubts are often expressed in the form of questions.

Aren't many human beings motivated by the opportunities for making choices? If so, how many choices are we really giving children when we use a basal program? If they had more choices, wouldn't they want to read more—and isn't that what we desire more than anything else?

Is there really a definite sequence that children should follow in learning reading skills? The research so far (Bond & Dykstra, 1967; Britten, 1975) seems to tell us that there is no magic sequence. Programs such as "language experience" and "library-book-individualized," which have no definite sequence, seem to allow children to achieve as well as basal reading programs do.

In controlling vocabulary, skill sequence, and content so tightly, are we sometimes damaging the very essence of reading—the desire between two individuals, reader and author, to communicate? If the next thing the reader will communicate about with an author is determined by what comes next in the reader, does that type of conditioning result in students who truly *want* to read? (It gives one pause.)

The other defect in basal programs is their abuse by the teachers who rely on them. Abuse is not the fault of a program, of course, but it can often lead to a limited degree of success, both for teacher and students. Here are two ways in which teachers may sometimes find themselves abusing a basal program:

1. By placing a child in a reader that is far too difficult or easy for him. (In defense of the teacher, this usually happens because most teachers find it difficult to handle more than three groups. And thus the dilemma: we can't drive teachers out of their minds in order to place every child in the right reader; yet if we don't place every child in the right reader, we may end up discouraging a large number of children.)

2. By assuming that basal readers teach, when in reality, the teachers have to do most of the teaching (and the children have to do all of the learning). In order to cover so many pages a day, many teachers skip a good portion of the skill-building exercises and reviews, as well as the enrichment experiences and the library-book reading that are so important for application and motivation. When "coverage" rather

than "mastery" becomes the goal, the basal reading program becomes both the horse and driver rather than the cart.

COMBINING A BASAL PROGRAM WITH LIBRARY BOOKS AND LANGUAGE EXPERIENCES

As I warned you at the beginning of Chapter 8, I'm now pushing you as hard as I can toward combining the three main approaches we've discussed toward teaching reading: language experience, trade book individualized reading, and basal reader. By taking the best of each of these approaches, I think you'll find that you and your students will experience more satisfaction, more success, less boredom, and less anxiety than you might experience using only one of the approaches.

As I've mentioned, the basal reader program provides security for you, your principal, the parents, and often the children. It provides you with lessons and practice materials that you can adapt to your students. It provides you with reading selections that can be used by several children at once—when you wish to guide them in the use of the four cueing systems and in the practice of inferential, critical, and creative thinking. As long as you realize that nothing horrible will happen to your students when you omit selections from the readers and lessons from the guides, you will be able to comfortably use an LEA and a TBIR approach along with your basal reader program.

Of course, this is the crux of the matter. Some teachers (and principals) are fearful of leaving unturned one page in the basal program. What a shame, for they have bought into the belief that basal readers and teachers' guides have been handed down from on high. That they are infallible. That they are "scientific." That when Michael misses one story, one worksheet, one lesson, he must make it up or "he'll get way behind." (On the contrary, Michael may have gotten ahead by lying in his sickbed reading a good book!)

But there's no point in my pushing this point any further, as I believe we're talking about a personality consideration here. Some teachers have an adventurous personality that allows them to try out new ways and not be anxious about skipping basal lessons now and then. "The boys and girls will get a review lesson on it, anyway," they'll say. Some teachers, on the other hand, who are just as good at teaching as the adventurous ones, shy away from adventurous approaches. Those of us who are between adventurous and timid have to find our own "happy medium."

So, basal reader programs offer security and handy materials. But a language experience approach offers children something a basal reader program can't—the opportunity to learn to read naturally through their own language. An LEA also offers them the opportunity to learn how to write at the same time. Research shows, by the way, that language experience approaches produce better spellers (Bond & Dykstra, 1967; Dykstra, 1968).

The trade book approach offers ample opportunities for children to practice *interactive reading* instead of mere worksheet completion. It also provides the perfect chance for teachers to get to know each child better through individual conferences and to inspire them in a more personal way.

In March of 1984 James Baumann published an article in *The Reading Teacher* that I think you ought to read. It's entitled "How to Expand a Basal Reader Program," and it tells you one way to combine the three major approaches. I'm so convinced you should read it, I've arranged to reprint it for you, so you won't have to track it down in the library. Besides, I have the ulterior motive of encouraging you to read *The Reading Teacher* and to become aware of the publications offered to you by the International Reading Association. So here is Baumann's article. I hope it will persuade you to try combining all three approaches.

HOW TO EXPAND A BASAL READER PROGRAM*

Consider the following scenario:

Ms. Murphy teaches a third grade class of 25 students. The school district has adopted a basal reader series that she is required to use. She has organized her class in three reading groups, the least capable, average, and most capable readers. Ms. Murphy writes separate daily lesson plans for each reading group and places this schedule on the chalkboard (Figure 1). She has introduced a reading kit and some games, but all her lessons center around the basal reader—the heart of each lesson consists of reading and discussing a basal story or participating in a related skill development activity.

Although the specifics may vary, the structure of Ms. Murphy's reading class is typical of countless elementary classrooms. The teacher introduces the basal reader story; students engage in a directed reading activity; stories are discussed and comprehension is assessed; and skill instruction and reinforcement exercises follow.

These procedures represent a sensible use of basal readers that requires careful planning and skillful instruction. But with time the pattern becomes repetitive and tedium sets in. The efficiency of instruction diminishes.

A classroom teacher can liven up a basal reader program. Suggestions of three types will be discussed here: (1) Involve additional persons; (2) add elements of language experience and individualized reading; (3) involve students in a wide variety of language arts activities. Inspect Figure 2 while reading the following sections, because the sample class schedules demonstrate how Ms. Murphy has incorporated these elements in her basal program.

READING HELPERS

One or more room parents, properly trained, can direct students in games or reading kits, accompany them to the school library and assist in book selection, conduct informal reading invento-

*James F. Baumann, in The Reading Teacher, *March, 1984. Reprinted with permission of James F. Baumann and the International Reading Association.*

Figure 1 Daily schedule for Ms. Murphy's third grade reading class

Panthers [*Slower readers*]	Tigers [*Average readers*]	Lions [*Better readers*]
Meet: Introduce "Mark and the Dinosaur."	Reread "The Friendly Fox" silently.	Do one story from the reading kits.
Finish reading silently then answer comprehension questions.	Meet: Discuss "The Friendly Fox." Skill review: Short vowels.	Finish book reports.
Work on sight word flash cards with your partner.	Complete short vowel work paper.	Meet: Discuss "Harriet Tubman" story from yesterday.

ries, or guide students in plays or special projects. The classroom teacher is freed to work more intensively with groups or individuals giving special instruction, either corrective or for gifted readers who need more challenge.

A peer tutoring program also helps expand a basal reader program. Students from higher grades can assist the classroom teacher. For example, peer tutors from fifth or sixth grade could drill primary students on basic sight vocabulary or listen to them read orally. Students from a teacher's own class can tutor younger students. This experience, though primarily for the tutee, can also be motivating for the tutor, especially if the student is not a skillful reader: Success in being the teacher can stimulate confidence and self-concept.

Another option is to involve secondary students. Many high schools have co-op programs in which students participate in community activities. For example, students from early childhood classes in high schools may want to tutor in elementary classrooms. They tend to be enthusiastic, reliable, and competent.

It must be remembered, however, that the responsibility for training all tutors lies with the classroom teacher. Success depends upon appropriate training in specific tasks. Training may be time consuming, but the benefits are potentially great, for the added help is essential in making other modifications of the basal program, as described below.

LEA AND INDIVIDUALIZED READING

Reading educators frequently profess the benefits of a language experience approach (LEA) or individualized reading program

Figure 2   Three examples of daily schedules for Ms. Murphy's expanded basal program

Panthers [Slower readers]	Tigers [Average readers]	Lions [Better readers]
Example 1		
Meet: Discuss "Alligator Story." Review sequence.	Silent reading of book you chose.	Go to the library with Ms. Smith to select a book.
Work with sixth grade tutors on oral reading and flash cards.	Meet: Rehearse "Mary the Marvelous Magician" play.	Silent reading. Tutors go and work with first graders.
Whole class vocabulary development activity: Homophones		
Example 2		
Write stories about yesterday's nature walk. Ms. Smith will help.	Work in classroom library kit.	Meet: Skill work: Distinguishing between fact and opinion.
Tape record your stories.	Meet: Plan next edition of the class newspaper.	Do workbook page 25. Silent reading of choice.
Meet with me individually: Read your story.	Work with editors on the paper.	
Whole class listening activity: Making mental pictures		
Example 3		
Whole class presents oral reports on nonfiction books		
Meet: Learn how to become kindergarten tutors.	Work with Ms. Smith constructing puppets for Wednesday's puppet play.	Go to library to work on "Famous Black Americans" reports.
Whole class watches TV program: "The Bird Book"		

but fail to appreciate the problems involved in managing these methodologies when implemented in their entirety. A compromise is to retain the basal reader as the core of the reading program, but incorporate elements of language experience and individualized reading.

Struggling readers may profit from a limited but regular exposure to LEA reading and writing. Two or three times a week, the teacher may require this group to write experience stories and add new vocabulary words to their word banks.

Other groups of students may benefit from self-selection and individualized reading activities. For example, a group of capable readers may set aside the basal for a week or two, read children's books of their choice, and participate in student-teacher conferences and book-sharing activities. This gives them a break from daily basal instruction and exposes them to good children's literature.

LANGUAGE ART ACTIVITIES

A third way to expand a basal reading program is to involve students in varied language arts activities in the reading class. Good examples are creative writing and creative dramatics, large and small group listening and vocabulary development activities, and literary programs on educational TV and radio.

The groupings for these language arts activities can be different from the usual basal groupings, since they allow mixing students of varying reading ability. The advantage is that students have opportunity to learn from peers who are not in their regular basal groups.

One activity that promotes reading is a class or school-wide Author's Day on which all children come dressed as their favorite storybook character. Author's Day can involve parades of characters, contests for best costume, and book talks by the characters. (What could be more stimulating than a prepared oral reading from *The Cat in the Hat* by the Cat himself?)

Most of all, students need time to practice reading, for pitifully little time in reading class is devoted to actual reading. Teachers must realize that it is perfectly legitimate—and necessary—to have children sit and read books of their own choosing. A daily silent reading period is an appropriate component of any reading program.

Infusing LEA and individualized reading activities into a basal program is beneficial in several ways. Students have a change of pace; these activities promote positive attitudes toward reading; and the teacher has unique ways to teach vocabulary and comprehension skills. But because these activities are incorporated into a basal program, a teacher can remain confident that basic skills development is being adequately addressed. Note, however, that adding these elements is possible only with the help of room parents and peer tutors, who free the teacher to initiate and direct the new approaches.

CONCLUSIONS

As the daily class schedules (Figure 2) show, Ms. Murphy now has parent and student helpers and students are engaged in language experience, individualized reading, and other language arts activities. The basal reader remains the foundation, but students are now exposed to other activities designed to develop specific skills and to deepen interest and appreciation of reading.

It would not be prudent to attempt to incorporate all these features into a basal program at once. Instead, introduce them one at a time, over the course of a semester or school year. By expanding and augmenting a standard basal program, a teacher can liven up reading instruction and make the tasks of teaching and learning more enjoyable and effective for all.

THE MAIN IDEAS IN THIS CHAPTER

Basal reader programs (series) include books of stories, poems, plays, and informative articles. They also include teacher's guides containing skill lessons, lesson plans, and other suggestions related to basal reader selections. Publishers of the series also offer a wide variety of supplementary materials.

Basal reader programs are the most popular of the three main approaches to reading instruction, the other two being LEA (Chapter 7) and TBIR (Chapter 8). Their popularity seems to stem from the security they offer teachers, administrators, and parents rather than from their scientific validity or superiority over other approaches.

High-quality basal readers contain illustrations and content that represent different groups and sexes without stereotyping them. The text is interesting and well written, the illustrations encourage an appreciation of artistic styles and media, and the selections represent a large variety of genre.

High-quality teacher's guides show the teacher how to have children use all four cueing systems and to think at inferential, critical, and creative levels. They also show how to use both oral and silent reading experiences for a variety of instructional purposes, how to teach reading in the context of the four language arts, and how to work with gifted, handicapped, and English-deficient students.

REFERENCES AND SUGGESTED READING

Aukerman, R. C. (1981). *The basal reader approach to reading.* New York: John Wiley & Sons.

Aukerman, R. C. (1984). *Approaches to beginning reading.* New York: John Wiley & Sons.

Barnard, D. P., & DeGracie, J. (1976). Vocabulary analysis of new primary reading series. *Reading Teacher, 30,* 177–180.

Baumann, J. F. (1984). How to expand a basal reader program. *Reading Teacher, 37,* 604–607.

Baxter, K. B. (1974). Combatting the influence of black stereotypes in children's books. *Reading Teacher, 27,* 540–544.

Bond, G. L., & Dykstra, R. (1967). The cooperative research program in first grade reading instruction. *Reading Research*

Quarterly, 2, 5–142.

Britten, G. E. (1975). Danger: State adopted texts may be hazardous to our future. *Reading Teacher, 29,* 52–58.

Britton, G., Lumpkin, M., & Britton, E. (1984). The battle to imprint citizens for the 21st century. *Reading Teacher, 37,* 724–733.

Durkin, D. (1978–79). Reading comprehension instruction. *Reading Research Quarterly, 14,* 495–527.

Dykstra, R. (1968). Summary of the second-grade phase of the cooperative research program in primary reading instruction. *Reading Research Quarterly, 1,* 49–70.

Engel, R. E. (1981). Is unequal treatment of females diminishing in children's picture books? *Reading Teacher, 34,* 647–652.

Ernst, S. B. (1977). *An investigation of students' interpretations of inclusionary and exclusionary gender generic language.* Unpublished doctoral dissertation, Washington State University, Pullman, Washington.

Frasher, R., & Walker, A. (1972). Sex roles in early reading textbooks. *Reading Teacher, 25,* 741–749.

Graebner, D. B. (1972). A decade of sexism in readers. *Reading Teacher, 26,* 52–58.

Harrison, L. (1975). Crow-magnon woman—in eclipse. *Science Teacher, 42,* 8–11.

Heinrich, J. S. (1976). Elementary oral reading: Methods and materials. *Reading Teacher, 30,* 10–15.

Kidd, V. (1971). A study of the images produced through the use of the male pronoun as the generic. *Moments in Contemporary Rhetoric and Communication, 1,* 25–29.

Litcher, J. H., & Johnson, D. W. (1969). Changes in attitudes towards negroes of white elementary students after use of multi-ethnic readers. *Journal of Educational Psychology, 60,* 148–152.

Meisel, S., & Glass, G. G. (1970). Voluntary reading interests and the interest content of basal readers. *Reading Teacher, 23,* 655–659.

Miller, H. B., & Hering, S. (1974). Teacher's ratings—Which reading group is number one? *Reading Teacher, 28,* 389–391.

National Council for Teachers of English. (1977). *Classroom practices in teaching English, 1976–1977: Responses to sexism.* Urbana, IL.

National Educational Association. (1977). *Sex role stereotyping in the schools.* Washington, DC.

O'Donnel, H. (1974). Cultural bias: A many headed monster. *Elementary English, 51,* 81–109.

Parker, L. D., & Campbell, E. K. (1971). A look at illustrations in multiracial first grade readers. *Elementary English, 48,* 67–74.

Rose, C., et al. (1972). Content counts: Children have preferences in reading textbook stories. *Elementary English, 49,* 14–19.

Rowell, E. H. (1976). Do elementary students read better orally or silently? *Reading Teacher, 29,* 367–370.

Rubin, R. A. (1975). A reading ability and assigned materials: Accommodation for the slow but not the accelerated. *Elementary School Journal, 75,* 373–377.

Schreiner, R., & Tanner, L. R. (1976). What history says about teaching reading. *Reading Teacher, 29,* 468–473.

Shake, M. C., & Allington, R. L. (1985). Where do teacher's questions come from? *Reading Teacher, 38,* 432–438.

Shannon, P. (1982). Some subjective reasons for teachers' reliance on commercial reading materials. *Reading Teacher, 35,* 884–889.

Stauffer, R. G. (1971). Slave, puppet or teacher? *Reading Teacher, 25,* 24–29.

Walker, C. M. (1979). High frequency word list for grades 3–9. *Reading Teacher, 32,* 803–812.

APPLICATION EXPERIENCES FOR THE TEACHER EDUCATION CLASS

A. *What's your opinion?* Use your own experiences as well as ideas in the textbook to justify your opinions.

1. The Joplin plan is better than the self-contained plan in allowing for individual differences and encouraging interactive reading.

2. With a basal reader program, teachers should feel secure in knowing that each child will be able to read at his level of ability.

3. The most important criterion for a good basal reading program is: "The teacher's guide shows ways of developing the ability to use all four cueing systems."

4. By using language experience approaches and portions of the TBIR approach, the teacher who uses a basal reader program can provide children with a better chance of perceiving reading as an enjoyable communication process.

5. Since there are 16 basal reader programs and 165 other programs that have proved "successful" (with some teachers), teaching kids to read must not be that difficult.

6. To compensate for the past, women and girls should be featured in basal readers more often than men and boys.

B. *Miscue Analysis:* Patrick, a second grader, reads a first-grade selection in the following way:

Mary has a dog. His name is Rex. He is little. He is brown. . . . He runs fast. Mary follows him . . . He shakes hands . . . He gets wet . . . He shakes himself. Then he is dry.*

Tell why you would or wouldn't place Patrick in a second-grade basal reader for instruction. What do you think is Patrick's concept of reading? Would language experience approaches or patterned books help Patrick in any way?

---

*Colin Dunkeld, Portland Informal Reading Inventory, Form P. Unpublished manuscript, Portland State University. Reprinted by permission of the author.

C. *Evaluating Basal Reading Programs*

1. With one or more partners, evaluate an up-to-date basal reading series. If the entire class is examining the same basal series, you may wish to concentrate on only one teacher's guide and its accompanying basal reader. Use the ten criteria on pages 291–292 for your evaluation. Or, each group can concentrate on only one of the criteria. Report to the rest of the class on your findings.

2. With a small group, compare a few teacher's guides from a modern basal series with a few from an old basal series. What differences do you notice in terms of the criteria from this chapter? Report on these differences to the rest of the class.

3. With a small group, compare the "male" vs. "female" words in Table 9.1 between two or more basal series. To do this, select two or three pages from each reader for your count; limit your count to *he* vs. *she*, *her* vs. *him*, and male nouns vs. female nouns (such as *father, mother, Jane, John, uncle, aunt, boy, girl, woman, man* combined). Be sure to count the total words on each page as well, so you can compare percentages rather than frequencies; for example, 40 male nouns divided by 1000 total words equals 4 percent; 20 female nouns divided by 1000 equals 2 percent. Report on your findings to the rest of the class.

4. Chapter 3 gave you several different strategies for producing questions that help children think more about what they have been reading. Evaluate the questions suggested in a basal reader teacher's guide. How well do they carry out those strategies? (You may wish to divide into groups, with each group taking a different strategy from Chapter 3.)

FIELD EXPERIENCES IN THE ELEMENTARY SCHOOL CLASSROOM

A. Teach a lesson by using the teacher's guide to a basal reader. In what ways did the guide limit you or your students? How would you modify the lesson next time? How did the guide help you?

B. Try planning and teaching your own lesson related to a selection in a basal reader. Do not look at the teacher's guide until after you have taught the lesson. How was your lesson similar and different? What did you lose by creating your own? What did you gain?

C. Examine a lesson plan in a teacher's guide to a basal reader. Then plan a way to teach the same skills or ideas through a language experience approach or with the library books your students are using. As an option, you may wish to plan a way to use all three approaches in combination.

IV SPECIAL CONCERNS OF THE CLASS-ROOM READING TEACHER

CHAPTERS

10 DIAGNOSIS AND EVALUATION: HELPING CHILDREN GROW IN READING

CHAPTER PREVIEW

Whether teachers use basal readers, library books, or even children's writing as the basic medium of instruction, there will be times when they need to group children for instruction. Grouping often involves estimating each child's instructional reading level, so that instructional materials are not too difficult or too easy. In this chapter we'll talk about the various ways that teachers make their decisions about children's instructional reading levels—through recommendations from previous teachers, standardized tests, tests by basal reader publishers, informal reading inventories, cloze-type or maze-type tests, miscue analysis, and special tests of graphophonic awareness. We'll also discuss the importance of looking not just at children's *levels* of reading but at their *concepts* of reading and their *strategies* for dealing with unfamiliar cues, because it is through understanding children's concepts and strategies that teachers can truly help children grow in reading.

Humans like to have friends but they don't like their friends to have smarter children.

CRITERIA FOR HELPFUL DIAGNOSTIC AND EVALUATION PROCEDURES

Sometimes when we test our students, we teachers may lose sight of *why* we're testing them. In our hurry to place each child in the right book for reading instruction, or in our rush to "cure" a child of his reading difficulties, for example, we may lose sight of the forest for the trees. We may begin to believe in the percentages and the other numbers we're producing more than we do in our intuitive understanding of the child. Or we may confuse *causes* of reading difficulty with symptoms, imagining that the child's inability to handle separate words is much more important than what she thinks reading is or what strategies she uses to gather meaning through the four cueing systems.

The main reason this confusion occurs is that it's relatively easy to test children on their sight words, or their graphophonic patterns, or the percentage of words they miss in a reading passage, and so difficult to test them on their ability to use the four cueing systems interactively, or on their awareness of reading as a communication process, or on the enjoyment they derive from reading. So, because of this difficulty, it's terribly tempting to grab onto whatever "solid" test data we can get, even though this data often tells us only about the child's symptomatic behavior and not the causes behind the behavior.

To help you keep this problem in mind, here are several criteria that may help you decide which diagnostic or evaluation procedures to use:

> **Diagnose:**   to carefully examine a student's problems in order to understand them

> **Evaluate:**   to determine the quantity or quality of a student's skill

Criterion 1:   The diagnostic (D) or evaluation (E) procedures should lead to better understanding of a child and not merely to labeling or placement.

Criterion 2:   The D/E procedures should treat each child as unique and not as a statistic.

Criterion 3:   The D/E procedures should increase a teacher's awareness of a child's concept of the reading process.

Criterion 4:   The D/E procedures should increase a teacher's understanding of a child's reading strategies.

Criterion 5:   The D/E procedures should increase a teacher's confidence in her ability to place a child in instructional materials that are challenging but not too difficult.

Criterion 6:   The D/E procedures should not bog a teacher down in the minutiae of tiny isolated subskills, but should help her gain broader perspective on a child's needs for reading instruction.

Criterion 7:   The D/E procedures should help a teacher examine and determine a child's ability to read interactively.

I hope that as you read this chapter, and engage in the experiences at the end of the chapter, you will apply these seven criteria and make your own judgments about the various diagnostic and evaluation procedures available.

THE CONCEPT OF READING LEVEL

Suppose you were assigned to teach a group of thirty randomly selected fifth graders. What range in reading levels (or abilities) would you expect to find? Would they all score at the fifth grade level (between 5.0 and 5.9) on a reading achievement test? Obviously not, but how many in the class would you expect to score above or below the fifth grade level: one or two? one fourth of them? one half? If you picked the last answer, you would probably come closest to being correct. Furthermore, the range of overall ability in reading may encompass second- through eighth-grade levels.

What if you were assigned to a first-grade class instead? The range may not seem as great, but it would be just as important as the range among fifth graders. A typical group of first graders would contain children who are already reading at the first- or even second-grade levels, some who are just beginning to read, and some who need considerable help in developing reading-readiness skills.

It's probably obvious, then, that a reading teacher shouldn't use the same instructional material for every child in the room. One book would be all right for some of the children, boring and unchallenging to others, and terribly frustrating to still others. Yet this is exactly the way many teachers taught reading not too many decades ago. And this is the way social studies, science, and other subjects are often taught today. (See Chapter 11.)

So how are you going to decide just what basal reader or other instructional materials to use for each child? How are you going to know how to help each child read better? These are some of the sources of information teachers use for these two purposes:

Recommendations from the previous teacher

Standardized test scores

Group administered tests developed by basal reader publishers

Informal reading inventories

Miscue analysis

The cloze technique

Special tests of graphophonic awareness

Let's look at each source to determine its strengths and weaknesses.

USING RECOMMENDATIONS FROM THE PREVIOUS TEACHER

Many teachers place their students in instructional materials according to the recommendation of the previous teacher. If Mrs. Fisher, who taught Nancy in the second grade, recommends on Nancy's cumulative folder that she be placed in the 3_2 reader at the beginning of third grade, Miss Green, the third-grade teacher, often does just that. And, on the surface, this seems like the logical thing to do in many cases. Since Mrs. Fisher knows that Nancy has completed the 3_1 reader by the end of second grade, it seems only rational to recommend the 3_2 reader for third grade and for Miss Green to follow that recommendation.

There are several flaws, though, in this logical rationale. First, Mrs. Fisher may have done what many teachers have done in the past: she may have decided on Nancy's instructional level at the beginning of second grade and then not tested Nancy in the middle of or at the end of the year to see what level of achievement she had reached. Thus, all she really had Nancy do during the year was to follow along with the group in which she was placed. Since Nancy's group finished the 3_1 reader, Mrs. Fisher recommended that she begin third grade at the 3_2 level. In other words, she ignored Nancy's individual progress and simply treated her as a group member—exactly like all the other children in Nancy's group.

A second flaw in this simplistic transition from Mrs. Fisher to Miss Green is that of ignoring the three summer months, as if no reading growth or decline could have taken place during that time. As just one example of how fallacious this attitude is, Aasen (1959) used various devices to encourage children to read during the summer months, thus improving their reading grade by 0.7 years, in contrast to no improvement for a control group.

A third flaw in the Fisher-to-Green transfer is the assumption that a recommendation by a former teacher is based on hard objective data about a child's actual reading performance. A study by Brown and Sherbenou (1981) demonstrates that this is often not the case. Their study showed that a teacher's perception of a child's reading abilities may strongly relate to how much he likes the child's nonacademic behavior in the classroom. In contrast, the relationship to the child's actual performance on reading tests may be quite low. To put it another way, it seems quite possible that many teachers judge a child's actual reading ability more on the basis of the child's cooperativeness and other such traits than on decoding and comprehension abilities.

What this means, in a practical sense, is that one should use the recommendation from the previous teacher as only one bit of information and only after determining the answer to three questions:

> What actual procedures did the teacher use to arrive at his recommendation?
>
> Do those procedures justify putting a great deal of faith in the recommendation?
>
> What did the child do during the summer that might possibly make a difference in her reading development?

STANDARDIZED TESTS: HOW ARE THEY STANDARDIZED?

Standardized tests have several things in common. For one thing, they are designed to be administered in the same way to each child or group of children taking the test. Directions are read from a manual, the exact time for each subtest is supposedly the same from group to group, and the same sequence of subtests is followed.

For another thing, standardized tests are *norm referenced,* which means that the test publishers first administer the tests to groups of children called *norm groups,* who supposedly represent the rest of the population. The average scores for children at different grade levels become the norms. For example, if the norm group of fourth graders gets an average score of 43 out of 60, the score of 43 then becomes a norm for all other fourth graders who later take the test.

Another common feature of standardized tests is the manner in which raw scores are translated into standardized scores. These standardized scores usually take the form of percentiles, stanines, or grade equivalency scores. The type teachers most often use is the grade equivalent score. The grade equivalency score for a raw score of 43 out of 60 may be anywhere from 4.0 to 4.9, depending upon when the norm group took the test. Theoretically, if the norm group took the test during the first week of school, the grade equivalency score for 43 would be 4.0, indicating the very beginning of fourth grade. If the norm group took the test in the fifth month of school, the grade equivalent score for 43 would be 4.5.

In actual practice, test publishers seldom spend time and money assembling a different norm group each month to determine a grade equivalency score of 4.1, 4.2, 4.3, and so on. Instead they do a great deal of mathematical predicting (Bauman & Stevenson, 1982). For example, to establish grade equivalency scores for a third-grade reading test, they may administer a test (made up by a reading educator) to children in second, third, and fourth grades. Let's say they give the test to this norm group in early September, and let's say that the third graders get an average score of 50 points. Therefore, a grade equivalency score of 3.0 would be assigned to this raw score of 50.

So far, so good; but what about those second and fourth graders who also had to take the third-grade test? Just to make our arithmetic simple, let's imagine that their average scores were 40 and 60 respectively. Then 40 would be assigned a grade equivalency of 2.0 and 60 a grade equivalency of 4.0. Now the publishers have only to divide the scores between 40 and 50 into ten divisions, so that a score of 41 would be 2.1, a score of 42 would be 2.2, and a score of 49 would be 2.9. Likewise the scores between 50 and 60 would be divided into ten divisions, so that a score of 51 would be given a grade equivalency of 3.1 and a score of 59 would be given a grade equivalency of 3.9. Actually the process is more complicated, but this gives you the general idea. For a more extensive description of this procedure, as well as an excellent comparison of grade equivalency scores with percentiles and stanines, you may want to read the article by James Baumann and Jennifer Stevenson in the March 1982 *Reading Teacher*.

MISINTERPRETATION OF THE TERM "GRADE LEVEL"

Frank Roberts, a fourth grader, was administered a standardized reading test, along with his classmates, during the first week of school. He scored a total of 48 and received a grade equivalency score of 3.6. His teacher, Mr. Jackson, was concerned because Frank was "reading below grade level." Teachers and administrators often express such concern; there seems to be an assumption that every child should be reading at his grade level or higher. However, this assumption is based on the lack of realization of how the grade-level norm was originally obtained. It was obtained, as we have

seen, by getting the average score of the norm group at a particular time during the school year. Since an *average score* means, roughly, "the score in the middle," 50 percent of the norm group had to score at or below the average score; 50 percent of the norm group had to score at or above the average score. Thus, if the norm group is representative of the total population, a teacher should theoretically expect half the children to score at or below "grade level" and half to score at or above grade level. Of course, it never works out this neatly, because a norm group can never come that close to representing every other group in the population. But the point should be clear, nevertheless: it is expecting much too much to have every child at or above grade level.

TYPES OF STANDARDIZED READING TESTS

There are four basic types of standardized reading tests:

Group survey tests that are part of a battery of school achievement tests; for example, the *Stanford Achievement Test*, the *California Achievement Test*, the *Metropolitan Achievement Test*, the *Iowa Test of Basic Skills*, and the *Sequential Tests of Education Progress* (STEP)

Group survey tests that measure only reading abilities; for example, the *Nelson Reading Test, Revised*, the *New Developmental Reading Tests*, the *Gates-MacGinitie Reading Tests*, and the *Iowa Silent Reading Test*

Group diagnostic tests; for example, *Silent Reading Diagnostic Tests*, the *Stanford Diagnostic Reading Test*, and the *Doren Diagnostic Reading Test*

Individual diagnostic tests; for example, the *Durrell Analysis of Reading Difficulty*, the *Gates-McKillop Reading Diagnostic Tests*, the *Diagnostic Reading Scales*, the *Gray Oral Reading Test*, and the *Woodcock Reading Mastery Test*

The major difference between the survey and diagnostic tests is in the degree to which the information gained about a child is specific. Whereas the survey tests usually provide only general scores on vocabulary, comprehension, and (sometimes) rate, the diagnostic tests provide scores related to more specific skills, such as phonic analysis, morphemic analysis, auditory discrimination, literal comprehension, inferential comprehension, and so on.

SELECTING APPROPRIATE STANDARDIZED READING TESTS

Any test, standardized or not, should have *validity;* that is, it should actually measure what you want it to measure. A test that calls for spelling, an encoding process, is not a valid test of decoding. A test that calls for the child to select the best from four synonyms for a word is not necessarily a valid test of his ability to understand that word in context. A test that calls for a child to read passages and answer questions related to the passages may be a valid test of reading comprehension, but it is not necessarily a valid test of decoding. A test written in the fifties or sixties may not be a valid test for children living in the eighties.

Any test, standardized or not, should have *reliability;* that is, it should give you consistent results from one testing time to the next and from one form to another. If Johnny ranks near the top of the group with Form A of the test, he should rank near the top with Form B. The *correlation coefficient* between the two forms should be high; acceptable coefficients are usually considered to be .80 or above, although some experts on testing prefer them to be .90 or above.

To determine the validity and reliability of a standardized test, one should examine the test manual that accompanies the test. For greater certainty, it is advisable to consult one of the following sources of test reviews:

Buros, Oscar K., ed. *Mental Measurements Yearbook.* Mt. Ranier, MD: Gryphon House, Inc., 1965, 1972, 1978, and 1984.

Grommon, Alfred H., ed. *Reviews of Selected Tests in English.* Urbana, IL: National Council of Teachers of English, 1976.

Tuinman, J. Jaap, ed. *Review of Diagnostic Reading Tests.* Newark, DE: International Reading Association, 1976.

Schell, Leo M., ed. *Diagnostic and Criterion-Referenced Reading Tests.* Newark, DE: International Reading Association, 1981.

Teachers and administrators need to be clear in their minds as to the purpose of administering a particular type of test. A standardized survey test, for instance, does some things well and other things poorly. It can tell you how well different groups or programs in a school are doing (on the average), but it is far less effective in telling you how well each individual is doing. (As we will discuss in the next section.) A standardized diagnostic test, of the individually-administered type, can yield a great deal of information about a particular child; however, these tests are usually much more difficult and time-consuming to administer and are therefore generally administered to only a small proportion of the children and by trained

reading specialists. A standardized diagnostic test, of the group-administered type, takes far less time to administer and provides several scores,
rather than the few scores provided by a survey test. Nevertheless, if one's
purpose is to get very specific information about each child's reading deficiencies, it is important to keep the test booklets, as well as the test scores.
By looking at the way a child responded to each item on the test, you can
get many insights into that child's specific strengths and weaknesses. Your
purpose, then, should determine the type of standardized test you use, if
any; it should also determine how you use the test scores and the test booklets.

SOME LIMITATIONS OF STANDARDIZED TESTS

Standardized tests usually have greater reliability because of their length
than more informal tests created by teachers, basal reader publishers, and
others. However, they often have less validity; that is, they less often measure exactly what the teacher wants to measure. These are some other lim-
itations:

> They are usually so long (to increase their reliability) that they are
> administered to groups instead of individuals. Thus the teacher is de-
> prived of observing each child "in action."

> They are usually timed, thus penalizing those who read well but
> slowly.

> They often present conditions that are not typical of the reading act.
> For example, they ask children to respond to multiple-choice ques-
> tions, which require recognition of the correct answer; reading, on the
> other hand, requires skill that is far more complex.

> They frequently overrate a child's reading level, thus encouraging
> some teachers to place a child in a reader that is too difficult and
> frustrating.

> Some children are good readers but poor test takers, particularly with
> standardized tests. Special forms are passed out, the right kind of pen-
> cil must be used, everyone in the room is sighing and moaning, the
> tension rises to fever pitch as the teacher looks at the clock and says,
> "Ready, begin." For some children, this kind of atmosphere is not con-
> ducive to clear thinking and careful reading.

> The reading passages in standardized tests are usually quite short. A
> child who does well on short passages requiring little retention may

not do as well on longer selections in basal readers and other materials.

The norm group quite likely will not truly represent the particular group of children you are instructing.

Standardized reading tests are often not accurate for those who are considerably below their grade level (Gunning, 1982). Let's look at a sixth-grade boy, for example, taking a sixth-grade test. This test may be designed in such a way that the lowest *possible* score would give him no less than a 3.2 grade equivalency. In reality, however, his level might be closer to, let's say, 1.8. Such an overestimate of his reading ability would cause a teacher to instruct him in materials that are much too difficult for him. To handle this kind of problem, some test publishers now use poor readers in special norm groups. Poor readers in sixth grade, for instance, might be administered a third-grade test, while average readers might be administered a sixth-grade test, thus providing two norm groups instead of one for sixth graders. Teachers can then give the easier test to their poor readers to get a more accurate indication of their reading ability. This procedure is called "out-of-level testing" and should only be used if the test publisher has actually developed out-of-level norms.

Standardized reading tests of the group-administered type (the type most commonly used in the schools) *meet none of the seven criteria* we discussed. By reexamining those criteria, you can see for yourself that such tests provide very little help for the teacher. Standardized scores need to be used as one of *several* D/E procedures for assessing *individual* growth in reading. Their main usefulness is for administrators and researchers who are comparing schools or other large groups of children.

GROUP ADMINISTERED TESTS DEVELOPED BY BASAL READER PUBLISHERS

Some publishers of basal readers have developed norm-referenced tests similar to standardized reading tests. Because of this similarity, they suffer from some of the same validity problems. On the other hand, they tend to be somewhat more valid than a regular standardized test, because the passages and words are similar to or the same as those used in the basal readers produced by the same publisher.

Other publishers develop criterion-referenced tests to use for placement of children in the readers. Rather than use a norm group, the publishing team has developed short objective-style tests that sample the various skills taught through the basal reader program. On each short test, the child is expected to score at a minimum level to demonstrate his reading competence. This minimum level, often 80 percent, is called a *criterion*. By administering these short skill tests in the same order as the skills are presented in the basal reader program, and by adding the scores on these tests, the teacher arrives at a score that can then be converted into an estimate of the child's instructional reading level. Because these tests are group-administered, however, they lack the validity that can be gained through individual administration. Also, because the tests are so short, they lack reliability. Furthermore, the nature of the objective-type tests, as well as their brevity, makes the testing situation quite different from the actual reading act.

INFORMAL READING INVENTORIES

An informal reading inventory (IRI) is a testing technique that allows a teacher to assess a child's reading levels individually by listening to him read several selections (usually from various levels of basal readers). General decoding skill is determined by counting miscues* noticed during the oral reading. General reading comprehension is determined by asking questions of the child, either after the oral reading or after he reads another selection silently.

The main purpose of an informal reading inventory (IRI) is to determine what book to place a child in for reading instruction. The informal reading inventory is not a standardized achievement test. It is a technique that experienced teachers have found useful in determining three levels of a pupil's reading: the *independent level* (the level at which the pupil can read easily with no help from others); the *instructional level* (the level at which the pupil can read with some fluency but with enough difficulty to make instruction necessary); and the *frustration level* (the level at which the pupil understands little of what is read and makes many miscues).

The informal reading inventory can help you determine, for example, that Alice can probably handle third-grade reading material independently,

---

*A miscue is simply the manner in which a child reads a word or sentence differently from the way the author wrote it. The author writes: "I love my big dog, Pat." The child reads, "I love the dog, Pat." Thus we have two miscues.

that fourth-grade material is about right for using during reading instruction, and that most fifth-grade material, unless she's extremely interested in it, will be too frustrating for her.

Preparing an Informal Reading Inventory

Many textbook publishers now provide teachers with an IRI that contains portions of stories and articles that are the same or similar to those in the publisher's basal reading series. If an informal reading inventory is not available to you from a basal reader publisher, you may wish to use one of those developed independently of a basal reader company: the *Ekwall Reading Inventory* (Ekwall & English, 1971) is an example of one of these; the *Classroom Reading Inventory* by Silvaroli (1979) is another.

Some teachers prepare their own informal reading inventories by finding *portions* of stories and articles (from 75 words at the preprimer level up to 200 words for fifth grade and up). These stories and articles are usually copied (without pictures) from the basal readers or other graded material they are using for reading instruction. While some teachers simply choose their story portions from the middle third of the book, others try to check the accuracy of their selections by applying a "readability formula" to them. You will find one of these formulas and the procedures for using it in Chapter 8. The use of a formula may be a good idea, if it hasn't already been done for you by the basal reader or test publisher. In the past, some basal readers have proved notoriously inconsistent in their reading levels from one selection to the next, varying by several grade levels (Bradley & Ames, 1976).

On the other hand, you probably would be better off using a readability *scale*, instead, such as the one I described. Personally, I wouldn't trust an informal reading inventory, whether it was one I developed myself or one developed commercially, without first comparing the selections with a readability *scale* (a set of graded selections). I would want to feel confident that each selection is a good indication of the grade level it's supposed to represent.

The problem with most readability *formulas* is that they are based only on sentence length and word difficulty. Thus, with the Fry formula, for example, you simply count the number of sentences and the number of syllables in a few samples of 100 words each. If you count syllables to show how difficult a word is, however, what happens when one selection uses the three-syllable word *Saturday*, which every child and teacher understands, and another selection uses the three-syllable word *saturant*, something very few people would understand? And if you simply count the number of sentences in a passage, you get only a measure of sentence *length*. Yet look at these three equally long sentences:

The boy sent his girl friend a letter.

The swain dispatched his love object an epistle.

To chérie baby he did post a missive.

Although each sentence has eight words, only the first one has the *language* that an elementary student would understand.

A readability *scale* normally works better than a formula, because the difficulty of a selection you are about to *use* with children is based on much more than word length and sentence length. It's based on the children's background of experiences, on their schemata development, on their reading vocabulary, and on the kind of syntax and style of language they are accustomed to hearing at home and school.

Let me demonstrate the need for a readability scale by showing you what happens to two selections that have exactly the same number of sentences and syllables. Both are rated by the Fry formula as "fifth-grade readability," but only Selection A, I'm sure you'll see, can be handled by a fifth grader. Whereas Selection A talks about Arthur's earning some money, something even a fifth grader can understand, Selection B is talking about Arthur's crimping some limeys (recruiting some British sailors for a sailing voyage).

Selection A
(Fry's Readability Level: fifth grade)

Arthur Finnington swung his thin legs out of bed and sat on the edge in a stupor. Suddenly he sat up straight.

"Hey, it's Saturday!" he said to himself. "My day for making some money!"

Absent-mindedly Arthur picked his clothes off the floor and began putting them on. His brain was sluggish from a good night's sleep, but he kept on trying to think anyway. He thought about last Saturday—a pretty good day selling homemade popsicles, but too much trouble trying to keep them from melting.

This time it had to be something *big*, he resolved.

Selection B
(Fry's Readability Level: fifth grade)

Arthur Finnington swung his lank legs out of bed and slumped on the edge in a stupor. He suddenly sat up straight.

To himself he moaned, "Jeze, Saturday." "My day for crimping some limeys."

Absent-mindedly he plucked his togs from the earthen floor and covered his flimsy frame. His brain, sluggish from sleep, wanted to shut down, but willpower won out in the end. Arthur thought about Saturday last—a blimey good day crimping hard up journeymen, but too much trouble trying to keep them from leaving.

This time he had to find other types, he resolved.

Both of these selections have the same readability rating on the Fry Scale, because both have the same number of sentences and syllables. But if they had been rated by a teacher or a readability scale, I'm sure you'd agree with me that Selection A would be about right for a fifth grader to understand but Selection B would be much too difficult. Before administering an informal reading inventory, then, I strongly urge you to check the "language-load" of each selection by means of a readability scale.

Miscues Counted During Administration of an IRI

Before we discuss the procedures for administering an informal reading inventory, you need to know what types of miscues to look for when a child is reading to you. Here are the miscues to count (but only when you're administering the test, not when you're scoring it):

Omission	(Then) she saw her mother coming.
Insertion	*In* ∧the forest was a big park.
Default	Child doesn't try the word. Teacher waits five seconds, then pronounces it, e.g., tea*d*cher.
Repetition	The boy $\overline{\text{went}}^{R}$ to school.
Substitution (real word or nonsense word)	She worked with him. He was a taskmaster. *them* *taskammer*
Self-correction	He (was saw his teacher.

These six types of miscues, according to the method I'm going to show you, should be counted only in determining an appropriate "stopping point" when a child is reading to you. As you'll see when we look at the *quality* of the miscues, we'll examine only the defaults, substitutions, and self-corrections.

ADMINISTERING AN INFORMAL READING INVENTORY

These suggestions for administering an informal reading inventory are based on numerous articles by other reading educators, on my own experience with children, and on the experience of the many teachers who have been kind enough to share their ideas with me. Later we'll discuss what research has to say about informal reading inventories, but right now I'd like to present an approach that has worked quite well for me and for colleagues in the public schools with whom I've worked.

1. Before having the pupil read the selections, try to develop a relaxed atmosphere. Make the test informal. (More specific suggestions appear under "Developing Good Testing Conditions.")

2. Have the student begin reading at least two full grade levels below the grade she's in. A fifth grader would begin by reading a third-grade selection, a fourth grader would start with a second-grade selection, and anyone in third grade or below would start with a preprimer selection. If you already know that a child is a very poor reader, no matter what grade she is in, start with the preprimer. It's better to start testing too low than too high, so the child can develop a feeling of self-confidence.

3. As she reads, count her miscues discreetly without discussing them. Just use tally marks on a pad in your lap.

4. When a child comes to a proper noun, such as a person's last name, pronounce it for her the first time she misses the word and count it as a miscue; however, don't count it as a miscue more than once in the same selection. Sometimes the same proper noun appears again and again in a selection, and it appears to be invalid to count these nouns more than once as a miscue.

5. Count omissions, insertions, repetitions, defaults, substitutions, and even self-corrections this time. (Later, when you score the IRI, you'll make *quality* judgments.) Most reading educators traditionally do *not* count punctuation errors, hesitations, and slow sounding-out of words.

6. Don't count dialect differences (such as "chimley" for "chimney" or "I don't be going" for "I'm not going"). (For a discussion of dialect differences, see Chapter 13—especially Tables 13.1 and 13.2.)

7. Check comprehension and memory by asking three literal and three inferential questions.

   Inferential questions usually require the reader to:
   a. Predict what's going to happen next (asked either at the end or halfway through a story)
   b. Decide what caused what (if the author did not explicitly explain it)
   c. Fill in information that an author has implied but not stated
   d. Determine the most important ideas implied by the author

Literal questions usually require the reader to:

a. Remember important details stated by the author
b. Remember the sequence of events
c. Translate written descriptions into oral ones (child's own words)

Some teachers test children's comprehension by giving new selections to read *silently* and then asking them questions. Research indicates, however, that the relationship between oral and silent reading is high enough to make this unnecessary—as well as time-consuming and fatiguing (Bond & Dykstra, 1967; Edwall & English, 1971; Elgart, 1978).

8. Stop the testing when the child finishes a selection that has been obviously frustrating. This nearly always occurs by the time she has missed 15 percent of the words in the selection or over 50 percent of the questions. To help you know when the child has reached this point, simply compute the "stopping point" for each selection before she reads. An objective stopping point can be obtained by multiplying the total number of words in each selection by 0.15. For instance, if the total number of words is 140, the estimated stopping point would be 21 miscues. Another check on the stopping point is to decide subjectively whether the child has reached frustration. This is shown by such behavior as heavy sighs, extreme fidgeting, pained expressions, not understanding your questions at the end of a selection, or even the request: "Can we stop now?" In this case, even though she has not missed 15 percent of the words or over 50 percent of the questions, stop the child at the end of the selection.

Developing Good Testing Conditions

There are several things you can do when administering an IRI to encourage a relaxed atmosphere and to increase the accuracy of the test. These are some suggestions:

Make sure the child is seated in such a way that he is not distracted by your keeping track of his miscues.

Take a few moments to develop rapport by talking about his reading interests—his favorite book, the kinds of books he likes, when he likes to read, where he likes to read, and so on.

Explain the reason and nature of your examination, perhaps like this: "Billy, I'd like to hear you read for a while so I can decide what book you should be reading. Do the best you can, but don't worry if you make mistakes, because your mistakes will help me see how I can help you this year. After you read each story, we'll talk about it for a few minutes."

Don't give the IRI during recess or any other time the student can't devote full attention to it. (If the test is viewed as a punishment, your results will not be valid.)

Administer the IRI where the child can't see his peers without turning around.

Make sure he is near enough to enable you to hear miscues clearly.

Allow for a minimum of distractions and interruptions. Tell the rest of the class that you shouldn't be disturbed while you're working with "Johnny." If necessary, allow time between each examination to work with other children.

Make sure the lighting on the reading passages is excellent. This may have a significant effect on the level of the book in which you place the child.

Allow a *full five seconds* for the child to decode a word before pronouncing it for him. (Try not to "jump the gun.")

Keep the testing situation "light and breezy." A formal, overserious approach may reduce the validity of an IRI.

SCORING AN INFORMAL READING INVENTORY

Many professors of education (including myself) were once reluctant to include directions for scoring an informal reading inventory in a general course on reading instruction, thinking that it might be too difficult for the students. After several years of teaching this topic at both the undergraduate and graduate levels, however, many of us have become convinced that preservice and inservice teachers want and need to understand the IRI scoring process.

Let me assure you, it's not that difficult. The information you need to understand the scoring of an IRI is nowhere as difficult as anything covered in your college-level mathematics courses. And as you are perhaps painfully aware, most education students today are required by state law to take from one to three courses in college level mathematics. Teachers today are using informal reading inventories in a great many regular elementary classrooms, thanks to their availability from basal reader publishers. Consequently, it only makes sense for teachers to understand what the scores on these inventories really mean.

The Traditional Quantity Method

For several decades informal reading inventories have been scored and interpreted according to the suggestions made by Emmett Betts (1946). Betts suggested that the percentage of words pronounced correctly during oral reading would serve nicely as a decoding score; the questions answered correctly would serve as a comprehension score. Therefore, if Clifford reads a passage of 100 words and miscues on 20 of these words, his decoding (word recognition) score would be 80 percent. If he answers four out of five questions to the teacher's satisfaction, his comprehension score would be 80 percent. What could be simpler?

But how should these scores be interpreted? While 80 percent might be a good score for comprehension, is 80 percent a good score for decoding? Probably every reading teacher in the country would say "No." When Clifford misses 20 out of a hundred words, he is missing one out of every five. Try reading the following paragraph with one out of every five words substituted with a nonsense word.

> "The lawyer-client *bedigglement*," Jones said. "You're in a *floureistyr* before you can make a *swinzoomer*. If you've got hard *bittledown* against your client, you're *quephrezondting* the commission of those *phenomenologicants* by keeping your *psychometrichosis*."

As you can see, a child who cannot *pronounce* one out of five words will be in trouble. In the first place, he usually can't understand what he can't pronounce. In the second place, the more words he can't pronounce in a passage, the more his comprehension of the entire passage suffers.

By a great deal of trial and error over the years, reading educators have come up with a fair amount of agreement about interpreting IRI scores. Although no two educators may have exactly the same percentages in mind when they interpret the scores, these percentages are about average:

Independent Reading Level: 98% of the words correct
90% of the questions correct

Instructional Reading Level: 94% of the words correct
60% of the questions correct

Frustrational Reading Level: below 90% of the words correct
below 50% of the questions correct

Thus, if Clifford were reading a selection from a fourth-grade basal reader and achieved a decoding score of 80 percent and a comprehension score of 80 percent, the teacher would probably conclude that fourth-grade reading material would be too difficult for instructional use. On the other hand, if he read a third grade passage with a decoding score of 95 percent and a comprehension score of 70 percent, the teacher would probably place him in a third grade basal reader for instruction.

So far this must seem terribly simple to you—and that's just the problem with it. It's a very simple way of looking at a process that is really quite complicated. We've been talking throughout this book about how reading involves four interacting processes, and now I'm showing you a testing device that relies primarily on the graphophonic process and largely ignores the three context processes (semantic, schematic, and syntactic). Although the traditional scoring procedure provides a decoding score, and thus an estimate of a child's ability to use graphophonic cues, it provides no real estimate of his ability to use context cues. You may wonder if the questions would provide such an estimate, but according to the research I'll describe in the next section, questions have several weaknesses. Clifford, for example, missed one out of every five words on his decoding score but managed to answer four out of five questions correctly. This kind of situation usually occurs under three conditions: (1) a child misses many of the words through default and the teacher tells him the words; (2) a child is bright enough to follow the general meaning of the selection because the teacher has provided him with most of the difficult words; and (3) a child can answer some of the questions because of his background of experiences rather than because of what he has read.

There are at least two ways out of this dilemma of using the traditional scoring methods. One is to avoid using the IRI altogether and to substitute the "cloze" or "maze" technique instead. The other way is to use a *qualitative* method instead of a quantitative method of scoring the IRI.

A Quality Approach Toward Scoring an IRI: What Research Tells Us

As I mentioned in the previous section, reading educators have traditionally counted only the *quantity* of miscues in an IRI. I'm sure you would agree, however, that we should be concerned with the *quality* of our students' miscues, not just the quantity. But what does research tell us about miscues? Let's review this research.

Good readers (those who comprehend what they're reading) make many miscues that actually *enhance* comprehension—meaningful substitutions, omissions, insertions, and self-corrections (Beebe, 1978–79;

Clay, 1968; D'Angelo, 1982). Our scoring of informal reading inventories should not penalize such positive reading behavior. We would get more accurate scores by giving *credit* for "positive miscues."

Poor readers do very little self-correcting; their substitutions are often not meaningful; and they frequently default on words by waiting for the teacher to pronounce them (D'Angelo, 1983; Goodman, 1969). These are "negative miscues." It doesn't make sense for our IRI scoring procedures to treat positive and negative miscues as equivalent—and as both negative. Nor does it make sense to place children in basal readers for instruction on the basis of such a simplistic quantity-type scoring procedure.

Counting whole-word omissions and insertions doesn't add significant information toward the decision as to which level is appropriate for instructing a student in reading (D'Angelo, 1983). Furthermore, both repetitions and hesitations are used primarily to allow time for readers to think (Goodman, 1969). Again, scoring procedures should not penalize positive miscues. Miscues that *consistently* provide reading educators with highly useful information are these:

> *Self-corrections* (usually showing that two or more of the cueing systems—syntactic, semantic, graphophonic, and schematic—are interacting)

> *Defaults* (showing that the student is afraid of attempting the word for fear of making a mistake, or that he is doing very little predicting, or that he does not recognize essential sight words, phonograms, vowel patterns, or suffixes)

> *Substitutions* (demonstrating comprehension when the miscue is relevant to the author's message or has the same meaning; demonstrating lack of comprehension *monitoring* when the miscue is a nonsense word, a partial word, or a word of a different syntactic class). Substitutions also provide information about the reader's use of graphophonic cues. By examining the graphic similarity between the author's word and the reader's word, we can get some idea of how effectively she is noticing graphophonic patterns (or at least single letters).

Studies on comprehension questions indicate that they are often not reliable indicators of how well a child has understood a selection during an informal reading inventory (McKenna, 1983). One set of questions on a selection will place a child at the instructional level; another set of questions on the same selection will place her at the frustration or independent level. Furthermore, they are more likely to measure *memory*—of what she has read, of what the teacher pronounced, of answers to similar questions, or of background experiences—than *comprehension* of what she read. Therefore, it is not advisable to base a child's instructional level solely on her response to questions, even though we call these questions a measure of "comprehension."

Suggested Recording Procedures

To prepare for a qualitative estimate of reading level the following recording procedures are recommended:

1. Tape-record the administration of an IRI so that miscues can be qualitatively scored later. After scoring the IRI, you will then be able to decide whether a student needs to read more selections for you, or whether you can now comfortably estimate the level of book she should be using during reading instruction. By using *qualitative* scoring, you will also have a much better idea of a child's reading concept and strategies. This information will in turn help you remediate his major reading problems, rather than only place him in a basal reader. (See the section on "Miscue Analysis.")

2. As you listen to the tape recording, mark the child's miscues on a copy of each selection. Figure 10.1 shows you how to do this.

3. As shown in Figure 10.1, substitutions are recorded by writing the substituted word over the author's word. When this substitution is then self-corrected, a large C is drawn around the two words. For example:

   permanent
   permit (substitution)   *only*
                                            ⌒ōwn (self-correction)

4. Whole-word omissions such as *station* and *a* are circled. Partial omissions such as *ranger* for *rangers* are treated as substitutions and are written above the author's word just as other substitutions are. (This will make your scoring easier later.) For example:

   ⬭station⬭ (whole-word omission)   *ranger*
                                            rangers (substitution)

5. Whole-word insertions such as the reader's word *it* between the author's words *cut* and *about* are shown with a caret. Partial insertions such as *trees* for *tree* are shown as substitutions. For example:

   it
   cut͜about (insertion)   *trees*
                                            tree (substitution)

6. Defaults are shown with a *d* above the word the teacher had to pronounce for the student after a five-second wait. If the student makes a

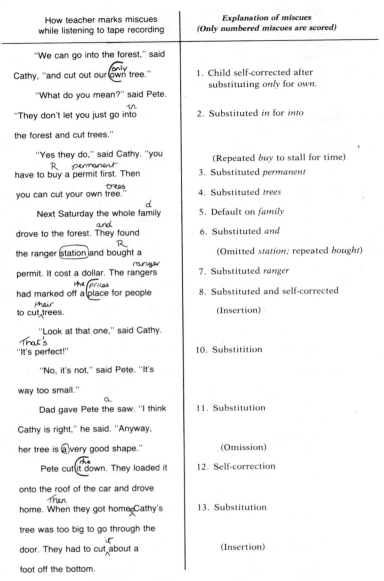

How teacher marks miscues while listening to tape recording	Explanation of miscues (Only numbered miscues are scored)
"We can go into the forest," said Cathy, "and cut out our ~~own~~ (only) tree."	1. Child self-corrected after substituting *only* for *own*.
"What do you mean?" said Pete. "They don't let you just go into the forest and cut trees."	2. Substituted *in* for *into*
"Yes they do," said Cathy. "you have to buy a permit first. Then you can cut your own tree."	(Repeated *buy* to stall for time) 3. Substituted *permanent* 4. Substituted *trees*
Next Saturday the whole family drove to the forest. They found the ranger station and bought a permit. It cost a dollar. The rangers had marked off a place for people to cut trees.	5. Default on *family* 6. Substituted *and* (Omitted *station;* repeated *bought*) 7. Substituted *ranger* 8. Substituted and self-corrected (Insertion)
"Look at that one," said Cathy. "It's perfect!"	10. Substitition
"No, it's not," said Pete. "It's way too small."	
Dad gave Pete the saw. "I think Cathy is right," he said. "Anyway, her tree is a very good shape."	11. Substitution (Omission)
Pete cut it down. They loaded it onto the roof of the car and drove home. When they got home Cathy's tree was too big to go through the door. They had to cut about a foot off the bottom.	12. Self-correction 13. Substitution (Insertion)

Figure 10.1 *Marking the Tape Recorded Miscues*

partial attempt, such as /ma/ for *magic* and then waits for the teacher to pronounce the word, write the partial attempt above the word and also a *d* to show that you had to pronounce it. If she says a word that is incorrect and gets you to pronounce the word by using a questioning tone *(much?)*, then write the word she suggests and also the letter *d*. For example:

d
family (no attempt)

farn (d)
family (partial attempt)

fancy? (d)
family (question)

7. Repeats are shown by writing an *R* above the word or phrase repeated. Use an *R* with a horizontal line for a repeated phrase. For example:

R
bought

$\overline{\quad R \quad}$
to buy

$\overline{\quad\quad R \quad\quad}$
to buy a farm

Suggested Scoring Procedures

Now you're ready to score each selection the child has read to you. As I mentioned, a child's omissions, insertions, and repetitions do not seem to give the teacher enough information to make them important in the scoring procedures. Therefore, you should examine them only when you need information in addition to what you'll get from these scoring procedures.

The qualitative procedure I'm recommending requires that you look only at the substitutions, self-corrections, and defaults. Rather than merely count these, you should *rate* each one on two qualitative scales, the Graphophonic Scale and the Context Scale. The Graphophonic Scale will give you an estimate of how well a student notices the *letters* of a word; the Context Scale will give you an estimate of how well she notices the context cues (semantic, syntactic, and schematic combined).

When you use the Graphophonic Scale, you'll give the student one point for each letter he gets correct on a substitution, self-correction, or default. When you use the Context Scale, however, the number of points you give will depend on the degree to which the student used context cues. For a self-correction, for example, give the maximum 6 points. For a substitution that is merely in the same syntactic class (for example, substituting a noun for a noun), you'll give only three points. The complete Context Scale, along with the Graphophonic Scale and a Question Scale, are shown in Figure 10.2. If you'll take a few minutes to examine it, you'll see that the scales are not too difficult to use. There is an application experience at the end of the chapter that will give you a chance to practice this qualitative scoring procedure.

Interpretation of the C-G-Q Scores

After you've obtained C-G-Q scores for each selection a child has read, you're ready to decide what grade level his instructional material should be. If Andy has done very well on a second-grade selection, moderately well on a third-grade selection, and poorly on a fourth-grade selection, you will probably want to instruct him with third-grade materials. Therefore you

Miscue	Scores		Explanation	Scales
	C	G		
only / o w n	6/6	3/3	C: Self-corrects; 6 out of 6 points G: 3 out of 3 letters	*Context Scale* (C) 0 = no attempt (default) 1 = nonsense substitution or partial attempt; teacher gives word 2 = substitution not in same syntactic class 3 = substitution merely in same syntactic class (e.g., noun for noun) 4 = substitution somewhat relevant to author's message and also in same syntactic class 5 = substitution gives about the same meaning to author's *message* 6 = self-correction
in / into	5/6	2/4	C Same meaning; 5 out of 6 points G: 2 out of 4 letters	
permanent / permit	3/6	5/6	C: Same syntax; 3 out of 6 points G 5 out of 6 letters	
trees / tree	5/6	4/4	C: Same meaning; 5 out of 6 points G: 4 out of 4 letters	*Graphophonic Scale* (G) 0 = no letter the same in substitution as in author's message 1 = one letter the same in substitution as in author's word 2 = two letters the same in substitution as in author's word N = number of letters the same in substitution as in author's word
d / family	0/6	0/6	C: Default; 0 out of 6 points G: 0 out of 6 letters	
and / They	5/6	0/4	C: Same meaning; 5 out of 6 points G: 0 out of 4 letters	
ranger / rangers	5/6	6/7	C: Same meaning; 5 out of 6 points G: 6 out of 7 letters	*Question Scale* (Q) Answering literal questions: 2 = remembers details, sequence, or description precisely 1 = remembers with moderate accuracy 0 = does not remember with accuracy
the / a	5/6	0/1	C: Same meaning; 5 out of 6 points G: 0 out of 1 letter	
prices / place	6/6	5/5	C: Self-corrects; 6 out of 6 points G: 5 out of 5 letters	Answering inferential questions: 3 = Very strong use of personal schemata: e.g., predicts future text with remarkable accuracy; fills in information that author left out or implied; or shows keen awareness of cause and affect that author only implied 2 = Moderately strong use of personal schemata 1 = Slight use of personal schemata; mostly relies on literal data 0 = No attempt to use personal schemata; can't really answer the question 15 = total possible points for 3 literal and 3 inferential questions
That's / It's	5/6	2/3	C: Same meaning; 5 out of 6 points G: 2 out of 3 letters	
a / the	5/6	0/3	C: Same meaning; 5 out of 6 point G: 0 out of 3 letters	
the / it	6/6	2/2	C: Self-corrects; 6 out of 6 points G: 2 out of 2 letters	
Then / When	4/6	3/4	C: Relevant; 4 out of 6 points G: 3 out of 4 letters	
Totals	60/78	32/52	C: 60 out of 78 G: 32 out of 52	**Note:** To determine Q score in percent, divide number of points earned by total number of possible points. For example, 9 earned points divided by 15 possible points results in a Q score of 9/15 or 60%.
Percents	77	62	C score: 77% G score: 62%	

Figure 10.2   *Demonstration of the C-G-Q Scoring Procedure*

need a quick method for interpreting the C-G-Q scores. From my experience and that of my graduate and undergraduate education students, I would recommend this form of interpretation: An IRI selection represents the instructional level only if all three C-G-Q scores add up to 180 percentage points or more. For example, if Andy's C score, G score, and Q score are each 60 percent on the third-grade selection, the total C-G-Q score equals 180 for that selection. Thus, we consider these results an indication that he could be instructed with third-grade materials.

A word of caution, however: even though a child's C-G-Q score equals 180 points, experience has taught us that the Question Score should not be below 50 percent and the Graphophonic and Context Scores should not be below 40 percent each. So essentially, a score of 180 points is the *minimum* for the instructional level. Here are some sample minimum scores for this level:

C Score	*G* Score	*Q* Score	*Total*
60	60	60	180
50	60	70	180
70	60	50	180
60	40	80	180
40	40	100	180

But what about the independent and frustration levels? How many points should they be? Again, relying on experience, I recommend these criteria:

Frustration Level: Below 50 percent on the Question Score or below 40 percent on either the Context Score or Graphophonic Score; or below 180 on the C-G-Q Score

Instructional Level: At least 50 percent on the Question Score, at least 40 percent on Context Score, at least 40 percent on the Graphophonic Score, and at least 180 on the C-G-Q Score

Independent Level: At least 80 percent on the Question Score and at least 240 points on the C-G-Q score

By looking at the *profile* of the three scores for each selection, the teacher can also learn something about the child's reading strategies, strengths, and weaknesses. Let's look at David's scores as an example:

	C	*G*	*Q*	*Total*
2_1 selection	57%	80%	80%	217
2_2 selection	53%	75%	73%	201
3_1 selection	45%	60%	53%	158

Notice how high the G scores are compared to the C scores. This comparison shows at a glance how much David relies on the graphophonic cueing system. Although David is about to go into third grade, he might be frustrated with third-grade materials until he gets more help on using context clues. The way he read the following sentence in the 3_1 selection may demonstrate his need for help:

$$\overset{\textit{late}}{\text{Albert turned on the light.}}$$

MISCUE ANALYSIS: UNDERSTANDING A CHILD'S CONCEPT AND STRATEGIES

Miscue analysis is a useful technique not only in scoring an informal reading inventory, but also in helping a teacher understand each student's reading concept and strategies. Miscue analysis can help a teacher discover answers to questions like these: What strategies is Jimmy using to decode unfamiliar words? Is he guessing wildly or is he using context clues? Is he relying too much on phonics? Is he ignoring graphophonic cues? Are some of his miscues a result of inadequate decoding skill or simply a result of a nonstandard dialect? Questions such as these are answered through analyzing the miscues a child makes during the time he is reading orally.

Do you remember from Chapter 1 these miscues that Tommy made?

Author: Roy saw a little boat pull a big boat.

Tommy: Roy was a little boat pulled by a big boat.

What you do when you carry on miscue analysis is simply to ask yourself why. Why did he make his first miscue? Why did he make the next one? And so on. By answering these questions you'll often be able to learn about a child's reading strategies and his notion of what reading is. Once you've discovered his strategies for reading and his concept of reading, you may have come much farther toward helping him become a better reader.

If we take Tommy's miscues as an example, we can speculate that Tommy's concept of reading is probably that "reading is a meaningful process." Imagine Tommy's defining it this way: "Reading is retelling a story in a way that makes sense." Since Tommy doesn't think it makes sense for a little boat to pull a big boat, he doesn't even see the way the author wrote the story. Therefore, he reads the sentence in a way that makes sense to him!

Now that we have a rough hypothesis for what Tommy's concept of reading is, let's see if we can discover his strategies for reading. Well, what's Tommy's first miscue? He sees the word *saw* as *was*, isn't that right? That tells us a little bit about his strategies. He predicts what words are coming next, for one thing. And that's a good strategy to have. But in this case he predicts *was* instead of *saw*.

Does he have a strategy for checking on his predictions? Does he glance at the first letter of the word he predicts, for instance, to see if it starts with the appropriate letter? Evidently not, for he goes right on reading. As a result, Tommy ends up with the idea that "Roy *was* a little boat." But this doesn't bother him, since after all, most people give their boat a name. So far, so good, as far as Tommy is concerned.

Now we come to the fifth word in the sentence. The author says "Roy saw a little boat pull a big boat." But Tommy, remember, is talking about a little boat named *Roy*. Naturally, then, he wouldn't say, "Roy was a little boat pull a big boat." That simply doesn't make good grammatical sense. To make good sense, one would have to say, "Roy was a little boat pulled by a big boat." We now know a little bit more about Tommy's reading strategies. As far as he's concerned, a sentence should make sense both semantically and syntactically.

So what do we *know* from listening to Tommy read just one sentence? Well, actually we *know* very little, but we can begin to make some hypotheses that we can check as he continues to read. We can hypothesize that Tommy perceives reading as a form of communication and not just a process of "sounding out" words. We can also hypothesize that his strategies for reading include the strategy of "go for broke." That is, he goes for the big message and doesn't concern himself very much with the little clues. He ignores the little clue of the second word in the sentence starting with *s* instead of *w*. He ignores the little clue that there is no suffix *ed* at the end of *pull*. (And, as I discovered later, he ignores little clues like periods, question marks, and capital letters as well.)

As we continue listening to Tommy read, we discover that our hypotheses are probably correct. He consistently goes for the big message and ignores the little clues. We now have a better idea of how to help him improve his reading. We don't want to spoil his perception that reading is a form of communication, but we do want to increase the accuracy of his reading by encouraging him to pay attention to the first letter in a word (*s* instead of *w*), to pay attention to phonograms such as *aw* (*saw, jaw, paw*), to notice whether a suffix is being used or not (*pull* vs. *pulled*), and to develop a better visual memory of important sight words like *was*.

USING MISCUE ANALYSIS AS A DIAGNOSTIC TEACHING TOOL

Now that you've seen a sample of miscue analysis in action, you can probably see how useful a device it can sometimes be to the teacher—whether she's using a basal reader program, a language experience approach, a trade-book individualized program, or some combination of these approaches. Whenever you have the opportunity to listen to a child read, you can listen to miscues and ask yourself why he's making them. In this way, as we did with Tommy, we can find out more about his concept of reading, his reading strategies, and what type of special instruction he needs.

What this means, of course, is that your concern when listening to a child read should be for the process rather than the product. Be concerned not so much for a perfect performance that you create by correcting every mistake Lisa makes, but rather for the processes she uses to perform for you. Does her performance signify that she perceives reading as a process of sounding out each word correctly for you? Does her performance signify that she perceives reading as a task to rush through as fast as possible in spite of mistakes?

You may wish to stop a child sometimes when her rendition doesn't make any sense ("That sentence didn't make sense, Lisa; would you try it again, please?"). Often, however, the child will gain more if you just listen to her read, and carry on miscue analysis while you listen.

Suppose, for example, that Mrs. Franklin sees this: "The dog ran over to Sammy and barked and barked at him." But Kevin reads this: "Da dog wen' over to Sammy and bock and bock at him." Mrs. Franklin knows that Kevin's mother tongue is Black English rather than Standard English. Therefore, she realizes that Kevin has performed a double translation—from print to Standard English to Black English—on the printed words *The* and *barked*. She also realizes that in substituting *went* for *ran* he has done little damage to his comprehension of the passage and simply used *went* because he had predicted that *went* would occur in that sentence slot. Mrs. Franklin decides not to stop Kevin.

On the other hand, suppose that Susan reads the same sentence like this: "Then Doug ran *other* to Sammy and *backed* and *backed* at her." Mrs. Franklin sees immediately that Susan is relying almost exclusively on minor graphophonic clues and is paying no attention to syntactic clues (*other* does not fit grammatically where *over* should be); or to semantic clues (*Sammy* and *her* don't match and people seldom *back* at others). Mrs. Franklin knows she has her work cut out for her. Susan needs to be taught to read for meaning rather than empty words. Mrs. Franklin knows this because she has carried on miscue analysis while Susan was reading.

She does not stop to correct her after each word that she reads incorrectly.

SOME POLITICAL AND EMOTIONAL MATTERS RELATED TO READING PLACEMENT

It's September and you've administered an IRI to Alice DeBoer. You've carefully scored her miscues by using the C-G-Q method, you've checked other data, and you've just made a professional decision to place her in the first reader for the first part of the year. Now let's make the problem more difficult. It so happens that Alice is in the second grade. Her first grade teacher recommended on her report card and in her cumulative folder that Alice be started in the 2_2 book at the beginning of second grade. Furthermore, her standardized test score for reading at the end of first grade was translated into a grade equivalent score of 2.6. Unfortunately many people interpret this to mean that the child is ready to read what the "normal" child in the sixth month of second grade is ready to read. (More about this erroneous interpretation later.) To make matters even worse, both Alice and her parents are upset because you're putting her "back" in the first reader.

You decide to talk to Miss McCloskey, her first grade teacher. She says: "Alice is one of those children who have been pushed a lot by her parents. According to her kindergarten teacher, she was even reading a bit before she got into kindergarten. As a result she was given reading instruction in kindergarten."

"That sounds okay to me," you say.

"Right," Miss McCloskey says. "But the trouble is, when Alice got her report card at the end of kindergarten, her teacher had recommended—in big bold letters—that she start first grade in the 2_1 book!"

"I begin to get the picture," you say.

"Yes. It turned out that Alice was good at memorizing words, but she couldn't really read them. She had no concept of phonics, for instance, or any other decoding skill. She was relying entirely on memory."

"So what did you do?" you ask her.

"I started her in the 2_1 book, but I had to move her quickly back to the first reader."

"How did she do in the first reader?"

"Quite well, but she knew the words from memory. I decided to pull her out of the basal series entirely for a while and had her work on a special phonics program."

"How did that work?"

"Fine, until the parents started complaining that I'd pulled her out of the 'top' reading group."

"Did you put her back in the 2_1 book?"

Miss McCloskey sighs. "Eventually, I did, after a running battle with the parents for months."

"And is that why you recommended her for the 2_2 book at the end of first grade?"

She shrugs her shoulders. "What else could I do? If I'd recommended her for anything lower, her parents would have been in the principal's office. And besides, I looked bad enough moving her up only one-half year. To most people looking at the report cards at the end of kindergarten and first grade, it would be obvious that I simply hadn't done my job—right?"

You pat her on the shoulder and nod your head with sympathy. Then you walk out of her room and wonder what in the world you're going to do. (Do you see now why this section is called "Some Political and Emotional Matters Related to Reading Placement"?)

Naturally I'd like to be able to give you a definite solution for this problem. But the solution will vary with each teacher and with each child. On the other hand, you can arrive at a solution (even though it isn't a perfect one) by finding answers to these questions:

How sure are you of your IRI results? Try using another set of selections from the same series and see if you get similar results.

How fair is the informal reading inventory? This question is often asked and is caused by a confusion as to the major purpose of the inventory. The main purpose of the IRI is to help you instruct each child at a level that is not too easy or too difficult. Probably the single most unfortunate mistake teachers make in teaching reading is to use instructional material that is too difficult for the child, thus causing frustration, anxiety, and a lowering of the child's self-concept.

Ekwall & English (1971) carried on a study of the anxiety level of children who reached the frustration level in reading. Their conclusions were somewhat alarming:

We are certainly doing students no favor by easing the criteria and thus placing them at a level in which they are physiologically frustrated. For example, students in the Ekwall polygraph study, when they became frustrated, exhibited the same signs as someone afraid of a crowd, or of someone about to get up to give a speech before a large audience, or of someone shaken by an automobile accident. Is it any wonder that students do not choose to read difficult material unless forced to? Can you imagine a situation in which every time you were forced to read you experienced the feelings of a person after an automobile accident? (p. 665)

You can see then how important it is to determine the child's instructional level and not to teach that child at a level of frustration. On the other hand, it could be very damaging to a child's self-concept to place her at a level that is too low for her. Here she is, doing everything good readers do; say, self-correcting her predictions, making meaningful substitutions, omissions, and insertions that actually enhance her comprehension, and she's placed in a book that is much too easy for her. To some children this is considerably degrading and also leads to boredom and a distaste for reading.

Why bother with an IRI? Why not just use the grade equivalent score of the standardized reading test? To emphasize the point made earlier, let's look at another opinion. Schwartz, a reading and test-construction expert, has this to say about the use of standardized tests:

One of the most blatant misuses of test results is the not infrequent practice of equating a grade level score with a graded reading text. So, for example, a child whose raw score on a survey test of reading converts to a grade level of 3.5, is given a 3_2 reader, the teacher erroneously assuming a connection between the grade level equivalent on the test and the level of difficulty of the reading text. No such connection exists! . . . a grade level equivalent for a given score is simply the average score achieved by all children at that grade level in the standardization sample, and has nothing whatsoever to do with graded texts. As a matter of fact, the level of difficulty represented in a 3_2 reader is usually higher than material that receives a third grade designation on a reading test. The poor youngster who is given a 3_2 reader on the basis of achieving such a score is surely in for trouble. (Schwartz, 1977, p. 367)

To put it another way: The grade equivalent scores for the particular standardized test used in your school district were not designed to match the grade levels of the particular basal reading series you are using. Such an assumption is made probably because we are sometimes fooled by numbers.

How much support do you have from your principal for the decision you would like to make? Have you explained the reasons for your decision? Will the principal support your decision and help explain it to the parents?

Are there any ways you can work with the parents to arrive at a decision that will be best for the child?

Have you used a qualitative scoring procedure by examining the miscues carefully?

USING THE CLOZE AND MAZE TECHNIQUES FOR DETERMINING INSTRUCTIONAL LEVELS

In previous chapters we've talked about using the cloze technique as an instructional device. Some teachers and researchers also use it as a group-administered test for determining students' reading levels. Rather than administer an informal reading inventory to one child at a time, they give a large group of children the same selection to read *silently*. Usually this selection omits every tenth word, and each student is to write down the exact word he thinks is missing. If he guesses at least 40 percent of the exact words missing, or 80 percent of the appropriate synonyms, the selection is considered representative of the instructional level for the child. Zintz (1972) recommends a more refined set of percentages:

Over 50 percent exact guesses = independent reading level

40 to 50 percent = instructional reading level

Fewer than 40 percent = frustration level

This procedure has distinct advantages and disadvantages when compared to an IRI. Perhaps the major advantage is that it can be administered to a group rather than to one individual at a time. The children merely write in the missing words, and the teacher ignores misspellings when she scores each child's inserted words. Another advantage is the way it emphasizes context cues rather than graphophonic cues. Yet, this is a major disadvantage as well, because it fails to provide separate measures of graphophonic awareness and context awareness. Nor does it provide an easy way to carry on miscue analysis, thus allowing you to ascertain reading strategies or reading concepts. Moreover, for this approach to be reliable, the selections must be several hundred words long. And, not least of all, scoring a cloze-type test can sometimes be horrendous, mainly because of children's handwriting and spelling when under stress.

To compensate for the scoring problem, some schools and school districts (New York, for example) use a maze-type test instead of a cloze-type test. With the maze technique, children are given the usual blanks about every ten words, but instead of writing in their word-guess, they select from multiple-choice responses. This is much more efficient, of course, but probably less valid, since it requires more testlike behavior than actual reading behavior. Actual reading behavior, as you know, requires one to predict the next word without the benefit of multiple-choice options.

Nevertheless, in spite of the disadvantages of cloze and maze techniques, they are a reasonably efficient way of quickly placing *intermediate grade* children in basal readers and work well for a "first-try-placement" procedure. When a child and instructional book don't seem to match, however (which you'll be able to determine in a week or two), I strongly recommend that you administer an informal reading inventory to that child and score it by the C-G-Q method.

MORE PRECISE ASSESSMENT OF GRAPHOPHONIC AWARENESS

Teachers of third grade and above sometimes feel the need for a special phonics test that will tell which letter patterns children still find confusing, even though the patterns have already been taught. Some teachers simply go through the alphabet, asking each child to tell "What sound does this letter make?" This isn't too bad an approach, since it tends to be less frightening than a more demanding test. It does lack precision, however, since it fails to test how well they can handle digraphs, such as *th* and *sh*, clusters such as *pl* and *cr*, vowel patterns such as *at* vs. *ate*, and phonograms such as those in *sit* and *cap*. As I mentioned in Chapter 5, patterns of letters are usually more important in learning to read (and spell) than are isolated letters.

Figure 10.3 is a Phonogram Test you might like to use. This test will give you a good idea of how well each student can recognize patterns of

Figure 10.3   High Frequency Phonogram Test

Name of Student _____   Grade _____

zab	zack	zace	zail	zay	zall	zed	zell	zeak
zear	zid	zick	zice	zight	zob	zock	zoke	zold
zout	zorn	zore	zub	zuck	zy	zad	zamp	zade
zain	zar	zen	zeal	zew	zend	zig	zill	zide
zag	zand	zake	zark	zaw	zam	zame	zang	zash
zan	zank	zet	zim	zent	zeam	zing	zime	zod
zong	zone	zud	zump	zunt	zap	zate	zest	zat
zane	zug	zeat	zin	zish	zint	zeep	zatch	zeed
zog	zum	zip	zink	zone	zope	zun	zut	zive
zot	zuff	zunk	zeet	zung	zow	zown	zab	zack

1. Read the first two words to your student and explain that most of these words are not real words. Tell the student you want to find out how well he knows the sounds of the letters.

2. Have him read the entire first row across the top of the page without help. Tell him to say "I don't know" whenever necessary.

3. Circle each one that he misses, using another copy for recording.

4. This test is recommended for grade 3 and up.

letters at the end of one-syllable words or at the end of syllables in multi-syllable words.

Since the phonogram test doesn't show how well a child recognizes consonant letters, digraphs, and clusters at the *beginning* of words, you may want to compensate by having the child tell you the sound each consonant letter, digraph, and cluster makes, or by pointing to each one and asking him to tell you a word that starts that way. Another way to accomplish the same thing, however, is to administer the "Baf Test" shown in Figure 10.4.

The "Baf Test" is a type of phonics test based on nonsense words. The advantage of nonsense words is that none or few of the words can be decoded on the basis of visual memory. Nearly all require recognition of phonic elements. For the Baf Test, the vowel pattern and phonogram are held constant for the consonant letters, digraphs, and clusters. The vowel patterns and phonograms change only for the second part. This test seems to work well with children who are already reading at least at the first-reader level and can understand the idea of "nonsense" words. First graders often find it puzzling, but children above second grade usually find it intriguing.

Figure 10.4 *The Baf Test*

Part I: Consonant letters, digraphs, and clusters

(For those whose instructional level is at least "First Reader")

This part of the inventory should be administered individually. You will need to reproduce a copy of this page for each child. The children should be encouraged to try decoding each nonsense word without your help. If they miss one, simply circle it and have them continue. Be sure to pronounce the first two for them *(băf and căf)* with a short /a/ and have them pronounce those two correctly before they continue.

Name of Student: _____

Directions to be Read or Told to the Student

These words are nonsense words. They are not real words. I'd like you to think about what sounds the letters have; then read each word out loud without my help. Don't try to go fast; read the list slowly. If you have any trouble with a word, I'll just circle it and you can go on to the next one. The first word is *băf*. Now you say it. The second is *căf*. Now you say it. . . . All right, now go on to the rest of the words in row 1.

A	B	C	D	E	F	G	H
Consonant Letters							
1. baf	caf	daf	faf	gaf	haf	jaf	
2. kaf	laf	maf	naf	paf	raf	saf	
3. taf	vaf	waf	yaf	zaf	baf	bax	caf
Consonant Digraphs							
4. chaf	phaf	shaf	thaf	whaf	fack	fang	fank
Consonant Clusters							
5. blaf	braf	claf	craf	draf	dwaf	flaf	fraf
6. glaf	fraf	fand	plaf	praf	quaf	scaf	scraf
7. skaf	slaf	smaf	snaf	spaf	splaf	spraf	squaf
8. staf	straf	swaf	thraf	traf	twaf		

Part II: Vowel letters, vowel digraphs, and clusters

(For those whose instructional level is at least "First Reader")

This part of the inventory should also be administered individually. You will need to reproduce a copy of this test for each child. The children should be encouraged to try decoding each nonsense word without your help. If they miss one, simply circle it and have them continue. Be sure to pronounce the first one for them *(băf)* and have them pronounce it correctly before they continue.

Name of Student _____

Directions to be Read or Told to the Student

"These words are nonsense words. They are not real words. I'd like you to think about what sounds the letters have; then read each word out loud without any help. Don't try to go fast; read the list slowly. If you have any trouble with a word, I'll just circle it and you can go on to the next one. The first word is *baf*. Now you say it. . . . All right, now go on to the rest of the words in row 1."

A	B	C	D	E	F	G
1. baf	bafe	barp	baif	bawf		
2. bef	befe	berf	beaf			
3. bof	bofe	borf	boaf	bouf	boif	boof
4. bif	bife	birf				
5. buf	bufe	burf				

THE MAIN IDEAS IN THIS CHAPTER

Children should learn to read with books that are not too difficult or too easy. This means that teachers who use basal readers need to place children in the correct basal, and that all reading teachers, no matter what medium of instruction they use, need to have a good idea of each child's instructional level.

Recommendations from children's previous teachers should be only one source of information in making a decision as to instructional levels. There are many reasons for not relying exclusively on such recommendations.

Standardized tests are norm-referenced. They are valid only to the extent that the norm group represents your students. The group-administered type is fairly accurate in comparing groups, but is not accurate in comparing individual students. Teachers should *not* use group-administered standardized test scores as the sole determiner of a child's placement in a book for instruction.

Getting "every child up to grade level" is a goal that matches neither reality nor the meaning of "grade level." "Grade level" refers to an *average* score of a norm group. By definition, some children will be above and some below average.

A child's miscues on an informal reading inventory should be examined for quality rather than quantity. The C-G-Q scoring method provides this opportunity.

Miscue analysis is a useful technique not only in scoring an informal reading inventory but also in helping a teacher understand each student's reading concept and strategies. Such an understanding can help the teacher move each child toward reading as communication rather than reading as isolated exercises.

Deciding what book to use for a child's instruction is sometimes a political and emotional matter as well as a diagnostic one.

For children above the third grade, the "cloze" or "maze" technique can be used to provide quick first-time estimates of instructional levels.

Special phonics tests can provide teachers with more precise information as to how well children recognize common graphophonic patterns.

REFERENCES AND SUGGESTED READING

Aasen, H. B. (1959). A summer's growth in reading. *Elementary School Journal, 60,* 70–74.

Baumann, J. F., & Stevenson, J. A. (1982). Understanding standardized reading achievement test scores. *Reading Teacher, 35,* 648–654.

Beebe, M. J. (1979–80). The effect of different types of substitution miscues on reading. *Reading Research Quarterly, 15,* 324–336.

Betts, E. A. (1946). *Foundations of reading instruction.* New York: American Book Co.

Bond, G. L., & Dykstra, R. (1967). The cooperative research program in first-grade reading instruction. *Reading Research Quarterly, 2,* 5–142.

Bradley, J. M., & Ames, W. S. (1976). The influence of intrabook readability variation on oral reading performance. *Journal of Educational Research, 70,* 101–105.

Brown, L. L., & Sherbenou, R. J. (1981). A comparison of teacher perceptions of student reading ability, reading performance, and classroom behavior. *Reading Teacher, 34,* 557–560.

Clay, M. (1968). A syntactic analysis of reading errors. *Journal of Verbal Learning and Verbal Behavior, 7,* 434–438.

D'Angelo, K. (1982). Correction behavior: Implications for reading instruction. *Reading Teacher, 35,* 395–398.

D'Angelo, K. (1983). Insertion and omission miscues of good and poor readers. *Reading Teacher, 36,* 778–782.

Dykstra, R. (1968). Summary of the second-grade phase of the cooperative research program in primary reading instruction. *Reading Research Quarterly, 1,* 49–70.

Ekwall, E. E., & English, J. (1971). *Use of the polygraph to determine elementary school students' frustration level.* Final Report, Project #OG078. Washington, DC: U.S. Dept. of Health, Education, and Welfare.

Elgart, D. B. (1978). Oral reading, silent reading, and listening comprehension: A comparative study. *Journal of Read-*

ing Behavior, 10, 203–207.

Englert, C. S., & Semmel, M. I. (1981). The relationship of oral reading substitution miscues to comprehension. *Reading Teacher, 35,* 273–280.

Goodman, K. S. (1969). Analysis of oral reading miscues: Applied psycholinguistics. *Reading Research Quarterly, 5,* 9–30.

Gunning, T. G. (1982). Wrong level test: Wrong information. *Reading Teacher, 35,* 902–905.

Johnston, P. H. (1982). *Reading comprehension assessment: A cognitive basis.* Newark, DE: International Reading Association.

McKenna, M. C. (1983). Informal reading inventories: A review of the issues. *Reading Teacher, 36,* 670–679.

Pikulski, J. J., & Shanahan, T. (Eds.). (1982). *Approaches to the informal evaluation of reading.* Newark, DE: International Reading Association.

Schwartz, J. I. (1977). Standardizing a reading test. *Reading Teacher, 30,* 346–368.

Silvaroli, N. J. (1979). *Classroom reading inventory.* Minneapolis, MN: William C. Brown Company.

Zintz, M. V. (1972). *Corrective reading.* Minneapolis, MN: William C. Brown Company.

APPLICATION EXPERIENCES FOR THE TEACHER EDUCATION CLASS

A. *What's your opinion?* Use the ideas in the textbook and your own experiences to justify your decision.

1. Placing a child in instructional materials that are too hard to read is worse than placing her in materials that are too easy.

2. Children should be placed in basal readers and reading groups according to their parents' wishes.

3. The previous teacher has the best idea of a child's reading level. After all, she spent almost a year with that child.

4. Standardized reading tests have the advantage of being scientifically developed and scored. They are an excellent indicator of each child's reading level and meet many criteria for helpful diagnosis and evaluation.

5. Getting every child up to grade level is a goal that matches neither reality nor the meaning of "grade level."

6. A child's miscues on an informal reading inventory should be examined for quality rather than quantity.

B. *Miscue Analysis:* Using Figures 10.5 and 10.6, compute C-G-Q scores for fifth-grader Victor on the fourth-grade selection he read. There are 182 words in the selection and Victor has 23 miscues (13%). Even if

Harriet Tubman never dreamed (that) she would become
famous. She had been born a slave and could (neither) read
nor write. When she was thirteen a slave boss struck her
(on the) head with a heavy iron weight. For the rest of her
life she carried an ugly scar.

She escaped from slavery and began helping others to
escape. People called her Moses because she would wait
outside a slave cabin and sing a little song, "Go down Moses."
It was a signal to get ready. She had come to help them
escape.

After a while she was so well known (that) the slave
owners offered a (large) reward for her capture. They offered
forty thousand dollars in gold for Harriet Tubman, whether
dead or alive.

One day she was sitting at a railroad station. Two men
walked by. She knew they were looking at her. She listened
carefully and overheard them talking about the reward. Quietly
she took out a book and pretended to read. They walked by
again and she heard one say, "That's not her. That can't be
Moses. Moses can't read."*

1. *Inferential:* (Asked after first paragraph) What is this going to be about? (I'm not sure. About a slave.)
2. *Literal:* Why did she have an ugly scar? (Her boss hit her.) What did he hit her with? (His pipe?)
3. *Inferential:* Did she help slaves or convicts to escape? (Slaves.) How do you know? (Because there were slave owners trying to catch her.)
4. *Literal:* How much was the reward for her capture? (Forty thousand dollars in gold.)
5. *Inferential:* Why did they offer so much money? (Because they were rich, I guess.) Any other reason? (They wanted to catch her real bad.)
6. *Literal:* What did she do to escape from the men who were looking for her? (She tried to look like she was reading.)

*Colin Dunkeld, Portland and Informal Reading Inventory, Form P, Page 6, Unpublished Manuscript, Portland State University, School of Education.

Figure 10.5 *Transcription of Victor's Miscues*

Selections Student Has Read

No.	Level =		Level =		Level =		Level =		Level =		Level =	
	C	G	C	G	C	G	C	G	C	G	C	G
1.												
2.												
3.												
4.												
5.												
6.												
7.												
8.												
9.												
10.												
11.												
12.												
13.												
14.												
15.												
16.												
17.												
18.												
19.												
Totals												
Percents												
Q scores												
CGQ total												

Figure 10.6   CGQ Evaluation Form for an IRI

you omit his two self-corrections, he still has 21 miscues (12%). By traditional quantitative standards, this selection represents his frustration level (traditionally considered to be above 10%). Do your results using the C-G-Q scales show him to be above or below this traditional frustration level? What can you tell from the miscues about his reading concept and strategies?

FIELD EXPERIENCES IN THE ELEMENTARY SCHOOL CLASSROOM

A. Using a tape recorder, administer an informal reading inventory to an elementary student. Write a professional report, describing the following:

1. Miscue data on three selections (similar to Figure 10.5)

2. C-G-Q data on the same three selections (similar to Figure 10.6)

3. An estimate of the student's concept of what reading is, using several miscues as examples

4. An estimate of the student's reading strategies (his use of the four cueing systems), using several miscues as examples

5. An estimate of the student's instructional level, using both miscue data and C-G-Q data as justification

B. Administer a phonics test to an elementary student, without the use of a tape recorder. Write a professional report describing your procedures, results, and conclusions.

11 THE CONTENT AREAS: CONTINUED GROWTH IN READING AND STUDY SKILLS

CHAPTER PREVIEW

Reading instruction may begin with basal readers, language experience stories, or self-selected library books. But from third or fourth grade on, the bulk of the practice in reading that most students get occurs during the reading of "content area" materials.

From third grade through twelfth, a student is expected to read at least 30,000 pages from science textbooks, social studies textbooks, math textbooks, literary anthologies, laboratory manuals, and so on. Let's imagine that each one of those pages is a stepping stone placed across a wide lake. If we place those stepping stones three feet apart, a student could reach the other side even if the lake were 17 miles wide!

That's a lot of reading! Yet, it's just a 50-yard dash compared to what those marathoners have to read who continue on through college, graduate school, and a lifetime profession that requires daily reading to keep up to date. Becoming a better, more efficient, more flexible, and more reflective reader is a learning process that may end at one's funeral, but certainly not at one's primary school graduation. This is why nearly every teacher becomes a reading teacher whether he wants to be or not. Nearly every subject that children and adults study today in our society must be partially learned through the process of reading.

Sometimes parents and teachers alike assume that once you teach a child the basic skills of reading, she should be able to read anything—a science text, a math text, whatever. Not so, of course. To take a simple illustration: even something as easy to use as a telephone book requires special skills that need to be learned. Tammie may be able to read a sixth grade basal reader, a library book about dinosaurs, and a long report on flying saucers that she wrote by herself, but still fail miserably in finding the telephone number of a good eye doctor whose office is not too far away.

Every type of reading material, as well as every content area, has its own peculiarities that have to be learned. Each content area has its own special vocabulary (and jargon), its own style of structuring sentences, its own logical organization, its own required reading speed, and its own assumptions about what experiences the reader has already had. In assuming what experiences the reader has already had, the author can so often go wrong. Writers cannot know what experiences every reader has had, nor can they accurately guess what schemata readers have invented on the basis of their experiences. Thus, while helping children learn how to deal with this problem, teachers need to understand why content area material is so much more difficult than experience stories, or basal reader stories, or most library books. They need to know how to develop children's schemata so they can cope with such difficult materials, learn to read different materials at different rates, learn to skim or scan for just the right information and no more, and, especially, learn to read material aggressively for specific purposes.

Most adults would think it unwise to send a child on a long, difficult journey with only a map and no instruction on how to use a map. In the same way, it is unwise to send a child through the communication maze he is expected to get through during his life without first explaining to him some of the keys to the map.

In *our* schools reading is the dessert.
In *Earth* schools reading is the main course.

WHY CONTENT AREA MATERIAL IS DIFFICULT TO READ

At least five factors have a major influence on the difficulty of textbooks and other content area materials: passage structure, vocabulary, sentence structure, paragraph structure, and imagery. Yet, when we boil these down even further, we find two underlying concerns: how much experience has the reader had with language, and how much experience has she had with the world?

Passage Structure

By the time they reach third grade, most children appear to be quite good at predicting what's going to happen next *in a story*. As mentioned in Chapter 3, they have learned to expect a main character who encounters a problem and does something about it. Their past experience provides them with a "top-level" schema (minitheory) about stories: there's going to be a setting, a main character, a conflict, and a resolution. When third graders are confronted with reading *content area* materials, they lack the kind of top-level schema that has helped them understand stories.

There's a vast difference between story passages and passages that explain things! Explanatory (exposition) passages usually give the reader no character to identify with, no setting, no conflict, no reaction to the conflict. Instead of leading the reader through a familiar and predictable structure, the writer instead tries to lead him through a twisted mass of information, which must seem to a child like a jungle, full of strange and frightening animals. Instead of encountering a main character or two, he encounters a series of abstract *ideas*. Instead of watching a character face a conflict, the reader himself must face strange monsters such as comparisons, contrasts, cause and effect, or, most hideous of all, the nine-headed water serpents called "lists" (Moore, Readence, & Rickelman, 1982). No, the schema he has for *stories* can't protect him from the "monsters of exposition."

To put it another way, content area reading is a very different ball-game. The teacher can't expect children to move from reading stories to reading social studies and science textbooks without a great deal of guidance. True, more and more basal readers provide informational articles as well as stories, which helps the transition to some extent, but it doesn't seem to be enough. Many children have had several years of training in story schemata by the time they reach third grade. It is unreasonable to think they will not need several years of training in exposition schemata. They will need to gradually learn the language of making comparisons and contrasts, of showing cause and effect, of developing main ideas through details.

Although we can often turn children loose to capture the butterflies called stories, we should not turn them loose with a butterfly net to capture the exposition monsters. The teacher needs to provide much more guidance and protection, leading children through a textbook assignment step by step, showing them *how* to separate cause from effect, how to make visual images of lists, and so on. There needs to be much more talking and writing about *informational* things, not just story things, as well; for example, "How can we compare these two things? How can we contrast these two things to show that they're different? What caused this to happen? Why?" Remember, through *talking* about informational matters, and through *writing* informational passages themselves, children can get a better feel for the informational language they are expected to *read*.

Vocabulary

All the content areas have their own specialized vocabulary, sometimes referred to as "jargon." It's difficult to talk about the social studies, for instance, without referring to the word *culture*, or to talk about the natural sciences without using the word *energy*. In mathematics we talk about *sets* and *operations*. To comprehend what they read in the content areas, children must rather quickly face these specialized words and be able to pronounce and understand them.

Sentence Structure

As children are given more and more content area materials to read, the number of dependent clauses (subordinate clauses) that they must face increases as well. Notice the dependent clauses (in italics) in the following sentences:

> Social Studies: The Zambezi is a river in Southern Africa, *flowing about 1,650 miles southeast through Rhodesia and Mozambique to the Indian Ocean.*
>
> Science: Moisture and heat are two agents of chemical change *that can create compounds from two or more elements.*
>
> Mathematics: *Because of the commutative principle,* the order in which certain operations are performed will not change the result.

The greater number of subordinate clauses is just one of many types of alterations and expansions of sentence patterns that make content area reading more difficult than many basal reader stories or library books.

Paragraph Structure

Guthrie (1979), after reviewing results of experimental studies, concluded that a highly readable paragraph contains two features: (1) a topic sentence at the beginning of the paragraph, and (2) coherence among the sentences in a paragraph. Unfortunately, many authors do not always write paragraphs with these two features. (Furthermore, such writing may become rather dull to mature readers.) The following are examples of paragraphs that are easy to read and more difficult to read.

> *Easy:* The skate is a strange looking fish. It's a flat fish with both eyes on top rather than one eye on each side of its head. As you look down on it, it appears a little like a diamond-shaped kite with a tail. The skate's tail looks as if it belongs to a snake rather than a fish.
>
> *More Difficult:* As you look down on it, it appears a little like a diamond-shaped kite with a tail. Its tail looks as if it belongs to a snake rather than a fish. But it's a fish, all right. It's a flat fish with both eyes on top rather than one eye on each side of its head. And with those eyes it searches constantly for food. The skate is a strange looking fish.

The second paragraph is more difficult to read for two reasons: (1) you have to wait until the end of the paragraph to find out the main idea the author wishes to express, and (2) the fifth sentence does not relate directly to the topic sentence or to the rest of the sentences. Research (Dupuis, 1984) shows that with this type of paragraph children find it more difficult to recall significant details. Yet one study (Donlan, 1980) found that in today's social studies textbooks, the topic sentence occurs as the first sentence of a paragraph only 13 percent of the time. In other words, in only one paragraph out of eight will you be likely to find the main idea by reading the first sentence.

Whether children *should* be taught to search for topic sentences is a moot point, since the research that justifies this activity is too sparse and inconclusive to give us any clear direction. Frankly, this has always seemed a rather mechanical, mindless way of looking for a main idea, anyway. Main ideas are seldom tucked neatly into one sentence. They are more dispersed throughout the entire paragraph or passage. Expecting to find the main idea in one sentence is like expecting to find the theme of an entire symphony in one measure. As most teachers and researchers will probably admit, main ideas are *often* difficult for students to determine (Berryhill, 1984). My hunch is that this is not because authors refuse to encapsulate their main ideas into the first sentence in each paragraph; it's because the material children are reading is too difficult in the first place, and thus they have difficulty bringing their schemata to bear upon the task—reading becomes a consumption of words rather than ideas. In a study involving 7,000 students in grades four, seven, and ten, the reading materials required in both the language arts and the social studies were found to be above the students' grade level (Kirkwood & Wolfe, 1980). My point is this: even though research may show that children can read paragraphs more easily when the first sentence broadcasts the main ideas, most authors don't write that way. (Nor do most people talk that way.) To help children grasp paragraphs better, we will first have to find some way to give them material at their level.

Imagery

When we read with comprehension, we have to create images in our minds: sights, sounds, smells, tactile sensations, muscular sensations, tastes. Reading in the content areas requires an enormous amount of intensive image making. With lightweight stories from basal readers or library books, image making becomes almost automatic, particularly when the child has been helped to find books and stories of the right difficulty. Furthermore, school-age children usually develop story schemata that help them predict "what's going to happen next." With content area material, however, children are often expected to slow down and "figure out" just what picture or sensation in the mind the author wants the reader to make. Let's look at the same three sentences again to see the extent of image making that is required:

Social Studies: The Zambezi is a river in Southern Africa, flowing about 1,650 miles southeast through Rhodesia and Mozambique to the Indian Ocean.

Science: Moisture and heat are two agents of chemical change that can create compounds from two or more elements.

Mathematics: Because of the commutative principle, the order in which certain operations are performed will not change the result.

Images, of course, are based on our own personal experiences and schemata. In the sentence about the Zambezi River, for example, we need

to have had experiences similar to the following in order for understanding to take place:

1. Seeing rivers in reality or in pictures

2. Seeing Africa on a map or globe or journey

3. Using directions (N, S, E, W, SE) on a map

4. Hearing the word *flowing* when referring to liquid

5. Traveling for many miles and noticing how long it takes

6. Seeing oceans in reality or in pictures

In an instructional sense, this means that teachers need to help children learn strategies for increasing their own image-making power. Such power in turn enables children to do a better job of allowing their own schemata to interact with semantic, syntactic, and graphophonic cues the author presents.

DEVELOPING CHILDREN'S CONTENT AREA READING STRATEGIES

Before children's image-making power can be used effectively in interactive reading, several related skills need to be developed. These skills, usually emphasized in the middle and upper grades, are:

1. Using a flexible reading rate

2. Using an appropriate speed set

3. Skimming and scanning

4. Developing a visual memory for sequential events

5. Finding reading materials at the right level of difficulty

6. Developing specialized vocabularies

7. Reading graphic materials

8. Locating information

9. Recording information

10. Using the PQ3R method

11. Reading content-area materials for a purpose

TOWARD A FLEXIBLE READING RATE

Research (McDonald, 1965) has shown that many people read various materials inflexibly—at the same speed—even though the content of the materials or their purposes for reading them vary considerably. Research (Spache & Spache, 1979) also shows, however, that students can be taught to vary their speed to match the materials. Many children who read a great many light, fictional books find themselves trying to read textbooks with the same rapid speed, even though they can't understand them at this speed. On the other hand, the small number of children who usually limit their reading to informational materials may attempt to read fiction at the same careful pace.

The task of helping some children read more flexibly, however, can't be successfully tackled until you've first helped them overcome their tendency to read everything too slowly. Obviously children can't be truly flexible until they are actually capable of reading at various speeds. So let's tackle this problem first. The following list describes some of the factors that usually account for habitually slow reading.

Materials too difficult. This is an obvious cause of some cases of slow reading, although one that is frequently ignored. In the past, science, social studies, and math textbooks have usually required children to read well beyond their personal reading level. This situation is getting better (Johnson, 1977) as authors attempt to relate their information to the schemata of today's children. However, school districts still tend to buy content area textbooks with the idea that every child in the same grade will be reading the same one. Since we know that children's reading levels vary tremendously within a single grade level, you can see what a burden this puts on some children. In a later section we'll address the procedures teachers can use to ease this burden.

Reading word-by-word. We've talked about this behavior several times already. It's encouraged by giving students material that's too difficult. It's fostered by teachers who have children concentrate on sounding out words rather than using all four cueing systems to determine an author's message. It's reinforced whenever children are praised merely for pronouncing each word correctly. It's also the result of insufficient right-hemisphere experiences that help children intuitively recognize letter patterns—phonograms, vowel patterns, affixes, compound words, and so on. As I mentioned earlier, research shows that word-by-word reading habits can continue into the college years; but it also shows that these habits can be changed even at this late stage in the learning process.

Weak image-making ability. Reading too slowly also seems to occur when children are not producing their own images as they read. It's as if the pronounced words are entities in themselves rather than symbols for events, places, things, and people. In other words, not only do overly slow readers read word-by-word, they aren't engaged in making pictures of what they're reading, in using their minitheories about life and language to help them find out what the author is saying. They'll often use their schemata quite readily in a listening situation, but they have yet to connect listening and reading as similar language processes. They need, no matter what their age, a language experience approach to help them get over this lack of insight. They need parallel listening-reading lessons in which thinking skills are first practiced in listening situations and then followed by similar practice in reading situations. They need many, many listening-talking experiences in which they have a chance to pantomime, draw, and discuss what they perceive another person is saying or reading aloud.

Vocal or subvocal reading. Vocal reading is simply reading out loud (usually by whispering) when silent reading is called for. This habit is fairly common with beginning readers, but usually disappears with practice in silent reading—although it may be more persistent with children who have not had opportunities for both vocal and silent reading from the very beginning of reading instruction. Subvocal reading is also quite common among beginners and even among some adults. The most primitive form of subvocal reading is moving the lips. Although this habit may be easily overcome, many people then progress to moving the muscles related to the tongue, throat, and vocal chords.

Whether vocal or subvocal reading is truly a disadvantage, though, has yet to be adequately demonstrated. Some teachers and researchers fear that the habit of vocal or subvocal reading limits students' reading speed to their talking speed, which is lower. Whereas a fast speaking speed is over 200 words per minute, fast readers can read up to 900 words per minute, and even faster than that if they omit many of the words and simply get "the gist of it." Sticht (1984) found that when most people read informational material, however, comprehension deteriorates rapidly after 200 or 300 words per minute.

It's doubtful that teachers should be overly concerned with children's subvocal reading. By fourth grade most children seem to have overcome their habits of whispering and lip moving. Generally all that's needed is to draw their attention to the habits. Some children may find the habits easier to overcome by putting their fingers on their lips or by holding something between their lips when they engage in silent reading. Research (Bruinsma, 1980) shows, however, that subvocalization may actually assist less able readers and should not be discouraged until comprehension has considerably improved. Probably one of the best long-range treatments is a steady diet of high-interest, low-vocabulary trade books—fictional or well-written informational accounts that sweep the reader along, causing him to devour books in large meaningful gulps rather than tiny meaningless nibbles.

Subvocal reading should not be viewed as some kind of disease to be stamped out once and for all. Many of us—if not all—who have overcome the habit of subvocal reading revert to it when material is hard to comprehend. In fact, sometimes a passage may be so difficult we'll find ourselves whispering in an attempt to understand it. Perhaps this is only one more illustration of what the linguists call the "primacy of speech."

Lack of purpose for reading. Many slow readers read slowly simply because they are not driven by any urge to find out something. For years Jimmy Miller, a slow reader, has been reading merely to please the teacher or to "get it done." He has little concept of what it means to communicate with an author because he's never learned that authors have much to say to him personally. His perception of reading is similar to that of Jack Jacob's perception of his painting job. Jack is a painter's apprentice and it's his job to scrape off the excess paint from the windows of the buildings his boss paints. He likes to start at the top and scrape off each window from left to right in the first row. Then he moves down to the second row and again scrapes off each window from left to right, and so on. In the same way, Jimmy Miller scrapes each word off the page and lets the letters fall to the floor.

If Jimmy had been offered some language experience approaches during his earlier years in school, and if he had been given numerous "directed-reading-thinking-activities" throughout his school years (as described in Chapter 3), perhaps he would not now be such a slow reader. He would understand that reading is a form of communicating (rather than merely getting a job done) and that one needs to read for specific purposes. Yet is is never too late for Jimmy to learn these two things. Language experience approaches may be used at any level of education, such as having him dictate stories about something important in his personal life or involving him in meaningful experiences that he and others can then describe to the teacher on a group chart. Other ideas for helping Jimmy will be described in the section, "Reading Content Area Materials for a Purpose."

Children *can* learn to read at a fast, slow, or medium pace depending upon their purposes and the difficulty of the materials. But before attempting such training, you should consider the five factors just discussed and apply appropriate remedies for each child. It does little good, and may even do harm, to put a child through rate-building exercises before the problems that account for slow reading are corrected.

Various mechanical devices such as tachistoscopes and pacers have been used for years with the intent of increasing students' reading speed. Results of these practices have been too inconsistent, however, to be very encouraging (although the devices do provide incentive for some children). A simpler approach, and one that seems to work as well, is a three-component program: The first component is that of diagnosing and treating the more basic reading problems such as inadequate word-recognition skills and insufficient awareness of cueing systems. The second component is that of encouraging a good deal of voluntary reading of easy trade books to develop fluency. The third component is a series of rapid-reading exercises, for which the children's words-per-minute and questions-answered-correctly are recorded.

Motivation for these exercises is enhanced by having the children keep a graphic record of both their reading rates and comprehension scores. (Or you may wish to have them keep only a rate graph, "fining" themselves thirty words per minute for each incorrect answer.) Numerous commercial materials are available for such exercises, including the *Standard Test Lessons in Reading* (Teachers College Press) for children above grade 3, *Developing Reading Efficiency* (Burgess) for children above grade 5, and the units called "Rate Builders" in the upper levels of the *SRA Reading Laboratories* (Science Research Associates).

METACOGNITIVE MONITORING OF APPROPRIATE SPEED SETS

In Chapter 3 we discussed the need for metacomprehension as well as comprehension when people read. Metacomprehension, you may remember, refers to knowing *what* we know and *when* we know. It also refers to knowing what we have to do to comprehend what we read. Reading flexibility can't exist without the reader's awareness both of his purposes for reading and his reading speed. To develop flexibility, teachers need to show children how to read for specific purposes and how to remind themselves of the reading speed necessary for those purposes.

A good way to remind them is through analogies. Analogies can be useful metacognitive aids because they provide a visual or imaginative trigger to memory. Every child who enjoys backseat driving in the family car for example, is aware of the need for different driving speeds. One speed is fine for freeway and turnpike driving but extremely hazardous for mountain roads with snakelike curves. Once the teacher has helped children develop the capacity to read at different speeds, it then becomes a matter of explaining to them the virtue of reading different materials at different speeds and of helping them establish a *speed set* for each type of material.

For example, the teacher can compare the importance of reading flexibly to the importance of eating different types of food at different rates. Whereas butterscotch pudding (light fiction) can be gobbled with gusto, one needs to chew raw carrots (informational material) in a thoughtful manner. Otherwise, digestion (understanding) is seriously hindered. A person doesn't need to chew butterscotch pudding, and ought not to gobble raw carrots. These explanations should be supplemented with occasional reminders that help the children establish the proper set before they begin to read. If they are about to read informational material, for instance, they could be reminded that they will now be dealing with "raw carrots" rather than "butterscotch pudding."

A more specific set can be established, however, by discussing with them their purposes for reading a particular selection. If Donald's purpose is simply to find out what an authority has to say about a very specific topic, it is often a waste of his time to read an entire chapter or even entire pages. By using an index and by scanning until he finds a key word related to the topic, he not only saves himself a lot of time, he reads actively rather than passively—varying his rate of reading according to his purposes. This manner of reading is the type of mature behavior a teacher should encourage.

Anthony Manzo (1975) recommends a "guided reading procedure" to encourage purpose setting and flexible reading. Although this procedure would be too difficult for primary grade children, it is evidently one that can work well with older children. These are the six steps of his procedure:

1. The teacher selects a short passage of about 500 words from a textbook the students are using and establishes with them a definite purpose for reading the passage.

2. When the students have finished reading the passage, they tell the teacher everything they can remember while she writes it on the board.

3. The students return to the passage to check the facts they've put on the board and to see if they can add more.

4. After correcting their facts and adding more, teacher and students organize the information, either in an outline or a diagram of some kind. (As long as the students *help* in creating the diagram, I've found it can be a useful visual device for remembering information. If the diagram is imposed on the students, though, it can easily confuse them.)

5. The teacher either presents a minilecture or leads a discussion on how this new information on the board relates to information they've learned previously. (New ideas are better learned when related to old ideas.)

6. The teacher may present a short quiz on this new information. (A quiz *can* be a metacognitive aid—or even a test on a student's use of metacognitive aids—but I recommend that you usually have them self-score the quiz rather than just hand it in for scoring. It is motivating for most students just to see how well they have learned something.)

PURPOSEFUL SKIMMING AND SCANNING

Another way to encourage children to develop a flexible reading rate is to teach them *how* to engage in skimming and scanning. People often do not need to read every word in a selection to get the information they need. The most obvious example, again, is the telephone book. One would hardly read the entire telephone book or even an entire page to find the name of someone you wish to call. This ability to find quickly one tiny bit of information is called *scanning* and is one that many children pick up quickly. Others (usually those, it seems, who have developed the perception of reading as a word-by-word, sounding-out process) find it difficult to acquire this skill.

The basic technique for teaching the scanning skill is to give children a limited time to find a specific bit of information in a fairly simple selection that they all read. Three types of scanning are usually taught this way. Thomas and Robinson (1977, p. 216) refer to these three types as levels:

Level 1: Scanning for a bit of information that stands out easily—the date of a historic discovery in science, or the university with which a noted author was affiliated

Level 2: Scanning for an answer that is worded like the question

Level 3: Scanning for an answer that is worded differently from the question

An example of a Level 1 scanning assignment might be this: "How long is the great white shark in the story you're about to read?" An example of a Level 2 scanning assignment might be: "Does the great white shark circle its prey when it hunts or does it go straight in for the kill?" An example of a Level 3 scanning assignment might be this: "Do you think a great white shark is a cautious hunter or a fearless one? Find something on this page that supports your opinion."

While the scanning skill is highly useful for finding specific facts, the skimming skill has another function. Through skimming, one tries to get the gist of a story or article rather than find a specific answer to a specific question. We often use skimming to decide whether or not a library book is going to be a good one to check out.

Skimming is often used for previewing a selection before actually reading it. By reading the first paragraph, the subheadings, and the last paragraph, you are engaged in skimming. If the purpose, though, is to make sure a book has the kind of information or story one wants, many people extend their skimming by reading for several pages. In other words, they look for a rough idea of what the author is going to say. Sometimes they extend their skimming further by glancing through the index and table of contents. Some people skim this way simply to "pick up ideas" without having to read an entire book. (Bookstore proprietors will tell you that many people go into bookstores just for this purpose without ever buying a single book.)

As when teaching scanning, to teach skimming the teacher needs to provide questions and tests that encourage rapid, selective reading rather than slow, compulsive reading. Questions that encourage skimming include these: "What is this book going to be about? What information do you think there will be in this article that will be useful or interesting to you? Is this book fiction or nonfiction? Will this book give you the information you need for your report on modern-day Eskimos?"

MONITORING THROUGH VISUAL IMAGERY

Much of what a child encounters in content area materials requires a good visual memory for sequential events for comprehension to occur. Let's take a story problem in mathematics as an illustration:

> Jim leaves his house with a pocketful of money. He buys a present for his mother for $8.95. When he gets home he has $6.35 left. How much money did he have in his pocket before he bought the present for his mother?

This is the kind of problem that often gives children (and some adults) "fits." Many children will see the word *left* in the problem and assume that to "get the answer" you must subtract $6.35 from $8.95. By doing this, they show that they're not reading with comprehension. They're not creating in their minds a visual image of what sequence is occurring. Instead, they should picture in their minds Jim leaving his house with a large wad of money in his pocket. Then they should see him giving some of that money to a storekeeper. Then they should picture this: wad of money in Jim's pocket . . . take away money for present . . . equals money left. Finally they should picture themselves adding the money left in Jim's pocket to the money he spent on the present in order to get right back to the money he had in his pocket in the first place: $6.35 plus $8.95 equals $15.30. In other words, they should form a visual sequence of a subtraction situation, but one that requires addition to solve it. (Alas, what they should picture and what they actually see are often entirely different. What they often see is simply the word *left*.)

The cure for this is sometimes quite simple. Rather than verbally explain the problem over and over to the children, the teacher can realize that the difficulty lies with faulty visual imaging and schemata development. By engaging in a bit of spontaneous drama—Jim leaving home with a wad of money in his pocket and so on—the children can learn to see what's really happening in a story problem.

This same need for comprehension self-monitoring (through visual imaging) occurs when children read science and social studies texts. Fortunately, in some of these texts, the publishers include pictures of the sequence that is being described. It's important, then, for the teacher to help the children examine the pictures before asking them to read. In this way they will have the pictured sequence in their minds as they read. Of course, this form of directing the children should not continue indefinitely. Eventually all you should have to say is, "Study the pictures first and then read the words." (As most students who have not been trained this way will tell you, "I like a book with pictures because I don't have to read as long.") In other words, they perceive the pictures as decorations rather than as aids to visual memory and schemata development.

A great deal of science can come alive for children if you have them draw their own pictures of what they read in science texts. By having them compare pictures they've drawn with pictures they later find in encyclopedias and other books, you not only motivate careful reading, but also teach them to read for images and not for words. A great deal of social studies can come alive if you have them recreate historical events, geographical customs, and economic transactions through spontaneous creative drama.

The ideas presented to children in social studies texts can often be made more visual and meaningful through creative dramatizations, as we see in this description of one teacher's use of creative drama in his fifth grade social studies program: Mr. Novick and his pupils were studying European exploration of the Americas. The class was divided into five groups, one that chose to study Coronado, one to study Columbus, and so on. Each group was given help in finding information from library sources and the textbook. Each group then planned a skit to present the major ideas about the explorer. The plans were presented by each small group to Mr. Novick. Mr. Novick praised them for their work but asked questions to show them where they still needed to do more research. After further research, the groups modified the plans for their skits and again presented their ideas to Mr. Novick. If Mr. Novick approved their plans, they were free to rehearse their skits in earnest.

After all five groups had their skits ready, they presented them in a theater-in-the-round fashion—skit in the middle of the room, audience in a circle. After each skit, the audience provided praise and specific suggestions for improvement. Further rehearsals prepared the groups for presenting the skits to another class.

Mr. Novick's approach was very well structured and certainly made the social studies reading more visual and real to the children. However, not all drama experiences related to the content areas need to be this elaborate. Once the children have become used to giving spontaneous skits, they can be invited at any time to dramatize something they've been reading. After one small group has tried it, another group can be asked to give an interpretation. Inviting another class into the room (or another group in a team-teaching situation) can be reserved for special occasions when the children have decided with you to polish a skit for a larger audience.

FINDING READING MATERIALS AT THE RIGHT LEVEL OF DIFFICULTY

Another strategy a student needs for increasing her retention and image-making power is to find reading materials that are challenging enough without being too difficult. Children who have been engaged in a trade-book-individualized-reading program (TBIR program) seem to have less difficulty with this than children who have been taught to read primarily through basal reading programs. They are used to looking for books that match their reading abilities.

Naturally, this strategy can't be taught if the teacher insists on having every child "doing social studies" in the same textbook. Of course, there's nothing wrong in having every child use the same textbook for studying pictures, maps, and indexes, and for developing scanning and skimming skills. What may be wrong is to expect every child to be able to read the same book. A more successful approach is to have a variety of textbooks and tradebooks available, in the room or the library, that offer similar information at different reading levels.

This means in actual practice that teachers need to be willing to have children read for specific *purposes* rather than to cover specific pages. Rather than assignments of definite pages to read in a definite textbook, their assignments look more like this:

> "Where did Columbus get the idea that it would be safe to sail westward to reach the East Indies? What made him so sure of himself? Why did he want to make the journey? Was he trying to get rich, or do you think he had other plans? If you had been a sailor at that time, do you think you would have gone with him?"

With open-ended assignments like this, children are encouraged to read in a variety of sources and to look for sources within their reading capabilities.

CHILDREN'S LITERATURE ONCE MORE TO THE RESCUE

Today's libraries are chock-full of trade books that can be used to supplement textbooks in the social, biological, and physical sciences. Books by Alvin and Virginia Silverstein, for example, can help children in grades three through six to a better understanding of humans and animals. Their series, *All About Them* and *Systems of the Body*, provide several books that are highly readable and informative. Another science author, Seymour Simon, has written more than fifty books designed to help young children understand, in everyday language, interesting facts and principles concerning the earth, space, and animals. His *Meet the Giant Snakes* and *Danger from Below: Earthquakes, Past, Present, and Future* are just two examples of the solid but easily digested "food" in this author's larder.

It would take several hundred pages to describe the thousands of trade books now available to elementary school teachers and students of the content areas. A good source for becoming aware of social studies trade books is the annual list, "Notable Children's Trade Books in the Field of Social Studies." You can obtain this list by writing to Children's Book Council, 67 Irving Place, New York, New York 10003. These are a sampling of useful books in the biological, physical, and social sciences:

The Biological Sciences

Aliki, *The Long-Lost Coelacanth and Other Living Fossils*

Amon, *Reading, Writing, Chattering Chimps*

Bendick, *The Mystery of the Loch Ness Monster*

Cole, *A Frog's Body*

Dowden, *The Blossom on the Bough: A Book of Trees*

Graves, *What Is a California Sea Otter?*

Halmi, *Zoos of the World*

Levine, *Lisa and Her Soundless World*

McClung, *How Animals Hide*

Silverstein, *Exploring the Brain*

The Physical Sciences and Mathematics

Adler, *Magic House of Numbers*

Branley, *Color: From Rainbows to Lasers*

Freeman, *Gravity and the Astronauts*

James and Barkin, *The Simple Facts of Simple Machines*

Lauber, *Tapping Earth's Heat*

Maestro, *Oil: The Buried Treasure*

National Geographic, *How Things Work*

Navarra, *Earthquake*

Nixon, *Glaciers: Nature's Frozen Rivers*

Watson, *Binary Numbers*

The Social Sciences

Aliki, *Mummies Made in Egypt*

Baker, *Settlers and Strangers: Native Americans of the Desert Southwest and History as They Saw It*

Bales, *Chinatown Sunday: The Story of Lillian Der*

Bernheim, *In Africa*

Cartwright, *What's in a Map?*

Clarke, *The American Revolution 1775–83: A British View*

Erdoes, *The Native Americans*

Fisher, *The Factories*

Foster, *The World of William Penn*

Fritz, *The Double Life of Pocahontas*

Kurelek, *Lumberjack*

Macaulay, *Underground*

Meyer, *Eskimos: Growing Up in a Changing Culture*

Rau, *The People of New China*

Steele, *Westward Adventure: The True Stories of Six Pioneers*

Singer, *We All Come from Puerto Rico, Too*

Warren, *Pictorial History of Women in America*

Wolf, *In This Proud Land: The Story of a Mexican American Family*

USING PEER WRITTEN AND TEACHER WRITTEN MATERIAL

There may be a few children in your class whose reading skills are so poor they have trouble with both textbooks and trade books. In this case you may wish to provide them with peer-written or teacher-written material. Peer-written material is obtained by asking certain children to contribute their written reports to the classroom or school library. Teacher-written material is obtained by paraphrasing textbook material in very simple language. In either case, it's a good idea to use some type of attractive binding (and even illustrations, if possible). It's also advisable to type these "home-made" materials with large type and to include no more than one paragraph on each page.

CONFRONTING SPECIALIZED VOCABULARY

In Chapter 4 we discussed the importance of verbal and nonverbal experiences to the acquisition of vocabulary. As you may recall, we examined the hypothetical case of a child's learning the phrase *rozaga hunt*. Using Dale's Cone of Experience as our model, we had David going on an actual rozaga hunt in order to get the deepest understanding of the phrase. Unfortunately teachers have neither the time nor money to explain most content area terms that well. Consequently, they have to resort to contrived experiences, creative dramatics, motion pictures, still pictures, verbal analogies, and other aids. All the ideas described in Chapter 4 for developing vocabularies through basal readers and library books apply equally well to content area textbooks.

The basic strategy the child must learn for dealing with specialized words in content areas is *not* to ignore them. This tends to be a strong habit for some children by the time they reach the intermediate grades—a habit that carries right on into adulthood. Their thinking, when you talk to them about it, seems to be something like this: "Oh, it's just a word we use a lot in science." If they can pronounce it, they are often content with that much success. Because of this attitude, it's often important for teachers to prepare children for reading a content area selection by discussing key words ahead of time. The word *energy*, for instance, may be placed on the chalkboard in sentences incorporating many context clues:

The horse had enough *energy* to pull a heavy wagon.

The chemical *energy* in a car battery is enough to run a starting motor.

By turning on the toaster you can change electrical *energy* into heat *energy* and toast your bread.

A door knob changes muscle *energy* into mechanical *energy*.

Then, after they've read the sentences, have them discuss what they think energy is. After a brief discussion, have each child write down her own definition in one simple sentence. Then she can look up the word in a dictionary, glossary, or science book to see how close she came. (Please refer to Chapter 4 for more ways to help children with vocabulary.)

READING GRAPHIC MATERIALS

When students see a graph or table they often say to themselves, "Oh boy, now I have less to read," *and then skip it.* I remember my own reluctance to give such visual aids anything more than "the briefest glance" until I suddenly realized they were more fun than the dull text that frequently accompanied them. A graph or table offers a student something that exposition seldom provides—the chance to get actively involved in "creating" his own information. Take the graph shown in Figure 11.1, for example. See how much information you can "create" without the need of any accompanying text. (Please look at Figure 11.1 before continuing.)

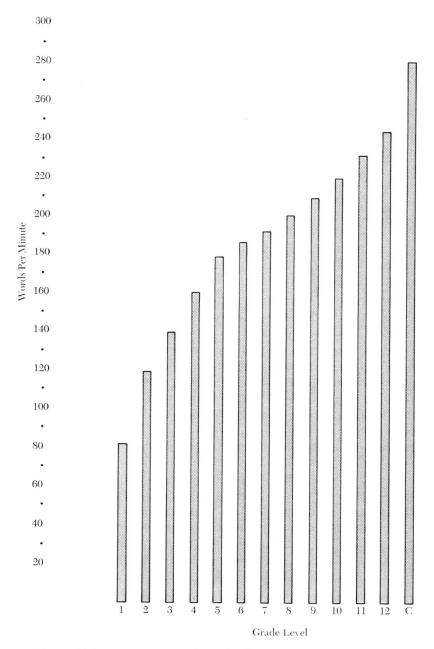

Figure 11.1 An Estimate of Student's Average Reading Rates of Informational Material Grades 1 through College. Based on information reported by Taylor, Frackenpohl, and Pettee (1960, p. 12).

Having "invented" your own facts and generalizations based on the graph in Figure 11.1, perhaps you would agree that graph reading is more fun than exposition like this: "Average reading rates seem to vary almost directly with grade level. In a study by Taylor, Frackenpohl, and Pettee (1960), they found that the average reading rate for first grade was eighty words per minute. For second grade, however, they found that the rate was one hundred fifteen words per minute. For third grade the rate was one hundred thirty-eight words per minute, while for fourth grade, the rate was one hundred fifty-eight words per minute. For fifth grade. . . ." Pretty dull and hard to assimilate this way, isn't it?

Now look at Table 11.1 and see what information you can generate on your own. Here, too, it can be seen that reading information presented in this manner would probably be more interesting than reading the same information in a long, fact-studded paragraph. By looking at graphs and tables you can usually *skip the dull reading!*

Maps can also be a fascinating way for children to gain information—witness the enthusiasm of children reading the map related to the journey of Bilbo Baggins in Tolkien's *Hobbit*. And so can diagrams and pictures, as shown by the eagerness displayed by children following diagrams for building model airplanes or studying pictures of dinosaurs.

If graphs, tables, maps, diagrams, and pictures can be so interesting, why are they often passed over with only the briefest glance? There are probably numerous reasons for this, including the possibility that they take more energy to read than simple exposition. But perhaps the biggest reason is that children have had too few opportunities to discover that reading them can be fairly easy and enjoyable. One way to bring about such a discovery is through having the children create graphs, maps, tables, diagrams, and informational pictures of their own. As a start you may wish to have them use simple information that you provide—such as average winter temperatures in various parts of the world, or other such statistical data found in almanacs. But as rapidly as possible, it is advisable to get them

Table 11.1 *Sex Differences between the Percentage of Boys and Girls Reading One Year or More Below Grade Level**

Grade	Boys	Girls
2	10%	4%
3	15%	7%
4	24%	12%
5	26%	12%

*Adapted from Arthur W. Heilman, *Principles and Practices of Teaching Reading*, 4th ed. (Columbus, OH: Charles E. Merrill, 1977), p. 74. Adapted with permission of the author and publisher.

involved in gathering their own information and translating that information into graphic or tabular form. There are almost limitless possibilities for such projects—a graph comparing the number of children in fifth grade who prefer vanilla, chocolate, and strawberry ice cream; a map of the classroom, the school, or the neighborhood; a diagram of "my dream house" or "how to make a simple glider"; a table showing school enrollment during the past ten years; a mural giving a reasonably accurate interpretation of village life in the Middle Ages.

All of these projects can be displayed for other children to read and discuss. This provides some of the guided practice necessary for learning to appreciate and understand "visuals"—and through the construction of these visuals, they will be able to discover for themselves the need for some type of scale on maps, graphs, diagrams, and informal pictures; the need for symbols such as color or special lines; and the need for accurate titles and labels.

LOCATING INFORMATION

For children to become adept at using content area materials, they need to learn how to locate precisely the information they want. The skill of locating information can be broken down like this:

1. Examining titles to determine appropriateness of books

2. Using a table of contents

3. Using an index

4. Using the glossary available in some books

5. Gaining information from appendixes

6. Finding appropriate visuals—maps, tables, graphs, pictures, and diagrams

7. Using the library card catalog

8. Using encyclopedias and other library reference books

Whereas most basal reader programs include useful exercises on many of the locational skills, these skills are usually mastered best through actual "research projects" in which children seek information in trade books, textbooks, encyclopedias, and other library references. Textbooks, though, such as those used for social studies or science, are often handy to use as raw material when the teacher wants to introduce or review locational skills with several students at the same time. Since several copies of a textbook are usually available, each child can look at the same example at the same time. Guided practice should not be limited to textbooks, however, as positive transfer is much more likely to take place when children also employ the locational skills with trade books and reference books they have found for themselves in the library.

As soon as children begin to use textbooks in science and social studies, they can begin to receive guided practice in "finding the secret treasures hidden within a book." Questions similar to the following are generally useful in helping children discover for themselves the utility of indexes, glossaries, illustrations, and so on. (To increase your own involvement and to gain a better understanding of the utility of such questions in aiding discovery, you can try answering these questions as they relate to the book you're reading right now.)

1. On what page can you find the beginning of an alphabetical list (called an *index*) of most of the things talked about in this book?

2. If you wanted to find out something in this book about how to increase children's reading speed, what topic would you look for in the index: children's reading speed? rate of reading? how to increase children's reading speed? reading rate? reading speed? Try those that you think may work and see which one is in the index.

3. On exactly what pages would you find information about children's reading speed?

4. On what page near the front of this book can you find a list of chapter titles?

5. On what page is there a table that might give you information about graphemes?

6. Between what pages is the chapter on phonics?

7. On what pages can you find suggestions for other books and articles to read on teaching phonics?

8. Looking only at the titles of articles suggested for additional reading on phonics, which one looks as if it may lead you to information on the so-called First Grade Studies. (Just indicate the number of the reference.)

9. If you were trying to find the library number of this book, which drawers would you look for in the card catalog? (Use letters.)

    a. The _____ drawer if I knew the first author's name.
    b. The _____ drawer if I knew the title.
    c. The _____ drawer if I only knew the subject of the book.

10. On what page in this book is the word *phonogram* defined?

11. Between what pages is there an appendix describing numerous "book projects?"

12. If you wanted to find out something about "how to teach deaf children to read," which two encyclopedia volumes would be most likely to contain the information you want? H T D C R

In addition to discovery questions, a teacher can also get children actively involved as "library detectives." A "detective's badge" or similar token can be given to those children who "find all the clues" or "solve the mystery." In this kind of activity, children are usually given clue cards or a list of clues and sent to the library ("the place in which the crime took place") singly, in pairs, or in supervised groups. The following "clues," though facetious in this instance, are the types of clues you could use:

1. The kind of weapon used in the crime was a revolver used by the Barsimians in the War of Tulips. What was the name of the weapon?

2. The main suspect in this case was last seen in the city of Atlantis. In what country is this?

3. The main suspect has the same name (or alias) as the man who wrote *Call of the Tame.* What is the suspect's name?

4. The motive for the crime probably had something to do with narcotics. From what you can find out about narcotics, why do you think the money was stolen, and who else besides the main suspect do you think was responsible for this crime?

A simpler form of this activity involves "clues" that are more direct, though less imaginative. With this form no "crime" has been committed; the clues are simply research problems geared to specific locational skills. For example:

Find in the card catalog the author of *Call of the Tame.*

What book in this library tells about the War of Tulips? You'll find it in the subject catalog under one of these topics: War of Tulips, Wars, Battles, or Tulips.

Use an encyclopedia to find the name of the revolver used by the Barsimians in the War of Tulips.

Some teachers also create the need for practicing locational skills by requiring children to prepare an oral or written report. If you take certain precautions (see the 1985 edition of *They All Want to Write* by Burrows,

Ferebee, Jackson, and Saunders), this is probably a worthwhile learning experience for most children. Requiring such a report without first providing specific training in locating, comprehending, and recording information, and without providing specific guidance during the preparation of the reports, however, generally leads to frustration for the teacher and negative reinforcement for the children.

RECORDING INFORMATION

When children read content area selections, they may sometimes wish to go no further than locating the appropriate material and comprehending it. On certain occasions, though, such as preparing for a report or gathering data for a hobby, children will need to record some of the information. This process seems to be burdensome and cumbersome to many students, perhaps as a result of numerous unguided attempts, leading to a negative attitude and to practicing clumsy techniques. Many teachers, it appears, ask children to "take notes" on what they read without first giving them the necessary training. As a result, the children usually copy information verbatim rather than jot down its essence. It is not a rare phenomenon to see high school and college students continue this habit.

There are at least two useful approaches to the training. One is the traditional outlining approach, which calls for two steps: (1) teaching children the procedure by actually outlining portions of textbooks with them, and (2) having them apply the outlining procedure to notetaking. For instance, take the previous portion of this chapter. The student who had received training in outlining might record the main ideas and important details like this:

I. Locating Information

    A. Specific skills related to use of

        1. Book titles
        2. Table of Contents
        3. Index
        4. Glossary
        5. Appendixes
        6. Visuals—maps, tables, graphs, pictures, diagrams
        7. Card catalog
        8. Encyclopedias and other references

    B. Teaching techniques

1. Basal reader exercises
2. Social studies or science textbooks
   a. "Secret treasure" for children to discover
   b. Discovery questions leading to use of A.1–A.8

3. Library detectives
   a. Detective's badge or other token
   b. Clues requiring use of A.1–A.8

4. Preparation for reports

II. Recording information

A. . . .

B. . . .

The outline approach is appropriate when students have a rather general assignment to learn all they can about a topic, or to read certain pages in a text, or when they are preparing for a report on a general topic. It is probably more common in out-of-school situations, however, to read informational sources for a specific purpose—to find the answer to a burning question, to learn how to do a particular thing related to a hobby, and so on. When this is the case, notetaking may be simply a matter of jotting down answers, rather than outlining a topic in logical arrangement.

Let's suppose, for instance, that you wished to read for the specific purpose of answering this question: How fast do high school students read? Using the graph in Figure 11.1, your notetaking may look like this:

1. 9th grade—about 214 w.p.m.—average for informational material

2. 10th grade—about 224 w.p.m.— "

3. 11th grade—about 237 w.p.m.— "

4. 12th grade—about 250 w.p.m.— "

To take an example closer to home, suppose you have to review for a test. You've heard through the grapevine that your instructor is going to make you "List ways of helping children learn the skills involved in locating information." (Let's hope this doesn't actually happen to you.) Instead of outlining what you've read on this, or covering three pages with yellow highlighter, you might take notes like these:

1. Use discovery-type questions to guide them through these skills with social studies or science textbooks

2. Use exercises provided in basal reader program

3. Have children become library detectives; give "clues" requiring use of locational skills

4. Have them use locational skills in preparing reports

These two approaches to notetaking—the outlining technique and the specific-purpose technique—can both be taught as soon as children have demonstrated their ability to decode and comprehend informational materials and to write well enough to read their own writing. For some children this will be during the third grade or even earlier; for others, it will be much later. It is doubtful, however, that teaching notetaking skills should be reserved for high school, since by that time too many bad habits will have developed.

PRE-RECORDING INFORMATION: GRAPHIC ORGANIZERS

Note taking is fine as long as children have the appropriate training for it. One of the problems children have in note taking, as well as in reading, however, is discerning which information is a main idea and which is detail that supports a main idea. Several educators have been trying to alleviate this problem with visual diagrams that parallel what the author is saying. Moore, Readence, and Rickelman (1982), for example, present an example of a graphic organizer for use with students who are reading about clothes and the types of fibers used to produce them, as shown in Figure 11.2.

Moore, Readence, and Rickelman recommend that the teacher present this type of diagram with an overhead projector and uncover it slowly from top to bottom. This method allows students to become directly involved. For example, the teacher might uncover the words *fibers*, *natural*, and *chemical* and say, "There are two main types of fibers for making clothes—

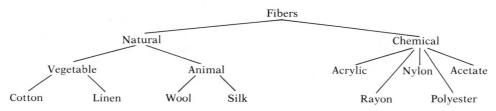

Figure 11.2 *Example of a Graphic Organizer (Moore, Readence, & Rickelman, 1982)*

natural and chemical. Nylon is one kind of chemical fiber. Do you know of any others?'' After gradually uncovering and discussing the diagram, as well as the students' ideas, the diagram can be left in view while they read the selection silently in their science or social studies textbook. The projector can be turned off afterward and a dittoed version passed out; leave several blanks on the ditto for them to fill in from memory, and then they can check their memory by referring back to the text. (The teacher should arrange other activities to enhance the students' schemata about fibers before they read the selection, such as passing out samples for them to feel, to examine with a magnifying glass, and to discuss.)

You can create other graphic organizers for passages that emphasize causes and effects, problems and solutions, sequence of events, and so on. A time line, for example, shows a sequence of important events. Rather than invent their own graphic organizers, however, some teachers use the diagrams, pictures, graphs, tables, or charts that are already included in the selection they're going to have the children read. The teacher first decides which visuals are most helpful in portraying the main ideas in the selection, then involves the students in examining the visuals and helping them decide the main ideas and supporting details they demonstrate. Next the students read silently to verify their ideas, and finally they check their ideas through discussion.

USING THE PQ3R METHOD

You've probably encountered the PQ3R (or SQ3R) method in your schooling. To refresh your memory, this approach can be summarized this way:

1. *Preview* the first paragraph or two, the subheadings, and the last paragraph or two.

2. Change each subheading into a *question* before reading a section.

3. *Read* the section to answer the question.

4. *Recite* to yourself the answer to the question.

5. *Review* the entire selection by repeating steps two and four *(question* and *recite)* for each section.

The PQ3R method has had a good track record and seems to help many people comprehend and retain content area reading material better than when they use no system whatever (Spache & Spache, 1979). In fact, some of the newer basal reader series are now introducing this method in middle-grade readers with selected informational articles. (It is not an appropriate method for fiction.)

The most effective means for introducing this approach is to have every child use the same book temporarily. You can give every child in the classroom a lower-grade social studies or science textbook for a few days. Rather than present the entire approach to the students in one session, it's best to introduce and practice one step at a time. Take two or three days to teach the preview step, for instance, before moving on to the question step. Before assigning them a few pages to read, have them use the preview step (first two paragraphs, subheadings, last two paragraphs). Then ask them questions like these: "What do you think this selection is going to be about? What else is it going to be about? What do you think the author will talk about first? What next? What we've just done is called a *preview*. Have you ever noticed how they use a preview on television—just before a movie or a show is going to start? Why do you think they do that? Why do you think it would be a good idea to preview something before you read it? Do you think it would get your mind ready for what the author is going to say to you?"

After they have learned the preview step well, introduce the question step. Go through an entire selection and show them how to change the subheadings into questions. Then go back and ask them again how they would change the first subheading into a question. As soon as they agree on an appropriate question (or questions) for that section, have them read for the purpose of answering the question. After they have agreed on the best answer to the question, move on to the next subheading and try the method again. Be sure when you're practicing the PQ3R method that you work on it only ten or fifteen minutes per day, so they get the idea that it's a snappy method that *works* rather than an additional burden they're now going to have to put up with in school.

Once they've learned the preview and question steps well, you're ready to "prove" to them how well the entire PQ3R method works. Give them a very short assignment; ask them this time not only to preview, question, and read, but to recite to themselves after each section, and then go back and review each section. Promise them they'll do very well on a short test you'll give them when they're finished. (Be sure the questions you write for the test are directly related to the most obvious questions into which they will most likely change the subheadings.)

The PQ3R method will quickly fall into disuse unless you give them opportunities to practice it frequently. Whenever an informational article appears in a basal reader that a small group is using, for example, you can use the opportunity to reinforce their skill in the method.

READING CONTENT AREA MATERIALS FOR A PURPOSE

Perhaps the most important strategy for children to develop in reading content area materials is to acquire a purpose for reading the material. There is nothing more wasteful of a student's time and natural curiosity than to attack a reading assignment with no motivation to learn anything in particular. As you may guess, this nonmotivation can reach epidemic proportions by the time children reach the sixth or seventh grade.

There are many reasons for this nonmotivation, of course, depending on the particular child. But two of the most likely causes for such a poor attitude toward reading content area materials are: (1) assigning too many pages for one assigment (Smith & Johnson, 1980), and (2) assigning pages to read without helping children develop any sense of excitement about what they will gain from reading them.

As for the number of pages in one assignment, it's far better to assign too few pages than too many. Remember, you're developing *habits* and not just covering material. The best way to develop the habit of not completing a reading assignment is to assign so many pages that children experience fatigue and give up. Ask any high school teacher; she'll tell you of the numerous students who have learned that the best way to handle a long reading assignment is simply not to read it.

As for assigning pages without developing a sense of purpose and excitement, probably no one is more guilty of this than college professors—the very people who serve as the "last-stop" models for those who become elementary and high school teachers. But, alas, this gives us no excuse to get even and do the same to children. Instead, we can use a variety of "interest getters" to make sure that most of our students will want to read the assignment in content area materials.

USING THE D-T-R-A APPROACH

Let's go back to the "directed-teaching-reading-activity" described in Chapter 3 for an example of creating motivation. The teacher wanted the children to read about the "Amazing Underground City" in New York; how the space under streets was filled with pipes and wires and other things; and how this underground city got started. She didn't say to the children. "For your social studies reading, I want you to read pages 257 to 265." Instead, she sparked their interest with an intriguing question: "Do you know what

kinds of things you can find underneath the streets here in New York City?" This led to some intelligent hypothesizing (pipes?) as well as to some imaginative guessing (monsters?) By the time they were through with their prereading discussion, the children were eager to read to find out two things: (1) What *is* under there? and (2) Was my guess right or not? In other words, the teacher used two types of "interest getters": first, sparking their curiosity about the unknown, and second, having them place their bets before the race begins (more mundanely known as "making predictions.")

USING INTEREST GETTERS

There are many other forms of "interest getters" you can try before asking children to read in content area materials. Here are just a few.

Believe it or not (before having them read an article about automobile manufacturing): "Would you like to own your own car someday? . . .

Do you think you could make your own car? . . . If you were going to make your own car, how many different kinds of parts do you think you'd have to put into it? . . . Did you know that to make a car today it takes 300 different kinds of parts . . . and not only that, those parts come from 56 countries! . . . As you read this article, see if you can find out what some of those different parts are and where they are made.''

Battle of the ages (before reading about one or both of the paired topics):

    a. "Who do you think was braver—the crew of astronauts who went to the moon, or the crews of the Nina, Pinta, and Santa Maria?"

    b. "Whose discovery was more important to people: Pasteur's or Einstein's?"

Puzzle appeal (before reading an article that attempts to solve the puzzle):

    a. "How can the richest nation on earth have so many poor people?"

    b. "What do you think you would find if you looked under the streets of New York City?"

Picture appeal (have them look at the picture related to an article they're going to read): "What do you think is happening in this picture? . . . What else? . . . Why do you think this is happening? . . . Does it happen anywhere else, do you think? . . . Read this article and see if your ideas are correct."

Prove me wrong (present a stereotype or another type of false statement, then have them read in order to prove you wrong):

    a. The commutative property works for addition, subtraction, multiplication, and division.

    b. Solar energy won't be useful to us for another thousand years!

    c. All monkeys are alike!

    d. Our sun is the biggest star in the whole universe!

Best prediction (don't let children know which article or section they're going to read, just give them the title): "From hearing the title, I'd like you to write down three things you think the author will say. Put your name on this sheet, fold it up, and place it in this prediction box. After you're finished reading, we'll see whose predictions came closest."

THE MAIN IDEAS IN THIS CHAPTER

Reading in the content areas requires specialized vocabulary and reading skills. Since children and adults spend so much time reading informational, nonfictional material, it's important that teachers prepare them for this type of reading.

Content area materials are difficult to read because of the abstractness of the writing and the reader's need for constant production of sensory images and associations related to previous experiences. Use of the schematic cueing system is required more than ever.

Teachers can assist children in comprehension monitoring by helping them learn how to produce visual images that fit individual schemata.

Teachers can help children develop strategies of reading at a flexible rate, aggressively interacting with tables, graphs, and other visual aids, and developing visual memory for sequential events—through a variety of instructional procedures.

Above all, children should learn to read with purpose. The teacher can help a great deal in encouraging purposeful reading by relating the reading to their main interests and by using a variety of "interest getters."

Content area materials should be available at each child's reading level. Multiple textbooks, trade books, peer-written materials, teacher-written materials, listening experiences—all can help accomplish this goal.

REFERENCES AND SUGGESTED READING

Askov, E. N., & Kamm, K. (1974). Map skills in the elementary school. *Elementary School Journal, 75,* 112–121.

Berryhill, P. (1984). Reading in the content area of social studies. In M. M. Dupuis (Ed.), *Reading in the content areas: Research for teachers* (pp. 66–74). Newark, DE: International Reading Association.

Braam, L. (1963). Developing and measuring flexibility in reading. *Reading Teacher, 16,* 247–254.

Bruinsma, R. (1980). Should lip movements and subvocalization during silent reading be directly remediated? *Reading Teacher, 34,* 293–396.

Davis, J. B. (1977). Improving reading and the teaching of science. *Clearing House, 50,* 390–392.

Donlan, D. (1980). Locating main ideas in history textbooks. *Journal of Reading, 24,* 135–140.

Dupuis, M. M. (Ed.). (1984). *Reading in the*

content areas: Research for teachers. Newark, DE: International Reading Association.

Guthrie, J. T. (1979). Paragraph structure. *Reading Teacher, 32,* 880–881.

Johnson, R. E. (1977). The reading level of elementary social studies textbooks is coming down. *Reading Teacher, 30,* 901–905.

Kirkwood, K. F., & Wolfe, R. C. (1980). *Matching students and reading materials: A cloze procedure method for assessing the reading ability of students and the readability of textual material.* Toronto: Ontario Ministry of Education.

Luffey, J. I. (Ed.). (1972). *Reading in the content areas.* Newark, DE: International Reading Association

Manzo, A. (1975). Guided reading procedure. *Journal of Reading. 18,* 287–291.

McDonald, A. S. (1965). Research for the classroom: Rate and flexibility. *Journal of Reading, 8,* 187–191.

Meyer, B. J. F., & Freedle, R. (1979). *The effects of different discourse types on recall.* Princeton, N.J.: Educational Testing Service.

Moore, D.W., Readence, J. E., & Rickelman, R. J. (1982). *Prereading activities for content area reading and learning.* Newark, DE: International Reading Association.

Robinson, H. A. (1975). *Teaching reading and study strategies: The content areas.* Boston: Allyn and Bacon.

Smith, R. J., & Johnnson, D. D. (1980). *Teaching children to read.* Reading, MA: Addison-Wesley.

Spache, G. D., & Spache, E. B. (1979). *Reading in the elementary schools.* Boston: Allyn and Bacon, 1979.

Sticht, T. G. (1984). Rate of comprehending by listening or reading. In J. Flood (Ed.), *Understanding reading comprehension* (pp. 140–160). Newark, DE: International Reading Association.

Taylor, S. E., et al. (1960). *Grade level norms for the components of the fundamental reading skill.* Research Information Bulletin No. 3, Educational Development Laboratories.

Thomas, E. L., & Robinson, H. A. (1977). *Improving reading in every class.* Boston: Allyn and Bacon.

Tyo, J. (1980). An alternative for poor readers in social science. *Social Education, 44,* 309–310.

APPLICATION EXPERIENCES FOR THE TEACHER EDUCATION CLASS

A. *What's your opinion?* Use your own experiences as well as the textbook to help you justify your decision.

1. Once you teach a child the basic skills of reading, she should be able to read anything—a science text, a math text, you name it.

2. Children should learn to read standard textbooks rather than relying on tradebooks.

3. Peer-written or teacher-written booklets can't possibly substitute for standard textbooks.

4. In this day and age, with copy machines everywhere, children really don't need to know how to take notes when they read.

5. Scanning and skimming are very different processes.

6. "Interest Getters" may be fine for children up to fifth grade, but after that they really shouldn't be necessary.

B. *Miscue Analysis:* Why is Jennie having trouble reading this textbook selection?

The first (hundred) [hunter] years in the history of[the] United States immigration [d]

had been, [d] in general, a period free [R] from [for] all restrictions [restaurants]. America had

become a refuge [referee] for the oppressed [opponents] of all lands.

C. *The PQ3R Method:* Use this method for a week or two with one of your college courses. Report to your education class on the effects you think this method is having on your retention of the materials you're supposed to be learning in that course.

D. *Preparing Students for Content Area Reading:* Divide the class into four groups: a math group, a natural science group, a physical science group, and a social studies group. Find two or three paragraphs from a textbook pertaining to your content area. Then decide on the following:

1. What "interest getter" would you use to get students to want to read them?

2. For what two key words will you help students develop stronger images and associations? Precisely how will you do this? Plan the exact procedures you will use.

3. In what way can you use creative dramatics with students to help them understand the paragraphs?

4. Try out your ideas with one of the other groups.

FIELD EXPERIENCES IN THE ELEMENTARY SCHOOL CLASSROOM

A. With one or more children, teach the Level 1 and Level 2 scanning skills described in this chapter. What different strategies did you have to use to help the children with the two different levels? What clues did you teach them to look for with Level 2 scanning that were different from the clues you taught them to look for with Level 1 scanning?

B. Plan and carry out a lesson based on Experience D under "Application Experiences for the Teacher Education Class." Try out your lesson with two or more children. Choose one of the children's textbooks and two or three pages rather than two or three paragraphs.

C. With one or more children, create an "elevation map" of the classroom. Help them decide on an appropriate scale, such as "one inch is equal to one foot," or whatever is appropriate for the size paper you will use. Help them decide on an appropriate key to show the height of different objects in the room (for example: green could be used for objects less than 12 inches tall). What concepts about maps were you able to teach through this experience? How could you have them apply these concepts to reading other elevation maps?

D. Teach a small group of children how to use the PQ3R method.

E. Try rewriting a selection from a textbook that is too difficult for a particular group of children, or help an advanced group of readers rewrite it for other students.

F. Help a group of students understand math story problems through creative dramatics.

12 INCREASING POSITIVE ATTITUDES: READING IN THE AFFECTIVE DOMAIN

CHAPTER PREVIEW

Which of these goals do you think is more important for a teacher of reading?

To teach children how to read

To teach children to want to read

Not an easy question to answer, is it? But you may want to think of it this way: if you teach Roger how to read, but in the process, he learns to hate reading, what have you gained? Will he go to books on his own for information and pleasure? If not, then what

have we lost? We've lost one important avenue toward Roger's success in life—toward his emotional maturity, his social awareness, his intellectual vigor, and maybe even toward his economic self-sufficiency.

But does reading instruction have anything to do with such broad concerns as emotional maturity, social awareness, intellectual vigor, and economic self-sufficiency? It can have, providing a teacher thinks of growth *through* reading as well as growth *in* reading as the ultimate goals of reading instruction. But growth through reading is only possible if children *want* to read about their social and natural environment and if they want to enjoy literature. If reading instruction is limited to workbook exercises and skill lessons, though, it's quite unlikely that such desires will flower in the classroom. Furthermore, it's quite unlikely that children will perceive reading as a process that involves pleasure as well as work.

Let's talk in this chapter, then, about ways to make sure that Roger's attitude toward reading is positive, that Marjorie's desire to learn to read better is strong, and that most of Pat's days of learning to read provide a sense of achievement and success and "growing up." The three approaches we'll concentrate on are (1) providing models, (2) providing motivation to learn, and (3) providing success through better retention. We'll also want to look at the important contributions that parents can make toward helping the teacher encourage positive attitudes toward reading.

READING ATTITUDE: HOW IMPORTANT FOR READING ACHIEVEMENT?

In a study by Heathington and Alexander (1984), a sample of 101 teachers were asked to rank nine categories of reading instruction in order of importance. The category of "comprehension" came out on top, but right behind, even ahead of "phonics," was the category called "attitude." On the other hand, when they were asked to estimate the amount of time they spent on each of the nine categories, "comprehension" was first, "phonics" was second, and "attitude" was *eighth*. Something to think about.

I wish I could tell you that research definitively supports teachers' beliefs that attitudes toward reading are highly important. Everyone who teaches reading knows that they are, but research doesn't often tell us which comes first—positive attitudes or positive achievement. Which causes which? Or is it impossible to tell? Some researchers (Puryear, 1975; Quandt & Selznick, 1984; Roswell, 1967) have found that children with negative attitudes toward reading tend to be those who have been unsuccessful at it. ("No surprise here," I'm sure you're saying.) Subjective observations from teachers also indicate, however, that those with negative attitudes tend to *learn* less than those with positive attitudes. (Again no surprise.) Three researchers (Neale, Gill, & Tismer, 1970) did find a significant correlation between children's attitudes toward reading and their reading achievement. But this still doesn't tell us whether positive attitudes lead to high achievement or high achievement leads to positive attitudes.

Newman (1982) got around this chicken-and-the-egg problem by doing a longitudinal study of twenty children. She studied a group of children who had scored low on the Metropolitan Readiness Test when they were about six years old. By ninth grade, though, these "low achievers" were now considered very high achievers in reading. In fact, they were much better readers than children who had scored *high* on reading readiness. So what made the difference between these slow-start-fast-finishers and their counterparts who showed so much promise but didn't do as well by ninth grade? According to Newman's findings, here is what made the difference:

Good models at home and school

A stimulating environment

Interest shown by parents and teachers

Good expectations expressed by parents and teachers

Encouragement to persevere

Low but positive pressure toward achievement

To put this succinctly, important adults spent time helping these high achievers develop positive attitudes toward reading! I have to conclude that positive attitudes *can* lead to positive achievement.

After examining the research on attitudes and reading, Alexander and Filler (1976) concluded that "a universal goal of reading instruction should be the fostering of positive attitudes toward reading" (p. 34). After reviewing 110 research reports between 1900 and 1977 on reading achievement and reading attitudes, Davis (1978) concluded that teachers need to be aware of students' attitudes when planning instruction. She also concluded that careful planning can help learners develop positive attitudes.

PROVIDING MODELS

Observations and research consistently point to this: children who want to learn to read better usually have adult models who like to read; children who feel the opposite about reading generally do not. Yet it is not unusual to find that parents want their children to be good readers but never crack a book in front of them. Nor is it unusual to find teachers who want their students to be good readers but never read for pleasure in front of them or talk about what they've read. (They're often so busy teaching reading they don't take time to read.)

At the risk of going off the deep end, let me throw out a hypothesis for you to consider: teachers who spend as much time on the "modeling approach" toward teaching reading as they do on skill instruction will have greater success than those who spend all their time on skill instruction. Why I make such a statement is this: we humans are emotional as well as rational creatures. Most of us long to be inspired as well as instructed. Most of us, particularly as we grow up, want to imitate others whom we admire. Let me hasten to comment, though, that I'm not advocating that teachers use only themselves as models. Other people will also serve as inspiration, including children's own classmates. Let's talk, then, about how teachers can promote themselves, parents, other adults, and children's peers as models.

First, the teacher herself. Mrs. Weaver obviously believes in the "modeling approach." For one thing, she reads to her class every day, even though they're in the fourth grade. She selects her "read-aloud books" very carefully—some with male heroes and some with female heroines, but all with literary quality and "an exciting plot." She reads a chapter every day just before they go home. "That way," she says, "I can end each day on a positive note and they're eager to return to school the next morning." Mrs. Weaver doesn't have a "Hollywood voice," but she reads with enjoyment and with just enough expression to display her excitement without trying to make "a big dramatic production of it."

For another thing, Mrs. Weaver shares her own personal reading experiences with her class. Once or twice a week, during her students' daily "Newstime," she talks about something she has read in a newspaper, magazine, or book. Often she brings that newspaper, magazine, or book to hold up while she talks to them, "not necessarily to show them a picture, but just to show them that here's something I like to read when I'm home." Furthermore, when the children have their customary thirty minutes on Monday, Wednesday, and Friday for library books, she usually sits right up in the front of the class and reads a book of her own. "It's tempting," Mrs. Weaver says, "to use the time for planning and so on, but most of the time I can resist the temptation, because I know how important it is for children to watch me enjoy the process that I so fervently teach every day. Actually I feel hypocritical if I don't read in front of them."

Miss Weingardt uses herself as a model for her second graders in much the same way. But she also tries to involve the parents in the modeling approach. In October, for her second "Teacher-to-Parent Newsletter" of the year, this is what she said:

Dear Parents,

I do know how busy you are, so let me assure you that what I'm going to suggest will take no more than an average of five minutes a day. And it's for a very worthy cause: your child. (I know that some of you are already doing the things I'm going to suggest, and to you let me just say thank you!)

From what we know about children, it appears that the good readers usually have parents who read themselves. These parents enjoy reading and like to share what they read with others. Their children evidently like to imitate them. Therefore, what I'm going to ask you to do (unless you already do it) is this:

1. Would you read something pleasurable to yourself—and in front of your child—at least once a week?
2. Would you read something pleasurable with your child at least twice a week? (It doesn't have to be at bedtime; anytime will do: before the bus comes, right after supper, anytime.)
3. Would you make sure all television sets, radios, tape recorders, and stereos are turned off for at least thirty minutes each evening, so that your child will be tempted to fill the time with pleasurable reading or creative play?

If you will do these three things (or continue doing them), I feel confident you will be helping me to help your child.

Sincerely,
Marianne Weingardt

P.S. If you would like me to send you a list of good books to read aloud with your child, please sign below and return the bottom portion of this sheet through your child.

Yes, I would like you to send me a list of good "read-aloud books."

Mrs. Weingardt decided this letter was so important that she sent it to each home by mail. "It cost me a few dollars postage," she said, "but my principal liked the idea so much, he's going to try to get some funds just for this purpose."

In some schools the classroom teachers have the assistance of "special teachers" such as the physical education teacher, the music teacher, and the art teacher. These teachers are asked to mention occasionally some information they have gotten from their own reading and to casually discuss the kinds of books and magazines they like. They are also asked to recommend specific children's books or magazines on sports, musicians, and artists. Even the principals get involved in some schools by visiting classrooms, talking about things they like to read, and recommending specific books for children. Schools fortunate enough to have librarians often set aside time for them to present "book chats" on new books that have arrived. In a few schools, the entire "community" gets involved, with the cook, janitor, nurse, secretary, principal, teachers, aides, and children all taking a twenty-minute "reading break" each day. In other schools, local celebrities are brought in to talk about topics of interest to children and to mention, without too much fanfare, the kinds of things they enjoy reading.

Mr. Peterson is a fifth grade teacher who likes to use "peer modeling" as well as adult modeling. Once a week the children in his class meet for forty minutes in "Book Clubs" of five or six children each. These clubs are not developed according to subject interest or already established friendships. Instead, membership is carefully planned by Mr. Peterson. "Each club," he says, "has two good readers, one or two average readers, and one or two poor readers. For the first twenty minutes they sit around the same

table and just read whatever interests them. For the last twenty minutes, they tell each other a little bit about what they've been reading. It's quite simple really, but it seems to motivate all of them to do more reading—especially the average and poor readers, who are inspired by the good readers."

Many other teachers, at all grade levels, use Mr. Peterson's approach. Some teachers also encourage book sharing and peer modeling by incorporating "book projects" into their reading programs. Two or three times a week, children get to sign up to share their book project, such as a dramatic skit, a brief reading, a television advertisement for the book, an advertising poster, and so on. When they complete their project, they tell where the book can be obtained and receive some type of "book certificate" or other symbol of accomplishment. Over 70 book projects are discussed in the next section and in Appendix F. For other ways to use peers as models and as teachers, see Chapter 13.

MAKING PARENTS ACTIVE PARTNERS IN THE READING PROGRAM

Children's attitudes toward reading are certainly influenced by the degree of success they have in learning to read. But their attitudes must also be a consequence of their parents' behavior and interests. Several studies have shown that parent involvement in their children's education has a rather direct effect on reading achievement (Niedermeyer, 1970). In one study, for example (Shuck, Ulsh, & Platt, 1983), 150 students from grades three through five who were behind in reading by at least two grade levels were placed in a parent tutoring program. Parents worked with their children at home by helping them read a book, do homework, practice word lists, and play games. This experimental group of students ended the year with an average grade equivalent score in reading of 3.8 as contrasted to 2.8 for the control group that was not in the parent tutoring program.

John McKinney (1977) found that by training 50 parents to tutor their third graders, the tutored children ended the year with an average score of 52 on a standardized reading test; the nontutored averaged a score of 37. Tutoring, though, is just one of many ways parents can get involved. Here are some others:

> Have a special collection of books in the school library that children can borrow and take home for their parents to read with them. These should be carefully-selected read-aloud books (Armstrong, 1981).

Use *The Read-Aloud Handbook* by Jim Trelease (1982) to help you select books for parents and children to read aloud (Penguin Books, 625 Madison Avenue, New York, NY, 10022).

Have a workshop for parents on the values and techniques of reading aloud with kids at home (Lautenschlager & Hertz, 1984).

Have a learning station in the classroom supervised by a parent; the parent can help children with basic sight words, skill lessons, writing language experience stories, and so on (Criscuolo, 1983).

Engage parents in producing a minilibrary of "thin books." These are made by cutting out interesting stories from old basals or other materials. The parents can then distribute them to the children, possibly read one aloud, and perhaps discuss them with children after the children have read them (Criscuolo, 1983).

If there is an extra room in the school building, arrange for parents to play educational reading and language games with the children during lunch periods and other times during the day. Arrange for the parents to check these games out to use with their own children at home (Criscuolo, 1983).

Recommend to parents special books and booklets developed by the International Reading Association (IRA) or the National Educational Association. Four booklets I especially recommend from the IRA are these:

How Can I Help My Child Build Positive Attitudes Toward Reading? by Susan Mandel Glazer, No. 879.
Why Read Aloud to Children? by Julie M. T. Chan, No. 877.
How Can I Help My Child Get Ready to Read? by Norma Rogers, No. 876.
How Can I Encourage my Primary-Grade Child to Read? by Molly Kayes Ransbury, No. 875.

These four booklets may be purchased for less than a dollar each and are available from: International Reading Association, P.O. Box 8139, 800 Barksdale Road, Newark, Delaware 19714.

From NEA I recommend these four books: *How to Prepare Your Child for School, Learning the Alphabet, How Letters Make Words,* and *Helping Your Child Read.* These books are designed so that parents can teach important concepts that will enable their children to achieve more readily at school. *Helping Your Child Read,* for example, has many stories for reading to children, with questions afterwards and picture cutouts for the child to paste in the book. The book encourages echo and choral reading and provides a list of poems and folktales at the end. These four books are available for around $2 each and can be obtained from: Avon Books, Department FP, 1790 Broadway, New York, NY 10019.

Start a summer reading program. Parents sign a pledge to get their children in the program, take them to the library during the summer, and to talk about the books with their children. The children receive a certificate at the end of the program (Criscuolo, 1974).

Develop a workshop to teach parents how to make simple but effective reading games to use with their children (Criscuolo, 1974). See the references at the end of Chapters 4 and 5 for ideas. Also see Appendixes A, B, and C.

Get more men to volunteer as reading models—fathers, principals, janitors, local businessmen, local athletes, physical education instructors. Get them to talk about a good book they recommend or how they use reading on their job or what reading has meant to them. According to a study by Downing and Thomson (1977), there is still a North American stereotype of reading as a feminine activity, which can influence some boys' attitudes. Downing and Thomson found that when children and adults were asked to decide whether the pictured activity of a person reading was more suitable for a boy or girl, the vast majority said, "For a girl."

PROVIDING MOTIVATION THROUGH THE USE OF LEARNING PRINCIPLES

Children's attitudes toward reading can be greatly influenced by how well teachers of reading employ basic psychological principles of motivation. These principles seem to be appropriate whether a person is teaching reading, mathematics, swimming, cooking, firefighting, janitoring, or even pickpocketing (judging from Fagin's success with Oliver and his other boys.) Let's look at four of these principles.

Principle One: Help Satisfy Their Basic Needs

According to Maslow's well-known "theory of motivation" (1970), human beings have basic types of needs: physiological comfort, physical and psychological safety, belonging and love, esteem from self and others, self-actualization, and knowledge and appreciation. The physiological needs for food, warmth, and sleep are generally dominant until they become at least partially satisfied. Once satisfied, however, they give way to the need for safety (security, stability, and structure). Having satisfied the physiological needs and the safety needs, human beings are then usually dominated by the need for belonging (love, companionship, friendship, affection).

As each set of needs is satisfied, the next set in the hierarchy takes over—after love, the need for esteem (importance, success, self-respect, recognition); after esteem, the need for self-actualization (self-fulfillment, satisfying one's potential, meeting one's self-ideal, doing what one is fitted for); and finally, after self-actualization, the needs that relate most to schooling (knowledge, understanding, and appreciation). This hierarchy of needs is shown graphically in Figure 12.1.

Generally speaking, then, the "lower" needs must be at least partially met before the "higher" needs of self-actualization and intellectual understanding will emerge. In a practical sense, this means that the teacher who ignores Bobby's lower needs will find it rather difficult to motivate him to learn something just to satisfy his intellectual curiosity or to satisfy his desire to become a more skilled person. These so-called lower needs must be dealt with during the entire school day, of course, but even during a

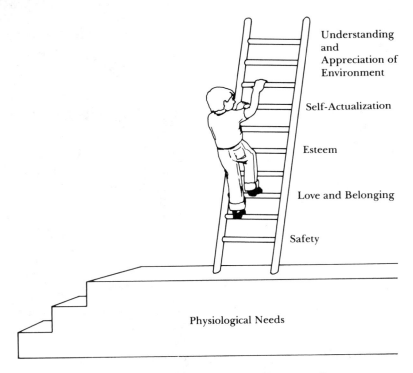

Figure 12.1   *The Ladder of Human Needs*

brief lesson a teacher who is conscious of them can be more successful than one who is ignorant of them.

Let's take, for example, the physiological needs of oxygen and exercise. Teachers may easily fall short of motivating children simply because they have failed to make sure that everyone has enough oxygen. Without a sufficient supply of oxygen, the brain becomes sluggish, curiosity dies, and boredom is the response to your frantic efforts to "teach them something." Making sure there is plenty of fresh air in your classroom is a help, of course, but it's often not enough. What some teachers have discovered is that some type of invigorating activity at periodic intervals throughout the day is essential to most children. Such activity, rather than interfering with learning, actually seems to enhance it.

This doesn't mean your classroom must be conducted like a three-ring circus, of course. It does mean, though, that large-muscle movement should be encouraged frequently. Even if you do no more than ask them to touch their toes before they sit down for a reading lesson, you stand a better chance of getting their intellectual attention. And during the lesson you can get them up to the board occasionally or have them pantomime a word or sentence. (A few teachers behave as though their students were bodiless minds: lavatory use is strictly scheduled, getting out of seats without permission is forbidden, and one intellectual activity follows another without any break for a physical activity.)

Which of these times would be best for having a session of dancing, rhythms, or dramatic play?

1. Just before recess so they can take their noise and excitement outside afterwards

2. Between two quiet intellectual sessions so they get the exercise they need

3. Right after recess because they'll be calmer then

It might be a good idea to use the dancing, rhythms, or dramatic play as an opportunity for plenty of movement—a chance for a physical break between two intellectual activities.

We've talked about a physiological need and how it can be met before and during your reading instruction. Now let's talk about the need for safety or security. This need can be met during your reading instruction in a number of ways—by providing each child with success, by accepting mistakes as natural allies of learning, and by assuring that instruction is carried on under reasonably orderly conditions. Obviously children are not going to feel secure if a lesson confronts them with a series of failures. To be motivated to engage in an intellectual exercise, they must experience success during that exercise. (More about success in a moment.) Nor will children feel secure if they perceive an intolerant attitude toward their mistakes. Nor will they feel secure if other children continually "misbehave" and things seem "out of control" to them.

Suppose you ask Jimmy to circle a VCE word and he circles a VC word. What would be your best response?

1. "Boys and girls, did Jimmy circle the right kind of word?"

2. "No, Jimmy, you weren't listening. You'd better sit down."

3. "Not quite, Jimmy. You've circled a VC word. See if you can circle a VCE word."

You may argue that Response 1 would be the best response because "it would keep the rest of the kids alert." That's true, it would. They'd be ready to pounce as soon as one of their "friends" went up to the board. But think of the harmful side effects that can occur—loss of security, loss of a sense of belonging, and loss of esteem, all in one blow. Response 2 would certainly not give the child a feeling of success; it would more than likely have a negative effect on his sense of security. Only when the teacher feels the need to use negative reinforcement with a "nonlistener" would this type of response be useful. Response 3 does give the child an opportunity for success without destroying his sense of security and thus would probably motivate him to continue learning.

Sarah is a second grader with a minor articulation problem. Her teacher feels that Sarah is a "needy child." Sarah's need for love (affection, warmth, friendliness, and sense of belonging), like the need for security and the physiological needs, has to be considered throughout the school day. But even during a single lesson it can be partially met by letting her know that her teacher and peers are on her side in her efforts to learn to read. To meet both the need for security and the need for a sense of belonging, the teacher should vigorously discourage children from making fun of those who make mistakes. This effort is considerably easier, of course, if the teacher refrains from careless smiles and sarcastic remarks.

Instead of reading, "I see three cookies on the table," Sarah reads, "I see free cookies on the table." What would be the best response for the teacher to make?

1. "Sarah, let me help you make the *th* sound in the word *three*. Watch my mouth."

2. "Sarah, I've told you many times—the *th* digraph is not pronounced /f/."

3. "Free! I didn't know the cookies were free. Did you, boys and girls?"*

---

*These responses are not fantasies; they are based on actual comments heard in classrooms.

You can meet the need for esteem during a lesson by making children feel important to you and their peers. A child who is rarely called upon, for example, won't feel very important. Yet this can easily happen when the teacher hurries to "cover the material" or calls on only the brightest students so as to save himself the effort of teaching the slower ones. (This may happen especially when the teacher is tired.)

Ms. Ronalds has decided to use a bit of team competition on a phonics game at the end of a lesson. Which would be the best way to select the teams?

1. Let two captains "choose up" the sides. This is the way they're used to doing it on the playground.

2. Ms. Ronalds should choose the teams, carefully balancing them with "strong" and "weak" players.

3. Let each child draw "blindly" from a set of cards labeled "Team A" and "Team B," because this is fairest.

If Ms. Ronalds lets captains choose the teams, how important will the last people chosen feel? Perhaps the playground approach should be reserved for the playground; Ms. Ronalds should be more concerned with human needs than with the "proper form." If Ms. Ronalds is skillful enough, she may be able to choose the teams herself without harming anyone's sense of importance. Sometimes, though, the chance approach works best, especially if you firmly discourage the children from cheering when the "good guys" get on their team and moaning about the "bad guys." (Some teachers feel that team competition on academic games is not worth the side effects and use individual or cooperative games instead.)

When teachers are aware of a child's physiological needs and her needs for security, belonging, and importance, the child is much more likely to be motivated toward self-actualization and intellectual understanding. The need for self-actualization, for most children, includes the desire to communicate better. Most children seem to perceive communication, including the act of reading, as "adult" and something they would like to be able to do as skillfully as adults do. Children who seem not to want to learn how to communicate better ("disadvantaged" children from all ethnic groups and economic strata) have frequently been unable to meet their "lower" needs. Attempts to motivate these children without taking their needs into account will often not succeed.

Principle Two: Teach at the Appropriate Level of Difficulty

Perhaps Principle Two is violated more often than any other principle of motivation. Most teachers learn quickly from experience that a learning task that is too easy for children will be boring, and one that is too hard will cause them to withdraw. This is easy enough to see, but what can you do about it? How can you select a learning task that will be just the right level of difficulty for each child?

Probably you can't. But to motivate children successfully, you have to try to come as close as possible to a task that will challenge them but not overly frustrate them. As an illustration, let's take Coach Cassidy, the track coach for Emerson High, working with a high jumper named Phil Peterson. Coach Cassidy puts the crossbar down fairly low the first time, so that Phil can clear it "with no sweat." Then he raises it slightly so that Phil has to expend a little more effort the next time. Then the coach raises it again— not so high that Phil misses and becomes frustrated, but just high enough to make him put a little more effort into the jump than he did the time before. This same gradual increase continues, making the task hard enough to be challenging but easy enough to be positively reinforcing: high enough to spur on the jumper to greater achievement, low enough to assure success. Success and difficulty go hand in hand to motivate the learner.

For the reading teacher, the task of finding the right level of difficulty is not as easy. A major step in the right direction is to teach diagnostically rather than with a shotgun approach. This means you must find out, through informal testing procedures, approximately what level each child is reading on and what specific reading deficiencies he has. Having assessed the levels and problems of each pupil, you will be able to teach them individually and to form small groups of pupils who are experiencing the same difficulties, or are on approximately the same developmental level.

But suppose the lesson you're teaching is obviously not at the right level: for some children it's too easy, and for some it's too hard. In this case, it's best to abbreviate your planned lesson and spend the extra time working with the children who are having trouble, while the rest move on to a follow-up activity or to reading in library books.

It is never advisable to ignore the difficulties some children may be having, thinking "they'll get it when they're older." Nothing is more dampening to motivation than to have one concept after another go by you and to fall farther behind. Nor is it advisable in your planning for the lesson to overlook its prerequisites. By carefully listing, mentally or on paper, the concepts the children need before they can understand the lesson, and by teaching those prerequisite concepts first, you can avoid a serious motivation problem.

Halfway through a lesson on finding the root in words with an *ed* suffix, you notice that Ronny understands it well and is looking quite bored. Which of these may be best to do?

1. Challenge him to find the root in some nonsense words such as *ruckled* or some hard words like *investigated*.

2. Do nothing special for him, as extra practice never hurt anyone.

3. Tell him that since he knows so much, perhaps he'd like to take over the lesson.

Principle Three: Provide Frequent and Specific Feedback

In brief, the procedure for following Principle Three is to present a small amount of information and follow this information with a request for some type of response from the student—answering a question, circling something on the board, completing a worksheet, taking a test. You then give the students feedback in the form of a nod of approval, the correct answer to compare with their own answer, a score, a token, or whatever will inform them about the adequacy of their understanding.

If you have been skillful in presenting information, the feedback you give the children will usually be positive reinforcement, and they will want to continue learning. With elementary school children, it is generally best to expose them to information for only a very brief period of time (often only a few seconds) before having them respond in some way and giving them feedback about their responses.

Which type of oral feedback for a worksheet would probably be the most motivating?

1. "Your grade on this was C−, John. You must try harder on the next one."

2. "You missed five out of twenty on this, John. Not bad . . . not bad . . . could be better, but not bad."

3. "You have a good understanding of the VCE pattern, John. You missed only one of the questions on that. Since you missed four of the words with a VV pattern, maybe I should help you a bit more on that. Now, do you see this word here? It has. . . ."

Principle Four: Add Novelty to Their Learning Experiences

This principle is perhaps so simple it needn't be discussed. But what about the children in some classrooms who daily suffer the tedium of teaching procedures and workbook formats that never vary? The novelty principle may be simple and obvious, but how often we teachers ignore it—although it's easy to understand why an overworked elementary school teacher may prefer the comfort of familiarity.

Following the novelty principle needn't be as time- and energy-consuming for the teacher as it sounds. Something as simple as having the children occasionally write on butcher paper with a felt pen instead of the usual chalkboard routine is often enough to cause a sharp rise in motivation. Or sitting on the floor instead of chairs. Or teaching a reading lesson in the afternoon instead of the morning. Or using sign language for part of the lesson. Or using a game for part of the lesson. Or giving a different piece of colored chalk to each child to use at the board: little things that take a bit of imagination but not much extra energy on the teacher's part.

If you'd like to remember these four principles of motivation you may want to make up some type of mnemonic (memory) device. Here's one that I like:

Novelty Needs Level Feedback.

By remembering that sentence, I can remember to think about novelty; concern myself with children's basic needs—especially for belonging and importance; teach at a level that is moderately challenging but not frustrating; and provide immediate and specific feedback whenever possible.

PROVIDING SUCCESS THROUGH BETTER RETENTION

The old adage that nothing succeeds like success applies to the development of reading skill as much as any other endeavor in life. The child who feels successful during the process of learning to read will generally have a positive attitude toward reading itself. The child who feels unsuccessful will often take out his frustration by misbehaving, refusing to read, and sabotaging the teacher's efforts to provide remedial instruction. (The child-saboteur may even go to such lengths as to purposely do poorly on tests to prove that he's "too dumb to learn to read anyway, so why try.")

For success to occur as she learns to read, a child must retain what she's learning long enough to practice it thoroughly in normal reading situations. If Millie learns several sight words during a reading lesson but then forgets them before she reads a basal reader story that contains those words, her sense of success will not be enhanced by the lesson.

It may be tempting for teachers to perceive success for a child in terms of how much praise or how many points he gets for performing non-interactive tasks, such as circling all the words that start with the /sh/ sound. Praise and worksheet points for isolated tasks may be necessary ingredients of success, but they're really only the peripheral measures. The real measure of success is whether the child, on his own, reading by himself, can holistically apply what he's learned in reading lessons, can enjoy the process of reading, and can communicate effectively with an author; thus, the absolute necessity for him to retain those skills and concepts he learns during reading lessons.

Let's assume that by concerning yourself with their basic needs and by using the principles related to novelty, feedback, and difficulty, you have now sufficiently motivated your students—they are ready to learn certain concepts necessary to skilled reading. How should these be taught? Is there any way for children to experience them so that they understand them quickly and well—so well that they don't forget them in a few days? To answer this question, we must consider four additional principles of learning.

Principle Five: Teach for Mastery

In a nutshell, this principle means to teach with thoroughness and meaningfulness. It means to avoid covering material for the sake of covering. It *sometimes* means to teach toward the accomplishment of specific performance objectives. And, it always means that what is taught should be clear and make sense to the learner.

Two of the following practices would be helpful in encouraging "learning for mastery." Which practice would not encourage learning for mastery?

1. Dividing the number of pages in a textbook by the number of school days and assigning that many pages each day.

2. Basing the content of a lesson on the children's previous experiences

3. Comparing and contrasting the concept you're teaching with other concepts

Method 1, believe it or not, is approximately the procedure used by some teachers—and understandably, too, if their goal is "coverage" rather than "mastery." Procedure 2 is one that adds meaning to the lesson, uses positive transfer from previous learning to new learning, and therefore aids in the goal of mastery. Procedure 3 is one of the best means of adding depth of meaning to a concept, thus making it easier to master.

But why teach for mastery? Who cares whether children master what you teach them? Isn't it enough simply to introduce them to something and let them master it later if they wish? These are appealing questions that often arise when the teacher is getting discouraged and ready to give up on Betty and Tommy. Undoubtedly, there are some things that should only be introduced rather than mastered—things that lie in the realm of appreciation such as listening to symphonic music or having an enjoyable craft experience. But what about a basic skill, such as reading, that one is expected to acquire and use throughout life; a skill that if not acquired often causes one to think of herself as a failure? Here, it seems, we're talking about something that should be learned very well indeed.

What happens to Christina when she doesn't master what is taught in one lesson, and another, and still another? That's right, her accumulated failures begin to interfere with future learning. Furthermore, she gradually develops a habit of not learning and forms a picture of herself as a person who is incapable of learning.

In brief, mastery is best obtained by not covering too much new information at once, which leads us to the next principle.

Principle Six: Provide Massed Practice Followed by Distributed Practice

You may think this principle means simply to "give them lots of practice and review often." But as usual it's not as simple as that. If Glenda has learned a word with quite a bit of meaning, such as *mother* or her own name, she'll remember it with little or no practice. But for less meaningful words like *the*, *there*, *here*, and *come*, it is likely that she'll need massed practice at first, followed by distributed practice later. Frequent, closely-spaced practice of only a few new words is provided at first, while making sure the child is decoding the words correctly. Follow this with practice distributed over several days or weeks, with the space between practice periods getting longer and longer.

There is no magic formula for distribution of practice. It will depend on how meaningful the material is, how motivated the child is, and what problems the child is having in learning the material. The main points to remember in developing a practice schedule are: (1) the student may need considerable guidance in the introductory session; (2) the practice sessions that immediately follow the introductory session should be brief, frequent, and closely spaced; and (3) the remaining practice sessions should be farther and farther apart.

Which of these do you think is the best schedule of practice for learning to decode long *a* with the VV spelling pattern?

1. During a twenty-minute lesson, with a ten-minute worksheet right after the lesson, for three minutes before going home, three minutes twice the next day, three minutes once the following day, three minutes once during the following week, and just occasionally for the rest of the year

2. During a forty-minute lesson, a twenty-minute worksheet, and a fifteen-minute review a month later

3. During a ten-minute lesson, a ten-minute worksheet, and a five-minute review once a week for the rest of the year

If you decided that the first schedule would provide the children with massed practice at first and distributed practice thereafter, you were right.

Schedule 2 is not as uncommon as it may seem, although frequently the review period is omitted. Mr. Rogers, for example, often uses this schedule, not because he is striving for mastery, but because he is striving for greater coverage. That is, he wants to cover as many concepts as possible in a single lesson. For instance, Mr. Rogers may try to teach a single lesson on decoding words with a VVC pattern, such as *boat*, *bait*, and *beat*, without first having three separate lessons—long /o/ in a VVC pattern, long /a/ in a VVC pattern, and long /e/ in a VVC pattern. Except for a review lesson, this would generally be too much to cover in one lesson, not only because of the overload of information but because of the fatigue factor.

Schedule 3 has the virtue of brevity, but probably doesn't allow for enough guided practice at first.

Principle Seven: Get Everyone Involved Each Step Along the Way

If you want maximum learning to take place, try to get each child involved in each problem you pose and each question you ask, each step along the way.

Which of these approaches in Mr. Sanchez's class would get the greatest number of students involved?

1. "John, would you please go to the board and circle a word with the VCE pattern?" (Mr. Sanchez watches John.)

2. "Now I'd like someone to go to the board and circle a word with the VCE pattern." (Mr. Sanchez looks from one child to the next.)

3. "Whose turn is it to go to the board? Mary? OK, you go to the board and circle a word with the VCE pattern." (Mr. Sanchez watches Mary.)

4. "Now, boys and girls, please watch while I circle the words that have a VCE pattern."

Approach 4 requires the responsibility of no one but the teacher, although he may hope that all the children will actually watch—and think about what they're watching. Unfortunately, this is often a vain hope. Very little tension or challenge has been developed; all the children have to do is tilt their heads in the direction of the board, thus fooling Mr. Sanchez into thinking that learning is taking place. Approaches 1 and 3 require the responsibility of one child, but the others are free to dream and scheme. The only approach that is likely to get them all involved is 2, since none of them is sure who's going to be called upon next. (Naturally this approach can't be used all the time or novelty would suffer.)

Now let's try another situation. Which of these would encourage the most involvement?

1. Present a little bit of information, give them a problem or question, present a little more information, give them a problem or question, present a little more information.

2. Present all your information at once and then ask if there are any questions. Then say, "Well, if there are no questions, I assume you understand it perfectly."

3. Present a problem or question, give them a little bit of information, present another problem or question, give them a little more information, present another problem or question.

Did you recognize method 2 as a familiar approach? It has been rumored that, occasionally, a college professor uses such an approach.

Either method 1 or 3 would work much better, with method 3 usually having the slight edge. For example, children would probably get more involved in the learning process if you began a lesson with a problem—"Who can tell me a word that has the same beginning sound as the word 'pet'?"—rather than beginning the lesson with information—"The three words on the board all begin with the /p/ sound."

Why does active involvement seem to increase learning and retention? For one thing, by getting a student personally involved, you've increased the amount of emotional impact of the instruction, and learning that takes place "with feeling" generally is retained longer. For another thing, the personal involvement results in the student's receiving a greater amount of feedback and reinforcement—usually of a positive nature, if you've done a good job of teaching. Positive reinforcement strengthens the desire to learn; feedback provides the learners with a check on how well they are doing.

Principle Eight: Help Positive Transfer Occur

Positive transfer is the effect that previous learning has in helping a person learn something new. Teachers and researchers have discovered, however, that positive transfer often does not take place automatically. Rather, it takes place only when the learner perceives the similarity between one learning situation and a subsequent one. And frequently the similarity has to be drawn to the learner's attention by the teacher.

In which of the following situations would positive transfer most likely take place?

1. Learning to decode *cat*, followed soon by learning to decode *mouse*

2. A lesson on decoding the letter *b*, followed soon by a lesson on decoding the letter *d*

3. Learning to decode *cat*, followed soon by learning to decode *cats*

4. A lesson on decoding long *a* in a VCE pattern (e.g., *bake*), followed soon by a lesson in decoding long *i* in a VCE pattern (e.g., *bike*)

Very little positive transfer can take place in alternative 1, since it would be difficult for the learner to perceive any similarity between the decoding of *cat* and *mouse*. In alternative 2, the learner may perceive the similarity between the two learning situations but that's just the problem. Rather than positive transfer, you are more likely to have negative transfer. In fact, children often get *b* and *d* confused, especially if one is introduced before the other is learned quite well. (Once the two have become confused, however, about all you can do is to bring them together in the same lesson and show the learner how the two differ.)

In alternative 3, learning the word *cat* will probably help the child learn the word *cats*, particularly if she learns the word *cat* quite well before the word *cats* is introduced—and particularly if the teacher helps the child see what makes the two words similar and different. Alternative 4 is also conducive to positive transfer, providing-again that the long *a* in a VCE pattern is first mastered and providing that the teacher helps the child see the essential similarity between the two situations (that the VCE pattern generally makes both the *i* and the *a* represent long sounds.)

Of course, there's one type of transfer the reading teacher wants more than any other: to have the children decode words they meet in books and on cereal boxes just the way they learned to decode them in a reading lesson. This is why most teachers try to provide practice in context during the course of a lesson. Reading whole passages, rich in context cues, not only provides vital practice in decoding the *words* in context; it also permits transfer from skill lessons to interactive reading. The teacher must keep these two ideas—contextual reading and interactive reading—constantly in mind if she wishes positive transfer of major importance to occur. If you make the practice during instruction similar to the long-range skill you're trying to develop, positive transfer is more likely to take place.

To remember these four principles of "success through retention," you may want to make up another mnemonic device. One that works well for me is this:

Involved Masters Practice Transfer.

This sentence reminds me to get every learner involved in every step of the lesson; to teach for mastery rather than coverage; to use massed practice during the lesson and follow with distributed practice over the next few days and weeks; and to teach in such a way that positive rather than negative transfer occurs.

USING ATTITUDE AND INTEREST INVENTORIES

Some educators feel that teachers should use some kind of attitude inventory to determine each child's basic attitude toward reading. This is certainly not a bad idea if you're not sure, especially if you think the child would rather fill out an inventory than just talk it over with you. Most experienced teachers I've discussed this with have told me they prefer to get this particular information from observing a child and from talking with him. My own experience with children has generally been the same.

Nonetheless, if you want to be more objective about your judgments, Figure 12.2 is one form of attitude inventory that might be useful because of its brevity and simplicity. It was developed in 1976 by the Right to Read Office in Washington, D.C.

For teachers in the elementary classroom, a more important type of inventory that provides specific help to the teacher seems to be an *interest* inventory. An interest inventory can tell you what kinds of books the child likes and what kinds of activities he engages in that he might also like to read and write about. To make an interest inventory about books, all we have to do is to borrow the ideas from Chapter 8. Make copies of the inventory in Figure 12.3 and read it to your students, one statement at a time, while they circle the appropriate number.

READING INTEREST/ATTITUDE SCALE

Right to Read Office, Washington, D.C., 1976

Date_____Grade_____Name_____

Directions: Read each item slowly twice to each child. Ask him or her to point to the face which shows how he or she feels about the *statement*. Circle the corresponding symbol. Read each item with the same inflection and intonation.

A
Strongly Agree
(Makes me feel good)

B
Undecided
(OK or don't know)

C
Strongly Disagree
(Makes me feel bad)

A B C 1. When I go to the store I like to buy books.
A B C 2. Reading is for learning but not for fun.
A B C 3. Books are fun to me.
A B C 4. I like to share books with friends.
A B C 5. Reading makes me happy.
A B C 6. I read some books more than once.
A B C 7. Most books are too long.
A B C 8. There are many books I hope to read.
A B C 9. Books make good presents.
A B C 10. I like to have books read to me.

Figure 12.2 *READING INTEREST/ATTITUDE SCALE (Right to Read Office, Washington, D.C., 1976)*

	A lot		A little		Not at all
1. I like to read about people that have real problems.	5	4	3	2	1
2. I like stories about finding clues and solving a mystery.	5	4	3	2	1
3. I like to read books of poems.	5	4	3	2	1
4. I like books with lots of pictures.	5	4	3	2	1
5. I like stories about people in love.	5	4	3	2	1
6. I like legends and tall tales.	5	4	3	2	1
7. I like funny stories.	5	4	3	2	1
8. I like books about animals.	5	4	3	2	1
9. I like make-believe stories about traveling in space.	5	4	3	2	1
10. I like books about important people.	5	4	3	2	1
11. I like sports stories.	5	4	3	2	1
12. I like to read plays.	5	4	3	2	1
13. I like science books.	5	4	3	2	1
14. I like stories about people of long ago.	5	4	3	2	1
15. I like adventure stories that take place outdoors.	5	4	3	2	1
16. I like fantasy stories about imaginary creatures and things that couldn't possibly happen.	5	4	3	2	1

Figure 12.3   *Reading Interest Inventory*

To make an interest inventory about activities the child enjoys, you can use a different format. For example:

1. What do you like to do in your free time?

2. Would you rather go to the science museum or the zoo?

3. Would you rather go to the library or to a music concert?

4. Would you rather write about an elf or about a space ship?

5. What's your favorite TV show?

6. What do you like to do that you would like to share with friends?

7. What do you do best?

These are just a few ideas. You can easily make up your own and change them as your experiences dictate. The point is that you now have useful information to help children find books they will like, to help them write about things that really interest them, to help them feel a sense of belonging and importance, and to help them develop a positive attitude toward reading, writing, and school.

THE MAIN IDEAS IN THIS CHAPTER

A child's attitude toward reading can greatly affect his reading achievement.

Parents can have a major influence on a child's attitude toward reading. They should be encouraged in a variety of ways to become involved in developing their children's reading skills and attitudes.

Success in reading growth may have as much to do with children's models as it does with the specific instruction they have.

Parents, teachers, and peers are all important models.

Children's attitudes toward reading can be influenced by the principles of motivation a teacher follows or doesn't follow.

Children's success in reading can be altered by the degree to which the teacher follows principles of retention.

Interest inventories can provide teachers with specific insights about their students. These insights can guide teachers in helping children engage in appropriate reading and writing experiences.

REFERENCES AND SUGGESTED READING

Alexander, J., & Filler, R. (1976). *Attitudes and reading*. Newark, DE: International Reading Association.

Armstrong, M. K. (1981). Petunia and beyond: Literature for the kindergarten crowd. *Reading Teacher, 35,* 192–195.

Criscuolo, N. P. (1974). Parents: Active partners in the reading program. *Elementary English, 51,* 883–884.

Criscuolo, N. P. (1983). Meaningful parent involvement in reading. *Reading Teacher, 36,* 446–447.

Cronbach, L. L. (1977). *Educational psychology*. New York: Harcourt, Brace, and World.

Davis, P. M. (1978). *An evaluation of journal published research on attitudes in reading, 1900–1977.* Unpublished doctoral dissertation. University of Tennessee.

Downing, J., & Thomson, D. (1977). Sex role

stereotypes in learning to read. *Research in the Teaching of English, 11,* 149–155.

Glaser, R. (1969). Learning. *Encyclopedia of Educational Research,* 4th ed. (pp. 706-733). New York: Macmillan.

Heathington, B. S., & Alexander, J. E. (1984). Do classroom teachers emphasize attitudes toward reading? *Reading Teacher, 37,* 484-489.

Hunter, M. (1967). *Motivation theory for teachers.* El Segundo, CA: TIP Publications.

Hunter, M. (1967). *Reinforcement theory for teachers.* El Segundo, CA: TIP Publications.

Hunter, M. (1967). *Retention theory for teachers.* El Segundo, CA: TIP Publications.

Hunter, M. (1969). *Teach More—Faster!* El Segundo, CA: TIP Publications.

Klausmeier, H. J., & Davis, J. K. (1969). Transfer of learning. In R. L. Ebel (Ed.), *Encyclopedia of Educational Research,* 4th ed. (pp. 1483–1493). New York: Macmillan.

Klausmeier, H. J., & Goodwin, W. (1985). *Learning and human abilities, educational psychology.* New York: Harper & Row.

Lautenschlager, J., & Hertz, K. V. (1984). Inexpensive, worthwhile, educational—parents reading to children. *Reading Teacher, 38,* 18–20.

Maslow, A. H. (1970). *Motivation and personality.* New York: Harper & Row.

May, F. B. (1969). An improved taxonomical instrument for attitude measurement. *College Student Survey, 2,* 31–35.

McKinney, J. A. (1977). *The development and implementation of a tutorial program for parents to improve the reading and mathematics achievement of their children.* (ERIC Document Reproduction Service, ED 113 703).

Neale, D. C., Gill, N., & Tismer, W. (1970). Relationship between attitudes toward school subjects and school achievement. *Journal of Educational Research, 63,* 232–237.

Newman, A. P. (1982). Twenty lives revisited—a summary of a longitudinal study. *Reading Teacher, 35,* 814–818.

Niedermeyer, F. C. (1970). Parents teach kindergarten reading at home. *Elementary School Journal, 70,* 438–445.

Puryear, C. (1975). *An investigation of the relationship between attitudes toward reading and reading achievement.* Unpublished doctoral dissertation. University of South Carolina.

Quandt, I., & Selznick, R. (1984). *Self-concept and reading.* Newark, DE: International Reading Association.

Roswell, C. G. (1967). *Change in attitude toward reading and its relationship to certain variables among children with reading difficulties.* Unpublished doctoral dissertation. George Peabody College for Teachers, Nashville.

Shuck, A., Ulsh, F., & Platt, J. S. (1983). Parents encourage pupils (PEP): An innercity parent involvement reading project. *Reading Teacher, 36,* 524–528.

Trelease, J. (1982). *The read-aloud handbook.* New York: Penguin.

White, W. F. (1969). *Psychosocial principles applied to classroom teaching.* New York: McGraw-Hill.

APPLICATION EXPERIENCES FOR THE TEACHER EDUCATION CLASS

A. *What's your opinion?* Use your own background as well as what you've learned from the textbook to defend your decision.

1. Adults can often be hypocritical with children about the importance of reading.

2. The most important models are the teachers, not the parents.

3. Encouraging parents to help teach children is a mistake. They'll abuse the power you give them.

4. Reading out loud to kids just interferes with the time they have for reading by themselves.

5. Whether a child enjoys reading or not has a little to do with motivation principles but not with retention principles.

6. Don't worry about a kid's reading attitude. Just teach her how to read successfully and she'll have a good attitude.

B. *Learning Principles:* Examine the following case studies with a partner or small group and decide what to do in each case. Decide what learning principle or principles you used in making each decision.

1. *Case Study One:* During a lesson on the VCE pattern you discover that all but two of the children have not yet mastered the long and short sounds of the vowel letters. What should you do?
   a. Postpone your lesson on the VCE pattern and teach all the long and short sounds of the vowel letters.
   b. Have the two children do something else while you teach the rest of the group the long and short sounds of the vowel letters.
   c. Continue the lesson as best you can; otherwise you may never cover what you're expected to cover in a year's time.

2. *Case Study Two:* You are planning to show a film to your fourth grade class to prepare them for some social studies reading they will be doing. Which of these procedures would be best?
   a. Show the film without stopping and give a test at the end of it.
   b. Stop the film once or twice, ask a question, have them write a brief answer, discuss the answer briefly before proceeding.
   c. Show the film without stopping, ask the children if they enjoyed it, tell them that maybe you'll show another film next week.

3. *Case Study Three:* Which of these presentations of a follow-up assignment may be the most motivating?
   a. "All right, boys and girls, please get out your workbooks and turn to page 186."
   b. "Well, as usual, boys and girls, the person who gets his worksheet all right will get a gold star on his paper."
   c. "Here's your airplane—I mean, your worksheet. Just unfold it, and we'll look at the directions together. I'll let you fly your airplanes as soon as you get everything correct on your worksheet."

4. *Case Study Four:* Suppose you have decided that Janice, a seven-year-old, needs to learn sixteen irregular words by sight. You provide her with a set of flash cards with the words printed on them and ask her to practice the words with a knowledgeable friend. How should she practice them for five or ten minutes a day so that she achieves mastery?

    a. Eight words the first day, eight more the second day, and all sixteen on the third day

    b. Four words the first day, the same four plus four more the second day, the same eight plus four more the third day, the same twelve plus four more the fourth day, all sixteen the fifth day, all sixteen three or four days later, only those she's having trouble with the next day, all sixteen the next day, all sixteen two weeks later

    c. All sixteen every day until she gets them all right

5. *Case Study Five:* Which of these will probably produce the greatest amount of learning? One of them is not so good, but it's a toss-up between the other two.

    a. "All of you close your eyes and put your finger on your chin whenever you hear a word with the sound of long *a* in it."

    b. "Jackie, will you help the girls and boys by putting up your hand whenever you hear a word with the sound of long *a* in it?"

    c. "All right, see if you can catch me. I'm going to say ten words after you close your eyes. The words that have a long *a* sound in them I'll say louder than the rest—but I may make a mistake. You put your finger on your chin when you think I've made a mistake."

C. *Interest Inventories:* Add to the interest inventory shown in Figure 12.2. Select questions that will give you more insights into what the children would like to read and write about. Compare your questions with others.

FIELD EXPERIENCES IN THE ELEMENTARY SCHOOL CLASSROOM

A. With one or more children, try out the attitude inventory shown in Figure 12.1. If possible, do this in an interview rather than passing it out as a checklist. This will give you more insights into why children feel the way they do about reading; use the interview questions as a foundation for a "frank discussion."

B. Find out the different ways the teacher you're working with uses the modeling approach toward improving children's attitudes toward reading. What are some other ways you can think of using the modeling approach?

C. What principles of learning does the teacher you're working with use to motivate the children and increase their retention? Precisely how does she do this? Are there some principles to which you would give greater attention?

D. Select three children and try to find out through observation and interview how much time they spend in one week reading just for their own pleasure or information. If possible, try to find out why the three children differ in the amount of personal reading they do at home and school.

E. Try out the interest inventory that you helped develop in your teacher education class.

13 CHILDREN WITH SPECIAL NEEDS: GIFTED, ENGLISH-DEFICIENT, HANDICAPPED

CHAPTER PREVIEW

We talked in Chapter 12 about increasing children's positive attitudes toward reading and reading instruction, but we left out a major influence on these attitudes—the degree to which the teacher relates to the special needs of gifted, English-deficient, and handicapped children. In an average classroom in our country, nearly half the students belong to one of these three categories; when it comes to reading attitudes, the teacher's approach to these students is a major factor indeed.

In this chapter we'll discuss the nature of "advanced learners" who are at least mildly gifted and some ways to match your reading program to their needs. We'll also discuss ways of teaching children whose culture and language may differ from yours. We'll also examine means of helping two types of handicapped learners, the slow and learning disabled. I have concentrated on these two types of handicapped students for two reasons: (1) they far outnumber children with emotional and physical handicaps, and (2) they have the cognitive handicaps that most elementary school teachers are at least moderately prepared to accommodate. At any rate, I hope as you read this chapter that you rediscover the need for teachers to be highly flexible in the materials and methods they use in working with a classroom of highly individual children.

When I first began my study of humans I thought they were all alike. But the more I got to know them as individuals, the more I realized how wondrously different they are.

DIVERSITY IN THE AMERICAN CLASSROOM

One of every six people in the United States does not use English as his or her first language (Bethell, 1976). One of nine people in the U.S. has a learning disability (Kirk et al., 1978). One of ten is at least mildly gifted or talented (Clark, 1983). One of seven is a slow learner (Kirk et al., 1978).

What do these approximate figures mean to the classroom teacher? It means that if you have a *typical* group of 30 children, you'll have five children who are deficient in English (and may not use it at home). It means you'll have three who are at least mildly gifted, three who are learning disabled and four who are intellectually slow. Even allowing for overlap, nearly half your class will have special needs. These estimates vary considerably from classroom to classroom, and I don't cite these figures to frighten you. Yet, I do want to remind you once again of the reality of human differences. These differences don't mean that a teacher must teach each child as a strange and isolated individual. After all, our similarities outnumber our differences. It does mean, though, that a teacher needs to be aware of differences and adjust her pace, methods, and materials. To make these adjustments, a teacher needs two kinds of information: (1) the nature of the differences, and (2) what methods and materials can be tried with various individuals and groups. We'll begin our examination of differences by talking first about children who are considered at least mildly gifted. Remember, though, that there are many ways for children to be gifted: some with words, some with numbers, some with music, some with muscle coordination. Gifted children, like their so-called average class-mates, vary enormously.

THE NATURE OF GIFTED LEARNERS

Most "intelligence tests" are designed so that the middle 50 percent of the population will achieve IQ scores of 90 to 110. The top two percent of the population will usually score above 131 and the bottom two percent below 69 (Clark, 1983). This means that about 10 percent will score around 120 or above. It is this figure of 120 (usually on *verbal* intelligence tests) that re-searchers have so often used in studying the effects of different "gifted child" programs in the schools.

All right, that gives us a very rough idea of what we mean by a "gifted learner" in a school setting—someone who verbal intelligence tests would tend to place in the top 10 percent as far as academic potential is con-cerned. Brain researchers claim that there are measurable *neurological* dif-ferences between gifted and "normal" individuals—such as faster move-ment between neurons which permits faster thinking (Thompson, Berger, & Berry, 1980); biochemically "richer" neurons that permit more complex thinking (Krech, 1969; Rosezweig, 1966); greater use of the prefrontal cor-tex, thus allowing for more foresight and more intuitive thinking (MacLean, 1978; Restak, 1979); more use of alpha wave activity, keeping the learner more relaxed, more capable of concentration and retention, and more likely to use the right and left sides of the brain in harmony (Lozanov, 1977; Mar-tindale, 1976).

These brain differences do not imply that heredity is the major factor in determining how advanced a student is, however. Numerous studies have shown that intelligence is also greatly influenced by environmental stimulation as well as by the child's personality characteristics. Further-more, IQ measures can change by 20 points or more depending upon the educational opportunities offered by the environment (Clark, 1983).

While high scores on intelligence tests and greater brain power are indicators of gifted-learner status, they are not the only indicators. Many, but not all, gifted learners are also highly creative as well. It is these chil-dren who probably suffer most in a school environment that encourages conformity and lock-step assignment production. These creative learners can perhaps be best identified through their personality characteristics. Re-search (Barron, 1962; Martindale, 1976) has shown that each of these chil-dren can be described with some of the following adjectives:

Autonomous—They make judgments without relying very much on the opinions of others. They have a high degree of self-confidence. They go against the crowd in the interest of trying to determine the truth.

Visionary—They desire change and perceive it as possible (when others may not). They feel that they are agents of change.

Goal-oriented—They have numerous ideas for keeping themselves occupied. They apply considerable effort toward projects that interest them.

Flexible—They show a high degree of adaptability in problem situations. They also use language flexibly and humorously.

Open—They demonstrate abundant curiosity and are reluctant to make judgments too quickly. They tolerate and seek new ideas and are willing to have closure/conclusion delayed.

Adventurous—They enjoy taking mild risks. They like to try new things. They enjoy the challenge of complex stimuli.

Unfortunately, some teachers perceive these characteristics differently:

Autonomous—This child is stubborn; conceited; can't follow directions.

Visionary—She's a rabble-rouser; daydreamer.

Goal-oriented—He can't apply himself to school work.

Flexible—This child is unprincipled; has an annoying sense of humor.

Open—She's always asking silly questions; can't make up her mind.

Adventurous—What a troublemaker he is; poor judgment.

As I mentioned, not all gifted learners are highly creative. Some may score high on intelligence tests but low on creativity tests. Furthermore, many teachers like to work with "high-IQ" children but not with high-creative children (Getzels & Jackson, 1960). One should not infer from this, however, that creativity and intelligence are unrelated. Some researchers (Getzels & Jackson, 1960) have tried to say that there is no relationship, but others have shown that the relationship is fairly strong (May & Ripple, 1962). Essentially, a certain degree of intelligence is necessary before creativity shows up on creativity tests. Those who score below 100 on verbal intelligence tests do not tend to do well on verbal creativity tests. When IQ scores rise above 115, however, intelligence no longer seems to determine how creative someone is (May & Ripple, 1962).

WORKING WITH GIFTED LEARNERS

Since creative gifted learners seem to be the most difficult for teachers to work with, I'm going to concentrate on ways of working with them. Because these children tend to be *autonomous* in temperament, they usually thrive on opportunities to make "important" decisions that affect their lives. They welcome opportunities to choose their own books to read rather than being limited to the next story in the basal reader. They like to decide on book projects for sharing the books with others; to plan their own schedule of work for the reading period; to present or write critical evaluations of books; and, in general, to guide their own ship whenever possible within the school setting. A trade-book-individualized-reading program often works well with these children (see Chapter 8).

Since these children tend to be *visionary*, they usually enjoy reading about important changemakers in our past and present, thus biographies should be a staple of their reading diet. Give them opportunities to talk and write about things that ought to be changed or improved in the world, in their classroom, in their private lives. The highly creative are fond of "make better" exercises and "what-if" exercises; for example, have them write about how they would improve such common things as pencils, chalkboards, shoes, and education. Then have them read their ideas aloud or read each other's ideas. Have them talk, write, and read about what-if situations: What if all boys had to prove they were men by cutting off their left little finger? What if we had such a severe shortage of sugar that only 100 pounds were available for the next six months?

Because these children are usually *goal-oriented*, they tend to enjoy individual projects, particularly if they get to choose what they will work on. Have an index-card box on your desk with ideas for extra projects in it, such as creating a new spelling game, or writing a history of Jefferson School, or looking in an unabridged dictionary for the word that has the most meanings. They usually like book projects, particularly if they get a "ticket" or other token for each book they read and share through a book project. Have a different-colored ticket for each type of book (mystery, biography, etc.) and encourage them to read at least one of each type of book. (See Appendix F for book project ideas.) Don't forget to let them make up their own ideas for projects as well.

In addition to being autonomous, visionary, and goal-directed, highly creatives tend to be flexible, open, and adventurous. Here are some ways to encourage these traits in your reading program:

Flexibility: Provide them with problem situations that require adaptability and more than one answer. For a language experience story, have them engage in an imaginary experience: lost in a huge city with no money—only a watch, a bag of lemons, and clothes—how to get home. Or try this one: stuck in a stalled elevator with your little brother who is crying—how to entertain him until help arrives—all you have in your pocket is a paper clip, a handkerchief, three pennies, and a pencil with no point. Don't forget to have them share their stories.

Openness: Give them five minutes to list as many things as they can think of that they want to find out about. Have them use the "hot water" method when they make their list: the hot water of ideas is the only faucet turned on. "Don't turn on the cold water of criticism while the hot water is on or you'll just get lukewarm water. Write down every idea you have no matter how silly it might seem." Then have them select the one they're most curious about. Develop a plan with them for locating reading material that will help them find out what they want to know.

Here's another idea for encouraging openness: have two or more children read the same book and then compare their ideas about the book. Who was the most important character? How would they have done something different from the way the main character did it? Could this story have taken place in any other setting? If so, how would that setting have affected what happened in the story? Could the main character have been different in age or personality? If the children agree with each other too readily, the teacher should try disagreeing with them, gently challenging their ideas.

Adventurousness: Remember, these children often like to take risks, to try something new and even dangerous, and they often enjoy things that are complex. Recommend books such as *Island of the Blue Dolphins, Call it Courage, My Side of the Mountain,* and *The Hobbit.* Encourage them to try book projects that have never been tried by anyone else in the class. Help them use books as starting points for writing their own adventures and reading them to others. Let them use a tape recorder to add sound effects to their stories. Encourage them to write their own riddles, such as this one: "You throw away the outside and cook the inside. Then you eat the outside and throw away the inside.* What is it?" Have them try out the riddles on their friends. Plan a "dangerous" adventure with them, perhaps something they want to do on the playground that they've been afraid to do before. Then have them write or dictate an experience story describing their feelings as well as their adventure.

I would suggest, for high-creative and other advanced learners, moving them out of a basal reader program as quickly as possible, either by having them move rapidly ahead in it or by omitting it entirely, depending upon the child's demonstrated abilities in reading and upon the policies of the school in which you're teaching. Generally speaking, these children need a strong supplement or alternate of a TBIR program (Chapter 8) and an LEA program (Chapter 7). Certainly this type of child needs more stimulating writing and reading experiences than those normally provided by a basal reader program. If for some reason you feel they should go through the basal program, by all means use the enrichment experiences suggested at the end of each unit. Many of these experiences include the use of library books. You may particularly want them to consider books with gifted children as characters. Tway (1980) provides an annotated discussion of several such books in the January, 1980 *Language Arts,* another journal besides *The Reading Teacher* that you'll find useful in your teaching. For many ideas on helping gifted children, look also at the journal called *Gifted Child Quarterly.* Isaacs (1973), for example, has a list of 100 ideas in the Summer, 1973 edition.

CHILDREN WHO DIFFER IN LANGUAGE AND CULTURE

As mentioned earlier, a large number of people in the United States do not speak Standard English in the home. Instead they speak a Spanish dialect, a Black dialect, a Chinese dialect, a Vietnamese dialect, a Native American

---

*Corn on the cob.

dialect, and so on. The instructional techniques for teaching reading to children whose home language is not Standard English are often quite similar to those used with other children. The major differences in instruction are usually in emphasis rather than in actual technique. We will get to this later; first, though, we should discuss a more important factor in the successful instruction of children who do not use Standard English in the home. This factor is the teacher's attitude. Several studies (Burg, 1975; Davison & Lang, 1960; Rosenthal & Jacobson, 1968) have shown that it may be this factor more than any other that determines how well children of minority subcultures learn to read.

This problem of attitude occurs all over the world. Children on the border between Brazil and Uruguay, for example, speak a dialect that is quite dissimilar from the dialect used in the schools. Eloisa (1975) says that these border children are typically way behind the other children in the schools. The problem, she says, is the teachers. Many of them refuse to treat the border dialect as a valid language with long roots in history and through which its users "can express their full personalities."

I hope you'll agree with me that all languages and dialects can be equally beautiful and useful. If you do have this attitude, I think it will be much easier for you to work with children who differ from you in culture, language, or dialect. Teachers who feel that their language, dialect, or culture is superior to those of their students are likely to have considerable difficulty teaching them to read.

> You will become a more successful teacher if you become a student too. If you try to learn as much as you can of the language and the customs of the person you will be teaching, both you and your student will have more success in learning a new language and new customs. (Johnson, 1975)

The point I'm trying to make, of course, is that teachers should not so much "help" children learn Standard English as they should share on an equal basis their different languages or dialects.

Dialect Defined

Most people know what is meant by a *language*, but what is a dialect? To the person who speaks it, it's the "mother tongue." To the person who speaks the same language but a different dialect, it's "sloppy speech," or "jibberish," or "lower-class speech," or "hoity-toity talk."

A dialect is a variation of a language. It differs from other variations in three ways. First, it differs *phonologically*; that is, it differs in the way people produce phonemes or in the particular phonemes used. For example, in some parts of the deep South, native speakers say /fee-ish/ for *fish*, adding a long *e* sound before the short *i* sound. People in the North, who use the short *i* sound, find that addition quite amusing (although some linguists say that the southern dialect comes closer to the English of the British Isles in colonial days).

Second, it differs *grammatically*. That is, it may differ in the way verb tense, negation, number, and other structural changes are signaled. For instance, someone speaking Black English may say, "From now on, I don't be playing," whereas someone speaking Standard English (or Anglo English) will say, "From now on, I'm not going to play."

Third, it differs *lexically*. That is, the actual words or vocabulary may differ. Someone speaking Black English may say, "Please carry me home," while someone speaking Anglo English will say, "Please take me home." Someone in certain parts of New England will call a toilet a "flush."

Dialect differences do not indicate sloppy speech, as some people claim. They are systematic variations of a common language. If you listen to two people speaking Black English, for instance, the differences between black and white dialects are consistent. If a person whose mother tongue is Black English is speaking to a person whose mother tongue is Standard English, there may be a tendency for the person speaking Black English (particularly a child) to switch back and forth between Black English and Standard English. This is especially true in a situation where speakers of Black English are made to feel that their dialect is inferior—which is sometimes the case in a school setting.

Table 13.1 shows some systematic differences between Black English and Standard English, and Table 13.2 shows some differences between English and Spanish.

What do the dialect differences shown in Tables 13.1 and 13.2 mean in practice? In general, they mean that speakers of Black English and of Spanish would probably benefit from a language experience approach combined with systematic instruction in the decoding processes. It further indicates that whereas an auditory phonics approach may be appropriate with children whose mother tongue is Black English, this approach may not work well with some Spanish-speaking children (Smith, 1975). In Spanish there is no sound of *h*, no final *nk*, and no initial-*s* consonant blend. "The pronunciations of many letters—the *j*, the *d*, the *v*, and the *r*—in many positions within words in English are significantly different even though the visual appearances are the same" (Thonis, 1976, p. 26). An approach that emphasizes visual differences rather than auditory differences, will probably be more appropriate for many Spanish-speaking children.

But before we look more thoroughly at instructional techniques, let's look at cultural differences that sometimes exist between minority children and majority children.

Table 13.1   *A Sample of Differences between Standard English and Black English*

Difference	Examples
Omission of the /s/ phoneme at the end of the third person singular, present tense verb	He *look* at the picture.
Omission of /s/ on plural nouns preceded by quantitative modifier	I got thirteen *pencil.* I got several *pencil.* I got many *pencil.*
Omission of /s/ in possessive case	Give me *Bill* pencil.
Addition of /s/ to first person or third person plural forms of verbs	I *sees* it. They *lets* us do it.
Omission of the /d/ phoneme at the end of words	*tole* for *told* *ba* for *bad*
Substitution of the /d/ phoneme for voiced /th/ at the beginning of words	*deh* for *the* *dat* for *that*
Use of present-tense form for past-tense verbs	He *ring* the bell yesterday. Yesterday I *jump* rope.
Variations on forms of *to be*	They *is readin'.* They *be readin'.* They *readin'.*
Double negative for emphasis	I *ain't* got *no* candy.
Omission of /r/ at the end of words and syllables	*foe* for *four* *Pass* for *Paris* *cat* for *carrot*
Omission of /l/ at the end of words or near the end of words	*foo* for *fool* *fought* for *fault* *hep* for *help*

Cultural Differences

Majority-culture children in our society are often taught to look to the future, to set goals for the future, and to set smaller subgoals that will help one reach the larger goals. "Some day you'll be a successful businessman like your father. But that means you're going to have to do well in high school so you can get into college. And that means you'll have to learn to read well and write and spell. So you had better get that homework done!" Although many minority children are taught exactly the same thing, some are not. Some minority children, as well as their parents, have had little experience with the type of success in which most school teachers believe.

Table 13.2 *Some Differences between Standard English and Some of the Spanish* Dialects*

Differences	Examples
The /th/ heard in *thanks* may be pronounced as /t/	*thanks* sounds like *tanks*
In some dialects the voiced /th/ may be pronounced /d/	*those* sound like *doze*
The /ch/ sound and the /sh/ sound may be interchanged	*chin* may be pronounced *shin* after child learns the /sh/ sound
Short /i/ sound may be pronounced like long /ē/	*tin* becomes *teen*
Voiced /s/ heard in *rise* and unvoiced /s/ heard in *rice* may be interchanged	*rise* becomes *rice* *police* becomes *please*
The /v/ sound heard in *very* may be pronounced more like /b/	*very* sounds like *berry*
The /b/ may become /v/ in medial positions	*havit* for *habit*
In words that have a *voiced* consonant sound at the end (sound made by vibrating the vocal chords while mouth is in a consonant position), the voiced sound may be omitted	*robe* becomes *rope* *five* becomes *fife* *dead* becomes *debt* *tug* becomes *tuck*
The /s/ sound at the beginning of a word may be preceded by a vowel sound if the /s/ sound is blended with a consonant	*stop* becomes *estop*
Noun determiners sometimes omitted	She is *doctor*.

*For more detail on dialect differences, see Ching (1976).

Instead they have experienced considerable failure as far as school-related tasks are concerned. They are therefore not used to the "goal-setting" approach that many teachers advocate.

This in no way means the children are "lazy," which is the label that some teachers attach to them. It does mean that the teacher has to try other means of motivating them to learn. Some teachers have been successful with behavioral-management techniques that require the teacher and child to establish short-range goals and the precise reinforcement that will motivate the child to reach those goals one at a time. The reinforcement varies with the child; it may mean the use of a playground ball at recess, or tokens that can be later turned in for prizes, or special time with the teacher—it depends on what the child considers to be a reward. But it does not mean vague promises, such as going on a field trip someday, or moving on to the next grade, or getting a job when you grow up.

Another major cultural difference is the way children look at achievement. Many "majority" children are taught to achieve on an individual basis—to have the best batting average, to be the best speller, to win a gold medal. Some minority children are not motivated to achieve in such an individualistic way. In some American cultures a child's identity is more closely related to the family's identity. Achievement for the family (or extended family group, including certain friends) is often more important than self-achievement. Siblings are considered extremely important and often act as substitute parents. The "good of the whole" is generally a strong value.

In other words, some American children are used to achieving for the benefit of a group, and the process of achieving is a group process. For them the learning process is better in a "human" setting, working either directly with the teacher or with other students, rather than working by themselves. For them, learning needs to be more a social affair in which peers work together, or older students help younger students, or the teacher works directly with the students. Lawrence (1975) described the successful use of sixth graders to help first graders learn to read after she had first trained the sixth graders in the language experience approach. Himmelsteib (1975) had ninth graders act as buddies to third graders in selecting library books and playing reading games. Boraks and Allen (1977) developed a more elaborate plan in which college students taught fourth and fifth graders to tutor each other in an inner-city school. The children were taught tutoring behavior such as promoting positive response patterns, keeping others on task, explaining the objectives, giving praise, and helping others verify their own responses. Breiling (1976) describes a program in which parents are trained by teachers to work with their own children—how to encourage their children, how to use reading games, and how to have the children read to them for ten minutes a day. Improvement in enthusiasm as well as sight vocabulary has been the reported result of this program.

To continue itemizing cultural differences between majority and minority children is to run the risk of establishing more false expectations than already exist for minority children. Minority children differ among themselves as much as majority children do. To expect every minority child to want to work with a buddy is as unsuitable as expecting all majority children to work on their own. The point I'm trying to make is that cultural differences do exist that will definitely affect the motivation each child brings to the learning task. When one motivational approach doesn't work with some children, the temptation for some teachers is to consider those children lazy, or "deprived," or in some way inferior. I'm urging instead that the teacher examine the possibility that cultural differences are interfering with the teaching-learning relationship.

You may remember from Chapter 12 that one of the principles of motivation is to help children satisfy their basic needs, including needs for affection and security. By understanding children's cultural background, by letting them know that you appreciate their culture and want to learn from it, and by gearing your motivational approaches to their cultural upbringing, you can help to make children feel secure and loved—and ready to learn.

WAYS OF DEALING WITH DIFFERENCES

We have learned that for a child to interact creatively and productively with education he must retain his personal integrity and be able to value what he and his family stand for. So one solution offered is that the Maori needs to feel proud of his heritage. . . . The child who enters school speaking Maori should be taught to read in Maori. (Clay, 1976, p. 339)

The Melting-Pot Approach

At the present time, three major approaches to helping minority children learn to read are in use. The first is the *melting-pot approach*. With this approach, you simply teach the child to read in Standard English, hoping that she will pick up enough understanding of Standard English through normal day-to-day communication in the classroom, on the playground, through television, and through other contacts with speakers of Standard English. That this approach sometimes fails is borne out by several reports (Saville & Troike, 1971; Thonis, 1976; U.S. Comm. on Civil Rights, 1974).

The ESL Approach

A second approach is the *English-as-a-second-language-approach*. With this approach, children are taught to speak in Standard English before or during the time they are expected to learn to read in Standard English. This approach has the theoretical virtue of building a child's language naturally from the oral skills of listening and speaking to the written skills of reading and writing. It also has the theoretical virtue of not labeling a child's language or dialect as "incorrect," seeking instead to teach Standard English as a second dialect or language—one that is necessary for all citizens to know in order to become "successful," both socially and financially.

There is a tendency, however, for some who advocate and use this method to look at those who do not speak Standard English as "handicapped." They often propose that Standard English be taught as soon as possible so that the "handicapped students" can function properly in a regular classroom (Donoghue, 1971). With this approach, it almost seems as though we are trying to drown out the children's earlier means of communicating by saturating them with Standard English. Instead of building upon the preschool language learning of these children, we tend to ignore that learning and start all over again. Children enter school and are encompassed by a strange new world of school language (Feeley, 1970). Is it any wonder that children whose home language is not Standard English often do poorly on tests of language skills?

One can certainly forgive and even applaud such sincere attempts to help minority children cope with the problem of reading Standard English. The English-as-a-second-language (ESL) approach is surely a more humane one than the melting-pot approach. However, with respect to the black children who have been put through an ESL program, the evidence is not very encouraging. Studies (Cagney, 1977; Eisenberg et al., 1968; Hall & Turner, 1974; Peisach, 1965; Weener, 1969) indicate that the problem some black students experience in learning to read is not in their inability to speak Standard English—or even to understand it. In Cagney's study (1977), for instance, a group of first graders who were fluent speakers of Black English and whose home language was Black English were exposed to a set of language experience stories written by other children. Half the stories were written in Standard Dialect, and half were written in a black dialect. They were read to the children by a teacher who was fluent in both Standard and Black English. The children were then asked questions about the stories designed to test their comprehension. On the average, the children made significantly more correct responses to questions about the stories written in Standard English than to questions about the stories written in Black English.

In other words, it would appear that most children who speak Black English as their native language have been sufficiently exposed to Standard English (via television and other sources) to understand it, even though they may not be fluent speakers of Standard English. The assumption that they must learn to speak Standard English fluently before they can learn to read it is probably erroneous. Furthermore, it is likely that attitudinal and cognitive variables are more important than dialect differences.

With respect to children dependent on another language, there appears to be no evidence they would benefit from learning to speak Standard English *fluently* any more than children who speak Black English. It is likely that they need abundant *exposure* to Standard English before they are expected to read it well, but fluent *speech* in Standard English is probably not necessary. What often happens, it appears, is that those of us who are attempting to provide assistance to minority children get our goals confused. If our goal is to have every child *speaking* fluent Standard English, then Kaplan's (1969) facetious suggestion may be applicable: adopt "sufficient totalitarian methods to disseminate it within the population." But if our goal is the more realistic one of teaching every child we can to *read*, and if our main concern is that they comprehend what they read, rather than "read orally with elegance," then the English-as-a-second-language approach is probably not the only one to use.

The Native Vernacular Approach

A third approach is the *native vernacular approach*. With this approach, minority children are first taught to read and write in their mother tongue, whether it be Puerto Rican Spanish, Cantonese Chinese, Sioux, or some other language. While they are learning to read and write in their native vernacular, they are exposed to Standard English through working with Standard English-speaking children in such activities as art, music, and physical education. Sometime before the end of third grade, they are given instruction in reading English as a second language.

The native vernacular approach has strong appeal to those who feel that a child's culture and vernacular should be respected and utilized in instructional programs. The teacher can start where each child is with respect to language development. Rather than start over, he can have the child reading as soon as majority children are, thus avoiding the stigma and devastation of failure.

Unfortunately, this type of program has serious drawbacks. The most serious drawback, of course, is that of resources, since this program requires skilled teachers who can communicate in Spanish, Vietnamese, Chinese, and so on. It also requires reading materials written in the various languages and dialects.

The problem of finding suitable reading materials can be handled partly through a language experience approach to reading instruction. According to Hall (1972), this approach is particularly appropriate for use with minority children because it makes it possible to have reading materials that match both their experiences and their language patterns. As Ruddell (1965) points out, reading comprehension is a function of the similarity between the patterns of language structure used by the person reading and those used in the reading materials. Since with the language experience approach, children read what they have written or dictated, this similarity is assured.

Besides language experience charts or stories, a supply of bilingual materials is gradually being developed, such as the Miami Linguistic Reader Series published by D. C. Heath. This series for English and Spanish languages is designed to teach Spanish-speaking children not only to read Standard English, but to pronounce it with precision. Several other publishers also have developed or are developing bilingual materials

(Thonis, 1976). It should be pointed out, however, that publication of Black English materials has tended to elicit quite negative reactions from both whites and blacks in the community. Black parents have been particularly incensed, because they feel their children need to learn the Standard English that will allow them to "get ahead" in our society.

The problem of finding suitable teachers may diminish as more universities train people to work in bilingual settings. Admittedly the greatest demand for these teachers is in population centers where minority children are concentrated. It is a rare school district that hires bilingual teachers when only a few minority children are present in the schools.

To make this problem more graphic, suppose you are teaching in a small town and in your classroom of first graders you have four children who speak Spanish, one who speaks with a black dialect, and two who speak with a Cantonese dialect. No other children in the school speak these vernaculars. The principal tells you to "do what you can with them." Unfortunately, you speak only Standard English. You understand only half of what the black child says and nothing of what the Chinese-speaking and Spanish-speaking children say. Many teachers today have children in their classrooms whose language they cannot understand.

The language experience approach may be called for in this situation, but there's no way you can take dictation, since you can't understand what they're saying. What should you do? Ignore them until they have picked up enough English? Not a very humane or professional solution. What about finding special tutors for them? Some teachers have been able to do this. By scouring the community, they have found volunteers who were shown how to use the language experience approach with the youngsters. (In a few cases they have been lucky enough to have state funds for hiring tutors.)

The solution to the dilemma teachers face is not easy or inexpensive. In fact, there is presently insufficient evidence to show that the bilingual approach actually works. Ching (1976) cites three studies in which the bilingual approach was compared with the traditional Standard English approach. In only one study did the researchers find that the bilingual approach was superior and in that case, both the schools and the teachers' training were superior at the start.

Most likely, a bilingual approach requires school settings in which teachers have extra training and motivation. So far, however, we have no assurances based on experimental research. Most of the present arguments for the bilingual approach are based on logic, politics, subjective observations, and humanitarian concern. Yet a concerted effort must be made to assist minority children, and the bilingual approach seems the most promising one at this point. As Nila Smith explains:

> There is a rapidly growing philosophy in regard to dialects and the teaching of reading which is widely advocated by many well-known linguists. These

linguists differ somewhat in regard to details, but fundamentally all of them agree to (1) accept the child's dialect as his native language; (2) provide him opportunities to read in his own dialect as a precedent to or along with reading in Standard English; and (3) combine teacher guidance, appropriate materials, teacher and peer associations to aid him in acquiring ability to speak and read with increasing fluency in Standard English as a second language while maintaining his native language. (Smith, 1975, p. 139)

Sources of Materials and Information on Bilingual and Bicultural Programs

International Reading Association
Executive Secretary
800 Barksdale Road
Newark, DE 19711

English as a Second Language Program
Center for Applied Linguistics
1717 Massachusetts Ave. N.W.
Washington, DC 20036

National Association for Bilingual Education
University of Texas at San Antonio
4242 Piedras Drive East
San Antonio, TX 78285

Teachers of English to Speakers of Other Languages (TESOL)
Executive Secretary
School of Languages and Linguistics
Georgetown University
Washington, DC 20007

Executive Secretary
National Council of Teachers of English
1111 Kenyon Road
Urbana, IL 61801

Bilingual-Bicultural Office
State Department of Public Instruction
Capital of your state, Your state

CHILDREN CONSIDERED SLOW OR DISABLED LEARNERS

We've been discussing children who need special help in learning to read because of cultural, dialect, or language differences. Now we'll look at other types of "minority" children who need special reading instruction.

These children are in the minority because they are either slow learners in general or disabled learners when it comes to reading and other communication skills. To oversimplify this for a moment, the difference between a "slow learner" and a "disabled learner," when it comes to reading, is really one of definition more than teaching practices. Techniques that prove useful for particular "disabled learners" often prove useful for particular "slow learners," and vice versa. By definition, though, a slow learner is one whose IQ is "well below average." A disabled learner's IQ is at least average but his ability to perform certain school tasks (such as reading and writing) is well below what would be expected of him.

The approximate proportion of so-called slow learners in the general school population is 16 percent (Kirk et al., 1978). Out of this total of slow learners, about 87 percent are considered "borderline children," with IQs ranging from roughly 70 to 85 percent. The other 13 percent of the slow learners (about 2 percent of the general school population) are generally classified as "retarded" and are often placed in highly specialized learning environments. In this chapter we'll talk only about slow learners who are considered "borderline," since these children experience much of their total instruction from regular classroom teachers.

The approximate number of so-called disabled learners in the general school population is more difficult to discover; some say 6 percent, some say 15 percent, some say higher. The problem is one of definition. If we were to agree, for instance, that over one-fourth of those children who speak Standard English in the home have problems learning to read, how many of those children will we say have trouble because of a learning disability, and how many because of a low intelligence quotient? If we arbitrarily say that 85 is a low IQ, then we could say that all children who have difficulty learning to read whose IQs are above 85 will be classified as "disabled" rather than "slow." If, on the other hand, we arbitrarily say that 95 is a low IQ, then we will come up with a lower number of disabled readers and a higher number of slow readers. You can see then what an arbitrary and sometimes meaningless distinction is made between groups of children who are having trouble learning to read.

Case Study of a Disabled Reader

Ralph is a nine-year-old boy who wears many invisible labels. He's been called a "nonreader," a "dyslexic," a "disabled reader," and a host of other things. Ralph has straight blond hair, blue eyes, and a smile that would melt all but the sternest of teachers. His above-average intelligence is demonstrated daily by his witty remarks and his ingenious ways of getting into trouble. Until recently he was considered hopeless by his regular classroom teachers and by his former "compensatory-program" teacher.

Although he is almost ten, he is only in the third grade, since he was held back a year. Until Miss Burnette came along, he was the number-one troublemaker in the school. Miss Burnette is the new third-grade teacher at Jefferson Elementary School, and Ralph is in love with her—as much as a nine-year-old boy can be in love with a twenty-five-year-old woman.

"Ralph has been a hyperactive child since birth," according to his mother. "He's always been more interested in fiddling with things or getting into mischief than in looking at books or talking to people. Even when he's watching TV, which is quite a lot, he's got his hands fiddling with things or he's climbing on something, or he's pestering someone. He's not like his sister at all. She's much quieter and likes to read. She's been saying real words since she was one year old, but Ralph—Ralph didn't say his first word until he was two. And he's always talked so fast and mushylike I still have trouble understanding him at times."

Ralph is not a typical disabled reader, because there is no such thing as a typical disabled reader. Ralph's particular symptoms have caused him to be labeled by his teachers and parents as "dyslexic," a label that doesn't help him much, since it simply refers to a child who shows difficulty in learning to read (despite average or above-average intelligence and despite a variety of normal instructional strategies employed by his teachers). Ralph not only reads very poorly, he also spells atrociously, writes illegibly, speaks haltingly with weak enunciation, and performs awkwardly in physical-education class. Some might say that Ralph is "discombobulated." Others would say he has "specific language disabilities," or "specific learning disabilities" (as if these longer labels somehow come closer to the truth).

The Nature of Ralph's Learning Disabilities

To explain the disabled reader's situation a little better, we'll continue to use Ralph as an example. In October Ralph's grade equivalent score on a standardized reading-achievement test was 2.1, although the norm was 4.2. On a standardized diagnostic inventory, his reading score was 1.5. Both standardized scores, as low as they were, estimated his reading performance at too high a level. On an informal reading inventory, for instance, he reached frustration level while reading a preprimer passage.

On weekly spelling tests Ralph was getting three or four out of fifteen correct, until Miss Burnette decided to give him only six words a week. Now he sometimes gets five or six correct. In mathematics he often surprises his teacher with his understanding of operations and with his reasoning ability, but he usually makes so many "silly" mistakes on his computations that he scores poorly on assignments and tests. "In science," Miss Burnette says, "Ralph is a whiz—as long as he can experiment with things instead of read about them." In creative writing he shows a mild degree of inventiveness, though he has to translate his illegible handwriting for his teacher.

Figure 13.1 shows a sample of Ralph's writing, in response to a field trip he took with several other children who work with Ms. Benjamin, the new compensatory-program teacher. These children went to Ms. Benja-

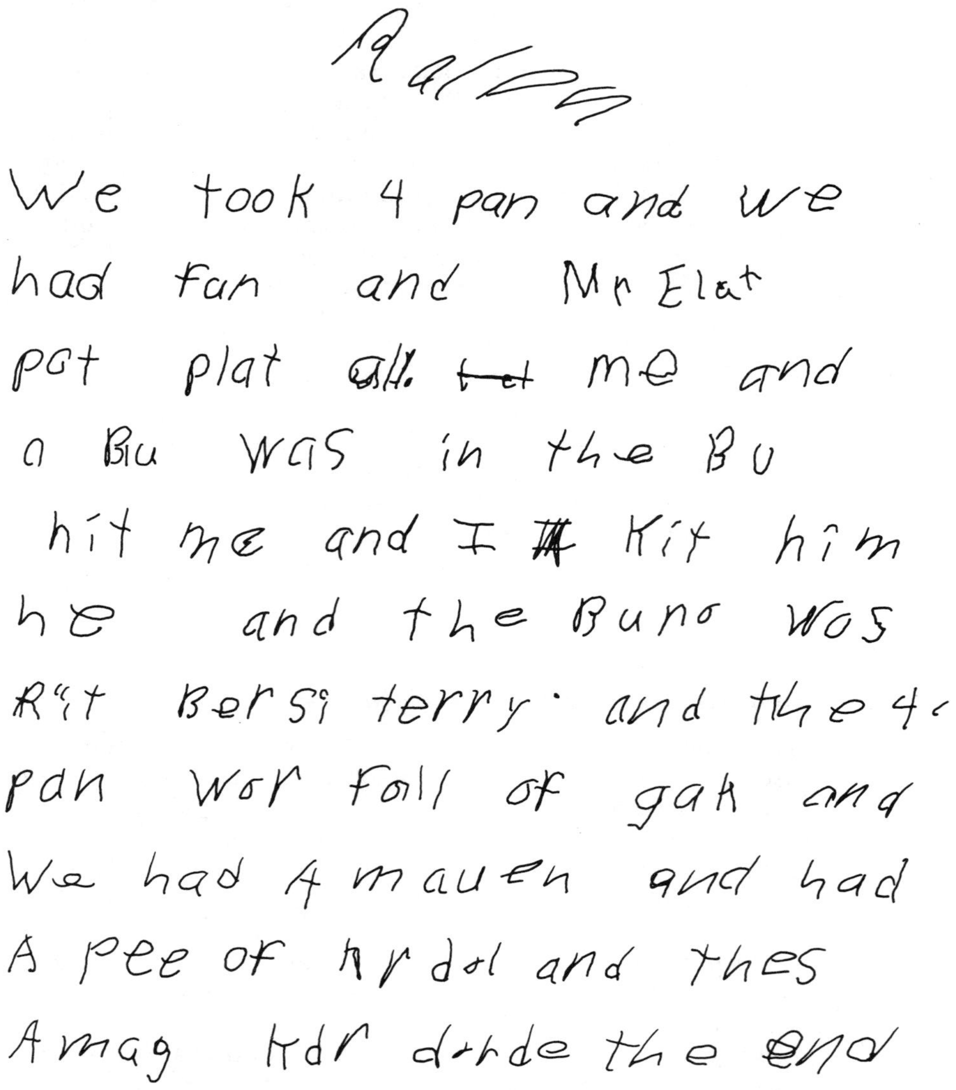

Ralph

We took 4 pan and we
had fan and Mr Elat
pot plat all tot me and
a Bu was in the Bu
hit me and I H Kit him
he and the Buno was
Rit Bersi terry· and the 4
pan wor foll of gah and
We had A mauen and had
A pee of hrdol and thes
Amag hdr drhde the end

Figure 13.1 *A Language Experience Story Created by Ralph.*

min's basement darkroom to develop photographs she had taken of them. Her friend, Mr. Eliot, had built the darkroom for her with black plastic. Ralph's story should be translated as follows:

> We took four pans and we had fun and Mr. Eliot put plastic all over me and a boogie monster was in the black. The boogie monster he hit me and I kicked

him and the boogie monster was right beside Terry. The four pans were full of junk and we had a machine and we had a piece of cardboard and there's a magic trick that put it on the cardboard. The end.

Here's how one group of children, all "compensatory readers," described the same field trip.

How We Made Our Pictures by Group 7

Ms. Benjamin took our pictures. Then she opened the film can in the darkroom. She took the film out of the can and wound it on the reel. Then she put it in the tank. Then we put the developer in the tank. We put the cover on the tank and shook it for seven minutes. We took the cap off and poured it out. We then poured in the stop-bath. We shook it for three minutes. Then we poured it out. We took the reel out of the tank and washed all the chemicals out. We hung it up to dry.

Then we went over to Ms. Benjamin's house on Friday afternoon. We went downstairs in the cellar to the darkroom. First we took off our coats and put them on a table. Then we went into the darkroom and found all these chemicals. We took the pictures out of a bag and put them in the enlarger. Then Ms. Benjamin took out the paper and put it in the enlarger. Ms. Benjamin cleaned the pictures. We timed them in the enlarger for four seconds. Then we put the picture in Mike's developer. Then we put it in Sandy's stop-bath. Sandy put it in Betty's fixer.

We went upstairs and had milk, peanut butter, and crackers. We put the pictures in the dryer. When the pictures were dry, we went back to school.

As seen in Figure 13.1, Ralph not only has difficulty with the mechanics of writing but also has difficulty expressing himself. His teachers feel that most of the problem comes from his inability to concentrate, especially when he is asked to write. Concentrating on the details of developing photographs, for example, may have been an arduous task, though he carried out his part with a reasonable degree of seriousness. When it came time to record his experience in writing, moreover, the additional concentration that it required seemed to be too much for him, and he resorted to a tale of a "boogie monster." In addition to the problem of concentration, Ralph may also have had difficulty perceiving and understanding the operations involved in developing the photographs. This would have resulted in a foggy memory of the experience.

Ralph's difficulty appears to be one of intake. The messages coming in from the environment seem to be weak and distorted. It's as if his nerves are like garden hoses that someone is standing on, partially obstructing the flow to the brain. This analogy is merely illustrative, of course, and not to be taken seriously. Exactly what causes this intake problem is not known, though we will consider possible explanations later.

In November, Ms. Benjamin administered the *Slingerland Tests for Identifying Children with Specific Language Disabilities* (1971). This battery of tests demonstrated to Ms. Benjamin that Ralph's visual memory and auditory memory were both quite poor.

His weaknesses in visual and auditory memory were particularly noticeable when he had to use his kinesthetic abilities to *write* the word rather than select from alternatives. When shown the word *thundering*, he wrote *t–h–u–e–n–d–r–o–n–b*. When presented with this phrase orally—"saw this first girl"—he wrote *scr ther gur feir*. It was clear to both Ms. Benjamin and Miss Burnette that Ralph was a child with severe learning disabilities.

Several studies cited by Klasen (1972) show that Ralph is not alone. The signs of severe reading disability, on the surface at least, seem to be neurological, according to Klasen.

Poor coordination—Ralph, for example, can't jump rope.

Lack of fine-motor control—He has great difficulty forming manuscript letters, although he does much better with cursive, since he can move from one letter to the next without removing his pencil from the paper.

Directional confusion—Ralph reverses, inverts, and transposes letters and words, for example:
   reversals: *b* for *d, d* for *b, q* for *p, p* for *q, saw* for *was, was* for *saw*
   inversions: *u* for *n, n* for *u, p* for *b, b* for *p*
   transpositions: *neihgbor* for *neighbor, s–p–r–t* for *s–t–p–r*
When he draws a circle, he sometimes draws it in a clockwise direction and sometimes in a counterclockwise direction.

Speech defects—Ralph's stuttering is quite mild, but he seems to be struggling to put his thoughts into words, resulting in words and syllables that seem jumbled; his enunciation is very weak, making it hard for others to understand him.

Visual and auditory perceptual disorders—Ralph often (though not always) shows these perceptual disorders when asked to rely on either his discrimination or memory abilities.

Concentration problems—Ralph is quite hyperactive, which in itself causes concentration problems. He often complains that words are confusing to him. In addition, he shows unwillingness to concentrate (perhaps because his past attempts at concentrating yielded little success in perceiving and understanding).

THE INACCURACY OF THE DYSLEXIA LABEL

The term *dyslexia,* although a short and once-popular term, is an inaccurate label for the condition we are discussing in this chapter. The original meaning of the word was simply "the inability to read." A dictionary definition of the word is "an impairment of the ability to read due to a brain defect" (Stein, 1973). However, this still does not capture the nature of the malady that Ralph and other children like him experience.

From a practical standpoint, what teachers generally notice are inabilities in reading, spelling, handwriting, speaking, and certain activities related to physical education—in roughly that order. The title of Clarke's book *Can't Read, Can't Write, Can't Talk Too Good Either* (1974) is perhaps the most sensible, down-to-earth definition.

Because of the confusion surrounding the word *dyslexia,* many researchers and teachers now refer to this condition as *learning disabled.* But no label comes close to describing the difficulties these youngsters experience. In fact, labels probably do more harm than good in some cases. Educators are seemingly making the same mistake that psychiatrists used to make by attempting to categorize disturbed people as manic depressives, hebephrenic schizophrenics, paranoics, and so on. Once people had been classified, the tendency was to treat everyone in the same category the same way and ignore individual differences. There is considerable danger that we will fall into the same trap.

There is also considerable danger in overusing the labels *dyslexic* or *learning disabled* to apply to anyone who is having trouble learning to read. Unfortunately, once children are so labeled, they are sometimes forgotten or rushed off to a specialist without first examining one's own teaching methods and one's way of relating to the particular child.

Allington (1975) presents several cogent arguments against the use of labeling.

Most of the labels simply do not have a single commonly accepted definition. For example, what is a *hyperactive* child? Is it one who disrupts the classroom? Is it the "normal," restless, active boy? Is a child *dyslexic* just because he reverses the *b* and the *d?* Many children do this for the first two grades.

Labels provide no useful information. Rather than label a child, it might be far better to determine the specific skills that are deficient and make plans for remediation.

Labels are often a feeble attempt to define the cause of the ailment (e.g., Poor Ralph can't spell because he has dyslexia). Knowing the causes is really not that useful in applying treatment anyway, according to Allington.

Assigning labels is beyond the professional skill of most teachers.

Labeling children only shifts the burden of failure to them. Perhaps a better label under which academic underachievers might be placed is *teaching disabled*. This term more adequately describes the situation. We are not faced with children who *cannot* learn, but with children who need instruction somewhat different from that provided in regular classrooms. These children can learn; it is the teaching that needs modification. (Allington, 1975, p. 367)

CLASSROOM DIAGNOSIS OF THE READING OR LANGUAGE DISABLED CHILD

It would appear that the earlier a person's disability is detected, the easier it is to treat (Jordan, 1977; Slingerland, 1970). But how does one determine whether a child is sufficiently disabled to require special instructional strategies in the classroom or perhaps special instruction by a compensatory teacher? By definition, a disabled child is one whose intelligence is average or above. But can we obtain a valid and reliable measure of intelligence? And what do we do with it when we get it? The decision as to when a child is sufficiently disabled to require special instruction is truly arbitrary. There are presently no standardized tests of reading disability, and it's doubtful that such norm-based tests would be useful for such an individual problem. Slingerland (1970) and Jordan (1977) have developed diagnostic tests for reading and language disabilities that can be administered by specialized teachers; however, both are quite time-consuming. For the classroom teacher I recommend the checklists in Appendix 0 and the RAD test in Appendix G.

WAYS OF WORKING WITH ENGLISH-DEFICIENT, SLOW, OR DISABLED LEARNERS

English-deficient, slow, and disabled learners have several things in common. They're generally in the minority and feel their minority status. They often experience a damaged self-concept in a school setting. They are often in a position of having to learn something through the medium of a written language they perceive as confusing and meaningless. They often feel left out, abandoned. Instruction for these children needs to compensate for these difficulties.

Help Improve Their Self-Concepts

Wattenburg and Clifford (1964) found that measures of children's self-concepts were better at predicting their reading achievement than the usual intelligence and readiness tests. But perhaps we don't need research reports to prove the obvious. It is readily apparent that people's conceptions of themselves influence and direct their behavior. If Janice feels she's a lousy cook, she's not likely to try hard at being a good cook, for fear of encountering more dismal failures. In fact, her negative self-concept in this case will probably influence her cooking behavior in such a way that she does burn the roast and lump the gravy. Similarly, if Sammy develops a concept of himself as a lousy reader, his chances for success are greatly reduced.

> Research conducted in the areas of self-concept and the role of teacher expectations as they correspond to academic achievement shows them to be interrelated. Poor achievement leads to a lowered self-image which results in continued poor achievement. (Clark, 1974, p. 361)

How can teachers help their special children improve their self-concepts? Quandt and Selznick, in *Self-Concept and Reading* (1984), offer several suggestions:

1. Praise those children who praise other children.

2. Whenever possible, avoid comparisons with other students. Help children see that they are valued not for their reading status but for their status as interesting and worthwhile human beings.

3. Use another basis for grouping children besides reading *ability*. Have reading *interest* groups as well that meet once a week for sharing.

4. Keep showing them their progress. Have an occasional individual conference with each child.

5. Help each child become a "junior expert" on something.

6. Change instructional approaches when one is not working. Don't expect the child to adjust to your approach.

7. Give them opportunities to demonstrate to others what they have learned rather than rushing on to the next skill.

8. Find materials easy enough for the child to feel success with.

9. Explain to parents the nature of self-concept and the value of parental praise.

In addition to these suggestions, I'd like to emphasize the importance of using the child's vernacular, whether it be another language or just another way of expressing himself in English. This means you must use a language experience approach for part of your instruction.

> If he hears, speaks, and feels what is already known to him, he is more comfortable than if he is bombarded by strange sounds and sights. Once he feels at ease or successful in reading his own language, he is more receptive to acquiring another language and the culture it represents. (Johnson, 1975, p. 236)

Another way to improve self-concept is through providing models that children can emulate. One reason that some children perceive themselves as nonreaders is that the people they identify with do not read. In a study by Nichols (1977), for instance, she found that none of the fathers of a group of "nonreading" black boys used reading in his daily activities to any appreciable extent. Furthermore, the fathers placed a low value on reading. In addition, Nichols found census figures showing that for the top five occupations engaged in by black men in this particular region, not one required reading or clerical skills. Nichols did discover, however, that many of the black men in this region were highly skilled storytellers and that the boys gained status through imitating these men. In fact, many of the boys were superb storytellers by the age of ten. She suggests that the language experience approach be used with students in this kind of situation so that their stories can be captured in print and then used to inspire reading.

In addition to language experience stories, Nichols suggests that men in the community who use reading in their work be brought in for short visits with the children. Others suggest that various adults be brought in to read to children, that biographies of famous minority people be read, and that their pictures be hung on the school walls for inspiration. In general, providing identification figures for children is an important way to help them improve their self-concepts.

Use a Multisensory Approach

One way to help children who are having trouble learning to deal with a written language is to employ as many of the senses as possible. Whether a child is an English-deficient, slow, or disabled learner, a multisensory approach can make the learning process easier. For example, when Miss Burnette wants Ralph to learn the letter *b*, she shows him the letter in print and says the letter to him. She then reminds him how to make the *b* on the chalkboard, using large movements, starting the letter at the top and producing it with one motion, without taking her chalk off the board. She then traces the letter and says it simultaneously. Next she has Ralph look at the letter and say it. Following this, he is expected to look at it, say it, and trace it with his hand simultaneously. Then he writes it on the board, using the full swing of his arm. He then traces it and says it simultaneously. Then he moves to his desk and writes it two or three times on his paper, saying it each time he writes it. And finally he circles any *b* he finds on a worksheet. A similar approach is used for learning sight words such as *the*, *there*, or *off*.

Chapter 12 emphasized the need for massed practice followed by distributed practice. If ever this principle were needed, it is in teaching slow, disabled, or English-deficient readers. Furthermore, not only should the massed practice (such as the lesson on *b* just described) be multisensory, but the distributed practice as well. Before Ralph goes to see Ms. Benjamin, he is shown the letter *b* by Miss Burnette; he says it ten times as she traces it on his back. When he arrives at Ms. Benjamin's door he hands her a note from Miss Burnette explaining what he has recently learned. Ms. Benjamin asks him to read the letter *b*, trace it, and even shout it. Not only does he trace the letter in the air, he traces it on fine sandpaper or felt or wet paint. The same is true of words. He writes the word *there* (for his two teachers) with chalk, with felt pen, with finger paint, with a wooden stylus on a "magic-erase" wax tablet. The correct sequence of letters in each word is accented again and again—visually, auditorily, kinesthetically, tactually.

Every conceivable device for keeping the multisensory approach from becoming drudgery must be used—novelty in writing tools, novelty in writing surfaces, novelty in praise, games as rewards for good work. The multisensory approach is slow and painstaking, but needn't be painful. Children, especially hyperactive ones, enjoy getting out of their seats to write words, trace them, circle them, find them, and manipulate them.

Spelling and reading need to go hand in hand during many of the learning experiences. Research demonstrates a strong interrelationship and interdependence between spelling and word-recognition skills (1981). Ms. Benjamin often has Ralph not only shout the words, but the letters as well. Spelling races, however, are never used since precision rather than speed is what children need to sharpen the images of what they receive.

Listening and reading should also go hand in hand whenever possible. The teacher should often read to the children while they follow along silently with their own copies. This procedure can be modified by using listening tapes in a reading or listening center. There is some evidence that this approach, when combined with other multisensory experiences, can lead to significant progress in reading. Marie Carbo (1981) found that *some* of the children she worked with increased their reading scores by one and one-half years in just three months through the use of homemade "talking books." Carbo recommends making your own listening tapes to go along with easy-to-read books, because she has found that the commercial tapes are often too fast for children who are having trouble learning to read. She also suggests providing many clear cues for turning pages and for looking at pictures and reminding the children to put their fingers under the words as they hear them being read.

Patterned Books as Multisensory Learning Experience

A significant multisensory experience can be provided through the use of patterned books. We've discussed these materials several times, so by this time you're probably wondering why I haven't mentioned them before in this chapter. They do seem like a natural medium of instruction for English-deficient, slow, or disabled learners, don't they? *The Bus Ride* (Scott, Foresman Reading Systems, Level 2, Book A, 1971) is a good example of an appropriate patterned book for these children. Part of the book goes like this:

> The girl got on the bus.
> Then the bus went fast.
>
> A boy got on the bus.
> Then the bus went fast.
>
> A fox got on the bus.
> Then the bus went fast . . .

A more challenging example is *The Great Big Enormous Turnip* by Alexei Tolstoy (Franklin Watts, 1968). Part of the book goes like this:

> The mouse pulled the cat.
> The cat pulled the dog.
> The dog pulled the granddaughter.
> The granddaughter pulled the old woman.

(For more patterned books, see Appendix P.)

Make Reading Experiences Meaningful through LEA

> From the very first dictated story, the blind child realizes, if he did not already know from home experience, that oral language can be *saved* in the form of Braille. Braille immediately has a *use* for him and learning to read and write it is not a chore detached from any purpose, but rather a discovery of how to help order his world of experiences. (Curry, 1975, p. 274)

I hope this analogy between a blind child and the special learners we're talking about is clear. All children who are learning to read, whether blind, English-deficient, average, gifted, slow, or disabled, need to feel the process is meaningful. One of the best ways to bring meaning into the process is through language experience approaches. Nothing is more meaningful to a child than his own experiences, his own way of looking at those experiences, his own way of expressing himself. By capitalizing on events that occur in the classroom, on the playground, in and out of school, the teacher can help children develop their own reading materials—materials that make sense. This may mean tape recording their stories and finding someone to type them in *both* languages, but it could well be worth it for your own success in teaching them to read.

Ralph is particularly fond of using the tape recorder to dictate his stories, having someone transcribe them, and then reading them the next day. (Smith [1976] describes this technique in considerable detail.) Like most children, Ralph seems genuinely thrilled to see his own creations "in print," and he invariably gets great pleasure out of reading them to others. Had the same stories been written by someone else and given to him to read, he would not have been able to read them. But because he has written them himself and because they are based on his own direct or imaginary experiences, he can read them with considerable skill (relative to his normal reading). Of course, much of this reading is based on memory, rather than on precise decoding. Nevertheless, Ralph is receiving excellent practice on the type of mature reading that we eventually want him to master—reading based primarily on comprehension. Even more important for Ralph now, reading is a meaningful act, it makes sense to him.

Make Reading a Personal Affair

As mentioned earlier, many so-called "problem readers" (alias English-deficient, slow, disabled, reluctant, dyslexic, remedial, compensatory) feel left out or even abandoned. Their sense of belonging is weak because of numerous failures to communicate with people, to achieve lasting friendships, and to achieve in the way their peers are achieving. Perhaps even more than children who are achieving at normal levels, they need someone who cares for them and is concerned enough to give them the extra time it takes to help them learn to read and write—someone who will help them stop feeling so inferior.

Their bad luck (in being a "problem reader" in the first place) often follows them to school, however. For, according to research (Miller & Hering, 1975) it appears that most teachers prefer teaching the better readers. Even without research studies, casual observation in classrooms demonstrates that some teachers have far less patience with poor readers than with good ones. And because of this, the children who need the most help are often those who get the least.

In fact, this may be the most serious problem of all for children like Ralph—simply not getting enough help of the right kind when they need it. As a result, their self-concept deteriorates; they withdraw rather than risk further failure, and learning to read becomes a meaningless, senseless, impersonal, and chaotic experience.

Yet teachers who care for people like Ralph can help. After his first successfully written experience story, Ralph read it with ease to his reading teacher, Ms. Benjamin. He was so thrilled by his success and the praise he received, he spruced up his courage and asked his regular classroom teacher, Miss Burnette, if he could read it to the class.

He read it beautifully. And the children—even those who had laughed at him before—were stunned. Spontaneously, without any signal from the teacher, they clapped loud and long. Some even slapped him on the back and told him what a good reader he was.

Ralph hasn't been the same since. He now considers himself a reader. And with the help of caring, affectionate teachers, some day he'll be just that.

THE MAIN IDEAS IN THIS CHAPTER

Advanced students (those who are at least mildly gifted) often have characteristics of creativity. They frequently exhibit one or more of these characteristics and may be autonomous, visionary, goal-oriented, flexible, open, adventurous. For teachers to be successful in motivating these youngsters, they must gear their materials and methods to those personality characteristics.

When working with children who do not speak Standard English, teachers should be able to appreciate their culture and vernacular and to communicate this appreciation to them. The teacher needs to be a learner as well as an instructor.

It is advisable to use a child's own vernacular as a temporary teaching medium and to treat Standard English as another useful language rather than as the "only" language.

Teachers must avoid thinking of children mainly according to labels such as "dyslexics" or "slow learners" or "disabled learners" and think of them as individuals with specific problems and instructional needs.

On the other hand, some of the methods of diagnosis and teaching used with "normal" readers can be modified for English-deficient, slow, and disabled learners.

Children who are English-deficient, slow, or disabled need multisensory learning experiences. But they also need, just as other children do, to perceive reading as a meaningful, communicative experience. Furthermore, they need, even more than other children, to experience reading instruction as a personal, friendly interaction with an affectionate, caring teacher.

REFERENCES AND SUGGESTED READING

Allington, R. I. (1975). Sticks and stones . . . but will names never hurt them? *Reading Teacher, 28,* 364–369.

Barron, F. (1962). The psychology of imagination. In S. J. Parnes & H. F. Harding (Eds.), *A source book for creative think-*

ing (pp. 227–237). New York: Charles Scribner's Sons.

Bethell, T. (1975, May 26). Becoming an American. *Newsweek*, p. 13.

Boraks, N., & Allen, A. R. (1977). A program to enhance peer tutoring. *Reading Teacher, 30*, 479–484.

Breiling, A. (1976). Using parents as teaching partners. *Reading Teacher, 30*, 187–192.

Burg, L. A. (1975). Affective teaching—Neglected practice in innercity schools? *Reading Teacher, 28*, 360–363.

Cagney, M. A. (1977). Children's ability to understand Standard English and Black dialect. *Reading Teacher, 30*, 607–610.

Carbo, M. (1981). Making books talk to children. *Reading Teacher, 35*, 186–189.

Ching, D. C. (1976). *Reading and the bilingual child*. Newark, DE: International Reading Association.

Clark, B. (1983). *Growing up gifted*. Columbus, OH: Charles E. Merrill.

Clark, L. (1974). *Can't read, can't write, can't talk too good either: How to recognize and overcome dyslexia in your child*. Baltimore: Penguin.

Clay, M. M. (1976). Early childhood and cultural diversity in New Zealand. *Reading Teacher, 29*, 333–342.

Curry, R. G. (1975). Using LEA to teach blind children to read. *Reading Teacher, 29*, 272–279.

Davison, H., & Lang, G. (1960). Children's perceptions of their teachers' feelings toward them related to self-perception, school achievement, and behavior. *Journal of Experimental Education, 29*, 107–118.

Donoghue, M. R. (1971). *The child and the English language arts*. Minneapolis: William C. Brown.

Eisenberg, L., et al. (1968). Class and race effects on the intelligibility of monosyllables. *Child Development*, 1077–1079.

Eloisa, M. G. D. (1975). Frontier dialect: A challenge to education. *Reading Teacher, 28*, 653–658.

Feeley, J. (1970). Teaching non-English-speaking first graders to read. *Elementary English*, 199–208.

Getzels, J. W., & Jackson, P. W. (1960). *The gifted student*. Cooperative Research Monograph No. 2. Washington: U.S. Department of Health, Education, and Welfare.

Hall, M. (1972). *The language experience approach for the culturally disadvantaged*. Newark, DE: International Reading Association.

Hall, V. C., & Turner, R. R. (1974). The validity of the "different language explanation" for poor scholastic performance by Black students. *Review of Educational Research, 44*, 69–81.

Himmelsteib, C. (1975). Buddies read in library program. *Reading Teacher, 30*, 32–35.

Isaacs, A. F. (1973). What to do when you discover a child is gifted and interested in language; or one hundred ways to tickle your fancy with language and linguistics. *Gifted Child Quarterly, 17*, 144–149.

Johnson, L. (1975). Bilingual bicultural education: A two-way street. *Reading Teacher, 29*, 231–239.

Jordan, D. R. (1977). *Dyslexia in the classroom*. Columbus: Charles E. Merrill.

Kaplan, R. B. (1969). On a note of protest (in a minor key). *College English, 30*, 386–389.

Kirk, S. A., et al. (1978). *Teaching reading to slow and disabled learners*. Boston: Houghton, Mifflin.

Klasen, E. (1972). *The syndrome of specific dyslexia*. Baltimore: University Park Press.

Krech, D. (1969). Psychoneurobiochemeducation. *Phi Delta Kappan, 50*, 370–375.

Lawrence, D. (1975). Sparta revisited. *Reading Teacher, 28*, 464–465.

Lozanov, G. (1977). A general theory of suggestion in the communications process and the activation of the total reserves of the learner's personality. *Suggesto-paedia-Canada, 1,* 1–4.

MacLean, P. (1978). A mind of three minds: Educating the triune brain. In J. Chall & A. Mirsky (Eds.), *Education and the brain.* Chicago: University of Chicago Press.

Martindale, C. (1976). What makes creative people different. *Psychology Today, 9* (2), 44–50.

May, F. B., & Ripple, R. E. (1962). Caution in comparing creativity and IQ. *Psychological Reports, 10,* 229–230.

Miller, H. B., & Hering, S. (1975). Teacher's ratings—Which reading group is number one? *Reading Teacher, 28,* 389–391.

Niaden, N. (1976). Ratio of boys to girls among disabled readers. *Reading Teacher, 29,* 439–442.

Nichols, P. C. (1977). A sociolinguistic perspective on reading and Black children. *Language Arts, 54,* 150–157.

Peisach, E. C. (1965). Children's comprehension of teacher and peer speech. *Child Development, 36,* 467–480.

Quant, I., & Selznick, R. (1984). *Self-concept and reading.* Newark, DE: International Reading Association.

Restak, K. (1979). *The brain: The last frontier.* New York: Doubleday.

Rosenthal, R., & Jacobson, L. (1968). *Pygmalion in the classroom.* New York: Holt, Rinehart, & Winston.

Rosezweig, M. (1966). Environmental complexity, cerebral change and behavior. *American Psychologist, 21,* 321–332.

Ruddell, R. B. (1965). The effect of oral and written patterns of language structure and reading comprehension. *Reading Teacher, 18,* 273.

Saville, M. R., & Troike, R. C. (1971). *A handbook of bilingual education.* Teaching English to speakers of other languages. Newark, DE: International Reading Association.

Slingerland, B. H. (1970). *Slingerland screening tests for identifying children with specific language disability.* Cambridge: Educators Publishing Service.

Slingerland, B. H. (1971). *A multi-sensory approach to language arts for specific language disability children, a guide for primary teachers.* Cambridge: Educators Publishing Service.

Smith, L. B. (1976). They found a golden ladder . . . Stories by children. *Reading Teacher, 29,* 541–545.

Smith, N. B. (1975). Cultural dialects: Current problems and solutions. *Reading Teacher, 29,* 137–141.

Stein, J. (Ed.). (1973). *The Random House dictionary of the English language.* New York: Random House.

Thompson, R., Berger, T., & Berry, S. (1980). An introduction to the anatomy, physiology, and chemistry of the brain. In M. Wittrock (Ed.), *The brain and psychology.* New York: Academic Press.

Thonis, E. W. (1976). *Literacy for America's Spanish-speaking children.* Newark, DE: International Reading Association.

Torrance, E. P. (1962). Guiding creative talent. Englewood Cliffs, NJ: Prentice-Hall.

Tway, E. (1980). The gifted child in literature. *Language Arts, 57,* 14–20.

U.S. Commission on Civil Rights. (1975). *A better chance to learn: Bilingual-biculture education* (Clearing House Publication #51). Washington, DC.

Wattenburg, W. W., & Clifford, C. (1964). Relation of self-concept to beginning achievement in reading. *Child Development, 35,* 461–467.

Weener, P. D. (1969). Social dialect differences and the recall of verbal messages. *Journal of Educational Psychology, 60,* 194–199.

Wilson, M. (1981). A review of recent research on the integration of reading and writing. *Reading Teacher, 34,* 896–901.

APPLICATION EXPERIENCES FOR THE TEACHER EDUCATION CLASS

A. *What's your opinion?* Use textbook ideas and your own ideas based on personal and professional experiences to defend your decision.

1. It doesn't really hurt gifted students to have to complete reading lessons on concepts they've already learned. This way they solidify their knowledge and also pick up things they might have forgotten.

2. Gifted students should not be put in special classrooms for reading and writing. They are important as models for average and slow learners.

3. When a child reads aloud in a black dialect, Spanish dialect, or other nonstandard dialect, it is a sign of a major reading deficiency.

4. Cultural differences should be an important factor in determining a teacher's methods for reading instruction.

5. The ESL approach is better than the native vernacular approach.

6. A learning disabled reader is "dyslexic," and there's not much a teacher can do about it.

B. *Miscue Analysis:* The following is an example of Ralph's miscues on a preprimer selection*:

Boys and girls run down~~to~~ the st~~d~~reet.

Run in, run~~to on~~ out.

Run up ~~far~~ and down.

Run up and down the street.

Two girls run. ~~get-go~~

Three boys run. ~~Trees~~

What strategies is Ralph (a "learning disabled" child) using?

---

*Bank Street College of Education. "Lunch on a Boat," in *Around the City* (New York: Macmillan, 1965). Reprinted with permission from the publisher.

C. *Looking at Prejudices:* Discuss with three or four others any prejudices you may have had (or still have) toward people who speak a dialect or language different from your own. Discuss how you have overcome these prejudices or how you might overcome them as a teacher.

D. *Views from Practicing Teachers:* Arrange for teachers who are working with gifted, handicapped, and English-deficient children to talk with your class. Ask them to discuss some of the children they're working with and the instructional procedures they use with the children.

FIELD EXPERIENCES IN THE ELEMENTARY SCHOOL CLASSROOM

A. Using the procedures you learned in Chapter 10, carry on miscue analysis with a child whose mother tongue is not Standard English. Which of his miscues are truly reading errors; which are dialect translations? What recommendations would you make for providing reading instruction to this child?

B. Be a "student" to one of the minority children in the school. Learn some of his dialect or language. Try to learn about some of his cultural behavior and values that differ from yours. Find ways to show your appreciation for his instruction.

C. Using the "Observation Checklist" in Appendix O, over a period of several days observe a child who has been classified as a disabled learner. If possible, do the same with a child who has been classified as a slow learner. What similarities and differences do you notice? Are these differences due to different *types* of children or simply to different individuals? What evidence do you have for your conclusions?

D. With a child who is considered a gifted student, informally discuss a library book that both of you have read. Using some of the ideas for questions that we've talked about, see what you can discover about his schemata related to the book. What effect do these schemata have on his interpretation of the book? How are these schemata developed by reading library books?

14 BECOMING A GOOD INSTRUCTIONAL MANAGER: A LOOK AT THE FUTURE

CHAPTER PREVIEW

We've come a long way together, you and I. All the way from a visit with those philosophers from Zania in Chapter 1 to this chapter—a visit with the future. We'll attempt to predict the future by looking at the changes that will probably happen (and are happening) in the way classroom teachers manage their reading and language arts programs. Looking into the future can be difficult for both the author and the reader, because it is sometimes discouraging to compare the future to the present, and great patience is called for. But looking ahead can be exciting too, as we see the possibilities for teachers to take greater responsibility for creative planning, teaching, and managing.

The way a teacher manages his or her instructional program greatly influences how well children learn to read. Research shows us that, but it doesn't show us exactly *how* teachers should allocate their instructional time and *what* resources they should utilize the most. Only teachers and administrators, using thoughtful judgments, can make these decisions. Their judgments will depend today and tomorrow on how we perceive the reading process. If we perceive it one way, we will allocate most instructional and practice time to isolated subskill practice. If we perceive it another way, we will have children spend more time on integrated interactive practice. The viewpoints and decisions of teachers and administrators will continue to make an enormous impact on what children learn in school. The challenges that face us all—teachers, administrators, and teacher educators—are both impressive and inspiring.

Humans *may* create havoc with their lives, but their potential for creating knowledge and beauty is very great indeed.

A LOOK AT RESEARCH BEFORE WE BEGIN

Berliner (1981) summarizes his research and that of his colleagues with several interesting conclusions:

> In many classrooms there is a lack of attention to classroom management that results in considerable inefficiency and reduced achievement. (p. 205)

> Classroom management definitely affects achievement, because learning time can be lost through poor management of time and students.

> Reading achievement is enhanced by two classroom ingredients: (a) a great deal of learning that is directly guided by the teacher, and (b) a businesslike environment that is also warm enough to enable students to meet their needs.

> Teachers' beliefs about what is important to learn greatly influence the way they manage the time available for reading instruction.

> Increasing the amount of time children spend with reading materials *that are easy enough* leads to higher scores on achievement tests, greater retention rates, and more positive attitudes toward school.

> Today's teachers have a complex job and need management training.

Guzetti and Marzano (1984), in their summary of research findings, conclude that effective reading teachers do these things:

1. Maintain and *communicate* high expectations of their students as part of their management strategy.

2. Rely on direct interaction between the teacher and the students as their *major* teaching and managing strategy. They do not rely on materials to *teach;* only to reinforce.

3. Manage instructional time to allow for practice in inferential thinking and other types of higher-level thinking.

4. Arrange time for frequent and specific feedback.

Singer, McNeil, and Furse (1984) wondered why some schools in Los Angeles had considerably higher scores on inferential reading comprehension than others. They hypothesized that the high scoring schools had a broader curriculum that included more time for social studies, science, and fine arts than did the other schools. Their hunch was based on the theory that children need these other areas to develop enough background knowledge (and schemata) to allow them to engage in inferential thinking. After examining the time allotments teachers provided in the high-scoring and low-scoring schools, they concluded that their hypothesis was valid.

Allington (1980) wondered if part of the reason for poor readers' not improving very fast was teachers' inappropriate management of time. In his study of first and second graders from four school districts, he found that teachers gave poor-reader groups and good-reader groups about the same amount of instructional time with the teacher. Thus the poor readers, because they read slower and because they were unfortunately stopped so often to have their "errors" corrected, got the chance to read far fewer words during small-group instruction time. The poor-reader groups read less than half as much as good-reader groups. Here are Allington's results:

	Words Read	Range
Good-reader groups	539 (average)	141-1306
Poor-reader groups	237 (average)	48-686

Furthermore, he found that teachers seldom asked poor readers to read silently, thus unconsciously denying them opportunities to read for meaning without fear of correction. When *good* readers made errors, the teachers tended to help correct them through context cues, with emphasis on the syntactic and semantic properties of the words. When poor readers made errors, the teachers tended to help correct them through graphophonic cues, with emphasis on visual and auditory properties of the words. Thus, without meaning to, they helped to exaggerate the poor readers' limited concept and strategies of reading.

Mason (1983) was concerned about the amount of time teachers spend in actual instruction when they teach reading. She found that teachers were not managing their instructional time in ways most conducive to learning. About three-fourths of the instructional time was used in giving directions for worksheets and other assignments, supervising the filling of worksheets, checking assignments with children, and having students examine isolated lists of words on the chalkboard. Only one-fourth of the time was spent actually reading "text."

Durkin (1979) unfortunately found a similar time allotment in her study. Furthermore, she found that the time spent on actual instruction tended to emphasize graphophonic cues rather than the interactive nature of the four cueing systems. Comprehension as a process, she found, was actually *taught* only one percent of the time. Teachers in general considered asking questions sufficient comprehension instruction.

MANAGERIAL CHANGES THAT NEED TO BE MADE

I don't know how you felt as you read the last section, but writing it made me feel just a little bit discouraged. The discouragement comes from realizing how much knowledge about the effective teaching of reading is available but never gets a chance to be applied. I'm not *thoroughly* discouraged, mind you, just mildly. In fact, my discouragement is probably nothing more than childish impatience, for I know that over the next few decades changes will gradually take place, just as they always have. As we communicate with each other in this last chapter, then, let's both keep in mind that change is bound to take place and that both of us will probably be involved in causing changes to occur.

One of the changes we can hope for is that more teachers will allot instructional time according to *goals* rather than available materials. What researchers see too often in elementary school classrooms is teachers' letting materials dictate what happens next. Suppose, for example, that the next lesson in the teacher's guide is "what is meant by the terms *short vowel sound* and *long vowel sound*." Yet, suppose the teacher has observed that a particular group of seven children is still reading word by word, without predicting ahead, without noticing the same kind of syntactic and semantic cues they notice when they listen. What management decisions, according to the research I've just cited, will most teachers make? Most will decide to push ahead in the teacher's guide, to teach the lesson on the terms *short vowel sound* and *long vowel sound*, to assign the worksheets that "teach these terms," and to assume that word by word reading will go away in time anyway.

This is sad, for the vast majority of teachers are conscientious, concerned people who *want* to help their students become highly successful readers. But for a variety of reasons, most of them "go by the book." Poor training? Often. Personal timidity? Certainly sometimes. Lack of encouragement from administrators? Unfortunately often. Many school systems do not encourage teachers to develop management skills that would allow them to make more reasonable decisions. Too often, instead, teachers are encouraged to let the teacher's guide and other materials determine both the goals and the time allotments. True, some schools have "management by objective" programs, but all of the ones I've seen are programs essentially imposed on teachers that allow very little flexible planning on the teacher's part. So you see, the change we're talking about involves not only teachers like you and teacher educators like me, but principals, reading coordinators, superintendents, and curriculum coordinators as well.

GETTING MANAGERIAL ADVICE FROM OTHERS

What can the classroom teacher do, meanwhile, if he or she feels "under the gun" to follow a teacher's guide or curriculum guide? One alternative is to follow the guide in the order dictated by children's needs. As I mentioned earlier, no research has been done that justifies a tight sequence dictated by page numbers in guides. Another alternative is to sit down with your principal or other supervisor and explain what your goals are and how you would like some flexibility to try carrying them out. This should be an open-minded discussion, of course; I'm not advocating a hot-tempered diatribe on your part. Instead, I'm suggesting that two heads are usually better than one. I have talked many teachers into this approach and nearly all of them have gained greater authority for making managerial decisions in their classrooms. Principals and coordinators are, after all, pursuing the same objectives you are.

In a moment, I'm going to talk specifically about time allotments. Naturally I'm going to try to bias you about this, just as I've done all through the book. The research reports, articles, and books I've sifted through, at the risk of poor vision and library mildew, have all pushed me toward an interactive view of reading (although, to be honest, much too slowly). My experiences with children and teachers through the years are also responsible—perhaps even more than research reports—for biasing me. If you don't agree with the views I've accumulated, I really won't feel as bad as you might think, because I know everyone has to find meaning in one's own way. I only hope you'll keep your mind open to what your experiences teach you and that you'll continue to *read* throughout your teaching career. And please, let some of your reading be other than those "how to" articles in teacher magazines that are overloaded with commercial advertisements for this set of stickers and that set of worksheets. Some of that kind of reading can be useful, I admit, but what about articles that can have even greater, longer-lasting use to you and your students? I've mentioned magazines, or "journals," that can have a real impact on your goals and procedures, such as *The Reading Teacher* and *Language Arts;* now I'm going to give you addresses and zip codes in case you wish these journals to come to your doorstep instead of reading them in libraries.

The Reading Teacher	*Language Arts*
International Reading Association	National Council for Teachers of
800 Barksdale Road	English
P.O. Box 8139	111 Kenyon Road
Newark, Delaware 19714	Urbana, Illinois 61801

Lest you fear that the articles in these journals deal only with large-scale issues, let me assure you that they're also full of very specific suggestions for your teaching. *The Reading Teacher,* for example, has an entire section in each issue called "The CLASSROOM Reading Teacher," consisting of creative ideas sent in by teachers. And most of the articles, no matter how large in scope, also relate the ideas to actual classroom teaching. I'm going to pick randomly one of the issues off my shelf right now and report on its contents:

The concept-text approach: Helping elementary students comprehend text

Supporting reading in the home—naturally: Selected materials for parents

Parents' attitudes toward reports of standardized reading test results

Linking logos with print for beginning reading success

Comprehensible Input PLUS the Language Experience Approach: Reading instruction for limited-English speaking students

Changing the role of reading specialists: From pull-out to in-class programs

Kindergarten teachers—members of a reading research lab in France . . .

Second graders answer the question "Why publish?"

Test review: Diagnostic Reading Scales

Remarkable books in Spanish for young readers

Letters

ERIC/RCS: The quality of textbooks

Critically speaking [Here's where you are introduced each month to new trade books published for children!]

Research Views: Homework: Is it worthwhile?

The CLASSROOM Reading Teacher [Highly practical ideas from teachers]

Have I convinced you yet? *The good classroom manager needs to keep up-to-date by reading professional journals.* In our hopes for changes over the next few decades, you may want to join me by participating in this kind of change. This one change in teachers' (and principals') reading habits could make a major difference in the quality of reading instruction. Neither of us, I'm sure, would mind picking up a research review, say in 1999, and reading a much less discouraging report than the one I gave you at the beginning of this chapter.

THE GREAT DEBATE OF TODAY: WHAT SHOULD BE PRACTICED THE MOST?

During the sixties, Jeanne Chall (1967) wrote a book entitled *The Great Debate*, in which she examined the perpetual debate among reading educators as to whether to emphasize "phonics," or whole words, or meaning, or something else. Every classroom manager is intimately involved in this debate whether she realizes it or not. As the research indicates, teachers' beliefs about what is important to learn greatly influence the way they manage the time available for reading instruction. But when you get right down to it, the great debate for the classroom teacher, involved each day in making managerial decisions, is not whole word vs. phonics, decoding vs. comprehension, or subskills vs. interactive reading. The debate is consciously or unconsciously one of whether to have the children practice reading skills in an isolated fashion (using worksheets and similar assignments) or to practice reading skills in an integrated, interactive fashion (using fictional or nonfictional text).

The Mason and Durkin studies indicate clearly which side of the debate most teachers are on, as judged by the actual amount of time allotted to explaining, distributing, and correcting worksheets. It's not that they necessarily *wish* to be on this side of the debate. When you ask teachers what they're most concerned about, they invariably put comprehension at the top—and when asked, they'll put "reading attitudes" very high on the list as well (see Chapter 12 for research on this). But what people are most concerned about and what they do about it are not always the same thing, as most dieters will tell you.

So, again looking into the future, what we can hope to see—very gradually—is a movement on the part of elementary school teachers toward making time-allotment decisions on the basis of their major concerns. If their major concerns are to get children to read with understanding and to enjoy reading, then they will eventually have to allot more time for real reading, with, say, 60–70 percent of it under the teacher's guidance and the remaining portion dictated solely by the students' interests and needs.

Furthermore, teachers of the future will have to become more time conscious rather than less. They'll have to ask themselves hard managerial questions, such as:

How much time each week do my students actually spend in teacher-guided reading of actual text?

How much time each week do my students spend in self-guided reading of actual text?

How much time do they spend on nonintegrated assignments? Although it's crucial that they understand assignments I give them, how crucial are the actual assignments? Which are worth the time to explain, distribute, and correct? Some are worth it, some are not; which provide the kind of practice that will lead to success on the interactive reading activities I have planned for them?

Are there some worksheet assignments that I feel lukewarm about, but assign because I feel that parents want to see their children bringing home worksheets? Is there some way to explain my program to parents so they will no longer expect so many worksheets as a sign of learning? What about sending home more of children's own writing? What about language experience stories they can read to their parents? What about patterned books and other library books they can actually *read* to their parents?

What kind of balance am I providing between context practice and graphophonic practice? Am I spending too much time on one cueing system (graphophonic) compared to the others? Even though graphophonic cues are not as familiar to beginning readers as the cueing systems used in oral language, am I spending so much time on isolated "phonics" lessons that my students are beginning to perceive reading as merely a graphophonic process? After I teach a graphophonics concept in isolation, do I allot time the same day, or at least the next day, for my students to apply this concept in interactive reading?

Have I actually allocated time for schematic development before I assign material to read? Do I only give lip service to "interactive reading" without helping children develop the schemata necessary for interactive reading to occur? (The interaction between the author and reader cannot take place unless the reader's background experiences at least *simulate* those of the author's; for example, the author may be talking about a snowman, while the reader may never have seen a snowman, so the teacher can simulate the author's background experience by showing the children a picture of a snowman and discussing it.)

Have I apportioned sufficient time for practice in inferential reading? Have I allowed instructional time for sitting down with children and helping them read between the lines—helping them fill in those empty slots that all authors leave for readers to bridge with their own background of experiences? Do I arrange to show them by modeling how to read inferentially? Or am I so eager to go through all the memory questions in the teacher's guide that I forget to *teach comprehension* by showing them what a reader does in order to comprehend?

Am I providing time for children to *enjoy* reading? Do they have time every day (or nearly every day) to read materials of their own choice? Do they get time to share the pleasure or inspiration they obtain from reading? Are they getting a variety of practice experiences, or are they getting the same old diet day after day after day? Am I providing time for a positive reading attitude to grow?

Do I allow time for writing and reading to work together? For all four of the language arts to work together? Or do I schedule my program so that little interaction among the language arts can occur? What about time for the language arts to interact with social studies? With science? With other areas?

Am I apportioning time according to the best information I can get concerning children and the reading process? Or, am I making time decisions on the basis of pages in workbooks, pages in basal readers, and pages in teacher's guides?

TIME ALLOTMENTS FOR ORAL AND SILENT READING

Another question we can hope more teachers will ask themselves is this: When do I want my students to practice the reading process silently, and when do I want them to practice it orally? Both research and casual observation show us that teachers have two "favorite" forms of reading instruction in the elementary schools. One is to have the children meet the teacher in small groups and take turns reading out loud, called the "round-robin approach." The other popular form, with children above third grade, is to assign a selection for children to read silently and have the children write answers to questions the teacher has written on the chalkboard. An observer in the schools often sees this form of "instruction" carried on right up through twelfth grade.

Obviously we need a more goal-oriented approach toward this managerial decision. There are different advantages to gain from silent and oral reading. When teachers decide on the form according to its advantages rather than according to tradition, I'm sure you'll agree that this provides a "plus" for both the teacher and the students.

Oral Reading

Let's start with oral reading. When would it be advantageous to use this form? I should first point out that there's good reason for this form to be somewhat more dominant in the primary than in the later grades. As Taylor and Connor (1982) point out, beginning readers seem to need more immediate feedback on their reading than do older children; a greater need to hear themselves speak the words; and more opportunity to read "like big people do" (those who have been read to think that reading is an out-loud kind of thing).

This does not mean, though, that young children should experience oral reading only. On the contrary, from the very first month of school, children should have chances to read silently on their own—guided sentence by sentence, if necessary, with a question or comment from the teacher: "So what did Bill do with the pencil? Have you ever used a pencil that didn't have to be sharpened? Here's the kind of pencil that Bill is using. Can someone show us how to get the lead to come out?" In this way they can be gradually introduced into the world of reading the way most people use it in everyday life, and they can read for meaning rather than only for correct pronunciation.

Another advantage of oral reading, however, is that it gives teachers an opportunity to carry on miscue analysis. As I mentioned in Chapter 10, miscue analysis is one of the best ways to determine a child's concept of reading and his main strategies for reading, whether his concern is mainly for meaning or for letter-by-letter translation from print to sound. This particular advantage of oral reading is true at all levels and is especially necessary now and then with problem readers.

A third advantage of oral reading experiences is that of providing a chance for children to prove a point they've made during a discussion following silent reading of a selection. This, in turn, provides teachers with a chance to teach literal, inferential, critical, and creative thinking operations that are necessary in the reading process (see Chapter 3).

A fourth advantage of oral reading is the opportunity it provides to practice reading with expression—to use different pitches and pauses and stress particular words the way the reader thinks "the author might have said it." This kind of expressive reading emphasizes the concepts of reading as communication, reading as sharing language and ideas, reading as entertaining or informing. It can also help develop a habit of reading for comprehension. Echo and choral reading, as mentioned several times in earlier chapters, are excellent for this type of oral reading. It is also effective to have children practice a portion of text silently and then read it to other children who have closed their books. And don't forget to have them read plays, or read dialogue in stories by taking roles and skipping the *he said* and *she said* parts. And what about having children share out loud part of a library book they're reading—right there in the basal reader group? Just have a different person share each time you meet (but make sure she has a chance to practice first).

I guess my only admonition about oral reading is this: don't bore children by having them read a selection silently and then, in round-robin fashion, read it orally. Use oral reading for one or more of its advantages, not for punishment. (Believe me, *you* would consider it punishment if you had to go through this procedure.) Oral reading should follow silent reading when children are engaged in a directed-reading-and-thinking-activity (pages 77–81), or when they're entertaining or informing others, but not as a way to check their reading errors after they've read it silently. If you're going to check their reading *strategies* (how much they rely on each of the cueing systems), it is generally better to omit the silent reading. In this way you can see how they attack something *new*. (I'll mention again, however, that during miscue analysis in small groups, the children should be discouraged from correcting each other's *words*. After the child has finished a sentence or larger portion, read it the same way he did and ask him to correct *you* so that *you* make sense.)

Silent Reading

As for silent reading, I've already mentioned one of its main advantages. The ability to read well silently, of course, is what most people need in our society. There are relatively few opportunities to read orally. Furthermore, as I mentioned, silent reading provides an even better opportunity to read for meaning than does oral reading. This is because children (and teachers) can so easily get lost in the *sounds* of words during oral reading. With silent reading, the teacher can guide the children with specific purposes for reading each sentence or paragraph or page, and then sit back and not even think about how well they're pronouncing the words as they read them to themselves. She can concentrate on helping the children arrive at the author's meaning!

Silent reading also gives children that wonderful opportunity to keep their miscues to themselves and to search for their own understanding (or at least for the answer to the teacher's question). When children are asked to read silently under the teacher's direction, they don't have to impress anyone with their fluency or their ability to pronounce each word. They can let their eyes drift ahead or behind, they can stutter and stammer inside their heads and mumble to their hearts content, *and no one cares!* Can you imagine what bliss this must be for some children? With silent reading, children are allowed to read as adults do—predicting, confirming, changing our hypotheses as we go, skipping a word here and there, throwing in a word now and then, self-correcting our miscues, even substituting words as long as the text still makes sense. *In silent reading, children can communicate with an author instead of an audience.*

MANAGING GROUP WORK AND INDIVIDUAL WORK

For a time during the sixties and seventies, it was fashionable to have children work on reading, mathematics, and spelling on their own, on the theory that each child has his own learning pace and style and shouldn't be held back or frustrated by a group of peers. This practice made good sense to some people, and there are still some who argue vehemently for "individualized learning." Results from an extensive research project, the "Beginning Teacher Evaluation Study," however, put a damper on others' enthusiasm. The BTE Study found that working alone for a large percentage of time was not conducive to learning; that group instruction, large or small, produced better results than instructing a child through "individualized materials" such as worksheets and programmed booklets (McDonald, 1976).

Why the advantage of group instruction? For one thing, having the learning experience directed by a teacher, rather than a booklet or worksheet, increases the "engagement rate"—the amount of time children stay on task. In fact, in the BTE Study the *conscious* nonattendance to a task averaged 16 percent of the time when children worked alone and only 5 percent of the time when they worked in groups with the teacher (Pearson, 1984).

Not that merely getting children together with a teacher makes the only difference; it also depends on what teachers *do* with children in those groups. As I mentioned earlier, teachers who are warm but task-oriented seem to help children achieve the most. Yet even task orientation isn't enough. Naturally, the more closely the learning tasks simulate real reading, the more difference they make in helping the learner increase reading achievement. Many teachers, for example, ask inferential comprehension questions, but it takes specific instruction in inferential thinking to really make a difference for children on reading achievement tests (Pearson, 1984). In other words, taking the time to *show* children, with actual text rather than an isolated worksheet, how to fill the slots between the lines, how to predict what's going to happen next, how to tell cause from effect, and how to tell the author's main ideas, is what pays off.

There may be yet another reason that children learn more when more of their time is spent working with a teacher in a group than by themselves. Anthropologists have been telling us for decades that human beings are social, cooperative creatures. Most of us are not like male bears, frogs, or fiddler crabs, which spend most of their lives alone. Ashley Montague tried to explain this back in 1950. In his book, *On Being Human*, he cites several examples of how cooperation among animals is quite common: white mice who live with groups grow stronger and faster than they do in isolation. Chimpanzees often pass food to each other through cage bars. Even goldfish survive better in groups, and humans generally can't maintain mental health without feeling that they're a member of *some* groups, no matter how small. (In fact, Montague contended that since human relations are so important to people's health, it ought to be taught in school as the "fourth R.") More recently, you've probably seen the articles in popular magazines telling how monkeys can learn more and faster when they're taught along with at least one other monkey. (Some say this is because the monkeys enjoy the competition, but anthropologists might point out that even competition is a form of cooperation, since it helps both monkeys meet their needs.)

Grouping and Scheduling Children for Reading

But how to group children for reading instruction? We've talked about using informal reading inventories and other measures to determine reading groups; however, we haven't discussed other managerial problems related to grouping, such as how many children to put in a group or how many groups to have. Unfortunately, solutions to this kind of problem are not nice and neat. On one occasion I asked a class of experienced teachers who were taking my advanced reading course to describe in writing how each divided students into groups and scheduled instruction and practice times for reading programs. Each approach was very different. Grouping and scheduling depend on many variables, two of which are the school's grouping plan and the number of reading levels.

School-Building Grouping Plan

In some school buildings, children in one room go to other rooms for reading and mathematics. In other buildings, the children stay with their homeroom teacher for all subjects except music and physical education. In still others, the primary grades stay with one teacher most of the day, but the intermediate grades move from one room to another for nearly every subject. Obviously, these systems can make quite a difference in your reading program.

Imagine that you're in a building that uses the "cross-graded plan" for reading. In this case, only some of the children in your homeroom will stay with you during the reading period. Each teacher will be assigned to teach a particular level or two. You've been assigned, let's say, to the two second grade levels and are expected to teach children using the 2_1 and 2_2 basal readers.

How are children assigned to teachers in the cross-graded plan? There are two basic ways: one is to have the homeroom teachers administer informal reading inventories during the first two weeks of school and decide what level to place each child in. Then, during the third week, the principal apportions the children to each teacher for reading instruction, attempting to limit each teacher to only one or two levels. The other common procedure is to use the previous teacher's recommendation (ignoring all the disadvantages of this method) and assign children to reading teachers during the *first* week of school. In either case, you will teach only one or two reading levels under this procedure. You may feel that this eliminates grouping problems, but most teachers find themselves grouping the children even when they're expected to use only one basal reader, because even within one assigned level, children soon differentiate themselves. Some children, even within this framework, seem more capable than others, and teachers try to accommodate for this difference.

Many teachers don't like the cross-graded plan and prefer to work more intimately with the same children all day long. In schools where this is the norm, children are theoretically apportioned to each "self-contained" classroom with an eye to the previous teacher's recommendations in each child's case. That is, they try not to give one teacher too many levels to teach, while at the same time trying to apportion fairly the number of good readers and poor readers. (Why principals get gray.) Theoretically, this method would give each teacher about three levels to teach—low, average, and high. But for a variety of reasons, most teachers end up with more than three levels, especially conscientious teachers who administer an informal reading test and discover that Nancy should be in the Grade 4 reader instead of the 3_2 reader as her former teacher recommended. And so on; you see what can happen. It is not unusual for a fourth-grade, self-contained classroom teacher to have children reading at six different levels.

Although this sounds as if I'm advocating the cross-graded (Joplin) plan, I'm not. I'm sympathetic toward those teachers and principals who use this procedure, but I can't really advocate it. When you don't have the same children in reading that you have in the content areas (math, science, social studies), you miss out on tremendous opportunities to help children *apply* what you've taught them personally during reading and writing instruction. On the other hand, if the principal helps the teachers establish procedures for getting together *frequently* and communicating about the children they teach in common, this disadvantage of cross-graded teaching is not quite as noticeable.

Nevertheless, as I said, there are many teachers who intuitively feel that children should not be bustled from room to room during the day and that as social creatures they will learn more in a more intimate environment. I wish I could tell you that research shows that one approach is better than the other, but so far research shows simply that it's the teacher that makes the difference and not the way the children are "herded."

Number of Reading Levels

It shouldn't be surprising, then, that the second variable to consider in determining grouping and scheduling procedures is the number of reading levels one is expected to accommodate. With a language experience program the teacher is free to make very rough groupings, usually into three groups. For example, by breaking a class of 30 into three groups of approximately ten each, she can more readily develop language experience charts and allow each child to participate in developing them. With a basal reader program, however, she often feels obligated to have one group for each level represented by test scores or recommendations from former teachers. Thus, some teachers in self-contained classrooms end up with four to seven groups. When this happens, teachers must be very good managers indeed.

Mrs. Beck, a very fine second grade teacher in Portland, Oregon, tells how *she* handles this situation:

> In my second grade classroom I have children with reading abilities ranging from high second-grade level (2_2) down to preprimer (PP). Altogether, I have six reading groups to manage without the assistance of an aide. Out of my group of 22 children, there are four children who leave the room for half an hour each day to go to Chapter I [a special program for problem readers].
>
> The only sane way I can manage six reading groups is to intermesh reading, spelling, and writing. I have a daily routine that we follow during a block of time from 9:00 a.m. to 11:00 a.m., with a ten-minute break at 10:00 a.m. With this management system I can meet with three reading groups each day. The following day, while I'm working with the remaining three reading groups, the groups from the previous day read their newly assigned stories and work on their workbook pages.
>
> During the time I'm working with the reading groups, other students are not allowed to interrupt. If a child needs help with a problem, he must go to a student helper or wait until the reading group changes, at which time students are given time to ask questions or get help from the teacher.
>
> We have a daily routine that we follow each week. Students are to do one page in their spelling workbooks each day. Once a week, on different days, they complete phonics worksheets, read comprehension worksheets, and make up and write their own sentences using all of their spelling words for that week. They also write down their weekly spelling list and dictation sentences which they take home and study for weekly tests on Thursday and Friday. I do not have reading groups on Fridays unless I have fallen off track during the week. Most Fridays, after the spelling tests, my entire class reads and discusses *Weekly Readers* together. We also complete the last page of the *Weekly Reader*, which covers comprehension, vocabulary words, and word-building skills. There are also times outside of the language arts time block in which, as a whole class, we work on phonics skills. During the week we also have time during which students have a free choice to read whatever they want, but they have to read without talking or walking around for ten minutes. Then I encourage the children to share what they have read.
>
> Overall, this management system works well for me, and I see my students progressing in their reading skills. But I know there is probably room for improvement, especially in the area of student-contact time, since I'm only able to meet with each group every other day.

As you can see from Mrs. Beck's description, working with six groups *can* be done. As admirable as her management solution is, however, it does lead to having children working on their own more than research seems to tell us to. If we now know that face-to-face contact with teachers produces better results than working individually on worksheets, wouldn't it be a good idea for Mrs. Beck to consider some way to increase the amount of teacher instruction and reduce the amount of worksheet instruction? Of course, if I were Mrs. Beck, I'd say, "Easier said than done." And yet, for someone creative enough to come up with a solution for working with six groups, one wonders if she wouldn't be willing to try an approach that would be even *more* satisfactory to her. These are some questions Mrs. Beck might ask herself:

1. Is there any way to cut the number of groups to four so that I can work with all four on four days a week, instead of two days a week? Could some children move up one level if I give them special help? With the extra time I would have for meeting with the children, wouldn't *I* be able to meet their individual needs *more* than worksheets can?

2. If I can't cut down the number of groups, is there some way of meeting for a shorter time with each group? I certainly wouldn't want to meet with all six groups every day for 20 minutes each group, because that would drive me crazy. But suppose I were to meet with my three advanced groups only twice a week and my three low groups four times a week? This would even allow me to have individual conferences (IC) on library books twice a week. I would have to train parent tutors and peer tutors, so I wouldn't have to help individuals between groups, but it would be worth it. My schedule would look something like this:

Monday	Tuesday	Wednesday	Thursday	Friday
PP—15 min.	PP—30 min.	PP—15 min.	PP—30 min.	*Weekly Reader*,
P—15	P—30	P—15	P—30	Language experience writing
1—15	1—30	1—15	1—30	rience writing
2_1—25	*IC—30	1—15	*IC—30	and reading,
2_2—25		2_1—25		Book sharing
3_1—25		2_2—25		
		3_1—25		

3. Is there some way to use our social studies and science time to apply what I'm teaching during the language arts period? That way I wouldn't feel the need to assign so many worksheets. What about using our phonics knowledge on new words that show up in social studies, science and math?

---

*Library book reading and individual conferences

4. Is there a way to introduce a greater *variety* of writing experiences in my program, since writing *can* be an important way to improve children's reading abilities? Since they've already written down their weekly spelling list and dictation sentences to take home and study, why have them also make up and write their own sentences using all of their spelling words for that week? Why not have them write individual language experience stories instead? Wouldn't this be more helpful in developing an appropriate concept of reading as a communication process? Besides, by writing experience stories they'll have plenty of spelling practice and also get additional reading experience by reading each other's stories.

5. How about a total-group language experience each Friday—something we do or talk about together and then produce a class chart or book? *Friday can be a very special day together.*

USING VOLUNTEER AIDES

In Chapter 12 I explained some of the ways that parents and other adults can act as tutors, both at home and at school. With tactful training, however, they can make excellent volunteer aides as well. Jack Cassidy, a former school district reading supervisor, found that senior citizens are excellent tutors, makers of instructional materials, and classroom aides. He mentions others who might also be called upon: "Groups often overlooked as volunteers are women . . . with grown children, men who do not frequent senior centers but may be involved in local clubs, and homebound persons who might help construct instructional materials" (Cassidy, 1981, p. 290).

If you'd like more information for you and your volunteer aides, write for the 1985 booklet, *Handbook for the Volunteer Tutor*, edited by Sidney Rausch and Joseph Sanacore, International Reading Association, 800 Barksdale Road, P. O. Box 8139, Newark, Delaware 19711. Another book on this topic is Edward Robbins's *Tutor Handbook*, available from the Government Printing Office, Washington, D.C.

Most of the teachers I talk to sing praises for their volunteer aides. As Beth DeVogele, a special reading teacher, said: "One success story I've had throughout my teaching career is the utilization of the volunteer tutor. Today is a time of larger numbers in the classroom, greater demands for individual needs, and record numbers of children with emotional and learning difficulties. The teacher can't possibly meet the demands placed on her. Salaried aides are often not feasible because of financial stress. We need to seek out capable willing volunteers. They *are* in existence, but they need to feel and *be* essential if they're going to work well with you."

I mentioned in Chapter 12 that volunteer aides can be used to supervise reading centers, an often vital function. They can also be extremely important in guiding and tutoring children who need your help *right now* when you're trying to work with reading groups. In addition, they can help you find and display appropriate library books and various materials related to science, social studies, and other units. When children need special help in learning sight words, phonograms, and vowel patterns, a volunteer aide can make the difference between their feeling of success or failure.

RESEARCH ON PEER TUTORING

When America became an urban instead of rural society, and one-room multigraded schoolhouses gave way to classrooms of children all the same age, we lost an important teaching concept. The concept was this: *teaching teaches the teacher.* You probably developed this notion yourself somewhere along the way—that when you teach someone younger or less skilled, you're the one who learns the most. Research verifies your experience. Nevi (1983) presents several studies showing that tutors improve as much or more than tutees. Allen (1976) examined more than 80 research reports and concluded that tutoring can lead to higher reading scores for both tutees and tutors. In fact, he found that all types of tutors can be effective: adult tutors, older-age students, students with behavioral problems, low achievers tutoring younger children, tutors of the opposite sex, untrained tutors, and trained tutors. He also found that no one method of training seemed to be definitely superior. Perhaps Ashley Montague was right: human beings *are* cooperative creatures.

Allen and Feldman had previously studied a group of low-achieving fifth graders. These children alternated between studying alone and teaching a third-grade tutee. When they were in the role of tutors, their reading test scores were higher than when they studied alone. Allen and Feldman explain the difference this way: "A substantial amount of empirical data demonstrates that role enactment does produce behavioral and attitudinal changes in the person enacting the role . . . It is necessary for a teacher to adopt a completely different point of view from that taken by a student" (1973, p. 1). Thus, they explain, when children play the role of teacher, and look at the material to be taught, it takes on a different and more understandable organization. Furthermore, assuming the role of teacher gives some children a feeling of importance they've been missing.

For fear that I've given the impression that only the tutor gains from tutoring, let me cite a few more studies showing specific effects on those tutored. King (1982) trained seventh graders to assist third graders with SRA comprehension labs, to make and use flash cards with them, to play educational games with them, to read to them, and to listen to them read. The tutors also learned to discuss what the third graders read and to ask them questions at various levels of thinking. After eight weeks of tutoring, 40 minutes a day, the experimental third graders were compared with a control group and a "placebo group." With the placebo group the tutors talked, played, and worked on art projects with the third graders. The control group was merely supervised in a 40-minute study period each day and worked by themselves. (Children were randomly assigned to the three different third-grade groups.) The results after only eight weeks were as follows:

Tutees (experimental)	4.6 grade equivalency score
Placebo group	3.3 grade equivalency score
Control group	3.1 grade equivalency score

No, you're not seeing a misprint. In this particular case, perhaps because of the excellent and enthusiastic training received by the tutors, there is a one-and-one-half year difference between the tutored children and the children who worked alone. King cites several similar studies that demonstrate the same effect, including one showing that learning-disabled children from special classrooms can benefit from in-class tutoring when they are mainstreamed into regular classrooms for reading instruction.

The city of Marshall, Minnesota developed a system of peer tutoring on school buses. MacDermot (1982) reports that in this school system, fourth and fifth graders acted as tutors to second and third graders. The tutors received five hours of training and were shown how to use tutoring packets. These packets contained short review lessons with five activities for each target skill. The packets were placed where the tutors could get them without disturbing teachers or classes. When a tutor felt that his pupil had learned a particular skill, he recorded this and put the pupil's folder in a box labeled "Ready for Testing." A teacher then administered a test to the second or third grader and gave the results to the tutor to pass on to the tutee. The outcome of this program? Improved test scores for the tutees and positive attitudes for the tutors, tutees, parents, and teachers, all at a very low cost.

Lehr (1984) summarizes the research on peer teaching this way:

Peer teaching is especially valuable in reading.

Peer teaching often leads to higher performance in reading skills, writing mechanics, and sight words.

Many types of activities seem to be effective: flashcards, word lists, worksheets, games, dictating spelling words, studying for a quiz or assignment together, simply discussing ideas already introduced by the teacher.

Tutor training can help avoid tutors' damaging tutees' self-concepts; it can also help teach tutors how to give directions, confirm correct responses, apply nonpunitive corrections, praise, gather and replace materials, measure and record performance, allocate time, and monitor progress.

Hiebert (1980) cites several studies that agree with the results reported so far. Moreover, she also cites studies showing that children who learn to read before school age have usually been taught by older brothers or sisters. Evidently, we humans are "natural-born teachers." Put someone younger (or at least innocent-looking) in our path and we can't resist teaching them something. It's too bad that many teachers do not take advantage of this natural compulsion. In fact, though, Hiebert cites studies showing that many teachers do their best to *prevent* peer interaction. In other words,

some teachers are so concerned that children *will* help each other with their work, they neglect to capitalize on the benefits that can come from their tutoring each other.

Since research shows that a great deal of wasted learning time occurs when children must wait around to ask the teacher a question (Hiebert, 1980, p. 879), it certainly behooves classroom teachers to plan ways to provide structured tutoring experiences instead. It also behooves them to arrange for cross-graded tutoring experiences to occur as well, since these experiences benefit both tutors and tutees. However, let me urge those who are considering such interaction among peers to consider materials in addition to flashcards, games, and worksheets for the tutoring media— namely books. As King's study showed, having the tutor read to her pupil and listen to her pupil read were also effective. Children who require tutoring need more practice in interactive reading, and this is where training will be crucial; your tutors may need to be trained to help their tutees read for *meaning* and to look for context clues as well as graphophonic clues. When tutors themselves have already been taught this way, it will be natural for them to follow suit.

MANAGING THE BIG EYE: MAKING TELEVISION WORK FOR YOU

While peer tutors and volunteer aides can be of great benefit to the teacher, especially as she attempts to work intensively with reading groups, two other resources are beginning to show promise: television and the computer. Television was of limited use in classrooms during the last two decades, since everyone had to drop what they were doing to watch a program scheduled by a local television station. Today, however, the courts have ruled in favor of noncommercial copying of television programs, thus freeing teachers to create videocassettes that might be useful in classrooms. In the near future, the VCR (videocassette recorder) could easily become one of the teacher's best friends.

Even today, the teacher with access to a VCR is fortunate; the videocassette is an incredibly easy way to bring the outside world into the classroom. A cassette can't beat a direct experience, perhaps, but it can often make the pages of science and social studies textbooks, as well as basal readers, come alive. Interactive reading can't occur unless the reader brings schemata to the page, and video recordings, *before* reading, can provide the background experience necessary for developing schemata.

So when you're despairing because of the four hours a day of television viewing your students engage in, remember—there's a nugget of gold inside that large mass of ugly rock. The trick is to learn what's available from television that you can use in your classroom. If you're not now a habitual viewer of public television, you might want to make the minimum contribution they request so you can receive the monthly guide, *Dial*, that will come to your home at least a week before the programs are aired, enabling you to anticipate your need for a VCR. Regular programs (those your children favor) can also be used to your advantage in teaching reading, since transcripts of both PBS and commercial programs are often available. You can use transcripts of children's favorite programs like a play, with children taking turns reading parts. The teacher can use transcripts of informational programs to create reading charts or dittos (based on small segments of a program) to read and discuss after children view the videotape. The reading charts or dittos can be based on the exact words from a transcript or made simpler by paraphrasing. The charts, dittos, or actual transcripts can be used as part of an activity for children to engage in while the teacher works with reading groups, or they can be used as a class activity under the teacher's direction. To obtain transcripts, write for the particular program from the specific network:

ABC, 7 West 66th Street, New York, N.Y., 10023.

CBS, 51 West 52nd Street, New York, N.Y. 10019.

NBC, 30 Rockefeller Plaza, New York, N.Y. 10027.

PBS, 475 L'Enfant Plaza S.W., Washington, D.C. 20024.

With a VCR a teacher can also tape segments of Sesame Street (for kindergarten and first grade) or Electric Company (for second through fifth grade). These two programs were designed to enhance children's success in learning to read. While Sesame Street emphasizes names and sounds of letters and a list of sight words, Electric Company emphasizes vowel patterns, suffixes, and other patterns. Both programs have been shown to be effective in accomplishing their specific goals. Research by Ball and Bogatz (1970) on Sesame Street showed that:

1. Steady viewers learned the letter names and sounds

2. Steady viewers learned the alphabet in order

3. Children who watched and learned more came from homes where Sesame Street was watched by both mother and child and where the mother talked with the child about the show

Ball and Bogatz (1972) also evaluated the Electric Company and its effects on 100 classes of children. Half these classes watched the show in their classroom; the other half watched it at home. The school watchers gained considerably more than the home watchers. We can thus predict that having a volunteer aide watch these programs with the children can have a positive influence. This kind of viewing can take place while the teacher works with reading groups.

PUTTING THE COMPUTER IN ITS PLACE: IN THE ELEMENTARY SCHOOL CLASSROOM

Another resource teachers can use while they work with reading groups is a "personal computer," especially one equipped for word processing. Personal computers were a novelty in schools not too long ago, but by 1984, there was one available for every 92 students in the United States (Hassett, 1984). By 1994, we should see that ratio greatly reduced. It may well be a rare classroom that does not have one. At any rate, "powerful microcomputers are now resident in many schools . . . Traditional textbook publishers, along with commercial software houses and some nonprofit organizations, have begun to produce reading lessons based on a variety of instructional paradigms. Instructional tools—word processors, spelling checks, and management systems—have assumed a stage center position in the educational software market and in the software inventories of many schools" (Mason et al., 1983, p.vii).

When you consider two facts, that (1) children enjoy operating computers, and that (2) the main process involved in *operating* computer programs is the reading process, you can see why I have some enthusiasm for installing a computer in every classroom, especially when the initial research on the effect of computer use is so positive (Mason et al., 1983). And especially when you consider how well a computer's word-processing capabilities allow a child to manipulate and generate words. How relatively easy it is for children to produce sentences, rearrange them, change them, add to them, and in general to create their own reading material. How painless it is for children to spend hours with computer games and simulations and not even realize how much effort they're putting into *reading*. And how relatively painless it is for teachers and aides to take dictation from children eager to tell their story and thereby create more reading text.

I certainly don't want to give you the impression that most of the computer games and simulations produced for schools are excellent; they're not. If you get a chance to read some of the software reviews in the computer journals, you'll discover that you have to be *very* selective. Before purchasing or recommending purchase of a game, simulation, or other software item, I strongly recommend that you check one of these journals for a review of the program:

The Reading Teacher (section called "Computer Software")

Educational Computer Magazine

Compute

Classroom Computer Learning

Computers, Reading and Language Arts

Classroom Computer News

Creative Computing

Personal Computing

Journal of Educational Technology Systems

The biggest flaw in many programs is that they imitate worksheets; students merely plug in answers and get feedback. These are not the kind of program that turns children into more avid readers. Programs that interest them are games and simulations that involve some kind of goal, such as reaching an important destination, accumulating wealth, getting rid of bad guys, finding the treasure, solving a puzzle as quickly as possible, and so on. Especially challenging are programs that require children to solve problems and make decisions.

Mason (1983) brings up another use for personal computers in the classroom that allows a computer to act as a nonthreatening teacher. The program, CADPP (Computer Assisted Diagnostic Prescriptive Program in Reading and Mathematics) permits a teacher to program specific prescriptions, which are then presented by the computer to a student who has completed a test (for example, "Do page 19 in Booklet D"). According to Mason, students perceive the test corrections as well as the prescriptions that follow as less threatening than those presented by a teacher. This is particularly true for children who already think of themselves as poor readers.

Mason also recommends programs that put the child in a position of superiority over the computer—programs, for example, that require the student to tutor the computer. The program *Animal* is one of these. In this game the computer tries to guess what animal the student has in mind by asking the student questions. Whenever the computer fails to guess the animal, it requests that the student type in a new question and answer that will help it determine the correct animal. For instance, if the student notices that the computer has not asked anything about ears, she types in a question and answer that will help this poor ignorant computer learn that the animal she has in mind has long ears. As the game goes on, the computer guesses more animals, and the student *reads and responds* to dozens of questions—and *writes* dozens of questions.

Many programs also require the student to proofread and get rid of "bugs" before the computer will give the student what he wants. This often leads to improved spelling as well as reading (Mason, 1983), but it also leads to a feeling of triumph when the student finds bugs. "This joy in accomplishment is so profound that it often shocks teachers who had thought nothing in school could excite these children" (Mason, 1983, p. 506).

With the right software, you can also use a personal computer as an aid to your recordkeeping system. If you choose to do so, your computer can be programmed to test students on their mastery of certain fundamentals, such as sight vocabulary, phonograms, or vowel patterns. It can also be programmed to maintain student files, to update their records, to list prescriptions for students, and even to generate reports for parents and administrators. For more information, write to Random House Management Systems, School Division, 201 East 50th Street, New York, NY 10022.

Most basal reader publishers now produce similar management systems, as well as numerous reading games that coincide with their basal reader programs. Remember, though, to make sure your school district is purchasing true games or simulations and not dull worksheet-style programs that are merely labeled "games." And don't restrict yourself to "Reading" programs; take a look, also, at social studies and science programs, which usually offer more interactive reading and practice in inferential thinking than many reading programs.

MANAGING BEHAVIORAL PROBLEMS THAT INTERFERE WITH LEARNING

All right now, you've got everything under control, right? You've carefully allocated your instructional time to match your concept of reading and your specific goals for a group of children. You've scheduled your time to allow for integrated interactive reading as well as isolated practice. You've arranged for children to choose books for themselves and to produce their own reading material through writing or dictation. And you've decided how you're going to handle the basal reader program you're expected to use. You know just how you're going to group your children for different kinds of experiences. And on paper, it looks just great.

There's only one problem. Children don't always behave the way you want them to. Well, I could take the easy way out and recommend that you take an ITIP course (Instructional Theory Into Practice) or some other type of "behavioral management" course—and I do recommend that—but in the meantime, let me give you some tips that have worked for a lot of teachers I've worked with.

Although I hate the term "behavioral management," people do need some kind of motivation. So, before you despair because of certain children's behavior and immediately try "behavioral management," you might ask yourself whether you've been violating any of the motivation principles I reminded you of in Chapter 12: Novelty . . . Needs . . . Level . . . Feedback. Are the children acting up because of the lack of new stimuli—new materials, new approaches, something new and different in the routine? I'm reminded of stage actors who often must repeat the same lines day after day for months on end. Even for these professionals, a director finds it necessary to introduce a surprise in the routine now and then—a new line, a change in costume, a new song—anything to keep the actors from dying of boredom.

Are the children misbehaving because their basic needs for oxygen, importance, and belonging are being ignored? When was the last time you opened a window, touched your toes with them (well, maybe your ankles), found a way to make James feel important, or helped Ginny find a friend? Are some children sullen because the work you're asking them to do is too easy and "babyish"; too difficult or confusing the way you've been presenting it; not at "the right height for the high jump"? Do some children need more readiness experiences for what you're trying to teach? Do some children need a peer tutor or more help from a volunteer aide?

And what about feedback? Does it occur every few seconds? Or does it come too late, way after the children have forgotten what they were doing in the first place? Quite often, children don't need a teacher with "behavior management" principles, they need a teacher with *learning* management principles.

The four motivation principles are crucial to successful management of an elementary school classroom. And so are the four retention principles; violation of these also can lead to children's misbehavior. (Do you recall them? Involved . . . Masters . . . Practice . . . Transfer?) Are you constantly on the lookout for ways to involve each child in each step of the learning process? Thinking of ways of keeping Joyce from drifting away into noninvolvement? Do you sometimes get each child to jot down his answer before calling on someone? Or sometimes have them tell a partner before telling the rest of the group? Or are you rushing your lessons and letting only a few energetic children do all the thinking? Are you teaching for mastery of concepts or coverage of pages? Are you increasing mastery through adding meaning to your lessons, relating new ideas to old ones, new words to schemata?

Do you sometimes assume that teaching is the same thing as learning? "I taught it to them last week, so they should have learned it." Or do you review or check the very next day, and a week later as well? How much time are you allotting for positive transfer of concepts? Are they really getting enough practice *applying* what you teach them? Do you *help* them make the necessary application of a "skill lesson" to interactive reading? Basically, do you help them feel successful (through principles of retention) so they want to learn more?

"All right," you say, "I've tried every single one of those ideas on motivation and retention, and I'm still having trouble with Jimmy and Cleo." If you really have tried those principles for more than a few days, *then* you may want to try one more set of management principles.

1. *Help the misbehaving child understand exactly what behavior you want.* When I was first a classroom teacher I spent a good deal of time telling my "discipline problems" what not to do: "Don't sharpen your pencil when I'm talking! Stop poking her! Stop talking! No eating in the classroom! Quit that humming!" It often never occurred to me to tell the offending child exactly what I wanted him to do during a lesson. Only gradually did I learn to say pleasantly but firmly: "You are here to learn, and I *want* you to learn. When I'm teaching you, Jimmy, I want you to do three things. I want you to sit up straight. I want you to keep your eyes on me or on the chalkboard. And I want you to try to answer every question. Now you tell me the three things I want you to do." This leads us to the second principle.

2. *Use positive reinforcement for the behavior you desire.* Having made it clear to Jimmy what behavior I considered "learning behavior," at least in a lesson situation, I then needed some way to help him achieve success. So I needed to praise him or make him feel important or liked whenever he accommodated me with "learning style behavior." If I said something like, "I really like the way Jimmy is sitting up straight with his eyes on me and waiting to answer *every* question," it usually worked. Not only did it reward Jimmy, it encouraged the laggards to get ready too. (But you know all this. You've seen it many times, haven't you? I hope so.)

3. *If possible, ignore misbehavior that is new to a child.* Suppose that talking to her neighbor during a reading lesson is a new type of behavior for Cleo, or one that occurs very infrequently. What would be the best thing to do when you see it occur?

Pretend you don't even notice it, while, at the same time, you praise others for listening so well.

Nip it in the bud. Let her know immediately that she is misbehaving. That way, the habit will never get started.

After she sees you looking at her, ignore her completely.

It might be tempting to select the second alternative and nip it in the bud. With negative responses of this sort you might be able to suppress her behavior temporarily, but you may not eliminate it. In fact, for some children, the attention you give them by scolding is a form of *positive reinforcement*. By scolding, you put them in the spotlight and perhaps even give them a bit of prestige.

If you chose the third alternative, you may be in for trouble, because essentially you're saying that even though you saw her misbehaving, it doesn't really matter to you. The first alternative is probably the best response—*if the behavior is new or very infrequent.* By ignoring the behavior, you may provide the opportunity for the behavior to go unrewarded (depending on how much reinforcement she gets from her neighbor).

4. *Use a negative response when positive reinforcement fails to get the desired result, but be aware of possible side effects.* Let's say that Cleo doesn't care whether you praise others for listening, that she gives you no opportunity for rewarding her in any way, and that your ignoring her seems to encourage her to talk louder and louder and to generally disrupt your instruction. What should you do?

Send her to the principal who is trained to handle problems like this.

Tell her that since she's missed part of the lesson by talking, she'll have to stay in for part of the recess to learn what she missed.

Warn her to stop talking or she'll be in trouble.

The first procedure is a way of telling the child that she's too much for you to handle. Sometimes one has to admit defeat like this, but obviously it's not solving your problem very well, particularly since Cleo is missing a lesson she needs. The third procedure may suppress the undesired behavior, but the warning is so vague it may have an undersirable side effect. Instead of paying attention to the rest of your lesson, she may spend several minutes wondering just what kind of trouble she might be in if she talks to her neighbor again.

The second procedure, or something like it, would clearly indicate not only what behavior you *don't* want but also what behavior you *do* want. In addition, it signals to her that the more she misses of the lesson, the more she'll miss a chance to talk to her friends during recess. Of course, it may also have the undersirable side effect of making her think of you as an "old meanie," the type of side effect that often occurs with a negative response. However, during the first few minutes of recess, you can cancel out some of this by briefly and kindly explaining to her what behavior is important during a lesson, by asking her to listen carefully while you briefly check her comprehension of the previous lesson, by praising her for correctly answering your questions, and by sending her out for the rest of recess *immediately* after reviewing the lesson—don't spoil the effect by scolding her once more before dismissing her. The approach advocated for Cleo is not the approach to use with all children who interrupt a lesson by talking to their neighbors. It is merely one illustration of how a negative response can be used, if necessary.

5. *Distribute the positive reinforcement.* Unfortunately, permanent behavior change seldom occurs during the course of a single lesson or other type of interaction between child and teacher. It takes time and distributed reinforcement. To help Cleo's behavior become more permanent, which should you do?

Praise her every time she pays attention in all future lessons.

Keep praise to a minimum and keep her in for recess whenever she talks to her neighbor.

Praise her frequently at first but gradually diminish your praise.

Continual praise (the first alternative) is too much of a good thing and may make the child dependent on you. What you want, eventually, is to have the learning of communication skills become its own reward or at least to have Cleo learning without constantly needing your emotional support. The second alternative (minimum reward and maximum punishment) will convince her you're an "old meanie" and may destroy her desire to relate to you and learn from you.

The third alternative (praise that is frequent at first but gradually diminishes) is more likely to succeed in the long run. By giving frequent praise at first, you will help to "set" the behavior you desire. Often, a smile, a friendly nod, or a quiet "Good thinking, Cleo" is sufficient. By gradually diminishing your praise, you will probably strengthen her desire for praise, her urge to learn from you in order to receive it, and eventually her chance to be rewarded just by learning itself.

THE MAIN IDEAS: ONE MORE ATTEMPT TO PREDICT THE FUTURE

Classroom management, involving decisions about time allotment, group work vs. individual work, peer tutors and adult aides, utilization of computers, television, and other resources, and the control of misbehavior, will continue to have a major impact on reading achievement.

As teaching becomes ever more complex, teachers will be increasingly better trained as managers of time, people, and resources.

While the average teacher allocates time more according to available materials than definite goals, this situation will most likely change as teachers and administrators learn more about the complex interactive nature of the reading process. Simplistic views of the past and debates over phonics vs. meaning will gradually fade as reading educators continue to grow in sophistication.

The "great debate" for the near future, when it comes to practical decisions in the classroom, will not be phonics vs. meaning but whether to have children spend most of their practice time with worksheets and arbitrary subskills or most of their practice time with real text in an interactive fashion.

A greater number of teachers will learn how to allocate time for silent vs. oral reading according to the specific values of each. Round-robin reading and testing of comprehension will give way to thoughtful modeling of comprehension, practice in integrating the four cueing systems, and sharing written materials to give information and pleasure.

The VCR and the computer will become two of the teacher's best friends.

Managing behavioral problems will become less of a nagging headache as teachers become more sophisticated in "learning management" through learning principles. There will gradually be less confusion in schools between teaching and learning.

Since research continually shows that teachers are more important than instructional materials, teachers will slowly gain more control over the instructional program, especially as they demonstrate both management ability and knowledge of the reading process. The tyranny of "teacher proof" materials will eventually become a quaint cultural and historical artifact, and teachers and children will become freer to interact as human beings.

REFERENCES AND SUGGESTED READING

Allen, V. L., & Feldman, R. S. (1973). Learning through tutoring: Low achieving children as tutors. *Journal of Experimental Education, 42,* 1–5.

Allen, V. L. (1976). Research on children tutoring children: A critical review. *Review of Educational Research, 46,* 355–386.

Allington, R. L. (1980). Poor readers don't get to read much in reading groups. *Language Arts, 57,* 872–876.

Ball, S., & Bogatz, G. A. (1970). *The first year of Sesame Street: An evaluation.* Princeton, N.J.: Educational Testing Service.

Ball, S., & Bogatz, G. A. (1972). *Research on Sesame Street: Some implications for compensatory education.* Baltimore: John Hopkins University Press.

Becker, G. J. (1973). *Television and the classroom reading program.* Newark, DE: International Reading Association.

Berliner, D. C. (1981). Academic learning time and reading achievement. In J. T. Guthrie (Ed.), *Comprehension and teaching: Research reviews* (pp. 203–226). Newark, DE: International Reading Association.

Cassidy, J. (1981). Grey power in the reading program—a direction for the eighties. *Reading Teacher, 35,* 287–291.

Chall, J. S. (1967). *Learning to read: The great debate.* New York: McGraw-Hill.

Durkin, D. (1979). What classroom observations reveal about reading comprehension instruction. *Reading Research Quarterly, 14,* 481–533.

Guzzetti, B. J., & Marzano, R. J. (1984). Correlates of effective reading instruction. *Reading Teacher, 37,* 754–758.

Hassett, J. (1984). Computers in the classroom. *Psychology Today, 18,* September, 22–28.

Hiebert, E. H. (1980). Peers as reading teacher. *Language Arts, 57,* 877–881.

Judd, D. H. (1981). *Partners in education: Instructional uses of the microcomputer.* Chicago: Follett.

Judd, D. H. (1982) Word processing in the classroom: Is it really practical? *Educational Computer Magazine, 2,* May–June, 18–19.

King, R. T. (1982). Learning from a PAL. *Reading Teacher, 35,* 682–685.

Lehr, F. (1984). Peer teaching. *Reading Teacher, 37,* 636–639.

MacDermot, H. G. (1982). Bus tutoring. *Reading Teacher, 35,* 481.

Mason, G. E. (1983). The computer in the reading clinic. *Reading Teacher, 36,* 504–507.

Mason, G. E., Blanchard, J. S., & Daniel, D. B. (1983). *Computer applications in reading.* Newark, DE: International Reading Association.

Mason, J. M. (1983). An examination of reading instruction in third and fourth grades. *Reading Teacher, 36,* 906–913.

McDonald, F. I. (1976). *Beginning teacher evaluation study, Phase II summary.* Princeton, NJ: Educational Testing Service.

Montague, A. (1950). *On being human.* New York: Henry Scribner.

Nevi, C. N. (1983). Cross-age tutoring: Why does it help the tutors? *Reading Teacher, 36,* 892–898.

Pearson, P. D. (1984). A context for instructional research on reading comprehension. In J. Flood (Ed.), *Promoting reading comprehension.* Newark, DE: International Reading Association.

Rausch, S., & Sanacore, J., (Eds.) (1985). *Handbook for the volunteer tutor.* Newark, DE: International Reading Association.

Robbins, E. L. (1971). *Tutor handbook.* Washington, D.C.: National Reading Center.

Singer, H., McNeil, J. D., & Furse, L. L. (1984). Relationship between curriculum scope and reading achievement in elementary schools. *Reading Teacher, 37,* 608–612.

Taylor, N. E., & Connor, U. (1982). Silent vs. oral reading: The rational instructional use of both processes. *Reading Teacher, 35,* 440–443.

APPENDIXES

APPENDIX A   MORE GAMES FOR LEARNING SIGHT WORDS

Word Chase

Materials: Game board, place markers such as plastic cars or buttons, one die. Home spaces should be four different colors (same four colors as markers). Rather than write the sight words on the game board, write them on tagboard strips about ¾″ × 1½″. Glue clear plastic holders to the squares on the game board and insert the tagboard strips. This allows you to change the sight words whenever you wish.

Object of game: First person to get from his home space all around the board and back to home space wins.

Procedures: (two to four may play)

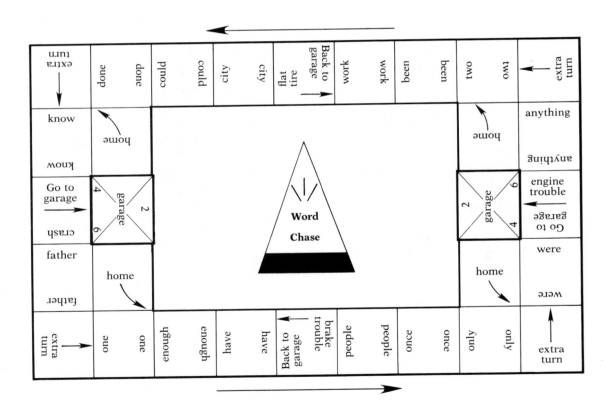

Figure A–1   *Word Chase game board*

1. Players roll die to see who goes first. Highest number goes first.

2. Each person rolls die and moves number of spaces indicated.

3. When person lands on a space, he must read word out loud.

4. If a player doesn't read word correctly (as decided by other players), he must move back to where he was.

5. Second person on same space bumps first person's marker all the way back to his home space.

6. After going all the way around, player must roll the exact number on the die to get back into home space and win.

7. Must roll a 2, 4, or 6 to get out of the garages.

Word Toss

Materials: four boards, each about 1″ by 6″ by 30″, twelve 2″ to 3″ nails, three rubber or plastic rings.

Procedures: (best for two to four players)

1. Each person tosses three rings. Person with highest score goes first.

2. Leader shows a word with flash card (about three seconds).

3. If player reads word correctly, gets to throw three rings.

4. Leader keeps score with tally marks.

5. Whoever has most points at end of ten minutes (or some other designated time) is the winner.

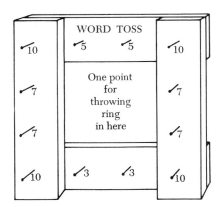

Figure A–2 *Word Toss playing board*

Steal the Words

Materials: 64 (3″ × 5″) cards with 16 different high-frequency irregular words printed on them; each word is printed twice on four different cards (once right-side up and once upside down).

Object of game: Person with biggest pile of cards at end of game wins.
Procedures: (two to four may play)

1. Draw a card to see who goes first. Person who draws word with most letters deals cards.

2. After shuffling cards, dealer gives four cards face down to each person.

3. Dealer then places row of four cards face up in middle of playing area.

4. Person to left of dealer goes first.

5. If player has card that is the same as a card in the middle of playing area, she picks it up and places both cards face up in a pile close to her. (This forms the pile of words that others may later steal.) Before picking it up, however, she must read word to satisfaction of other players.

6. If player does not have a card that is the same as one in the middle, she must place one of her cards in the middle, thus adding to the selection in the middle.

7. If a player has a card that is the same as the top card of another player's pile, she must first read the word on the card out loud and then say STEAL THE WORDS as she takes the other player's entire pile and places it on top of her own.

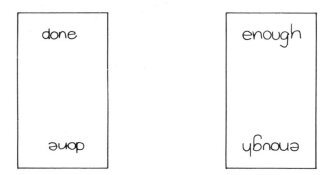

Figure A–3   *Steal the Words game cards*

8. A person may steal a pile of words only at the time of that person's regular turn!

9. After all players have used up their four cards, the dealer deals out four more cards to each; this time, however, the dealer does *not* place any more in the middle of the playing area.

10. Dealer places extra cards in center during her final deal.

11. When the final cards have been dealt and played, the game is over.

12. Last person to take a card with her card gets all the rest of the cards in the middle.

Word Checkers

Materials: Inexpensive or homemade checkerboard; set of checkers; paper labels slightly smaller than the squares on the checkerboard. Print a different word on each label—twice—so that each player can see the word right-side-up.

Object of game: First person to get all of other person's checkers wins; or the person who has the most checkers at the end of a designated time, such as ten minutes.

Procedures: Two people may play. Follow same procedures as with regular checkers, except:

Before person can move his checker, he must say the word or words that are on his path, including the word he finally lands on.

When a person cannot decode (pronounce) a word correctly, he loses his turn.

Boggle

A game that combines spelling and decoding; 16 lettered cubes. Purchase from Warren's Educational Supplies, 7715 Garvey Avenue, Rosemead, CA 91770.

Context Clues Game

A game that develops vocabularies through the use of context clues. Purchase from Lakeshore Curriculum Materials, 2695 E. Dominguez Street, P.O. Box 6261, Carson, CA 90749.

Crossword Puzzles

Laminated colorful puzzles at different levels of difficulty. Purchase from Ideal School Supply, 11000 South Lavergne, Oak Lawn, IL 60453.

Educational Password Game

A game based on the popular television show. Purchase from Milton Bradley, 74 Park Street, Springfield, MA 01101.

Picture Words for Beginners

An activity of matching words and pictures. Purchase from Milton Bradley, 74 Park Street, Springfield, MA 01101.

Rummy-Nyms

A game similar to rummy; one deck for synonyms; one for antonyms. Purchase from Little Brown Bear Associates, Box 561167, Miami, FL 33156.

Synonym Puzzles

A set of "jigsaw puzzles" allowing children to match synonyms. Purchase from Incentives for Learning, 600 West Van Buren Street, Chicago, IL 60607.

Word Cover

A game similar to Bingo for learning high-frequency words. Purchase from Houghton Mifflin, One Beacon Street, Boston, MA 02107.

The Language and Thinking Program

Readiness materials for developing vocabulary and language skills. Purchase from Follett Educational Corporation, 1010 West Washington Blvd., Chicago, IL 60607.

Peabody Language Development Kits

Pictures, puppets, and lessons for development of oral vocabulary and language skills. Purchase from American Guidance Service, Publishers' Building, Circle Pines, MN 55014.

APPENDIX B MORE GAMES FOR LEARNING GRAPHOPHONIC PATTERNS

e-Boat Adventure

Materials: Game board (see below), place markers such as buttons or cardboard boats, one die.

Object of game: First one to get onto the Isle of *e* wins the game.

Procedures: (best for two to four players)

1. Roll die to see who goes first. Highest number goes first.

2. Each person rolls die and moves number of spaces indicated.

3. When player lands on a word, she must read the word out loud as it is, then cover up the final *e* and read it out loud again.

4. If player doesn't read word correctly both ways (and in the correct order), player must move back to where she was. (Other players decide.)

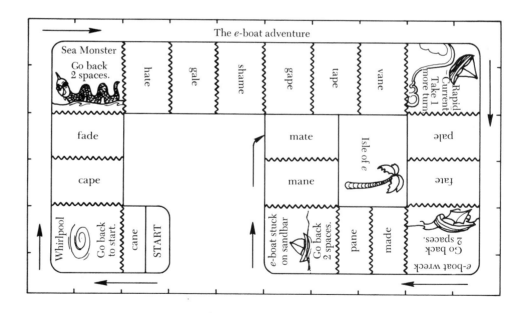

Figure B–1 *e-Boat Adventure game board*

5. It is all right to have more than one *e*-boat on a space.

6. To land on the Isle of *e*, player must roll the exact number on the die.

Values of game:

Practice in decoding VC words

Practice in discriminating between VC and VCE patterns

Development of positive feelings about "reading" as a school subject

Indirect practice in spelling VC and VCE words

Practice in reading common phonograms such as *ad, an, at*

Adaptations of game: Use other VC-VCE contrasts such as *pin-pine, bit-bite,* and *rip-ripe.*

Wild Things

Materials: A deck of 52 (3" × 5") cards with words having *r*-controlled vowels written on them (except for eight "wild cards"). There should be five "suits": *ar, er, ir, or,* and *ur.*

Object of game: First one to get rid of all cards in hand wins.

Procedures:

1. Deal five cards to each player face down.

2. Place rest of deck face down in center of the table.

3. Turn top card face up on the side of the deck to form discard pile.

4. Person to left of dealer begins play.

Figure B–2 *Wild Things game cards*

Figure B–3 *Adaptation of Wild Things game cards*

5. Each player plays (discards) only one card; then it's the next person's turn.

6. In order to play, each player must be able to discard one card from hand by following suit *(ar, er, ir, or, ur)*. Player must read word out loud to the approval of other players or lose turn. Example: If *hurt* is top card on discard pile, player must discard a *ur* word.

7. If player does not have a word that follows suit, he may play a card having a word beginning with the same first letter as the top card on discard pile. This now changes the suit. Example: If *hurt* was down and next player discarded *harm*, next player must play an *ar* word or another *h* word.

8. A player may change suit anytime by playing a wild card and calling out the suit he wishes to change to. Example: Plays wild card and says, "I want to change it to *e-r* words."

9. If player does not have a playable card, he must draw one card from deck and lose turn.

Values of game:

Practice in decoding words with *r*-controlled vowels

Practice in discriminating among words with *r*-controlled vowels

Adaptations of game: Use the five basic vowel patterns as suits: VC, VCE, VVC, CV, and VCC. The player not only reads the word but calls out the pattern as well. Another adaptation is the use of phonograms as suits, such as *at, ack, am, an,* and *ap.*

Figure B–4 *Phonograms as Wild Things game cards*

Animal Race

With this gameboard, the child matches pictures and beginning sounds after choosing his track to race against one to three other children. Purchase from Houghton Mifflin, One Beacon Street, Boston, MA 02107.

Build It

A game that teaches decoding of consonant letters and short-vowel letters. Purchase from Remedial Education Press, Kingsbury Center, 2138 Bancroft Place, N.W., Washington, DC 20008.

Phonetic Quizmo

A lotto-type game designed to teach the decoding of consonant letters and clusters. Purchase from Milton Bradley, 74 Park Street, Springfield, MA 01101.

Split Words

An activity for building words from wooden blocks with consonant letters, consonant clusters, and phonograms printed on them. Purchase from American Teaching Aids, Box 1652, Covina, CA 91722.

Blend Dominoes

A game designed to have children build words containing consonant digraphs and consonant clusters. Purchase from Lakeshore Curriculum Materials, 2695 E. Dominguez Street, P.O. Box 6261, Carson, CA 90749.

Ugly Oogly

A card game requiring the blending of consonant letters or clusters with phonograms. Purchase from Little Brown Bear Associates, Box 561167, Miami, FL 33156.

Autophonics

Games similar to bingo involving "vehicles" to drive. Teach decoding of vowel letters, vowel digraphs, and diphthong clusters. Purchase from Warren's Educational Supplies, 7715 Garvey Avenue, Rosemead, CA 91770.

Sea of Vowels

Children travel by "submarine" in search of treasure; teaches "long and short vowels." Purchase from Ideal School Supply, 11000 South Lavergne, Oak Lawn, IL 60453.

Quiet Pal Game

Children build words with "silent letters" in them. Purchase from Warren's Educational Supplies, 7715 Garvey Avenue, Rosemead, CA 91770.

Tick-Tack-Go

Board games on decoding vowel letters and patterns. Purchase from Little Brown Bear Associates, Box 561167, Miami, FL 33156.

Vowel Wheels

Five activities in which children move discs to produce words. Purchase from Milton Bradley, 74 Park Street, Springfield, MA 01101.

Advanced Prefix and Suffix Puzzles

Three-piece "jigsaw" puzzles requiring children to match prefix and suffix with root. Order from Developmental Learning Materials, 7440 Natchez Avenue, Niles, IL 60648.

Compound Word Game

Children use cards to form compound words. Purchase from Developmental Learning Materials, 7440 Natchez Avenue, Niles, IL 60648.

Mousetrap

A card game in which compound words are analyzed and synthesized. Order from Little Brown Bear Associates, Box 561167, Miami, FL 33156.

Syllable Scoreboard

Children use a basketball gameboard and move across the board according to the number of syllables in words drawn from a "ball bin." Purchase from Developmental Learning Materials, 7440 Natchez Avenue, Niles, IL 60648.

Durrell-Murphy Phonics Practice Program

Picture cards which can be used by the child without adult supervision. Purchase from Harcourt Brace Jovanovich, 757 Third Avenue, New York, NY 10017.

Get Set Games

Various games on decoding skills. Purchase from Houghton Mifflin, One Beacon Street, Boston, MA 02107.

APPENDIX C   MORE COMPREHENSION GAMES

Main Idea Travel Game

Both the primary and the intermediate editions of this game use a playing board, one die, six colored markers, 110 story cards, and other materials to help children learn how to detect main ideas in reading selections. Purchase from Comprehension Games Corporation, 63–110 Woodhaven Blvd., Rego Park, NY 11374.

Drawing Conclusions

A game containing five bingo cards, one spinner, 80 plastic markers, 110 story cards, and other materials designed to help children learn how to draw conclusions. Purchase from Comprehension Games Corporation.

Fact or Opinion

A game containing a playing board, one die, six markers, 110 story cards, and other materials related to learning this comprehension skill. Purchase from Comprehension Games Corporation.

Reading for Detail

A game that contains two spinners, a playing board, six plastic horses, 72 story cards, and other materials. Purchase from Comprehension Games Corporation.

Reading Rx

This is a box of activity cards with hundreds of games and activities for reinforcing decoding, comprehension, and reference skills. Purchase from Tarmack/Tac, 8 Baird Mountain Road, Asheville, NC 28804.

APPENDIX D MORE IDEAS FOR LANGUAGE EXPERIENCE STORIES AND OTHER TYPES OF WRITING

1. Have the children see how long they can make this sentence: "The bear chased the girl." They may change the sentence or the words in any way they wish. After they have made the sentence as long as they wish, they may also add more sentences.

2. Ask them to think of ideas for making the classroom more attractive.

3. Ask pupils to choose one picture (from a large set of pictures) to tell or write a story about. Give them a day or two to think about their idea. Then have them come one at a time to a quiet corner to tell you the story (or to tell it into a tape recorder). Let the child hold the picture while telling the story.

4. Find pictures that tell a story, for example, a crying child who is obviously lost. Have children tell or write (or both) what is happening now, what happened just before the picture, and what is going to happen after the picture.

5. Make a "touch book" with a different texture on each page: sandpaper, wax paper, silky fabric, etc. Number each page and pass around the book. When a child has a turn with the book, she is to write down the page number and also at least five words that describe how the material feels. The child then hands in the paper to the teacher and passes on the book. (This is an excellent activity for a learning center.) Some children may need help from a large chart of "touch words" to select words for their own lists.

6. Ask pupils to make up one or two sentences that describe you, the teacher. Have fun reading them aloud, while at the same time discussing the kinds of words and phrases that can be used to describe a person's appearance and personality. Have the children use suggestions from your discussion to develop a paragraph about themselves.

7. Have the children make up a story or just tell about their own drawings or paintings. Take dictation during the telling or use a tape recorder. Or have them write up their story after telling it.

8. Develop a class story based on an event that occurs during the school day, such as an unusual fire drill or an animal that gets into the room. The teacher takes dictation from the class.

9. Read two or three Dr. Seuss books to the children and discuss the imaginary animals he created. Have them create their own imaginary animals on paper and tell or write about them.

10. Have the children close their eyes and imagine an imaginary character, such as a strange animal or funny person. Have them describe their characters one at a time and help weave them together into a story as they describe them. You may either stop here or write the characters' names on the board and have the children make up a story about them. They may use part of the story already created if they wish.

11. Have some of the children bring in toys to explain to the others. Have them pretend they are toy manufacturers and, together, think of ways to improve the toys. Accept even their wildest impossible ideas; in fact, encourage such ideas. If you wish, you can then have them write a story about a toymaker and how he tried to make the "best toy in the world."

12. Have children read each other's palms. Encourage them to tell exactly what adventures their partners will have, exactly how they will make their fortune, etc.

13. Each person writes a detailed description of a character from a familiar story—one they've all read in class, favorite bedtime stories, etc. Then each person reads her description and the rest of the class guesses who was described.

14. Make up "balloon adventures" about a helium-filled balloon and its travels around the world. An effective "starter" is to bring such a balloon to school and release it.

15. Have the children get in groups of four or five. Put several words on the chalkboard that might suggest a story, such as *sailboat*, *waves*, *rocks*, and *beach*. Each person in a group starts a story and then passes it on to another person in his group until the teacher says "time." When each person has added something to each of the stories, have the children read the stories to see how similar and different they are.

16. Give each child a newspaper funny with the words cut out. Have them write their own dialogue.

17. Have a class puppet who talks to the children every day. Have him tell about an adventure he had (the teacher had), about something he

saw one of them doing that he didn't think was such a good idea, about how proud he is of them, etc. Let the children make up adventures for him.

18. After practicing with some What-if questions (such as What if all the trees in the world were cut down?), have them write their own What-if story.

19. After a period of spontaneous drama, have them write up the story they created.

20. Write a title on the board, such as "The Danger Zone" or "Flying Is for the Birds." Have each person write three sentences as a beginning of a story. Then have them put their names on their papers, fold the papers in half twice, and put them in a large box. They will then blindly pick one from the box and finish the story. Finally they will hand the story to the person who began the story, so that all may see how their story turned out.

21. Give each child five 3″ × 5″ index cards or other small pieces of paper. Have them write WHO, WHEN, WHAT, WHERE, and WHY on the five cards. After WHO they are to write the name and description of a character they have created. After WHAT they should tell something the character did. After WHEN and WHERE they should tell the time and place of the action. After WHY they should explain why the character did what he or she did (the motive).

    For example: WHO, Bill Robertson, a jeweler, age 40, tired-looking, graying hair, nail biter; WHAT, stole some of his own jewelry; WHEN, during a summer day when no customers were in the store; WHERE, in his own jewelry store in Chicago in a run-down shopping area; WHY, he wanted to claim he was robbed and collect the insurance money so he could send his daughter to college.

    Have the children put the cards in separate boxes: a WHO box, a WHAT box, a WHEN box, a WHY box, and a WHERE box. Mix the contents in the boxes and let the children each select five new cards—one from each box. They are to use their new cards, but only the ones that help them think of a story.

22. Have them create a story from a single Where sentence. Give each child a sentence on a piece of paper, for example, "I went to the circus," or "I went to a farm," or "I went to a grocery store." It is all right if several children have the same sentence, but they should all begin with "I went to. . . ."

    Show them how to create a "story" from a sentence. Put this sentence on the board: "I went to the new shopping mall." Under the sentence write the words: *when, who, what, why.* Then show them how to ask questions that will help them describe their trip. For instance: When did you go? Whom did you see or go with? What did you do there? Why did you do these things?

23. Have them create a story from a single Who sentence. This is similar to 22. Work with Who sentences such as "I saw Mrs. Twilliger, that lady who sells strange things." Ask questions about where, when, what, and why. For example, where did you see Mrs. Twilliger? When did you see her? What was she doing when you saw her? Why was she doing it?

24. Have them create a story from a single What sentence, e.g., "He was dropping cotton balls from an airplane." Ask who, when, where, and why questions.

25. Have them create a story from a single When sentence, e.g., "It was on a dark, foggy night at the beginning of summer vacation." Ask where, who, what, and why questions.

26. Have them create a story from a single Why sentence, e.g., "She was tired of having those kids tramp across her lawn and pick her flowers." Ask who, where, what, and when questions.

27. Have them create new adventures for their favorite cartoon characters such as Snoopy and Charlie Brown. This is especially good shortly after they have seen a Charlie Brown TV special.

28. Have them create new adventures for their favorite TV character.

29. Have them create a newspaper story about a game they have played on the playground. Be sure to have them include the who, what, when, and where in their story, and the why, if it's appropriate.

30. Have the children make up Crazy Titles and put them in a grab box for other children to pick from blindly. An example of a Crazy Title would be: "The Lion Who Ran the People Zoo" or "The Girl Who Walked Backwards."

APPENDIX E   SOURCES OF HIGH-INTEREST LOW-VOCABULARY BOOKS FOR CHILDREN

Publisher	Title	Reading Grade Level*	Interest Grade Level
Addison-Wesley Publishing Reading, MA 01867	Checkered Flag Series	2–4	6–12
	The Morgan Bay Mysteries	2–4	4–11

Publisher	Title	Reading Grade Level*	Interest Grade Level
Annmaur Corporation 500 74th Street North Bergen, NJ 07047	The Hip Reader	1–3	4–9
Children's Press 1224 West VanBuren St. Chicago, IL 60607	True Book Series	2–3	3–6
Field Publications 245 Long Hill Rd. Middletown, CT 06457	Know Your World	3–5	4–8
Franklin Watts, Inc. 387 Park Ave. S. New York, NY 10016	Let's Find Out Series	2–4	5–6
Garrard Publishing 1607 N. Market Street Champaign, IL 61820	American Folktales	3–4	2–6
Pitman Learning 19 Davis Drive Belmont, CA 94002	Getting Along Series Pacemaker True Adventures	3–5 2–3	4–8 5–12
Reader's Digest Services Educational Division Pleasantville, NY 10570	Reading Skill Builders	1–4	2–5
Santillana Publishing 257 Union Street Northvale, NJ 07647	I Want to Be Series	2–4	4–6
Scholastic 730 Broadway New York, NY 10003	Action Libraries	2–3	4–8

*Reading level estimated by formula and not by scale.

APPENDIX F BOOK PROJECTS FOR CHILDREN AND TEACHERS

Oral Projects

1. Try to interest others in a book you have read by reading an interesting part to the class. Practice before you read to them.

2. Read an exciting part to the class. Stop reading right in the middle of the action. Practice before you read to them.

3. Tell about one character in the book. Tell why he is such an interesting person. Make the others in the class want to know more about him.

4. Show on a globe or map how you would get from your home to where the story took place. Tell how you would travel there. Then tell something about this place. Tell a little bit about why the place was important to the story. Make the others in the class wish they could go there.

5. Pretend you are one of the characters in the book. Describe yourself and tell one or two things you do in the story. If others have already read the book, ask them to guess who you are.

6. Find an important object in the book you just read. Show it to the class and have them guess what it is and why it might be important in the story. Give them a few hints, but don't tell them too much.

7. Play "Twenty Questions" with the class. Have them think of the object or person you have in mind that was important in the story. First tell them whether it is "animal, vegetable, or mineral." After the game give them some hints as to why the object or person was important, but don't tell them too much.

8. Tell the class some interesting facts you learned about a country you read about. Then ask them three or four questions to see what facts they can remember.

9. Tell how you would have done something differently than the way a person in the story did it.

10. Prepare and present a TV commercial for your book. Try to interest others in "buying" your book.

11. Read to the class two or three poems from a book of poems you have read. Be sure to practice several times before you do this. You may wish to use the tape recorder for practicing.

12. Find someone else who has read the same book of poetry. Together, read two or three poems to the class. You might try different arrangements, as with a song; for example, one person could read the first verse, the other person could read the second verse, and both could read the third verse together.

13. See if you can recite from memory a favorite poem from a poetry book you have just read.

14. Dress up as a character in the book and tell about yourself or about one of the adventures you had.

15. After reading a book of folktales, see if you can learn one of the stories well enough to tell to the class.

16. Look up an author in *The Junior Book of Authors* or *More Junior Authors* (in the reference section of the library). Tell the class a few interesting things about him.

17. Make up another adventure for one of the characters. Tell us the adventure.

18. Make up a new ending for the book. Tell your ending to the class after you first tell a little bit about the beginning and the middle. Don't tell them the real ending, though.

19. Have a panel discussion about a book that three or four of you have read. Tell how you agree and disagree about some of the characters or about part of the story.

20. Tell about an adventure you had that was similar to one a character in the book had.

21. Meet in small groups to chat about books you have read.

Drama Projects

1. Pantomime a scene from your book. Have the class guess what you were doing. Tell them only enough to get them interested in the book.

2. Plan so that you and a friend read the same book, then prepare and present a skit about part of the book. You may have to make up some of your own dialogue, or you can say what the characters said in the book.

3. Tape record a skit based on the book. You may have to make up some of your own dialogue and make your voice sound like several different people. Play the tape recording to the class.

4. Put on a puppet play about one part of the book.

5. Play "Meet the Author." Find someone who has read the same book. One person pretends to be the author and the other interviews him. The interviewer asks questions about the book, about the author's life (if you can find information about his life), etc.

6. Pretend you are the author of the book and are trying to get someone to publish it. Tell the "publishing staff" (your class) why it would be a good book to publish. Let them ask you questions.

7. Play charades with the class. Act out each word of the title. See how long it takes for the class to guess the title.

8. If several others have read this book, pantomime a scene from the book *by yourself*. Then ask the class to guess the *title* of the book. See if they can also guess the author.

9. Pretend you are a character in the book you have read. Find someone who will pretend he is a character in a different book. In front of the class, carry on a conversation between the two characters. You might tell each other about some of your adventures or about some of the people you know (those who were described in the books).

10. Put on a play by yourself in which you play two or three parts. Make name cards for each character. Each time you switch parts, hold up one of the cards.

11. Find some dolls you can use to represent characters in your book. Put on a doll play about one part of your book.

12. Put on a play with one or two others. Have the class guess the title and author of the book.

Written Projects

1. Write an advertisement for the book you have read. Put the ad on the bulletin board. Be sure to tell where the book can be found and a few things about why it's a "marvelous" book.

2. Write a letter to a friend and try to persuade her to read the book.

3. Make up a new table of contents for your book. Use your imagination to invent chapter titles that would interest someone else in reading the book.

4. Read two or three chapters of the book. Then write down what you think will happen in the next chapter. Then write briefly about how close your guess was.

5. Make a brief outline of your book. For example:

Tom Sawyer

I. Tom plays, fights, and hides
   A. Tom tricks Aunt Polly
   B. Siddy gets Tom in trouble
   C. Tom fights with a new boy
   D. Tom returns home late at night
II. The glorious whitewasher

6. Write about something that happened in the book in the same way a newspaper reporter would describe it. A reporter tries to answer these questions: Who? What? When? Where? Why? Don't forget to make up a snappy headline for your newspaper article.

7. Write a pretend letter to a character in the book. Tell the character how his or her life is the same or different from yours.

8. Write a real letter to the author of the book. Send the letter in care of the publisher.

9. Make a short diary for one of the characters in the book. Describe three or four days as if you were the person in the book.

10. Pretend you are one of the characters in the book. Write a letter to another character in the book.

11. Add another chapter to the book. Tell what happened next, or what adventure was left out.

12. Write an ending to the book that is quite different from the one the author wrote.

13. Write about *two* books you have read about the same topic. Tell how the books are similar and different.

14. See how good your memory is. Describe the important details in one chapter. Draw a line under your description, then reread that chapter. Write down any important details you left out.

15. Write about an adventure you had that was like an adventure a character in the book had. Tell how the two adventures were alike and different.

16. Read in an encyclopedia or in another factual book about a person, place, or thing described in your book. Write down some of the things you learned this way that you did *not* learn from the book itself.

17. Try to make a list from memory of all the characters in the book. List both their first and last names. Draw a line under your list. Now skim through the book to see if you remembered all of them. Write down any you didn't remember. How good was your memory for names?

18. Write about the character in the story that you would most like to have for a friend. Tell why he or she would be a good friend. Also write about the character that you would *not* like to have for a friend. Tell why.

19. Write about how you would have solved a problem differently from the way a character in the book did.

20. Pick two characters from the story. Write about how they were alike and how they were different.

21. Make a list of words or phrases in the story that helped you almost be able to see or hear or smell or feel or taste something described in the story.

22. Write a poem that tells about one adventure in the book.

Arts and Crafts Projects

1. Make clothes for a doll to match a character in the book. Display it for the rest of the class to see. Make sure you put a card by it with the name of the book, the author, and your name.

2. Make an object that is important in the book you just read. Have the class guess what it is and why it might be important in the story. Give them a few hints, but don't tell them for sure.

3. Make a flannel board or bulletin board display about your book.

4. Make a comic strip about one of the scenes in your book. Put it on the bulletin board.

5. Make a diorama (a small stage) that describes a scene in the book. Use a cardboard box for the stage. Make the objects and people in your scene out of clay, cardboard, pipe cleaners, papier-mâché, or any other material.

6. Make a mobile representing five or six characters in the book.

7. If the book doesn't have a book jacket, make one for it. Be sure to put a picture on it and all the necessary information. A manila folder might be good to use.

8. Make a "movie" of one scene in your book. Use a long piece of butcher paper. After you draw a sequence of several pictures, roll the butcher paper. Then ask two people to unroll it as you describe the scene to the class.

9. Make a picture of one scene in the book. Put it on the bulletin board. Below it put the title and author and two or three questions about the scene. Try using crayon, chalk, or charcoal.

10. Same as 9. Use tempera or watercolor.

11. Same as 9. Use collage materials: bits of paper, cloth, or other materials.

12. Study the illustrations in the book. What techniques did the artist use? See if you can illustrate a part of the book that was not illustrated. Try to use some of the same techniques the artist did. Put your illustration on the bulletin board. Be sure to name the illustrator that you imitated.

13. Make a time line of the story showing main events rather than dates. Draw pictures to illustrate the main events.

14. Read half or more of the book. Then draw three pictures to show three different ways the book might end. Put them on the bulletin board,

along with a card giving the title, author, your name, and "Three Ideas on How this Book Might End."

15. Make a scrapbook of things related to the book. Be sure to label what you put in your scrapbook.

16. Make a map to show where the characters went in the story.

Demonstration Projects

1. Demonstrate a science principle you learned from your book by performing an experiment in front of the class.

2. Show the class how to make something you learned to make from reading your book.

3. Show the class how to do something you learned to do from reading your book.

APPENDIX G   THE RAD TEST—RAPID ASSESSMENT OF A DISABLED READER

Directions for Administration

Note: This test is not a diagnostic test. Its purpose is to provide you with a means of quickly determining which children in a group may have "specific language disability."

Part A: Visual-Kinesthetic Memory
Directions: Print the following words or letters at least 1½ inches high with heavy black felt pen on white cardboard about 3″ × 8″:

1. bad	6. hobby
2. your	7. eighty
3. top	8. minnow
4. nuts	9. whenever
5. JKBF	10. stumbles

Show each card one at a time in the order given. (Do not print the number on the card. Just say the number as you show it.) Expose the card for about ten seconds while the students hold their pencils high over their heads.

After you have turned the card over, count five more seconds and say "Write word number one." The children are then to write the word next to the number one on their sheet of paper. Give them about fifteen seconds to write the word; then ask them to raise their pencils above their heads again.

Repeat this procedure for each of the ten words. Do not show a word again after you have turned over the card.

Part B: Auditory Memory and Visual Discrimination
Directions: Have the following words and letters ready to read to the students:

11. quick	16. mommy
12. fyqt	17. thought
13. saw	18. surround
14. bedc	19. running
15. bubbles	20. everyone

Say each word or series of letters. Say each one twice. While you are saying each one, the students should have their paper turned over. After you have said a word or series of letters twice, count five seconds and say, "Turn over your paper and find the words or letters in row one. Draw a circle around the word or letters I just said."

Allow about ten seconds for them to circle a word or series of letters. Then say, "Put your pencil down and turn over your paper. Listen for the next word or letters."

Repeat this procedure for each of the ten words or series of letters. Do not say a word or series of letters more than twice.

RAD Test

Student's Name _____ Grade _____
Teacher's Name _____ Date _____

Part A:
1. _____ 6. _____
2. _____ 7. _____
3. _____ 8. _____
4. _____ 9. _____
5. _____ 10. _____

Part B:

11. puick	qnick	quick	pnick	kciuq
12. fypt	tqyf	ftyq	fyqt	tyqf
13. was	saw	sam	mas	zaw
14. dceb	dbce	bedc	peqc	becd
15. buddles	dubbles	selbbub	bubbles	bnbbles
16. mommy	wowwy	ymmom	mymmo	mowwy
17. thought	tghuoht	thought	thuoght	thuohgt
18. snrronud	surround	dnuorrus	sunnourd	surruond

19.	nurring	runners	running	gninnur	rurring
20.	evyerone	oneevery	evenyoue	everyone	evenyone

Directions for Scoring RAD Test

To derive a score from this test, simply add the number of correct items in the twenty-item test. Now compare the papers in the bottom third of the group with those in the top third. Disabled learners will usually stand out. This is not a precise assessment, but it gives you a way to determine quickly which children need closer observation.

To be somewhat more precise about your assessment, place a check mark to designate the type of error or errors exhibited, then derive a total for each type of error. Do you find several reversals, transpositions, inversions, substitutions, insertions, omissions? Do the test results coincide with your observations on the Observation Checklist in Appendix O? If so, you have candidates for special instruction.

APPENDIX H PHONICS TESTS

Phonics Test 1: The BAF Test

The BAF Test uses nonsense words and is not suitable for children who have not yet succeeded at the Primer level or above. It consists of two parts and must be administered individually. Normally this test would be given to children above grade two who are considered "remedial readers."

Part I: Consonant Letters, Digraphs, and Clusters

The children should be encouraged to try decoding each nonsense word without your help. If they miss one, simply circle it and have them continue. Be sure to pronounce the first one for them /băf/ and have them pronounce it correctly before they continue. It is also a good idea to correct the second one if they miss it (*caf* is pronounced /kăf/).

Name of Student _____

Directions to be read or told to the student:

"These words are nonsense words. They are not real words. I'd like you to think about what sounds the letters have; then read each word out loud without my help. Don't try to go fast; read the list slowly. If you have any trouble with a word, I'll just circle it and you can go on to the next one. The first word is /băf/. Now you say it. . . . All right, now go on to the rest of the words in row 1."

	A	B	C	D	E	F	G
Consonant Letters							
1.	baf	caf	daf	faf	gaf	haf	jaf
2.	kaf	laf	maf	naf	paf	raf	saf
3.	taf	vaf	waf	yaf	zaf	baf	bax

	A	B	C	D	E	F	G	H
Consonant Digraphs								
4.	chaf	phaf	shaf	thaf	whaf	fack	fang	fank
Consonant Clusters								
5.	blaf	braf	claf	craf	draf	dwaf	flaf	fraf
6.	glaf	graf	fand	plaf	praf	quaf	scaf	scraf
7.	skaf	slaf	smaf	snaf	spaf	splaf	spraf	squaf
8.	staf	straf	swaf	thraf	traf	twaf		

Part II: Vowel Letters, Vowel Digraphs, and Vowel Clusters
(For those whose instructional level is at least "Primer")
This part of the inventory should also be administered individually. You will need to reproduce a copy of this test for each child. The children should be encouraged to try decoding each nonsense word without your help. If they miss one, simply circle it and have them continue. Be sure to pronounce the first one for them /băf/ and have them pronounce it correctly before they continue.

Directions to be read or told to the student

"These words are nonsense words. They are not real words. I'd like you to think about what sounds the letters have; then read each word out loud without any help. Don't try to go fast; read the list slowly. If you have any trouble with a word, I'll circle it and you can go on to the next one. The first word is /băf/. Now you say it. . . . All right, now go on to the rest of the words in row 1."

	A	B	C	D	E	F	G
1.	baf	bafe	barp	baif	bawf		
2.	bef	befe	berf	beaf			
3.	bof	bofe	borf	boaf	bouf	boif	boof
4.	bif	bife	birf				
5.	buf	bufe	burf				

Phonics Test 2: The Phonogram Phonics Test

For a description of this test, as well as instructions for administration, please see pages 365–366.

APPENDIX I A STARTER LIST OF GOOD BOOKS FOR CHILDREN*

Picture Books

Stone Soup, Marcia Brown
Mike Mulligan and His Steam Shovel, Virginia Lee Burton
The Snowy Day, Ezra Jack Keats
Make Way for Ducklings, Robert McCloskey
Where the Wild Things Are, Maurice Sendak
Millions of Cats, Wanda Gag
Horton Hatches the Egg, Dr. Seuss
People, Peter Spier
Goodnight Moon, Margaret Wise Brown
Alexander and the Terrible, Horrible, No Good, Very Bad Day, Judith Viorst
The Day Jimmy's Boa Ate the Wash, Stephen Kellogg
The Wingdingdilly, Bill Peet

Folk Tales and Myths

Grimm's Fairy Tales, Jakob and Wilhelm Grimm
East of the Sun and West of the Moon, Peter Christian Asbjornsen and Jorgen E. Moe
English Fairy Tales, Joseph Jacobs
Tall Tale America, Adrien Stoutenberg
The Magic Orange Tree, Diane Wolkstein
Tales for the Third Ear, Verna Aardema
Zlateh the Goat, Isaac Bashevis Singer
The Book of Greek Myths, Edgar and Ingri Parin D'Aulaire
Norse Gods and Giants, Edgar and Ingri Parin D'Aulaire
And It Is Still That Way, Byrd Baylor
Grandfather Tales, Richard Chase

Realism

Durango Street, Frank Bonham
The House of Sixty Fathers, Meindert DeJong
Dragonwings, Laurence Yep

---

*Compiled by Eric A. Kimmel, Doris A. Kimmel, and Frank B. May. The order of the titles in each category is according to the degree of importance the compilers gave to each book. All the books, however, are considered either proven or future classics.

Are You There, God? It's Me, Margaret, Judy Blume
Bridge to Terabithia, Katharine Paterson
It's Like This, Cat, Emily Neville
The Big Wave, Pearl Buck
Words by Heart, Ouida Sebestyen
Homecoming, Cynthia Voigt
Tex, S. E. Hinton
Roll of Thunder, Hear My Cry, Mildred Taylor

Outdoor Adventure

Swiss Family Robinson, Johann Wyss
Island of the Blue Dolphins, Scott O'Dell
Julie of the Wolves, Jean C. George
My Side of the Mountain, Jean C. George
Call It Courage, Armstrong Sperry

Biography

Amos Fortune, Free Man, Elizabeth Yates
Daniel Boone, James Daugherty
Carry On, Mr. Bowditch, Jean Lee Latham
America's Paul Revere, Esther Forbes
Will You Sign Here, John Hancock? Jean Fritz
Freedom Train, The Story of Harriet Tubman, Dorothy Sterling
A Day of Pleasure, I. B. Singer
Homesick, Jean Fritz
The Road From Home, David Kherdian
Ben & Me, Robert Lawson

Historical Fiction

The Witch of Blackbird Pond, Elizabeth Speare
The Courage of Sara Nobel, Alice Dalgliesh
Otto of the Silver Hand, Howard Pyle
Johnny Tremain, Esther Forbes
The Little House In The Big Woods, Laura Ingalls Wilder
Treasure Island, Robert Louis Stevenson
Little Women, Louisa May Alcott
Warrior Scarlet, Rosemary Sutcliff
The King's Fifth, Scott O'Dell
Robin Hood, J. Walker McSpadden
My Brother Sam Is Dead, James L. Collier

Fantasy

The Enormous Egg, Oliver Butterworth
Rabbit Hill, Robert Lawson
Mary Poppins, P. L. Travers
The Borrowers, Mary Norton
The Wind In The Willows, Kenneth Grahame
Alice in Wonderland, Lewis Carroll
Pinocchio, Carlo Collodi
The Wizard of Oz, L. Frank Baum
Mrs. Frisby and the Rats of NIMH, Robert C. O'Brien
The Hobbit, J. R. R. Tolkien
The Lion, the Witch and the Wardrobe, C. S. Lewis
Lizard Music, D. Manus Pinkwater
House of Stairs, William Sleator
Charlie and the Chocolate Factory, Roald Dahl
Tuck Everlasting, Natalie Babbit
Bunnicula, Debra and James Howe
The Indian In The Cupboard, Lynn Reid Banks

Science Fiction

A Wrinkle in Time, Madeleine L'Engle
The Wonderful Flight to the Mushroom Planet, Eleanor Cameron
A Wizard of Earthsea, Ursula K. Le Guin
The White Mountains, John Christopher
Dragonsong, Anne McCaffrey
Tunnel in the Sky, Robert Heinlein
Dandelion Wine, Ray Bradbury
The Book of Three, Lloyd Alexander

Humor

How to Eat Fried Worms, Thomas Rockwell
Henry Huggins, Beverly Cleary
"B" Is For Betsy, Carolyn Haywood
Mrs. Piggle-Wiggle, Betty MacDonald
The Great Brain, John D. Fitzgerald
Henry Reed, Inc., Keith Robertson
Homer Price, Robert McCloskey
Anastasia Krupnick, Lois Lowry

Poetry

In a Spring Garden, Richard Lewis
Beastly Boys and Ghastly Girls, William Cole
Nightmares, Jack Prelutsky
Tirra Lirra, Laura Richards
Songs of Childhood, Eugene Field
It Doesn't Always Have to Rhyme, Eve Merriam
The First Book of Poetry, Isabel J. Peterson
The Monster Den, John Ciardi
The Peaceable Kingdom, Elizabeth Coatsworth
Peacock Pie, Walter De la Mare
Like Nothing at All, Aileen Fishter
Rainbows Are Made, Carl Sandburg
Ashanti to Zulu: African Traditions, Margaret Musgrove
A Child's Garden of Verses, Robert Louis Stevenson
The World of Christopher Robin, A. A. Milne
Don't You Turn Back, Langston Hughes
Where the Sidewalk Ends, Shel Silverstein
A Light in the Attic, Shel Silverstein
Random House Book of Poetry, Jack Prelutsky, ed.

Information

Pagoo, H. C. Holling
Frontier Living, Edwin Tunis
The Birth of Sunset's Kittens, Carla Stevenson
Dinosaurs, Herbert Zim
The Art of Ancient Greece, Shirley Glubok
How Far Is Far?, Alvin Tresselt
A Tree Is a Plant, Clyde Robert Bulla
The Story of Ants, Dorothy Shuttlesworth
101 Science Experiments, Illa Podendorf
The Game of Baseball, Sam and Beryl Epstein
The Courtship of Animals, Millicent E. Selsam
The Weaver's Gift, Kathryn Lasky
Chicken's Aren't the Only Ones, Ruth Heller
Castle, David Macaulay

Animals

The Incredible Journey, Sheila Burnford
Bambi, Felix Salten

Along Came a Dog, Meindert DeJong
Gentle Ben, Walt Morey
The Yearling, Marjorie Rawlings
Misty of Chincoteague, Marguerite Henry
Old Yeller, Frederick B. Gipson
Black Beauty, Anna Sewell
Where the Red Fern Grows, Wilson Rawls
Big Red, Jim Kjelgaard
King of the Wind, Marguerite Henry
Rascal, Sterling North

Mystery

The Egypt Game, Zilpha Keatley Snyder
The House With the Clock in Its Walls, John Bellairs
Encyclopedia Brown, Donald Sobol
Secret of the Emerald Star, Phyllis Whitney
The Alley, Eleanor Estes
The Witch's Daughter, Nina Bawden
The Mystery of the Hidden Hand, Phyllis Whitney
The Mysterious Christmas Shell, Eleanor Cameron
The Case of the Cat's Meow, Crosby Bonsall
From the Mixed Up Files of Mrs. Basil E. Frankweiler, E. L. Konigsburg
Summer of Fear, Lois Duncan
The View From the Cherry Tree, Willo Davis Roberts

Sports

All American, John R. Tunis
The Trouble with Francis, Beman Lord
Rookie First Baseman, Cary Paul Jackson
First Serve, Mary Towne
Matt Gargan's Boy, Alfred Slote

Plays

100 Plays for Children, edited by A. S. Burack
Short Plays for Children, Helen Louise Miller
Thirty Plays for Classroom Reading, Donald D. Durrell and B. Alice Crossley
Children's Plays from Favorite Stories, Sylvia E. Kamerman
Dramatized Folk Tales of the World, Sylvia E. Kamerman

APPENDIX J   NEWBERY AND CALDECOTT AWARD BOOKS

Newbery Books

Year	Title	Author	Publisher
1922	*The Story of Mankind*	van Loon	Liveright
1923	*The Voyages of Dr. Dolittle*	Lofting	Lippincott
1924	*The Dark Frigate*	Hawes	Little, Brown
1925	*Tales from Silver Lands*	Finger	Doubleday
1926	*Shen of the Sea*	Christmas	Dutton
1927	*Smoky the Cowhorse*	James	Scribner
1928	*Gay Neck*	Mujkerji	Dutton
1929	*Hitty, Her First Hundred Years*	Field	McMillan
1930	*The Trumpeter of Krakow*	Kelly	Macmillan
1931	*The Cat Who Went to Heaven*	Coatsworth	Macmillan
1932	*Waterless Mountain*	Armer	McKay
1933	*Young Fu of the Upper Yangtze*	Lewis	Holt
1934	*Invincible Louisa: Anniversary Edition*	Meigs	Little, Brown
1935	*Dobry*	Shannon	Viking
1936	*Caddie Woodlawn*	Brink	Macmillan
1937	*Roller Skates*	Sawyer	Viking
1938	*The White Stag*	Seredy	Viking
1939	*Thimble Summer*	Enright	Holt
1940	*Daniel Boone*	Daugherty	Viking
1941	*Call It Courage*	Sperry	Macmillan
1942	*Matchlock Gun*	Edmonds	Dodd, Mead
1943	*Adam of the Road*	Gray	Viking
1944	*Johnny Tremain*	Forbes	Houghton Mifflin
1945	*Rabbit Hill*	Lawson	Viking
1946	*Strawberry Girl*	Lenski	Lippincott
1947	*Miss Hickory*	Bailey	Viking
1948	*The Twenty-One Balloons*	du Bois	Viking
1949	*King of the Wind*	Henry	Rand McNally
1950	*The Door in the Wall*	de Angeli	Doubleday
1951	*Amos Fortune, Free Man*	Yates	Dutton
1952	*Ginger Pye*	Estes	Harcourt Brace
1953	*The Secret of the Andes*	Clark	Viking
1954	*And Now Miguel*	Krumgold	Crowell
1955	*The Wheel on the School*	de Jong	Harper & Row

Year	Title	Author	Publisher
1956	*Carry On, Mr. Bowditch*	Latham	Houghton Mifflin
1957	*Miracles on Maple Hill*	Sorensen	Harcourt Brace
1958	*Rifles for Waitie*	Keith	Crowell
1959	*Witch of Blackbird Pond*	Speare	Houghton Mifflin
1960	*Onion John*	Krumgold	Crowell
1961	*Island of the Blue Dolphins*	O'Dell	Houghton Mifflin
1962	*Bronze Bow*	Speare	Houghton Mifflin
1963	*A Wrinkle in Time*	L'Engle	Farrar, Straus & Giroux
1964	*It's Like This, Cat*	Neville	Harper & Row
1965	*Shadow of a Bull*	Wojciechowska	Antheneum
1966	*I, Juan De Pareja*	de Trevino	Farrar, Straus & Giroux
1967	*Up a Road Slowly*	Hunt	Follett
1968	*From the Mixed-up Files of Mrs. Basil E. Frankweiler*	Konigsburg	Atheneum
1969	*The High King*	Alexander	Holt, Rinehart & Winston
1970	*Sounder*	Armstrong	Harper & Row
1971	*Summer of the Swans*	Byars	Viking
1972	*Mrs. Frisby and the Rats of NIMH*	O'Brien	Atheneum
1973	*Julie of the Wolves*	George	Harper & Row
1974	*The Slave Dancer*	Fox	Bradbury
1975	*M. C. Higgins, The Great*	Hamilton	Macmillan
1976	*The Grey King*	Cooper	Atheneum
1977	*Roll of Thunder, Hear My Cry*	Taylor	Dial
1978	*Bridge to Terabithia*	Paterson	Crowell
1979	*The Westing Game*	Raskin	Dutton
1980	*A Gathering of Days: A New England Girl's Journal, 1830–1832*	Blos	Scribner
1981	*Jacob Have I Loved*	Paterson	Crowell
1982	*William Blake's Inn*	Willard & Provenson	Harcourt Brace Jovanovich
1983	*Dear Mr. Henshaw*	Cleary	Monroe

Year	Title	Author	Publisher
1984	*Dicey's Song*	Voigt	Atheneum
1985	*Hero and the Crown*	McKinley	Greenwillow

Caldecott Books

Year	Title	Author	Publisher
1938	*Animals of the Bible*	Lathrop	Lippincott
1939	*Mei Li*	Handforth	Doubleday
1940	*Abraham Lincoln*	d'Aulaire	Doubleday
1941	*They Were Strong and Good*	Lawson	Viking
1942	*Make Way for Ducklings*	McCloskey	Viking
1943	*Little House*	Burton	Houghton Mifflin
1944	*Many Moons*	Thurber & Slobodkin	Harcourt Brace Jovanovich
1945	*Prayer for a Child*	Field & Jones	Macmillan
1946	*Rooster Crown*	Petersham	Macmillan
1947	*Little Island*	MacDonald & Weisgard	Doubleday
1948	*White Snow, Bright Snow*	Tresselt & Duvoisin	Lothrop
1949	*Big Snow*	Hader	Macmillan
1950	*Song of the Swallows*	Politi	Scribner
1951	*The Egg Tree*	Milhous	Scribner
1952	*Finder Keepers*	Nicolas	Harcourt
1953	*The Biggest Bear*	Ward	Houghton
1954	*Madeline's Rescue*	Bemelmans	Viking
1955	*Cinderella*	Brown	Scribner
1956	*Frog Went A-Courtin'*	Langstaff & Rojankovsky	Harcourt Brace Jovanovich
1957	*A Tree is Nice*	Udry & Simont	Harper & Row
1958	*Time of Wonder*	McCloskey	Viking
1959	*Chanticleer and the Fox*	Cooney	Crowell
1960	*Nine Days to Christmas*	Ets & Labastida	Viking
1961	*Baboushka and the Three Kings*	Robbins	Parnassus
1962	*Once a Mouse*	Brown	Scribner
1963	*The Snowy Day*	Keats	Viking
1964	*Where the Wild Things Are*	Sendak	Harper
1965	*May I Bring a Friend?*	de Regniers	Atheneum
1966	*Always Room for One More*	Leadhas & Hogrogian	Holt, Rinehart & Winston
1967	*Sam Bangs & Moonshine*	News	Holt, Rinehart & Winston

Year	Title	Author	Publisher
1968	*Drummer Hoff*	Emberley	Prentice-Hall
1969	*Fool of the World and the Flying Ship*	Ransome	Farrar, Straus & Giroux
1970	*Sylvester and the Magic Pebble*	Steig	Simon & Schuster
1971	*A Story, a Story*	Haley	Atheneum
1972	*One Fine Day*	Hogrogian	Macmillan
1973	*The Funny Little Woman*	Mosel	Dutton
1974	*Duffy and the Devil*	Zemach	Farrar, Straus & Giroux
1975	*Arrow to the Sun*	McDermott	Viking
1976	*Why Mosquitoes Buzz in People's Ears*	Aardema	Dial
1977	*Ashanti to Zulu: African Traditions*	Musgrove	Dial
1978	*Noah's Ark*	Spier	Doubleday
1979	*The Girl Who Loved Wild Horses*	Goble	Bradbury
1980	*The Ox-Cart Man*	Hall and Cooney	Viking
1981	*Fables*	Lobel	Harper & Row
1982	*Jumanji*	Van Allsburg	Houghton Mifflin
1983	*Shadow*	Brown	Scribner
1984	*The Glorious Flight*	Provenson	Viking
1985	*Saint George and the Dragon*	Hodges & Human	Little, Brown

APPENDIX K   BASAL READER PUBLISHERS

Addison-Wesley Publishing Company, Jacob Way, Reading MA 01867

Allyn and Bacon, 7 Wells Avenue, Boston, MA 02210

American Book Company, 135 West 50th Street, New York, NY 10020

Economy Company, 1901 North Walnut, P.O. Box 25308, Oklahoma City, OK 73125

Ginn and Company, 191 Spring Street, Lexington, MA 02173

Harcourt Brace Jovanovich, Inc., 1250 Sixth Avenue, San Diego, CA 92101

Harper & Row, Publishers, Inc., 10 East 53rd Street, New York, NY 10022

Holt, Rinehart, and Winston, 521 Fifth Avenue, New York, NY 10017

Houghton Mifflin Company, One Beacon Street, Boston, MA 02108

Laidlaw Brothers, Thatcher and Madison, River Forest, IL 60305

J. B. Lippincott Company, East Washington Square, Philadelphia, PA 19105

Macmillan Company, 866 Third Avenue, New York, NY 10022

Charles E. Merrill Publishing Company, 1300 Alum Creek Drive, Columbus, OH 43216

Open Court Publishing Company, 1058 Eighth Street, La Salle, IL 61301

Scott, Foresman and Company, 1900 East Lake Avenue, Glenview, IL 60025

Silver Burdett, 250 James Street, Morristown, NJ 07960

APPENDIX L   COMPREHENSION PRACTICE ACTIVITIES

These activities are designed to be used during interactive reading experiences or to be followed by interactive applications.

Practice in Developing Images or Associations

1. When reading a story aloud to children, occasionally have them close their eyes and picture what you're reading. Once in a while you may wish to pause to discuss their "pictures" or to write a descriptive word or phrase on the board.

2. Have them first read a passage silently and then draw a picture of what they see "in their heads."

3. Ask the children first to read a passage silently and then tell what they "saw."

4. Have them first read a passage silently and then tell what personal experiences it made them remember.

5. Arrange for them first to read a passage silently and then pantomime what they "saw."

6. Have one child read a passage aloud while other children pantomime the picture they "see."

Practice in Following a Sequence

1. Have the children work in pairs. Each member of the pair should read silently the same set of directions. Then one person should attempt to follow the directions while the other person judges whether he followed the directions correctly.

2. Provide children with directions for making things—paper airplanes, paper costumes for dolls, cookies, et cetera. Have them work in pairs so they can check each other's comprehension of the directions.

3. Have them read a story, then decide in what order to place pictures depicting events in the story.

4. Ask them to read a story, then tell it or act it out to some other children.

5. Provide a child with a set of directions for a game, then have her explain the game in sequence to some other children.

6. Ask the children to read informative passages about sequential occurrences, such as the water cycle or the cycle of life for a butterfly, then explain the cycle to some other children or depict the cycle in a sequential drawing.

Practice in Finding Important Details

1. Help the children change a story into a brief newspaper report. Help them write it as a reporter does, telling who, what, where, and when. The same activity can be used for an historical event described in a social studies book.

2. Help the children change a story into a telegram of twenty-five words or less. Show them how to include only the most important details. You can use the same activity for an historical event described in a social studies book.

3. After they have decided on the main idea for a passage, have them find or remember details that support their decision.

4. Ask them to scan a reading selection from a basal reader, social studies book, or science text to find highly factual information. This is best done orally in small groups, with the first child to find it reading the answer.

5. Develop their appreciation for literary devices by having them read aloud some sentences, phrases, or words that "help paint a picture for the reader."

Practice in Drawing Inferences

This thinking process can be practiced even on reading passages as simple as this:

One hot day Roy went on a boat ride.
He went with his teacher and his school friends.

To give children practice at *literal thinking*, the teacher might simply ask, "What kind of a day was it when Roy went on a boat ride?" But to give children practice at *inferential thinking*, the teacher could ask, "What season of the year do you think it is—winter, summer, spring, or fall?" To answer this question, they would have to make inferences based on the words *hot, teacher,* and *school*. Robert may say "summer" because of the word *hot*. Jill may say, "No, it can't be summer because Roy is going with his teacher and school friends." Frank may then say, "I'll bet it's either spring or fall." All three children will be engaged in inferential thinking.

The teacher has helped them to communicate with the author rather than merely absorbing the author's words.

Practice in Determining Main Ideas

Try reading the following selection and then choose the best title for it:

> In 1888 a terrible snowstorm hit New York City. Tall poles snapped, and electric wires fell into the street. People were killed by electric shock. Some were killed by the falling poles. And nearly a thousand died in the fires that broke out.
>
> The mayor saw that he must do something to make his city a safe place to live. He asked electricians to put electric wires safely underground. Then the mayor sent men out to take down the wooden poles.
>
> These electric wires were the beginning of America's amazing underground city in New York. Today the narrow streets and the sidewalks hide more than four million miles of wire. In some places there are so many wires and pipes that two fingers cannot be pushed between them. . . .*

1. A terrible snowstorm

2. How some people were killed

3. Putting wires underground

4. How an amazing underground city began

Since the first three ideas all lead up to the fourth one, perhaps you would agree that #4 is the best title. This type of exercise gives children specific practice in determining main ideas. Other types of experiences include these:

1. After they read a selection, ask them questions such as these:
   "What do you think the author was trying to tell you?"
   "What was this story really about?"
   "Was there one big idea the author was talking about?"
   "If you were the author, what is the one thing you'd want the readers to remember from this article more than anything else?"

2. Have children read a selection and then create a title for it.

3. After they've read a story or an article, have them "capture the big idea" with a two-line or four-line verse. You'll need to do this together

---

*From page 250 of "Air Pudding and Wind Sauce," *Keys to Reading* (Oklahoma City, OK: Economy Company, 1972), adapted from "Amazing Underground City," by Edward Hymoff (*Boys' Life*, August 1963).

a few times before they can do it on their own. Here's an example for "Goldilocks and the Three Bears":

Goldilocks bothered the bears.
She even broke one of their chairs.
But she'll never do that again.
Not even now and then.

4. After older children have read a story, let them decide on the "basic theme": (a) people against nature; (b) people against people; or (c) people against themselves.

5. After they have read a selection, have them decide whether the title "tells what the story was really about." Or you might ask them if it "tells what the author was really trying to say." Then have them create a "better" title.

Practice in Recognizing Details that Support Main Ideas

Let's look again at the article on New York City's amazing underground city. Mr. Hymoff, the author of this article, didn't simply tell the reader, "Now I'm going to tell how an amazing underground city began." Instead he chose to present as many details as he thought necessary to illustrate and lead up to this idea. To help children realize what the author has done, the teacher will often need to have children "reconstruct" the author's purpose and procedures. You can do this with questions like these:

1. Why do you think this article is called "Amazing Underground City?"

2. What can you find in this article that seems to be "amazing"?

3. Was the author, Mr. Hymoff, trying to just tell about the underground city or was he trying to tell you how this underground city began? Or was he doing both? What can you find in the article to prove your point?

4. Mr. Hymoff tells us that in 1888 a terrible snowstorm hit New York City. Can you find anything in the first paragraph that would explain why he used the word "terrible"?

5. How did the amazing underground city begin?

Practice in Predicting

1. After they have read part of a story, have them guess what is going to happen next.

2. Let them draw or pantomime what's coming next, after they have read a certain portion of a story.

3. Have them continue the story in writing; then read the rest of the story and discuss how their endings differed.

4. Have older children read a dittoed portion of a newspaper editorial or other passage presenting an argument, then have them discuss what they think the author would have said next. Then read the rest of the editorial to them so they can see how well they predicted. (You can do the same thing with an informative passage rather than an argumentative one.)

Practice in Understanding Cause and Effect

Cause-and-effect relationships are the nuclei of many stories and articles. Event B happens because of Event A; Event F occurs because of the personality of Character D; and so on. Unless children recognize such relationships, their understanding of an article or story will have little depth. In "The Amazing Underground City," for example, they would not really understand why the "mayor saw that he must do something to make his city a safe place to live" unless they connect this with the electric wires falling into the street.

The teacher's role is again one of asking thoughtful questions—this time questions that encourage children to notice the cause-and-effect relationships, such as these:

1. Why did the mayor see that he must do something to make his city a safe place to live?

2. What caused the electric wires to fall into the street in the first place?

3. Why did so many people die in the snowstorm of 1888?

4. Why did the mayor have the electricians put the wires under the ground?

5. What kind of person do you think the mayor was? Do you think this had anything to do with what he decided to do after the storm of 1888?

Practice in Distinguishing between the Factual and Nonfactual

This form of critical thinking can be practiced through at least eight types of activities:

1. Distinguishing between literal and figurative expressions

2. Distinguishing between real-life stories and fantasies

3. Distinguishing between real-life stories and satire

4. Distinguishing between factual statements and opinions

5. Recognizing differences between observations an author is making and inferences she is making

6. Recognizing differences between observations an author is making and judgments he is making

7. Detecting an author's bias and how this influences her statements

8. Deciding on the author's competence and how this may influence the accuracy of his statements

Here are some corresponding sample learning activities for the critical thinking activities:

1. Discuss the meaning of figurative phrases such as "shouting my head off" or "pulling my leg." Have the children think of others they have heard. Have them picture in their heads or on paper "what the words seem to mean and what they really mean." The same type of thing can be done with metaphors you and the children discover in descriptive passages. For example, in the sentence "John flew down the hallway to his classroom," what does *flew* seem to mean and really mean? (Other examples: Bill didn't get the *point* of my poem. That book is hard to *swallow*. I *plowed* right through my homework.)

2. After they've read a fanciful story in their basal readers or library books, ask them whether it was a "real-life" story or a "make-believe" one. Have them explain their answers.

3. Read aloud to the children *The Enormous Egg* by Oliver Butterworth. This book includes satire that most children in third through sixth grades will enjoy and understand. Ask them to discover how the author satirizes ("makes fun of" or "pokes fun at") advertisers, politicians, and others. Another book useful for this type of experience is Merrill's *The Pushcart War*. Discuss how Jean Merrill creates imaginary characters and situations that are very like real people and real situations. Help them understand that authors sometimes do this to avoid criticizing people directly.

4. Show them how to tell the difference between factual statements and opinions. Use these nonsense statements as illustrations:

   a. A snurtzle has two eyes and three fleb pads. (factual)
   b. Snurtzles are very good at swinking. (opinion)

    c. A snurtzle can swink 50 gallons a day. (factual)
    d. It is clear that snurtzles are always flumptuous. (opinion)

Ask them what makes them sure that statements b and d are opinions. Then present them with a list of actual statements and have them decide which statements seem factual and which seem to be opinions. Have them justify their answers. (Note: for this type of exercise, a "factual" statement is not necessarily a "truthful" statement.) Then have them look for factual statements and opinions in their basal readers, library books, or social studies textbooks.

5. Have them learn to distinguish between observations and inferences by discussing two-part statements such as these:

Noticing: Jimmy Smith took the milk out of Mrs. Jones's refrigerator. (Observation)

Guessing: Jimmy *stole* the milk. (Inference)

Noticing: Jimmy Smith took the milk out of Mrs. Jones's refrigerator. (Observation)

Guessing: Mrs. Jones asked Jimmy to keep her milk while she was on vacation. (Inference)

6. Have them learn to distinguish between observations and judgments by discussing three-part statements such as these:

Noticing: Jimmy Smith took the milk out of Mrs. Jones's refrigerator. (Observation)

Guessing: Jimmy *stole* the milk. (Inference)

Judging: Jimmy is a *thief*. (Judgment)

Noticing: Jimmy Smith took the milk out of Mrs. Jones's refrigerator.

Guessing: Mrs. Jones asked Jimmy to keep her milk while she was on vacation.

Judging: Jimmy is a nice kid.

After they complete exercises such as these, have them look for examples of when the author is "noticing, guessing, or judging" in their basal readers, library books, or social studies books.

7. Have the children study magazine ads with the intention of detecting these three propaganda tricks:

    a. *Expert Appeal:* "Four out of five doctors recommend No-Ache Aspirin."

     b. *Winner Appeal:* "More people buy Shuvvy than any other car."

     c. *Star Appeal:* "Hefty Breakneck, star tackle for the Podunk Tigers, uses Left Tackle Deodorant. Shouldn't you?"

Ask them why the advertisers use these tricks. Have them talk about the times they have used these tricks in their own lives. For instance: *Expert Appeal*—"If you don't believe me, just ask my mother." *Winner Appeal*—"But Mom, all the kids are wearing Squishtight Jeans." *Star Appeal*—"Frankie Hackshaw is in sixth grade and he wears 'em." Ask them whether authors may sometimes use tricks like these to get them to believe something or do something. If possible, demonstrate this technique through the use of a basal reader, library book, or social studies text.

8. Have the children compare information in two science books or encyclopedias, one published recently and one published several decades ago; have them see how many disagreements they can find about topics such as Mars or atoms. Show them where to find the copyright date in books. Discuss the importance of currency for some information.

Practice in Creative Thinking

1. Ask the children, before or during the reading of a story, to imagine how they might solve the main character's problem. Then, when they have finished the story, have them discuss or write about how they might have solved the problem in a different way.

2. Have them discuss how the main character's problem was similar to one they have right now. Encourage them to tell how they might solve those personal problems. At a later date, encourage them to tell how they actually did solve them.

3. Encourage them to share their feelings about stories or books through drama, poetry, painting, and other media. For instance, a child can pretend she's one of the characters in the story; she can describe herself and tell about one or two things she did in the story. Two children who have read the same book may enjoy dramatizing a scene from the book. Another child may decide to make a diorama (a small stage) describing a scene in his book. (For other ideas, see Appendix F.)

4. Give them time to construct things (castles, dragons, rockets, etc.) they have read about.

5. Let them share their favorite passages from stories by reading aloud to each other. Give them practice time and assistance so the experience will be a positive one for both the audience and the readers. Encourage them to give their own original interpretation to the reading.

APPENDIX M   EXAMPLES OF SIX COMMON SENTENCE PATTERNS

Here are some examples of Pattern 1 (read them aloud if possible):

Noun + Be verb + Prepositional phrase

The girl was inside the house.
My friend was outside the car.
The bear was in the zoo.
Bob was behind the door.
The doctor was in the hospital.
His doctor was under the table.
A nurse was near the bed.
The flebonk was in the malps.

Now you make up two or three.

Here are examples of Pattern 2 (read them aloud, if possible):

Noun + Intransitive verb + (Adverb)*

The boy walked slowly.
The boy walked.
Susan walked.
That girl played under the house.
This girl played in the park.
My mother worked in the morning.
The giant spoke grumpily.
That flebonk lived in the malps.

Now it's your turn. Make one of them nonsensible if you can.

These are examples of Pattern 3:

Noun + Linking verb + Adjective

The candy seemed sweet.
That candy was sweet.
His shirt looked dirty.

---

*Notes: An adverb is not always needed. Also, a prepositional phrase may be used instead of an adverb.

Your dress was pretty.
The monkey seemed clever.
That child was cruel.
Alice appeared snobbish.
The flebonk was masty.
That flebonk smelled yucky.
My flebonk tasted delicious.

Here are examples of Pattern 4:

Noun + Linking verb + Noun

The dog was his friend.
The dog became his friend.
The dog remained his friend.
Bob was a snob.
That girl became my sweetheart.
Her brother remained a fink.
Your costume was a scream.
My flebonk became a skiddle.
His skiddle remained a nurgle.

These are examples of Pattern 5:

Noun + Transitive verb + Noun

The monkey climbed the ladder.
My father drove a car.
This motor ran the pulley.
Jim owned this place.
The train jumped the track.
Your sister liked my brother.
Her flebonk zagged his delbur.
His delbur zagged a flurtop.

Here are examples of Pattern 6:

Noun + Transitive verb + Noun + Noun

The woman gave her dog a bone.
The woman fed her son a steak.
My father spared the beggar a dime.
The king granted Columbus an audience.
The club awarded Felix a prize.
Mr. Jones offered Mother a hand.
My uncle left my sister a fortune.

APPENDIX N   IDEAS FOR TEACHING DICTIONARY USE

A Sample Lesson on the Front, Middle, and Back of a Dictionary

Print the letters of the alphabet near the top of the chalkboard, with a wide space between the *e* and *f* and the *p* and *q*. Write the words *front, middle,* and *back* above these three divisions.

front   *middle*   *back*
a b c d e   f g h i j k l m n o p   q r s t u v w x y z

Write these words on the chalkboard under the label *front,* and ask the children what letters they begin with: *apple, boy, car dog, elephant.* Tell them these words can be found in the *front part* of the dictionary. Prove this to them by telling them on what page of their school dictionary to find each word. After they have found each word, ask them whether the word was in the front part of the dictionary, the middle part, or the back part. (If they don't understand this, review the terms *front, middle,* and *back* as they apply to things like the *top* of their desks or a *row* of desks.)

Write *fox, girl,* and *hat* on the board under *middle* and tell them these words can be found in the middle part of the dictionary. Point to the letters on the chalkboard and ask them how you knew that. Then ask them to think of other words they could find in the middle part of the dictionary (words like *ink, jump, king, log, mop, nap, off,* and *pan*). As they dictate them, write them on the board under the label *middle.* Prove it with two or three of the words by telling them on what page to find them.

Write *queen* under the label *back* and tell them that *queen* can be found in the back part of the dictionary. Point to the letters on the chalkboard and ask them how you knew that. Then ask them to think of other words they would find in the back part of the dictionary (words like *rabbit, sun, tiger, umbrella, visit, wish, X-ray, yard,* and *zebra*). As they dictate them, write them on the board under the label *back.* Prove it with two or three of the words by telling them on what page to find them.

Write several words on the board and ask them in what part of the dictionary they would expect to find each one—the front part, the middle part, or the back part.

Give them a worksheet that contains a list of words each followed by a blank. Have them write *front, middle,* or *back* in each blank. Before they complete their worksheet, review the three parts of the dictionary by presenting this verse:

The front is *a* to *e.*
The middle is *f* to *p.*

And so, as you can see,
The back is *q* to *z*.

Ideas for Teaching Alphabetical Order

To look up *fatigue*, Henry needs a good grasp of alphabetical order. Suppose he decides that *fatigue* is in the middle part of the dictionary and he happens to turn to page 203. On page 203 he finds words that begin with the letter *h*. Now what does he do? He has to realize that *h* is too far and that he needs to move toward the front of the dictionary until he gets to the *f*s. Once he gets to the *f*s, though, he needs to look for words that begin with *fa*. And once he gets there, he needs to look for words that begin with *fat*, and so on.

There are practice exercises on alphabetical order in most reading workbooks. Or you can create your own. Just select some words from the teacher's guides to basal readers or from school dictionaries. For the first type of exercise, select words that begin with different first letters. For the second type of exercise, select words that begin with the same letter but have different second letters. For the third and fourth types of exercise, of course, the third and fourth letters would differ. After you teach the children how to alphabetize these types of lists, you're ready to teach them how to use "guide words" in a dictionary.

A Sample Lesson on Guide Words

Say something like this to your students: "Now that you've learned how to alphabetize, you're ready to learn how to use guide words. Let's look at some guide words in your dictionary. At the top of page 216 are the words *fast* and *fatten*. Can you find them? These are the guide words for page 216. These two words tell you that all the words on this page begin with the letters *f-a*. Can you tell me why I know that's true? Can you prove it to me?"

"These two guide words tell you that some of the words on this page start with *f-a-s* and some of them start with *f-a-t*. Can you prove this to me?"

"These two guide words tell you that none of the words on this page starts with *f-a-s-s*. How do I know that? Can you prove this to me?"

"These two guide words tell you that none of the words on this page starts with *f-a-t-u*. How do I know that? Can you prove this to me?"

Write *father*, *fatal*, *fashion*, and *favor* on the board. Then ask, "Would you expect to find the word *father* on this page? Why? Prove it. Would you expect to find the word *fatal*? Why? Prove it. Would you expect to find the word *fashion*? Why not? Can you prove it? Would you expect to find the word *favor*? Why not? Can you prove it?"

"What guide words do you find on page 285? What things do these two guide words tell you? Do you see the word I've just written on the chalkboard? Would you expect to find this word on this page? Prove it. What guide words do you find on page 95? What things do these two guide words tell you? Without looking at the page, tell me one word that you think will be there. Tell me one word you're sure will not be there."

"On this worksheet is a list of words. After each word, I'd like you to write the two guide words you find in the dictionary on the page where the word appears. Let's do the first one together."

Ideas for Teaching the Use of a Pronunciation Key

Now that Henry has learned to look in the right part of the dictionary and to use guide words, he's ready to learn how to use the pronunciation key at the bottom of every dictionary page (or every other page). This key is used in conjunction with the "respelling" shown in parentheses right after a word. Take the word *feign*, for example. Right after the word *feign*, Henry is likely to find (fān). He would now know that this word rhymes either with *pan* or with *pain*. If he already knows his diacritical marks, he will know it rhymes with *pain*. But if he doesn't know his diacritical marks, he should look down at the bottom of the page (or the adjacent page) at the "Pronunciation Key" or the "Concise Pronunciation Key." This key is nothing but a list of words that serve as examples. Since Henry is not sure how to pronounce the middle sound in (fān), he should look for a word in the key that also has a macron over the *a*, such as *āce*. Now, assuming he knows how to pronounce *ace*, he would know that (fān) rhymes with pain.

A major technique for teaching Henry and others to use the Concise Pronunciation Key is to use the key with them on a few words each day until they understand it. Some children may need extra drill with workbook exercises, but unless the workbook exercises are followed up with actual use of the dictionary, they won't be very useful.

APPENDIX O OBSERVATION CHECKLIST FOR READING AND LANGUAGE DISABILITIES

General Behavior

_____ 1. Shows average or above-average intelligence in some way, e.g., does well in science reasoning or mathematical reasoning, shows sense of humor, or has ingenious ways of getting into trouble

_____ 2. Often has trouble expressing himself/herself
_____ 3. Often shows poor eye-hand coordination
_____ 4. Appears nervous or anxious in many situations
_____ 5. Tends to get frustrated easily
_____ 6. Withdraws when things get too difficult
_____ 7. Has far too much energy (or sometimes far too little)
_____ 8. Has trouble concentrating
_____ 9. Has trouble remembering directions, names, or other details
_____ 10. Has trouble making lasting friendships

Reading Behavior

_____ 1. Standardized reading achievement score: at least one year below grade level in grades 2–3 and two years below in later grades
_____ 2. Standardized individual diagnostic score: at least one year below grade level in grades 2–3 and two years below in later grades
_____ 3. Informal reading inventory: at least one year below grade level in grades 2–3 and two years below in later grades
_____ 4. Baf Test: 30-percent error in grades three and above (see Appendix H).
_____ 5. Essential Reading Vocabulary: 50-percent error in grades three and above (see Chapter 4).
_____ 6. Has considerable trouble concentrating on reading task even when working directly with teacher
_____ 7. Frequently guesses wildly at words rather than using word-analysis skills
_____ 8. Forgets words shortly after learning to read them
_____ 9. Asks teacher to decode words rather than using word-analysis skills
_____ 10. Transposes letters or words or syllables while reading
_____ 11. Loses place in reading passage easily
_____ 12. Often does not seem to know the meaning of what he or she has read
_____ 13. Usually a word-by-word reader
_____ 14. Makes many errors on worksheets

Writing Behavior

_____ 1. Does very poorly on spelling tests, usually getting more words wrong than right
_____ 2. Creative writing has 30 percent or more of the words spelled wrong
_____ 3. Transposes words, letters, or syllables
_____ 4. Reverses letters such as _b_ and _d, p_ and _q_
_____ 5. Inverts letters such as _n_ and _u_ or _p_ and _b_
_____ 6. Usually guesses at spelling rather than using phonics
_____ 7. Forgets how to spell a word shortly after learning it
_____ 8. Has considerable trouble concentrating on learning how to spell words
_____ 9. Does not remember how to spell common prefixes or suffixes
_____ 10. Substitutes one suffix for another
_____ 11. Draws circles inconsistently counterclockwise and clockwise
_____ 12. Has considerable difficulty drawing a circle that is round and connected
_____ 13. Usually makes letters with one stroke if possible; lifting pencil tends to cause confusion
_____ 14. Writes as little as possible

_____ 15. Writing that requires memory of sequence and details is quite difficult
_____ 16. Writing is very laborious
_____ 17. Uses personal abbreviations for long difficult words
_____ 18. Has particular trouble with letter size and shape but also shows inconsistent spacing, alignment, and slant

APPENDIX P TWO HUNDRED PATTERNED BOOKS FOR TEACHING WRITING AND READING

Adams, Pam. *This Old Man*
Alain. *One, Two, Three, Going to Sea*
Aliki. *Go Tell Aunt Rhody*
Aliki. *Hush Little Baby*
Aliki. *My Five Senses*
Asch, Frank. *Monkey Face*
Balian, Lorna. *The Animal*
Balian, Lorna. *Where in the World Is Henry?*
Barohas, Sarah, E. *I Was Walking Down the Road*
Barrett, Judi. *Animals Should Definitely Not Wear Clothing*
Barton, Byron. *Building a House*
Barton, Byron. *Buzz, Buzz, Buzz*
Baskin, Leonard. *Hosie's Alphabet*
Battaglia, Aurelius. *Old Mother Hubbard*
Baum, Arline, and Joseph Baum. *One Bright Monday Morning*
Baylor, Byrd. *Everybody Needs a Rock*
Becker, John. *Seven Little Rabbits*
Beckman, Kaj. *Lisa Cannot Sleep*
Bellah, Melanie. *A First Book of Sounds*
Berenstain, Stanley, and Janice Berenstain. *The B Book*
Bonne, Rose, and Alan Mills. *I Know an Old Lady*
Brand, Oscar. *When I First Came to This Land*
Brandenberg, Franz. *I Once Knew a Man*
Briggs, Raymond. *Jim and the Beanstalk*
Brooke, Leslie. *Johnny Crow's Garden*
Brown, Marcia. *The Three Billy Goats Gruff*
Brown, Margaret Wise. *A Child's Good Night Book*
Brown, Margaret Wise. *Do You Know What I'll Do?*
Brown, Margaret Wise. *Four Fur Feet*
Brown, Margaret Wise. *The Friendly Book*
Brown, Margaret Wise. *Goodnight Moon*
Brown, Margaret Wise. *Home for a Bunny*

Brown, Margaret Wise. *The Important Book*
Brown, Margaret Wise. *Where Have You Been?*
Burningham, John. *Mr. Gumpy's Outing*
Cameron, Polly. *I Can't Said the Ant*
Carle, Eric. *The Grouchy Ladybug*
Carle, Eric. *The Mixed Up Chameleon*
Carle, Eric. *The Very Hungry Caterpillar*
Charlip, Remy. *Fortunately*
Charlip, Remy. *What Good Luck!*
Cook, Bernadine. *The Little Fish that Got Away*
de Paola, Tomie. *If It's My Brother*
de Regniers, Beatrice Schenk. *Catch a Little Fox*
de Regniers, Beatrice Schenk. *The Day Everybody Cried*
de Regniers, Beatrice Schenk. *How Joe the Bear and Sam the Mouse Got Together*
de Regniers, Beatrice Schenk. *The Little Book*
de Regniers, Beatrice Schenk. *May I Bring a Friend?*
de Regniers, Beatrice Schenk. *Willy O'Dwyer Jumped in the Fire*
Domanska, Janina. *If All the Seas Were One Sea*
Duff, Maggie. *Jonny and His Drum*
Duff, Maggie. *Rum Pum Pum*
Edens, Cooper. *Caretakers of Wonder*
Einsel, Walter. *Did You Ever See?*
Emberly, Barbara. *Drummer Hoff*
Emberly, Barbara. *Simon's Song*
Emberly, Barbara, and Ed Emberly. *One Wide River to Cross*
Emberly, Ed. *Klippity Klop*
Ets, Marie Hall. *Elephant in a Well*
Ets, Marie Hall. *Play with Me*
Flack, Marjorie. *Ask Mr. Bear*
Galdone, Paul. *Henny Penny*
Galdone, Paul. *The Little Red Hen*
Galdone, Paul. *The Three Bears*
Galdone, Paul. *The Three Billy Goats Gruff*
Galdone, Paul. *The Three Little Pigs*
Ginsburg, Mirra. *The Chick and the Duckling*
Greenburg, Polly. *Oh Lord, I Wish I Was a Buzzard*
Gwynne, Fred. *The King Who Rained*
Higgins, Don. *Papa's Going to Buy Me a Mockingbird*
Hoffman, Hilde. *The Green Grass Grows All Around*
Hutchins, Pat. *Good-Night Owl*
Hutchins, Pat. *Rosie's Walk*
Hutchins, Pat. *Titch*
Ipcar, Dahlov. *I Love my Anteater with an A*

Joslin, Sesyle. *What Do You Do, Dear?*
Joslin, Sesyle. *What Do You Say, Dear?*
Joyce, Irma. *Never Talk to Strangers*
Katz, Bobbie. *Nothing but a Dog*
Keats, Ezra Jack. *Over in the Meadow*
Kellogg, Steven. *Can I Keep Him?*
Kellogg, Steven. *The Mysterious Tadpole*
Kent, Jack. *The Fat Cat*
Klein, Lenore. *Brave Daniel*
Kraus, Robert. *Good Night Little ABC*
Kraus, Robert. *Whose Mouse Are You?*
Krauss, Ruth. *Bears*
Krauss, Ruth. *A Hole Is to Dig*
Langstaff, John. *Frog Went A-Courtin'*
Langstaff, John. *Gather My Gold Together: Four Songs for Four Seasons*
Langstaff, John. *Oh, A-Hunting We Will Go*
Langstaff, John. *Over in the Meadow*
Laurence, Ester. *We're Off to Catch a Dragon*
Lexau, Joan. *Crocodile and Hen*
Lobel, Anita. *King Rooster, Queen Hen*
Lobel, Arnold. *A Treeful of Pigs*
Mack, Stan. *10 Bears in My Bed*
Mars, W. T. *The Old Woman and Her Pig*
Martin, Bill. *Brown Bear, Brown Bear*
Martin, Bill. *Fire! Fire! Said Mrs. McGuire*
Martin, Bill. *Freedom Books*
Martin, Bill. *A Ghost Story*
Martin, Bill. *The Haunted House*
Martin, Bill. *Instant Readers*
Martin, Bill. *Little Owl Series*
Martin, Bill. *Monday, Monday, I Like Monday*
Martin, Bill. *Sounds of Language*
Martin, Bill. *Wise Owl Series*
Martin, Bill. *Young Owl Series*
Mayer, Mercer. *If I Had . . .*
Mayer, Mercer. *Just for You*
Mayer, Mercer. *What Do You Do with a Kangaroo?*
McGovern, Ann. *Too Much Noise.*
Memling, Carl. *Riddles, Riddles from A to Z*
Memling, Carl. *Ten Little Animals.*
Mizumura, Kazue. *If I Were a Cricket*
Moffett, Martha. *A Flower Pot Is Not a Hat*
Nodset, Joan. *Who Took the Farmer's Hat?*
O'Neill, Mary. *Hailstones and Halibut Bones*
Patrick, Gloria. *A Bug in a Jug*

Peppe, Rodney. *The House that Jack Built*

Petersham, Maud, and Miska Petersham. *The Rooster Crows: A Book of American Rhymes and Jingles*

Pinkwater, Daniel. *The Big Orange Splot*

Polushkin, Maria. *Mother, Mother, I Want Another*

Preston, Edna Mitchell. *Where Did My Mother Go?*

Quackenbush, Robert. *Poems for Counting*

Quackenbush, Robert. *She'll Be Comin' Round the Mountain*

Quackenbush, Robert. *Skip to My Lou*

Raskins, Ellen. *Spectacles*

Rokoff, Sandra. *Here Is a Cat*

Rossetti, Christina. *What Is Pink?*

Scheer, Julian, and Marvin Bileck. *Rain Makes Applesauce.*

Scheer, Julian, and Marvin Bileck. *Upside Down Day.*

Schulz, Charles. *You're My Best Friend Because*

Sendak, Maurice. *Chicken Soup with Rice*

Sendak, Maurice. *Where the Wild Things Are*

Seuss, Dr. *Dr. Seuss's ABC*

Sharmat, Marjorie. The Terrible Eater

Shaw, Charles B. *It Looked Like Spilt Milk.*

Shulevitz, Uri. *One Monday Morning*

Skaar, Grace. *What Do the Animals Say?*

Sonneborn, Ruth A. *Someone Is Eating the Sun*

Spier, Peter. *The Fox Went Out on a Chilly Night*

Stover, JoAnn. *If Everybody Did*

Tolstoy, Alexei. *The Great Big Enormous Turnip*

Viorst, Judith. *Alexander and the Terrible, Horrible, No Good, Very Bad Day*

Viorst, Judith. *I Used to Be Rich Last Sunday*

Viorst, Judith. *If I Were in Charge of the World*

Viorst, Judith. *I'll Fix Anthony*

Waber, Bernard. *Dear Hildegarde*

Watson, Clyde. *Father Fox's Pennyrhymes.*

Welber, Robert. *Goodbye, Hello.*

Wildsmith, Brian. *Brian Wildsmith's ABC*

Wildsmith, Brian. *The Twelve Days of Christmas*

Wildsmith, Brian. *What the Moon Saw*

Withers, Carl. *A Rocket In My Pocket*

Wolkstein, Diane. *The Visit*

Wondriska, William. *All the Animals Were Angry*

Wright, H. R. *A Maker of Boxes*

Zaid, Barry. *Chicken Little*

Zemach, Harve. *The Judge*

Zemach, Margot. *Hush, Little Baby*

Zemach, Margot. *The Teeny Tiny Woman*

Zolotow, Charlotte. *Do You Know What I'll Do?*

Index

ABOUT THE AUTHOR

Dr. May is the author of four textbooks for preservice and inservice teachers: *Teaching Language as Communication, To Help Children Read, To Help Children Communicate,* and *Reading as Communication.* He has been a Professor of Education at the University of Wisconsin—Madison, Washington State University, the University of Puget Sound, the University of North Carolina—Greensboro, and is now a Professor of Education at Portland State University in Portland, Oregon. His teaching experience also includes all the grades from one through twelve and in a variety of locations from East to West: Pelham, New Hampshire; New York, New York; Greensboro, North Carolina; Dayton, Ohio; Chicago, Illinois; and Pullman, Washington. Dr. May's informal but insightful style has made him a much-sought-after speaker and consultant across the country—particularly in the areas of reading, writing, and learning processes.

Photograph by Evelyn Liu-Eliot